RC Perfection

A Complete Guide to Perfecting the Reading Comprehension Section for all LSAT Students

DRAGON
TEST

To all my students, may you conquer life as you have conquered the LSAT, through introspection and devotion.

Table of Contents

Introduction: The Four Paths to Perfection

The Skills Required for RC Perfection

Unlike the Logic Games or the Logical Reasoning section, getting a perfect score on RC (or just one or two questions wrong) can be an elusive goal. In all my time working as an LSAT teacher, the Reading Comprehension section was what students struggled with the most by far. Students fought with a myriad of different issues: some couldn't finish in the allotted time; some were able to narrow the answer choices down to two but consistently picked the wrong one; others did not know how to deal with rarer question types; still others would blast through the passage without much deeper reflection, only to stare blankly at the questions, not knowing where to begin.

As of early 2023, no comprehensive and in-depth work focusing on RC exists. Some books give a basic and rudimentary overview of RC and list the most commonly seen question types. Online test-taking websites that might require a subscription will have explanations for different passages and different questions. But nothing offers the student systematic training on the core skills needed. My goal in writing this book is to provide an easily accessible, in-depth, and complete guide that can accompany you on your journey to acing the Reading Comprehension section.

Success in RC depends on four different things. This book will look at each of these skills in turn. They are:

1. The ability to reorganize the passage structurally while reading and remember key details.

2. The ability to draw hints from the questions and anticipate what the correct answer might look like.

3. The ability to examine answer choices, compare them, and rank them in preferability.

4. The ability to do all this within the allotted time.

The book is divided into four parts, each corresponding to one of these skills.

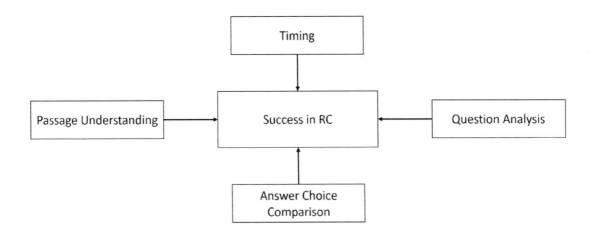

Isolating Your Weakness

As we work through this book and during your regular RC practice, it is crucial to look back on your work and critically evaluate your own performance. After completing each passage/section and the questions, stop and reflect. Ask yourself, *"What did I find most troubling about this passage and its questions?"* Is it because your understanding of the passage wasn't deep enough to tackle the questions? Is it because you were not analyzing the questions and coming up with a potentially correct answer choice? Perhaps you could narrow your selection to two answer choices but kept selecting the wrong one? In that case, were you conducting keyword analysis on the answer choices or ranking the answers? Was it because you don't have enough time?

Isolating our areas of weakness and focusing on overcoming these weaknesses is the only way to improve. As we progress through the book, we will look at the specific problems and issues haunting students and what drills and habits we can apply to solve these problems.

LR Skills Carry Over

Throughout this book, we will borrow specific ideas and concepts from my other book, LR Perfection. As we will soon see, certain core habits like reading for structure, answer choice keyword analysis, and ranking answers are helpful in both LR and RC.

In fact, many RC Questions can be approached in a manner similar to their LR counterparts. Purpose Questions can be treated like LR Role Questions, According to the Passage Questions can be treated as Must be True Questions, Inference Questions as Most Strongly Supported Questions, etc. Don't hesitate to find inspiration from LR even as we embark on our RC journey.

Cultivating Your Reading Ability

Unlike LR, where pattern recognition and habit finetuning alone are sometimes enough for the advanced student; RC performance is often dependent on our inherent reading ability. In other words, you can be familiar with all the strategies pertaining to different question types and answer choice selection yet still have a hard time simply because you didn't understand the passage, along with its subtleties and nuances.

For many students, it can be beneficial to use outside readings to strengthen our reading ability. What readings you chose should largely depend on the passages you find the most challenging. For instance, if you are consistently having trouble with art-themed passages, why not take an hour to research the basic tenets of art theory? If you are being butchered by abstract humanities passages, reading up on topics in philosophy will work wonders. If passages about Dworkin and legal positivism are too difficult, sit down, take a deep breath, and spend a few days delving over Dworkin's original essays.

Unlike my previous book, LR Perfection, which focused on the hardest questions and was tailored toward advanced students (160+), this book can be easily accessed by students of all levels and abilities. I sincerely hope that this can serve as a useful guide on your road to the elusive goal of RC Perfection! I apologize for any errors or typos you may encounter. This project was a one-person job until Sabrina, my editor, came bravely to the rescue. If you spot any issues, have any advice for improvement, or any LSAT-related questions or comments, do email me at joshua@dragontest.org. If you would like additional information or guidance, you can also check my website www.dragontest.org or join my discord group where I try to provide help and advice. Chinese speaking students may opt to add me on WeChat (作者微信号)：Lsatdragon （可获取一节免费一对一答疑课）

Lastly, I'd like to thank Yibo Zhang for giving me the courage to embark upon this project; and Sabrina Musgrave, my editor, who tirelessly sought out the shortcomings I could not see.

Part I: The Passage

Chapter 1: Engaging with the Passage

<u>Why</u> is the author writing this passage, and <u>what</u> did they do to accomplish this goal?

Anticipating the Author's Purpose

The first and foremost thing to remember about approaching an RC passage is a core skill we have already learned when practicing Logical Reasoning Questions: We must be aware of the passage structurally.

Most LR stimuli consisted of arguments. In an argument, there will be a main conclusion and supporting premises. When approaching an LR argument, we consistently ask ourselves, "what is the author's main point?" or "what is the main conclusion of this argument?" This applied not only to Find the Conclusion Questions but to every question type from the Assumption Family (Flaw, SA, NA, Strengthen, Weaken, etc.) and more. When reading an RC passage, we should take the same approach. As we go through the passage, we are constantly asking ourselves, *"What is the Main Point of this passage? What is the author trying to convey, and what kind of supporting information are they using?"*

On the other hand, RC passages are much longer than the arguments we see in LR. As a result, many of us end up mindlessly reading/browsing through the passage without really thinking about what the author is trying to say. We end up finishing the passage but can't remember anything. The bits and pieces of information we recall are fragmented and piecemeal. When we finally get to the questions, we have no specific evidence to lean on and rely on our intuition instead.

Because time is so limited on the RC section, we don't have the luxury of wasting any of it. We must engage with the passage from the beginning and practice **active reading**. Rather than mindlessly wander through the passage as we read, we need to be asking ourselves questions, find the answers in the passage, and reorganize the information we just read structurally.

But how?

We start by **anticipating** the Author's Purpose. In other words, as soon as we begin reading a passage, we ask ourselves, "why is the author writing this passage?" Just like how each LR argument will contain a main conclusion, and all that information will start to make sense once you have isolated what the conclusion is; if we can figure out the main point/conclusion of a passage, then reading and understanding the passage will become so much easier.

To illustrate my point, look at the following passage. As soon as you finish, try to recollect what it's about without referring back. For realism's sake, try to limit yourself to 3 minutes.

<u>PT29 Passage 4</u>

Until about 1970, anyone who wanted to write a comprehensive history of medieval English law as it actually affected women would have found a dearth of published books or articles concerned with specific legal topics relating to women and derived from extensive research in actual court records. This is a serious deficiency, since court records are of vital importance in discovering how the law actually affected women, as opposed to how the law was intended to affect them or thought to affect them. These latter questions can be answered by consulting such sources as treatises, commentaries, and statutes; such texts were what most scholars of the nineteenth and early twentieth centuries concentrated on whenever they did write about medieval law. But these sources are of little help in determining, for example, how often women's special statutory privileges were thwarted by intimidation or harassment, or how often women managed to evade special statutory limitations. And, quite apart from provisions designed to apply only, or especially, to women, they cannot tell us how general law affected the female half of the population—how women defendants and plaintiffs were treated in the courts in practice when they tried to exercise the rights they shared with men. Only quantitative studies of large numbers of cases would allow even a guess at the answers to these questions, and this scholarly work has been attempted by few.

One can easily imagine why. Most medieval English court records are written in Latin or Anglo-Norman French and have never been published. The sheer volume of material to be sifted is daunting: there are over 27,500 parchment pages in the common plea rolls of the thirteenth century alone, every page nearly three feet long, and written often front and back in highly stylized court hand. But the difficulty of the sources, while it might appear to explain why the relevant scholarship has not been undertaken, seems actually to have deterred few: the fact is that few historians have wanted to write anything approaching women's legal history in the first place. Most modern legal historians who have written on one aspect or another of special laws pertaining to women have begun with an interest in a legal idea or event or institution, not with a concern for how it affected women. Very few legal historians have started with an interest in women's history that they might have elected to pursue through various areas of general law. And the result of all this is that the current state of our scholarly knowledge relating to law and the medieval Englishwoman is still fragmentary at best, though the situation is slowly improving.

That was a dense passage. When I went over this passage with my students, many were so focused on the details that they forgot to think about the passage's main point. So, go ahead; without looking back at the passage, can you summarize what the author talked about?

***

Students with strong reading skills can probably come up with a good response. But for the rest of us, it was probably quite a struggle. Chances are that you forgot as quickly as you read, there were some keywords and bits and pieces of information that you remembered, but if I asked you to summarize the passage in two to three sentences, you'd have to go back and look at the passage again.

Remember what we talked about before. If by some miracle you already knew what the author's main point was as soon as you started reading, then everything will automatically make sense. Armed with that knowledge, you can now categorize each sentence as you read them, and by the time you finish the passage, your understanding of the passage will be organized and coherent.

So let's try that again, go back and re-read the passage, but this time I will tell you the author's main point/thesis:

Because of the scarcity of scholarship based on real cases, we know little about how the law actually affected women from the Middle Ages. This situation arose because most legal historians are more interested in general ideas rather than how real women were affected.

***

Once you know what the passage was going to talk about, reading all that convoluted information became much easier, right? Now, you can process the details as soon as you read them, you can organize them in your mind, you can categorize them based on what you knew about the passage.

The Author's Purpose

But wait, you say, on the actual exam itself; we have no way of knowing what the author's main point is until the very end! We still have no choice but to read through the passage, all muddled and confused, hoping that clarity and understanding will eventually come to us. We will still get lost in the details, unable to retain the information we've just read, and still unable to organize all that information coherently.

You are right. There's no way to know what the author's main point is for sure until we've finished reading the entire passage. Sometimes it's stated outright near the end of the passage, but most times, we need to derive it ourselves. So we can't use the author's main point as an aid as we read through the passage. But we have the next best thing:

The Author's Purpose

Simply put, the Author's Purpose tells us WHY the author wrote the passage. None of the passages that appear on the LSAT are there randomly. Each passage and even the paragraphs within each passage are there for a reason. Think about real-life situations; we give speeches or write essays to explain, persuade, incite, attack opponents, defend a position, or justify and provide a rationale for our actions. All writers write with a purpose in mind, unless you are making a shopping list/laundry list, and even then, we make lists to help us remember things. **In other words, there is a purpose behind every piece of writing**.

If the main point/thesis is WHAT the author is trying to get across to the readers, the Author's Purpose is WHY the author is penning this passage in the first place. As you are reading the passage, constantly ask yourself WHY? Why is the author writing this passage, why is the author giving us an example in paragraph 2? Why is the author choosing to use a negatively connotated word like "*unfortunately*?"

As we read through the passage, hints and clues will be scattered or hidden, giving us a rough idea of the WHY. When approaching a passage, our first task is to constantly ask ourselves why the author is writing what they did.

Let's return to PT29 Passage 4; only this time we will ask ourselves the question "WHY?"

Until about 1970, anyone who wanted to write a comprehensive history of medieval English law as it actually affected women would have found a <u>dearth</u> of published books or articles concerned with specific legal topics relating to women and derived from extensive research in actual court records.

<u>Dearth</u>: so there is a lack of material. Why is the author pointing this out? Why is the author writing this passage in the first place?

Hmmm, I'm not too sure; maybe the author wants to offer a solution to this by proposing alternative sources? Maybe they will tell us why there is so little scholarship. Maybe they are drawing awareness to the issue by calling for more focus on this field. I guess I will keep on reading to find out.

This is a <u>serious deficiency</u>, since court records are of vital importance in discovering how the law actually affected women, as opposed to how the law was intended to affect them or thought to affect them. These latter questions can be answered by consulting such sources as treatises, commentaries, and statutes; such texts were what most scholars of the nineteenth and early twentieth centuries concentrated on whenever they did write about medieval law. But these sources <u>are of little help</u> in determining, for example, how often women's special statutory privileges were thwarted by intimidation or harassment, or how often women managed to evade special statutory limitations. And, quite apart from provisions designed to apply only, or especially, to women, they <u>cannot tell us</u> how general law affected the female half of the population—how women defendants and plaintiffs were treated in the courts in practice when they tried to exercise the rights they shared with men. Only quantitative studies of large numbers of cases would allow even a guess at the answers to these questions, and this scholarly work has <u>been attempted by few</u>.

So the lack of scholarship is a "*serious deficiency*," and what materials that are available are "*of little help.*"

Ok, so the situation is pretty bad. But WHY is the author saying this?

So far, the author has only highlighted the problems; is that their purpose? To highlight the problems plaguing an academic field? Or is it something more? Perhaps the author will propose a solution in the next paragraph?

One can easily imagine <u>why</u>.

Nice! So the author is going to tell us why scholarship is so limited. Maybe this is the Author's Purpose after all.

Most medieval English court records are written in Latin or Anglo-Norman French and have never been published. The sheer volume of material to be sifted is daunting: there are over 27,500 parchment pages in the common plea rolls of the thirteenth century alone, every page nearly three feet long, and written often front and back in highly stylized court hand.

Is it because there are too many inaccessible sources?

But the difficulty of the sources, while it might appear to explain why the relevant scholarship has not been undertaken, <u>seems actually to have deterred few</u>:

Nope, that's not the reason. Let's see what the author thinks the *real* reason is.

the fact is that <u>few historians have wanted to write</u> anything approaching women's legal history in the first place. Most modern legal historians who have written on one aspect or another of special laws pertaining to women have begun with an interest in a legal idea or event or institution, <u>not with a concern for how it affected</u>

women. Very few legal historians have started with an interest in women's history that they might have elected to pursue through various areas of general law. And the result of all this is that the current state of our scholarly knowledge relating to law and the medieval Englishwoman is still fragmentary at best, though the situation is slowly improving.

This is unfortunate. The real reason is that historians don't care enough about the issue.

As it should be clear by now, the Author's Purpose in this passage is to highlight a problem in an academic field and explain how it came to pass. I'm amazed that the author didn't propose a tentative solution to the problem. Most RC passages that highlight a problem will usually offer a potential solution.

Compare this to the main point of the passage:

> *The scarcity of scholarship based on real cases meant we know little about how the law actually affected women from the Middle Ages, this situation arose because most legal historians are more interested in general ideas rather than how women were affected.*

Notice how closely related the Author's Purpose is to the passage's Main Point? As we read the passage and try to figure out the purpose, the main point should also come naturally to us. (More on this later)

The Hypothesis-Validation Framework

Notice how as we read through the passage, we were constantly asking ourselves WHY the author wrote this passage, and we were also constantly coming up with potential answers? At first, as soon as we realized that the first paragraph was talking about a problematic situation, we started to propose potential answers to the WHY question. We thought it might be to offer a way to solve the problem; maybe the author is simply highlighting the problem to bring awareness to it or explain how this problem arose in the first place?

By the second paragraph, we realized that the author is going to tell us the reason behind this problematic situation. So the author isn't simply highlighting a deficiency. Similarly, the author never provided a solution to this problem, so that can't be the purpose of this passage.

Think about RC reading as a **scientific experiment**. In a scientific experiment, we would develop an initial hypothesis, and with additional evidence, we would either modify, confirm, or replace our hypothesis. RC reading is very similar. As soon as we start reading a passage, we ask ourselves what's the Author's Purpose in writing this passage. As we keep reading, we find details and words that serve as our scientific evidence. We continuously modify, confirm, or even replace our initial hypothesis entirely. Eventually, by the time we have finished reading the passage, we will have a much better understanding of the Author's Purpose, the passage's main point, and the role of the rest of the information we've just read.

This is a reading habit that I've named the **Hypothesis-Validation Framework**, and it has worked wonders for both my students and me, especially in the most complex passages. In short, we start the reading and try to brainstorm some of the reasons why the author is writing the passage, or what the passage will talk about (hypothesis). As we read through the passage, we use the additional information to validate our initial hypothesis. If the hypothesis isn't fully validated, then we modify it accordingly.

This framework also works in non-LSAT readings. In my RC class and privately, I tried it with dense passages from Clifford Geertz, Kant, Foucault, Habermas, and jurists like Hart and Dworkin. The results were extraordinary.

What is the Author Doing? (CEER)

As we read the passage, a second vital question to ask ourselves is this: **"What is the author doing?"**

As we mentioned previously, a cardinal sin of RC reading is scanning the passage without thinking, and getting bogged down in the details without actively reflecting on what you just read and how the ideas relate.

You have probably heard countless exhortations telling you to "read actively," but such vague advice doesn't really help anyone. We all know what we are supposed to do, but when it comes to challenging passages, we can't just magically begin to read, reflect, and connect the dots, especially when time is limited.

So how do we train our active reading ability? We do this by repeatedly asking ourselves, as we are reading, "What is the author doing in this specific passage/paragraph/sentence?" If we can figure out what the author is doing, then realizing why they are doing it and how it relates to the entire passage's thesis becomes much easier. Ask yourself, after every few sentences or so, "What is the author doing now?"

In preparation for this book, I went back to the PTs and tried to categorize every passage from PT1 to PT90 and their associated questions. In every passage, the author will be doing one or more of the following: they can be **comparing** different concepts/positions; **explaining** something like a theory, **evaluating** the merits of an idea or practice; or **recommending** a course of action.

As we read through each passage, if you ever find yourself drifting off, stop and ask yourself whether the author is comparing, explaining, evaluating, or recommending something. Constantly ask yourself this question until you are comfortable engaging with the material you've just read.

Comparison

In a comparison-themed passage, the author will compare two or more things, list their similarities and differences, their pros and cons, and perhaps end up choosing one. Pure comparison passages are relatively rare. Quite often, a passage will start by comparing two different scientific theories, two legal practices, or two schools of thought and then recommending one over the other.

> We must note here that while heavy on the comparison element between Passages A and B, comparative passages do not necessarily fall under the Comparison framework. Each passage must be considered independently. We will look at Comparative Passages in more depth later in the book.

Look at the following passage and try to use the hypothesis-validation framework to aid your understanding. What's being compared in this passage? What's the Author's Purpose in writing this passage? What's its main point?

Intellectual authority is defined as the authority of arguments that prevail by virtue of good reasoning and do not depend on coercion or convention. A contrasting notion, institutional authority, refers to the power of social institutions to enforce acceptance of arguments that may or may not possess intellectual authority. The authority wielded by legal systems is especially interesting because such systems are institutions that nonetheless aspire to a purely intellectual authority. One judge goes so far as to claim that courts are merely passive vehicles for applying the intellectual authority of the law and possess no coercive powers of their own.

In contrast, some critics maintain that whatever authority judicial pronouncements have is exclusively institutional. Some of these critics go further, claiming that intellectual authority does not really exist—i.e., it reduces to institutional authority. But it can be countered that these claims break down when a sufficiently broad historical perspective is taken: Not all arguments accepted by institutions withstand the test of time, and some well-reasoned arguments never receive institutional imprimatur. The reasonable argument that goes unrecognized in its own time because it challenges institutional beliefs is common in intellectual history; intellectual authority and institutional consensus are not the same thing.

But, the critics might respond, intellectual authority is only recognized as such because of institutional consensus. For example, if a musicologist were to claim that an alleged musical genius who, after several decades, had not gained respect and recognition for his or her compositions is probably not a genius, the critics might say that basing a judgment on a unit of time— "several decades"—is an institutional rather than an intellectual construct. What, the critics might ask, makes a particular number of decades reasonable evidence by which to judge genius? The answer, of course, is nothing, except for the fact that such institutional procedures have proved useful to musicologists in making such distinctions in the past.

The analogous legal concept is the doctrine of precedent, i.e., a judge's merely deciding a case a certain way becoming a basis for deciding later cases the same way—a pure example of institutional authority. But the critics miss the crucial distinction that when a judicial decision is badly reasoned, or simply no longer applies in the face of evolving social standards or practices, the notion of intellectual authority is introduced: judges reconsider, revise, or in some cases throw out the decision. The conflict between intellectual and institutional authority in legal systems is thus played out in the reconsideration of decisions, leading one to draw the conclusion that legal systems contain a significant degree of intellectual authority even if the thrust of their power is predominantly institutional.

Here's my take on the passage:

Intellectual authority is defined as the authority of arguments that prevail by virtue of good reasoning and do not depend on coercion or convention. A contrasting notion, *institutional authority*, refers to the power of social institutions to enforce acceptance of arguments that may or may not possess intellectual authority. The authority wielded by legal systems is especially interesting because such systems are *institutions that nonetheless aspire to a purely intellectual authority*. One judge goes so far as to claim that courts are merely passive vehicles for applying the intellectual authority of the law and possess no coercive powers of their own.

Right away, two competing concepts should stand out: Intellectual authority vs. institutional authority. The author will probably go more in-depth into each and compare the two.

We are also told that legal systems "aspire to purely intellectual authority." So which is it then, are legal systems intellectual, institutional, or a mix of both?

*In contrast, *some critics maintain* that whatever authority judicial pronouncements have is exclusively institutional. Some of these critics go further, claiming that intellectual authority does not really exist—i.e., it reduces to institutional authority. But it can be countered that these claims break down when a sufficiently broad historical perspective is taken: Not all arguments accepted by institutions withstand the test of time, and some well-reasoned arguments never receive institutional imprimatur. The *reasonable argument* that goes unrecognized in its own time because it challenges institutional beliefs is common in intellectual history; intellectual authority and institutional consensus *are not the same thing*.*

More comparisons of different views here. The argument has shifted somewhat, but the comparison element is still relevant. We are now comparing some critics' views on the nature of judicial authorities and that of the author.

So some critics think judicial authority is exclusively institutional. The author didn't explicitly refute this; instead, they argue that intellectual authority is separate from institutional authority.

At this point, we might hypothesize that the Author's Purpose might be to argue that intellectual authority does exist, and that judicial authority derives largely from it.

But, the critics might respond, intellectual authority is only recognized as such because of institutional consensus. For example, if a musicologist were to claim that an alleged musical genius who, after several decades, had not gained respect and recognition for his or her compositions is probably not a genius, the critics might say that basing a judgment on a unit of time— "several decades"—is an institutional rather than an intellectual construct. What, the critics might ask, makes a particular number of decades reasonable evidence by which to judge genius? The answer, of course, is nothing, except for the fact that such institutional procedures have proved useful to musicologists in making such distinctions in the past.

Aha, we are back again to the critics' argument. Remember that the critics oppose the author in their belief that judicial authority is purely institutional, and that intellectual authority is a pseudo-construction. We know already that this is something the author disagrees with, so it's highly likely that the author will offer a final refutation in the last paragraph.

*The analogous legal concept is the doctrine of precedent, i.e., a judge's merely deciding a case a certain way becoming a basis for deciding later cases the same way—a pure example of institutional authority. *But the critics miss the crucial distinction* that when a judicial decision is badly reasoned, or simply no longer applies in the face of evolving social standards or practices, the notion of intellectual authority is introduced: judges reconsider, revise, or in some cases throw out the decision. The conflict between intellectual and institutional authority in legal systems is thus played out in the reconsideration of decisions, leading one to draw the conclusion that *legal systems contain a significant degree of intellectual authority* even if the thrust of their power is predominantly institutional.*

Indeed, that's exactly what the author does. Decisions based on institutional authority can be overturned. So intellectual authority must be in play here. Does the author argue that legal authorities are purely intellectual? Nope, they do concede a point to the critics and believe them to be a hybrid of both types of authorities.

The passage starts by comparing and contrasting two types of authorities, intellectual and institutional. It then goes off into a back-and-forth between certain critics and the author. The comparison framework works well in this passage for both. It forces us to acknowledge the two parties central to this argument and gives us a clearer picture of the Author's Purpose.

Note how this passage is more than just comparing and contrasting two schools of thought. The author is explicitly committed to one position. One can say that their purpose in this passage is to defend the idea that judicial authority contains elements of intellectual authority. By making two comparisons, first between institutional and intellectual authority, and secondly between the author and the critics, we come to a much clearer understanding of the passage.

Let's look at another passage where detecting comparisons play an oversized role in understanding the passage. Again, try to do this in three minutes if you can.

***

PT22 Passage 2

In recent years, a growing belief that the way society decides what to treat as true is controlled through largely unrecognized discursive practices has led legal reformers to examine the complex interconnections between narrative and law. In many legal systems, legal judgments are based on competing stories about events. Without having witnessed these events, judges and juries must validate some stories as true and reject others as false. This procedure is rooted in objectivism, a philosophical approach that has supported most Western legal and intellectual systems for centuries. Objectivism holds that there is a single neutral description of each event that is unskewed by any particular point of view and that has a privileged position over all other accounts. The law's quest for truth, therefore, consists of locating this objective description, the one that tells what really happened, as opposed to what those involved thought happened. The serious flaw in objectivism is that there is no such thing as the neutral, objective observer. As psychologists have demonstrated, all observers bring to a situation a set of expectations, values, and beliefs that determine what the observers are able to see and hear. Two individuals listening to the same story will hear different things, because they emphasize those aspects that accord with their learned experiences and ignore those aspects that are dissonant with their view of the world. Hence there is never any escape in life or in law from selective perception, or from subjective judgments based on prior experiences, values, and beliefs.

The societal harm caused by the assumption of objectivist principles in traditional legal discourse is that, historically, the stories judged to be objectively true are those told by people who are trained in legal discourse, while the stories of those who are not fluent in the language of the law are rejected as false.

Legal scholars such as Patricia Williams, Derrick Bell, and Mari Matsuda have sought empowerment for the latter group of people through the construction of alternative legal narratives. Objectivist legal discourse systematically disallows the language of emotion and experience by focusing on cognition in its narrowest sense. These legal reformers propose replacing such abstract discourse with powerful personal stories. They argue that the absorbing, nonthreatening structure and tone of personal stories may convince legal insiders for the first time to listen to those not fluent in legal language. The compelling force of personal narrative can create a sense of empathy between legal insiders and people traditionally excluded from legal discourse and, hence, from power. Such alternative narratives can shatter the complacency of the legal establishment and disturb its tranquility. Thus, the engaging power of narrative might play a crucial, positive role in the process of legal reconstruction by overcoming differences in background and training and forming a new collectivity based on emotional empathy.

In recent years, a growing belief that the way society decides what to treat as true is controlled through largely unrecognized discursive practices has led legal reformers to examine the complex interconnections between <u>narrative</u> and <u>law</u>.

Ok, so the "complex interconnections between narrative and law." Hmmm, perhaps the author will compare these two ideas or talk about the role of narrative in the legal field? Not too sure at this point; let's read on.

In many legal systems, legal judgments are based on competing stories about events. Without having witnessed these events, judges and juries must validate some stories as true and reject others as false. This procedure is rooted in <u>objectivism</u>, a philosophical approach that has supported most Western legal and intellectual systems for centuries. Objectivism holds that there is a <u>single neutral description</u> of each event that is unskewed by any particular point of view and that has a privileged position over all other accounts. <u>The law's quest for truth</u>, therefore, consists of <u>locating this objective description</u>, the one that tells what really happened, as opposed to what those involved thought happened.

So the law is based on locating the objective description of what really happened. There's a single version of what constitutes the truth.

The <u>serious flaw</u> in objectivism is that there is no such thing as the neutral, objective observer. As psychologists have demonstrated, all observers bring to a situation a set of expectations, values, and beliefs that determine what the observers are able to see and hear. Two individuals listening to the same story will hear different things, because they emphasize those aspects that accord with their learned experiences and ignore those aspects that are dissonant with their view of the world. <u>Hence there is never any escape in life or in law from selective perception, or from subjective judgments</u> based on prior experiences, values, and beliefs.

The author's view is apparent here. They disagree with the objective view. The author thinks that we cannot escape subjective judgments. So the conflict/comparison isn't between narrative and law, as we had initially thought. **Instead, it's between an objective and subjective view of the world.**
Furthermore, we now know what the author believes. They are attacking the belief in objectivism in legal procedures and defending subjectivism. That is probably the Author's Purpose here.

The <u>societal harm</u> caused by the assumption of objectivist principles in traditional legal discourse is that, historically, the stories judged to be objectively true are those told by <u>people who are trained in legal discourse</u>, while the stories of those <u>who are not fluent in the language of the law</u> are rejected as false.

Wow, a third pairing: people who have legal training and people who don't. How does this play into our comparison between objective and subjective views?

We are told that the objectivist view has this negative implication. It disadvantages those who have no legal training. Ok, so this fits in with our previous understanding of the passage. The author is further attacking the objective view.

Legal scholars such as Patricia Williams, Derrick Bell, and Mari Matsuda have sought empowerment for the latter group of people through the construction of alternative legal narratives.

So all three are on the same team here; maybe the author will talk about the nuanced differences between the three in this paragraph. But either way, all three are on team subjective.

Objectivist legal discourse systematically disallows the language of emotion and experience by focusing on cognition in its narrowest sense. These legal reformers propose <u>replacing</u> such abstract discourse with powerful personal stories. They argue that the absorbing, nonthreatening structure and tone of personal stories may <u>convince legal insiders for the first time to listen</u> to those not fluent in legal language. The compelling force of personal narrative <u>can create a sense of empathy</u> between legal insiders and people traditionally excluded from legal discourse and, hence, from power.

The three scholars want to use personal stories and experiences to replace abstract legal discourse. The author thinks this can empower those with no legal training.

Thus, the engaging power of <u>narrative</u> might play a crucial, positive role in the process of legal reconstruction by overcoming differences in background and training and forming a new collectivity based on emotional empathy.

The word "narrative" appears again. So by "narrative," the author meant "subjective personal stories." I didn't realize that before, but it all makes sense now. The Author's Purpose is to advocate for the role of personal narratives in legal discourse. Why are they doing it? Because the world is fundamentally subjective, and holding on to an objective view excludes the disenfranchised.

We are reorganizing and re-categorizing the information we've just read by focusing on the contradictions between almost dialectically opposed concepts in the passage (objective vs. subjective; legally trained vs. untrained). By grasping these key concepts, we are forced to come to a much clearer understanding of what the passage is talking about, its purpose and central thesis.

This passage is also typical of many other comparison-themed essays in that it starts by comparing and contrasting different concepts and positions, but eventually ends up recommending one over the other. We will look at another hybrid passage now.

PT85 Passage 4

According to the generally accepted theory of plate tectonics, the earth's crust consists of a dozen or so plates of solid rock moving across the mantle-the slightly fluid layer of rock between crust and core. Most earthquakes can then be explained as a result of the grinding of these plates against one another as they collide. When two plates collide, one plate is forced under the other until it eventually merges with the underlying mantle. According to this explanation, this process, called subduction, causes an enormous build-up of energy that is abruptly released in the form of an earthquake. Most earthquakes take place in the earth's seismic "hot zones" – regions with very high levels of subduction. Contrary to expectations, however, global seismic data indicate that there are also regions with high levels of subduction that are nonetheless nearly free of earthquakes. Thus, until recently, there remained a crucial question for which the plate tectonics theory had no answer-how can often intense subduction take place at certain locations with little or no seismic effect?

One group of scientists now proposes that the relative quiet of these zones is tied to the nature of the collision between the plates. In many seismic hot zones, the plates exhibit motion in opposite directions-that is, they collide because they are moving toward each other. And because the two plates are moving in opposite directions, the subduction zone is relatively motionless relative to the underlying mantle. In contrast, the plate collisions in the quiet subduction zones occur between two plates that are moving in the same general direction-the second plate's motion is simply faster than that of the first, and its leading edge therefore becomes subducted. But in this type of subduction, the collision zone moves with a comparatively high velocity relative to the mantle below. Thus, rather like an oar dipped into the water from a moving boat, the overtaking plate encounters great resistance from the mantle and is forced to descend steeply as it is absorbed into the mantle. The steep descent of the overtaking plate in this type of collision reduces the amount of contact between the two plates, and the earthquake-producing friction is thereby reduced as well. On the other hand, in collisions in which the plates move toward each other the subducted plate receives relatively little resistance from the mantle, and so its angle of descent is correspondingly shallow, allowing for a much larger plane of contact between the two plates. Like two sheets of sandpaper pressed together, these plates offer each other a great deal of resistance.

This proposal also provides a warning. It suggests that regions that were previously thought to be seismically innocuous-regions with low levels of subduction-may in fact be at a significant risk of earthquakes, depending on the nature of the subduction taking place.

According to the generally accepted theory of plate tectonics, the earth's crust consists of a dozen or so plates of solid rock moving across the mantle-the slightly fluid layer of rock between crust and core. Most earthquakes can then be explained as a result of the grinding of these plates against one another as they collide. When two plates collide, one plate is forced under the other until it eventually merges with the underlying mantle. According to this explanation, this process, called subduction, causes an enormous build-up of energy that is abruptly released in the form of an earthquake. Most earthquakes take place in the earth's seismic "hot zones" – regions with very high levels of subduction.

The "generally accepted" theory of plate tectonics is introduced. Will the author go on to talk about a newer renegade theory?

The paragraph then goes into a detailed **explanation** of this general theory and how earthquakes occur. Basically, one plate gets pushed under the other, and friction causes earthquakes.

Contrary to expectations, however, global seismic data indicate that there are also regions with high levels of subduction that are nonetheless nearly free of earthquakes. Thus, until recently, there remained a crucial question for which the plate tectonics theory had no answer-how can often intense subduction take place at certain locations with little or no seismic effect?

Bingo! So there are regions where plates get pushed under, but no earthquakes occur. This doesn't make sense; the traditional theory can't explain this. Why would the author tell us this? Probably to introduce a new theory/explanation, right?

One group of scientists now proposes that the relative quiet of these zones is tied to the nature of the collision between the plates. In many seismic hot zones, the plates exhibit motion in opposite directions-that is, they collide because they are moving toward each other. And because the two plates are moving in opposite directions, the subduction zone is relatively motionless relative to the underlying mantle. In contrast, the plate collisions in the quiet subduction zones occur between two plates that are moving in the same general direction-the second plate's motion is simply faster than that of the first, and its leading edge therefore becomes subducted.

Here is the new theory and more detailed explanations. So when two plates move toward each other, there is lots of friction and earthquakes. When they move away from each other, there is no friction and no earthquakes. Finally, when two plates move in the same direction, and the second plate catches up from behind, it gets pushed under the first one.

But in this type of subduction, the collision zone moves with a comparatively high velocity relative to the mantle below. Thus, rather like an oar dipped into the water from a moving boat, the overtaking plate encounters great resistance from the mantle and is forced to descend steeply as it is absorbed into the mantle. The steep descent of the overtaking plate in this type of collision reduces the amount of contact between the two plates, and the earthquake-producing friction is thereby reduced as well. On the other hand, in collisions in which the plates move toward each other the subducted plate receives relatively little resistance from the mantle, and so its angle of descent is correspondingly shallow, allowing for a much larger plane of contact between the two plates. Like two sheets of sandpaper pressed together, these plates offer each other a great deal of resistance.

Exactly what we thought: greater friction and earthquakes occur when two plates move toward each other. When they move in the same direction, the one behind gets pushed under, so there is less friction and fewer earthquakes.

This proposal also provides a warning. It suggests that regions that were previously thought to be seismically innocuous-regions with low levels of subduction-may in fact be at a significant risk of earthquakes, depending on the nature of the subduction taking place.

In this passage, the author both compares and explains two different plate tectonics theories. The traditional theory can't explain why subduction doesn't automatically lead to earthquakes. In other words, in some regions, one plate gets pushed under another, but no earthquakes occur. The new theory explains this phenomenon better: the plates are moving in the same direction, and the plate coming in from behind sinks deep below the first one.

In Passage 2 of PT22, we used a hybrid of the Comparison-Recommendation framework to anticipate and understand the passage. Here, Comparison-Explain might be better suited. Most of the passage explains the respective theories, but at its core, the passage compares the two theories.

The author is fairly neutral in tone and attitude; they don't explicitly pick one theory over the other, although we do sense that they are receptive to the new theory.

We will return to this passage at the end of the book when we talk about tips related specifically to science-based passage types, but for now, let's look at Explain type passages in more detail.

Explain

As we saw in PT85 Passage 4, the author went into great detail to explain how the traditional plate tectonics theory worked in explaining subduction and how earthquakes occurred. It also explained the newer theory, even using the analogy of an oar dipping into the ocean to demonstrate how the second plate is likely to sink deeper into the mantle.

Many passages, especially scientific ones, will devote large portions to explaining an abstract concept or theory. Many students, especially under the pressure of test day, are terrified of this type of writing. They read through the passage, but nothing really registers. Even worse, many will get bogged down in the details, thus losing focus on WHY the author is explaining this stuff in the first place. Sometimes the author is explaining something simply for its own sake, and the purpose of the passage is to introduce a new concept/theory. But more often, the author may compare two ideas, evaluate them, and perhaps recommend one over the other.

When we come to these passages, you must strive to do your best to simplify the concepts the author is trying to explain. As we said before, do not miss the forest for the trees. Also, think about the cause/effect relationships, if any, that appear in these passages.

Look at the following passage, test your understanding, and then see my thinking process and how we differ.

PT28 Passage 2

Long after the lava has cooled, the effects of a major volcanic eruption may linger on. In the atmosphere a veil of fine dust and sulfuric acid droplets can spread around the globe and persist for years. Researchers have generally thought that this veil can block enough sunlight to have a chilling influence on Earth's climate. Many blame the cataclysmic eruption of the Indonesian volcano Tambora in 1815 for the ensuing "year without a summer" of 1816—when parts of the northeastern United States and southeastern Canada were hit by snowstorms in June and frosts in August.

The volcano-climate connection seems plausible, but, say scientists Clifford Mass and Davit Portman, it is not as strong as previously believed. Mass and Portman analyzed global temperature data for the years before and after nine volcanic eruptions, from Krakatau in 1883 to El Chichón in 1982. In the process they tried to filter out temperature changes caused by the cyclic weather phenomenon known as the El Niño-Southern Oscillation, which warms the sea surface in the equatorial Pacific and thereby warms the atmosphere. Such warming can mask the cooling brought about by an eruption, but it can also mimic volcanic cooling if the volcano happens to erupt just as an El Niño induced warm period is beginning to fade.

Once El Niño effects had been subtracted from the data, the actual effects of the eruptions came through more clearly. Contrary to what earlier studies had suggested, Mass and Portman found that minor eruptions have no discernible effect on temperature. And major, dust-spitting explosions, such as Krakatau or El Chichón, cause a smaller drop than expected in the average temperature in the hemisphere (Northern or Southern) of the eruption—only half a degree centigrade or less—a correspondingly smaller drop in the opposite hemisphere.

Other researchers, however, have argued that even a small temperature drop could result in a significant regional fluctuation in climate if its effects were amplified by climatic feedback loops. For example, a small temperature drop in the northeastern U.S. and southeastern Canada in early spring might delay the melting of snow, and the unmelted snow would continue to reflect sunlight away from the surface, amplifying the cooling. The cool air over the region could, in turn, affect the jet stream. The jet stream tends to flow at the boundary between cool northern air and warm southern air, drawing its power from the sharp temperature contrast and the consequent difference in pressure. An unusual cooling in the region could cause the stream to wander farther south than normal, allowing more polar air to come in behind it and deepen the region's cold snap. Through such a series of feedbacks a small temperature drop could be blown up into a year without a summer.

Long after the lava has cooled, the effects of a major volcanic eruption may linger on. In the atmosphere a veil of fine dust and sulfuric acid droplets can spread around the globe and persist for years. Researchers have generally thought that this veil can block enough sunlight to have a chilling influence on Earth's climate. Many blame the cataclysmic eruption of the Indonesian volcano Tambora in 1815 for the ensuing "year without a summer" of 1816—when parts of the northeastern United States and southeastern Canada were hit by snowstorms in June and frosts in August.

So volcano eruptions lead to dust in the atmosphere, which will cool the climate even a year later. That's all you need to know from this paragraph.

The volcano-climate connection seems plausible, but, say scientists Clifford Mass and Davit Portman, it is not as strong as previously believed. Mass and Portman analyzed global temperature data for the years before and after nine volcanic eruptions, from Krakatau in 1883 to El Chichón in 1982. In the process they tried to filter out temperature changes caused by the cyclic weather phenomenon known as the El Niño-Southern Oscillation, which warms the sea surface in the equatorial Pacific and thereby warms the atmosphere. Such warming can mask the cooling brought about by an eruption, but it can also mimic volcanic cooling if the volcano happens to erupt just as an El Niño induced warm period is beginning to fade.

Two scientists are challenging this connection. They did a bunch of studies and found that the cooling previously thought to have been caused by volcanic eruptions might be due to El Nino fading.

Remember in LR Perfection, we talked about causal relationships? A can cause B, but alternative causes like C or D can also cause B. So here, the scientists think that the atmosphere cooled not because of volcanic eruptions but because the warming effects of El Nino are wearing off.

Once El Niño effects had been subtracted from the data, the actual effects of the eruptions came through more clearly. Contrary to what earlier studies had suggested, Mass and Portman found that minor eruptions have no discernible effect on temperature. And major, dust-spitting explosions, such as Krakatau or El Chichón, cause a smaller drop than expected in the average temperature in the hemisphere (Northern or Southern) of the eruption—only half a degree centigrade or less—a correspondingly smaller drop in the opposite hemisphere.

So volcanic eruptions have a smaller and even negligible effect on temperature. The major culprit is El Nino ending.

Other researchers, however, have argued that even a small temperature drop could result in a significant regional fluctuation in climate if its effects were amplified by climatic feedback loops. For example, a small temperature drop in the northeastern U.S. and southeastern Canada in early spring might delay the melting of snow, and the unmelted snow would continue to reflect sunlight away from the surface, amplifying the cooling. The cool air over the region could, in turn, affect the jet stream. The jet stream tends to flow at the boundary between cool northern air and warm southern air, drawing its power from the sharp temperature contrast and the consequent difference in pressure. An unusual cooling in the region could cause the stream to wander farther south than normal, allowing more polar air to come in behind it and deepen the region's cold snap. Through such a series of feedbacks a small temperature drop could be blown up into a year without a summer.

What another group of researchers think is introduced. Be sure to compare the two schools of thought.

What does the other group think? It sounds like a counterargument to me. They think that even if the drop in temperature is smaller than previously thought, it can snowball into a much bigger influence down the road. Does the author take a position? Not really.

So this passage, once you have simplified the concepts and grasped what at its core is a scientific debate, is fairly straightforward.

Some scientists believe that the effects of volcanic eruptions on climate cooling are negligible.

Other researchers think that even if the initial change is small, that can greatly impact climate cooling down the road.

In this passage, the author explains the belief of some scientists and gives us the response of another group of scientists.

We will go into more detail on how to tackle a passage that is full of abstract concepts and excruciating details down the road, but for now, just remember that if a passage contains scientific explanations, try to simplify the concept that the author is trying to explain, and ask yourself why such an explanation is warranted?

Evaluation

Now we are moving into passages where the author's viewpoint/opinion is even more explicit. In Evaluation themed passages, the author will make a judgment call about the pros and cons of a position or idea they have previously discussed. Does the author think the position is a good one? Do they agree with it?

Knowing what the author's attitude is will help immensely with many question types, so it's crucial to note if what you are reading is simply the author stating the facts, or an expression of their opinion.

Let's look at a few passages where the author makes a judgment call. There may be parts of the passage where the author is **comparing** or **explaining** something, with the **evaluation** coming in during another part of the passage. So, it's essential to remain flexible as you are reading.

PT32 Passage 3

In studying the autobiographies of Native Americans, most scholars have focused on as-told-to life histories that were solicited, translated, recorded, and edited by non-Native American collaborators—that emerged from "bicultural composite authorship." Limiting their studies to such written documents, these scholars have overlooked traditional, preliterate modes of communicating personal history. In addition, they have failed to address the cultural constructs of the highly diverse Native American peoples, who prior to contact with nonindigenous cultures did not share with Europeans the same assumptions about self, life, and writing that underlie the concept of an autobiography— that indeed constitute the English word's root meaning.

The idea of self was, in a number of pre-contact Native American cultures, markedly inclusive: identity was not merely individual, but also relational to a society, a specific landscape, and the cosmos. Within these cultures, the expression of life experiences tended to be oriented toward current events: with the participation of fellow tribal members, an individual person would articulate, reenact, or record important experiences as the person lived them, a mode of autobiography seemingly more fragmented than the European custom of writing down the recollections of a lifetime. Moreover, expression itself was not a matter of writing but of language, which can include speech and signs. Oral autobiography comprised songs, chants, stories, and even the process whereby one repeatedly took on new names to reflect important events and deeds in one's life. Dance and drama could convey personal history; for example, the advent of a vision to one person might require the enactment of that vision in the form of a tribal pageant.

One can view as autobiographical the elaborate tattoos that symbolized a warrior's valorous deeds, and such artifacts as a decorated shield that communicated the accomplishments and aspirations of its maker, or a robe that was emblazoned with the pictographic history of the wearer's battles and was sometimes used in re-enactments. Also autobiographical, and indicative of high status within the tribe, would have been a tepee painted with symbolic designs to record the achievements and display the dreams or visions of its owner, who was often assisted in the painting by other tribal members.

A tribe would, then, have contributed to the individual's narrative not merely passively, by its social codes and expectations, but actively by joining in the expression of that narrative. Such intercultural collaboration may seem alien to the European style of autobiography, yet any autobiography is shaped by its creator's ideas about the audience for which it is intended; in this sense, autobiography is justly called a simultaneous individual story and cultural narrative. Autobiographical expressions by early Native Americans may additionally have been shaped by the cultural perspectives of the people who transmitted them.

In studying the autobiographies of Native Americans, <u>most scholars</u> have focused on as-told-to life histories that were solicited, translated, recorded, and edited <u>by non-Native American collaborators</u>—that emerged from "bicultural composite authorship." Limiting their studies to such written documents, these scholars have <u>overlooked</u> traditional, preliterate modes of communicating personal history. In addition, they have <u>failed to address</u> the cultural constructs of the highly diverse Native American peoples, who prior to contact with nonindigenous cultures did not share with Europeans the same assumptions about self, life, and writing that underlie the concept of an autobiography— that indeed constitute the English word's root meaning.

Right off the bat, the author talks about a problem plaguing most scholars. Their focus has been devoted to autobiographies written in partnership with non-native Americans. The author's tone is quite obvious. They disagree with this practice.

What will the author do next? Talk about ways to remedy this? Compare this with a minor faction of writers? Explain the cause behind this narrow-mindedness? We have to keep on reading to find out.

The <u>idea of self</u> was, in a number of pre-contact Native American cultures, markedly <u>inclusive</u>: identity was not merely individual, but also relational to a society, a specific landscape, and the cosmos. Within these cultures, the expression of life experiences tended to be oriented toward current events: with the participation of fellow tribal members, an individual person would articulate, reenact, or record important experiences as the person lived them, a <u>mode of autobiography seemingly more fragmented</u> than the European custom of writing down the recollections of a lifetime. Moreover, expression itself was not a matter of writing but of language, which can include speech and signs. <u>Oral autobiography</u> comprised songs, chants, stories, and even the process whereby one repeatedly took on new names to reflect important events and deeds in one's life. <u>Dance and drama</u> could convey personal history; for example, the advent of a vision to one person might require the enactment of that vision in the form of a tribal pageant.

The author talks about how Native American cultural practices differ from European ones. The concept of an autobiography is alien as fellow tribe members can equally articulate one's life experience. Oral history, dance, and ceremonies are all equally valid forms of re-enacting one's life.

Think about the differences between Native American and European practices here. The comparison framework works well.

One can view as autobiographical the elaborate <u>tattoos</u> that symbolized a warrior's valorous deeds, and such artifacts as a decorated <u>shield</u> that communicated the accomplishments and aspirations of its maker, or a <u>robe</u> that was emblazoned with the pictographic history of the wearer's battles and was sometimes used in reenactments. Also autobiographical, and indicative of high status within the tribe, would have been a <u>tepee</u> painted with symbolic designs to record the achievements and display the dreams or visions of its owner, who was often assisted in the painting by other tribal members.

Here, the author lists objects that we wouldn't normally associate with an autobiography and argues that they are autobiographical in nature. This is a further development of the idea presented in the previous paragraph.

A <u>tribe</u> would, then, have <u>contributed</u> to the individual's narrative not merely passively, by its social codes and expectations, but <u>actively</u> by joining in the expression of that narrative. Such intercultural collaboration may seem alien to the European style of autobiography, yet any autobiography is shaped by its creator's ideas about the audience for which it is intended; in this sense<u>, autobiography is justly called a simultaneous individual story and cultural narrative</u>. Autobiographical expressions by early Native Americans may additionally have been shaped by the cultural perspectives of the people who transmitted them.

In the last paragraph, the author argues that an autobiography is not simply a traditional, European-styled work written by the individual; collective experiences and objects can also constitute an autobiographical expression.

If we were to tie everything together, then the evaluative nature of this passage becomes evident:

Chapter 1: Engaging with the Passage

- Paragraph 1: Scholars ignored Native American cultural practices by focusing on Eurocentric autobiographies.

- Paragraph 2: Native American cultural practices meant that there were many ways to express one's life than a simple work in writing.

- Paragraph 3: Objects and shared experiences within the tribe can also be considered autobiographical.

- Paragraph 4: A repetition and summary of the ideas expressed in paragraphs 2 and 3.

The author's position/attitude is quite clear from the very beginning. They are critical of the current scholarly practice, as it ignores traditional cultural practices and trends. They then delineate the differences between Native American and European conceptualizations and expressions of self. (Comparison)

Recommendation

We have already seen recommendations in several of the previous passages. The author has spoken in favor of a specific course of action, advocating one practice over another. A recommendation-themed passage is similar to an evaluation one in that the author is making their position clear. But the difference will be that in an Evaluation themed passage, the author simply points out the good and bad of an action or practice. In contrast, the author will deliberately vouch for a certain course of action in a recommendation-themed passage.

In simpler terms, if the author is evaluating something, they are listing its good and bad; but if the author is recommending something, then we know that the author is telling us to do or believe something.

PT38 Passage 4

One of the greatest challenges facing medical students today, apart from absorbing volumes of technical information and learning habits of scientific thought, is that of remaining empathetic to the needs of patients in the face of all this rigorous training. Requiring students to immerse themselves completely in medical coursework risks disconnecting them from the personal and ethical aspects of doctoring, and such strictly scientific thinking is insufficient for grappling with modern ethical dilemmas. For these reasons, aspiring physicians need to develop new ways of thinking about and interacting with patients. Training in ethics that takes narrative literature as its primary subject is one method of accomplishing this.

Although training in ethics is currently provided by medical schools, this training relies heavily on an abstract, philosophical view of ethics. Although the conceptual clarity provided by a traditional ethics course can be valuable, theorizing about ethics contributes little to the understanding of everyday human experience or to preparing medical students for the multifarious ethical dilemmas they will face as physicians. A true foundation in ethics must be predicated on an understanding of human behavior that reflects a wide array of relationships and readily adapts to various perspectives, for this is what is required to develop empathy. Ethics courses drawing on narrative literature can better help students prepare for ethical dilemmas precisely because such literature attaches its readers so forcefully to the concrete and varied world of human events.

The act of reading narrative literature is uniquely suited to the development of what might be called flexible ethical thinking. To grasp the development of characters, to tangle with heightening moral crises, and to engage oneself with the story not as one's own but nevertheless as something recognizable and worthy of attention, readers must use their moral imagination. Giving oneself over to the ethical conflicts in a story requires the abandonment of strictly absolute, inviolate sets of moral principles. Reading literature also demands that the reader adopt another person's point of view—that of the narrator or a character in a story— and thus requires the ability to depart from one's personal ethical stance and examine moral issues from new perspectives.

It does not follow that readers, including medical professionals, must relinquish all moral principles, as is the case with situational ethics, in which decisions about ethical choices are made on the basis of intuition and are entirely relative to the circumstances in which they arise. Such an extremely relativistic stance would have as little benefit for the patient or physician as would a dogmatically absolutist one. Fortunately, the incorporation of narrative literature into the study of ethics, while serving as a corrective to the latter stance, need not lead to the former. But it can give us something that is lacking in the traditional philosophical study of ethics—namely, a deeper understanding of human nature that can serve as a foundation for ethical reasoning and allow greater flexibility in the application of moral principles.

One of the greatest challenges facing medical students today, apart from absorbing volumes of technical information and learning habits of scientific thought, is that of remaining empathetic to the needs of patients in the face of all this rigorous training. Requiring students to immerse themselves completely in medical coursework risks disconnecting them from the personal and ethical aspects of doctoring, and such strictly scientific thinking is insufficient for grappling with modern ethical dilemmas. For these reasons, aspiring physicians need to develop new ways of thinking about and interacting with patients. Training in ethics that takes narrative literature as its primary subject is one method of accomplishing this.

The passage starts off with an evaluative claim: current medical education disconnects future doctors from patients. Doctors are losing touch on a personal and ethical level.

The author then makes a recommendation to remedy the situation: incorporate narrative literature into ethics training.

Although training in ethics is currently provided by medical schools, this training relies heavily on an abstract, philosophical view of ethics. Although the conceptual clarity provided by a traditional ethics course can be valuable, theorizing about ethics contributes little to the understanding of everyday human experience or to preparing medical students for the multifarious ethical dilemmas they will face as physicians. A true foundation in ethics must be predicated on an understanding of human behavior that reflects a wide array of relationships and readily adapts to various perspectives, for this is what is required to develop empathy. Ethics courses drawing on narrative literature can better help students prepare for ethical dilemmas precisely because such literature attaches its readers so forcefully to the concrete and varied world of human events.

Again, in the author's evaluation of traditional training, theoretical training in ethics falls short because it's not grounded in reality. The author recommends narrative literature as an alternative because it's more connected to the "world of human events."

The act of reading narrative literature is uniquely suited to the development of what might be called flexible ethical thinking. To grasp the development of characters, to tangle with heightening moral crises, and to engage oneself with the story not as one's own but nevertheless as something recognizable and worthy of attention, readers must use their moral imagination. Giving oneself over to the ethical conflicts in a story requires the abandonment of strictly absolute, inviolate sets of moral principles. Reading literature also demands that the reader adopt another person's point of view—that of the narrator or a character in a story—and thus requires the ability to depart from one's personal ethical stance and examine moral issues from new perspectives.

This paragraph is evaluative. The author lists all the benefits of reading narrative literature: it forces you to use your moral imagination, adopt flexible ethical thinking, and put yourself in another's shoes.

It does not follow that readers, including medical professionals, must relinquish all moral principles, as is the case with situational ethics, in which decisions about ethical choices are made on the basis of intuition and are entirely relative to the circumstances in which they arise. Such an extremely relativistic stance would have as little benefit for the patient or physician as would a dogmatically absolutist one. Fortunately, the incorporation of narrative literature into the study of ethics, while serving as a corrective to the latter stance, need not lead to the former. But it can give us something that is lacking in the traditional philosophical study of ethics—namely, a deeper understanding of human nature that can serve as a foundation for ethical reasoning and allow greater flexibility in the application of moral principles.

In the last paragraph, the author starts with an evaluative defense of narrative literature, saying that it does not lead to absolute moral relativism. The passage concludes with a reiteration of the author's central recommendation, namely that narrative literature should be incorporated into training in medical ethics for the benefits listed above.

PT57 Passage 2

An effort should be made to dispel the misunderstandings that still prevent the much-needed synthesis and mutual supplementation of science and the humanities. This reconciliation should not be too difficult once it is recognized that the separation is primarily the result of a basic misunderstanding of the philosophical foundations of both science and the humanities.

Some humanists still identify science with an absurd mechanistic reductionism. There are many who feel that the scientist is interested in nothing more than "bodies in motion," in the strictly mathematical, physical, and chemical laws that govern the material world. This is the caricature of science drawn by representatives of the humanities who are ignorant of the nature of modern science and also of the scientific outlook in philosophy. For example, it is claimed that science either ignores or explains away the most essential human values. Those who believe this also assert that there are aspects of the human mind, manifest especially in the domains of morality, religion, and the arts, that contain an irreducible spiritual element and for that reason can never be adequately explained by science.

Some scientists, on the other hand, claim that the humanist is interested in nothing more than emotion and sentiment, exhibiting the vagrant fancies of an undisciplined mind. To such men and women the humanities are useless because they serve no immediate and technological function for the practical survival of human society in the material world. Such pragmatists believe that the areas of morality, religion, and the arts should have only a secondary importance in people's lives.

Thus there are misconceptions among humanists and scientists alike that are in need of correction. This correction leads to a much more acceptable position that could be called "scientific humanism," attempting as it does to combine the common elements of both disciplines. Both science and the humanities attempt to describe and explain. It is true that they begin their descriptions and explanations at widely separated points, but the objectives remain the same: a clearer understanding of people and their world. In achieving this understanding, science in fact does not depend exclusively on measurable data, and the humanities in fact profit from attempts at controlled evaluation. Scientific humanism can combine the scientific attitude with an active interest in the whole scale of human values. If uninformed persons insist on viewing science as only materialistic and the humanities as only idealistic, a fruitful collaboration of both fields is unlikely. The combination of science and the humanities is, however, possible, even probable, if we begin by noting their common objectives, rather than seeing only their different means.

An effort should be made to dispel the misunderstandings that still prevent the much-needed synthesis and mutual supplementation of science and the humanities. This reconciliation should not be too difficult once it is recognized that the separation is primarily the result of a basic misunderstanding of the philosophical foundations of both science and the humanities.

So the author is calling for a synthesis of the science and humanities. I'm not too sure what that means; maybe both should be taught together in a multidisciplinary setting? Perhaps we should have science majors learn the classics, and have art majors learn some STEM subjects as well? We shall see. But this is definitely a recommendation.

Some humanists still identify science with an absurd mechanistic reductionism. There are many who feel that the scientist is interested in nothing more than "bodies in motion," in the strictly mathematical, physical, and chemical laws that govern the material world. This is the caricature of science drawn by representatives of the humanities who are ignorant of the nature of modern science and also of the scientific outlook in philosophy. For example, it is claimed that science either ignores or explains away the most essential human values. Those who believe this also assert that there are aspects of the human mind, manifest especially in the domains of morality, religion, and the arts, that contain an irreducible spiritual element and for that reason can never be adequately explained by science.

The author introduces a humanist view toward science, a view that the author doesn't agree with, as they feel it is too simplified.

Some scientists, on the other hand, claim that the humanist is interested in nothing more than emotion and sentiment, exhibiting the vagrant fancies of an undisciplined mind. To such men and women the humanities are useless because they serve no immediate and technological function for the practical survival of human society in the material world. Such pragmatists believe that the areas of morality, religion, and the arts should have only a secondary importance in people's lives.

Here, the author introduces what some scientists think of the humanities. In these two paragraphs, the author compares what could be considered biased views from opposite camps. Some humanists take an oversimplified view of science, while some scientists think the humanities are useless.

Thus there are misconceptions among humanists and scientists alike that are in need of correction. This correction leads to a much more acceptable position that could be called "scientific humanism," attempting as it does to combine the common elements of both disciplines. Both science and the humanities attempt to describe and explain. It is true that they begin their descriptions and explanations at widely separated points, but the objectives remain the same: a clearer understanding of people and their world. In achieving this understanding, science in fact does not depend exclusively on measurable data, and the humanities in fact profit from attempts at controlled evaluation. Scientific humanism can combine the scientific attitude with an active interest in the whole scale of human values. If uninformed persons insist on viewing science as only materialistic and the humanities as only idealistic, a fruitful collaboration of both fields is unlikely. The combination of science and the humanities is, however, possible, even probable, if we begin by noting their common objectives, rather than seeing only their different means.

After pointing out the shortcomings of both sides, the author continues with their comparison of the science and humanities. Noting their similarities and similar objectives, the author then goes on to reiterate the call to combine the two, emphasizing their similarities rather than differences.

Understanding of this passage can be improved if we remember to note the recommendation the author makes, the comparison between the sciences and humanities, as well as the author's evaluation of the scientists and humanists who couldn't see the bigger picture. As you read through a passage, constantly ask yourself if the author is making a comparison, explaining something, evaluating a claim, or suggesting a recommendation. This will help you immensely on your path to developing the habit of active reading.

Summary

- Engaging with the passage as you read is the first step to improving performance in the RC section. If blindly wandering through the information is something you tend to do, it must be fixed at all costs!

- A key question to ask yourself from the beginning is why the author is **writing this passage?** Every passage was written with a goal in mind. As you read the passage, the answer to this question should become clear.

- Use the **Hypothesis-Validation Framework** to become more involved in the reading process. As you read, try to come up with potential answers to the passage's purpose, or what the author will say next. Use subsequent information to confirm or modify your hypothesis. This process is beneficial in the most difficult readings, and we will look at this framework in more detail near the end of the book.

- Also, whenever new concepts appear in the passage, try to connect them to ideas we have already seen. **Conceptual link-backs** will help us build on what we have read, make sense of the passage's overall message, and prevent us from forgetting what we have just read.

- Another way to force yourself to engage with the passage is to try to decipher what move the author is making throughout the passage. We use CEER to constantly remind ourselves what the author is doing as we are reading.

  - Is the author making a **comparison**? If so, between what? Why is the author making this comparison?

  - Is the author **explaining** a concept or theory? Can the author's explanation be simplified so I can better grasp what they are trying to express?

  - Is the author making an **evaluative** claim? What is the author's opinion? Are they for or against it, and why?

  - Is the author making a **recommendation**? Or is their stance more neutral?

Practice these habits as you read in the subsequent exercises from this book and on your own. Eventually, the process should come more naturally.

Next, we will look at ways to structurally reorganize the paragraphs/passage as we read.

An Excerpt from LR Perfection: STRUCTURE

An Excerpt from LR Perfection: STRUCTURE

What is an Argument? What is a Conclusion?

Before we dive into Find the Conclusion/Main Point Questions, it is important to remember that behind every conclusion, there is an argument. The word "argument" often appears on the LSAT; too often, we don't think too much about it, but it's a word not to be taken lightly.

So what is an argument?

An argument is an author's viewpoint, opinion, or decision supported by additional premises and evidence.

An argument is not simply a statement of fact or opinion without any support.

> An argument will always contain a premise, main conclusion, and maybe an intermediate conclusion.

Elements of a Logical Reasoning Stimulus

So now that we have taken a closer look at how facts, opinions, decisions, principles and generalizations can all make up an LR argument, let's look at how arguments are structured in the LR stimulus.

At the core of most LR stimuli will be an argument (I would say > 80% of all LR stimuli contain an argument). An argument will consist of premises and a conclusion, and if that's the only information presented in a stimulus, our job would be so much easier.

But instead, most LR stimuli will also contain many peripheral elements.

When reading a LR stimulus, our job is to *separate* the **core information** (premise, intermediate conclusion, and main conclusion) from the **peripheral information** (background information, opposing viewpoints, and concessions).

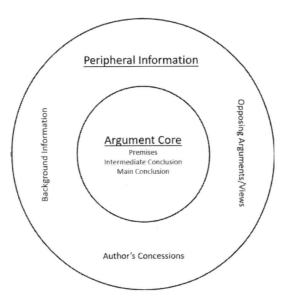

Let's look at each of these elements in detail:

The Argument Core:

Main Conclusion:

Hands down the most important part of any LR stimulus. *It is the point the author is trying to get across.* The conclusion is supported by premises and sometimes the intermediate conclusion. Every time we approach a question that is NOT a Must be True, Most Strongly Supported, Explain a Result, and Agree/Disagree questions, I'm always sifting through the stimulus and asking myself, what is the author's conclusion?

Premise:

The premise *directly* supports the conclusion, the information presented in the premise/premises should *make the conclusion more believable.* An LR stimulus can contain a single premise or multiple premises.

Premises also independently support the conclusion; it's different from the intermediate conclusion. *Many students confuse a multi-premise argument with one that has both premises and an intermediate conclusion.* We will now look at this.

Intermediate Conclusion:

The intermediate conclusion is a statement that is supported by the premise/premises, which in turn, supports the conclusion. It is a part of a chain of reasoning which starts with the premise and ends with the main conclusion.

Let's look at a few different examples and clear up any confusion:

Electric vehicles are so much more enjoyable to drive than traditional cars, more and more people will buy electric cars in the future.

Here we have a simple premise-conclusion format argument. *EVs being more enjoyable to drive* is a premise being used to support the conclusion that *EV sales will grow in the future.*

Now let's mix it up a little:

Electric vehicles are so much more enjoyable to drive than traditional cars. The price of gas is going through the roof. More and more people will buy electric cars in the future.

Here the argument consists of three statements, with two *independent* premises and a main conclusion. Note that each of the two premises independently supports the conclusion. There isn't really any logical connection between statements 1 and 2.

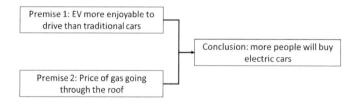

While in the above example, Premise 1 and Premise 2 are independent supporting statements for the conclusion, the LR stimulus has another trick up its sleeve, the intermediate conclusion:

Look at the following example:

The price of gas is going through the roof, more and more people will buy electric cars, the internal combustion engine car is doomed.

We have borrowed Premise 2 and the Conclusion from the previous example and added a new piece of information to the argument.

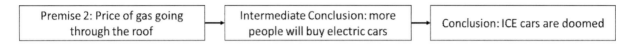

Here, we have taken the logic chain a step further and come up with the main conclusion of *internal combustion engine cars being doomed.* How is this conclusion supported? By the statement *more people will buy electric cars.*

But wait, wasn't this statement the conclusion itself in the previous example? If it is now used to support another conclusion, doesn't this make it a premise as well?

Absolutely.

> The **intermediate conclusion** serves a *dual function* in an argument: it is a **premise** used to support the main conclusion, while simultaneously being a **conclusion** that is supported by another premise.

And that is how we distinguish an intermediate conclusion from a regular premise or main conclusion. We ask ourselves; *does it sit in the middle of an argument's logic chain in such a way that it is both a premise AND a conclusion?* Does a piece of information support it, and is in turn used to support another piece of information?

Let's try a final variation of the previous example and see if you can identify the function of each statement:

Electric vehicles are so much more enjoyable to drive than traditional cars. The price of gas is going through the roof. More and more people will buy electric cars in the future. Governments across the world are increasingly restricting the sale of internal combustion engine cars, the ICE car is doomed.

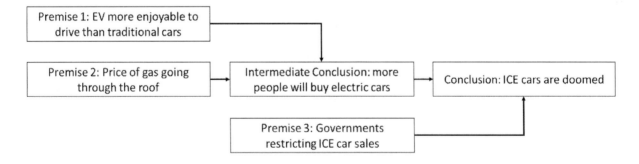

Here, we have a third premise, *governments restricting ICE car sales,* being used to support the main conclusion. It is an independent piece of information that supports only the main conclusion, and as a result, it is simply another premise.

So in summary, *the core of any LR stimulus is its argument.* Three components of any argument are its premises, intermediate conclusion, and main conclusion. When we are reading through any Find the Conclusion Questions, we are essentially identifying the author's argument, figuring out which statement is the premise, which is the intermediate conclusion, and which is the main conclusion.

Peripheral Information Found in a Stimulus (Not Part of the Argument!):

Outside of the argument core, we must be aware of another three types of statements. They are opposing viewpoints, concessions, and background information.

Opposing Viewpoints:

Often, the LR stimulus is structured so that the author is responding to another person's claim, which may or may not be explicitly stated. Sometimes the author will agree with the other person's view or claim, but more frequently, they will disagree. Let's look at two quick examples:

William: The law school admissions process should take a more holistic approach and place less weight on standardized tests.

Harry: I disagree. Standardized testing is the only way to ensure that candidates meet a high standard for facing the rigorous challenges of law school.

Here, Harry disagrees with William's viewpoint, and provides evidence to support his own perspective. Harry would conclude that *Law schools should NOT place less weight on standardized tests;* his premise is that standardized tests are the only way to ensure students are ready for law school. William's view, in this example, would be the OPPOSING VIEWPOINT, and does not constitute a core part of the argument. (Note also that William only provides an opinion, and does not provide support for it, therefore William's statement is not an argument in itself.)

Sometimes the opposing viewpoint is not explicitly stated, as seen in the example below:

Harry: Contrary to what many people believe, standardized testing should form an integral part of the law school admissions process. Standardized testing is an important indicator of whether a student is ready to face the rigorous challenges of law school.

Here, the opposing viewpoint can be inferred from Harry's argument, but it is not a core part of it.

Concession:

In an LR stimulus, the author will sometimes concede a point before defending their conclusion/main point. In a concession, the author's voice is discernible, so sometimes students will mistake a concession for the argument's conclusion. So remember that the author will often make a concession before bringing out their main point.

Here is an example of what concessions look like:

While it may be true that pulling an all-nighter writing a paper will get you a pass with the least amount of time spent, the best way to write a paper for a class would be to start early, conduct meticulous research, and revise iterative drafts until the final version is completed.

In short, a concession is where the author seemingly takes a step back and acknowledges that the opposing view has some valid points.

But granting the opponent a valid point is not the same as admitting defeat. Quite the opposite: a concession is ALWAYS followed by the author's actual viewpoint. So every time we sense that the author is conceding a point, be prepared for the author's actual main point.

An Excerpt from LR Perfection: STRUCTURE

Background Information:

Lastly, background information is any piece of information that appears in the stimulus to explain the importance, relevancy, or setting of the issue discussed in the argument. It could be used to define key terms that appear in the argument or provide us with a better understanding of what is being argued. Background information usually appears as statements of fact and are always peripheral to the author's argument.

When we read through the stimulus of an LR question, a habit we must foster and turn into second nature is the ability to **categorize**. We must constantly be asking ourselves, what is the nature of the sentence I just read, and what's its job in the author's argument? There are six types of statements; three are crucial to the argument, and three are not. Which of them am I looking at now?

***

Finally, let's wrap up the theoretical section with the step-by-step construction of a detailed example.

Step 1: Let's start with the conclusion, the very heart and soul of any argument, and by extension, any LR question:

The Industrial Revolution led to the turmoil of World War II.

Step 2: Hmmm…that seems like a somewhat far-fetched idea, can we add in a premise to support our claim?

The Industrial Revolution led to the turmoil of World War II. As gaps in income and living standards widened due to industrialization, many people flocked to demagogues who promised a better life through extreme means.

Step 3: There seems to be a gap between our premise and conclusion, how does popular support for demagogues lead to war? I think an intermediate conclusion is needed:

The Industrial Revolution led to the turmoil of World War II. As gaps in income and living standards widened due to industrialization, many people flocked to demagogues who promised a better life through extreme means. As a result, wealth disparity caused people to embrace ideologies that espoused war and persecution of minorities as a means of solving their problems.

Note here that the intermediate conclusion is the last sentence of the paragraph. It's also preceded by the words "as a result." **The LSAT uses this common tactic to throw test-takers off balance**. Too often, undiscerning test takers would assume this to be the main conclusion, when it is in fact only the intermediate conclusion. More on this later.

Steps 1-3 conclude the argument phase of the stimulus. This is the core of any LR stimulus and what we should focus on when tackling the majority of LR questions.

Step 4: Let's add in some background information to explain the topic at hand better:

The Industrial Revolution, which spread from Britain across Europe during the nineteenth century, was a period of rapid change. The Industrial Revolution led to the turmoil of World War II. As gaps in income and living standards widened due to industrialization, many people flocked to demagogues who promised a better life through extreme means. As a result, wealth disparity caused people to embrace ideologies that espoused war and persecution of minorities as a means of solving their problems.

Step 5: Let's add in an opposing viewpoint to the mix:

The Industrial Revolution, which spread from Britain across Europe during the nineteenth century, was a period of rapid change. <u>Some historians have argued that the Industrial Revolution provided only benefits to humanity, bringing the world into modernity.</u> The Industrial Revolution led to the turmoil of World War II. As gaps in income and living standards widened due to industrialization, many people flocked to demagogues who promised a better life through extreme means. As a result, wealth disparity caused people to embrace ideologies that espoused war and persecution of minorities as a means of solving their problems.

Step 6: Finally, let's include a concession from the author:

The Industrial Revolution, which spread from Britain across Europe during the nineteenth century, was a period of rapid change. Some historians have argued that the Industrial Revolution provided only benefits to humanity, bringing the world into modernity. <u>Although it's true that the rapid industrialization of Europe in the nineteenth century saw the introduction of many new technologies and improvements to life</u>, it also indirectly led to the turmoil of World War II in the twentieth century. As gaps in income and living standards widened due to industrialization, many people flocked to demagogues who promised a better life through extreme means. As a result, wealth disparity caused people to embrace ideologies that espoused war and persecution of minorities as a means of solving their problems.

There you have it! The entire stimulus is complete with the argument (premise, intermediate conclusion, conclusion); and the peripheral information (background information, opposing viewpoint, concession). Read it over one more time and try to categorize every statement as it comes up:

The Industrial Revolution, which spread from Britain across Europe during the nineteenth century, was a period of rapid change. Some historians have argued that the Industrial Revolution provided only benefits to humanity, bringing the world into modernity. Although it's true that the rapid industrialization of Europe in the nineteenth century saw the introduction of many new technologies and improvements to life, it also indirectly led to the turmoil of World War II in the twentieth century. As gaps in income and living standards widened due to industrialization, many people flocked to demagogues who promised a better life through extreme means. As a result, wealth disparity caused people to embrace ideologies that espoused war and persecution of minorities as a means of solving their problems.

***

That's it for the information you'll need to analyze a passage/paragraph's structure. Of course, you won't be able to examine each paragraph of an RC passage as carefully as you would an LR stimulus. But as you read through a paragraph an even an entire passage, try to pretend that it's an LR stimulus, and see if you can spot the conclusion and premises within it.

Chapter 2: Paragraph Structure

In the previous chapter, we looked at the elements making up an LR argument. The core information will consist of premises, a main conclusion, and possibly an intermediate conclusion. The peripheral information will be made up of background information, opposing viewpoints, and concessions.

When reading through individual paragraphs in an RC passage, **we can sometimes try to think of each paragraph as an individual, stand alone LR argument**. This can help us decipher the structure of a passage's individual paragraphs and force us to come to a deeper understanding of the reading. See if each paragraph contains a mini-argument of its own, and if so, what are its premises and conclusions. We should also be on the lookout for peripheral statements as well: are there background information, opposing viewpoints, and concessions in a paragraph too?

Not all paragraphs will contain an argument; some may consist purely of background or factual information. But trying to categorize what we are reading is an essential habit to have while reading for RC, just like it was for LR.

When the paragraph **does not contain an argument**, we won't be able to find premises and a conclusion. In that case, we should still try to break down the paragraph by sub-points or sections. If there are different ideas or views, we can list them separately. If the paragraph talks about a historical event's different phases, we can divide it chronologically. If the paragraph talks about the three benefits of a recommended action, outline those three benefits…you get the idea.

Let's look at a few dense paragraphs from real RC passages and try to clarify their internal structure.

Read the following paragraph, try to break it down into sections for easier understanding.

Various theoretical approaches have been developed to account for both the evidence gleaned from samples of Moon rock collected during lunar explorations and the size and distribution of craters on the Moon. Since the sizes of LHB craters suggest they were formed by large bodies, some astronomers believe that the LHB was linked to the disintegration of an asteroid or comet orbiting the Sun. In this view, a large body broke apart and peppered the inner solar system with debris. Other scientists disagree and believe that the label "LHB" is in itself a misnomer. These researchers claim that a cataclysm is not necessary to explain the LHB evidence. They claim that the Moon's evidence merely provides a view of the period concluding billions of years of a continuous, declining heavy bombardment throughout the inner solar system. According to them, the impacts from the latter part of the bombardment were so intense that they obliterated evidence of earlier impacts. A third group contends that the Moon's evidence supports the view that the LHB was a sharply defined cataclysmic cratering period, but these scientists believe that because of its relatively brief duration, this cataclysm did not extend throughout the inner solar system. They hold that the LHB involved only the disintegration of a body within the Earth- Moon system, because the debris from such an event would have been swept up relatively quickly.

We deliberately chose a paragraph from the middle of a passage, so you won't have a clear idea of the topic being discussed. But that shouldn't stop us:

The passage discusses/compares three different theories that attempt to explain some geological features of the moon, possibly craters.

The <u>first</u> theory believes that the craters are caused by a large asteroid or comet which broke up and struck the inner solar system.

What is the support offered for the first theory? We are told that the craters seemed to have been created by large bodies.

The <u>second</u> theory believes the craters to have been formed over a long period of time. Newer strikes erased evidence of earlier strikes.

Is there any evidence offered for the second theory here? Not really.

Finally, the <u>third</u> theory is closer to the first theory, it posits that the bombardment was relatively short, but instead of hitting the inner solar system, it struck only the Earth and Moon.

So we have three separate theories, all mentioned in a single paragraph; let's keep on going.

New support for the hypothesis that a late bombardment extended throughout the inner solar system has been found in evidence from the textural features and chemical makeup of a meteorite that has been found on Earth. It seems to be a rare example of a Mars rock that made its way to Earth after being knocked from the surface of Mars. The rock has recently been experimentally dated at about four billion years old, which means that, if the rock is indeed from Mars, it was knocked from the planet at about the same time that the Moon was experiencing the LHB. This tiny piece of evidence suggests that at least two planetary systems in the inner solar system experienced bombardment at the same time. However, to determine the pervasiveness of the LHB, scientists will need to locate many more such rocks and perhaps obtain surface samples from other planets in the inner solar system.

So a piece of rock was knocked from Mars and found on Earth. We know this is potential support for one of the theories mentioned in the previous paragraph. But which one?

We know it's not theory 3, because that theory thinks the bombardment happened only to the Earth and Moon.

Does it support theory 2? I don't think so, because theory 2 was talking about the moon getting hit over a long period of time. How does a rock from Mars help this theory?

All that's left is theory 1. Theory 1 thinks the inner solar system was struck extensively, and Mars is a planet in the inner solar system.

Is this conclusive proof? No. In fact, the author even says that we need more evidence. The author didn't side with any of the theories, but at least they are receptive to theory 1.

Let's look at the passage in its entirety, and note how much easier comprehension becomes once you've grasped the structure of each individual paragraph:

PT51 Passage 2

A vigorous debate in astronomy centers on an epoch in planetary history that was first identified by analysis of rock samples obtained in lunar missions. Scientists discovered that the major craters on the Moon were created by a vigorous bombardment of debris approximately four billion years ago—the so-called late heavy bombardment (LHB). Projectiles from this bombardment that affected the Moon should also have struck Earth, a likelihood with profound consequences for the history of Earth since, until the LHB ended, life could not have survived here.

Various theoretical approaches have been developed to account for both the evidence gleaned from samples of Moon rock collected during lunar explorations and the size and distribution of craters on the Moon. Since the sizes of LHB craters suggest they were formed by large bodies, some astronomers believe that the LHB was linked to the disintegration of an asteroid or comet orbiting the Sun. In this view, a large body broke apart and peppered the inner solar system with debris. Other scientists disagree and believe that the label "LHB" is in itself a misnomer. These researchers claim that a cataclysm is not necessary to explain the LHB evidence. They claim that the Moon's evidence merely provides a view of the period concluding billions of years of a continuous, declining heavy bombardment throughout the inner solar system. According to them, the impacts from the latter part of the bombardment were so intense that they obliterated evidence of earlier impacts. A third group contends that the Moon's evidence supports the view that the LHB was a sharply defined cataclysmic cratering period, but these scientists believe that because of its relatively brief duration, this cataclysm did not extend throughout the inner solar system. They hold that the LHB involved only the disintegration of a body within the Earth-Moon system, because the debris from such an event would have been swept up relatively quickly.

New support for the hypothesis that a late bombardment extended throughout the inner solar system has been found in evidence from the textural features and chemical makeup of a meteorite that has been found on Earth. It seems to be a rare example of a Mars rock that made its way to Earth after being knocked from the surface of Mars. The rock has recently been experimentally dated at about four billion years old, which means that, if the rock is indeed from Mars, it was knocked from the planet at about the same time that the Moon was experiencing the LHB. This tiny piece of evidence suggests that at least two planetary systems in the inner solar system experienced bombardment at the same time. However, to determine the pervasiveness of the LHB, scientists will need to locate many more such rocks and perhaps obtain surface samples from other planets in the inner solar system.

Background Info

Bombardment of the moon four billion years ago created many craters

---

3 Hypothesis:

1. happened throughout solar system, late period only, when asteroid or comet disintegrated

2. continuous bombardment of the moon, not limited to four billion years ago

3. late period only, but only occurred to moon and earth

Found Rock from Mars

Can be tentative support for Theory 1

Need for additional evidence to know for sure

Chapter 2: Paragraph Structure   57

By breaking down each paragraph structurally, the passage becomes much easier to understand and remember. Let's try that with a few more paragraphs/passages.

Yet the academic study of jurisprudence has seldom treated common law as a constantly evolving phenomenon rooted in history; those interpretive theories that do acknowledge the antiquity of common law ignore the practical contemporary significance of its historical forms. The reasons for this omission are partly theoretical and partly political. In theoretical terms, modern jurisprudence has consistently treated law as a unified system of rules that can be studied at any given moment in time as a logical whole. The notion of jurisprudence as a system of norms or principles deemphasizes history in favor of the coherence of a system. In this view, the past of the system is conceived as no more than the continuous succession of its states of presence. In political terms, believing in the logic of law is a necessary part of believing in its fairness; even if history shows the legal tradition to be far from unitary and seldom logical, the prestige of the legal institution requires that jurisprudence treat the tradition as if it were, in essence, the application of known rules to objectively determined facts. To suggest otherwise would be dispiriting for the student and demoralizing for the public.

In this paragraph, we are told that academic studies of law tend to ignore the influences of history. We are then given two reasons for this, one theoretical and one political.

Theoretically, the law is studied as a coherent whole, as a logical and unified system of rules. Historical influences that might not fit in with the logic behind a legal system might be conveniently ignored. Politically, for us to believe in the fairness of the law, we must believe it to be something logical. If some legal traditions arose from historical contingencies, that makes them fallible, and we may lose our respect for the law.

So, in this relatively dense and abstract paragraph, the author highlights a phenomenon and gives us two explanations. That's how we should break down this paragraph structurally.

If we were taking notes for this paragraph, then they could potentially look something like this:

Why is history ignored in the study of law?

Theoretical: historical influences don't fit in with our unified/logical vision of the law

Political: If we emphasize historical influences, people might realize that the law isn't logical, unified, and fair

Let's look at another passage now. This time, try to break down individual paragraphs structurally for better understanding.

PT33 Passage 3

Experts anticipate that global atmospheric concentrations of carbon dioxide (CO_2) will have doubled by the end of the twenty-first century. It is known that CO_2 can contribute to global warming by trapping solar energy that is being reradiated as heat from the Earth's surface. However, some research has suggested that elevated CO_2 levels could enhance the photosynthetic rates of plants, resulting in a lush world of agricultural abundance, and that this CO_2 fertilization effect might eventually decrease the rate of global warming. The increased vegetation in such an environment could be counted on to draw more CO_2 from the atmosphere. The level of CO_2 would thus increase at a lower rate than many experts have predicted.

However, while a number of recent studies confirm that plant growth would be generally enhanced in an atmosphere rich in CO_2, they also suggest that increased CO_2 would differentially increase the growth rate of different species of plants, which could eventually result in decreased agricultural yields. Certain important crops such as corn and sugarcane that currently have higher photosynthetic efficiencies than other plants may lose that edge in an atmosphere rich in CO_2. Patterson and Flint have shown that these important crops may experience yield reductions because of the increased performance of certain weeds. Such differences in growth rates between plant species could also alter ecosystem stability. Studies have shown that within rangeland regions, for example, a weedy grass grows much better with plentiful CO_2 than do three other grasses. Because this weedy grass predisposes land to burning, its potential increase may lead to greater numbers of and more severe wildfires in future rangeland communities.

It is clear that the CO_2 fertilization effect does not guarantee the lush world of agricultural abundance that once seemed likely, but what about the potential for the increased uptake of CO_2 to decrease the rate of global warming? Some studies suggest that the changes accompanying global warming will not improve the ability of terrestrial ecosystems to absorb CO_2. Billings' simulation of global warming conditions in wet tundra grasslands showed that the level of CO_2 actually increased. Plant growth did increase under these conditions because of warmer temperatures and increased CO_2 levels. But as the permafrost melted, more peat (accumulated dead plant material) began to decompose. This process in turn liberated more CO_2 to the atmosphere. Billings estimated that if summer temperatures rose four degrees Celsius, the tundra would liberate 50 percent more CO_2 than it does currently. In a warmer world, increased plant growth, which could absorb CO_2 from the atmosphere, would not compensate for this rapid increase in decomposition rates. This observation is particularly important because high-latitude habitats such as the tundra are expected to experience the greatest temperature increase.

Experts anticipate that global atmospheric concentrations of carbon dioxide (CO_2) will have doubled by the end of the twenty-first century. It is known that CO_2 can contribute to global warming by trapping solar energy that is being reradiated as heat from the Earth's surface. <u>However</u>, some research has suggested that elevated CO_2 levels could enhance the photosynthetic rates of plants, resulting in a lush world of agricultural abundance, and that this CO_2 fertilization effect might eventually decrease the rate of global warming. The increased vegetation in such an environment could be counted on to draw more CO_2 from the atmosphere. The level of CO_2 would thus increase at a lower rate than many experts have predicted.

The paragraph starts with some background information. Carbon Dioxide causes global warming.

However, some seem to think that increased CO_2 leads to more plants, which may actually slow down CO_2 increase and global warming.

However, while a number of recent studies confirm that plant growth would be generally enhanced in an atmosphere rich in CO_2, they also suggest that increased CO_2 would <u>differentially increase the growth rate of different species of plants</u>, which could eventually result in <u>decreased agricultural yields</u>. Certain important crops such as corn and sugarcane that currently have higher photosynthetic efficiencies than other plants may lose that edge in an atmosphere rich in CO_2. Patterson and Flint have shown that these <u>important crops may experience yield reductions</u> because of the <u>increased performance of certain weeds</u>. Such differences in growth rates between plant species could also <u>alter ecosystem stability</u>. Studies have shown that within rangeland regions, for example, a weedy grass grows much better with plentiful CO_2 than do three other grasses. Because this weedy grass predisposes land to burning, its potential increase <u>may lead to greater numbers of and more severe wildfires</u> in future rangeland communities.

The second paragraph tells us some of the more detailed implications of increased CO_2.

Increased CO_2 may lead to more weeds and less crop plants, alter ecosystem stability, and potentially lead to more wildfires.

It is clear that the CO_2 fertilization effect does not guarantee the lush world of agricultural abundance that once seemed likely, but what about the potential for the increased uptake of CO_2 to <u>decrease the rate of global warming?</u> Some studies suggest that the changes accompanying global warming will not improve the ability of terrestrial ecosystems to absorb CO_2. Billings' simulation of global warming conditions in wet tundra grasslands showed that the level of <u>CO_2 actually increased</u>. Plant growth did increase under these conditions because of warmer temperatures and increased CO_2 levels. But as the permafrost melted, more <u>peat</u> (accumulated dead plant material) began to decompose. This process in turn <u>liberated more CO_2 to the atmosphere</u>. Billings estimated that if summer temperatures rose four degrees Celsius, the tundra would liberate 50 percent more CO_2 than it does currently. In a warmer world, increased plant growth, which could absorb CO_2 from the atmosphere, <u>would not compensate for this rapid increase in decomposition rates</u>. This observation is particularly important because high-latitude habitats such as the tundra are expected to experience the greatest temperature increase.

So at the end of the day, the increase in plants didn't lead to a decrease in CO_2; moreover, peat decomposition due to global warming actually released even more CO_2.

Each subsequent paragraph is a direct response to the hypothesis stated in the first paragraph. In paragraph 2, the author argues against the idea that more CO_2 means more plants. Evidence is provided that even though more plants flourish, many are weeds, which has disastrous consequences.

In paragraph 3, the author argues against another idea presented in the first paragraph. Even though CO_2 may lead to more plants, global warming is not necessarily slowed down due to faster absorption of CO_2. Because as the climate warms, even more CO_2 is released, and that would offset whatever CO_2 absorbed by the plants.

Experts anticipate that global atmospheric concentrations of carbon dioxide (CO_2) will have doubled by the end of the twenty-first century. It is known that CO_2 can contribute to global warming by trapping solar energy that is being reradiated as heat from the Earth's surface. However, some research has suggested that elevated CO_2 levels could enhance the photosynthetic rates of plants, resulting in a lush world of agricultural abundance, and that this CO_2 fertilization effect might eventually decrease the rate of global warming. The increased vegetation in such an environment could be counted on to draw more CO_2 from the atmosphere. The level of CO_2 would thus increase at a lower rate than many experts have predicted.

> We know
>
> CO_2 Trap Heat $\Rightarrow$ Global Warming
>
> But maybe
>
> $CO_2 \Rightarrow$ More Plants $\Rightarrow$ Decreased $CO_2 \Rightarrow$ Less Global Warming?

However, while a number of recent studies confirm that plant growth would be generally enhanced in an atmosphere rich in CO_2, they also suggest that increased CO_2 would differentially increase the growth rate of different species of plants, which could eventually result in decreased agricultural yields. Certain important crops such as corn and sugarcane that currently have higher photosynthetic efficiencies than other plants may lose that edge in an atmosphere rich in CO_2. Patterson and Flint have shown that these important crops may experience yield reductions because of the increased performance of certain weeds. Such differences in growth rates between plant species could also alter ecosystem stability. Studies have shown that within rangeland regions, for example, a weedy grass grows much better with plentiful CO_2 than do three other grasses. Because this weedy grass predisposes land to burning, its potential increase may lead to greater numbers of and more severe wildfires in future rangeland communities.

> CO_2 does lead to more plants, but weeds benefit more than nutritious plants
>
> More weeds can lead to more wild fires

It is clear that the CO_2 fertilization effect does not guarantee the lush world of agricultural abundance that once seemed likely, but what about the potential for the increased uptake of CO_2 to decrease the rate of global warming? Some studies suggest that the changes accompanying global warming will not improve the ability of terrestrial ecosystems to absorb CO_2. Billings' simulation of global warming conditions in wet tundra grasslands showed that the level of CO_2 actually increased. Plant growth did increase under these conditions because of warmer temperatures and increased CO_2 levels. But as the permafrost melted, more peat (accumulated dead plant material) began to decompose. This process in turn liberated more CO_2 to the atmosphere. Billings estimated that if summer temperatures rose four degrees Celsius, the tundra would liberate 50 percent more CO_2 than it does currently. In a warmer world, increased plant growth, which could absorb CO_2 from the atmosphere, would not compensate for this rapid increase in decomposition rates. This observation is particularly important because high-latitude habitats such as the tundra are expected to experience the greatest temperature increase.

> More CO_2 does NOT lead to agricultural abundance
>
> Neither does it decrease global warming:
>
> - Plant growth did increase
> - But melting led to more peat decomposition
> - Which led to even more CO_2
>
> Net increase in CO_2 still increased global warming

Take a look at the following paragraph, how would you break it down structurally?

Recent studies have confirmed the ability of leading questions to alter the details of our memories and have led to a better understanding of how this process occurs and, perhaps, of the conditions that make for greater risks that an eyewitness's memories have been tainted by leading questions. These studies suggest that not all details of our experiences become clearly or stably stored in memory—only those to which we give adequate attention. Moreover, experimental evidence indicates that if subtly introduced new data involving remembered events do not actively conflict with our stored memory data, we tend to process such new data similarly whether they correspond to details as we remember them, or to gaps in those details. In the former case, we often retain the new data as a reinforcement of the corresponding aspect of the memory, and in the latter case, we often retain them as a construction to fill the corresponding gap. An eyewitness who is asked, prior to courtroom testimony, "How fast was the car going when it passed the stop sign?" may respond to the query about speed without addressing the question of the stop sign. But the "stop sign" datum has now been introduced, and when later recalled, perhaps during courtroom testimony, it may be processed as belonging to the original memory even if the witness actually saw no stop sign.

This paragraph tells us that leading questions can alter our memories. How does this happen? Three separate points go on to support this assertion.

One, some of our experiences are not clearly stored if we don't pay enough attention to them, leading to gaps in our memory.

Two, if new details are introduced and don't conflict with our existing memories, we can make them a part of our memory and use them to reinforce what we remember.

Three, if the new details introduced don't correspond to what we remember, we can use them to fill in the gaps.

If we were to treat this paragraph as a long, convoluted LR stimulus, the first sentence could be construed as the **conclusion/main point**, while the three points listed could be considered **premises**.

Let's look at one final passage as a whole. Try structurally dividing each paragraph into sections to make it more manageable as you read.

PT43 Passage 4

Faculty researchers, particularly in scientific, engineering, and medical programs, often produce scientific discoveries and invent products or processes that have potential commercial value. Many institutions have invested heavily in the administrative infrastructure to develop and exploit these discoveries, and they expect to prosper both by an increased level of research support and by the royalties from licensing those discoveries having patentable commercial applications. However, although faculty themselves are unlikely to become entrepreneurs, an increasing number of highly valued researchers will be sought and sponsored by research corporations or have consulting contracts with commercial firms. One study of such entrepreneurship concluded that "if universities do not provide the flexibility needed to venture into business, faculty will be tempted to go to those institutions that are responsive to their commercialized desires." There is therefore a need to consider the different intellectual property policies that govern the commercial exploitation of faculty inventions in order to determine which would provide the appropriate level of flexibility.

In a recent study of faculty rights, Patricia Chew has suggested a fourfold classification of institutional policies. A supramaximalist institution stakes out the broadest claim possible, asserting ownership not only of all intellectual property produced by faculty in the course of their employment while using university resources, but also for any inventions or patent rights from faculty activities, even those involving research sponsored by non-university funders. A maximalist institution allows faculty ownership of inventions that do not arise either "in the course of the faculty's employment [or] from the faculty's use of university resources." This approach, although not as all encompassing as that of the supramaximalist university, can affect virtually all of a faculty member's intellectual production. A resource-provider institution asserts a claim to faculty's intellectual product in those cases where "significant use" of university time and facilities is employed. Of course, what constitutes significant use of resources is a matter of institutional judgment.

As Chew notes, in these policies "faculty rights, including the sharing of royalties, are the result of university benevolence and generosity. [However, this] presumption is contrary to the common law, which provides that faculty own their inventions." Others have pointed to this anomaly and, indeed, to the uncertain legal and historical basis upon which the ownership of intellectual property rests. Although these issues remain unsettled, and though universities may be overreaching due to faculty's limited knowledge of their rights, most major institutions behave in the ways that maximize university ownership and profit participation.

But there is a fourth way, one that seems to be free from these particular issues. Faculty-oriented institutions assume that researchers own their own intellectual products and the rights to exploit them commercially, except in the development of public health inventions or if there is previously specified "substantial university involvement." At these institutions industry practice is effectively reversed, with the university benefiting in far fewer circumstances.

Faculty researchers, particularly in scientific, engineering, and medical programs, often produce scientific discoveries and invent products or processes that have potential commercial value. Many institutions have invested heavily in the administrative infrastructure to develop and exploit these discoveries, and they expect to prosper both by an increased level of research support and by the royalties from licensing those discoveries having patentable commercial applications. However, although faculty themselves are unlikely to become entrepreneurs, an increasing number of highly valued researchers will be sought and sponsored by research corporations or have consulting contracts with commercial firms. One study of such entrepreneurship concluded that "if universities do not provide the flexibility needed to venture into business, faculty will be tempted to go to those institutions that are responsive to their commercialized desires." There is therefore a need to consider the different intellectual property policies that govern the commercial exploitation of faculty inventions in order to determine which would provide the appropriate level of flexibility.

> Researchers in universities make discoveries and invent stuff that have commercial value.
>
> Commercial companies will try to lure them away to work for them.
>
> Universities should be sensitive to these needs.
>
> We should examine university intellectual property policies towards faculty research, discoveries, and inventions

In a recent study of faculty rights, Patricia Chew has suggested a **fourfold classification** of institutional policies. A **supramaximalist** institution stakes out the broadest claim possible, asserting ownership not only of all intellectual property produced by faculty in the course of their employment while using university resources, but also for any inventions or patent rights from faculty activities, even those involving research sponsored by non-university funders. A **maximalist** institution allows faculty ownership of inventions that do not arise either "in the course of the faculty's employment [or] from the faculty's use of university resources." This approach, although not as all encompassing as that of the supramaximalist university, can affect virtually all of a faculty member's intellectual production. A **resource-provider** institution asserts a claim to faculty's intellectual product in those cases where "significant use" of university time and facilities is employed. Of course, what constitutes significant use of resources is a matter of institutional judgment.

> Four Types of University Policies:
>
> 1. Supramaximalist: everything belongs to the university, even research funded by outsiders
>
> 2. Maximalist: faculty can keep research results discovered outside of faculty employment and didn't use university resources
>
> Author thinks 2 is still really broad
>
> 3. Resource Provider: if significant resources of the university have been used, then it belongs to the university.

As Chew notes, in these policies "faculty rights, including the sharing of royalties, are the result of university benevolence and generosity. [However, this] presumption is contrary to the common law, which provides that faculty own their inventions." Others have pointed to this anomaly and, indeed, to the uncertain legal and historical basis upon which the ownership of intellectual property rests. Although these issues remain unsettled, and though universities may be overreaching due to faculty's limited knowledge of their rights, most major institutions behave in the ways that maximize university ownership and profit participation.

> 1-3 are all contrary to the law, but they are the most common practices

But there is a **fourth way**, one that seems to be free from these particular issues. Faculty-oriented institutions assume that researchers own their own intellectual products and the rights to exploit them commercially, except in the development of public health inventions or if there is previously specified "substantial university involvement." At these institutions industry practice is effectively reversed, with the university benefiting in far fewer circumstances.

> 4. everything belongs to the faculty member, unless there is substantial university involvement or is related to public health
>
> Both the author and Chew seems to think #4 is the most suitable way to uphold the rights of faculty members.

Summary

Once you become more confident engaging with the passage during reading, it's time to pay more attention to the **structure of individual paragraphs**. Some of the shorter paragraphs (especially at the beginning or end of the passage) may be more straightforward, so reading them simply for meaning is fine.

But the longer and more dense paragraphs in RC passages can easily lead you astray if you do not have a clear awareness of its structure. So when you come across a big paragraph, **break it down into segments**.

Thinking about an RC paragraph like an LR argument can help us in many ways. An LR argument will have a main conclusion and supporting premises. When approaching a paragraph in an RC passage, ask yourself **what the main point and support are in this particular paragraph**.

Finally, if the author makes a **list** of several distinct concepts (three hypotheses in PT51 Passage 2, or the four different university policies in PT43 Passage 4, for example), note each one! You can highlight or take notes, whichever you prefer. This will make tackling the questions a much easier process.

Chapter 3: Passage Structure

Bringing it all together

Now it's time to look at the structure of the **entire passage**. If you remember from school, a typical persuasive essay will include an introduction with a thesis statement, maybe three paragraphs further explaining the points that support your thesis, and a concluding paragraph. In other words, each paragraph has a particular role to play in the essay you wrote.

While in a given RC passage, the role of each paragraph won't be as clearly cut out for you, it helps to think about the role played by each paragraph in a passage as a whole. This will help with "Organization" type questions down the road and reinforce our understanding of the passage.

We have briefly touched upon this concept earlier in the book. When we practiced active reading/passage engagement using the CEER framework, we saw that once we have deciphered the Author's Purpose in writing a particular passage, it's much easier to see what the author is doing in individual paragraphs. For example, the author can compare two theories in the first paragraph, evaluate them in the second, and recommend one over the other in the third.

Similarly, the peripheral components of an LR argument (background information, concession, opposing viewpoint) can also guide us when reading the passage. There will be paragraphs or parts where the author presents background information on the topic to be discussed, conceding a point to an opponent, or describing the opponent's stance/argument in greater detail. Similar to how we approach an LR argument, our job is to separate the author's core argument from the peripheral information, if the author is in fact making an argument in the passage.

In the last chapter, we pretended each individual paragraph is an LR argument. This made us look for "main points" and "premises" in each paragraph.

Now, repeat the process but for the entire passage. What is the "main point" of the passage, which paragraphs are the premises, and which paragraphs are the peripheral information?

***

Let's look at a few passages in detail, and I'd like you to answer the following three questions.

1. Try to give a **one-sentence summary** of each paragraph.

2. Why is the author writing this passage (**purpose**), and what is their central thesis (**main point**)?

3. What **role** does each paragraph play relative to the author's main point?

PT25 Passage 4

Scientists typically advocate the analytic method of studying complex systems: systems are divided into component parts that are investigated separately. But nineteenth-century critics of this method claimed that when a system's parts are isolated its complexity tends to be lost. To address the perceived weaknesses of the analytic method these critics put forward a concept called organicism, which posited that the whole determines the nature of its parts and that the parts of a whole are interdependent.

Organicism depended upon the theory of internal relations, which states that relations between entities are possible only within some whole that embraces them, and that entities are altered by the relationships into which they enter. If an entity stands in a relationship with another entity, it has some property as a consequence. Without this relationship, and hence without the property, the entity would be different— and so would be another entity. Thus, the property is one of the entity's defining characteristics. Each of an entity's relationships likewise determines a defining characteristic of the entity.

One problem with the theory of internal relations is that not all properties of an entity are defining characteristics: numerous properties are accompanying characteristics—even if they are always present, their presence does not influence the entity's identity. Thus, even if it is admitted that every relationship into which an entity enters determines some characteristic of the entity, it is not necessarily true that such characteristics will define the entity; it is possible for the entity to enter into a relationship yet remain essentially unchanged.

The ultimate difficulty with the theory of internal relations is that it renders the acquisition of knowledge impossible. To truly know an entity, we must know all of its relationships; but because the entity is related to everything in each whole of which it is a part, these wholes must be known completely before the entity can be known. This seems to be a prerequisite impossible to satisfy.

Organicists' criticism of the analytic method arose from their failure to fully comprehend the method. In rejecting the analytic method, organicists overlooked the fact that before the proponents of the method analyzed the component parts of a system, they first determined both the laws applicable to the whole system and the initial conditions of the system; proponents of the method thus did not study parts of a system in full isolation from the system as a whole. Since organicists failed to recognize this, they never advanced any argument to show that laws and initial conditions of complex systems cannot be discovered. Hence, organicists offered no valid reason for rejecting the analytic method or for adopting organicism as a replacement for it.

Scientists typically advocate the analytic method of studying complex systems: systems are divided into component parts that are investigated separately. But nineteenth-century critics of this method claimed that when a system's parts are isolated its complexity tends to be lost. To address the perceived weaknesses of the analytic method these critics put forward a concept called organicism, which posited that the whole determines the nature of its parts and that the parts of a whole are interdependent.

Two different schools are presented in the first paragraph: typical scientists, who study a phenomenon by dividing it into parts, and Organicists, who insist on studying it in its entirety.

Make sure you note the COMPARISON being made in the first paragraph.

Organicism depended upon the theory of internal relations, which states that relations between entities are possible only within some whole that embraces them, and that entities are altered by the relationships into which they enter. If an entity stands in a relationship with another entity, it has some property as a consequence. Without this relationship, and hence without the property, the entity would be different— and so would be another entity. Thus, the property is one of the entity's defining characteristics. Each of an entity's relationships likewise determines a defining characteristic of the entity.

This paragraph is famous for its difficulty, the author is EXPLAINING two core traits of organicism (internal relations). Remember, organicism is all about understanding a problem as a whole; you can't divide a problem into sub-components.

The first trait is that *"relations between entities are possible only within some whole."* So if you have a system that has two sub-entities, A, and B; you can't understand the relationship between A and B without taking into consideration the entire system. In other words, you can't go about learning about A, then B, and then magically understand the entire system.

The second trait builds on this first point: *"Entities are altered by the relationships into which they enter."* So back to our original system, both A and B are changed by being together. So if you learned about A or B independently, that still doesn't give you a true understanding of the entire system.

To use a really crude example, let's say that a Tesla consists of wheels, seats, a battery, and a computer. Knowing how these four things work separately is not going to make you understand how a Tesla works.

Together, these two points are basically telling us that you can't take the sub-components out of a system if your goal is to try to understand the whole system.

One problem with the theory of internal relations is that not all properties of an entity are defining characteristics: numerous properties are accompanying characteristics—even if they are always present, their presence does not influence the entity's identity. Thus, even if it is admitted that every relationship into which an entity enters determines some characteristic of the entity, it is not necessarily true that such characteristics will define the entity; it is possible for the entity to enter into a relationship yet remain essentially unchanged.

The author is EVALUATING internal relations/organicism now. They have some issues with it.

Remember in the previous paragraph, we are told that entities/sub-components are changed once they are joined together. Here, the author says, "Yes, there are characteristics that will change, but some of these changes have no effect on the entity itself."

The ultimate difficulty with the theory of internal relations is that it renders the acquisition of knowledge impossible. To truly know an entity, we must know all of its relationships; but because the entity is related to everything in each whole of which it is a part, these wholes must be known completely before the entity can be known. This seems to be a prerequisite impossible to satisfy.

The author is again EVALUATING the theory of internal relations and providing additional criticism.

If the theory of internal relations is true, then we can't know anything. To know something, we must know all of its relationships, and we have to know all the relationships of these relationships, etc.

Organicists' criticism of the analytic method arose from <u>their failure to fully comprehend the method</u>. In rejecting the analytic method, organicists <u>overlooked</u> the fact that before the proponents of the method analyzed the component parts of a system, they first determined both the <u>laws applicable</u> to the whole system and the <u>initial conditions of the system</u>; proponents of the method thus <u>did not study parts of a system in full isolation from the system as a whole</u>. Since organicists failed to recognize this, they never advanced any argument to show that laws and initial conditions of complex systems cannot be discovered. Hence, organicists offered <u>no valid reason</u> for rejecting the analytic method or for adopting organicism as a replacement for it.

A final attack/criticism of the organicists. The author says that in the traditional scientific method, even when we are studying the parts, it's not done in full isolation from the system. The initial conditions of the system and the laws applicable to the whole must also be known. Thus, the position advocated by the organicists is flawed, and their understanding is ignorant.

- Paragraph 1: Scientists break systems down into components to study them, but organicists believe that you can't understand parts without understanding the whole.
- Paragraph 2: Organicists believe in the theory of internal relations, which states that you can't take the parts out of a whole when trying to understand a problem. (Parts are defined by their relationship to the whole, and parts change when they interact as a part of a whole.)
- Paragraph 3: A problem with this theory is that even though parts can change, these changes may be inconsequential.
- Paragraph 4: This theory also creates a slippery slope that makes acquiring knowledge impossible.
- Paragraph 5: The scientific method doesn't really study parts in full isolation; the organicists overlook this and were wrong.

Overall, the relationship between each paragraph and the whole passage is pretty clear. Paragraph 1 provides background information. Paragraph 2 explains the theory underlining the organicists' argument (opposing viewpoint). Paragraphs 3-5 critique the organicists' position, with the passage's main point being the last sentence.

If this passage was a massive LR argument, then paragraph 1 would be background information, paragraph 2 the opposing viewpoint, paragraphs 3-4 the argument's premises, and paragraph 5 containing an additional premise and the main conclusion. This passage's purpose is relatively straightforward: to provide a critique/attack of the organicists' position.

Let's try another passage; think about the main points of each paragraph and their relationship to the passage's overall main point/purpose. Give yourself 3 minutes if practicing under realistic conditions.

PT26 Passage 3

Between June 1987 and May 1988, the bodies of at least 740 bottlenose dolphins out of a total coastal population of 3,000 to 5,000 washed ashore on the Atlantic coast of the United States. Since some of the dead animals never washed ashore, the overall disaster was presumably worse; perhaps 50 percent of the population died. A dolphin die-off of this character and magnitude had never before been observed; furthermore, the dolphins exhibited a startling range of symptoms. The research team that examined the die-off noted the presence of both skin lesions and internal lesions in the liver, lung, pancreas, and heart, which suggested a massive opportunistic bacterial infection of already weakened animals.

Tissues from the stricken dolphins were analyzed for a variety of toxins. Brevetoxin, a toxin produced by the blooming of the alga Ptychodiscus brevis, was present in eight out of seventeen dolphins tested. Tests for synthetic pollutants revealed that polychlorinated biphenyls (PCBs) were present in almost all animals tested.

The research team concluded that brevetoxin poisoning was the most likely cause of the illnesses that killed the dolphins. Although P. brevis is ordinarily not found along the Atlantic coast, an unusual bloom of this organism—such blooms are called "red tides" because of the reddish color imparted by the blooming algae— did occur in the middle of the affected coastline in October 1987. These researchers believe the toxin accumulated in the tissue of fish and then was ingested by dolphins that preyed on them. The emaciated appearance of many dolphins indicated that they were metabolizing their blubber reserves, thereby reducing their buoyancy and insulation (and adding to overall stress) as well as releasing stores of previously accumulated synthetic pollutants, such as PCBs, which further exacerbated their condition. The combined impact made the dolphins vulnerable to opportunistic bacterial infection, the ultimate cause of death.

For several reasons, however, this explanation is not entirely plausible. First, bottlenose dolphins and P. brevis red tides are both common in the Gulf of Mexico, yet no dolphin die-off of a similar magnitude has been noted there. Second, dolphins began dying in June, hundreds of miles north of and some months earlier than the October red tide bloom. Finally, the specific effects of brevetoxin on dolphins are unknown, whereas PCB poisoning is known to impair functioning of the immune system and liver and to cause skin lesions; all of these problems were observed in the diseased animals. An alternative hypothesis, which accounts for these facts, is that a sudden influx of pollutants, perhaps from offshore dumping, triggered a cascade of disorders in animals whose systems were already heavily laden with pollutants. Although brevetoxin may have been a contributing factor, the event that actually precipitated the die-off was a sharp increase in the dolphins' exposure to synthetic pollutants.

Between June 1987 and May 1988, the bodies of at least 740 bottlenose dolphins out of a total coastal population of 3,000 to 5,000 washed ashore on the Atlantic coast of the United States. Since some of the dead animals never washed ashore, the overall disaster was presumably worse; perhaps 50 percent of the population died. A dolphin die-off of this character and magnitude had never before been observed; furthermore, the dolphins exhibited a startling range of symptoms. The research team that examined the die-off noted the presence of both skin lesions and internal lesions in the liver, lung, pancreas, and heart, which suggested a massive opportunistic bacterial infection of already weakened animals.

So a significant proportion of bottlenose dolphins died. This is potentially due to a bacterial infection.

The first paragraph lays the groundwork for subsequent developments. This is background information. The passage can really go anywhere from here. Perhaps the author will talk about how man-made causes led to this unfortunate event, and recommend environmental protection measures be implemented; perhaps the author will describe how the scientists finally discovered what caused the die off; or perhaps we will find out that it's not due to the bacterial infection after all.

Tissues from the stricken dolphins were analyzed for a variety of toxins. Brevetoxin, a toxin produced by the blooming of the alga Ptychodiscus brevis, was present in eight out of seventeen dolphins tested. Tests for synthetic pollutants revealed that polychlorinated biphenyls (PCBs) were present in almost all animals tested.

So brevetoxin was found in 8/17 dolphins, and PCBs were found in all the dolphins tested.

It's important to note that brevetoxins and PCBs are two different things. Once we realize that, the next logical question would be, "Well, was it the brevetoxin or the PCBs? Maybe it was both? Maybe neither?"

The research team concluded that brevetoxin poisoning was the most likely cause of the illnesses that killed the dolphins. Although P. brevis is ordinarily not found along the Atlantic coast, an unusual bloom of this organism—such blooms are called "red tides" because of the reddish color imparted by the blooming algae—did occur in the middle of the affected coastline in October 1987. These researchers believe the toxin accumulated in the tissue of fish and then was ingested by dolphins that preyed on them. The emaciated appearance of many dolphins indicated that they were metabolizing their blubber reserves, thereby reducing their buoyancy and insulation (and adding to overall stress) as well as releasing stores of previously accumulated synthetic pollutants, such as PCBs, which further exacerbated their condition. The combined impact made the dolphins vulnerable to opportunistic bacterial infection, the ultimate cause of death.

The research team believes that the brevetoxins weakened the dolphins, who were subsequently killed by the bacterial infection talked about in the first paragraph.

To support this argument, there was a spike in brevetoxins in the algae at the start of the dolphin die off in 1987. The dolphins ate fish containing the brevetoxins, got sick, and got really weak in conjunction with the PCBs. Bacterial infections ultimately finished them off.

Note how the research team, even though they believe brevetoxins to be the main cause, are not denying the effect of PCBs.

For several reasons, however, this explanation is not entirely plausible. First, bottlenose dolphins and P. brevis red tides are both common in the Gulf of Mexico, yet no dolphin die-off of a similar magnitude has been noted there. Second, dolphins began dying in June, hundreds of miles north of and some months earlier than the October red tide bloom. Finally, the specific effects of brevetoxin on dolphins are unknown, whereas PCB poisoning is known to impair functioning of the immune system and liver and to cause skin lesions; all of these problems were observed in the diseased animals. An alternative hypothesis, which accounts for these facts, is that a sudden influx of pollutants, perhaps from offshore dumping, triggered a cascade of disorders in animals whose systems were already heavily laden with pollutants. Although brevetoxin may have been a contributing factor, the event that actually precipitated the die-off was a sharp increase in the dolphins' exposure to synthetic pollutants.

The author offers a different opinion: rather than brevetoxins being the main cause and PCBs being a minor cause, they think it's the opposite. PCBs are the main cause, and perhaps brevetoxins were a contributing factor.

The author lists three reasons for this: first, algae blooms associated with brevetoxin spikes have happened before, but dolphins didn't die then. Second, the algae bloom started after the dolphins started to die. Lastly, we don't know how brevetoxins affect dolphins, but PCBs definitely can lead to the result we are seeing.

In paragraph 2, when the author mentioned the discovery of brevetoxins and PCBs, I honestly thought the rest of the passage would talk about why it's one and not the other. But that would be too simple. The real arguments are much more nuanced than that. The researchers believed a bacterial infection killed the dolphins, but before that, brevetoxins severely weakened them, with PCBs being a contributing factor. The author, on the other hand, thinks PCBs to be the main culprit.

Paragraphs 1 and 2 contain background information preparing us for the core of the argument. Paragraph 3 outlines the researchers/opponents' argument and their supporting information. Paragraph 4, finally, presents us with the author's argument and its premises.

What is the Author's Purpose here? To attack one explanation for the dolphin die-off and propose an alternative explanation.

And the Main Point of the passage? Rather than brevetoxins from algae weakening dolphins who were subsequently killed by a bacterial infection, synthetic pollutants (PCBs) are more likely.

Let's move on to a humanities-themed passage, this time, pay special attention to the ideas discussed in the first paragraph and how they relate to subsequent paragraphs.

PT27 Passage 2

Personal names are generally regarded by European thinkers in two major ways, both of which deny that names have any significant semantic content. In philosophy and linguistics, John Stuart Mill's formulation that "proper names are meaningless marks set upon…persons to distinguish them from one another" retains currency; in anthropology, Claude Lévi-Strauss's characterization of names as being primarily instruments of social classification has been very influential. Consequently, interpretation of personal names in societies where names have other functions and meanings has been neglected. Among the Hopi of the southwestern United States, names often refer to historical or ritual events in order both to place individuals within society and to confer an identity upon them. Furthermore, the images used to evoke these events suggest that Hopi names can be seen as a type of poetic composition.

Throughout life, Hopis receive several names in a sequence of ritual initiations. Birth, entry into one of the ritual societies during childhood, and puberty are among the name-giving occasions. Names are conferred by an adult member of a clan other than the child's clan, and names refer to that name giver's clan, sometimes combining characteristics of the clan's totem animal with the child's characteristics. Thus, a name might translate to something as simple as "little rabbit," which reflects both the child's size and the representative animal.

More often, though, the name giver has in mind a specific event that is not apparent in a name's literal translation. One Lizard clan member from the village of Oraibi is named Lomayayva, "beautifully ascended." This translation, however, tells nothing about either the event referred to—who or what ascended—or the name giver's clan. The name giver in this case is from Badger clan. Badger clan is responsible for an annual ceremony featuring a procession in which masked representations of spirits climb the mesa on which Oraibi sits. Combining the name giver's clan association with the receiver's home village, "beautifully ascended" refers to the splendid colors and movements of the procession up the mesa. The condensed image this name evokes—a typical feature of Hopi personal names—displays the same quality of Western Apache place names that led one commentator to call them "tiny imagist poems."

Hopi personal names do several things simultaneously. They indicate social relationships—but only indirectly—and they individuate persons. Equally important, though, is their poetic quality; in a sense they can be understood as oral texts that produce aesthetic delight. This view of Hopi names is thus opposed not only to Mill's claim that personal names are without inherent meaning but also to Lévi-Strauss's purely functional characterization. Interpreters must understand Hopi clan structures and linguistic practices in order to discern the beauty and significance of Hopi names.

Personal names are generally regarded by European thinkers in <u>two major ways</u>, both of which <u>deny</u> that names have any <u>significant semantic content</u>. In philosophy and linguistics, <u>John Stuart Mill's</u> formulation that "proper names are meaningless marks set upon...persons to <u>distinguish</u> them from one another" retains currency; in anthropology, Claude Lévi-Strauss's characterization of names as being primarily instruments of <u>social classification</u> has been very influential. Consequently, interpretation of personal names in societies where names have <u>other functions and meanings</u> has been neglected. Among the Hopi of the southwestern United States, names often refer to historical or ritual events in order both to <u>place individuals within society</u> and to confer an <u>identity</u> upon them. Furthermore, the images used to evoke these events suggest that Hopi names can be seen as a type of poetic composition.

Different concepts are introduced in the first paragraph, we must pay extra attention to these as they will be discussed again in subsequent paragraphs.

Mill believes that names are marks to distinguish us from one another, while Levi-Strauss believes them to be marks of social classification. Both deny that names have significant semantic content (meaning in the actual words themselves).

The author's voice shines through in the middle of the paragraph: "*consequently, interpretation of personal names in societies where names have other functions and meanings has been neglected.*"

So does the author agree with Mill and Levi-Strauss' definition? No. The author believes names can have other functions and meanings. We also know from the first sentence that European thinkers deny that names have "semantic content." So perhaps the author will argue that names do have semantic meaning, after all?

You see, the writers of the test love to drop hints about how the subsequent passage will develop, even from the very beginning. **It's our job to read the first paragraph with extra attention, and try to connect the different ideas, and anticipate potential movements in subsequent paragraphs.**

The last sentence of the first paragraph is imperative. Hopi names do three things. They place individuals within society and confer an identity upon them. They also act as poetic compositions.

Think about what we read at the beginning of the paragraph:

Mill thinks names distinguish one from another. So in other words, they *confer an identity*. Levi-Strauss thinks names are instruments of social classification; in other words, they *place individuals within society*.

So in the last sentence of the paragraph, the author is really saying that Hopi names satisfy both Mill's and Levi-Strauss's definition of names, but contrary to their views that names have no innate meaning, Hopi names can be seen as a type of poetic composition.

 Throughout a passage, the author loves to express a previously talked about concept but in different wording. It's our job to find the recurring themes and concepts in a passage even when different terms and vocabulary are used.

I'll give a short example:

The <u>Russian</u> invasion of the Ukraine in 2022 was based on flawed reasoning. Emboldened by its endeavors in other operations, <u>Moscow</u> thought the war would be over in a few quick months. Fed by faulty intelligence and hubris, the <u>Kremlin</u> decided to go to war.

Here, "Moscow," and "the Kremlin" refer to the same thing: the Russian government/Putin. Different nouns/subjects/ideas are used interchangeably, but the concept is the same. This is similar to the author's writing style in many RC passages. Different terms are used interchangeably, but they might just be referring to the same thing.

A great habit to have in the more complicated passages is to link what we've already read with ideas or words that seem to be new. Ask yourself, is the author using a new term to refer to an old concept? **Practice the habit of conceptual link-backs discussed in Chapter 1.**

Throughout life, Hopis receive several names in a sequence of ritual initiations. Birth, entry into one of the ritual societies during childhood, and puberty are among the name-giving occasions. Names are conferred by an adult member of a clan other than the child's clan, and names refer to that name giver's clan, sometimes combining characteristics of the clan's totem animal with the child's characteristics. Thus, a name might translate to something as simple as "little rabbit," which reflects both the child's size and the representative animal.

So Hopis receive names during ritual initiations, which will refer to the child's clan (social classification?) and the child's characteristics. Remember that both Mill and Levi-Strauss argue that names don't have meaning. So perhaps this is direct evidence contrary to that? Let's read on.

More often, though, the name giver has in mind a specific event that is not apparent in a name's literal translation. One Lizard clan member from the village of Oraibi is named Lomayayva, "beautifully ascended." This translation, however, tells nothing about either the event referred to—who or what ascended—or the name giver's clan. The name giver in this case is from Badger clan. Badger clan is responsible for an annual ceremony featuring a procession in which masked representations of spirits climb the mesa on which Oraibi sits. Combining the name giver's clan association with the receiver's home village, "beautifully ascended" refers to the splendid colors and movements of the procession up the mesa. The condensed image this name evokes—a typical feature of Hopi personal names—displays the same quality of Western Apache place names that led one commentator to call them "tiny imagist poems."

In this paragraph, the author talks about the meaning behind Hopi names. In the example given, even though the name itself has linkages to both the name giver's clan and the receiver's home village, we cannot tell judging from the name itself. Instead, the author emphasizes the images and connotations invoked by this name, comparing it to a "tiny imagist poem."

Let us for a second return to the first paragraph – remember the predominantly Western view that names have no semantic meaning. Now that we know Hopi names evoke condensed images and describe a person's tribe and social connections, can we still argue that names have no meaning in themselves? Probably not. We see that the author has cited the case of Hopi naming conventions to challenge the European view deliberately.

We should strive to attempt this in every paragraph we read. When you incorporate new information, ask yourself, "what is the role of this new information/new paragraph in relation **to what was discussed previously?**"

Hopi personal names do several things simultaneously. They indicate social relationships—but only indirectly—and they individuate persons. Equally important, though, is their poetic quality; in a sense they can be understood as oral texts that produce aesthetic delight. This view of Hopi names is thus opposed not only to Mill's claim that personal names are without inherent meaning but also to Lévi-Strauss's purely functional characterization. Interpreters must understand Hopi clan structures and linguistic practices in order to discern the beauty and significance of Hopi names.

This paragraph gives us a very nice conclusion to the passage as a whole. This paragraph's message should not surprise us if we had been actively reading the passage and making connections between the different ideas.

Hopi names indicate social relationships (name of clan, clan's totem animal, clan of name giver), and they individuate persons (the child's characteristics). So they satisfy the requirements as listed by Levi-Strauss and Mill. But contrary to the theory of these two, Hopi names do have semantic meaning.

Let's try to summarize each paragraph with a brief sentence and think about their respective roles in this passage:

Paragraph 1: Westerners view names as tools to distinguish people from each other or labels of social classification, they also think that names don't have meaning in themselves. Hopi names, however, can be understood as having all three qualities.

The first paragraph, in my opinion, provides the opposing viewpoint as well as the main point of the passage.

Paragraph 2: Hopis receive several names in life, these can refer to their clans, clan of the person who named them, and distinguishing features of the person.

This paragraph shows us how Hopi names fulfill the requirement listed by Mill (differentiation) and Levi-Strauss (social classification). We can think about this paragraph as a premise to the passage's main point.

Paragraph 3: Hopi names are poems. There is a story behind them, and they evoke beautiful images. So in other words, Hopi names have semantic content. This is the second premise to the passage's main point.

Paragraph 4: The main point of the passage is reiterated. Hopi names serve to differentiate individuals, they serve to classify one in relation to one's society, and they are poetic compositions with semantic meaning.

Why is the author writing this passage? What is their purpose? Why did the author go into a long discussion on the nature of Hopi naming practices?

One sentence from the middle of the first paragraph provides us with the clearest hint: "*Consequently, interpretation of personal names in societies where names have other functions and meanings has been neglected.*" Students often overlook this sentence, but it sheds light on the Author's Purpose. The author describes Western understanding of naming conventions, but consequently goes on to use Hopi names as a counterexample of an instance where names are much more than that. They can have innate semantic content.

***

In this passage, two habits are invaluable in helping us reach a more coherent understanding of the passage quickly. **First, try to think about the role played by each paragraph in relation to the passage as a whole.** If the passage's main point was the main conclusion, then which paragraphs can be considered premises, and which paragraphs can be considered background information or opposing viewpoints?

Secondly, although in different wording, a few key concepts popped up repeatedly. Early in the passage, the author talked about the different traits of names (differing people, social classification, semantic content). **We can use these concepts as road signs to guide our reading**. For instance, when the author is talking about Hopi names as poetic compositions rich in imagery, that's actually hinting at them having semantic content. When the author is talking about Hopi names telling us the tribe the person came from, and the tribe from which the name giver came from, that can be interpreted as telling us that Hopi names work as a tool of social classification as well.

PT40 Passage 3

According to the theory of gravitation, every particle of matter in the universe attracts every other particle with a force that increases as either the mass of the particles increases, or their proximity to one another increases, or both. Gravitation is believed to shape the structures of stars, galaxies, and the entire universe. But for decades cosmologists (scientists who study the universe) have attempted to account for the finding that at least 90 percent of the universe seems to be missing: that the total amount of observable matter—stars, dust, and miscellaneous debris—does not contain enough mass to explain why the universe is organized in the shape of galaxies and clusters of galaxies. To account for this discrepancy, cosmologists hypothesize that something else, which they call "dark matter," provides the gravitational force necessary to make the huge structures cohere.

What is dark matter? Numerous exotic entities have been postulated, but among the more attractive candidates—because they are known actually to exist—are neutrinos, elementary particles created as a by-product of nuclear fusion, radioactive decay, or catastrophic collisions between other particles. Neutrinos, which come in three types, are by far the most numerous kind of particle in the universe; however, they have long been assumed to have no mass. If so, that would disqualify them as dark matter. Without mass, matter cannot exert gravitational force; without such force, it cannot induce other matter to cohere.

But new evidence suggests that a neutrino does have mass. This evidence came by way of research findings supporting the existence of a long-theorized but never observed phenomenon called oscillation, whereby each of the three neutrino types can change into one of the others as it travels through space. Researchers held that the transformation is possible only if neutrinos also have mass. They obtained experimental confirmation of the theory by generating one neutrino type and then finding evidence that it had oscillated into the predicted neutrino type. In the process, they were able to estimate the mass of a neutrino at from 0.5 to 5 electron volts.

While slight, even the lowest estimate would yield a lot of mass given that neutrinos are so numerous, especially considering that neutrinos were previously assumed to have no mass. Still, even at the highest estimate, neutrinos could only account for about 20 percent of the universe's "missing" mass. Nevertheless, that is enough to alter our picture of the universe even if it does not account for all of dark matter. In fact, some cosmologists claim that this new evidence offers the best theoretical solution yet to the dark matter problem. If the evidence holds up, these cosmologists believe, it may add to our understanding of the role elementary particles play in holding the universe together.

According to the theory of gravitation, every particle of matter in the universe attracts every other particle with a force that increases as either the mass of the particles increases, or their proximity to one another increases, or both. Gravitation is believed to shape the structures of stars, galaxies, and the entire universe. But for decades cosmologists (scientists who study the universe) have attempted to account for the finding that at least 90 percent of the universe seems to be missing: that the total amount of observable matter—stars, dust, and miscellaneous debris—does not contain enough mass to explain why the universe is organized in the shape of galaxies and clusters of galaxies. To account for this discrepancy, cosmologists hypothesize that something else, which they call "dark matter," provides the gravitational force necessary to make the huge structures cohere.

In a scientific-themed passage, we must fully understand the information we read before moving on. I've had countless students who tried to rush science passages but had to return to an earlier part of the passage. This is because science-based passages will become more complicated as they go on. Concepts and ideas in the latter half of the passage will usually build upon what we learned earlier. So even though it may sound counter-intuitive, slow down before you speed up. This is a strategy we shall explore fully in Chapter 20: Topic Specific Reading Strategies.

The first paragraph tells us that the bigger/closer the particles, the stronger the gravitational force. But then we are also told that a large proportion of the universe seems missing.

Remember in the previous passage (PT27 Passage 2), we discussed trying to find the connection between the information we've already read and new, incoming information?

So here, as we are reading through the first paragraph, we already know that there is a positive correlation between mass/proximity and gravity. We are also told that a large majority of the universe seems to be missing.

So if mass/proximity ~ gravitational force, why would we think there's more mass to the universe?

It can only mean one thing: the gravitational force currently in existence is strong. Only when the gravitational force is really strong, would we assume there to be more mass of particles in the universe.

We just discovered a hidden inference/assumption belonging to the author. These rarely appear in the questions, but when they do, you can be sure that they show up in the hardest questions. **Being able to anticipate hidden inferences, assumptions, and synthesize details as we read** is a habit common to all my superstar students, those who ended up in the 175+ range.

The author finally states this at the very end of the paragraph: *"...provides the gravitational force necessary to make the huge structures cohere."* For the universe to form into galaxies, we need an insane amount of gravitational force, and that requires a lot of mass, but we can only find 10% of what mass is required. That's where the scientists' hypothesis regarding dark matter comes in.

Connecting the dots between different concepts and drawing our own inferences are necessary tools of an active reader. It's not enough to simply understand the material on a surface level, but we should strive to pose questions to ourselves and use the passage to answer them as we read.

What is dark matter? Numerous exotic entities have been postulated, but among the more attractive candidates—because they are known actually to exist—are neutrinos, elementary particles created as a by-product of nuclear fusion, radioactive decay, or catastrophic collisions between other particles. Neutrinos, which come in three types, are by far the most numerous kind of particle in the universe; however, they have long been assumed to have no mass. If so, that would disqualify them as dark matter. Without mass, matter cannot exert gravitational force; without such force, it cannot induce other matter to cohere.

Here, we should pay special attention to all the properties of neutrinos. These may come in handy in a detail-oriented question down the road! So we know that neutrinos actually exist, are by-products of reactions between other particles, come in three types (we don't know what they are), are the most numerous kind of particles in the universe, and are, finally, assumed to have no mass. (But do they?)

But <u>new evidence</u> suggests that a neutrino <u>does have mass</u>. This evidence came by way of research findings supporting the existence of a long-theorized but <u>never observed phenomenon called oscillation</u>, whereby each of the three neutrino types can <u>change into one of the others</u> as it travels through space. Researchers held that the transformation is possible only if neutrinos also have mass. They obtained experimental confirmation of the theory by generating one neutrino type and then finding evidence that it had oscillated into the predicted neutrino type. In the process, they were able to estimate the mass of a neutrino at from 0.5 to 5 electron volts.

Again, more details! Some of these are very subtle. Evidence suggests that neutrinos have mass. Evidence was found that one neutrino transformed into another type. This is oscillation. Notice how the transformation was never directly observed. Only experimental evidence supporting it are present. Oscillation occurs only if neutrinos have mass. Evidence shows that oscillation probably occurs, so neutrinos probably have mass.

While slight, even the lowest estimate would yield a lot of mass given that neutrinos are so numerous, especially considering that neutrinos were previously assumed to have no mass. Still, even at the highest estimate, neutrinos could only account <u>for about 20 percent</u> of the universe's "missing" mass. Nevertheless, that is enough to alter our picture of the universe even if it does not account for all of dark matter. In fact, some cosmologists claim that this new evidence offers the <u>best theoretical solution yet</u> to the dark matter problem. If the evidence holds up, these cosmologists believe, <u>it may add to our understanding</u> of the role elementary particles play in holding the universe together.

Lastly, we are told that even if neutrinos have a mass of 5v each (highest estimate), at least 70% of the mass required to explain why gravity is so strong are still missing. (At the beginning of the passage, we are told at least 90% are missing.)

Even though neutrinos don't provide a complete solution to our problem, the author and some cosmologists believe it's the best theory we've got.

Let's summarize each paragraph quickly, followed by the Author's Purpose and the main point of the passage.

- Paragraph 1: The universe is held together by very strong gravitational force, meaning there's much mass involved. But we've only discovered 10% of that. Where's the rest of it? Scientists call the missing matter "dark matter."
- Paragraph 2: What makes up "dark matter?" Maybe it's neutrinos. But neutrinos are thought to contain no mass.
- Paragraph 3: But maybe neutrinos do have mass. If neutrinos can oscillate, then they must have mass. We don't have directly observed proof that oscillation happens, but evidence suggests it does.
- Paragraph 4: Unfortunately, even if this is the case, neutrinos can't make up for all the missing pieces, but it's a good starting point.

Purpose: to explain how neutrinos may be some of the missing pieces behind the universe's unaccounted mass.

Main Point: There is a very high likelihood that neutrinos constitute some of the dark matter/missing mass that would be required for the level of gravitational force in the universe.

Two takeaways from this passage:

In many science-based passages, concepts will build upon each other and become more complicated. So we need a strong foundation before moving forward in the passage.

Secondly, with science-based passages, we must pay special attention to "science words" such as hypothesis, theory, evidence, etc. Scientists "hypothesize" that dark matter exists, which means we don't know for sure, and it's only a theory. "Evidence" suggest that oscillation occurs and neutrinos have mass; again, we are not 100% certain. **Remember to distinguish between the facts, hypotheses, theories, and opinions in a science-based passage.**

PT41 Passage 4

Although philanthropy—the volunteering of private resources for humanitarian purposes—reached its apex in England in the late nineteenth century, modern commentators have articulated two major criticisms of the philanthropy that was a mainstay of England's middle-class Victorian society. The earlier criticism is that such philanthropy was even by the later nineteenth century obsolete, since industrialism had already created social problems that were beyond the scope of small, private voluntary efforts. Indeed, these problems required substantial legislative action by the state. Unemployment, for example, was not the result of a failure of diligence on the part of workers or a failure of compassion on the part of employers, nor could it be solved by well-wishing philanthropists.

The more recent charge holds that Victorian philanthropy was by its very nature a self-serving exercise carried out by philanthropists at the expense of those whom they were ostensibly serving. In this view, philanthropy was a means of flaunting one's power and position in a society that placed great emphasis on status, or even a means of cultivating social connections that could lead to economic rewards. Further, if philanthropy is seen as serving the interests of individual philanthropists, so it may be seen as serving the interests of their class. According to this "social control" thesis, philanthropists, in professing to help the poor, were encouraging in them such values as prudence, thrift, and temperance, values perhaps worthy in themselves but also designed to create more productive members of the labor force. Philanthropy, in short, was a means of controlling the labor force and ensuring the continued dominance of the management class.

Modern critics of Victorian philanthropy often use the words "amateurish" or "inadequate" to describe Victorian philanthropy, as though Victorian charity can only be understood as an antecedent to the era of state sponsored, professionally administered charity. This assumption is typical of the "Whig fallacy": the tendency to read the past as an inferior prelude to an enlightened present. If most Victorians resisted state control and expended their resources on private, voluntary philanthropies, it could only be, the argument goes, because of their commitment to a vested interest, or because the administrative apparatus of the state was incapable of coping with the economic and social needs of the time.

This version of history patronizes the Victorians, who were in fact well aware of their vulnerability to charges of condescension and complacency, but were equally well aware of the potential dangers of state managed charity. They were perhaps condescending to the poor, but—to use an un-Victorian metaphor—they put their money where their mouths were, and gave of their careers and lives as well.

Although philanthropy—the volunteering of private resources for humanitarian purposes—reached its apex in England in the late nineteenth century, <u>modern</u> commentators have articulated <u>two major criticisms</u> of the philanthropy that was a mainstay of England's middle-class Victorian society. The <u>earlier</u> criticism is that such philanthropy was even by the later nineteenth century <u>obsolete</u>, since industrialism had already created social problems that were beyond the scope of small, private voluntary efforts. Indeed, these problems required substantial legislative action by the state. Unemployment, for example, was not the result of a failure of diligence on the part of workers or a failure of compassion on the part of employers, nor could it be solved by well-wishing philanthropists.

The first paragraph is always crucial because it allows us to situate the topic and scope of the subsequent discussion. On the actual exam, with the added pressure of time and stress, many students cannot "get into the zone" and focus on the passage. Instead, they end up quickly reading through the passage, highlighting mindlessly without retaining or understanding, skipping over making inferences and linkages all together.

We have already discussed ways to get into "active reading" mode. We start by anticipating the Author's Purpose, use CEER to determine what the author is doing at a particular stage in a passage, and try to structurally divide the passage/paragraphs to better understand the author's argument.

Another thing we can do to start off on the right foot is to **slow down** our reading speed in the first paragraph **deliberately**. Read one or two sentences at a time, stop, think about what is being discussed and what the author will potentially discuss down the road. Slowing down has two marked benefits: one, it can help calm our nerves and prevent us from rushing forward aimlessly, avoiding wasted time; two, by taking the time to grasp the scope of the discussion and basic concepts fully, we will have an easier time understanding the rest of the passage, especially if subsequent discussions build upon earlier ones.

So let's take a look at this first paragraph.

The paragraph starts off discussing Victorian philanthropy. The structure of the paragraph is straightforward enough: the author notes two main criticisms. However, there are two things that I would like to note: first, both criticisms are *modern*. We are told that there is an earlier and later criticism, so some students, naturally, assumed that the earlier one was espoused by commentators during the Victorian age, and the latter by people of the modern era. This is not the case. Even though one is earlier and one is later, both are modern criticisms.

Secondly, the first paragraph is devoted entirely to the earlier criticism. Typically, if the paragraph starts off by talking about two things, both will be included in that paragraph. Not so in this case. This just goes to show that we should always be aware of how each paragraph and the passage as a whole is developing structurally.

The earlier criticism is that Victorian philanthropy is obsolete. Given the scale of the problem, private contributions are not enough to address the issues at hand.

The <u>more recent</u> charge holds that Victorian philanthropy was by its very nature a <u>self-serving exercise</u> carried out by philanthropists at the expense of those whom they were ostensibly serving. In this view, philanthropy was a means of <u>flaunting</u> one's power and position in a society that placed great emphasis on status, or even a means of cultivating <u>social connections</u> that could lead to economic rewards. Further, if philanthropy is seen as serving the interests of individual philanthropists, so it may be seen as serving the <u>interests of their class</u>. According to this "<u>social control</u>" thesis, philanthropists, in professing to help the poor, were encouraging in them such values as prudence, thrift, and temperance, values perhaps worthy in themselves but also designed to <u>create more productive members</u> of the labor force. Philanthropy, in short, was a means of <u>controlling the labor force</u> and ensuring the continued dominance of the management class.

The second, more recent criticism calls Victorian philanthropy a "self-serving exercise." In other words, the philanthropists did good deeds to show off and network with other wealthy elites. Their true purpose was not altruistic. It is also said that philanthropy was designed to keep the laborers in check, to foster an agreeable and docile workforce for the capitalists.

So far, the author has described both criticisms in detail; what will they do next? A likely prediction is that they will EVALUATE the merits of both criticisms. Are these criticisms justified?

Modern critics of Victorian philanthropy often use the words "amateurish" or "inadequate" to describe Victorian philanthropy, as though Victorian charity can only be understood as an antecedent to the era of state sponsored, professionally administered charity. This assumption is typical of the "Whig fallacy": the tendency to read the past as an inferior prelude to an enlightened present. If most Victorians resisted state control and expended their resources on private, voluntary philanthropies, it could only be, the argument goes, because of their commitment to a vested interest, or because the administrative apparatus of the state was incapable of coping with the economic and social needs of the time.

Who are the modern critics? Remember that both the earlier and later critics are modern, so the author is talking about both. This paragraph is easily confusing because it's the first time the author's voice/opinion shines through. Does the author agree with the modern critics? No: in this paragraph, the author is actually criticizing the critics.

What is the author's criticism? This is where things get really confusing. But we do have a few pieces of information to go by, and it is our job to infer from them what we can.

According to the author, the critics are suspicious of Victorian philanthropy due to faulty assumptions. For the critics, Victorian philanthropy "can only be understood as an antecedent to the era of state-sponsored, professionally administered charity." Remember what was the criticism of Victorian philanthropy mentioned in the first paragraph? Namely that it is inadequate compared to later, large-scale, state-sponsored welfare.

So the author is criticizing the critics for comparing Victorian philanthropy to state-sponsored welfare of the modern era. The author is basically saying, "you only found problems with the Victorians because you are comparing it to something better which came along later…you shouldn't be doing that!"

This information makes the "Whig fallacy" discussion much more comprehensible. What is the Whig fallacy? What does it mean to "*read the past as an inferior prelude to an enlightened present?*"

My understanding is this: we are so caught up in the belief that the world is a better place now, it's more equal and enlightened, so that the past must have been a brutish and nasty place. Because current society is better, the past must be filled with suffering and inequality and ignorance. In other words, I think the author is trying to tell us to view the past on its own terms, rather than relative to the present.

This paragraph is famously tricky, mainly due to the discussion about the "Whig fallacy," which threw off a lot of students. But that's no reason to panic. Remember that one of the criticisms was that Victorian philanthropy was inadequate compared to modern efforts. The author's view is suddenly that much clearer: they are arguing that we shouldn't criticize Victorian philanthropy in light of improved modern efforts, and we shouldn't judge the past based on our understanding of the present.

When we come across a challenging section/paragraph, one of the first things we can try is to tie it to the things we've already read earlier. (**Conceptual Link-Back**)

It also helps to know the **author's stance** if you are confused. We know that the author is criticizing the critics. So what is the position of the critics? How is the author finding fault with them? Why?

Let's keep on going:

If most Victorians resisted state control and expended their resources on private, voluntary philanthropies, it could only be, the argument goes, because of their commitment to a vested interest, or because the administrative apparatus of the state was incapable of coping with the economic and social needs of the time.

Remember our example about Russia, Moscow, and the Kremlin earlier? The authors of RC passages love to refer to the same concept but with different terms. So whenever seemingly new ideas are introduced, always ask yourself, is the author simply using a different term to refer to an old idea?

What is the author referring to by "*vested interest*?" In the second paragraph, more recent criticism talked about philanthropists serving the *interest of their class* by using philanthropy as a tool to maintain their control over workers. Why is the author talking about the state "*incapable of coping*" with the needs of the time? Remember that in the first paragraph, the author talked about Victorian philanthropy being obsolete, because they could not solve the problems created by industrialization, problems that the state couldn't even deal with.

This version of history <u>patronizes</u> the Victorians, who were in fact <u>well aware of their vulnerability</u> to charges of condescension and complacency, but were <u>equally well aware of the potential dangers of state managed charity.</u> They were perhaps condescending to the poor, but—to use an un-Victorian metaphor—they put their money where their mouths were, and gave of their careers and lives as well.

The author finishes off with a concession, whilst still defending the efforts of the Victorian philanthropists.

By now, we should have a relatively clear idea of the Author's Purpose. They are defending Victorian philanthropy by pointing out the flawed assumptions behind its two major criticisms. The passage's first half **explains** the critics' position, while the second half is the author's **evaluation**.

We can try to synthesize the passage's Main Point from what we already know about the Author's Purpose, and the information that we've just read:

Contrary to its critics, and despite its shortcomings, Victorian philanthropy represented an authentic and significant effort to make their society a better place.

Let's look at two more passages that may not have as clearcut a structure as the previous passages, but try your best to summarize each paragraph, break them down structurally, think about the Author's Purpose and main point, and finally, the relationship of each paragraph to that purpose/main point.

If practicing under realistic conditions, give yourself around 3 minutes per passage.

PT52 Passage 3

Traditional theories of animal behavior assert that animal conflict within a species is highly ritualized and does not vary from contest to contest. This species-specific model assumes that repetitive use of the same visual and vocal displays and an absence of escalated fighting evolved to prevent injury. The contestant that exhibits the "best" display wins the contested resource. Galápagos tortoises, for instance, settle contests on the basis of height: the ritualized display consists of two tortoises facing one another and stretching their necks skyward; the tortoise perceived as being "taller" wins.

In populations of the spider Agelenopsis aperta, however, fighting behavior varies greatly from contest to contest. In addition, fighting is not limited to displays: biting and shoving are common. Susan Riechert argues that a recently developed model, evolutionary game theory, provides a closer fit to A. aperta territorial disputes than does the species specific model, because it explains variations in conflict behavior that may result from varying conditions, such as differences in size, age, and experience of combatants. Evolutionary game theory was adapted from the classical game theory that was developed by von Neumann and Morganstern to explain human behavior in conflict situations. In both classical and evolutionary game theory, strategies are weighed in terms of maximizing the average payoff against contestants employing both the same and different strategies. For example, a spider may engage in escalated fighting during a dispute only if the disputed resource is valuable enough to warrant the risk of physical injury. There are, however, two major differences between the classical and evolutionary theories. First, whereas in classical game theory it is assumed that rational thought is used to determine which action to take, evolutionary game theory assumes that instinct and long-term species advantage ultimately determine the strategies that are exhibited. The other difference is in the payoffs: in classical game theory, the payoffs are determined by an individual's personal judgment of what constitutes winning; in evolutionary game theory, the payoffs are defined in terms of reproductive success.

In studying populations of A. aperta in a grassland habitat and a riparian habitat, Riechert predicts that such factors as the size of the opponents, the potential rate of predation in a habitat, and the probability of winning a subsequent site if the dispute is lost will all affect the behavior of spiders in territorial disputes. In addition, she predicts that the markedly different levels of competition for web sites in the two habitats will affect the spiders' willingness to engage in escalated fighting. In the grassland, where 12 percent of the habitat is available for occupation by A. aperta, Riechert predicts that spiders will be more willing to engage in escalated fighting than in the riparian habitat, where 90 percent of the habitat is suitable for occupation.

Let's break down this passage.

Traditional theories of animal behavior assert that animal conflict within a species is <u>highly ritualized</u> and does not vary from contest to contest. This species-specific model assumes that repetitive use of the same visual and vocal displays and an absence of escalated fighting evolved to prevent injury. The contestant that exhibits the "best" display wins the contested resource. Galápagos tortoises<u>, for instance</u>, settle contests on the basis of height: the ritualized display consists of two tortoises facing one another and stretching their necks skyward; the tortoise perceived as being "taller" wins.

The author starts by talking about "traditional theories." Right away that got me wondering, will the author be making a comparison to newer theories down the road? Keep this in mind as we read.

We learn that according to traditional theories, animals compete (for mates, territory, etc.) in nonviolent manners to prevent injury. Two animals want the same resources, but if they actually fought, the winner might be injured or weakened too, so it's not good for anybody. So what ends up happening is that animals show off in non-violent competitions instead.

In populations of the spider Agelenopsis aperta, <u>however</u>, fighting behavior varies greatly from contest to contest. In addition, fighting is not limited to displays: <u>biting and shoving are common</u>. Susan Riechert argues that a recently developed model, <u>evolutionary game theory, provides a closer fit</u> to A. aperta territorial disputes than does the species specific model, because it explains variations in conflict behavior that may result from varying conditions, such as differences in size, age, and experience of combatants.

Just as we predicted, a new theory is introduced. AA spiders, unlike other animals, actually fight! The "traditional theory" doesn't explain this well. Is there a better theory? Yes, Susan Riechert seems to think so. It's called the Evolutionary Game Theory; let's read on to learn more about it.

Evolutionary game theory was adapted from the classical game theory that was developed by von Neumann and Morganstern to explain human behavior in conflict situations. In both classical and evolutionary game theory, strategies are weighed in terms of maximizing the average payoff against contestants employing both the same and different strategies. For example, a spider may engage in escalated fighting during a <u>dispute only if the disputed resource is valuable enough to warrant the risk of physical injury</u>.

What is Evolutionary Game Theory? It derives from Classical Game Theory. Exactly what it is the author doesn't say. But we can learn from the passage that for both theories, multiple strategies are compared to determine which one brings the most benefit.

The information in the passage is a little abstract, but the example the author gives can be insightful. Remember the topic we are discussing is why do AA spiders actually fight instead of limiting their fighting to ceremonial displays? We learn that it's potentially because the resources they are fighting over is actually worth risking injury.

If we can connect the dots and expand on the ideas developed in the passage a little, the subsequent reading will become much easier. So the spiders fight when resources are super valuable. Perhaps when there's not enough food, the spiders will actually fight for food; but when food is plenty, the spiders will refrain from fighting and limit their competition to non-violent means?

There are, however, <u>two major differences</u> between the classical and evolutionary theories. First, whereas in classical game theory it is assumed that rational thought is used to determine which action to take, evolutionary game theory assumes that instinct and long-term species advantage ultimately determine the strategies that are exhibited. The other difference is in the payoffs: in classical game theory, the payoffs are determined by an individual's personal judgment of what constitutes winning; in evolutionary game theory, the payoffs are defined in terms of reproductive success.

In the last third of this paragraph, we are told the differences between classical and evolutionary game theories.

In traditional game theory, people choose their strategies based on rational thought, whereas in evolutionary game theory, the spiders decide whether to fight based on instinct and advantage. What these instincts and advantages are, the author doesn't say, but I'm going to assume that since the theory is called "evolutionary game theory," they will have something to do with survival and the ability to pass their genes to their offspring.

And this is exactly what the author says: reproductive success is considered a payoff.

But what is the difference between the advantages, instincts, and payoffs? We are still not too sure. **Being aware of what the passage has failed to explain is equally important as knowing what it did explain.** Because this will easily allow us to catch **out of scope** answer choices down the road. This is another habit of superstar test-takers.

In studying populations of A. aperta in a grassland habitat and a riparian habitat, Riechert <u>predicts</u> that such factors as the <u>size of the opponents</u>, the potential <u>rate of predation</u> in a habitat, and the probability of <u>winning a subsequent site</u> if the dispute is lost will all affect the behavior of spiders in territorial disputes.

So what factors determine whether spiders will fight each other for a nesting site? Three factors are listed: size of opponents, rate of predation, and how likely you are to win if you lose this fight. So in other words, if there are a lot of predators around, your opponent is formidable, and the risks of loss are high, you will most likely refrain from fighting.

A second important thing to note is that these are Riechert's predictions, do these predictions come true? Is Riechert's hypothesis validated?

In addition, she predicts that the markedly different levels of <u>competition for web sites</u> in the two habitats will affect the spiders' willingness to engage in escalated fighting. In the grassland, where 12 percent of the habitat is available for occupation by A. aperta, Riechert predicts that spiders will be more willing to engage in escalated fighting than in the riparian habitat, where 90 percent of the habitat is suitable for occupation.

An additional factor: the availability of web sites. So if there are a lot of suitable homes, then spiders won't fight; but if locations are limited, they are more likely to fight.

Let's put all this information into outline form:

Paragraph 1:

- o   Traditional Theory says that animals don't actually fight in competitions for resources because of the risk of injury

Paragraph 2:

- o   But AA spiders do fight, so the traditional theory does not offer a good explanation for their behavior
- o   SR thinks evolutionary game theory is a better fit
- o   Evolutionary Game Theory is similar to Classical Game Theory in that subjects choose the strategies with the most payoff
- o   They are different in that Evolutionary Game Theory has a different calculus (instincts, advantages, and payoffs)

Paragraph 3:

- o   SR predicts 4 factors that will determine whether spiders fight (size of enemy, predators, risk of loss, and availability of nesting sites)

By now, you probably have a good idea of this passage's purpose, main point, and each paragraph's main point and role.

It is important to note that the author does not evaluate SR's evolutionary game theory and its accuracy in explaining spider behavior. Similarly, no recommendations are made. The author compares the traditional theory with evolutionary game theory; and classical game theory with evolutionary game theory. But I think the most important thing the author does is explain what evolutionary game theory is, and how one scientist has used it to explain spider behavior.

Purpose: to introduce a new theory and shed light on how it might better explain spider behavior.

Main Point/Thesis: Evolutionary Game Theory explains animal behavior based on calculated strategies, and it may explain why spiders choose to engage in actual fighting.

Paragraph 1 talks about the traditional theory, it is used to introduce Evolutionary Game Theory, so I think it qualifies as background information.

Paragraph 2 introduces Evolutionary Game Theory and compares it to Classical Game Theory, so it can be considered the core of the passage.

Paragraph 3 is harder to categorize, but it further details the specific factors that may determine whether Evolutionary Game Theory applies to spiders. It provides additional details to further explain the information stated in the second paragraph.

This is one of the hardest scientific-themed passages, but if you had a clear idea of what the traditional species theory, Classical Game Theory, and Evolutionary Game Theory are, respectively, it is rather straightforward.

Lastly, because the author isn't making an explicit argument, we couldn't categorize each paragraph as premises, counter-arguments, or conclusions. But the very exercise of thinking about the passage's main point and the role each paragraph plays in relation to that main point can help us better understand the passage's organizational structure as a whole.

Let's look at another rather difficult passage that may not have a clear organizational structure. Again, try to read the whole passage, identify its purpose/main point, and describe the content and role of each paragraph.

PT21 Passage 1

Musicologists concerned with the "London Pianoforte school," the group of composers, pedagogues, pianists, publishers, and builders who contributed to the development of the piano in London at the turn of the nineteenth century, have long encountered a formidable obstacle in the general unavailability of music of this "school" in modern scholarly editions. Indeed, much of this repertory has more or less vanished from our historical consciousness. Granted, the sonatas and Gradus ad Parnassum of Muzio Clementi and the nocturnes of John Field have remained familiar enough (though more often than not in editions lacking scholarly rigor), but the work of other leading representatives, like Johann Baptist Cramer and Jan Ladislav Dussek, has eluded serious attempts at revival.

Nicholas Temperley's ambitious new anthology decisively overcomes this deficiency. What underscores the intrinsic value of Temperley's editions is that the anthology reproduces nearly all of the original music in facsimile. Making available this cross section of English musical life—some 800 works by 49 composers—should encourage new critical perspectives about how piano music evolved in England, an issue of considerable relevance to our understanding of how piano music developed on the European continent, and of how, finally, the instrument was transformed from the fortepiano to what we know today as the piano.

To be sure, the concept of the London Pianoforte school itself calls for review. "School" may well be too strong a word for what was arguably a group unified not so much by stylistic principles or aesthetic creed as by the geographical circumstance that they worked at various times in London and produced pianos and piano music for English pianos and English markets. Indeed, Temperley concedes that their "variety may be so great as to cast doubt on the notion of a 'school.'"

The notion of a school was first propounded by Alexander Ringer, who argued that laws of artistic survival forced the young, progressive Beethoven to turn outside Austria for creative models, and that he found inspiration in a group of pianists connected with Clementi in London. Ringer's proposed London Pianoforte school did suggest a circumscribed and fairly unified group—for want of a better term, a school—of musicians whose influence was felt primarily in the decades just before and after 1800. After all, Beethoven did respond to the advances of the Broadwood piano—its reinforced frame, extended compass, triple stringing, and pedals, for example—and it is reasonable to suppose that London pianists who composed music for such an instrument during the critical phase of its development exercised no small degree of influence on Continental musicians. Nevertheless, perhaps the most sensible approach to this issue is to define the school by the period (c. 1766–1873) during which it flourished, as Temperley has done in the anthology.

Let's look over this passage one paragraph at a time:

Musicologists concerned with the "London Pianoforte school," the group of composers, pedagogues, pianists, publishers, and builders who contributed to the development of the piano in London at the turn of the nineteenth century, have long encountered a <u>formidable obstacle</u> in the general unavailability of music of this "school" in modern scholarly editions. Indeed, much of this repertory has more or less <u>vanished</u> from our historical consciousness. Granted, the sonatas and Gradus ad Parnassum of Muzio Clementi and the nocturnes of John Field have remained familiar enough (though more often than not in editions lacking scholarly rigor), but the work of other leading representatives, like Johann Baptist Cramer and Jan Ladislav Dussek, has <u>eluded serious attempts at revival</u>.

In the first paragraph, the author presents us with a problem. Many significant composers from the "London Pianoforte School" have been forgotten. Perhaps the author will explain why we no longer remember them; perhaps the author will provide a recommendation or a way to bring more publicity to them.

Nicholas Temperley's ambitious new anthology decisively <u>overcomes this deficiency</u>. What underscores the <u>intrinsic value</u> of Temperley's editions is that the anthology <u>reproduces nearly all</u> of the original music in facsimile. Making available this cross section of English musical life—some 800 works by 49 composers— should encourage <u>new critical perspectives</u> about how piano music evolved in England, an issue of considerable relevance to our understanding of how piano music developed on the European continent, and of how, finally, the instrument was transformed from the fortepiano to what we know today as the piano.

The author introduces NT's new work. The author speaks favorably of it. The author lists several positive points about this work: 1. It's comprehensive and all-encompassing. 2. It should encourage new perspectives on how piano music evolved in England and Europe, as well as shed light on the historical evolution of the piano.

To be sure, the concept of the London Pianoforte school itself calls for review. <u>"School" may well be too strong a word</u> for what was arguably a group unified not so much by stylistic principles or aesthetic creed as by the <u>geographical circumstance</u> that they worked at various times in London and produced pianos and piano music for English pianos and English markets. Indeed, Temperley <u>concedes</u> that their "variety may be so great as to cast doubt on the notion of a 'school.'"

This paragraph tells us that what we initially thought of as a school of musicians may not be definable as such. Different musicians had different principles and ideas; their only connection may be that they all worked in London.

This paragraph put me off a little initially. It sounds like a concession. But how does it fit into the overall argument? So far, the author has been talking about how great NT's new work is at emphasizing a previously forgotten group. So what's NT's stance on the concept of the London Piano Forte school?

The author finally tells us at the very end of the paragraph: "*Temperley concedes…cast doubt on the notion of a school.*" So NT thinks that strictly speaking, the LPS isn't really a school. The first part of this paragraph is supporting NT's idea also. It's not a concession after all, but rather, information that further supports NT.

The notion of a school was first propounded by <u>Alexander Ringer</u>, who argued that laws of artistic survival forced the young, progressive Beethoven to turn outside Austria for creative models, and that he found inspiration in a group of pianists <u>connected with Clementi in London</u>. Ringer's proposed London Pianoforte school did suggest <u>a circumscribed and fairly unified group</u>—for want of a better term, a school—of musicians whose influence was felt primarily in the decades just before and after 1800. After all, Beethoven did respond to the advances of the Broadwood piano—its reinforced frame, extended compass, triple stringing, and pedals, for example—and it is reasonable to suppose that London pianists who composed music for such an instrument during the critical phase of its development exercised no small degree of influence on Continental musicians. <u>Nevertheless</u>, perhaps the most sensible approach to this issue is <u>to define the school by the period</u> (c. 1766– 1873) during which it flourished, <u>as Temperley has done</u> in the anthology.

Here we are presented with an opposing argument by AR. It's an opposing argument because we already know that the author and Temperley believe the group is not strictly definable as a "school."

What is Ringer's argument? Why does he think this group of musicians should be categorized as a school? Ringer's argument is twofold: in the first place, this is a connected group of musicians based in London, with Clementi as a central figure. So they were all working together, rather than just chancing to be in the same place. Secondly, they were all composing music for an early iteration of the piano (the Broadwood piano), and they had a collective influence on European musicians and composers such as Beethoven.

Nevertheless, the author still stands by their original stance: it's hard to define this group as a school with a unified style. Categorizing these musicians by their years active, rather than any personal or stylistic connections is still the suitable way to go, as Temperley had done.

Let's put everything together:

- Paragraph 1: The author presents us with an issue/scenario/shortcoming: many composers of the LPS have been forgotten, and their works are unavailable.
- Paragraph 2: NT's new work remedies this problem. The author then goes into a positive evaluation of NT's work; it is comprehensive and sure to encourage new perspectives.
- Paragraph 3: The author supports NT's view that the LPS cannot be categorized strictly as a "school."
- Paragraph 4: The author presents an opposing viewpoint/counter-argument, but reiterates his or her support for how and who NT chose to include in his anthology.

So what is the Author's Purpose here? Why is the author writing this passage? In large part, it's to give a positive review on NT's new anthology: it's comprehensive, it will encourage new perspectives, and even how Temperley defined this group of musicians (by period) is more accurate than the traditional depiction of them as a school.

To derive the main point of the passage, let's try to unify the key points from each paragraph into one coherent sentence:

Nicholas Temperley's new anthology is a comprehensive, valuable, and accurate compilation that sheds light on a hitherto unavailable/inaccessible group of musicians.

Summary

Once we are comfortable actively engaging with the passage in our readthrough and can navigate incredibly dense/complicated paragraphs, it's time to bring everything together. It's often helpful to think of an entire passage **as one giant argument**. As you are reading, try to figure out the passage's main point, and what parts of the passage, or which paragraphs are the author's premises (supporting information).

After reading through every passage, always try to come up with the Author's Purpose (why this passage was written) and the author's thesis statement (main point). Then, quickly think about the role played by each paragraph in relation to the author's main point. Do they provide background information, highlight an opponent's position/argument, or support the main point?

Another good habit is to link newly appeared concepts with what has already been discussed (**Conceptual Link-Back**). This can happen in two ways:

- One, the author will use slightly different words to refer to a concept/idea discussed earlier.

- Two, a new idea is introduced, but you can synthesize additional inferences by combining it with earlier information.

In addition, it helps to be **aware of the limits/boundaries of the author's discussion**. If all the author did was to introduce two concepts, A and B, in the passage, be sure to make a note of that. Be aware that the author never said A caused B, or A is similar to B, etc. Practice delineating the scope of the passage's discussion when we are reading it, so that out-of-scope answers can be easily spotted down the road.

These are all reading habits I've witnessed in my superstar students throughout years of teaching.

It also helps to fight the urge to rush headlong into a passage. When under stress, we are naturally inclined to try to take in as much information as possible, without reflecting upon what we have just read. What ends up happening is that about halfway through the passage, you come to the dreadful realization that you have no idea what the passage is talking about. By then, you must either go back to the beginning to re-read everything, or double down and keep on going, hoping things will become clearer later.

Usually, you'll just end up even more stressed because now you know you've messed up and wasted a few precious minutes.

Instead, we want to **deliberately start each passage at a slower pace**, read, understand, and retain the information thrown at you. Try to make inferences or brainstorm about the possible implications of the information you just read. Use the first few sentences to mentally prepare yourself for the rest of the passage, think about the discussion's scope, and anticipate the Author's Purpose.

Unfortunately, some passages will defy categorization. Some passages that simply explain an idea, or extremely complicated passages, do not have a clearly cut-out argumentative structure. Nonetheless, try to summarize each paragraph in a short, concise sentence. This will help us figure out the Author's Purpose/main point when you have finished reading the entire passage.

Chapter 4: The Details

Going Deeper

In the previous three chapters, we have practiced **engaging with the passage via active reading** (anticipating the Author's Purpose, using CEER to determine what moves the author is making, linking back concepts); **breaking down a paragraph along structural lines** (treating each paragraph as a mini-LR argument, making a list of the key points); and **organizing the passage as a whole structurally** (treating the whole passage as a big LR argument, watching out for recurring ideas, connecting new ideas with existing ideas).

These three things are all habits we want to practice until they come naturally to us. Initially, you might have to constantly remind yourself to do them. But the more you practice, the better you will get at organizing the information presented in a passage and discovering the relationship between different paragraphs and ideas.

Our goal in RC is to read a passage in approximately three minutes (four minutes if it's an especially difficult passage). In these 3-4 minutes, you must come up with a potential answer to the Author's Purpose, the passage's main point, what each paragraph is chiefly discussing, and the relationship between each paragraph and the passage's main point.

Once you can do this consistently, it's time to shift more of your attention to the **details**. Certain details that can appear in an RC passage are of extreme interest to us because they can serve as the basis for different question types. Thus, it is our job to have a holistic understanding of the passage as a whole and an awareness of key details within the passage.

> Therefore, training for passage reading on the LSAT is a **two-stage process**.
>
> In the **first stage**, we focus on all the skills we covered in the first three chapters. We practice these until they can be automated. We can consistently break down paragraphs and passages, reorganize them along a unified theme, and articulate the purpose and main point.
>
> In the **second stage**, we watch for the details that appear in the passage. These details will clarify our comprehension of the passage, giving us a deeper understanding, and ultimately be the critical factors in successfully navigating more complex questions.

There are **two reasons** why we practice becoming proficient at coming to a general understanding of the passage before turning our eyes to the details:

First of all, untrained students will use all their mental capacity to understand a passage, leaving little energy to focus on the more intricate and subtle points. In a more complex science-themed passage, for instance, we must first strive to understand the issue at hand before turning our attention to the disagreements between two researchers in the field. If we do not have a confident grasp of the passage, additional details will just further confuse us.

Secondly, understanding the details will only help us if we situate them as a part of the bigger picture. A technical detail will be much easier to understand if we know its function within context. If we cannot make the mental connection between what the author is saying and the over-arching theme of the passage, then we are left with a bunch of broken pieces of information and are even more confused as we approach the questions.

However, you should strive to do both on the actual passage read itself **simultaneously**. Reading the passage once for structure and again for details will take up too much time. The goal is to become so proficient at passage structural analysis so that you can devote more of your attention and energy to the details of a passage.

So if you are uncomfortable with the skills we've covered so far, review them and try to implement them in your passage reading endeavor. Only proceed if you are entirely comfortable.

Now we will look at five types of details that occur in RC passages, each of which should be of special interest to the advanced student.

Author's Opinion/Attitude

We should always strive to discover what the author thinks when reading a passage. Students will be familiar with questions that ask us about the "*author's attitude*," or POV questions that ask us "*with which of the following statements would the author most likely agree*." In these question types, we must grasp what the author, the writer of the passages, thinks about the topic they have just described.

The author's attitude is fairly easy to discern in passages with Evaluation or Recommendation themed sections. Here, the author will explicitly take a position and go on to defend their view. However, in other passages, the author's attitude can be less visible.

In passages where the author gives us a lot of Comparisons or Explanations, or if the author is describing something in explicit detail, it's much harder to determine their personal opinion about the issue at hand. In such cases, we need to search the text for **opinion words** or phrases that give us a clearer picture of what the author thinks.

It is also possible that the author avoids taking a position in the passage. Neutral passages also appear frequently on the LSAT. But before we decide that the author's attitude/tone is neutral, we must be confident that we haven't simply overlooked the hidden indicators that may be sprinkled throughout the passage.

Take a look at the following passages, try to determine what the author's stance/attitude is towards what they are discussing:

PT84 Passage 4

It might reasonably been expected that the adoption of cooking by early humans would not have led to any changes in human digestive anatomy. After all, cooking makes food easier to eat, which means that no special adaptions are required to process cooked food. However, current evidence suggests that humans today are capable of living on raw food only under unusual circumstances, such as a relatively sedentary lifestyle in a well supported urban environment. Important theoretical obstacles to living on raw food in the wild today include both the low digestibility of much raw plant food, and the toughness of much raw meat. These points suggest that humans are so evolutionary constrained to eating foods that are digestible and easily chewed that cooking is normally obligatory. Furthermore, the widespread assumption that cooking could not have had any impact on biological evolution because its practice is too recent appears to be wrong. (Various European and Middle Eastern sites that go back more than 250,000 years contain extensive evidence of hominid use of fire and apparent "earth ovens.") The implication is that the adoption of cooked food created opportunities for humans to use diets of high caloric density more efficiently. Selection for such efficiency, we suggest, led to an inability to survive on raw-food diets in the wild.

Important questions therefore arise concerning what limits the ability of humans to utilize raw food. The principal effect of cooking considered to date has been a reduction in both tooth and jaw size over evolutionary time. Human tooth and jaw size show signs of decreasing approximately 100,000 years ago; we suggest that this was a consequence of eating cooked food. Subsequent population variation in the extent and timing of dental reduction is broadly explicable by regional variation in the time when improvements in cooking technology were adopted. It is also possible that the earliest impact of cooking was the reduction of tooth and jaw size that accompanied the evolution of *Homo ergaster* approximately 1.9 million years ago. If so, the decrease in tooth and jaw size that started around 100,000 years ago may prove to result from late modifications in cooking technique, such as the adoption of boiling.

The evolution of soft parts of the digestive system is harder to reconstruct because they leave no fossil record. Human digestive anatomy differs from that of the other great apes in ways that have traditionally been explained as adaptions to a high raw-meat diet. Differences include the smaller gut volume, longer small intestine, and smaller colon. All such features are essentially adaptions to a diet of relatively high caloric density, however, and may therefore be at least as well explained by the adoption of cooking as by eating raw meat. Testing between the cooking and raw-meat models for understanding human digestive anatomy is therefore warranted.

It <u>might reasonably been expected</u> that the adoption of <u>cooking</u> by early humans <u>would not have led</u> to any <u>changes in human digestive anatomy</u>. After all, cooking makes food easier to eat, which means that no special adaptions are required to process cooked food.

This first sentence situates the subsequent scope of the discussion, so let's use it to prepare ourselves for the subsequent reading.

The phrase "it might reasonably been expected" should stand out to us. The author doesn't seem to be fully on board with this theory, which states that the introduction of cooking did not lead to changes in our digestive system. This leads us to wonder: will the author present an opposing view? Is the author more accepting of the opposing view, namely that cooking did lead to digestive changes?

<u>However</u>, current evidence suggests <u>that humans today</u> are capable of living on raw food <u>only under</u> <u>unusual</u> circumstances, such as a relatively sedentary lifestyle in a well supported urban environment.

So we can't live on raw foods anymore. How does this relate to the idea presented earlier? If we can't eat raw foods anymore, did cooking change our digestive system? This sounds like potential support for that opposing theory.

Thinking about the implications of new information and how they can combine with existing information to create inferences can help us anticipate subsequent developments in the passage and make our understanding of the reading a little easier. (Conceptual Link-Back)

Important theoretical obstacles to living on raw food in the wild today include both the low digestibility of much raw plant food, and the toughness of much raw meat. These points suggest that humans are so <u>evolutionary</u> <u>constrained</u> to eating foods that are digestible and easily chewed that cooking is normally obligatory. Furthermore, the widespread assumption that cooking could not have had any impact on biological evolution because its practice is too recent <u>appears to be wrong</u>. (Various European and Middle Eastern sites that go back more than 250,000 years contain extensive evidence of hominid use of fire and apparent "earth ovens.")

Again, this is also talking about why we can no longer live on raw foods. The author believes this to be an "evolutionary constraint." In other words, we evolved to be unable to eat raw foods; what caused this change? Think back on the information presented at the very beginning of the paragraph, the author is casting doubt on the theory that the adoption of cooking did not lead to digestive changes.

So by now, I'm more and more confident that this passage will talk about how the adoption of cooking led to evolutionary changes in our digestive system, which in turn prevents us from processing raw meat.

The passage's anticipated topic/purpose is further strengthened by the subsequent statements in the paragraph: the author removes another obstacle to the idea that cooking leads to biological changes. Cooking has been occurring for a long time, enough time to have an impact on biological evolution.

*The implication is that the adoption of cooked food created opportunities for humans to use diets of high caloric density more efficiently. Selection for such efficiency, **we suggest**, led to an inability to survive on raw-food diets in the wild.*

The last statement of the last paragraph essentially confirms our anticipation. In this paragraph, we have used the Hypothesis-Validation framework to great effect. The author believes that the Adoption of cooked foods ➔ Anatomical changes to process high caloric density more efficiently ➔ Inability to survive on raw foods.

An additional thing to note is the phrase "we suggest." Typically, in a science-themed passage, such words can point to either one of the author's main points or a hypothesis. There is a crucial distinction here. Behind a hypothesis, there is no experimental evidence to back up the claim. It's just an idea thrown out there waiting to be confirmed or modified based on experimental evidence. So whenever the author presents a view in a science-based passage, we must ask ourselves whether the author has **backed it up with experimental data, or is it simply a hypothesis still to be confirmed?**

Chapter 4: The Details

Let's read on to find out:

*Important questions therefore arise concerning <u>what limits the ability</u> of humans to utilize raw food. The principal effect of cooking considered to date has been a reduction in both <u>tooth</u> and <u>jaw size</u> over evolutionary time. Human tooth and jaw size show signs of decreasing approximately 100,000 years ago; **we suggest** that this was a consequence of eating cooked food. Subsequent population variation in the extent and timing of dental reduction is **broadly explicable** by regional variation in the time when improvements in cooking technology were adopted. **It is also possible** that the earliest impact of cooking was the reduction of <u>tooth</u> and <u>jaw size</u> that accompanied the evolution of Homo ergaster approximately 1.9 million years ago. If so, the decrease in tooth and jaw size that started around 100,000 years ago **may prove to result** from late modifications in cooking technique, such as the adoption of boiling.*

Remember the author's proposed causal relationship: Cooking ➔ Changes to the digestive system ➔ Cannot process raw food. Look at the first sentence: now we are talking about *"what limits the ability of humans to utilize raw food."* So this is probably talking about the specific changes to the digestive system?

Reductions in tooth and jaw size are considered. The author believes these to be the changes in our anatomical features resulting from the adoption of cooking and leading to our inability to process raw foods.

Slight modification of our earlier hypothesis here: tooth and jaw size changes are not part of changes to our digestive system, but rather, our bone structure/anatomy. Nonetheless, the author is still going into more detail about the causal relationship posited in the first paragraph.

Look at the bolded keywords: notice the level of certainty in the wording chosen by the author. Words like *"suggest," "also possible,"* and *"may prove to result"* all point to the likelihood that the author is positing a potential explanation here. In other words, we are dealing with the author's hypothesis, rather than the typical science passage, which can consist of a conclusion backed up by experimental results.

But perhaps the author will provide experimental evidence in the final paragraph, let's read on to find out.

*The evolution of <u>soft parts of the digestive system</u> is <u>harder to reconstruct</u> because they leave no fossil record. Human digestive anatomy differs from that of the other great apes in ways that have <u>traditionally been explained as adaptions to a high raw-meat diet</u>. Differences include the smaller gut volume, longer small intestine, and smaller colon. All such features are essentially adaptions to a diet of <u>relatively high caloric density</u>, however, and **may therefore be at least as well explained** by the adoption of cooking as by eating raw meat. **Testing** between the cooking and raw-meat models for understanding human digestive anatomy is therefore **warranted**.*

Now we are finally talking about the digestive system. Remember our causal relationship in the first paragraph and the questions it raises. What kind of digestive changes were caused by the adoption of cooking that in turn led to our inability to process raw meat?

Notice the **comparison** element in this paragraph. Again, we are presented with a traditional theory and another theory proposed by the author. What is the traditional theory?

Raw Meat ➔ Digestive Changes ("traditionally been explained as adaptions to a high raw-meat diet")

And the author's theory?

Cooking ➔ Digestive Changes

So in other words, the author proposes an **alternative cause** that lead to the digestive changes.

Notice the strength and certainty of the author's language. In using terms such as *"may therefore be at least as well explained,"* *"testing,"* and *"warranted,"* the author still hasn't offered any concrete evidence/proof for their preferred theory. It remains an alternative hypothesis.

There are several takeaways from this passage, a few of which we have emphasized previously.
First, it's essential to **mentally situate ourselves** within the topic of discussion and think about the scope of the passage right off the bat. We do this by reading the first sentences of the passage with extra attention. If we kept on reminding ourselves that the passage will discuss the relationship between cooking and changes to the digestive system as we read along, there's a lesser chance that we will get bogged down and get lost.

Second, **coming up with a hypothesis** of what the author will discuss in the passage and using subsequent text to confirm/modify that will help make our reading flow and our attempt to understand what is going on much more engaging. (See Chapter 1, Hypothesis-Validation Framework)

Third, whenever we encounter unclear information, **think back** on what we have encountered previously. Ask ourselves how the new information relates to the old? To give you an example, when the author began to talk about changes in jaw and tooth size, if we remembered that the author also discussed how cooking led to changes in our anatomical structure, we can then ask ourselves whether the jaw and tooth changes can be attributable to the adoption of cooking? If we did ask this question at the beginning of paragraph two, then getting through that paragraph has suddenly become so much easier. (Conceptual Link-Back)

Lastly, and keeping on topic with the theme of this chapter, **details matter** once we have grasped the passage's argument structure. Seemingly unimportant words like *"we suggest,"* *"may prove,"* or *"it is also possible"* tell us that the author is simply hypothesizing. They haven't proven anything. So if an answer choice said *"the author has proven that the adoption of cooking has led to changes in the digestive system,"* that would be too strong of an answer and wrong.

Let's do a quick summary/overview of this passage, as usual:

- Paragraph 1: Traditional theory states that cooking did not lead to human bodily changes, but that may be false. It's possible that cooking led to changes that made people unable to eat raw food.
- Paragraph 2: It's possible that the adoption of cooking led to a reduction in tooth and jaw size.
- Paragraph 3: While some believe that the digestive system changed due to a diet of raw meat, it's equally possible that this is due to the adoption of cooking.

Author's Purpose: To present an alternative hypothesis explaining the anatomical and digestive evolution of the human body.

Passage Main Point: We hypothesize that the adoption of cooking led to evolutionary changes in human physical and digestive systems, which in turn led to our inability to eat raw meat.

PT26 Passage 4

In England before 1660, a husband controlled his wife's property. In the late seventeenth and eighteenth centuries, with the shift from land-based to commercial wealth, marriage began to incorporate certain features of a contract. Historians have traditionally argued that this trend represented a gain for women, one that reflects changing views about democracy and property following the English Restoration in 1660. Susan Staves contests this view; she argues that whatever gains marriage contracts may briefly have represented for women were undermined by judicial decisions about women's contractual rights.

Shifting through the tangled details of court cases, Staves demonstrates that, despite surface changes, a rhetoric of equality, and occasional decisions supporting women's financial power, definitions of men's and women's property remained inconsistent— generally to women's detriment. For example, dower lands (property inherited by wives after their husbands' deaths) could not be sold, but "curtesy" property (inherited by husbands from their wives) could be sold. Furthermore, comparatively new concepts that developed in conjunction with the marriage contract, such as jointure, pin money, and separate maintenance, were compromised by peculiar rules. For instance, if a woman spent her pin money (money paid by the husband according to the marriage contract for the wife's personal items) on possessions other than clothes she could not sell them; in effect they belonged to her husband. In addition, a wife could sue for pin money only up to a year in arrears-which rendered a suit impractical. Similarly, separate maintenance allowances (stated sums of money for the wife's support if husband and wife agreed to live apart) were complicated by the fact that if a couple tried to agree in a marriage contract on an amount, they were admitting that a supposedly indissoluble bond could be dissolved, an assumption courts could not recognize. Eighteenth- century historians underplayed these inconsistencies, calling them "little contrarieties" that would soon vanish. Staves shows, however, that as judges gained power over decisions on marriage contracts, they tended to fall back on pre-1660 assumptions about property.

Staves' work on women's property has general implications for other studies about women in eighteenth-century England. Staves revises her previous claim that separate maintenance allowances proved the weakening of patriarchy; she now finds that an oversimplification. She also challenges the contention by historians Jeanne and Lawrence Stone that in the late eighteenth century wealthy men married widows less often than before because couples began marrying for love rather than for financial reasons. Staves does not completely undermine their contention, but she does counter their assumption that widows had more money than never-married women. She points out that jointure property (a widow's lifetime use of an amount of money specified in the marriage contract) was often lost on remarriage.

In England before 1660, a husband controlled his wife's property. In <u>the late seventeenth</u> and <u>eighteenth</u> centuries, with the shift from land-based to commercial wealth, marriage began to incorporate certain features of a contract. Historians have <u>traditionally argued</u> that this trend represented a gain for women, one that reflects changing views about democracy and property following the English Restoration in 1660. <u>Susan Staves</u> <u>contests</u> this view; she argues that whatever gains marriage contracts may briefly have represented for women were undermined by judicial decisions about women's contractual rights.

We will soon look at how keeping an eye on important dates and timelines in an RC passage can enhance our understanding. But for now, realize that the "late seventeenth century" is just about the late 1600s. Combine that with the first sentence, and you realize that the paragraph is talking about changes *after 1660.*

So before 1660, a wife's property was controlled by the husband. After 1660, and into the 1700s, marriage began to involve more contractual obligations. Two opposing views are introduced here; the traditional view believes that women gained more rights because of this development. Staves, on the other hand, takes a more negative view.

It's important not to over-simplify these positions. It's not hard to notice the two different views in the first paragraph, but some students, after seeing that the traditional view called the incorporation of contractual elements into a marriage a "*gain for women,*" quickly assume that Staves believed such gains non-existent.

But Staves' position is more nuanced than that. She concedes that there may have been momentary gains, but these were subsequently lost due to unfavorable court cases. (Undermined by judicial decisions)

*Shifting through the tangled details of court cases, Staves **demonstrates** that, despite surface changes, a rhetoric of equality, and occasional decisions supporting women's financial power, <u>definitions of men's and women's property remained inconsistent— generally to women's detriment.</u> For example, dower lands (property inherited by wives after their husbands' deaths) could not be sold, but "curtesy" property (inherited by husbands from their wives) could be sold. Furthermore, comparatively new concepts that developed in conjunction with the marriage contract, such as jointure, pin money, and separate maintenance, were <u>compromised by peculiar rules</u>. <u>For instance</u>, if a woman spent her pin money (money paid by the husband according to the marriage contract for the wife's personal items) on possessions other than clothes she could not sell them; in effect they belonged to her husband. <u>In addition</u>, a wife could sue for pin money only up to a year in arrears-which rendered a suit impractical. <u>Similarly</u>, separate maintenance allowances (stated sums of money for the wife's support if husband and wife agreed to live apart) were complicated by the fact that if a couple tried to agree in a marriage contract on an amount, they were admitting that a supposedly indissoluble bond could be dissolved, an assumption courts could not recognize. Eighteenth- century historians <u>underplayed</u> these inconsistencies, calling them "little contrarieties" that would soon vanish. **Staves shows, however**, that as judges gained power over decisions on marriage contracts, they tended to fall back on pre-1660 assumptions about property.*

This is a long paragraph, but if we apply the skillsets developed in Chapter 2, we shouldn't have too many problems with it. There are a lot of examples and illustrations in this paragraph. **Remember, whenever you see the author providing an example, that example is ALWAYS used to illustrate a specific point.** If we are sometimes confused about the exact meaning of an example, refer back to the point that the example is trying to illustrate.

What are the key points that this paragraph is trying to express? Remember, Staves thinks that marriage taking on elements of a contract did not ultimately benefit women due to hostile judicial decisions.

One, a double standard was applied to men and women's property. Men's property and women's property could have different names and the court was more restrictive concerning women's property.

Two, there were particular rules and restrictions on a woman's assets, despite purported protection by the marriage contract.

Lastly, even contractual obligations in the event of separation were not recognized by the court in some instances because planning for such outcomes challenges the very Christian sanctity of marriage.

Overall, we are given more details on exactly how the courts have placed further restrictions on women's properties even with marriage contracts in place.

Let's now turn to the Author's Opinion/Attitude. Like in the previous passage, it's also very subtle here. We must remember that while this passage is primarily about Stave's views, it's not Stave herself who is speaking. Instead, it's our author who is describing Stave's position.

It's important to distinguish what Stave thinks and what the author thinks. If we are confronted with different questions asking us about Stave's and the author's positions, we must not confuse the two. Stave's position is reasonably clear in the passage. But what the author thinks is less so.

But some hints tell us what the author thinks about Stave's position. I've bolded these indicator words in the paragraph above. Words like "*Stave shows*" and "*Stave demonstrates*" all indicate that Stave has convinced our author. As we mentioned previously, in EXPLANATION-themed passages where the author is mainly describing someone's view or position, it's rare to find significant sections devoted to the author's own opinion. Instead, we must sift through the passage for these little hints of where the author stands.

Staves' work on women's property has <u>general implications</u> for other studies about women in eighteenth-century England. Staves <u>revises</u> her previous claim that separate maintenance allowances proved the weakening of patriarchy; she now finds that an oversimplification. She also <u>challenges the contention</u> by historians Jeanne and Lawrence Stone that in the late eighteenth century wealthy men married widows less often than before because couples began marrying for love rather than for financial reasons. Staves <u>does not completely undermine</u> their contention, but she does <u>counter their assumption</u> that widows had more money than never-married women. She points out that jointure property (a widow's lifetime use of an amount of money specified in the marriage contract) was often lost on remarriage.

Two additional traits of Stave's work are described in the last paragraph. In the first place, spousal support does not necessarily mean the weakening of the patriarchy. Secondly, she believes the view that men married wealthy widows less because more people began to marry for love has a problematic assumption behind it. Perhaps widows weren't that wealthy after all. In other words, men married widows less often not because of love, but because widows were not as prosperous as once thought.

PT35 Passage 4

Ronald Dworkin argues that judges are in danger of uncritically embracing an erroneous theory known as legal positivism because they think that the only alternative is a theory that they (and Dworkin) see as clearly unacceptable—natural law. The latter theory holds that judges ought to interpret the law by consulting their own moral convictions, even if this means ignoring the letter of the law and the legal precedents for its interpretation. Dworkin regards this as an impermissible form of judicial activism that arrogates to judges powers properly reserved for legislators.

Legal positivism, the more popular of the two theories, holds that law and morality are wholly distinct. The meaning of the law rests on social convention in the same way as does the meaning of a word. Dworkin's view is that legal positivists regard disagreement among jurists as legitimate only if it arises over what the underlying convention is, and it is to be resolved by registering a consensus, not by deciding what is morally right. In the same way, disagreement about the meaning of a word is settled by determining how people actually use it, and not by deciding what it ought to mean. Where there is no consensus, there is no legal fact of the matter. The judge's interpretive role is limited to discerning this consensus, or the absence thereof.

According to Dworkin, this account is incompatible with the actual practice of judges and lawyers, who act as if there is a fact of the matter even in cases where there is no consensus. The theory he proposes seeks to validate this practice without falling into what Dworkin correctly sees as the error of natural law theory. It represents a kind of middle ground between the latter and legal positivism. Dworkin stresses the fact that there is an internal logic to a society's laws and the general principles they typically embody. An interpretation that conforms to these principles may be correct even if it is not supported by a consensus. Since these general principles may involve such moral concepts as justice and fairness, judges may be called upon to consult their own moral intuitions in arriving at an interpretation. But this is not to say that judges are free to impose their own morality at will, without regard to the internal logic of the laws.

The positivist's mistake, as Dworkin points out, is assuming that the meaning of the law can only consist in what people think it means, whether these people be the original authors of the law or a majority of the interpreter's peers. Once we realize, as Dworkin does, that the law has an internal logic of its own that constrains interpretation, we open up the possibility of improving upon the interpretations not only of our contemporaries but of the original authors.

Ronald Dworkin argues that judges are in danger of uncritically embracing an erroneous theory known as legal positivism because they think that the only alternative is a theory that they (and Dworkin) see as clearly unacceptable—natural law. The latter theory holds that judges ought to interpret the law by consulting their own moral convictions, even if this means ignoring the letter of the law and the legal precedents for its interpretation. Dworkin regards this as an impermissible form of judicial activism that arrogates to judges powers properly reserved for legislators.

Ah, the famous passage on jurisprudence, here we go:

The first paragraph introduces two distinct parties and two distinct theories. The two theories are legal positivism and natural law. The two parties we must note are Dworkin and the judges.

What is legal positivism? The paragraph doesn't say. On the other hand, natural law believes that judges should consult their own moral compass when making judgment, even if that means ignoring the law itself.

What do the judges and Dworkin think of natural law? They think it unacceptable.

What about legal positivism? Dworkin thinks it's erroneous. He also thinks that the judges perceive it to be the only acceptable alternative to natural law.

What are the judges' position on legal positivism? If we accept Dworkin's position, then the judges are accepting of it. But is Dworkin correct?

Legal positivism, the more popular of the two theories, holds that law and morality are wholly distinct. The meaning of the law rests on social convention in the same way as does the meaning of a word. Dworkin's view is that legal positivists regard disagreement among jurists as legitimate only if it arises over what the underlying convention is, and it is to be resolved by registering a consensus, not by deciding what is morally right. In the same way, disagreement about the meaning of a word is settled by determining how people actually use it, and not by deciding what it ought to mean. Where there is no consensus, there is no legal fact of the matter. The judge's interpretive role is limited to discerning this consensus, or the absence thereof.

According to legal positivism, law and morality are wholly distinct (contrary to natural law). The law is a social convention or accepted social standard. This is found in the paragraph's first and second sentences and the author's view. In other words, laws derive from social norms and rules governing human behavior.

Notice the subtle shift starting in the third sentence! The author is no longer giving a direct, factual representation of legal positivism; but rather, what we see here is the author's descriptions of Dworkin's view on legal positivism. Remember that Dworkin thinks the theory to be erroneous. What's Dworkin's view of legal positivism?

The passage doesn't directly represent Dworkin's characterization of the positivist view of the law. Instead, we are given a few fragmented statements, from which we must reconstruct Dworkin's view.

Remember, positivists believe the law is a "*social convention*" and not inherently moral. In other words, if there was a piece of legislation against hunting endangered animals, it's not because hunting lions is wrong per se, but because society has come to the agreement/acceptance that such behavior should be prohibited.

Similarly, suppose a law that limited senators to single terms came into place. In that case, that's not because it's immoral to serve two terms or more, but because society or a social institution with authority has willed it so. In other words, the law is valid as long as it is accepted, and its validity has nothing to do with its content.

*According to Dworkin, this account is incompatible with the actual practice of judges and lawyers, who act as if there is a fact of the matter even in cases where there is no consensus. The theory he proposes seeks to validate this practice without falling into what Dworkin **correctly** sees as the error of natural law theory. It represents a kind of middle ground between the latter and legal positivism. Dworkin stresses the fact that there is an internal logic to a society's laws and the general principles they typically embody. An interpretation that conforms to* *these principles may be correct <u>even if it is not supported by a consensus</u>. Since these general principles may involve such moral concepts as justice and fairness, judges may be called upon to <u>consult their own moral intuitions</u> in arriving at an interpretation. But this is not to say that judges are free to impose their own morality at will, without regard to the internal logic of the laws.*

Remember how Dworkin said that the positivists believed the law to be nothing more than a set of rules society accepts. If society did not accept or recognize a set of rules, it would not be law. But Dworkin argues that in the actual practice of judges and lawyers, they also apply other standards. Judges and lawyers do not depend exclusively on legal rules, statutes, established bodies of reasoning empowered by legislation, or the judiciary. Instead, they bring other concepts into their arguments.

For Dworkin, principles with moral undertones can also serve a role in the law. They may be considered to decide a case, even if they are not recognized explicitly as laws authorized by society.

Principles "may involve moral concepts such as justice and fairness," and since Dworkin believes principles have a place in the law, then so does morality.

The positivist's mistake, as Dworkin points out, is assuming that the meaning of the law can only consist in what people think it means, whether these people be the original authors of the law or a majority of the interpreter's peers. **Once we realize, as Dworkin does**, *that the law has an <u>internal logic</u> of its own that constrains interpretation, we open up the possibility of improving upon the interpretations not only of our contemporaries but of the original authors.*

In the last paragraph, the author reiterates Dworkin's argument that the law consists of more than social convention. We have the discretion to interpret laws, guided by principles and other considerations.

To be honest, I was not too fond of this passage. I feel like the test makers did not do a good job summarizing Dworkin's arguments criticizing Hart and legal positivism. I tried to explain the concepts the best I could, based solely on the information given in the passage. As such, key points in Dworkin's argument are lost upon us. The interested student should take a look at Dworkin's seminal paper, "<u>A Model of Rules</u>," published in 1967.

But I deliberately selected this passage to show yet again that the author's stance/attitude can easily be lost to us. Two hints are given to us in this passage: in the second to last paragraph, the author states *"...what Dworkin correctly sees...,"* and again, in the last paragraph: *"Once we realize, as Dworkin does...."* Judging from these two pieces of subtle information, we can sense that the author agrees with Dworkin.

Like we mentioned previously, in passages where the author's position is not explicitly made clear (no evaluations or recommendations), **we should try our best to find these circumstantial details**, hidden away in the passage, hinting at what the author thinks or where they stand. If a question regarding the author's attitude came along, being mindful of such details will prove invaluable.

Dates and Chronology

I like to keep a clear grasp of years and specific dates. Sometimes, when the author presents a series of facts in quick succession, it's easy to lose track of them all. If the date/year in which something occurred was given, then we can try to arrange the events in chronological order. This can help make our understanding more transparent.

PT25 Passage 2

While a new surge of critical interest in the ancient Greek poems conventionally ascribed to Homer has taken place in the last twenty years or so, it was nonspecialists rather than professional scholars who studied the poetic aspects of the Iliad and the Odyssey between, roughly, 1935 and 1970. During these years, while such nonacademic intellectuals as Simone Weil and Erich Auerbach were trying to define the qualities that made these epic accounts of the Trojan War and its aftermath great poetry, the questions that occupied the specialists were directed elsewhere: "Did the Trojan War really happen?" "Does the bard preserve Indo- European folk memories?" "How did the poems get written down?" Something was driving scholars away from the actual works to peripheral issues. Scholars produced books about archaeology, and gift exchange in ancient societies, about the development of oral poetry, about virtually anything except the Iliad and the Odyssey themselves as unique reflections or distillations of life itself—as, in short, great poetry. The observations of the English poet Alexander Pope seemed as applicable in 1970 as they had been when he wrote them in 1715: according to Pope, the remarks of critics "are rather Philosophical, Historical, Geographical . . . or rather anything than Critical and Poetical."

Ironically, the modern manifestation of this "nonpoetical" emphasis can be traced to the profoundly influential work of Milman Parry, who attempted to demonstrate in detail how the Homeric poems, believed to have been recorded nearly three thousand years ago, were the products of a long and highly developed tradition of oral poetry about the Trojan War. Parry proposed that this tradition built up its diction and its content by a process of constant accumulation and refinement over many generations of storytellers. But after Parry's death in 1935, his legacy was taken up by scholars who, unlike Parry, forsook intensive analysis of the poetry itself and focused instead on only one element of Parry's work: the creative limitations and possibilities of oral composition, concentrating on fixed elements and inflexibilities, focusing on the things that oral poetry allegedly can and cannot do. The dryness of this kind of study drove many of the more inventive scholars away from the poems into the rapidly developing field of Homer's archaeological and historical background.

Appropriately, Milman Parry's son Adam was among those scholars responsible for a renewed interest in Homer's poetry as literary art. Building on his father's work, the younger Parry argued that the Homeric poems exist both within and against a tradition. The Iliad and the Odyssey were, Adam Parry thought, the beneficiaries of an inherited store of diction, scenes, and concepts, and at the same time highly individual works that surpassed these conventions. Adam Parry helped prepare the ground for the recent Homeric revival by affirming his father's belief in a strong inherited tradition, but also by emphasizing Homer's unique contributions within that tradition.

While a new surge of critical interest in the ancient Greek poems conventionally ascribed to Homer has taken place in <u>the last twenty years</u> or so, it was <u>nonspecialists</u> rather than professional scholars who studied the <u>poetic aspects</u> of the Iliad and the Odyssey between, roughly, <u>1935 and 1970</u>. During these years, while such nonacademic intellectuals as Simone Weil and Erich Auerbach were trying to define the qualities that made these epic accounts of the Trojan War and its aftermath great poetry, the questions that occupied the <u>specialists</u> were directed elsewhere: "Did the Trojan War really happen?" "Does the bard preserve Indo- European folk memories?" "How did the poems get written down?" Something was driving scholars away from the actual works to <u>peripheral issues</u>. Scholars produced books about archaeology, and gift exchange in ancient societies, about the development of oral poetry, about virtually anything except the Iliad and the Odyssey themselves as unique reflections or distillations of life itself—as, in short, great poetry. The observations of the English poet Alexander Pope seemed as applicable in <u>1970</u> as they had been when he wrote them in 1715: according to Pope, the remarks of critics "are rather Philosophical, Historical, Geographical . . . or rather anything than Critical and Poetical."

Assuming this passage was from the nineties, the "last twenty years or so" would bring us back to the 1970s. So there was a surge of critical interest in Homer's poetry from the 1970s until the 1990s.

But from 1935 until 1970, the author distinguishes between the "specialists" and the "non-specialists." The specialists, or professional academics, were not interested in Homer's poetry's literary qualities. It was the amateur, non-academic intellectuals, who were interested in Homer's poetry itself.

Ironically, the modern manifestation of this <u>"nonpoetical"</u> emphasis can be traced to the profoundly influential work of <u>Milman Parry</u>, who attempted to demonstrate in detail how the Homeric poems, believed to have been recorded nearly three thousand years ago, were the products of a long and highly developed tradition of oral poetry about the Trojan War. Parry proposed that this tradition built up its diction and its content by a process of <u>constant accumulation and refinement over many generations of storytellers</u>. <u>But after Parry's death in 1935</u>, his legacy was taken up by scholars who, unlike Parry, forsook intensive analysis of the poetry itself and focused instead on only one element of Parry's work: the creative limitations and possibilities of oral composition, concentrating on fixed elements and inflexibilities, <u>focusing on the things that oral poetry allegedly can and cannot do</u>. The dryness of this kind of study drove many of the more inventive scholars <u>away from the poems</u> into the rapidly developing field of Homer's archaeological and historical background.

Here, the author traces the origins of this "nonpoetical" trend. Remember, the nonpoetical emphasis describes the focus placed by specialists on cross-disciplinary studies.

How did the work of Milman Parry eventually lead to a shift away from pure literary analysis? Parry's work focused on both analysis of the poetry itself as well as the limitations of oral poetry. But after Parry's death in 1935 (also marking the beginning of the recent trend among specialists that lasted until 1970), scholars began to lose focus in the poetry itself, and many scholars shifted their focus away to archaeological and historical research.

Appropriately, Milman Parry's son Adam was among those scholars responsible for a <u>renewed interest in Homer's poetry as literary art.</u> Building on his father's work, the younger Parry argued that the Homeric poems exist both within and against a tradition. The Iliad and the Odyssey were, Adam Parry thought, the beneficiaries of an inherited store of diction, scenes, and concepts, and at the same time highly individual works that surpassed these conventions. Adam Parry <u>helped prepare the ground for the recent Homeric revival</u> by affirming his father's belief in a strong inherited tradition, but also by emphasizing Homer's unique contributions within that tradition.

In the last paragraph, the author describes the return of interest among scholars in the literary qualities of Homer's poetry. For Parry Junior, Homer's poetry was not only classified as a highly developed oral tradition but also remarkable for its own sake. The author doesn't tell us when Parry Junior worked, but since we know that the rekindled interest in Homer began in 1970, it's probably around this time that Parry Junior led the revival.

***

This passage is best understood if we organized everything along chronological lines:

- Pre-1935: Milman Parry studied Homer, both its literary qualities and as a developing oral tradition.
- 1935: Milman Parry dies, scholars began to focus exclusively on the limitations of oral poetry.
- 1935-1970: Academic scholars lose interest in Homeric poetry's literary qualities, focusing instead on archaeological and historical research. Amateur critics undertake studies of the poems themselves.
- Around the 1970s, Adam Parry reaffirms Homeric poetry's value as oral traditions and re-emphasizes the poems' value.
- The 1970s – 1990s: More scholars became interested in the literary content of Homeric poems.

In this passage, the author primarily focuses on tracing the origins and ending of a trend in the study of Homeric poetry. We don't really find any hints of what the author's own attitude is, their voice is fairly neutral throughout the passage.

The Author's Purpose can look something like this: "to describe the factors leading to the rise and fall in a trend in the study of Homeric poetry."

Our pre-phrased main point answer will be more detailed: "While Milman Parry's work led to a turning away from the poetic qualities of Homer's works among professional academics, it was his son's effort that saw a rekindled focus on the same subject."

PT44 Passage 4

The proponents of the Modern Movement in architecture considered that, compared with the historical styles that it replaced, Modernist architecture more accurately reflected the functional spirit of twentieth-century technology and was better suited to the newest building methods. It is ironic, then, that the Movement fostered an ideology of design that proved to be at odds with the way buildings were really built.

The tenacious adherence of Modernist architects and critics to this ideology was in part responsible for the Movement's decline. Originating in the 1920s as a marginal, almost bohemian art movement, the Modern Movement was never very popular with the public, but this very lack of popular support produced in Modernist architects a high-minded sense of mission—not content merely to interpret the needs of the client, these architects now sought to persuade, to educate, and, if necessary, to dictate. By 1945 the tenets of the Movement had come to dominate mainstream architecture, and by the early 1950s, to dominate architectural criticism— architects whose work seemed not to advance the evolution of the Modern Movement tended to be dismissed by proponents of Modernism. On the other hand, when architects were identified as innovators—as was the case with Otto Wagner, or the young Frank Lloyd Wright—attention was drawn to only those features of their work that were "Modern"; other aspects were conveniently ignored.

The decline of the Modern Movement later in the twentieth century occurred partly as a result of Modernist architects' ignorance of building methods, and partly because Modernist architects were reluctant to admit that their concerns were chiefly aesthetic. Moreover, the building industry was evolving in a direction Modernists had not anticipated: it was more specialized and the process of construction was much more fragmented than in the past. Up until the twentieth century, construction had been carried out by a relatively small number of tradespeople, but as the building industry evolved, buildings came to be built by many specialized subcontractors working independently. The architect's design not only had to accommodate a sequence of independent operations, but now had to reflect the allowable degree of inaccuracy of the different trades. However, one of the chief construction ideals of the Modern Movement was to "honestly" expose structural materials such as steel and concrete. To do this and still produce a visually acceptable interior called for an unrealistically high level of craftmanship. Exposure of a building's internal structural elements, if it could be achieved at all, could only be accomplished at considerable cost— hence the well-founded reputation of Modern architecture as prohibitively expensive.

As Postmodern architects recognized, the need to expose structural elements imposed unnecessary limitations on building design. The unwillingness of architects of the Modern Movement to abandon their ideals contributed to the decline of interest in the Modern Movement.

The proponents of the Modern Movement in architecture considered that, compared with the <u>historical styles</u> that it replaced, <u>Modernist architecture</u> more accurately reflected the functional spirit of twentieth-century technology and was better suited to the newest building methods. It is ironic, then, that the Movement fostered an ideology of design that proved to be at odds with the way buildings were really built.

We always read the first paragraph with great attention, to mentally prepare ourselves for the subsequent discussion and find guidance on ways to organize the rest of the passage. Although this first paragraph is extremely short, it contains a fundamental idea. Modernists believe their architecture is more functional and better suited to newer building methods. But that's not how the buildings were really built. In other words, the author does not think Modernist buildings more functional or better suited to newer building methods.

The tenacious adherence of Modernist architects and critics to this ideology was in part responsible for the Movement's decline. <u>Originating in the 1920s</u> as a marginal, almost bohemian art movement, the Modern Movement was never very popular with the public, but this very lack of popular support produced in Modernist architects a <u>high-minded sense of mission</u>—not content merely to interpret the needs of the client, these architects now sought to <u>persuade, to educate, and, if necessary, to dictate</u>. By <u>1945</u> the tenets of the Movement had come to <u>dominate mainstream architecture</u>, and by the <u>early 1950s</u>, to dominate <u>architectural criticism</u>— architects whose work seemed not to advance the evolution of the Modern Movement tended to be dismissed by proponents of Modernism. On the other hand, when architects were identified as innovators—as was the case with Otto Wagner, or the young Frank Lloyd Wright—attention was drawn to only those features of their work that were "Modern"; other aspects were conveniently ignored.

In this paragraph, the author gives us a timeline of Modernism. Again, it's important not to mix up the dates. **The test makers can easily throw in a few trap answers that mix up the dates and their associated details.** Time permitting, I would list the dates and what happened then:

The 1920s: Beginning of Modernism

1945: Modernism dominates mainstream architecture

The early 1950s (1950-1955): Modernism dominates architectural criticism

Other than the timeline, the author also offers two criticisms of Modernism: one, it sought to force its views upon the public. Two, the eventual growth in Modernism's importance overshadowed other features of celebrated architects.

The <u>decline</u> of the Modern Movement <u>later in the twentieth century</u> occurred partly as a result of Modernist architects' <u>ignorance of building methods</u>, and partly because Modernist architects were <u>reluctant to admit that their concerns were chiefly aesthetic</u>. Moreover, the building industry was evolving in a direction Modernists had not anticipated: it was <u>more specialized</u> and the process of construction was much <u>more fragmented</u> than in the past. <u>Up until the twentieth century</u>, construction had been carried out by a relatively small number of tradespeople, but as the building industry evolved, buildings came to be built by many specialized subcontractors working independently. The architect's design not only had to accommodate a sequence of independent operations, but now had to reflect the <u>allowable degree of inaccuracy of the different trades</u>. However, one of the chief construction ideals of the Modern Movement was to "honestly" expose structural materials such as steel and concrete. To do this and still produce a visually acceptable interior called for an <u>unrealistically high level of craftmanship</u>. Exposure of a building's internal structural elements, if it could be achieved at all, could only be accomplished at <u>considerable cost</u>— hence the well-founded reputation of Modern architecture as prohibitively expensive.

The author describes the reasons behind Modern architecture's decline in the third paragraph. While we don't know exactly when this happened, we do know that it's post the 1950s, and later in the twentieth century.

Remember how we practiced connecting earlier ideas with new information in previous chapters? This skill will come in handy now. In the first paragraph, the author thought Modernist architecture was neither functional nor suited to newer building methods. Let's see if they expand upon either one of those points.

The author gives three reasons for the decline of the Modern Movement. The first is the Modernist's ignorance of building methods. The second is that the Modernist is reluctant to admit "*their concerns were chiefly aesthetic.*" If an architect's concerns are chiefly aesthetic, could it be possible that they ignored some of the functional elements of architecture? Maybe. The third reason for the decline of the Modern Movement is more fully developed in the latter half of the paragraph. Despite the specialization of building construction and increasing inaccuracy, the Modern Movement demanded an "unrealistically high level of craftmanship, this made Modernist architecture economically unfeasible.

Thus, Modernist architecture is unsuited to modern building methods, this echoes what the author has already mentioned earlier.

As <u>Postmodern</u> architects recognized, the need to expose structural elements imposed unnecessary limitations on building design. The unwillingness of architects of the Modern Movement to abandon their ideals <u>contributed to the decline of interest</u> in the Modern Movement.

Here, the author is giving a quick summary of the shortcomings of the Modern Movement, and why these shortcomings contributed to the decline of the Modernist Movement.

In this passage, the author is primarily concerned with the reasons behind the decline of the Modernist Movement. While the first part of the passage outlines the history and rise of Modernism, the author takes a critical view from the very beginning. The author's intentions are also made clear to us in the very first paragraph. They state that the ideology of Modernism was at odds with the actual construction of buildings.

As for the Main Point of the passage, we can formulate that based on the Author's Purpose. If the author is concerned with why the Modernist Movement declined, then their Main Point would be a one or two sentence statement stating the reasons. A good answer to the Main Point of this passage would be, "The Modernist Movement became unsustainable because of its overemphasis on aesthetics, lack of functionality, and inability to adapt to evolving building methods."

PT66 Passage 4

Advances in scientific understanding often do not build directly or smoothly in response to the data that are amassed, and in retrospect, after a major revision of theory, it may seem strange that a crucial hypothesis was long overlooked. A case in point is the discovery of a means by which the nuclei of atoms can be split. Between 1934, when a group of Italian physicists including Enrico Fermi first bombarded uranium with neutrons, and 1939, when exiled Austrian physicist Lise Meitner provided the crucial theoretical connection, scientists compiled increasing evidence that nuclear fission had been achieved, without, however, recognizing what they were witnessing.

Earlier, even before the neutron and proton composition of atomic nuclei had been experimentally demonstrated, some theoretical physicists had produced calculations indicating that in principle it should be possible to break atoms apart. But the neutron-bombardment experiments were not aimed at achieving such a result, and researchers were not even receptive to the possibility that it might happen in that context. A common view was that a neutron's breaking apart a uranium nucleus would be analogous to a pebble, thrown through a window, causing a house to collapse.

In Berlin, Meitner pursued research related to that of the Italians, discovering a puzzling group of radioactive substances produced by neutron bombardment of uranium. Fermi and others achieved numerous similar results. These products remained unidentified partly because precise chemical analyses were hampered by the minute quantities of the substances produced and the dangers of working with highly radioactive materials, but more significantly because of the expectation that they would all be elements close to uranium in nuclear composition. In 1938 Meitner escaped from Nazi Germany and undertook related research in Sweden, but her research partner Otto Hahn kept her informed of his continuing experimentation. Late in that year he wrote to her of a surprising result: one of the substances resulting from the neutron bombardment of uranium had been conclusively identified as barium, an element whose structure would have made it impossible to produce through any mechanism he envisaged as being involved in the experiments. Hahn even remarked that, despite the clear chemical evidence of what had occurred, it went "against all previous experiences of nuclear physics," but he also noted that together the number of protons and neutrons in the nuclei of barium and technetium, the accompanying product of the experiment, added up to the number of such particles that compose a uranium nucleus.

It was Meitner who finally recognized the significance of the data in relation to underlying theoretical considerations: the researchers had actually been splitting uranium atoms. Coining the term "nuclear fission," she quickly submitted her conclusion for publication in a paper coauthored with physicist Otto Frisch. When scientists in Europe and North America rushed to corroborate the findings, it became clear that the relevant evidence had been present for some time, lacking mainly the right conceptual link.

Advances in scientific understanding often do not build directly or smoothly in response to the data that are amassed, and in retrospect, after a major revision of theory, it may seem strange that a crucial hypothesis was long overlooked. A <u>case in point</u> is the discovery of a means by which the <u>nuclei of atoms can be split</u>. Between 1934, when a group of Italian physicists including Enrico Fermi first bombarded uranium with neutrons, and 1939, when exiled Austrian physicist Lise Meitner provided the crucial theoretical connection, scientists compiled increasing evidence that nuclear <u>fission</u> had been achieved, without, however, recognizing what they were witnessing.

As usual, pay extra attention to the opening statements of a passage. Here, it will serve as a helpful guide for subsequent developments.

The first sentence tells us that our scientific understanding does not increase proportionately to experimental data increases. Instead, sometimes we may have all the data without knowing what they are trying to explain. It's only after finally coming up with a theory that we look back and realize that the new theory does well to explain the previous data.

The keywords "*a case in point*" are crucial here. **This is a phrase often seen in RC passages**. A brief glance across the passage tells me that the rest of it all deals with physicists' experiments. So this passage is most likely the author providing an example to illustrate their earlier point.

From there, even though I don't know much about the experiments just yet, having only read the first paragraph, I can venture to guess that the physicists were conducting some kind of experiment, but could not adequately explain the data. It was only after a new theory was formulated later that the earlier data finally became explainable.

Armed with this knowledge, we can examine the content more thoroughly. The experiment in question involves the splitting of atomic nuclei. So scientists were basically splitting atoms but not realizing what was happening until the theory of nuclear fission was formulated.

Earlier, even before the neutron and proton composition of atomic nuclei had been experimentally demonstrated, some theoretical physicists had produced calculations indicating that <u>in principle it should be possible to break atoms apart</u>. But the neutron-bombardment experiments were not aimed at achieving such a result, and researchers <u>were not even receptive to the possibility</u> that it might happen in that context. A common view was that a neutron's breaking apart a uranium nucleus would be analogous to a pebble, thrown through a window, <u>causing a house to collapse</u>.

So theoretically, it was possible to split atomic nuclei. But in reality, researchers didn't think it would actually happen. Just as breaking a window wouldn't cause a house to collapse, so they thought shooting a neutron at an atomic nucleus wouldn't cause it to split.

<u>In Berlin</u>, Meitner pursued research related to that of the Italians, discovering a puzzling group of <u>radioactive substances produced by</u> neutron bombardment of uranium. Fermi and others achieved numerous similar results. These products <u>remained unidentified</u> partly because precise chemical analyses were hampered by the minute quantities of the substances produced and the dangers of working with highly radioactive materials, but more significantly because of the expectation that they would all be elements close to uranium in nuclear composition. <u>In 1938</u> Meitner escaped from Nazi Germany and undertook related research in Sweden, but her research partner Otto Hahn kept her informed of his continuing experimentation. Late in that year he wrote to her of a surprising result: one of the substances resulting from the neutron bombardment of uranium had been conclusively identified as <u>barium</u>, an element whose structure would have made it impossible to produce through any mechanism he envisaged as being involved in the experiments. Hahn even remarked that, despite the clear chemical evidence of what had occurred, it went "against all previous experiences of nuclear physics," but he also noted that together the number of protons and neutrons in the nuclei of <u>barium</u> and <u>technetium</u>, the accompanying product of the experiment, <u>added up to the number of such particles</u> that compose a uranium nucleus.

This paragraph goes into greater detail on the experiments and their results. The events are presented in chronological order. Again, it's helpful to have a timeline of what happened.

1934: Enrico Fermi began bombarding uranium atoms with neutrons. (From the first paragraph)

Between 1934 and 1938: Meitner is in Germany and discovers, just like Fermi, that if you bombard uranium with neutrons, you get an unidentified by-product.

1938: Meitner escapes to Sweden but continues her research; Otto Hahn figures out the by-products are barium and technetium and tells Meitner.

1939: Meitner and Otto Frisch formulate the theory of Nuclear Fission (From the first paragraph)

It was Meitner who finally recognized the significance of the data in relation to underlying theoretical considerations: the researchers had actually been splitting uranium atoms. Coining the term "nuclear fission," she quickly submitted her conclusion for publication in a paper coauthored with physicist Otto Frisch. When scientists in Europe and North America rushed to corroborate the findings, it became clear that the relevant evidence had been present for some time, lacking mainly the right conceptual link.

In the last paragraph, the author details how Meitner came to discover Nuclear Fission. The evidence for it was there all along. The by-products were barium and technetium, and shooting a neutron at a uranium atom splits it into two new elements. The evidence for Nuclear Fission was staring her right in the face, it was only afterward that she came up with a theory to explain it.

Overall, a fairly straightforward passage. The author tells us that often, in scientific experiments, the theory only comes belatedly, after we've had the data for some time. They then use Meitner's discovery of nuclear fission as an example to illustrate this scientific phenomenon.

The timeline of Meitner's discovery can be a little tricky, and this was something the test makers exploited in the subsequent questions. But being aware of the chronological sequence of what happened will make our understanding of the passage much clearer.

***

Different POV

Another area of confusion during passage reading occurs when different views, perspectives, or schools of thought are presented in quick succession. One speaker will have one point of view, the second speaker a slightly different point of view, and a third person yet another view.

When we encounter passages like this, you will likely find trap answers that mix up the speakers and their respective POVs. A challenging question type associated with these details will ask us to compare and contrast the views held by different speakers. These questions take a lot of time because they require us to return to the passage, summarize the respective views, and think about their differences before attempting the question. So it's vital to clearly understand each speaker's view, or at least where to find such evidence.

When you see a series of different point of views, you can either jot the views of each person down on paper if timing is not an issue; or if you prefer, use color-coded highlighting to accentuate the differences between each person. (For example, I would use the yellow highlighter for Speaker A's views, green for Speaker B, etc.)

Take a look at the following passages:

PT75 Passage 1

Having spent several decades trying to eliminate the unself-conscious "colonial gaze" characteristic of so many early ethnographic films, visual anthropologists from the industrialized West who study indigenous cultures are presently struggling with an even more profound transformation of their discipline. Because inexpensive video equipment is now available throughout the world, many indigenous peoples who were once examined by the Western ethnographer 's camera have begun to document their own cultures. Reaction to this phenomenon within Western anthropological circles is sharply divided.

One faction, led by anthropologist James Weiner, sees the proliferation of video and television as the final assault of Western values on indigenous cultures. Weiner argues that the spread of video represents "a devaluation of the different," culminating in the replacement of genuine historical, linguistic, social, and cultural difference with superficial difference among electronic images. He believes that video technologies inevitably purvey a Western ontology, one based on realism, immediacy, and self-expression. Thus, Weiner concludes, using video technology costs indigenous peoples the very cultural identity they seek to record. Moreover, he maintains that anthropologists who attribute a paramount truth value to these films simply because they are made by indigenous peoples are theoretically naive.

But Weiner's opponents contend that his views betray a certain nostalgia for the idea of the "noble savage." One such opponent, anthropologist Faye Ginsburg, concedes that no Western object that has entered cultural circulation since the fifteenth century has been neutral, but she considers it little more than boilerplate technological determinism to argue that using a video camera makes one unwittingly Western. Unlike Weiner, Ginsburg maintains that non-Western indigenous peoples can use Western media without adopting the conventions of Western culture. In fact, Ginsburg and many other anthropologists believe that video affords societies-especially oral ones-an invaluable opportunity to strengthen native languages and traditions threatened by Western exposure.

The Brazilian fieldwork of anthropologist Terence Turner, who studies the relationship between traditional Kayapo culture and Kayapo videotapes, lends credence to Ginsburg's position. Primarily an oral society, the Kayapo use video to document both ceremonial performances and transactions with representatives of the Brazilian government (this latter use is intended to provide legally binding records of the transactions). In contrast to Weiner's argument that video foists a Western ontology onto its users, Turner has found that the representations of Kayapo ceremonies, including everything from the camerawork to the editing, conform to the same principle of beauty embodied in the ceremonies themselves, one rooted in a complex pattern of repetition and sequential organization. The videos aesthetically mirror the ceremonies. The camera is not so at odds with Kayapo culture, it seems, that it transforms any Kayapo who uses it into a Westerner.

Having spent several decades trying to eliminate the un-self-conscious "colonial gaze" characteristic of so many early ethnographic films, <u>visual anthropologists from the industrialized West</u> who study indigenous cultures are presently struggling with an even more profound transformation of their discipline. Because inexpensive video equipment is now available throughout the world, many indigenous peoples who were once examined by the Western ethnographer 's camera have <u>begun to document their own cultures</u>. Reaction to this phenomenon <u>within Western anthropological circles</u> is sharply divided.

The first paragraph gives us background information for the subsequent discussion. Western anthropologists use video cameras to record indigenous peoples and cultures for their studies. But as video cameras become more widespread, indigenous peoples are now using them to record themselves. Western anthropologists are sharply divided in their reactions.

One faction, led by anthropologist <u>James Weiner</u>, sees the proliferation of video and television as the final <u>assault</u> of Western values on indigenous cultures. Weiner argues that the spread of video represents "a devaluation of the different," culminating in the <u>replacement</u> of genuine historical, linguistic, social, and cultural difference with <u>superficial difference among electronic images</u>. He believes that video technologies inevitably purvey a Western ontology, one based on realism, immediacy, and self-expression. Thus, Weiner concludes, using video technology <u>costs indigenous peoples the very cultural identity they seek to record.</u> Moreover, he maintains that <u>anthropologists</u> who attribute a paramount truth value to these films simply because they are made by indigenous peoples are <u>theoretically naive</u>.

The first school of thought, represented by James Weiner, believes that Indigenous video camera use represents a further invasion of Western technology on Indigenous values.

Furthermore, JW calls his opponents (those who take a more positive view of this practice), "*theoretically naïve.*"

But <u>Weiner's opponents</u> contend that his views betray a certain nostalgia for the idea of the <u>"noble savage."</u> One such opponent, anthropologist <u>Faye Ginsburg</u>, concedes that no Western object that has entered cultural circulation since the fifteenth century has been neutral, but she considers it <u>little more than boilerplate</u> technological determinism to argue that using a <u>video camera makes one unwittingly Western</u>. <u>Unlike Weiner</u>, Ginsburg maintains that non-Western indigenous peoples <u>can use Western media without adopting the conventions of Western culture</u>. In fact, Ginsburg and many other anthropologists believe that video affords societies-especially oral ones-an invaluable <u>opportunity to strengthen native languages and traditions</u> threatened by Western exposure.

The second school of thought, represented by Faye Ginsburg, holds the opposite view. They believe using Western technology can "*strengthen native languages and traditions.*"

What are Ginsburg's views toward Weiner? She thinks his views betray an almost patronizing, condescending fetishization of indigenous cultures. Using advanced technology somehow pollutes a pure and simple culture is a mistaken view held by JW and associates.

Ginsburg further states that using a video camera does not mean that you have to adopt the conventions of Western culture (the opposite of JW).

*The Brazilian fieldwork of anthropologist <u>Terence Turner</u>, who studies the relationship between traditional Kayapo culture and Kayapo videotapes, <u>lends credence to Ginsburg's position</u>. Primarily an oral society, the Kayapo use video to document both ceremonial performances and transactions with representatives of the Brazilian government (this latter use is intended to provide legally binding records of the transactions). <u>In contrast to Weiner's argument</u> that video foists a Western ontology onto its users, Turner has found that the representations of Kayapo ceremonies, including everything from the camerawork to the editing, <u>conform to the same principle of beauty embodied in the ceremonies themselves</u>, one rooted in a complex pattern of repetition and sequential organization. The videos aesthetically mirror the ceremonies. The camera is not so at odds with Kayapo culture, **it seems**, that it transforms any Kayapo who uses it into a Westerner.*

A third person is introduced into the debate, Terence Turner, who agrees with Ginsburg. Turner found that Kayapo recordings confirm their original principles of beauty, and the act of using a video camera has not diluted their original aesthetic principles or made them somehow more Western.

The last statement, voiced by the author of the passage, sheds light on the author's position. It appears that they generally agree with the position held by Turner and Ginsburg.

If we were to summarize the views held by each respective party quickly, it would look something like this:

Weiner	Ginsburg	Turner
Using video cameras represents an assault of Western culture upon Indigenous customs Using Western technology makes one a Westerner and is a loss of traditional values Thinks opponents naive	Using a camera does not automatically make one Western Opponent's beliefs betray erroneous biases and prejudices Cameras can strengthen Indigenous customs	Agrees with Ginsburg Kayapo use of cameras show us their traditional standards of beauty are still intact

PT21 Passage 2

What is "law"? By what processes do judges arrive at opinions, those documents that justify their belief that the "law" dictates a conclusion one way or the other? These are among the oldest questions in jurisprudence, debate about which has traditionally been dominated by representatives of two schools of thought: proponents of natural law, who see law as intertwined with a moral order independent of society's rules and mores, and legal positivists, who see law solely as embodying the commands of a society's ruling authority.

Since the early 1970s, these familiar questions have received some new and surprising answers in the legal academy. This novelty is in part a consequence of the increasing influence there of academic disciplines and intellectual traditions previously unconnected with the study of law. Perhaps the most influential have been the answers given by the Law and Economics school. According to these legal economists, law consists and ought to consist of those rules that maximize a society's material wealth and that abet the efficient operation of markets designed to generate wealth. More controversial have been the various answers provided by members of the Critical Legal Studies movement, according to whom law is one among several cultural mechanisms by which holders of power seek to legitimate their domination. Drawing on related arguments developed in anthropology, sociology, and history, the critical legal scholars contend that law is an expression of power, but not, as held by the positivists, the power of the legitimate sovereign government. Rather, it is an expression of the power of elites who may have no legitimate authority, but who are intent on preserving the privileges of their race, class, or gender.

In the mid-1970s, James Boyd White began to articulate yet another interdisciplinary response to the traditional questions, and in so doing spawned what is now known as the Law and Literature movement. White has insisted that law, particularly as it is interpreted in judicial opinions, should be understood as an essentially literary activity. Judicial opinions should be read and evaluated not primarily as political acts or as attempts to maximize society's wealth through efficient rules, but rather as artistic performances. And like all such performances, White argues, each judicial opinion attempts in its own way to promote a particular political or ethical value.

In the recent Justice as Translation, White argues that opinion-writing should be regarded as an act of "translation," and judges as "translators." As such, judges find themselves mediating between the authoritative legal text and the pressing legal problem that demands resolution. A judge must essentially "re-constitute" that text by fashioning a new one, which is faithful to the old text but also responsive to and informed by the conditions, constraints, and aspirations of the world in which the new legal problem has arisen.

What is "law"? By what processes do judges arrive at opinions, those documents that justify their belief that the "law" dictates a conclusion one way or the other? These are among the oldest questions in jurisprudence, debate about which has traditionally been dominated by representatives of two schools of thought: <u>proponents of natural law</u>, who see law as intertwined with a moral order independent of society's rules and mores, and <u>legal positivists</u>, who see law solely as embodying the commands of a society's ruling authority.

What is the law?

Two parties and their views are presented: proponents of natural law, who believe laws contain moral standards; and legal positivists, who see laws as a tool to control society.

Since the early 1970s, these familiar questions have received some new and surprising answers in the legal academy. This novelty is in part a consequence of the increasing influence there of academic disciplines and intellectual traditions previously unconnected with the study of law. Perhaps the most influential have been the answers given by the <u>Law and Economics school</u>. According to these legal economists, law consists and ought to consist of those rules that maximize a society's material wealth and that abet the efficient operation of markets designed to generate wealth. More controversial have been the various answers provided by members of the <u>Critical Legal Studies</u> movement, according to whom law is one among several cultural mechanisms by which holders of power seek to legitimate their domination. Drawing on related arguments developed in anthropology, sociology, and history, the critical legal scholars contend that law is an expression of power, <u>but not, as held by the positivists</u>, the power of the legitimate sovereign government. Rather, it is an expression of the power of elites who may have no legitimate authority, but who are intent on preserving the privileges of their race, class, or gender.

Two more schools of thought and their perspectives on "what is law" are introduced: one, the Law and Economics School, which believes the law's purpose is to maximize a society's material wealth and ensure the efficient operation of markets. Two, the Critical Legal Studies movement, which believes the law is a tool of the elites to control society.

The CLS movement is contrasted with the view held by legal positivists. While both believe the law to be a tool of power held by authority, legal positivists believe such authority to be legitimate; for CLS proponents, it doesn't have to be.

In the mid-1970s, <u>James Boyd White</u> began to articulate yet another interdisciplinary response to the traditional questions, and in so doing spawned what is now known as the <u>Law and Literature movement</u>. White has insisted that law, particularly as it is interpreted in judicial opinions, should be understood as an essentially literary activity. Judicial opinions should be read and evaluated not primarily as political acts or as attempts to maximize society's wealth through efficient rules, but rather as artistic performances. And like all such performances, White argues, each judicial opinion attempts in its own way to promote a particular political or ethical value.

A fifth perspective is introduced, the Law and Literature movement. The law is a literary activity/performance aimed at promoting specific values.

In the recent Justice as Translation, White argues that opinion-writing should be regarded as an act of "<u>translation</u>," and judges as "translators." As such, judges find themselves mediating between the authoritative legal text and the pressing legal problem that demands resolution. A judge must essentially <u>"re-constitute" that text by fashioning a new one</u>, which is faithful to the old text but also responsive to and informed by the conditions, constraints, and aspirations of the world in which the new legal problem has arisen.

The author further expands on White's beliefs. Judges must translate the law from text into new interpretations adapted to their environment and conditions.

Let's look at one more passage, try to keep track of all the different views.

PT21 Passage 3

Since the early 1920s, most petroleum geologists have favored a biogenic theory for the formation of oil. According to this theory, organic matter became buried in sediments, and subsequent conditions of temperature and pressure over time transformed it into oil.

Since 1979 an opposing abiogenic theory about the origin of oil has been promulgated. According to this theory, what is now oil began as hydrocarbon compounds within the earth's mantle (the region between the core and the crust) during the formation of the earth. Oil was created when gases rich in methane, the lightest of the hydrocarbons, rose from the mantle through fractures and faults in the crust, carrying a significant amount of heavier hydrocarbons with them. As the gases encountered intermittent drops in pressure, the heavier hydrocarbons condensed, forming oil, and were deposited in reservoirs throughout the crust. Rock regions deformed by motions of the crustal plates provided the conduits and fractures necessary for the gases to rise through the crust.

Opponents of the abiogenic theory charge that hydrocarbons could not exist in the mantle, because high temperatures would destroy or break them down. Advocates of the theory, however, point out that other types of carbon exist in the mantle: unoxidized carbon must exist there, because diamonds are formed within the mantle before being brought to the surface by eruptive processes. Proponents of the abiogenic theory also point to recent experimental work that suggests that the higher pressures within the mantle tend to offset the higher temperatures, allowing hydrocarbons, like unoxidized carbon, to continue to exist in the mantle.

If the abiogenic theory is correct, vast undiscovered reservoirs of oil and gas—undiscovered because the biogenic model precludes their existence—may in actuality exist. One company owned by the Swedish government has found the abiogenic theory so persuasive that it has started exploratory drilling for gas or oil in a granite formation call the Siljan Ring—not the best place to look for gas or oil if one believes they are derived from organic compounds, because granite forms from magma (molten rock) and contains no organic sediments. The ring was formed about 360 million years ago when a large meteorite hit the 600- million-year-old granite that forms the base of the continental crust. The impact fractured the granite, and the Swedes believe that if oil comes from the mantle, it could have risen with methane gas through this now permeable rock. Fueling their optimism further is the fact that prior to the start of drilling, methane gas had been detected rising through the granite.

Since the early 1920s, most petroleum geologists have favored a biogenic theory for the formation of oil. According to this theory, organic matter became buried in sediments, and subsequent conditions of temperature and pressure over time transformed it into oil.

Most geologists subscribe to the biogenic theory, which holds that oil comes from organic matter.

Since 1979 an opposing abiogenic theory about the origin of oil has been promulgated. According to this theory, what is now oil began as hydrocarbon compounds within the earth's mantle (the region between the core and the crust) during the formation of the earth. Oil was created when gases rich in methane, the lightest of the hydrocarbons, rose from the mantle through fractures and faults in the crust, carrying a significant amount of heavier hydrocarbons with them. As the gases encountered intermittent drops in pressure, the heavier hydrocarbons condensed, forming oil, and were deposited in reservoirs throughout the crust. Rock regions deformed by motions of the crustal plates provided the conduits and fractures necessary for the gases to rise through the crust.

Opponents believe that oil comes from hydrocarbons that rose out of the earth's mantle and subsequently condensed.

Opponents of the abiogenic theory charge that hydrocarbons could not exist in the mantle, because high temperatures would destroy or break them down. Advocates of the theory, however, point out that other types of carbon exist in the mantle: unoxidized carbon must exist there, because diamonds are formed within the mantle before being brought to the surface by eruptive processes. Proponents of the abiogenic theory also point to recent experimental work that suggests that the higher pressures within the mantle tend to offset the higher temperatures, allowing hydrocarbons, like unoxidized carbon, to continue to exist in the mantle.

Opponents of the abiogenic theory (believers of the biogenic theory): hydrocarbons cannot exist in the mantle, it's too hot.

Proponents of the abiogenic theory: carbons such as diamonds can exist in the mantle, and the higher pressure in the mantle may cancel out the effects of hot temperatures.

If the abiogenic theory is correct, vast undiscovered reservoirs of oil and gas—undiscovered because the biogenic model precludes their existence—may in actuality exist. One company owned by the Swedish government has found the abiogenic theory so persuasive that it has started exploratory drilling for gas or oil in a granite formation call the Siljan Ring—not the best place to look for gas or oil if one believes they are derived from organic compounds, because granite forms from magma (molten rock) and contains no organic sediments. The ring was formed about 360 million years ago when a large meteorite hit the 600- million-year-old granite that forms the base of the continental crust. The impact fractured the granite, and the Swedes believe that if oil comes from the mantle, it could have risen with methane gas through this now permeable rock. Fueling their optimism further is the fact that prior to the start of drilling, methane gas had been detected rising through the granite.

The last paragraph discusses an implication of the abiogenic theory. If oil came from hydrocarbons rising from the earth's mantle, then there may be many more undiscovered oil reserves than we had previously thought. Cautious optimism is expressed as methane has been found in such a potential site.

Let's simplify the content of this passage:

Biogenic: oil comes from organic material.

Abiogenic: oil comes from hydrocarbons rising out of the earth's mantle.

Biogenic: hydrocarbons cannot exist in the mantle. It's too hot.

Abiogenic: but the mantle is not too hot to contain some carbon (diamonds), and the pressure in the mantle may cancel out the high temperature's effects on hydrocarbons.

The author: if the abiogenic view is correct, there will be a lot of undiscovered oil. One Swedish company is doing such explorations, and the initial results look promising.

In this passage (Author's Purpose), the author has outlined a debate between the proponents of the biogenic theory and the proponents of the abiogenic theory.

Given the relatively neutral stance of the author, who deliberately avoids taking a position, except for the tone of cautious optimism at the very end of the passage, our main point for the passage should look something like this:

Contrary to the biogenic view, which holds that oil is derived from organic materials, the abiogenic view believes that oil comes from hydrocarbons rising out of the earth's mantle, with far-reaching implications for the oil industry.

***

Abstract Words and Descriptions

When a passage contains abstract, vague, or complex language, we can be easily thrown off-track. The author may be describing the setup of an experiment, exploring a philosophical debate, or defining a difficult-to-understand concept. Many students fear abstract descriptions, and rightfully so, because not only can we lose sight of the bigger picture when we are bogged down in these details, but more often, we struggle to understand them and see their relevance.

We can do several things when faced with abstract sentences and descriptions in a passage. We can try to pause and think about the meaning of these abstract terms, coming up with our own examples and analogies. We can try to simplify what the author is saying by translating it into simple English. We can also connect these ideas to what we have already learned from the passage.

For the subsequent three passages, read through them and seek to understand as much as possible. Take notes if you need to. But more importantly, look at my subsequent explanations to see how I broke down the abstractions and details in these passages.

PT53 Passage 4

Sometimes there is no more effective means of controlling an agricultural pest than giving free rein to its natural predators. A case in point is the cyclamen mite, a pest whose population can be effectively controlled by a predatory mite of the genus Typhlodromus. Cyclamen mites infest strawberry plants; they typically establish themselves in a strawberry field shortly after planting, but their populations do not reach significantly damaging levels until the plants' second year. Typhlodromus mites usually invade the strawberry fields during the second year, rapidly subdue the cyclamen mite populations, and keep them from reaching significantly damaging levels.

Typhlodromus owes its effectiveness as a predator to several factors in addition to its voracious appetite. Its population can increase as rapidly as that of its prey. Both species reproduce by parthenogenesis—a mode of reproduction in which unfertilized eggs develop into fertile females. Cyclamen mites lay three eggs per day over the four or five days of their reproductive life span; Typhlodromus lay two or three eggs per day for eight to ten days. Seasonal synchrony of Typhlodromus reproduction with the growth of prey populations and ability to survive at low prey densities also contribute to the predatory efficiency of Typhlodromus. During winter, when cyclamen mite populations dwindle to a few individuals hidden in the crevices and folds of leaves in the crowns of the strawberry plants, the predatory mites subsist on the honeydew produced by aphids and white flies. They do not reproduce except when they are feeding on the cyclamen mites. These features, which make Typhlodromus well-suited for exploiting the seasonal rises and falls of its prey, are common among predators that control prey populations.

Greenhouse experiments have verified the importance of Typhlodromus predation for keeping cyclamen mites in check. One group of strawberry plants was stocked with both predator and prey mites; a second group was kept predator-free by regular application of parathion, an insecticide that kills the predatory species but does not affect the cyclamen mite. Throughout the study, populations of cyclamen mites remained low in plots shared with Typhlodromus, but their infestation attained significantly damaging proportions on predator-free plants.

Applying parathion in this instance is a clear case in which using a pesticide would do far more harm than good to an agricultural enterprise. The results were similar in field plantings of strawberries, where cyclamen mites also reached damaging levels when predators were eliminated by parathion, but they did not attain such levels in untreated plots. When cyclamen mite populations began to increase in an untreated planting, the predator populations quickly responded to reduce the outbreak. On average, cyclamen mites were about 25 times more abundant in the absence of predators than in their presence.

Sometimes there is no more effective means of controlling an <u>agricultural pest</u> than giving free rein to its <u>natural predators</u>. <u>A case in point</u> is <u>the cyclamen mite</u>, a pest whose population can be effectively controlled by a predatory mite of the genus <u>Typhlodromus</u>. Cyclamen mites infest strawberry plants; they typically establish themselves in a strawberry field <u>shortly after planting</u>, but their populations do not reach significantly damaging levels <u>until the plants' second year</u>. Typhlodromus mites usually invade the strawberry fields <u>during the second year</u>, rapidly subdue the cyclamen mite populations, and keep them from reaching significantly damaging levels.

The first sentence hints at what this passage is about. It's about using natural predators to control an agricultural pest. As the second sentence tells us, the rest of the passage is about a specific case that illustrates this. Remember the words "*case in point?*"

Typhlodromus is a natural predator of the cyclamen mite, and the passage will talk about how Typhlodromus is used to keep cyclamen mites in check.

Cyclamen mites invade strawberry fields "shortly after planting," meaning they show up in the first year, but don't do significant damage until the second year. Typhlodromus arrive in the second year.

Typhlodromus owes its effectiveness as a predator to <u>several factors in addition to its voracious appetite</u>. Its population can <u>increase as rapidly as that of its prey</u>. Both species reproduce by parthenogenesis—a mode of reproduction in which unfertilized eggs develop into fertile females. Cyclamen mites <u>lay three eggs per day over the four or five days</u> of their reproductive life span; Typhlodromus lay <u>two or three eggs per day for eight to ten days</u>. <u>Seasonal synchrony</u> of Typhlodromus reproduction with the growth of prey populations and ability to <u>survive at low prey densities</u> also contribute to the predatory efficiency of Typhlodromus. During winter, when cyclamen mite populations dwindle to a few individuals hidden in the crevices and folds of leaves in the crowns of the strawberry plants, the predatory mites subsist on the honeydew produced by aphids and white flies. They do not reproduce except when they are feeding on the cyclamen mites. These features, which make Typhlodromus well-suited for exploiting the seasonal rises and falls of its prey, are common among predators that control prey populations.

Several reasons for why Typhlodromus is effective are listed:

- Voracious appetite

- Can increase as rapidly as that of the prey (cyclamen mites)
    - Cyclamen mites lay 3 eggs per day for 4-5 days (12-15 eggs in total)
    - Typhlodromus lay 2-3 eggs per day for 8-10 days (16-30 eggs in total)

- Seasonal synchrony of predator reproduction with prey population
    - So, if prey increases in spring, Typhlodromus will reproduce in the spring, etc.

- Typhlodromus can survive at low prey densities.
    - When cyclamen mites dwindle in the winter, Typhlodromus survive on alternate food sources.

- Typhlodromus only reproduce when feeding on cyclamen mites.

<u>Greenhouse experiments have verified the importance of Typhlodromus</u> predation for keeping cyclamen mites in check. <u>One group</u> of strawberry plants was stocked with both predator and prey mites; a <u>second group</u> was kept predator-free by regular application of parathion, an insecticide that kills the predatory species but does not affect the cyclamen mite. Throughout the study, populations of cyclamen mites remained low in plots shared with Typhlodromus, but their infestation attained significantly damaging proportions on predator-free plants.

A study is conducted; one plot had cyclamen mites and Typhlodromus and the other had only cyclamen mites. Cyclamen mites were under control when Typhlodromus was present, but caused significant damage when the predator was removed.

Applying parathion in this instance is a clear case in which using a pesticide would do far more harm than good to an agricultural enterprise. The <u>results were similar in field plantings of strawberries</u>, where cyclamen mites also reached damaging levels when predators were eliminated by parathion, but they did not attain such levels in untreated plots. When cyclamen mite populations began to increase in an untreated planting, the predator populations quickly responded to reduce the outbreak. On average, cyclamen mites were about 25 times more abundant in the absence of predators than in their presence.

As we learned in the previous chapters, we should always try to compare the information discussed in each paragraph. In the previous paragraph, the author tells us that Typhlodromus was an effective check on cyclamen mites in *greenhouse experiments;* here, we are shown that they are equally effective in the real world (*field plantings of strawberries.*)

Typhlodromus effectively kept cyclamen mites in check because the Typhlodromus was not killed by parathion. If they were killed by parathion, cyclamen mites were about "25 times more abundant."

The tricky thing about this passage, for most of my students, was to have a clear grasp of the concepts discussed. Cyclamen mites were the parasites. Typhlodromus, also mites, were the beneficial predators. Parathion, a pesticide, was actually bad for the strawberry plants, as it killed the beneficial predators without harming the parasites. Some of this might sound counter-intuitive if you did not fully grasp the full implications behind each concept. **That's why we must pause and pay extra attention to the parties, objects, or concepts whose role may not be apparent at first glance.**

Secondly, remember how we often translated abstract or vague statements in LR stimuli into more comprehensible sentences? That habit can be constructive in RC passages as well. **Translating abstract ideas into simple language and pausing to think about that idea's implications will help us better understand the passage as a whole.**

Take a look at the information presented in the second paragraph. Cyclamen mites lay 3 eggs per day for 4-5 days; while Typhlodromus mites lay 2-3 eggs for 8-10 days. In other words, cyclamen mites lay 12-15 eggs while Typhlodromus lay 16-30 eggs in total. A Typhlodromus mite will always lay more eggs than a cyclamen mite, possibly twice as many. Rather than simply skimming over the numerical data in the passage, if we paused and did a little calculation of our own, the idea that the author is trying to convey becomes much easier to see.

Similarly, **trying to come up with our own examples** that correspond with the author's description can help us reach a more intimate understanding of what they are trying to express. When the author stated that Typhlodromus reproduction is seasonally synchronized with the prey population growth, that got me thinking. We know that the prey population (cyclamen mites) dwindles during the winter, so whichever season sees cyclamen mites increase in population (I'm guessing Spring or Summer), we will see a similar uptick in Typhlodromus reproduction.

Let's look at another science-based passage that contains abstract ideas and descriptions. Try to simplify abstract descriptions by coming up with our own concrete examples of what the author is describing. Think about the implication behind each idea rather than simply acknowledging their existence. Try to translate vague or abstract language into our own words.

PT65 Passage 4

As part of an international effort to address environmental problems resulting from agricultural overproduction, hundreds of thousands of acres of surplus farmland throughout Europe will be taken out of production in coming years. Restoring a natural balance of flora to this land will be difficult, however, because the nutrients in soil that has been in constant agricultural use are depleted. Moreover, much of this land has been heavily fertilized, and when such land is left unplanted, problem weeds like thistles often proliferate, preventing many native plants from establishing themselves. While the quickest way to restore heavily fertilized land is to remove and replace the topsoil, this is impractical on a large scale such as that of the European effort. And while it is generally believed that damaged ecological systems will restore themselves very gradually over time, a study underway in the Netherlands is investigating the possibility of artificially accelerating the processes through which nature slowly re-establishes plant diversity on previously farmed land.

In the study, a former cornfield was raked to get rid of cornstalks and weeds, then divided into 20 plots of roughly equal size. Control plots were replanted with corn or sown with nothing at all. The remaining plots were divided into two groups: plots in one group were sown with a mixture of native grasses and herbs; those in the other group received the same mixture of grasses and herbs together with clover and toadflax. After three years, thistles have been forced out of the plots where the broadest variety of species was sown and have also disappeared from mats of grass in the plots sown with fewer seed varieties. On the control plots that were left untouched, thistles have become dominant.

On some of the plots sown with seeds of native plant species, soil from nearby land that had been taken out of production 20 years earlier was scattered to see what effect introducing nematodes, fungi, and other beneficial microorganisms associated with later stages of natural soil development might have on the process of native plant repopulation. The seeds sown on these enriched plots have fared better than seeds sown on the unenriched plots, but still not as well as those growing naturally on the nearby land. Researchers have concluded that this is because fields farmed for many years are overrun with aggressive disease organisms, while, for example, beneficial mycorrhiza— fungi that live symbiotically on plant roots and strengthen them against the effects of disease organisms—are lacking. These preliminary results suggest that restoring natural plant diversity to over farmed land hinges on restoring a natural balance of microorganisms in the soil. In other words, diversity underground fosters diversity aboveground. Researchers now believe that both kinds of diversity can be restored more quickly to damaged land if beneficial microorganisms are "sown" systematically into the soil along with a wide variety of native plant seeds.

As part of an international effort to address environmental problems resulting from agricultural overproduction, hundreds of thousands of acres of surplus farmland throughout Europe will be taken out of production in coming years. Restoring a natural balance of flora to this land will be difficult, however, because the nutrients in soil that has been in constant agricultural use are depleted. Moreover, much of this land has been heavily fertilized, and when such land is left unplanted, problem weeds like thistles often proliferate, preventing many native plants from establishing themselves. While the quickest way to restore heavily fertilized land is to remove and replace the topsoil, this is impractical on a large scale such as that of the European effort. And while it is generally believed that damaged ecological systems will restore themselves very gradually over time, a study underway in the Netherlands is investigating the possibility of artificially accelerating the processes through which nature slowly re-establishes plant diversity on previously farmed land.

The first part of the paragraph describes a problem, which can be simplified into a long causal chain: Farming + Fertilization ➜ Loss of Soil Nutrients + Weeds ➜ Native Plants Cannot Return

Consequently, the passage explores artificial ways to accelerate the restoration of former farmland, the fastest way is to replace the topsoil, but that would be too impractical. So we need to find other alternatives.

In the study, a former cornfield was raked to get rid of cornstalks and weeds, then divided into 20 plots of roughly equal size. Control plots were replanted with corn or sown with nothing at all. The remaining plots were divided into two groups: plots in one group were sown with a mixture of native grasses and herbs; those in the other group received the same mixture of grasses and herbs together with clover and toadflax. After three years, thistles have been forced out of the plots where the broadest variety of species was sown and have also disappeared from mats of grass in the plots sown with fewer seed varieties. On the control plots that were left untouched, thistles have become dominant.

It's crucial to realize that the twenty plots are divided into **four** different types of plots here. This may come in handy in the subsequent reading or when taking on the questions. There are two types of control plots (corn vs. empty), and two types of testing plots (native grass and herbs vs. native grass and herbs + clover and toadflax).

After three years, both testing plots have no thistles left; but the empty control plot has been covered in thistles.

On some of the plots sown with seeds of native plant species, soil from nearby land that had been taken out of production 20 years earlier was scattered to see what effect introducing nematodes, fungi, and other beneficial microorganisms associated with later stages of natural soil development might have on the process of native plant repopulation. The seeds sown on these enriched plots have fared better than seeds sown on the unenriched plots, but still not as well as those growing naturally on the nearby land. Researchers have concluded that this is because fields farmed for many years are overrun with aggressive disease organisms, while, for example, beneficial mycorrhiza— fungi that live symbiotically on plant roots and strengthen them against the effects of disease organisms—are lacking. These preliminary results suggest that restoring natural plant diversity to over farmed land hinges on restoring a natural balance of microorganisms in the soil. In other words, diversity underground fosters diversity aboveground. Researchers now believe that both kinds of diversity can be restored more quickly to damaged land if beneficial microorganisms are "sown" systematically into the soil along with a wide variety of native plant seeds.

Soil from land that hasn't been farmed for 20 years were scattered on some of the testing plots. Be careful that we are not replacing the topsoil, we are just scattering some soil into the mix!

The soil has beneficial microorganisms, and the results were positive for native plants.
In terms of the best environment for native plants,

Nearby land where plants grew naturally > Test plots with unfertilized soil scattered > Regular test plots

Let's pause for a moment and think about what we have learned so far.

We know that re-introducing native plants into disused fields will prevent the proliferation of weeds. We also know that scattering soil rich in beneficial micro-organisms will help native plants grow better.

If we really think about it, there's a causal chain between the information presented in the second and third paragraphs:

Scattering unfertilized soil → Introduces beneficial microorganisms → Increases native plants' defenses against disease → Native plants grow better → Weeds/Thistles are prevented from coming back

This is essentially the message of the passage. When we pause and think about the relationship between different ideas and concepts, what they each represent, and attempt to find any connections between them, a seemingly dense and abstract passage can become much more straightforward.

***

PT22 Passage 4

What it means to "explain" something in science often comes down to the application of mathematics. Some thinkers hold that mathematics is a kind of language—a systematic contrivance of signs, the criteria for the authority of which are internal coherence, elegance, and depth. The application of such a highly artificial system to the physical world, they claim, results in the creation of a kind of statement about the world. Accordingly, what matters in the sciences is finding a mathematical concept that attempts, as other language does, to accurately describe the functioning of some aspect of the world.

At the center of the issue of scientific knowledge can thus be found questions about the relationship between language and what it refers to. A discussion about the role played by language in the pursuit of knowledge has been going on among linguists for several decades. The debate centers around whether language corresponds in some essential way to objects and behaviors, making knowledge a solid and reliable commodity; or, on the other hand, whether the relationship between language and things is purely a matter of agreed-upon conventions, making knowledge tenuous, relative, and inexact.

Lately the latter theory has been gaining wider acceptance. According to linguists who support this theory, the way language is used varies depending upon changes in accepted practices and theories among those who work in a particular discipline. These linguists argue that, in the pursuit of knowledge, a statement is true only when there are no promising alternatives that might lead one to question it. Certainly this characterization would seem to be applicable to the sciences. In science, a mathematical statement may be taken to account for every aspect of a phenomenon it is applied to, but, some would argue, there is nothing inherent in mathematical language that guarantees such a correspondence. Under this view, acceptance of a mathematical statement by the scientific community— by virtue of the statement's predictive power or methodological efficiency—transforms what is basically an analogy or metaphor into an explanation of the physical process in question, to be held as true until another, more compelling analogy takes its place.

In pursuing the implications of this theory, linguists have reached the point at which they must ask: If words or sentences do not correspond in an essential way to life or to our ideas about life, then just what are they capable of telling us about the world? In science and mathematics, then, it would seem equally necessary to ask: If models of electrolytes or $E = mc^2$, say, do not correspond essentially to the physical world, then just what functions do they perform in the acquisition of scientific knowledge? But this question has yet to be significantly addressed in the sciences.

What it means to "explain" something in science often comes down to the application of mathematics. Some thinkers hold that mathematics is a kind of <u>language</u>—a systematic contrivance of <u>signs</u>, the criteria for the authority of which are <u>internal coherence, elegance, and depth</u>. The application of such a highly artificial system to the physical world, they claim, results in the creation of a kind of statement about the world. Accordingly, what matters in the sciences is finding a mathematical concept that attempts, as other language does, to accurately describe the functioning of some aspect of the world.

A LOT of information in the first paragraph: Math is essential to the sciences, math is a language. A language is a system of internally coherent, elegant, and deep signs. Languages describe things, and since math is also a language, science is about finding the most suitable math to describe the physical world.

At the center of the issue of scientific knowledge can thus be found <u>questions about the relationship between language and what it refers to</u>. A discussion about the role played by language in the pursuit of knowledge has been going on among <u>linguists</u> for several decades. The debate centers around whether language corresponds in some essential way <u>to objects and behaviors</u>, making knowledge a solid and reliable commodity; or, on the other hand, whether the relationship between language and things is purely <u>a matter of agreed-upon conventions</u>, making knowledge tenuous, relative, and inexact.

This passage is especially tricky because of the sudden shift in scope between the first paragraph and the rest of the passage. The first paragraph had me thinking that the rest of the passage will discuss the relationship between math and science, or how math is a language. But instead, we are now discussing the relationship between language and the objects it's referring to.

This shows that while we should always try to predict what the passage is about right from the beginning, we need to constantly readjust our prediction/hypothesis as we move through the passage and encounter new information. Refer back to the **Hypothesis-Validation Framework** we discussed in Chapter 1.

The debate centers around two views on what language refers to. Again, this is pretty abstract stuff. Does language refer to objects and behaviors, or is language purely a matter of convention?

These abstract descriptions can be problematic for even the most discerning students. Given the time constraints in RC, we are often tempted to read something without really stopping to try to understand what it means. After reading this paragraph, we can probably remember that the debate is about whether language refers to concrete objects, or correspond largely with agreed-upon conventions.

But what does this actually mean? Being able to repeat/regurgitate what was stated in a passage doesn't count as true understanding. What can we say in response if someone had asked us to explain the differences between the two views?

This is where **trying to come up with our own examples or analogies** can really help. Coming up with examples is one of the best ways to achieve a deeper, more personal level of understanding of difficult topics. They are also much easier to remember when we are confronted with too much information.

So can we come up with an example to flesh out the essence of the two parties to the debate?

What if language referred to real objects and behaviors? Take the word "dog," for example. If this theory holds true, then the letters of "d," "o," and "g," when joined together, has a direct link to the four-legged furry canine. You can't just use a different word.

But if the language between language and things is purely a matter of agreed-upon conventions? Back to our "dog" example, if the word "dog" is used to refer to puppies and golden retrievers and pugs simply because that's what everybody uses, then if everybody woke up the next day and decided to use the word "cat" to refer to these animals, then it shouldn't matter. All that matters is that there is consensus.

Given the limited information in the passage, I've come up with this half-baked example. At this point, I don't know if my example is on point or accurate yet, but that shouldn't deter me. Because the very act of trying to come up with an example or analogy in the face of difficult concepts will **always** help make them more understandable. The examples may not be perfect, but they will improve our understanding.

*Lately the <u>latter theory</u> has been gaining wider acceptance. According to linguists who support this theory, the way language is used <u>varies depending upon changes</u> in accepted practices and theories among those who work in a particular discipline. These linguists argue that, in the pursuit of knowledge, a statement is <u>true only when there are no promising alternatives</u> that might lead one to question it. Certainly this characterization **would seem to be applicable to the sciences**. In science, a <u>mathematical statement</u> may be taken to account for every aspect of a phenomenon it is applied to, but, some would argue, there is <u>nothing</u> inherent in mathematical language that <u>guarantees</u> such a correspondence. Under this view, acceptance of a mathematical statement by the scientific community— by virtue of the statement's predictive power or methodological efficiency— transforms what is basically an analogy or metaphor into an explanation of the physical process in question<u>, to be held as true until another, more compelling analogy takes its place.</u>*

The "*latter theory*," of course, refers to the "*agreed upon convention*" theory. Always know exactly what the author is referring to.

The advocates believe a statement is "*true only when there are no promising alternatives*." Remember their position on language? Language is an agreed-upon convention. It derives its meaning from social consensus. In other words, the definition no longer holds true if there are better alternatives.

Notice how we have connected the original position of the theorists with their views on when a statement is true?

Continuing with the paragraph, the author is now talking about math. We know that math is a language, and the theorists believe that a statement/definition is no longer true when there are better alternatives. So similarly, a mathematical theorem or explanation is only true until a better theorem or explanation comes along.

As we read through conceptually difficult passages, we always try to link newly presented information with what we have already learned or summarized. In especially abstract passages, we must build upon our previous understanding as we move through the passage, otherwise we'll soon be lost. (**Conceptual Link-Back**)

A few words that seem to betray the author's attitude appears in the paragraph's middle: "*would seem to apply to the sciences*." I suppose that the author agrees with the second side of the debate. But I can't be sure, I'll need to read further to reach a more definitive conclusion.

In pursuing the <u>implications</u> of this theory, linguists have reached the point at which they must ask: If words or sentences do not correspond in an essential way to life or to our ideas about life, <u>then just what are they capable of telling us about the world?</u> In science and mathematics, then, it would seem equally necessary to ask: If models of electrolytes or E = mc2, say, do not correspond essentially to the physical world, then <u>just what functions do they perform in the acquisition of scientific knowledge?</u> But this question has yet to be significantly addressed in the sciences.

In abstract passages, always try to recollect what had just been discussed, even as we start a new paragraph. We know that these theorists think language is a social convention, math is a language, so math is also an agreed-upon convention.

So if a math theorem isn't universally true, and only true because we have agreed to it, then can we really know what is true and what isn't? How would we ever obtain objective, true knowledge; when the language used to describe it, and by extension, the math used in scientific discoveries, are just temporary principles held in place by social consensus and popularity?

This is what this paragraph is trying to suggest. In the example given, E =MC2, Einstein's equation is mathematical, making it a part of language. In turn, it doesn't refer to fixed objects and identities but is a matter of "*agreed upon convention*." So is scientific knowledge itself subjective?

Finally, the last sentence further hints at the author's attitude. From the previous paragraph, it appears that the author is somewhat convinced of the validity of this theory. Combined with this information, we know that they are not fully convinced, as additional unresolved questions remain.

***

Key Persons

Let's examine one final, albeit less common detail that can confuse students. In some passages, the author will not only present the different POV of various speakers, but also throw out a bunch of names of scientists, scholars, artists, or musicians. In the questions section, the test makers will then ask you about the subtle differences between some of these key personages, even when little details were given.

Let's return to a previously seen passage for this exercise. This time, think about all the musicians and scholars mentioned in the passage and what we know about each of them.

PT21 Passage 1

Musicologists concerned with the "London Pianoforte school," the group of composers, pedagogues, pianists, publishers, and builders who contributed to the development of the piano in London at the turn of the nineteenth century, have long encountered a formidable obstacle in the general unavailability of music of this "school" in modern scholarly editions. Indeed, much of this repertory has more or less vanished from our historical consciousness. Granted, the sonatas and Gradus ad Parnassum of <u>Muzio Clementi</u> and the nocturnes of <u>John Field</u> have remained familiar enough (though more often than not in editions lacking scholarly rigor), but the work of other leading representatives, like <u>Johann Baptist Cramer</u> and <u>Jan Ladislav Dussek</u>, has eluded serious attempts at revival.

<u>Nicholas Temperley's</u> ambitious new anthology decisively overcomes this deficiency. What underscores the intrinsic value of Temperley's editions is that the anthology reproduces nearly all of the original music in facsimile. Making available this cross section of English musical life—some 800 works by 49 composers—should encourage new critical perspectives about how piano music evolved in England, an issue of considerable relevance to our understanding of how piano music developed on the European continent, and of how, finally, the instrument was transformed from the fortepiano to what we know today as the piano.

To be sure, the concept of the London Pianoforte school itself calls for review. "School" may well be too strong a word for what was arguably a group unified not so much by stylistic principles or aesthetic creed as by the geographical circumstance that they worked at various times in London and produced pianos and piano music for English pianos and English markets. Indeed, Temperley concedes that their "variety may be so great as to cast doubt on the notion of a 'school.'"

The notion of a school was first propounded by <u>Alexander Ringer</u>, who argued that laws of artistic survival forced the young, progressive Beethoven to turn outside Austria for creative models, and that he found inspiration in a group of pianists connected with Clementi in London. Ringer's proposed London Pianoforte school did suggest a circumscribed and fairly unified group—for want of a better term, a school—of musicians whose influence was felt primarily in the decades just before and after 1800. After all, <u>Beethoven</u> did respond to the advances of the Broadwood piano—its reinforced frame, extended compass, triple stringing, and pedals, for example—and it is reasonable to suppose that London pianists who composed music for such an instrument during the critical phase of its development exercised no small degree of influence on Continental musicians. Nevertheless, perhaps the most sensible approach to this issue is to define the school by the period (c. 1766–1873) during which it flourished, as Temperley has done in the anthology.

Seven names were dropped in this passage. In order of appearance, they are Muzio Clementi, John Field, Johann Baptist Cramer, Jan Ladislav Dussek, Nicholas Temperley, Alex Ringer, and Beethoven. Here is what we know about each of them based on information gathered from the passage:

- Muzio Clementi: significant figure in the London Pianoforte School, his works are still remembered today.

- John Field: similar to Clementi, some of his works are still remembered.

- Johann Baptist Cramer: of the London Pianoforte School, most of his works forgotten.

- Jan Ladislav Dussek: same as Johann Baptist Cramer

- Nicholas Temperley: the author in discussion in the passage, the author approves of his new anthology

- Alexander Ringer invented the term "London Pianoforte School," a definition that Temperley might not agree with.

- Beethoven: cited as evidence by Alexander Ringer to show the existence of the London Pianoforte School and its influence on continental European musicians.

***

With so many names in play, it's easy to overlook the subtle differences between some of them. For instance, if a question asked us why the author mentioned John Field, we might easily have gotten it wrong.

We know that the first paragraph also talks about the London Pianoforte School being forgotten, and since John Field is a member of this school, we might have easily assumed that he was one of the composers that have faded from our collective consciousness.

So the takeaway from this is to keep an eye out for key persons or groups that appear in the passage. Even though the author might not go into much details about them, they can still be the source of tricky questions.

Chapter 5: A Quick Word on Highlighting

Highlighting with a sense of purpose

The modern LSAT is taken on the computer and a variety of electronic tools are available to annotate and markup the passage as we read. There are three highlighter colors and an underline option.

There are many ways to use these tools to our benefit. I've always found that using different colors to represent different views and concepts to be helpful in accentuating our understanding. For instance, if in the passage the author shifts back and forth rapidly between descriptions of natural law proponents and legal positivists, who they are and what views they hold, then I would use one color to highlight exclusively the traits and views associated with the natural law proponents; and another color just for the legal positivists.

In other words, we want to use the highlighter function to remind ourselves of the structural divides within a passage or to organize and clarify confusing details.

But what I really wanted to focus on in this chapter is to introduce us to a drill that will improve our efficiency and accuracy when using highlights. Take a look at the following passage, and highlight/underline the passage as you normally would:

PT77 Passage 2

How severe should the punishment be for a corporate crime- e.g., a crime in which a corporation profits from knowingly and routinely selling harmful products to consumers? Some economists argue that the sole basis for determining the penalty should be the reckoning of cost and benefit: the penalty levied should exceed the profit that accrued to the corporation as a result of committing the crime. For example, if a corporation made a profit of $6 million from selling an unsafe product and the fine were, say, $7 million, these economists would feel that justice had been done.

In arguing thus, the economists hold that the fact that a community may find some crimes more abhorrent than others or wish to send a message about the importance of some values-such as, say, not endangering citizens' health by selling tainted food should not be a factor in determining penalties. The law, the economists argue, should affect corporations' earnings rather than try to assess their morality.

But this approach seems highly impractical if not impossible to follow. For the situation is complicated by the fact that an acceptable reckoning of cost and benefit needs to take into account estimated detection ratios-the estimated frequency at which those committing a given type of crime are caught. Courts must assume that not all corporate crimes are detected, and legal wisdom holds that penalties must be higher as detection ratios decrease. Otherwise, a corporation might calculate that since it has only, say, a 1-in-10 chance of being caught committing a crime, even if the potential penalty is somewhat larger than the profit to be gained from violating the law it may still ultimately be more profitable to repeatedly commit the crime. A true reckoning of cost and benefit would therefore have to take estimated detection ratios into account, but this means that, in the above scenario, if the profit resulting from a crime were $6 million, the penalty would have to be not $7 million but at least $60 million, according to the economists' definition, to be just.

The economists' approach requires that detection ratios be high enough for courts to ignore them (50 percent or more), but recent studies suggest that ratios are in fact closer to 10 percent. Given this, the astronomical penalties necessary to satisfy the full reckoning of cost and benefit might arguably put convicted corporations out of business and throw thousands of people out of work. Thus, some other criterion in addition to the reckoning of cost and benefit-such as the assignment of moral weight to particular crimes - is necessary so that penalties for corporate crimes will be practical as well as just.

***

Now, take the words that you have highlighted or underlined, and list them in chronological order on a piece of paper:

Now, using ONLY the words that you've listed, and NOT referring back to the passage, try to answer the following questions:

Paragraph 1 Key Points:

Paragraph 2 Key Points:

Paragraph 3 Key Points:

Paragraph 4 Key Points:

Passage Main Point:

Author's Purpose and Attitude:

How severe should the <u>punishment</u> be for a <u>corporate</u> <u>crime</u>- e.g., a crime in which a corporation profits from knowingly and routinely selling harmful products to consumers? Some <u>economists</u> argue that the <u>sole basis</u> for determining the penalty should be the reckoning of <u>cost and benefit</u>: the penalty levied should exceed the profit that accrued to the corporation as a result of committing the crime. For example, if a corporation made a profit of $6 million from selling an unsafe product and the fine were, say, $7 million, these economists would feel that justice had been done.

In arguing thus, the economists hold that the fact that a community may find some crimes more <u>abhorrent</u> than others or wish to send a message about the <u>importance of</u> some <u>values</u>-such as, say, not endangering citizens' health by selling tainted food <u>should not be a factor</u> in determining penalties. The law, the economists argue, should affect corporations' earnings rather than try to assess their morality.

But this approach seems <u>highly impractical</u> if not <u>impossible</u> to follow. For the situation is complicated by the fact that an acceptable reckoning of cost and benefit needs to take into account estimated <u>detection</u> <u>ratios</u>-the estimated frequency at which those committing a given type of crime are caught. Courts must assume that not all corporate crimes are detected, and legal wisdom holds that <u>penalties must be higher</u> as detection ratios decrease. Otherwise, a corporation might calculate that since it has only, say, a 1-in-10 chance of being caught committing a crime, even if the potential penalty is somewhat larger than the profit to be gained from violating the law it may still ultimately be more profitable to repeatedly commit the crime. A true reckoning of cost and benefit would therefore have to <u>take estimated detection ratios into account</u>, but this means that, in the above scenario, if the profit resulting from a crime were $6 million, the penalty would have to be not $7 million but at least $60 million, according to the economists' definition, to be just.

The economists' approach requires that detection ratios be high enough for courts to ignore them (50 percent or more), but recent studies suggest that ratios are in fact closer to 10 percent. Given this, the <u>astronomical penalties necessary</u> to satisfy the full reckoning of cost and benefit might arguably put convicted corporations <u>out of business</u> and throw thousands of people <u>out of work</u>. Thus, <u>some other criterion</u> in addition to the reckoning of cost and benefit-such as the assignment of moral weight to particular crimes - is necessary so that penalties for corporate crimes will be practical as well as just.

Here is my take:

Keywords from Paragraph 1:

Punishment
Corporate crime
Economists
Sole Basis
Cost and Benefit

Keywords from Paragraph 2:

Abhorrent
Importance of values
Should not be a factor

Keywords from Paragraph 3:

Highly impractical
Impossible
Detection ratios
Penalties must be higher
Take estimated detection ratios into account

Keywords from Paragraph 4:

Astronomical penalties necessary
Out of business
Out of work
Some other criterion

Take a look at just my highlighted keywords, without referring back to the passage, can you re-paint a representative picture of what the passage was talking about?

Paragraph 1 talks about how severe the punishment of corporate crimes should be. Some economists believe that the sole basis for the severity of punishment should be a cost-and-benefit analysis. (Introduces the cost-and-benefit analysis calculus.)

Paragraph 2 tells us that according to the cost-and-benefit analysis, abhorrent deeds or the wish to emphasize certain values should not factor into our decision-making process when determining the punishment. (An implication of the calculus)

Paragraph 3 points out a weakness of the cost-and-benefit calculus. It's highly impractical and maybe even impossible. Because not all crimes are detected, we must have higher penalties that take into account estimated detection ratios.

Paragraph 4 tells us that when detection ratios are considered, the penalties will be massive, this will put the companies out of business and people out of work. So an additional criterion is needed.

We know that the author's attitude is critical towards the cost-and-benefit analysis. Their purpose would be to point out a weakness in the analysis and call for additional criteria in determining how to calculate corporate crime penalties.

Finally, we can synthesize the passage's main point from all the information that we have gathered: *The impracticality of using the cost-and-benefit analysis in determining corporate penalties means that additional criterion is needed.*

***

We should be tactical and selective in highlighting information from the passage. We want to use the highlighter sparingly, so that the entire page is not covered in highlights, which is the same as not having highlighted anything at all. By limiting our highlights, we are also forcing ourselves to **prioritize** the most important elements of each paragraph and ultimately, the entire passage.

We want to use the highlights as **signposts** for the structural elements of the passage. If we were coming back to the passage to find an elusive detail associated with a particular individual or view, we want to know exactly where to look, and our highlights should serve as a guide.

We are given different colored highlighters on the actual LSAT itself, and I will use different colors to represent **different POVs** throughout the passage. This way, if a certain question is asking about someone specific, I know exactly where to look for the relevant material.

The advanced student will be able to detect **potential traps** (such as complex details or subtle nuances) that may form the source of tricky questions, we can also make a note of these parts in anticipation of potential difficult questions (see the "Red Car Theory" in the next chapter).

Finally, we want our highlights to be **representative**. That was the whole point of the drill in this chapter. Can you recall the passage's content by looking at your highlighted words? Our highlights should help us understand, categorize, and retain the information in the passage.

Occasionally practice this drill on a passage that you have just read. Extract your highlights and try to regurgitate the whole passage based only on these keywords.

Signpost Words

Before we conclude the chapter I just wanted to draw your attention to certain words that can help us in our grasp of the passage. These are known as "signposting words" and are essential in helping the reader follow your argument and understand the relationship between the ideas which you are trying to explain.

Making a note of these words, when they appear in the passage, can guide us through the author's argument as we proceed through the readings, give us a stronger sense of direction, and help us better and more effeciently grasp the structure of the argument itself.

Now I do not highlight these words personally, preferring to focus on the content of the argument itself. But I will definitely make a mental note when these words appear in the passage, and use my understanding of these words to better organize my thoughts and prepare myself for the information that follows these words.

But that's just me. If you find highlighting signposting words in your readings better help you grasp the passage's structure and make the argument more coherent, then by all means do so.

Listing ideas

- First/Firstly
- To begin with
- Second/Secondly
- Afterwards
- Subsequently
- Following this
- Finally

Further developing an idea

These words can be used to further build upon a point made earlier, but they can also form a part of a list, similar to the words listed above.

- As well as
- In addition/Additionally
- What is more
- Another
- Besides
- Furthermore
- Moreover

Similar ideas

- Similarly
- Likewise
- In the same way

Contrasting ideas or opposing viewpoints

- In contrast
- In comparison

- However
- Conversely
- Whereas
- On the other hand
- Alternatively
- Despite this
- Nonetheless/Nevertheless
- Yet
- On the contrary

Examples/illustration

- For example
- For instance
- To illustrate
- In particular
- One way
- Such as
- Namely
- Notably
- Exemplifies

Causal relationships or concluding

- Therefore
- Consequently
- Accordingly
- Thus
- As a result
- This causes
- Hence
- For this reason
- Because of this
- In view of this
- Resulting from this
- Subsequently
- This suggests that

Different way of explaining

- In other words
- Stated otherwise
- That is to say
- Put simply

Emphasis on a piece of information

- In particular
- Especially
- Indeed

- Most importantly
- In fact
- Chiefly
- Mainly
- Mostly

Summarizing/making concluding remarks

- In summary
- In conclusion
- In short/In brief
- Overall

Chapter 6: Reading Ability Diagnostic

Do you play any sports?

Working from home during COVID had many benefits. I was getting more rest, better managing my time, and saving some money. But simultaneously, the inability to travel or live a normal life was hard mentally and emotionally. I stopped exercising, I ate more and more junk food, I became really unfit.

I joined a boxing gym in 2022 to force myself to exercise more. I enjoyed the sport, and gradually got better at boxing techniques. I practiced my jabs, crosses, and hooks; I worked on my footwork and balance. I was slowly getting better.

But what really held me back was my conditioning. I'd be out of breath after a round, I'd get weak and have to pause to catch my breath. Eventually, my coach pulled me aside and told me to work on things that seemed unrelated to boxing. He told me to work on my balance, flexibility, strength, and most importantly, cardio conditioning.

As a result, I stopped boxing for a bit and began to focus more on my strength and conditioning in my training. To my amazement, my boxing began to improve even when I stopped practicing it deliberately. I saw more improvements than I did when I was only focusing on technique.

If you used to play sports or still do so, this example will resonate with you. In many sports performance at the top level requires more than just technique. You can be the most technical player, the best shooter/dribbler, but you will be severely disadvantaged if you were not running or lifting weights or stretching as well.

Performance on the LSAT Reading Comprehension section is very much like playing a sport at the highest level. Our **general reading ability**, together with our **RC-specific skills**, come together to help us succeed in this section. Most of this book is devoted to RC-specific skills. We have already looked at how to analyze a passage structurally; we will soon go on to study how to tackle different question types, anticipate the correct answer choice, and compare and rank attractive answer choices.

But it doesn't matter how good we are at breaking down a passage or how competent we are at analyzing question stems to anticipate the correct answer choice; if we *cannot* understand the passage or what the author is trying to convey, all these skills are useless.

Similarly, a student with strong reading ability must still be aware of the LSAT-specific quirks and traits of different questions and answers. To succeed in RC, both our general reading ability and RC-specific techniques must be strong. These two skillsets complement each other and are both crucial.

***

Unfortunately, the RC prep materials you see on the market will not tell you this, but it makes perfect sense in a way. A boxing coach will tell you to work on your strength and conditioning on your own time, but during boxing class, your coach will not make you lift weights or run intervals. He is going to teach you how to box. An RC tutor or RC prep book is *not* going to teach you how to read properly or even how to become a better reader in general. They might not even tell you to read more outside of class time, they might just have you learning the specific RC-related techniques.

In fact, improving our *general reading ability* is something that could benefit the majority of LSAT test takers. Back when I used to teach the LSAT, many of my students were non-native speakers of English. What had held them back the most was a general weakness in reading ability. Even after they learned how the rules and steps to properly answer a question, they were still making mistakes. Because the correct answer depended on a piece of information they completely overlooked or didn't understand.

Reading ability can be improved upon even if time is limited. If you are willing to put in the effort, drastic improvements can be seen. We will devote an entire chapter at the end of this book to the art of using outside reading to supplement our RC practice.

But for now, the more relevant question to ask yourself is this:

"How strong is your reading ability/level, and is it enough to successfully navigate the RC section?"

Even among native speakers of English, some of us will have stronger reading ability than others. Some of us read vociferously growing up, some still enjoy reading more than others, and some may have studied or worked in fields from which certain RC passages were drawn. If this was the case, then a passage about a topic with which you were familiar with was no doubt a much easier read than another topic you knew nothing about. So we know that prior experience and knowledge can go a long way when it comes to Reading Comprehension.

And this brings us to the core of this chapter, a four-part diagnostic to test how strong your current reading ability really is. Four of the most challenging passages from RC history have been placed below, one each from the law, the sciences, humanities, and the arts; the four recurring subjects in RC passages. Look at the following passages and complete the outlines I've prepared for you. After you have completed ALL four passages, compare your answers to mine at the end of the chapter.

Read the following passage in 3 minutes, do NOT go over time! We are testing your reading ability here, DON'T CHEAT.

PT30 Passage 3

Philosopher Denise Meyerson views the Critical Legal Studies (CLS) movement as seeking to debunk orthodox legal theory by exposing its contradictions. However, Meyerson argues that CLS proponents tend to see contradictions where none exist, and that CLS overrates the threat that conflict poses to orthodox legal theory.

According to Meyerson, CLS proponents hold that the existence of conflicting values in the law implies the absence of any uniquely right solution to legal cases. CLS argues that these conflicting values generate equally plausible but opposing answers to any given legal question, and, consequently, that the choice between the conflicting answers must necessarily be arbitrary or irrational. Meyerson denies that the existence of conflicting values makes a case irresolvable, and asserts that at least some such cases can be resolved by ranking the conflicting values. For example, a lawyer's obligation to preserve a client's confidences may entail harming other parties, thus violating moral principle. This conflict can be resolved if it can be shown that in certain cases the professional obligation overrides ordinary moral obligations.

In addition, says Meyerson, even when the two solutions are equally compelling, it does not follow that the choice between them must be irrational. On the contrary, a solution that is not rationally required need not be unreasonable. Meyerson concurs with another critic that instead of concentrating on the choice between two compelling alternatives, we should rather reflect on the difference between both of these answers on the one hand, and some utterly unreasonable answer on the other—such as deciding a property dispute on the basis of which claimant is louder. The acknowledgment that conflicting values can exist, then, does not have the far-reaching implications imputed by CLS; even if some answer to a problem is not the only answer, opting for it can still be reasonable.

Last, Meyerson takes issue with the CLS charge that legal formalism, the belief that there is a quasi- deductive method capable of giving solutions to problems of legal choice, requires objectivism, the belief that the legal process has moral authority.

Meyerson claims that showing the law to be unambiguous does not demonstrate its legitimacy: consider a game in which participants compete to steal the item of highest value from a shop; while a person may easily identify the winner in terms of the rules, it does not follow that the person endorses the rules of the game. A CLS scholar might object that legal cases are unlike games, in that one cannot merely apply the rules without appealing to, and therefore endorsing, external considerations of purpose, policy, and value. But Meyerson replies that such considerations may be viewed as part of, not separate from, the rules of the game.

Now, without going back to the passage, try to answer the following questions:

Paragraph 1 Main Point:

Paragraph 2 Main Point:

Paragraph 3 Main Point:

Paragraph 4 Main Point:

Paragraph 5 Main Point:

Author's Purpose:

Passage Main Point:

Any details you may feel relevant and can still remember:

Again, read this passage in 3 minutes, take notes if needed:

PT31 Passage 4

Some of the philosophers find the traditional, subjective approach to studying the mind outdated and ineffectual. For them, the attempt to describe the sensation of pain or anger, for example, or the awareness that one is aware, has been surpassed by advances in fields such as psychology, neuroscience, and cognitive science. Scientists, they claim, do not concern themselves with how a phenomenon feels from the inside; instead of investigating private evidence perceivable only to a particular individual, scientists pursue hard data—such as the study of how nerves transmit impulses to the brain—which is externally observable and can be described without reference to any particular point of view. With respect to features of the universe such as those investigated by chemistry, biology, and physics, this objective approach has been remarkably successful in yielding knowledge. Why, these philosophers ask, should we suppose the mind to be any different?

But philosophers loyal to subjectivity are not persuaded by appeals to science when such appeals conflict with the data gathered by introspection. Knowledge, they argue, relies on the data of experience, which includes subjective experience. Why should philosophy ally itself with scientists who would reduce the sources of knowledge to only those data that can be discerned objectively?

On the face of it, it seems unlikely that these two approaches to studying the mind could be reconciled. Because philosophy, unlike science, does not progress inexorably toward a single truth, disputes concerning the nature of the mind are bound to continue. But what is particularly distressing about the present debate is that genuine communication between the two sides is virtually impossible. For reasoned discourse to occur, there must be shared assumptions or beliefs. Starting from radically divergent perspectives, subjectivists and objectivists lack a common context in which to consider evidence presented from each other's perspectives.

The situation may be likened to a debate between adherents of different religions about the creation of the universe. While each religion may be confident that its cosmology is firmly grounded in its respective sacred text, there is little hope that conflicts between their competing cosmologies could be resolved by recourse to the texts alone. Only further investigation into the authority of the texts themselves would be sufficient.

What would be required to resolve the debate between the philosophers of mind, then, is an investigation into the authority of their differing perspectives. How rational is it to take scientific description as the ideal way to understand the nature of consciousness? Conversely, how useful is it to rely solely on introspection for one's knowledge about the workings of the mind? Are there alternative ways of gaining such knowledge? In this debate, epistemology—the study of knowledge—may itself lead to the discovery of new forms of knowledge about how the mind works.

***

Now, without looking at the passage, repeat the process from the previous passage. Take a piece of blank paper and write down the key-points for each paragraph, the author's purpose, the passage's main point, and any details you may feel to be relevant.

Now, take a look at the following Science passage, do not go over 3 minutes.

<u>PT50 Passage 4</u>

One of the foundations of scientific research is that an experimental result is credible only if it can be replicated—only if performing the experiment a second time leads to the same result. But physicists John Sommerer and Edward Ott have conceived of a physical system in which even the least change in the starting conditions—no matter how small, inadvertent, or undetectable—can alter results radically. The system is represented by a computer model of a mathematical equation describing the motion of a particle placed in a particular type of force field.

Sommerer and Ott based their system on an analogy with the phenomena known as riddled basins of attraction. If two bodies of water bound a large landmass and water is spilled somewhere on the land, the water will eventually make its way to one or the other body of water, its destination depending on such factors as where the water is spilled and the geographic features that shape the water's path and velocity. The basin of attraction for a body of water is the area of land that, whenever water is spilled on it, always directs the spilled water to that body.

In some geographical formations it is sometimes impossible to predict, not only the exact destination of the spilled water, but even which body of water it will end up in. This is because the boundary between one basin of attraction and another is riddled with fractal properties; in other words, the boundary is permeated by an extraordinarily high number of physical irregularities such as notches or zigzags. Along such a boundary, the only way to determine where spilled water will flow at any given point is actually to spill it and observe its motion; spilling the water at any immediately adjacent point could give the water an entirely different path, velocity, or destination.

In the system posited by the two physicists, this boundary expands to include the whole system: i.e., the entire force field is riddled with fractal properties, and it is impossible to predict even the general destination of the particle given its starting point. Sommerer and Ott make a distinction between this type of uncertainty and that known as "chaos"; under chaos, a particle's general destination would be predictable but its path and exact destination would not.

There are presumably other such systems because the equation the physicists used to construct the computer model was literally the first one they attempted, and the likelihood that they chose the only equation that would lead to an unstable system is small. If other such systems do exist, metaphorical examples of riddled basins of attraction may abound in the failed attempts of scientists to replicate previous experimental results—in which case, scientists would be forced to question one of the basic principles that guide their work.

***

Now, without looking at the passage, repeat the process from the previous passage. Take a piece of blank paper and write down the key-points for each paragraph, the author's purpose, the passage's main point, and any details you may feel to be relevant.

Final passage, this one is about art. Take no more than 3 minutes:

PT79 Passage 2

Best known for her work with lacquer, Eileen Gray (1878-1976) had a fascinating and multifaceted artistic career: she became a designer of ornaments, furniture, interiors, and eventually homes. Though her attention shifted from smaller objects to the very large, she always focused on details, even details that were forever hidden. In Paris she studied the Japanese tradition of lacquer, employing wood surfaces-e.g., bowls, screens, furniture-for the application of the clear, hard-drying liquid. It is a time-consuming craft, then little known in Europe, that superimposes layer upon layer, sometimes involving twenty layers or more. The tradition of lacquer fit well with her artistic sensibilities, as Gray eschewed the flowing, leafy lines of the Art Nouveau movement that had flourished in Paris, preferring the austere beauty of straight lines and simple forms juxtaposed.

In addition to requiring painstaking layering, the wood used in lacquer work must be lacquered on both sides to prevent warping. This tension between aesthetic demands and structural requirements, which invests Gray's work in lacquer with an architectural quality, is critical but not always apparent: a folding screen or door panel reveals more of the artist's work than does a flat panel, which hides one side. In Gray's early work she produced flat panels; later she made door panels and even unfolded the panels into screens. In a screen she made for the lobby of an apartment, she fully realizes the implications of this expansion from two to three dimensions: the screen juts out from a wall, and that wall visually disintegrates into panels of lacquered bricks on the screen. The screen thus becomes a painting, a piece of furniture, and an architectural element all at once. She subsequently became heavily invested in the design of furniture, often tailoring pieces to fit a particular interior environment. She often used modem materials, such as tubular steel, to create furniture and environments that, though visually austere, meet their occupants' needs.

Gray's work in both lacquer and interior design prefigures her work as an architect. She did not believe that one should divorce the structural design of the exterior from the design of the interior. She designed the interior elements of a house together with the more permanent structures, as an integrated whole. Architecture for her was like work in lacquer: it could only be achieved from the inside out. But in architecture we discover the hidden layers; in fact we inhabit them. We find storage cabinets in the recesses of a staircase, desks that are also cabinets, and tables that are set on pivots to serve different functions in different contexts. One such table can be positioned either outside, on a balcony, or inside the house. Gray placed a carpet underneath it in each location, as though to underscore that there is no important distinction between exterior and interior.

***

Now, without looking at the passage, repeat the process from the previous passage. Take a piece of blank paper and write down the key-points for each paragraph, the author's purpose, the passage's main point, and any details you may feel to be relevant.

Now, go back to each of the passages, re-read them untimed, and fill in any missing information in your notes. This time with a different colored pen/pencil.

Okay, in terms of RC passages, those were as difficult as they come. It was probably quite a struggle to try to come up with something within three minutes, and probably also a little challenging even after revisiting the passage with no time constraints.

Take a look now at my notes for each of the passages, and compare both versions of your notes (timed and untimed), with what I had come up with:

My Notes:

30-3

Philosopher <u>Denise Meyerson</u> views the <u>Critical Legal Studies</u> (CLS) movement as seeking to debunk orthodox legal theory by exposing its contradictions. However, Meyerson argues that CLS proponents tend to see contradictions <u>where none exist</u>, and that CLS <u>overrates</u> the threat that conflict poses to <u>orthodox legal theory</u>.

Right in the first paragraph, we are introduced to multiple subjects: Denise Meyerson, CLS, and orthodox legal theory. CLS attacks orthodox legal theory; while Denise Meyerson attacks CLS. I anticipate that the rest of the passage will be about Denise Meyerson's criticisms of CLS (seeing non-existent contradictions; overrating the threats posed by conflict).

According to <u>Meyerson</u>, CLS proponents hold that the existence of <u>conflicting values</u> in the law implies the <u>absence of any uniquely right solution</u> to legal cases. CLS argues that these conflicting values generate equally plausible but opposing answers to any given legal question, and, consequently, that the choice between the conflicting answers must necessarily be <u>arbitrary or irrational</u>. Meyerson <u>denies</u> that the existence of conflicting values <u>makes a case irresolvable</u>, and asserts that at least some such cases can be resolved by <u>ranking the conflicting values</u>. For example, a lawyer's obligation to preserve a client's confidences may entail harming other parties, thus violating moral principle. This conflict can be resolved if it can be shown that in certain cases the professional obligation <u>overrides</u> ordinary moral obligations.

So the CLS proponents believe this: there are conflicting values in law, so there are no objective right solutions. Legal decisions are arbitrary or irrational.

On the other hand, Meyers believes this: even though there are conflicting values in law, we can rank these conflicting values and still come to a preferable solution.

In addition, says Meyerson, even when the two solutions <u>are equally compelling</u>, it <u>does not follow</u> that the choice between them <u>must be irrational</u>. On the contrary, a solution that is not rationally required need not be unreasonable. Meyerson concurs with another critic that instead of concentrating on the choice between two compelling alternatives, we should rather reflect on the difference between both of these answers on the one hand, and some utterly unreasonable answer on the other—such as deciding a property dispute on the basis of which claimant is louder. The acknowledgment that conflicting values can exist, then, does not have the far-reaching implications imputed by CLS; even if some answer to a problem is <u>not the only answer</u>, opting for it <u>can still be reasonable</u>.

Remember the CLS view from the previous paragraph? Choices made between conflicting answers are irrational.

In the previous paragraph, Meyerson said that with conflicting answers, you can still have one preferable solution.

Here, Meyerson goes a step further in the argument: even when no solution is preferable to the other; choosing between the two isn't necessarily irrational. Making a choice between two equally compelling options, A, and B; doesn't mean the choice is unreasonable. Both can be reasonable choices, and randomly picking one of them is still a reasonable choice.

Last, Meyerson takes issue with the CLS charge that legal formalism, the belief that there is a quasi- deductive method capable of giving solutions to problems of legal choice, requires objectivism, the belief that the legal process has moral authority.

CLS believes that if you think the law is capable of giving solutions, you must believe that the law has moral authority. Meyerson attacks this view.

Meyerson claims that showing the law to be unambiguous <u>does not demonstrate</u> its legitimacy: consider a game in which participants compete to steal the item of highest value from a shop; while a person may <u>easily identify the winner</u> in terms of the rules, <u>it does not follow that the person endorses the rules</u> of the game. A CLS scholar might <u>object</u> that legal cases are unlike games, in that one cannot merely apply the rules without appealing to, and therefore endorsing, external considerations of purpose, policy, and value. But Meyerson <u>replies</u> that such considerations may be viewed as part of, not separate from, the rules of the game.

Meyerson says that a clear law doesn't mean it's the right law. Just because the rules are clear doesn't mean you approve of the rules.

The CLS scholar might respond by saying that in games you can be clear of the rules without approving of the game; but in law, its different. If you apply the rules you are endorsing its external considerations.

Meyerson rebuts this by saying that the distinction between the rules and external considerations is moot. They are all one and the same.

This passage was difficult because we had to be aware not only of CLS proponents' criticisms of orthodox legal theory, but also how Meyerson in turn criticizes these criticisms. There were also a few abstract ideas that we had to explore and link together throughout the passage.

Paragraph 1: Meyerson sees two issues with CLS views of orthodox legal theory: seeing contradictions and overemphasizing the threat of conflicts.

Paragraph 2: Meyerson believes that, unlike the CLS proponents, even though there are contradictions in the law, you can still come to a rational decision by ranking the values behind your options.

Paragraph 3: Meyerson further believes that, even if we can't rank two choices in terms of their preferability; arbitrarily choosing one of them doesn't mean the decision is unreasonable. Both choices could have been reasonable.

Paragraph 4: Meyerson disagrees with the CLS view that applying legal reasoning means that you automatically endorse the law's moral authority.

Paragraph 5: Meyerson believes that you can be clear about the rules without endorsing them.

Author's Purpose: To list Meyerson's key criticisms of the CLS movement.

Main Point: Meyerson believes that, unlike the CLS proponents; contradictions in the law don't make legal decisions irrational or unreasonable; and the process of applying legal reasoning doesn't mean that you are automatically endorsing that law.

***

Take a look at your notes from previously, how do they compare to mine? Was there a significant gap between your notes from the timed reading of the passage and mine? What about the notes that you made when you went back to the passage a second time, untimed?

Keep this in mind, and let's look at the next passage.

31-4

Some of the <u>philosophers</u> find the <u>traditional, subjective approach</u> to studying the mind outdated and ineffectual. For them, the attempt to describe the sensation of pain or anger, for example, or the awareness that one is aware, has been surpassed by advances in fields such as psychology, neuroscience, and cognitive science. Scientists, they claim, do not concern themselves with how a phenomenon feels from the inside; instead of investigating private evidence perceivable only to a particular individual, <u>scientists pursue hard data</u>—such as the study of how nerves transmit impulses to the brain—which is <u>externally observable</u> and can be described <u>without reference to any particular point of view</u>. With respect to features of the universe such as those investigated by chemistry, biology, and physics, this objective approach has been remarkably successful in yielding knowledge. Why, these philosophers ask, should we suppose the <u>mind</u> to be any different?

Science studies the objective rather than the subjective. Scientists pursue hard data and externally observable information rather than subjective accounts.

Some philosophers believe this is how we should also study the mind.

But <u>philosophers loyal to subjectivity</u> are not persuaded by appeals to science when such appeals conflict with the data gathered by introspection. Knowledge, they argue, relies on the data of experience, which <u>includes subjective experience</u>. Why should philosophy ally itself with scientists who would reduce the sources of knowledge to only those data that can be discerned objectively?

Conversely, opposing philosophers believe that subjective experience is also important and should not be ignored.

On the face of it, it seems <u>unlikely</u> that these two approaches to studying the mind <u>could be reconciled</u>. Because philosophy, unlike science, does not progress inexorably toward a single truth, disputes concerning the nature of the mind are bound to continue. But what is particularly <u>distressing</u> about the present debate is <u>that genuine communication between the two sides is virtually impossible</u>. For reasoned discourse to occur, there must be <u>shared assumptions or beliefs</u>. Starting from radically divergent perspectives, <u>subjectivists and objectivists lack a common context</u> in which to consider evidence presented from each other's perspectives.

So the author thinks that the divide between objective and subjective philosophers is too great. Furthermore, the two groups lack any common ground to even start a conversation. The author calls this "distressing," an indicator of their attitude.

The situation may be likened to a debate between adherents of <u>different religions</u> about the <u>creation of the universe.</u> While each religion may be confident that its cosmology is firmly grounded in its respective sacred text, there is little hope that conflicts between their competing cosmologies could be resolved by <u>recourse to the texts alone</u>. Only further investigation into the <u>authority of the texts</u> themselves would be sufficient.

Here, the author uses an analogy in further explanation. Remember that the author had said that a main reason for the divide was the lack of common ground between the two parties. That's what this analogy is trying to better explain.

Let's say there are two religions, one that worships burgers and another that worships fries. The adherents of the burger religion believe that the earth was made by a hamburger god, because that's what the hamburger bible says; while believers of the fries religion believe that the world was made by fry gods; because that's what the fries bible says.

Two believers from these two religions will not find common ground. Each will hold on to their respective bibles and beliefs while ignoring the opponent's views.

What would be required to resolve the debate between the philosophers of mind, then, is <u>an investigation into the authority of their differing perspectives</u>. How <u>rational</u> is it to take <u>scientific description</u> as the ideal way to understand the nature of consciousness? Conversely, how <u>useful</u> is it to rely solely on <u>introspection</u> for one's *knowledge about the workings of the mind? Are there <u>alternative ways of gaining</u> such knowledge? In this debate, epistemology—the study of knowledge—may itself lead to the discovery of new forms of knowledge about how the mind works.*

Since no common ground can be found between the subjectivists and the objectivists, the author is calling for an examination into the validity/efficacy of both methods. In other words, what are the merits of each practice? The author also advocates looking at alternative ways to gain knowledge.

A passage with a lot of comparisons in it. To fully understand this passage, it helps to have a clear understanding of the two schools of thought. Subjectivists believe that personal experiences, memories, sensations, and feelings are all valid sources of knowledge in studying the mind; while objectivists believe that only hard data, evidence that's measurable and quantifiable, should be considered.

The author then argues that since the two groups have reached an impasse, we should evaluate each school individually, as well as see if there are alternative options that we have yet to consider.

Paragraph 1: Objectivists believe that studies of the mind should be based on hard data and evidence, just like in the sciences.

Paragraph 2: The subjectivists' view is introduced.

Paragraph 3: The author talks about the conflict between the two groups, and that there is no common ground between the two.

Paragraph 4: The author uses a debate between proponents of two different religions as an analogy for the current state of affairs between the objectivists and the subjectivists.

Paragraph 5: The author calls for a separate evaluation of the merits of both approaches, as well as looking into other approaches to the study of the mind.

While the author goes into detail comparing the objectivist and subjectivist views, the author's voice really shines through in the second half of the passage. The author is advocating a new way to break the impasse between the two parties. The **Author's Purpose**, in this passage, is to recommend specific actions that should be taken.

The **Main Point** of the passage, as we have seen in many previous passages, can be derived through a rewording of the Author's Purpose: "given the current impasse between advocates of the objectivist and subjectivist approach to studying the mind, it is crucial that we examine the merits of each perspective individually."

<u>50-4</u>

One of the <u>foundations of scientific research</u> is that an experimental result is <u>credible</u> <u>only if</u> it can be <u>replicated</u>—only if performing the experiment a second time leads to the same result. But physicists John <u>Sommerer</u> and Edward <u>Ott</u> have conceived of a physical system in which even the least <u>change</u> in the starting conditions—no matter how small, inadvertent, or undetectable—can <u>alter results radically</u>. The system is represented by a computer model of a mathematical equation describing the motion of a particle placed in a particular type of force field.

In science, experimental results must be replicable. That is, when we conduct the experiment again, the results must be the same.

Sommerer and Ott, however, describe conditions where the results may not be fully replicable. Tiny, undetectable changes to the starting conditions may lead to drastically different results. Surely this can have a massive impact on how science is conducted!

Sommerer and Ott based their system on an <u>analogy</u> with the phenomena known as <u>riddled basins of</u> <u>attraction</u>. If two bodies of water bound a large landmass and <u>water is spilled somewhere on the land</u>, the water will eventually make its way <u>to one or the other body of water</u>, its destination depending on such factors as <u>where</u> the water is spilled and <u>the geographic features</u> that shape the water's path and velocity. The <u>basin of</u> <u>attraction</u> for a body of water is the area of land that, whenever water is spilled on it, always directs the spilled water to that body.

S and O's scientific model is based on the riddled basins of attraction. So when you spill water on land, it will eventually flow into a river and ultimately into the ocean. If you spill water in New York, it will flow into the Atlantic Ocean, while if you spill water in California, it will flow into the Pacific. The basin of attraction for the Pacific Ocean, therefore, would be all the areas of land where the water will always flow to the Pacific.

In some geographical formations it is <u>sometimes impossible to predict</u>, not only the <u>exact destination</u> of the spilled water, but even which <u>body of water</u> it will end up in. This is because the boundary between one basin of attraction and another is riddled with fractal properties; in other words, the boundary is permeated by an extraordinarily <u>high number of physical irregularities</u> such as notches or zigzags. Along such a <u>boundary</u>, the only way to determine where spilled water will flow at any given point is <u>actually to spill it and observe its</u> <u>motion</u>; spilling the water at any immediately adjacent point could give the water an entirely different path, velocity, or destination.

So continuing with our example, it's pretty clear that water spilled in NYC will flow into the Atlantic; while water spilled in LA will flow into the Pacific. But the further we go from the oceans, the less obvious it becomes. Water spilled in Missouri will probably end up in the Mississippi and end up in the Gulf of Mexico/Atlantic; and water spilled in Chicago will probably end up in the Great Lakes, the St. Lawrence, and eventually flow into the Atlantic as well.

But what about water that's spilled in Colorado or Wyoming? Will it end up in the Pacific or Atlantic?

Along the boundaries of these basins, there will be such irregularities that we can't know for sure where the water will end up. We need to spill the water and actually observe. If the Rockies were the border between the Pacific basin of attraction and the Atlantic basin of attraction, then spilling water inches away on either side of the boundary can mean that the water will end up in one ocean as opposed to the other.

In the system posited by the two physicists, <u>this boundary expands to include the whole system</u>: i.e., the entire force field is riddled with fractal properties, and <u>it is impossible to predict even the general destination</u> of the particle given its starting point. Sommerer and Ott make a distinction between this type of uncertainty and that known as "chaos"; under <u>chaos</u>, a particle's general destination would be predictable but its path and exact destination would not.

We now return from the analogy of the water basins back to O and S's model. So in their model, the entire system is like the boundary of a basin of attraction. Remember what we know about these boundaries? We don't really know where the water will end up, and water spilled just inches away can end up in a completely different ocean.

So in this model, we won't even know where the destination is.

The author distinguishes this from "chaos," which gives us the general destination, but not the path or the exact destination. Under S and O's model, we don't know anything.

There are <u>presumably other such systems</u> because the equation the physicists used to construct the computer model was literally the first one they attempted, and the likelihood that they chose the only equation that would lead to an unstable system is small. If other such systems do exist, metaphorical examples of riddled basins of attraction <u>may abound in the failed attempts of scientists</u> to replicate previous experimental results—in which case, scientists would be <u>forced to question one of the</u> <u>basic principles that guide their work.</u>

Remember the first paragraph? In tradition science, we need to be able to replicate the experimental results in order to "prove" a hypothesis. But in S and O's model, we may not be able to recreate the results, not because the theory is wrong, but because of undetectable changes to the starting conditions.

In the final paragraph, the author is hinting at the possibility that the conditions described by S and O may be frequent in the field of sciences. An implication of that would be a need to re-examine not only past failures to replicate experimental results, but also a need to re-evaluate this central tenet of scientific experimentation. If we can't really control the starting conditions, does it make sense to try to replicate experiment results?

***

This was one of the hardest science passages to appear on the LSAT. The descriptive passages about the riddled basins of attraction were especially abstract and hard to fully grasp under limited time. With scientific passages, as we shall see again, it can be immensely helpful to think of real-world examples to supplement the content provided as we read along.

Paragraph 1: While science requires that we be able to replicate our experimental results; S and O's model seems to suggest that this may not be as straightforward as we'd like to think.

Paragraph 2: The basins of attraction is a concept in geology, where if water was to spill in a basin, it is sure to flow to an associated body of water.

Paragraph 3: The boundaries of these basins of attraction have many uncertainties, so if water is spilled here, you won't even know where it will end up.

Paragraph 4: S and O's model is like the boundaries of the basins of attraction. A slight change in location where you spill the water can lead to a new destination; so a slight change in starting conditions can lead to drastically different experimental results.

Paragraph 5: The implications of S and O's model is widespread for the study of science.

Author's Purpose: In this passage, the author is primarily concerned with explaining S and O's model, and an implication it may have for scientific research.

Main Point: Like the boundaries of a basin of attraction, S and O has proposed a model where even a slight change in starting conditions can lead to drastically different results, with far reaching implications for science.

79-2

Best known for her work with lacquer, Eileen Gray (1878-1976) had a fascinating and multifaceted artistic career: she became a designer of ornaments, furniture, interiors, and eventually homes. Though her attention shifted from smaller objects to the very large, she always focused on details, even details that were forever hidden. In Paris she studied the Japanese tradition of lacquer, employing wood surfaces-e.g., bowls, screens, furniture-for the application of the clear, hard-drying liquid. It is a time-consuming craft, then little known in Europe, that superimposes layer upon layer, sometimes involving twenty layers or more. The tradition of lacquer fit well with her artistic sensibilities, as Gray eschewed the flowing, leafy lines of the Art Nouveau movement that had flourished in Paris, preferring the austere beauty of straight lines and simple forms juxtaposed.

Eileen Gray has had a multifaceted career. She has worked in ornaments, furniture, interiors, and eventually homes. But she ALWAYS focused on the details, especially hidden details.

She started with lacquer (ornaments and furniture), which had simple forms and straight lines.

In addition to requiring painstaking layering, the wood used in lacquer work must be lacquered on both sides to prevent warping. This tension between aesthetic demands and structural requirements, which invests Gray's work in lacquer with an <u>architectural quality, is critical but not always apparent</u>: a <u>folding screen or door panel</u> reveals more of the artist's work than does a flat panel, which <u>hides one side</u>. In Gray's early work she produced flat panels; later she made door panels and even unfolded the panels into screens. In a screen she made for the lobby of an apartment, she fully realizes the implications of this expansion from two to three dimensions: the screen juts out from a wall, and that wall visually disintegrates into panels of lacquered bricks on the screen. <u>The screen thus becomes a painting, a piece of furniture, and an architectural element all at once.</u> She subsequently became heavily invested in the design of <u>furniture</u>, often tailoring pieces to <u>fit a particular interior environment</u>. She often used modem materials, such as tubular steel, to create furniture and environments that, though visually austere, meet their <u>occupants' needs</u>.

The second paragraph continues to outline Gray's artistic evolution. Hidden details, something mentioned in the first paragraph, appears in her folding screens and panels.

Gray subsequently began to design furniture. Her furniture, like her lacquer, both had hidden architectural qualities. Furthermore, her furniture was built with the occupants' needs in mind.

Gray's work in both lacquer and interior design prefigures her work as an <u>architect</u>. She did not believe that one should divorce the <u>structural design of the exterior</u> from the <u>design of the interior</u>. She designed the interior elements of a house together with the more permanent structures, as an <u>integrated whole</u>. Architecture for her was like work in lacquer: it could only be achieved from the inside out. But in architecture we discover <u>the hidden layers</u>; in fact we inhabit them. We find storage cabinets in the recesses of a staircase, desks that are also cabinets, and tables that are set on pivots to serve different functions in different contexts. One such table can be positioned either outside, on a balcony, or inside the house. Gray placed a carpet underneath it in each location, as though to underscore that there is no important distinction between exterior and interior.

So Gray eventually moved to architecture. We knew that her lacquer and furniture had architectural qualities; and now her architecture had the qualities of her furniture and lacquer.

Just like her lacquer and furniture, her architecture also has hidden layers.

***

This was one of the harder art themed passages. Many students had trouble making sense of the myriad of details in this passage, as the overarching theme of this passage was very subtle.

The passage retraces Gray's artistic journey from lacquer to furniture to architecture. In the process her work all possessed a hidden quality. Her lacquer work and furniture had an architectural element to them, which was hidden; while there were hidden components built into the interior and exterior of her architectural projects.

Paragraph 1: Gray's career, which encompassed ornaments, furniture, interior and exterior design; were filled with hidden details. She began her career in lacquer work.

Paragraph 2: Her lacquer work, as well as her furniture, had a hidden, architectural quality.

Paragraph 3: Gray's architecture, like her lacquer work, also saw the merging of the interior and the exterior. Her architecture, like her lacquer and furniture, also contained a hidden layer.

Author's Purpose: To outline Gray's artistic development in different phases and to highlight the common themes connecting these phases.

Main Point: In Gray's lacquer, furniture, and architecture; we discover the merging of the interior and the exterior, as well as the prevalence of hidden elements.

Diagnostic:

So now that we have compared my notes to yours, how do you feel? Were you able to cover most of the points that I've discovered in your initial, timed, readthrough? If so, congratulations! Your reading ability is strong enough to tackle the hardest RC passages. There isn't really any need to supplement this RC book with additional outside reading. Just focus on the techniques and strategies specific to the question types that you struggle with and the answer choice traps that you might have a hard time avoiding. (We cover these in the next two parts of the book.)

But again, perhaps you did struggle a little in the initial read of the passage. This is absolutely normal. Most untrained students won't be able to get all the key points out of these four passages in a time window of only 3-4 minutes. But if during your second read of the passage, when it was untimed, you were able to discover all the key points that I've listed, then congratulations to you also! Your reading ability is good enough, it just needs some finetuning. I would go back and re-read Part I, and practice becoming a more efficient reader: learn to extract and link key information from a passage at a faster pace. Your biggest concern will be timing. So practice reading at a faster pace without diluting your level of understanding.

For you, outside reading is optional. But if there were certain passages where you clearly struggled more than others, I would consider using outside reading to supplement a subject with which you are not familiar, be it the arts, humanities, law, or sciences.

Finally, for those of us who couldn't fully comprehend the passage even on their second readthrough, when the timing restraint was removed; I regret to say that your current reading ability might not be enough to tackle the more difficult RC passages.

At the end of this book there is a chapter devoted explicitly to using outside reading to boost our reading ability in a limited amount of time. It was a drill that I used with my ESL students to great effect. So go take a look at that, do a bit of outside reading everyday, just as you are learning the technical elements of RC from this book.

The Red Car Theory and How to Read More Efficiently for RC

For students unfamiliar with the "Red Car Theory," imagine that upon returning home from class, I ask you, *"how many red cars did you see on the road today?"* Chances are you won't really remember. Because you were not actively looking for red cars. But had I posed the question prior to you leaving for class, you would no doubt have been more attentive to red cars on the road. Perhaps you still wouldn't have made an accurate count of all the red cars you saw, but at least they would have stood out to you, and you would have not only spotted more red cars on the road, but every time a red car came along, you would also have remembered my question.

The moral of the story is that when we have an idea of what we are supposed to look for, such things (red cars or certain types of information in a passage) will become much more visible. We are also more likely to remember them afterwards. In Part I of the book, we learned how to remain engaged throughout the reading, how to break down individual paragraphs and entire passages structurally, and to watch out for details scattered throughout the passage that may become useful when we encounter the questions.

Reading for the LSAT, at its heart, is an exercise in **categorizing** and **retaining** information. We build up a framework and delineate the relationships between all the concepts we are introduced to so we have a better grasp of each passage's argument. As we encounter new information, we can then weave them into our pre-existing understanding of the passage, rather than being taken along for the ride. As we approach the questions, we will have a clearer idea of the type of information required to solve that particular question as well as its general location in the passage, sometimes even before examining the answer choices. As we shall see in Part II, the high scorer will not only be aware of the nuances and subtleties of different question types (much like LR), the steps we must take to solve them, but also know where to look for such information back in the passage.

This is where the Red Car Theory comes into play. We have already tried to consistently figure out the Main Point and Purpose of the passage, the organization of individual paragraphs/entire passage, the author's attitude, etc. as we are reading. We are doing this **not only** because being aware of the answers to these questions will enhance our understanding of the passage, **but also** because these will most likely appear as questions on the passage itself. In other words, we are anticipating what kind of questions may be asked, and we are reading not simply to understand, but to *prepare* for the questions coming.

We saw how certain passage details matter in Chapter 4. They are often the source for many difficult questions. But we don't want to be lost in the details either, if that's to the detriment of our holistic understanding of the passage. So train your reading ability to grasp the answers to the main questions (Main Point, Purpose, etc.), and once you can do that consistently and without effort. You can focus more of your attention on the details and subtleties of the passage.

Time is of the essence on RC. The advanced student and beginner student both have about three minutes to read the same passage. But while the beginner student may be spending two of those three minutes trying to understand what is going on, and the remaining minute thinking about the main point; the advanced student has automated this process so that they can devote their active thinking to more advanced information – things that may appear in harder questions down the road. To give you an example: if a novice/intermediate student saw a causal relationship in a passage, they might not even recognize it. Even if they did, all their attention would be devoted to identifying the cause and effect, as well as trying to link it to pre-existing information from earlier on. Now, whenever I see a causal relationship in a passage, I am contemplating ways to strengthen or weaken it instead. I have enough time to do this because all the other stuff comes like second nature to me after incessant practice. True, a strengthen/weaken question may not even appear later, but if it did, I would be fearless.

Imagine an author criticizing three different views throughout a passage, calling views A and B "mistaken" or "erroneous," but when they come to view C, their criticism becomes more muted. Imagine if the author declared, "View C is not without issues of its own." The typical student will read this and think, "pretty straightforward passage, the author evaluates and criticizes A, B, and C!" But upon reading this, my reactions will be slightly different: *This would make great source material for an inference question! If there will be a MSS/Most likely agree/Inference Question down the road, perhaps the correct answer would say "if forced to choose between the three, the author would most likely go with C."*

In other words, as I read, I am using my familiarity with typical RC Questions and Answers to anticipate what may become relevant down the road. Of course, there's no way to anticipate all or even most of the questions, but its not unusual to catch one or two this way. Again, I am only able to do this because I no longer need to actively think about the more macroscopic questions like Organization, MP, or Purpose. After so much practice, they have become intuitive.

Occasionally I come upon parts of a passage that I won't understand either. But this doesn't really matter, because I am confident in my grasp of the rest of the passage. For instance, if the latter half of paragraph 3 was really convoluted and I couldn't figure it out in my initial passage read, as I approach the questions, I am aware that if I have any issues, that's where the source will most likely be. If I didn't understand an answer choice or if I am unsure about a question, the latter half of paragraph 3 is the first place where I will check. To paraphrase Donald Rumsfeld, there are things that we don't know but we are not aware of their existence (unknown unknowns), and things that we are ignorant of but we can identify and know where to look (known unknowns). Even when my understanding falls short, my ignorance are firmly situated in the second camp. Being aware of your ignorance, combined with the Reverse Confirmation Technique (Chapter 17), can work miracles.

As you practice more questions in RC, you will have a more intimate understanding of the relationship between information from the passage and the questions. As you master the steps we learned in Part I, try to ask yourself this: *"if the information you are reading can become the source of potential trick questions, and if so, how?"*

For the advanced test taker, these will be your red cars.

Part II: The Questions

Part II: The Questions

Chapter 7: Four Types of Purpose Questions

One: Purpose of Passage:

Let's start with a question type that we have already encountered countless times before, even as we were analyzing the passage structure in previous chapters.

Throughout Part I of the book, we learned the skills on how to actively read, how to engage with the content of the passage, and how to break the passage down in terms of its structure. A fundamental question that we repeatedly asked ourselves was "**Why is the author writing this passage?**"

As we saw, there's always a reason to compose a piece of writing. You write a shopping list to prevent yourself from forgetting things at the supermarket; you scribble in your diary to record what has happened during the day; you write an argumentative essay to arguing for a specific position or to attack someone else's position. You write a love letter to express your feelings and infatuation for someone who will probably ghost you.

In Chapter 1, we used the CEER framework to figure out what the author is trying to do throughout the passage. Whenever we feel that our mind is beginning to wander or that we are struggling to processing what we've just read, CEER is a powerful tool for a reality check. Force yourself to answer this question: "What is the author doing? Are they making a **comparison** between two issues; **explaining** how something complicated works; **evaluating** the pros and cons; or **recommending** a position/course of action?"

The CEER framework can even be stretched to fit the entire passage in many instances. As you read through the passage, and when you have completed reading the passage, ask yourself,

"Why did the author write this passage? Was it to compare, explain, evaluate, recommend, or something else?"

Let's revisit a passage that we've already seen before, this time with a Purpose of Passage question included:

PT27 S3 Q14 (PT27 Passage 2)

Personal names are generally regarded by European thinkers in two major ways, both of which deny that names have any significant semantic content. In philosophy and linguistics, John Stuart Mill's formulation that "proper names are meaningless marks set upon…persons to distinguish them from one another" retains currency; in anthropology, Claude Lévi-Strauss's characterization of names as being primarily instruments of social classification has been very influential. Consequently, interpretation of personal names in societies where names have other functions and meanings has been neglected. Among the Hopi of the southwestern United States, names often refer to historical or ritual events in order both to place individuals within society and to confer an identity upon them. Furthermore, the images used to evoke these events suggest that Hopi names can be seen as a type of poetic composition.

Throughout life, Hopis receive several names in a sequence of ritual initiations. Birth, entry into one of the ritual societies during childhood, and puberty are among the name-giving occasions. Names are conferred by an adult member of a clan other than the child's clan, and names refer to that name giver's clan, sometimes combining characteristics of the clan's totem animal with the child's characteristics. Thus, a name might translate to something as simple as "little rabbit," which reflects both the child's size and the representative animal.

More often, though, the name giver has in mind a specific event that is not apparent in a name's literal translation. One Lizard clan member from the village of Oraibi is named Lomayayva, "beautifully ascended." This translation, however, tells nothing about either the event referred to—who or what ascended—or the name giver's clan. The name giver in this case is from Badger clan. Badger clan is responsible for an annual ceremony featuring a procession in which masked representations of spirits climb the mesa on which Oraibi sits. Combining the name giver's clan association with the receiver's home village, "beautifully ascended" refers to the splendid colors and movements of the procession up the mesa. The condensed image this name evokes—a typical feature of Hopi personal names—displays the same quality of Western Apache place names that led one commentator to call them "tiny imagist poems."

Hopi personal names do several things simultaneously. They indicate social relationships—but only indirectly—and they individuate persons. Equally important, though, is their poetic quality; in a sense they can be understood as oral texts that produce aesthetic delight. This view of Hopi names is thus opposed not only to Mill's claim that personal names are without inherent meaning but also to Lévi-Strauss's purely functional characterization. Interpreters must understand Hopi clan structures and linguistic practices in order to discern the beauty and significance of Hopi names.

The author's primary purpose in writing the passage is to

    A.   present an anthropological study of Hopi names
    B.   propose a new theory about the origin of name
    C.   describe several competing theories of names
    D.   criticize two influential views of names
    E.   explain the cultural origins of names

Let's think back on what we had come up with as the Author's Purpose in Chapter 3, where we last saw this passage. We know that the author briefly describes Mill and Levi-Strauss' theory of names but goes on to say that *the other functions and meanings of names have been ignored by these Eurocentric views.* The author then goes into detail describing Hopi names, showing us how they can be miniature poems full of meaning and imagery, a quality of names not considered by Mill or Levi-Strauss.

So what is the Author's Purpose? We are concerned with the "why," rather than the "what" in Passage Purpose questions. In these questions, the test-makers will frequently throw in wrong answer choices that *do actually describe something that the author does in the passage.* But such an answer, unfortunately, is not describing the **overarching purpose** behind the passage as a whole.

Let me use an example to illustrate: Why are you studying for the LSAT? Obviously, it's to apply to law school and attend law school eventually. During this process, you may have improved your reading ability, your ability to refute a fallacious argument, or spot conditional statements. But none of these are the reason *why* you are studying for the LSAT, they are simply effects.

Similarly, while studying for the LSAT you may have read a bunch of books, mine included; you may have registered for an account on a test prep website; you may have hired a tutor. These are things that you did, but they are not *why* you are studying for the LSAT.

So on Purpose of Passage questions, always try to think about the *why,* rather than the *what.* We want an answer that tells us why the author wrote the passage, not recount what the author did in the passage.

With this in mind, let's look at the answer choices:

 A.   *present* an *anthropological study* of Hopi names

So there are **two questions** that we must ask ourselves in a **Purpose of the Passage** question whenever we see an answer choice:

1. Does the author actually do this?

2. Is this why the author wrote the passage?

Does the author present an "anthropological study" of Hopi names? I suppose the author does talk about Hopi names in detail, in that sense it could maybe be considered an "anthropological study." But the verb "present" is also suspicious. "Presenting an anthropological study" sounds like you are presenting a paper at a conference or presenting a new discovery to a group of peers…it has the connotation of something organized, structured, and academic.

I think the author does present some unique features of Hopi names, but to call it "presenting an anthropological study" is a little too far fetched. So I wouldn't say that the author actually does this in the passage. I don't like this answer all that much.

 B.   *propose a new theory* about the origin of name

The author does mention that the traditional, European theories are not adequate. But is a new theory presented? If so, what is that new theory, and where is it mentioned in the passage?

I'd say that the author is more pointing out a glaring gap in existing theories, rather than propose a new theory. Perhaps the author thinks that a new theory is in order, but they never propose it.

Compared to Answer Choice A, I like this even less.

C. *describe several competing theories of names*

Does the author do this? Sure. Mill's theory is described, Levi-Strauss' theory is also described (all in the first paragraph). The rest of the passage talks about Hopi names, and I'm not too clear whether there is a theory that encompasses Hopi names or that such theory is described.

This answer is typical of the trap we just described. It does describe something the author did, but it's not the reason why this passage was written.

D. *criticize two influential views of names*

This answer choice, on the surface, feels a little off topic. The majority of the passage is devoted to describing Hopi names, there's barely any criticism levelled at anyone.

But on the other hand, if we had a strong grasp of the passage's structure and content and had done our best to anticipate what the correct answer might look like, then answer choice D may make more sense. Remember how the passage starts by talking about two theories of names, but then goes on to describe an important quality of names that these theories have overlooked. The rest of the passage goes on to talk about the meaning and semantic content of Hopi names, which is exactly what the two European theories overlook. In other words, the author is using the example of Hopi names as a *counterexample* to demonstrate the shortcomings of Mill and Levi-Strauss' theories. Indeed, the author mentions this in the very last paragraph: "*This view of Hopi names is thus opposed not only to Mill's claim that personal names are without inherent meaning but also to Lévi-Strauss's purely functional characterization.*"

If we think about the passage in this light, then we will realize that the author was trying to highlight a shortcoming in both Mill's and Levi-Strauss' theories.

E. *explain the cultural origins of names*

Does the author do this? Tell us where names come from culturally? For Hopi names, they do: we are told that they originate from one's tribal affiliation, specific events in one's life, and from a specific name giver. These are things that the author tells us about Hopi names.

But is this why we must differentiate what the author did in the passage and why the author wrote the passage. It is so very easy to get lost in the details of the answer choices, or be led astray by answer choices that sound reasonable on a first glance.

The biggest single helpful tip one can give when approaching RC questions is to **anticipate, as much as you can, what the correct answer might look like before you tackle the answer choices.**

Of course, this is not always possible. But for questions asking us about the Purpose of the Passage, this is usually doable.

We also saw how important it was to **read the very first paragraph in detail**.

The sentence where the author points out a shortcoming in Mill's and Levi-Strauss' theories is subtle and easily missed. If we had seen that sentence, it would guide our subsequent approach to the rest of the passage. If we had missed it, then we might have very easily thought the passage's whole point was to describe Hopi names per se.

Lastly, get into the habit of **ranking answer choices**.

Because the differences between the answer choices can be extremely subtle, especially on the harder questions; we must try to develop the subconscious habit of not being caught up on the truth/falsity of a single answer choice, but rather, to find the best possible answer choice out of five potential candidates.

This is where ranking answers will come in handy. For this question, I'd say that Answer Choice D > C > A/E > B.

The correct answer is D.

***

Let's look at another passage and an associated question that asks us for the Author's Purpose. Think about what we've learned so far, remember to read the first paragraphs of the passage in detail, and try to anticipate what the Author's Purpose might be as you read through the passage:

PT21 S4 Q7 (PT21 Passage 1)

Musicologists concerned with the "London Pianoforte school," the group of composers, pedagogues, pianists, publishers, and builders who contributed to the development of the piano in London at the turn of the nineteenth century, have long encountered a formidable obstacle in the general unavailability of music of this "school" in modern scholarly editions. Indeed, much of this repertory has more or less vanished from our historical consciousness. Granted, the sonatas and Gradus ad Parnassum of Muzio Clementi and the nocturnes of John Field have remained familiar enough (though more often than not in editions lacking scholarly rigor), but the work of other leading representatives, like Johann Baptist Cramer and Jan Ladislav Dussek, has eluded serious attempts at revival.

Nicholas Temperley's ambitious new anthology decisively overcomes this deficiency. What underscores the intrinsic value of Temperley's editions is that the anthology reproduces nearly all of the original music in facsimile. Making available this cross section of English musical life—some 800 works by 49 composers— should encourage new critical perspectives about how piano music evolved in England, an issue of considerable relevance to our understanding of how piano music developed on the European continent, and of how, finally, the instrument was transformed from the fortepiano to what we know today as the piano.

To be sure, the concept of the London Pianoforte school itself calls for review. "School" may well be too strong a word for what was arguably a group unified not so much by stylistic principles or aesthetic creed as by the geographical circumstance that they worked at various times in London and produced pianos and piano music for English pianos and English markets. Indeed, Temperley concedes that their "variety may be so great as to cast doubt on the notion of a 'school.'"

The notion of a school was first propounded by Alexander Ringer, who argued that laws of artistic survival forced the young, progressive Beethoven to turn outside Austria for creative models, and that he found inspiration in a group of pianists connected with Clementi in London. Ringer's proposed London Pianoforte school did suggest a circumscribed and fairly unified group—for want of a better term, a school—of musicians whose influence was felt primarily in the decades just before and after 1800. After all, Beethoven did respond to the advances of the Broadwood piano—its reinforced frame, extended compass, triple stringing, and pedals, for example—and it is reasonable to suppose that London pianists who composed music for such an instrument during the critical phase of its development exercised no small degree of influence on Continental musicians. Nevertheless, perhaps the most sensible approach to this issue is to define the school by the period (c. 1766–1873) during which it flourished, as Temperley has done in the anthology.

The author of the passage is primarily concerned with

    A. Explaining the influence of the development of the pianoforte on the music of Beethoven
    B. Describing Temperley's view of the contrast between the development of piano music in England and the development of piano music elsewhere in Europe
    C. Presenting Temperley's evaluation of the impact of changes in piano construction on styles and forms of music composed in the era of the London Pianoforte school
    D. Considering an alternative theory to that proposed by Ringer concerning the London Pianoforte school
    E. Discussing the contribution of Temperley's anthology to what is known of the history of the London Pianoforte school

So the first thing that we should have done was to try to anticipate what the Author's Purpose might be even as we are reading the passage. It doesn't really matter if such a question exists or not; simply figuring out what might be the Author's Purpose for writing this passage will help us engage with the rest of the material.

For instance, if we realize that the author is primarily comparing two positions, we will look extra carefully for what these two positions are as we read. If we had figured out that the author is making an evaluation, then we would know to look for the author's attitude, whether it's positive or negative, and to ask ourselves why.

So back to the passage, what does the author do throughout the passage, and *why* are they doing it?

We know from the passage that the author presents a situation in the first paragraph: the music of the LPS has largely faded from our consciousness. The author then introduces Temperley's new anthology, telling us that it addresses this deficiency (lack of exposure of LPS composers). The author then describes Temperley's new book, its views, and its merits. The author finally defends Temperley's categorization of LPS musicians based on time period, rather than to treat them as a closely knit group.

We know that the author looks upon Temperley's work favorably. But *why* is the author writing this passage? I think it's to do two things: one, to introduce the audience to Temperley's new anthology; and two, to give it a favorable review.

With this in mind, let's look at the answer choices:

   A.   *Explaining the influence of the development of the pianoforte on the music of Beethoven*

Again, whenever we are looking at Purpose of the Passage answers, two questions to ask: does this happen, and is this the reason why the *entire* passage was written.

Does the author explain the influence of pianoforte development on Beethoven?

Alexander Ringer kind of touches upon this. But what exactly that influence entails wasn't made clear. Further, it was a view held by an academic mentioned by the author, it's not the whole purpose behind why the author wrote this passage.

   B.   *Describing <u>Temperley's view</u> of the <u>contrast</u> between the development of piano music in England and the development of piano music elsewhere in Europe*

Is there contrast between the development of English piano music and continental piano music? I suppose that a case can be made that the English and the subsequent Broadwood piano were influential on the continent. But "contrast" means difference. What was the difference between the two styles of music? We don't really know for sure.

   C.   *Presenting Temperley's evaluation of <u>the impact of changes in piano construction</u> on <u>styles</u> and <u>forms</u> of music composed in the era of the London Pianoforte school*

Let's break down this answer choice:

So changes in piano construction caused the styles and forms of music to change.

And Temperley made an evaluation of these changes (e.g. are the changes positive or negative).

The passage is presenting Temperley's evaluation, which means that it's basically making a list of Temperley's views on how changes in piano construction changed the style and form of music.

The passage must satisfy these three requirements in order for this answer choice to be a contender.

This doesn't happen in the passage.

> D. *Considering an alternative theory to that proposed by Ringer concerning the London Pianoforte school*

Does Ringer propose a theory concerning the LPS? I believe so. Ringer calls this group of composers and musicians a "school." On the other hand, Temperley may believe that this group is less tight-knit than Ringer had believed. So in that sense, perhaps the content can be construed as an "alternative theory."

But this is really only the focus of the last two paragraphs. To think about the author's overarching purpose in writing the passage, we really must consider the entirety of the passage. We know that in the first two paragraphs, the author introduces Temperley's new work and how it addresses a current shortcoming in scholarship. If we think about this aspect of the passage as well, then we will realize that the passage's purpose is to provide a favorable review of Temperley's new work.

> E. *Discussing the contribution of Temperley's anthology to what is known of the history of the London Pianoforte school*

This answer is the closest match to our anticipated answer. The word "discussing" is fairly bland and neutral. I would have preferred something like "highlighting the contribution of Temperley's anthology," but I suppose the author is, after all, "discussing" Temperley's contribution too.

So what are Temperley's contributions? He provides an encompassing and holistic overview of the music that has been forgotten and overlooked. (Discussed in Paragraphs 1 and 2)

He also categorizes these musicians and composers as a loosely affiliated group based on chronology rather than a tight-knit cohort. (Discussed in Paragraphs 3 and 4)

E is the correct answer.

At the end of the day, E wins over the other answer choices because it satisfies the few requirements we would consider when looking at a Purpose of the Passage answer choice.

In the first place, what was discussed in answer choice E **actually takes place in the passage**. Secondly, it is the closest match to our anticipated answer, based on our close reading of the first paragraph, our hypothesis, and our confirmation after reading the entire passage. (Re-read Chapter 1 if you need on refresher on the general approach to a passage)

Common trap answers include answer choices describing things that did not happen in the passage; or things that did occur in the passage, but is not the reason why the author wrote the passage in the first place.

Two: Purpose of Paragraph

We just saw questions that asked us for the purpose of the entire passage. Now, we go one step deeper. The second type of Purpose Questions will ask us what the purpose of a specific paragraph is in the passage as a whole.

Think back on Chapter 3, where we discussed how different paragraphs fit into the passage as a whole. We saw that just like how an LR argument can contain a main conclusion, supporting premises, background information, opposing viewpoints, and concessions; so different paragraphs can play similar roles in a passage.

For example, a paragraph can introduce background information and lay the groundwork for our subsequent understanding of the topic being discussed. A paragraph can introduce one side of the debate or compare the positions of two schools of thought. A paragraph can provide experimental evidence to back up the author's main point. A paragraph can even be a concession the author gives to their opponent.

For these types of questions, it is essential to know what the passage's main point is as a whole, as well as the role played by the paragraph in question vis a vis the passage's main point.

Let's look at a few such examples:

PT25 S1 Q17 (PT25 Passage 3)

Even in the midst of its resurgence as a vital tradition, many sociologists have viewed the current form of the powwow, a ceremonial gathering of native Americans, as a sign that tribal culture is in decline. Focusing on the dances and rituals that have recently come to be shared by most tribes, they suggest that an intertribal movement is now in ascension and claim the inevitable outcome of this tendency is the eventual dissolution of tribes and the complete assimilation of native Americans into Euro-American society. Proponents of this "Pan-Indian" theory point to the greater frequency of travel and communication between reservations, the greater urbanization of native Americans, and, most recently, their increasing politicization in response to common grievances as the chief causes of the shift toward inter-tribalism.

Indeed, the rapid diffusion of dance styles, outfits, and songs from one reservation to another offers compelling evidence that inter-tribalism has been increasing. However, these sociologists have failed to note the concurrent revitalization of many traditions unique to individual tribes. Among the Lakota, for instance, the Sun Dance was revived, after a forty-year hiatus, during the 1950's. Similarly, the Black Legging Society of the Kiowa and the Hethuska Society of the Ponca—both traditional groups within their respective tribes—have gained new popularity. Obviously, a more complex societal shift is taking place than the theory of Pan-Indianism can account for.

An examination of the theory's underpinnings may be critical at this point, especially given that native Americans themselves chafe most against the Pan- Indian classification. Like other assimilationist theories with which it is associated, the Pan-Indian view is predicated upon an a priori assumption about the nature of cultural contact: that upon contact minority societies immediately begin to succumb in every respect—biologically, linguistically, and culturally—to the majority society. However, there is no evidence that this is happening to native American groups.

Yet the fact remains that intertribal activities are a major facet of native American culture today. Certain dances at powwows, for instance, are announced as intertribal, others as traditional. Likewise, speeches given at the beginnings of powwows are often delivered in English, while the prayer that follows is usually spoken in a native language. Cultural borrowing is, of course, old news. What is important to note is the conscious distinction native Americans make between tribal and intertribal tendencies. Tribalism, although greatly altered by modern history, remains a potent force among native Americans: It forms a basis for tribal identity, and aligns music and dance with other social and cultural activities important to individual tribes. Intertribal activities, on the other hand, reinforce native American identity along a broader front, where this identity is directly threatened by outside influences.

The primary function of the third paragraph is to

A. Search for evidence to corroborate the basic assumption of the theory of Pan-Indianism
B. Demonstrate the incorrectness of the theory of Pan-Indianism by pointing out that native American groups themselves disagree with the theory
C. Explain the origin of the theory of Pan-Indianism by showing how it evolved from other assimilationist theories
D. Examine several assimilationist theories in order to demonstrate that they rest on a common assumption
E. Criticize the theory of Pan-Indianism by pointing out that it rests upon an assumption for which there is no supporting evidence

So if you had been reading/taking notes using the habits and tips we talked about in the first part of the book, then you would have done the following upon reading this passage.

1. You would have tried to anticipate why the author is writing this passage (**Purpose** of Passage).
2. You would have inferred the **Main Point** of the Passage based on its purpose and the passage's content.
3. You would have a short **summary** of the sub-points of each of the four paragraphs.

Let's take a quick look at the passage:

Even in the midst of its resurgence as a vital tradition, many <u>sociologists</u> have viewed the current form of the <u>powwow</u>, a ceremonial gathering of native Americans, as a sign that <u>tribal culture is in decline</u>. Focusing on the dances and rituals that have recently come to be shared by most tribes, they suggest that an <u>intertribal movement</u> is now in ascension and claim the inevitable outcome of this tendency is the <u>eventual dissolution of tribes</u> and the <u>complete assimilation</u> of native Americans into Euro-American society. Proponents of this "Pan-Indian" theory point to the greater frequency of travel and communication between reservations, the greater urbanization of native Americans, and, most recently, their increasing politicization in response to common grievances as the chief causes of the shift toward inter-tribalism.

Many sociologists believe that the powwow is a sign that tribal culture is in decline. More travel and communication between tribes, increased urbanization and increased political responses are a sign of inter-tribalism, which they believe will lead to the dissolution of tribes, and ultimately the assimilation of native Americans.

Paragraph 1 talks about a commonly held belief. Does our author agree with it? Let's find out.

Indeed, the rapid diffusion of dance styles, outfits, and songs from one reservation to another offers compelling evidence that <u>inter-tribalism has been increasing</u>. However, these sociologists have failed to note the concurrent <u>revitalization of many traditions unique to individual tribes</u>. Among the Lakota, for instance, the Sun Dance was revived, after a forty-year hiatus, during the 1950's. Similarly, the Black Legging Society of the Kiowa and the Hethuska Society of the Ponca—both traditional groups within their respective tribes—have gained new popularity. Obviously, a more complex societal shift is taking place than the theory of Pan-Indianism can account for.

The author concedes that inter-tribalism has been increasing, but argues against the view described in the first paragraph.

The author is saying that the growth in inter-tribalism has not weakened individual tribes; there's been a revitalization of individual tribal culture as well.

An examination of the <u>theory's underpinnings</u> may be critical at this point, especially given that native Americans themselves chafe most against the Pan- Indian classification. Like other assimilationist theories with which it is associated, the Pan-Indian view is predicated upon an a priori <u>assumption</u> about the nature of cultural contact: that upon contact minority societies immediately begin to <u>succumb</u> in every respect— biologically, linguistically, and culturally—<u>to the majority society</u>. However, there is no evidence that this is happening to native American groups.

Which theory are we talking about? The Pan-Indian Theory is mentioned in the first paragraph. What does that theory espouse? Inter-tribalism is speeding up the assimilation of native Americans into mainstream society and weakening individual tribal identity.
Whenever the author refers to an idea from earlier on in the passage, always remind ourselves what exactly we are discussing. This will help us engage in active reading. (We call this **conceptual link-back**.)

The author argues that the Theory is based on faulty assumptions.

The theory assumes that minor societies always lose to major societies upon contact.

So basically, according to the Pan-Indian Theory, native American societies will lose to mainstream European society upon contact. Inter-tribalism and more travel are giving indigenous peoples more exposure to mainstream society, which in turn will weaken/destroy indigenous tribal culture.

The author states that this assumption is problematic as no evidence supports it.

Yet the fact remains that intertribal activities are a major facet of native American culture today. Certain dances at powwows, for instance, are announced as intertribal, others as traditional. Likewise, speeches given at the beginnings of powwows are often delivered in English, while the prayer that follows is usually spoken in a native language. Cultural borrowing is, of course, old news. What is important to note is the conscious distinction native Americans make between tribal and intertribal tendencies. Tribalism, although greatly altered by modern history, remains a potent force among native Americans: It forms a basis for tribal identity, and aligns music and dance with other social and cultural activities important to individual tribes. Intertribal activities, on the other hand, reinforce native American identity along a broader front, where this identity is directly threatened by outside influences.

The author states their own view on the roles of tribal culture and inter-tribalism. They don't believe that inter-tribalism is weakening individual tribal culture; rather, they are both fulfilling distinctive roles in safeguarding Indigenous culture and identity. Tribalism forms a basis for identity among individual tribes, while inter-tribal activities defend against outside influence.

Let's look at the key questions that we should have answered upon finishing reading the passage:

What is the Author's Purpose? I would say that the author is criticizing the Pan-Indian Theory and proposing an alternative way to look at the effects of inter-tribalism on tribal identity.

Main Point? I would propose something like this:

Contrary to the belief of Pan-Indian theorists, the rise of inter-tribalism will not weaken tribal identity and lead to complete assimilation; tribalism and intertribal activities both have their roles in reinforcing native American identity and defending its integrity.

Paragraph 1: Introduces the view of Pan-Indian theorists.

Paragraph 2: Pan theorists overlook the concurrent growth of tribal identity and inter-tribal activities. (Points out a weakness in the theory)

Paragraph 3: The theory is based upon a mistaken assumption, one that's not backed by evidence.

Paragraph 4: Instead of the Pan-Indian theory. Here is a better alternative explanation of the roles and relationships of tribalism and inter-tribal activities. (Author's own view)

***

Let's go back to our question, which asks us, what is the *primary function* of the third paragraph?

A question that asks us for the "primary function" of a particular paragraph is the same as a question that asks us what role it plays. In other words, what is the paragraph's relationship to the passage's main point/central thesis?

From what we have gathered in the passage, we know that Paragraph 3 forms a part of the author's attack upon the Pan-Indian Theory. The author points out a mistaken assumption underlying the Pan-Indian Theory.

With that in mind, let's quickly look at the answer choices:

   A.   *Search for evidence to corroborate the basic assumption of the theory of Pan-Indianism*

Chapter 7: Four Types of Purpose Questions

Corroborate means to support. The author is not supporting this assumption but attacking it.

  B. *Demonstrate the incorrectness of the theory of Pan-Indianism by pointing out that native American*
      groups themselves disagree with the theory

Nothing too terrible with the first part of the answer; maybe it's a little stronger than I'd like. What's messed up
with this answer is in the second half. The author attacks the theory by pointing out its erroneous underlying
assumption, not by suggesting that native Americans disagree with it.

  C. *Explain the origin of the theory of Pan-Indianism by showing how it evolved from other assimilationist*
      theories

We are told in passing that this theory shares assumptions with other assimilationist theories. But that doesn't
mean this theory evolved from other assimilationist theories.

I'll give an example: Let's say that Einstein's Theory of General Relativity and Darwin's Theory of Evolution
both share the assumption that the scientific method is the best way to arrive at the truth.

But this doesn't mean one theory evolved from the other.

  D. *Examine several assimilationist theories in order to demonstrate that they rest on a common*
      assumption

The author does state that the several assimilationist theories (we weren't told what they are, besides the Pan-
Indian Theory) rest on a common assumption.

But they never examine these theories in detail to show that they rest on a common assumption.

Again, this answer choice describes something that didn't happen in the passage.

  E. *Criticize the theory of Pan-Indianism by pointing out that it rests upon an assumption for which there*
      is no supporting evidence

Does the author do everything this answer choice says they did? Yes, the author is attacking Pan-Indianism. The
author highlights its mistaken assumption and tells us that "there is no evidence" at the very end of the
paragraph.

This answer is also the closest match we have to our anticipated answer. E is the correct answer.

Let's look at a passage that we have encountered many times previously, this time with a new question:

PT27 S3 Q11 (PT27 Passage 2)

Personal names are generally regarded by European thinkers in two major ways, both of which deny that names have any significant semantic content. In philosophy and linguistics, John Stuart Mill's formulation that "proper names are meaningless marks set upon…persons to distinguish them from one another" retains currency; in anthropology, Claude Lévi-Strauss's characterization of names as being primarily instruments of social classification has been very influential. Consequently, interpretation of personal names in societies where names have other functions and meanings has been neglected. Among the Hopi of the southwestern United States, names often refer to historical or ritual events in order both to place individuals within society and to confer an identity upon them. Furthermore, the images used to evoke these events suggest that Hopi names can be seen as a type of poetic composition.

Throughout life, Hopis receive several names in a sequence of ritual initiations. Birth, entry into one of the ritual societies during childhood, and puberty are among the name-giving occasions. Names are conferred by an adult member of a clan other than the child's clan, and names refer to that name giver's clan, sometimes combining characteristics of the clan's totem animal with the child's characteristics. Thus, a name might translate to something as simple as "little rabbit," which reflects both the child's size and the representative animal.

More often, though, the name giver has in mind a specific event that is not apparent in a name's literal translation. One Lizard clan member from the village of Oraibi is named Lomayayva, "beautifully ascended." This translation, however, tells nothing about either the event referred to—who or what ascended—or the name giver's clan. The name giver in this case is from Badger clan. Badger clan is responsible for an annual ceremony featuring a procession in which masked representations of spirits climb the mesa on which Oraibi sits. Combining the name giver's clan association with the receiver's home village, "beautifully ascended" refers to the splendid colors and movements of the procession up the mesa. The condensed image this name evokes—a typical feature of Hopi personal names—displays the same quality of Western Apache place names that led one commentator to call them "tiny imagist poems."

Hopi personal names do several things simultaneously. They indicate social relationships—but only indirectly—and they individuate persons. Equally important, though, is their poetic quality; in a sense they can be understood as oral texts that produce aesthetic delight. This view of Hopi names is thus opposed not only to Mill's claim that personal names are without inherent meaning but also to Lévi-Strauss's purely functional characterization. Interpreters must understand Hopi clan structures and linguistic practices in order to discern the beauty and significance of Hopi names.

The primary function of the second paragraph is to

    A. Present reasons why Hopi personal names can be treated as poetic compositions
    B. Support the claim that Hopi personal names make reference to events in the recipient's life
    C. Argue that the fact that Hopis receive many names throughout life refutes European theories about naming
    D. Illustrate ways in which Hopi personal names may have semantic content
    E. Demonstrate that the literal translation of Hopi personal names often obscures their true meaning

Remember how this passage is about how the European theories of names (Mill/Levi-Strauss) overlook that names can have semantic content. The author then uses the example of Hopi names as a counter-example.

Let's take a look at paragraph 2.

There are three key features of Hopi names that are discussed in the second paragraph. One, names are given during key events of a person's life. Two, the name itself will demonstrate a connection to the name-giver. Three, the name will also describe the child's characteristics.

Let's take a look at the answer choices:

A.   *Present reasons why Hopi personal names can be treated as poetic compositions*

The author talks about this, but in a later paragraph.

B.   *Support the claim that Hopi personal names make reference to events in the recipient's life*

Very tricky! Names are given during events in the recipient's life. But they don't make reference to these events! They reference the name giver's tribe and a characteristic of the child.

Be especially careful of answer choices that take an idea that is semi-related to what was described in the passage and then **subverts** it.

C.   *Argue that the fact that Hopis receive many names throughout life refutes European theories about naming*

Think carefully about this answer choice. Now think back on the content of the passage.

We know that the author's issue with European theories is that those theories don't account for the semantic content in names.

Why would Hopis receiving many names refute the European theories? Only if the European theories held that a person can only receive one name in their lifetime, then showing that Hopis receive many names would refute that theory.

The European theories didn't care how many names a person had; they simply held that names were tools and had no inherent meaning.

D.   *Illustrate ways in which Hopi personal names may have <u>semantic content</u>*

This answer doesn't really stand out to us initially. So it's important to dig deeper into the exact wording of the answer choice. What does it mean to have "semantic content?"

Semantic content means having inherent meaning in the words of the names. That is what the majority of the second paragraph is telling us. We are told that the name giver's tribal affiliation can be expressed in the name; as well as a personal characteristic of the person being named.

In other words, Hopi names have meaning/semantic content.

E.   *Demonstrate that the <u>literal translation</u> of Hopi personal names often <u>obscures</u> their <u>true meaning</u>*

Again, one of the ways in which we eliminate purpose answer choices is by asking ourselves whether this truly happens in the passage. A great way to do this is by trying to match up the keywords in the AC with what actually happened in the passage.

Does Paragraph 2 talk about the "true meaning" behind Hopi names? If so, where? What is the "literal translation" of these names? The author gives an example, "little rabbit." Does "little rabbit" obscure the true meaning of the name? No, it doesn't. Because the name is representative of the child's size and the clan totem animal. Nothing is "obscured."

The correct answer is D.

***

Ultimately, when it comes to questions asking you for a paragraph's function/purpose/role, even before looking at the answer choices, we should already know the answers to the following three questions:

What that specific paragraph talked about
What is the main point/central thesis of the passage
The role the paragraph plays relative to the main point.

Use these three questions to anticipate the correct answer choice; it is crucial to have at least a general idea of the correct answer before we start to go over the answer choices. This way, we are less likely to be subverted by trap answers.

Regarding tricky trap answers, beware of answer choices describing something that didn't happen; answer choices that are subverting the passage's original meaning; or even a partially correct answer. We will discuss the art of answer choice comparison in greater detail in Part III of the book. But for now, get into the habit of nitpicking answer choices for flaws and ranking them in order of preference.

Three: Purpose of a Sentence/Idea

Let's go another step further into the passage. We have looked at questions that asked us for the purpose of the entire passage and questions which asked us for the function/purpose of a paragraph. Now let's look at questions that are asking us for the purpose behind a single sentence.

In these questions, we need to focus on the specific statement/idea the question is concerned with. We need to isolate it within the passage. From there, we need to read the paragraph in which this statement is located. Pay extra attention to the sentences immediately before and after the statement in question. Finally, we can think about the passage's main point as a whole; and what, if any, connections exist between the sentence in question and the passage's main point.

How we approach these questions is very similar to how we approach Role Question on the LR section. In my other book, LR Perfection, I discuss the approach to Role Questions in greater detail. You can also check my website for a free preview of that book as well as additional musings on the relationship between LR and RC.

So in short, do the following:

1. Identify and isolate the sentence within the passage. Understand its meaning.

2. Re-read the location (and before/after) where the sentence was found.

3. Quickly scan the paragraph from which the sentence was found and think about the relationship between the sentence and the main point of the paragraph.

4. If you can, think about the relationship between the sentence and the passage as a whole.

Let's take a look at such a question:

PT25 S1 Q11 (PT25 Passage 2)

While a new surge of critical interest in the ancient Greek poems conventionally ascribed to Homer has taken place in the last twenty years or so, it was non-specialists rather than professional scholars who studied the poetic aspects of the Iliad and the Odyssey between, roughly, 1935 and 1970. During these years, while such non-academic intellectuals as Simone Weil and Erich Auerbach were trying to define the qualities that made these epic accounts of the Trojan War and its aftermath great poetry, the questions that occupied the specialists were directed elsewhere: "Did the Trojan War really happen?" "Does the bard preserve Indo- European folk memories?" "How did the poems get written down?" Something was driving scholars away from the actual works to peripheral issues. Scholars produced books about archaeology, and gift exchange in ancient societies, about the development of oral poetry, about virtually anything except the Iliad and the Odyssey themselves as unique reflections or distillations of life itself—as, in short, great poetry. The observations of the English poet Alexander Pope seemed as applicable in 1970 as they had been when he wrote them in 1715: according to Pope, the remarks of critics "are rather Philosophical, Historical, Geographical . . . or rather anything than Critical and Poetical."

Ironically, the modern manifestation of this "nonpoetical" emphasis can be traced to the profoundly influential work of Milman Parry, who attempted to demonstrate in detail how the Homeric poems, believed to have been recorded nearly three thousand years ago, were the products of a long and highly developed tradition of oral poetry about the Trojan War. Parry proposed that this tradition built up its diction and its content by a process of constant accumulation and refinement over many generations of storytellers. But after Parry's death in 1935, his legacy was taken up by scholars who, unlike Parry, forsook intensive analysis of the poetry itself and focused instead on only one element of Parry's work: the creative limitations and possibilities of oral composition, concentrating on fixed elements and inflexibilities, focusing on the things that oral poetry allegedly can and cannot do. The dryness of this kind of study drove many of the more inventive scholars away from the poems into the rapidly developing field of Homer's archaeological and historical background.

Appropriately, Milman Parry's son Adam was among those scholars responsible for a renewed interest in Homer's poetry as literary art. Building on his father's work, the younger Parry argued that the Homeric poems exist both within and against a tradition. The Iliad and the Odyssey were, Adam Parry thought, the beneficiaries of an inherited store of diction, scenes, and concepts, and at the same time highly individual works that surpassed these conventions. Adam Parry helped prepare the ground for the recent Homeric revival by affirming his father's belief in a strong inherited tradition, but also by emphasizing Homer's unique contributions within that tradition.

The author of the passage most probably quotes Alexander Pope in order to

    A. Indicate that the Homeric poems have generally received poor treatment at the hands of English critics
    B. Prove that poets as well as critics have emphasized elements peripheral to the poems
    C. Illustrate that the nonpoetical emphasis also existed in an earlier century
    D. Emphasize the problems inherent in rendering classical Greek poetry into modern English
    E. Argue that poets and literary critics have seldom agreed about the interpretation of poetry

Let's find where the author is quoting Alexander Pope.

The author mentions Pope at the end of the first paragraph:

> *The observations of the English poet Alexander Pope seemed as applicable in 1970 as they had been when he wrote them in 1715: according to Pope, the remarks of critics "are rather Philosophical, Historical, Geographical . . . or rather anything than Critical and Poetical."*

So we know from this sentence that Pope made a comment about critics in 1715, which is hundreds of years before the passage's discussion of Homer and Homerian critics. So Pope is probably talking about some other critics, perhaps his own.

According to Pope, these critics in the eighteenth century are focused on all these subjects, just not on the actual poetry itself.

What was the author's issue with Homerian critics in the twentieth century? It's the same problem Pope had with his critics two hundred years ago. The critics focused on all these topics and subjects, rather than on the actual merit of the poetry itself.

So consider both the statement about Pope and the author's main point in the first paragraph, what is the relationship between the two?

Perhaps the author is drawing a parallel between what happened to Pope in the past, and what is happening to Homer in the present? Perhaps by showing that a great poet like Pope had faced a similar situation in the past, the author is adding legitimacy to their observation of the present state of Homeric criticism? These are all potential pre-phrased answers that we can come up with upon reading the question.

Let's look at the answer choices:

> A.   *indicate that the Homeric poems have generally received poor treatment at the hands of English critics*

This answer deliberately mixes up the issues. Pope's complaint wasn't about critics of Homer. The author is complaining about the critics of Homer, how they are more concerned with peripheral topics rather than Homer's poetry itself. Pope was complaining about another set of critics, but his criticism was the same as the author's.

Having a clear grasp of the chronology (something we discussed in Chapter 4) would help us to avoid this answer choice. Pope lived in the 1700s. The Homeric critics being discussed are present in the 1900s. Two separate issues.

> B.   *prove that <u>poets</u> <u>as well as critics</u> have emphasized elements peripheral to the poems*

The comparison isn't between poets and critics, but between critics of Pope in the past and critics of Homer in the present.

> C.   *illustrate that the nonpoetical emphasis also existed in an earlier century*

This answer is fairly basic and safe. It does take into account the temporal distinction between Pope and present-day Homeric critics. It still falls a little short of my anticipated answer, since I feel like quoting Pope is somewhat supportive of the author's observations. But let's keep it for now.

> D.   *emphasize the problems inherent in <u>rendering</u> classical Greek poetry into modern English*

"Rendering" here means to translate. So this answer is essentially saying that the author quoted Pope to show how hard it is to translate Homer into English.

This answer is out of scope.

    E.   *argue that poets and literary critics have <u>seldom</u> agreed about the interpretation of poetry*

I suppose this answer can be tempting. But if we look deeper, then it falls short on many aspects.

Pope claimed that the critics were not interested in the poetry itself; but rather, the philosophical, geographical, and historical backgrounds associated with the poems. In other words, the critics are not coming up with alternative interpretations of the poetry – they are not interested in the poems themselves to begin with.

Secondly, the word "seldom" sounds too aggressive to me. We know that Pope's critics didn't focus on his poetry; neither did Homer's. Does that mean most critics of most poems chose not to focus on the poetry itself? We cannot know for sure.

The correct answer is C.

PT25 S1 Q15 (PT25 Passage 3)

Even in the midst of its resurgence as a vital tradition, many sociologists have viewed the current form of the powwow, a ceremonial gathering of native Americans, as a sign that tribal culture is in decline. Focusing on the dances and rituals that have recently come to be shared by most tribes, they suggest that an intertribal movement is now in ascension and claim the inevitable outcome of this tendency is the eventual dissolution of tribes and the complete assimilation of native Americans into Euro-American society. Proponents of this "Pan-Indian" theory point to the greater frequency of travel and communication between reservations, the greater urbanization of native Americans, and, most recently, their increasing politicization in response to common grievances as the chief causes of the shift toward inter-tribalism.

Indeed, the rapid diffusion of dance styles, outfits, and songs from one reservation to another offers compelling evidence that inter-tribalism has been increasing. However, these sociologists have failed to note the concurrent revitalization of many traditions unique to individual tribes. Among the Lakota, for instance, the Sun Dance was revived, after a forty-year hiatus, during the 1950's. Similarly, the Black Legging Society of the Kiowa and the Hethuska Society of the Ponca—both traditional groups within their respective tribes—have gained new popularity. Obviously, a more complex societal shift is taking place than the theory of Pan-Indianism can account for.

An examination of the theory's underpinnings may be critical at this point, especially given that native Americans themselves chafe most against the Pan- Indian classification. Like other assimilationist theories with which it is associated, the Pan-Indian view is predicated upon an a priori assumption about the nature of cultural contact: that upon contact minority societies immediately begin to succumb in every respect—biologically, linguistically, and culturally—to the majority society. However, there is no evidence that this is happening to native American groups.

Yet the fact remains that intertribal activities are a major facet of native American culture today. Certain dances at powwows, for instance, are announced as intertribal, others as traditional. Likewise, speeches given at the beginnings of powwows are often delivered in English, while the prayer that follows is usually spoken in a native language. Cultural borrowing is, of course, old news. What is important to note is the conscious distinction native Americans make between tribal and intertribal tendencies.

Tribalism, although greatly altered by modern history, remains a potent force among native Americans: It forms a basis for tribal identity, and aligns music and dance with other social and cultural activities important to individual tribes. Intertribal activities, on the other hand, reinforce native American identity along a broader front, where this identity is directly threatened by outside influences.

The author most likely states that "cultural borrowing is, of course, old news" primarily to

    A. Acknowledge that in itself the existence of intertribal tendencies at powwows is unsurprising
    B. Suggest that native Americans' use of English in powwows should be accepted as unavoidable
    C. Argue that the deliberate distinction of intertribal and traditional dances is not a recent development
    D. Suggest that the recent increase in intertribal activity is the result of native Americans borrowing from non Native American cultures
    E. Indicate that the powwow itself could have originated by combining practices drawn from both native and non-native American cultures

"Cultural borrowing is, of course, old news" appears at the end of Paragraph 4. Let's take a look at that paragraph:

> *Yet the fact remains that intertribal activities are a major facet of native American culture today. Certain dances at powwows, for instance, are announced as intertribal, others as traditional. Likewise, speeches given at the beginnings of powwows are often delivered in English, while the prayer that follows is usually spoken in a native language.* <u>*Cultural borrowing is, of course, old news.*</u> *What is important to note is the conscious distinction native Americans make between tribal and intertribal tendencies.*

In this paragraph, the author is continuing the discussion that began in the previous paragraph. Recall that the Pan-Indian theorists believe that inter-tribalism is hurting individual tribal identity. The author declared that the Pan-Indian Theory rests on a mistaken assumption.

In this paragraph, the author is talking about the peaceful coexistence of tribal and inter-tribal tendencies. Remember how the whole passage is really about how inter-tribalism is not hurting individual tribal identity? That's the direction in which the author is taking this. The author is saying here that there are many instances of inter-tribal expressions, and that has been going on for a long time. But native Americans separate the two, and it would be unfair and overly simplistic to argue that inter-tribalism is weakening tribal identities.

So by suggesting that *"cultural borrowing is old news,"* the author is supporting the idea that inter-tribal activities and foreign influences should not be automatically considered damaging to a tribe's identity.

Let's take a look at the answer choices:

> A. *Acknowledge that in itself the existence of intertribal tendencies at powwows is unsurprising*

This answer seems like another safe choice. If something is "old news," then it has happened for a long time, and it shouldn't be surprising. Furthermore, the passage is talking about the presence of inter-tribal activities in tribal life and in activities at powwows.

An analysis of the text of the answer choice doesn't reveal any glaring issues. Let's keep it for now.

> B. *Suggest that native Americans' use of English in powwows should be accepted as <u>unavoidable</u>*

This is a tempting choice, but there are two things that I am not so sure about.

First of all, the word "unavoidable" sounds too strong for my taste. If cultural borrowing is old news, perhaps a more reasonable thought would be that the use of English should be accepted as "unsurprising?"

Saying something is "unavoidable" gives it a sense of necessity or finality, and I'm not sure if something has happened in the past makes it "unavoidable."

Secondly, while the sentence immediately preceding the quoted statement is talking about the use of English at powwows, the paragraph as a whole is about something more general. So if I were to guess, I'd want to connect the statement about cultural borrowing being old news to the topic of the paragraph as a whole, which is about inter-tribalism.

> C. *Argue that the deliberate <u>distinction</u> of intertribal and traditional dances is not a recent development*

This is the opposite of what we want. The author is suggesting that the intermingling of inter-tribal and tribal practices is not a recent development.

D. *Suggest that the recent increase in intertribal activity is the result of native Americans borrowing from non Native American cultures*

Another untenable extrapolation. The author suggests that cultural borrowing has occurred in the past, and that inter-tribal activities are increasing. These are two separate issues. But did cultural borrowing cause an increase in inter-tribal activity? This was never something the author hinted at.

E. *Indicate that the powwow itself could have <u>originated</u> by combining practices drawn from both native and non-native American cultures*

The paragraph is telling us that the powwow contains intertribal and English elements and that cultural borrowing has occurred in the past. But to suggest that the powwow originated as a fusion of indigenous and European cultures is too much of a stretch.

Answer choice A is the correct answer.

LR Role Questions

We mentioned at the very beginning of the book that LR skills carry over into RC. This is especially true when we examine "According to the Passage" and "Inference" question types; It's also true when we go into detail on the process of answer choice elimination.

But for Purpose Questions, especially questions asking us what the purpose of a sentence is, our understanding of LR can be immensely helpful too. In fact, how we approach Role questions can provide a lot of inspiration when it comes to these RC Purpose questions.

As we know from the chapter on Role Questions from LR Perfection, the three steps to approaching a Role question are to isolate the statement in question; find the main conclusion; and ask yourself what the relationship is between the statement in question and the main conclusion of the argument. This is very similar to how we approach these "local" purpose questions. We identify the statement, we find what the paragraph/passage is talking about, and we ask ourselves what is the relationship between the two.

Another thing that we can learn from Role questions is the ability to dissect vague and abstract answer choices. In LR Perfection we practiced the art of extracting keywords from unclear answer choices and matching them up with the stimulus. This is something that we should try to do for RC answer choices as well. Think about whether the AC is describing something that truly happened in the passage, before asking yourself whether it's indeed the purpose of the sentence/statement.

Four: Purpose of a Word

We now come to the last type of Purpose Questions. We have looked at questions that asked us for the purpose of a passage, paragraph, and sentence. This last type of purpose questions will ask us what is the purpose of a specific word that appears in the passage.

When the question asks us "what is the reason why the author uses word X in the last paragraph?" or "the author uses the term X most probably to do which one of the following?" We need to think of the following things:

In the first place, we must examine the **actual word itself**. What does the word mean? Does it have any special connotations? What are some synonyms for this word, and why did the author pick this specific word and not one of its synonyms?

Second, we need to expand our horizons and look at the **sentence in which the word itself is found**. What idea is the sentence trying to convey, and does the word have a special role in conveying that idea?

Lastly, an optional step that may enhance our understanding if we are stuck: we can also examine the issue on an **even broader level**, and take a look at that paragraph as a whole. What is the main idea of that paragraph? What about the main point of the passage? Does the author choosing to use a specific word help advance their argument in any way? If so, how?

Take a look at the following passages and questions and try to come up with some potential answers before looking at the ACs.

PT31 S4 Q20 (PT31 Passage 3)

Donna Haraway's Primate Visions is the most ambitious book on the history of science yet written from a feminist perspective, embracing not only the scientific construction of gender but also the interplay of race, class, and colonial and postcolonial culture with the "Western" construction of the very concept of nature itself. Primatology is a particularly apt vehicle for such themes because primates seem so much like ourselves that they provide ready material for scientists' conscious and unconscious projections of their beliefs about nature and culture.

Haraway's most radical departure is to challenge the traditional disjunction between the active knower (scientist/historian) and the passive object (nature/history). In Haraway's view, the desire to understand nature, whether in order to tame it or to preserve it as a place of wild innocence, is based on a troublingly masculinist and colonialist view of nature as an entity distinct from us and subject to our control. She argues that it is a view that is no longer politically, ecologically, or even scientifically viable. She proposes an approach that not only recognizes diverse human actors (scientists, government officials, laborers, science fiction writers) as contributing to our knowledge of nature, but that also recognizes the creatures usually subsumed under nature (such as primates) as active participants in creating that knowledge as well. Finally, she insists that the perspectives afforded by these different agents cannot be reduced to a single, coherent reality—there are necessarily only multiple, interlinked, partial realities.

This iconoclastic view is reflected in Haraway's unorthodox writing style. Haraway does not weave the many different elements of her work into one unified, overarching Story of Primatology; they remain distinct voices that will not succumb to a master narrative. This fragmented approach to historiography is familiar enough in historiographical theorizing but has rarely been put into practice by historians of science. It presents a complex alternative to traditional history, whether strictly narrative or narrative with emphasis on a causal argument.

Haraway is equally innovative in the way she incorporates broad cultural issues into her analysis. Despite decades of rhetoric from historians of science about the need to unite issues deemed "internal" to science (scientific theory and practice) and those considered "external" to it (social issues, structures, and beliefs), that dichotomy has proven difficult to set aside. Haraway simply ignores it. The many readers in whom this separation is deeply ingrained may find her discussions of such popular sources as science fiction, movies, and television distracting, and her statements concerning such issues as nuclear war bewildering and digressive. To accept her approach one must shed a great many assumptions about what properly belongs to the study of science.

The author uses the term "rhetoric" most probably in order to do which one of the following?

A. Underscore the importance of clear and effective writing in historiographical works
B. Highlight the need for historians of science to study modes of language
C. Emphasize the fact that historians of science have been unable to put innovative ideas into practice
D. Criticize the excessive concern for form over content in the writing of historians of science
E. Characterize the writing style and analytical approach employed by Haraway

This is a passage that we haven't encountered before, so let's read through it together for clarity.

Donna Haraway's <u>Primate Visions</u> is the <u>most ambitious book</u> on the history of science yet written from a <u>feminist perspective</u>, embracing not only the scientific construction of gender but also the interplay of race, class, and colonial and postcolonial culture with the "Western" construction of the very concept of nature itself. <u>Primatology</u> is a particularly apt vehicle for such themes because primates seem so much like ourselves that they provide ready material for scientists' conscious and unconscious projections of their beliefs about nature and culture.

There's a lot of information in the first paragraph, and it gets a little confusing. The author has a very favorable impression of DH's new book, Primate Visions. What do we know about the book?

It's a book on the history of science written from the feminist perspective. But it's also a book about primatology. That's the study of apes and gorillas, etc. So how is a book about monkeys also a book about the history of science written from the feminist perspective? I am not too sure, but I guess we shall find out.

The first paragraph also tells us that scientists project their beliefs about nature and culture unto the primates.

Haraway's <u>most radical departure</u> is to challenge the traditional disjunction between the active <u>knower</u> (scientist/historian) and the passive <u>object</u> (nature/history). In Haraway's view, the desire to understand nature, whether in order to tame it or to preserve it as a place of wild innocence, is based on a troublingly <u>masculinist and colonialist view of nature</u> as an entity distinct from us and subject to our control. She argues that it is a view that is no longer politically, ecologically, or even scientifically viable. She <u>proposes an approach</u> that not only recognizes diverse human actors (scientists, government officials, laborers, science fiction writers) as contributing to our knowledge of nature, but that also recognizes the <u>creatures</u> usually subsumed under nature (such as primates) <u>as active participants in creating that knowledge as well.</u> Finally, she insists that the perspectives afforded by these different agents cannot be reduced to a single, coherent reality—there are necessarily only <u>multiple, interlinked, partial realities.</u>

DH believes the separation of student and subject, knower and object, is inappropriate. It thinks of nature as something distinct and subject to our control.

DH proposes an alternative where not only human actors but even monkeys and gorillas will create knowledge; and that there isn't a standard version of reality; but multiple versions of reality depending on whose perspective we are taking.

This iconoclastic view is reflected in Haraway's <u>unorthodox writing style</u>. Haraway does not weave the many different elements of her work into one unified, overarching Story of Primatology; they remain <u>distinct voices</u> that will not succumb to a master narrative. This fragmented approach to historiography is familiar enough in historiographical theorizing but has rarely been put into practice by historians of science. It presents a complex alternative to traditional history, whether strictly narrative or narrative with emphasis on a causal argument.

DH's views are seen in her writing style, which is distinct and fragmented, having many voices speak rather than having a unified master narrative.

*Haraway is <u>equally innovative</u> in the way she incorporates <u>broad cultural issues</u> into her analysis. Despite decades of **rhetoric** from historians of science about the need to unite issues deemed "<u>internal</u>" to science (scientific theory and practice) and those considered "<u>external</u>" to it (social issues, structures, and beliefs), that <u>dichotomy has proven difficult</u> to set aside. Haraway simply <u>ignores</u> it. The many readers in whom this separation is deeply ingrained may find her discussions of such popular sources as science fiction, movies, and television distracting, and her statements concerning such issues as nuclear war bewildering and digressive. To accept her approach one must shed a great many assumptions about what properly belongs to the study of science.*

More praise for Haraway's unorthodox approach. The author calls her "innovative." There's been the goal of uniting scientific theory and practice with social issues and beliefs in the scientific community, but it has been difficult. Haraway ignores this distinction. Finally, the author says that readers may find Haraway's work "bewildering," and we must keep an open mind.

The Author's Purpose in writing this passage is fairly straightforward. A favorable review is provided for Haraway's book.

The Main Point of the passage can be derived from the Author's Purpose, but with more content from the passages: Haraway's new book, Primate Visions, offers us not only an innovative view exemplified by an unorthodox writing style; but also an ambitious presentation of the history of science from the feminist perspective.

The first paragraph introduces DH's book Primate Visions, tells us what's special about it, and why the topic chosen is especially suitable.

The second paragraph highlights the most unique feature of DH's book. DH sees knowledge as being created by both humans and primates; and that there are different versions of reality.

The third paragraph tells us that DH's unique views are reflected in her writing style.

The last paragraph tells us that DH ignores the distinction between the science and its social impacts, being able to write about both in her book (incorporating broad cultural issues). We are also told that we must keep an open mind.

*****

Let's take a look at the question:

The author uses the term "rhetoric" most probably in order to do which one of the following?

The word "rhetoric" appears in the last paragraph. The author is talking about historians of science who want to unite science with the associated social policies/impacts. We also know that the word "rhetoric" can have multiple meanings. It can mean oration or speeches given in public; or it can mean something that is expressed but not put into practice, such as empty talk.

What do we know about these historians from the paragraph? We know that they have been trying to unite the two distinct issues; but have been unable to do so. In that sense, the word "rhetoric" seems to mean that the historians have been talking the talk, but have not been able to walk the walk.

A potentially correct answer would probably say that the author uses the term "rhetoric" in order to show that the historians of science have been unable to execute their goals in reality.

Let's look at the answer choices:

   A.   *Underscore the importance of <u>clear and effective writing</u> in historiographical works*

How would using a word like "rhetoric" stress the importance of clear and effective writing? We know that the historians of science spoke of the need to combine scientific theory and science's social impacts; although they were unable to do so. We do not know if the writing of historians is clear and effective. This answer choice is out of scope.

   B.   *Highlight the need for historians of science to study <u>modes of language</u>*

I am unclear as to what the "modes of language" are. Perhaps DH's writing style constitutes one of them. But the author never really calls on historians to study certain subjects, either explicitly or implied.

C.   Emphasize the fact that historians of science have been unable to put <u>innovative ideas</u> into practice

This answer touches upon the dichotomy between theory and practice. I like that. We know that our goal answer choice would discuss the historians unable to overcome the distinction between science and its implications.

So the first part of the answer choice looks good.

One thing that we have to double check are the keywords "innovative ideas." If the answer had read that it "emphasized the fact that historians of science have been unable to *unite the issues internal to science and external to it,*" then it would have been perfect.

So what we have to figure out now is what is meant by "putting innovative ideas into practice." Does that mean the same thing as "uniting the issues internal and external to science?"

I'm not too sure at this point, so I'll keep this answer choice and move on.

D.   Criticize the excessive concern for <u>form over content in the writing</u> of historians of science

Are the historians overly concerned with form, at the expense of content? Are these historians sacrificing the quality of their essays and books because they want to write the most structured or most beautifully formatted works? This is never mentioned in the paragraph/passage.

The historians would like to unite distinct issues but have not been able to do so. Do not get carried away by answer choices that are talking about issues that seem related, but are wholly separate. This is why it's crucial to have an anticipated answer that you can compare the answer choices to; rather than blindly reading through the ACs and trying to pick one that works.

E.   Characterize the writing style and analytical approach employed by <u>Haraway</u>

Again, we are talking about the historians of science, not Haraway. This answer is out of scope.

So all that remains is to double-check answer choice C. If I was pressed for time I would probably have gone with it and hoped for the best. But let's take a closer look at it.

Historians have not been able to set aside the differences between internal and external scientific issues. But Haraway has been able to do so. How did she do it? She ignores it. This is the "innovative approach" mentioned by the author. So when we say that the historians have been unable to "put innovative ideas into practice," what we are really saying is that the historians have not been able to do what Haraway did. They have not been able to set aside the distinction, they have not been able to ignore it. The historians have been talking about uniting these issues, but despite all their rhetoric, they have been unable to do so, failing to come up with an innovative solution, as Haraway did.

In the end, we made answer choice C work. But be really careful about what we did here. We made additional inferences based entirely on the content of the paragraph, rather than throwing in assumptions of our own.

We were not sure what "innovative ideas" meant, but we know that the paragraph also calls Haraway's approach "innovative." So based on the paragraph, we can safely argue that these are referring to the same thing.

So in other words, what this AC is really saying is this:

Emphasize the fact that historians of science have been unable to put <u>ideas that sidestep the distinction between internal and external scientific issues</u> into practice.

This may seem overly complicated and too nuanced to grasp at the moment, but there's a specific set of drills and tricks to apply when it comes to comparing and ranking vague answer choices. In fact, it will be the primary focus of Part III of this book. Just progress through the book at a steady pace for now.

C is the correct answer.

Let's look at one more Purpose of a Word question, this time, from a passage with which we are already very familiar:

PT27 S3 Q9 (PT27 Passage 2)

Personal names are generally regarded by European thinkers in two major ways, both of which deny that names have any significant semantic content. In philosophy and linguistics, John Stuart Mill's formulation that "proper names are meaningless marks set upon…persons to distinguish them from one another" retains currency; in anthropology, Claude Lévi-Strauss's characterization of names as being primarily instruments of social classification has been very influential. Consequently, interpretation of personal names in societies where names have other functions and meanings has been neglected. Among the Hopi of the southwestern United States, names often refer to historical or ritual events in order both to place individuals within society and to confer an identity upon them. Furthermore, the images used to evoke these events suggest that Hopi names can be seen as a type of poetic composition.

Throughout life, Hopis receive several names in a sequence of ritual initiations. Birth, entry into one of the ritual societies during childhood, and puberty are among the name-giving occasions. Names are conferred by an adult member of a clan other than the child's clan, and names refer to that name giver's clan, sometimes combining characteristics of the clan's totem animal with the child's characteristics. Thus, a name might translate to something as simple as "little rabbit," which reflects both the child's size and the representative animal.

More often, though, the name giver has in mind a specific event that is not apparent in a name's literal translation. One Lizard clan member from the village of Oraibi is named Lomayayva, "beautifully ascended." This translation, however, tells nothing about either the event referred to—who or what ascended—or the name giver's clan. The name giver in this case is from Badger clan. Badger clan is responsible for an annual ceremony featuring a procession in which masked representations of spirits climb the mesa on which Oraibi sits. Combining the name giver's clan association with the receiver's home village, "beautifully ascended" refers to the splendid colors and movements of the procession up the mesa. The condensed image this name evokes—a typical feature of Hopi personal names—displays the same quality of **Western Apache place names** that led one commentator to call them "tiny imagist poems."

Hopi personal names do several things simultaneously. They indicate social relationships—but only indirectly—and they individuate persons. Equally important, though, is their poetic quality; in a sense they can be understood as oral texts that produce aesthetic delight. This view of Hopi names is thus opposed not only to Mill's claim that personal names are without inherent meaning but also to Lévi-Strauss's purely functional characterization. Interpreters must understand Hopi clan structures and linguistic practices in order to discern the beauty and significance of Hopi names.

The author most likely refers to Western Apache place names in order to

    A. Offer an example of how names can contain references not evident in their literal translations
    B. Apply a commentator's characterization of Western Apache place names to Hopi personal names
    C. Contrast Western Apache naming practices with Hopi naming practices
    D. Demonstrate that other names besides Hopi names may have some semantic content
    E. Explain how a specific Hopi name refers subtly to a particular Western Apache site

As we are no doubt intimately familiar with the content of this passage, let's go straight to the question:

The author most likely refers to Western Apache place names in order to

Let's take a look at the paragraph where the author refers to Western Apache place names:

> *More often, though, the name giver has in mind a specific event that is not apparent in a name's literal translation. One Lizard clan member from the village of Oraibi is named Lomayayva, "beautifully ascended." This translation, however, tells nothing about either the event referred to—who or what ascended—or the name giver's clan. The name giver in this case is from Badger clan. Badger clan is responsible for an annual ceremony featuring a procession in which masked representations of spirits climb the mesa on which Oraibi sits. Combining the name giver's clan association with the receiver's home village, "beautifully ascended" refers to the splendid colors and movements of the procession up the mesa. The condensed image this name evokes—a typical feature of Hopi personal names—displays the same quality of **Western Apache place names** that led one commentator to call them "tiny imagist poems."*

We know that in this paragraph, the author is going into detail about the content of Hopi names. Hopi names have meaning in themselves, contrary to the theories proposed by Mill and Levi-Strauss.

Let's take a look at the exact sentence where the quoted words appear:

> *The condensed image this name evokes—a typical feature of Hopi personal names—displays the same quality of **Western Apache place names** that led one commentator to call them "tiny imagist poems."*

Hopi names contain beautiful imagery. Western Apache place names *also* contain beautiful imagery. This is rather straightforward.

Now for a slightly trickier question: what is the commentator calling "tiny imagist poems?" Hopi names or Western Apache place names?

The commentator is calling Western Apache place names "tiny imagist poems."

So if we arrange the information in this sentence, what we get is this:

> Western Apache place names contain beautiful imagery, one commentator calls them "tiny imagist poems." Hopi personal names, similar to Western Apache place names, also evoke condensed images.

So why is the author referring to Western Apache place names in this paragraph?

Remember the main point of this paragraph. The author is trying to demonstrate that the Hopi names contain meaning and imagery. So by quoting a commentator's views on Apache names, and by demonstrating the similarity between Apache names and Hopi names, the author is trying to legitimize their own observations. It is a form of support for the author's main point in this paragraph.

Let's take a look at the answer choices:

   A.   Offer an example of how names can contain references not evident in their literal translations

The paragraph does talk about references not evident in their literal translations in the very first sentence. But we must remember that the purpose of this paragraph is to describe in detail how Hopi names can contain beautiful imagery. The statement about Apache names is used to support this view.
While what answer choice A describes is something that appears in the paragraph, it is not why the author has mentioned Apache place names.

Remember that the correct answer choice must satisfy **two requirements**. It must truly describe something that actually occurred in the paragraph or passage, and it must be the real purpose behind the author's use of the specific word/sentence.

> B. _Apply_ a commentator's characterization of Western Apache place names to Hopi personal names

So the author is definitely trying to suggest that a commentator's characterization of Western Apache names is also an apt description of Hopi names. Is "apply" too strong a word? The author definitely thinks there are similarities between the two (Apache and Hopi). I suppose you can say that in the author's mind, the commentator's characterization of Apache names is also _applicable_ to Hopi names. If we look at it that way, this answer choice could work.

Let's see if there are better answers first.

> C. _Contrast_ Western Apache naming practices with Hopi naming practices

This is the opposite of what we want. To "contrast" two things is to discover how they are different. If we were "comparing" Apache place names with Hopi personal names, that would be a great choice.

But we are not trying to figure out the differences between how the Apache come up with names, and how the Hopi come up with their names. We know enough about Hopi naming practices; but nothing about Apache naming practices.

> D. Demonstrate that other names besides Hopi names may have some semantic content

This answer is certainly true. We know that Apache names have semantic content. But is this _why_ the author is referring to Apache names?

Remember that in our initial anticipation of what the correct answer might look like, we are hoping to find an answer that tells us the author mentioned Apache names because Apache names are like tiny imagist poems, and since they are similar to Hopi names, that's what Hopi names are, too.

So the author's primary purpose is to strengthen their view of Hopi names; rather than to show the non-exclusivity of Hopi names as image-filled words.

> E. Explain how a specific Hopi name _refers subtly_ to a particular Western Apache site

This answer is basically saying that a Hopi name is named after an Apache location.

The correct answer is B. We deliberated for a bit about whether it's too strong a characterization of the author's intent. But the use of the word "apply" is justifiable. It is also the closest to what we had anticipated, and as a result, the best available answer.

Summary

In this chapter, we saw four types of Purpose Questions, each of which addresses a component of the passage. There are questions that ask us for the whole purpose of the passage, the purpose of a paragraph within a passage, the purpose of a sentence or statement within a paragraph, or the purpose of a single word or phrase.

Collectively, these questions constitute one of the most frequently appearing question families in RC, so it's important to have a clear pathway to attacking them.

For Purpose questions, it's *crucial* to try to anticipate what the correct answer may look like prior to tackling the answer choices. As we saw time and time again, tricky answer choices that mention issues discussed in the passage; or obfuscate different ideas will abound in the harder questions. If our understanding of the relationships between different components isn't clear, then it's very easy to be led astray by these trap answer choices.

When examining answer choices, there are two questions that we must ask ourselves:

First, does what the answer choice describes occur in the passage?

Second, even if what the answer choice describes is a part of the passage, is it the purpose of the passage/paragraph/sentence/word?

Only when an answer choice satisfies both requirements, can we be confident that it is the correct answer.

Another tip I have for those who found these questions challenging is to take a closer look at Role Questions. How we approach these LR questions is very similar to how we approach Purpose questions. In both instances, we are considering the relationship between different elements of a stimulus/passage.

Chapter 7: Four Types of Purpose Questions

Chapter 8: Main Point

From Purpose to Main Point

Let's move to another common question type, Main Point Questions. Four types of questions (Purpose, Main Point, According to the Passage, and Inference) constitute the majority of RC questions you will encounter. Collectively, we shall call them the **big four**. We now look at the second of these four question types.

We have placed the Main Point chapter right after the Purpose chapter because most of the time, it's easier to find the passage's main point after you have figured out the Author's Purpose. Although in more straightforward passages, the Main Point can be plainly stated either in the first or the last paragraph, in more difficult passages, we need to come up with our own version of the passage's MP.

Think back on the passages that we have seen so far. We were able to make an educated guess on what the Author's Purpose was based on the first paragraph and information that appeared very early on. We would come up with our own hypothesis on what the passage is about and why the author wrote this passage, and we would finetune this hypothesis as we moved through the passage.

Once we have a rough idea of why the author is writing a particular passage, we can simply rephrase the Author's Purpose by including specific ideas mentioned in the passage. This may be a little hard to grasp, so let's use a few hypotheticals to illustrate the practice.

Let's use CEER as a rough framework. Remember that whenever we are reading a difficult passage, paragraph, or sentence, we can ask ourselves *"What is the author doing?"* to help us better engage with the content. Is the author comparing, explaining, evaluating, or recommending something?

We saw also that not only can CEER help us improve our active reading ability, it can also work as a basic guide to predicting the Author's Purpose. It doesn't work for every passage, but for many, the Author's Purpose is to compare, explain, evaluate, or to recommend. Sometimes it's a combination of several of these.

Let's pretend that there's a passage where the Author's Purpose is comparing the writing of Hemingway and Steinbeck. The Main Point of that passage will include the similarities and differences between the two authors. It will probably be along the lines of *"Hemingway and Steinbeck are similar in respect A, but different in B and C."*

If the Purpose of the passage is to explain a new theory, such as the Theory of Evolution, Then the Main Point can simply tell us what the theory entails. It can say that *"The Theory of Evolution states that the process of natural selection favors the continuation of traits that maximize survivability. Over long periods of time it leads to significant changes."*

If the Author's Purpose is to evaluate the pros and cons of a position or theory, the Main Point of the passage will naturally lay these out in more explicit detail. Similarly, if the author is making a recommendation in the passage, then the Main Point will tell us exactly what it is that the author is advocating.

Always try to come up with your own version of what the passage's Main Point might be. I like to do that as soon as I've finished reading the passage. I first think about what the Author's Purpose is, then try to come up with the MP.

There is another reason why we always try to think about the Author's Purpose *before* the Main Point of the passage.

In a passage where the author's position, opinion, or attitude is made clear, the correct main point answer choice will always reflect **what the author thinks**.

For instance, if the author spends the majority of the passage describing a position only to tell us in the last sentence of the passage that the position is erroneous; the correct MP answer *will have to include* the information about the position being wrong.

Similarly, if throughout the most part of a passage, the author is comparing the merits of two courses of action, only making a recommendation in the last paragraph; then the correct answer choice *will have to include* the author's recommendation, or what the author thought about the issues they just described.

In short, if the author's position or stance is neutral or unclear, then we have nothing to worry about. But if we do find evidence in the passage pointing to what the author personally thinks, then that must be included in the correct Main Point answer.

***

Main Point ≠ Laundry List

An important thing to note about a passage's Main Point is the MAIN in Main Point. The correct MP answer choice will not necessarily cover all the points made by the author.

Let's say that we have just read an essay. We don't know the topic or the thesis statement of this essay. It has three paragraphs. The first paragraph tells us that a democratic political system is more adaptable and flexible than an authoritarian system. The second paragraph tells us a democratic political system has a higher respect for individual rights and freedoms. The final paragraph tells us democratic countries do not go to war as easily as authoritarian ones. We are not given a conclusion or any hint of what the main point is.

In a case like this the main point would need to be inferred. A suitable answer would be that *"democratic systems of government are superior to authoritarian ones."* This is straightforward enough, and most students will have no difficulty recognizing this, even though the passage never explicitly states this.

A more complete answer may say that *"democratic governments are superior to authoritarian ones because they are more flexible, have more respect for rights and freedoms, and are more peaceful."* Such an answer touches upon each of the key points the author made, as well as the over-arching main point of the entire essay.

If an answer choice just said *"democratic governments are more adaptable, has higher respect for rights and freedoms, and are more peaceful,"* it can still work, even though it's not ideal. Laundry list answer choices that simply summarize or describe what happens in the passage without connecting the dots or drawing inferences can be correct in limited instances, but only when answers like the first two are not available. Most of the times, a simple regurgitation of what each paragraph talked about will be wrong as an answer choice.

Most students will understand why the first two choices are more suitable as MP answers than the third one. We want an answer that really gives us the central idea behind the author's argument, and not a mechanical summary/regurgitation of it. But when it comes to real RC passages, many students end up choosing the "laundry list" answer, especially when the Main Point of the passage isn't spelled out for us explicitly.

This happens for many reasons. The chief among them being that the student is not confident enough in their own reading ability. As a result, trying to play it safe, they memorize and regurgitate only what was explicitly stated in the passage. To make the inferences needed to answer many questions, we must be actively thinking about what we have just read. Rather than being passive recipients of the information in RC passages, we need to engage, compare, categorize, and even question what we have read.

Part I of the book is all about developing our reading skills; don't be afraid to go back and re-read those chapters if you feel like an inability to practicing active reading is what's holding you back.

You don't have to cover everything

In more recent PTs (70+), I have been noticing a sinister trend developing in MP Questions. I will address it here before we look at real questions, so that you may recognize the trap when you see it and avoid it accordingly.

Let's think back on our Democracy vs. Authoritarian systems hypothetical. You are faced with the following two answer choices for a Main Point Question:

Option 1: *Democratic governments are superior to authoritarian ones because they have greater respect for human rights and are less prone to go to war.*

Option 2: *More people prefer democracies to authoritarian governments because they are more adaptable and flexible, have greater respect for rights and responsibilities, and are less prone to go to war.*

Which one would you choose?
***

Let's look at both of these, what exactly are the issues with them, respectively?

Option 1 is missing one of the key points. In our hypothetical essay/passage, the first paragraph talks about democracies being more adaptable and flexible than authoritarian systems. But this is nowhere to be found in this answer choice.

Option 2 makes a subtle shift on the topic of discussion. Our hypothetical essay is talking about the advantages democracies have over authoritarian governments; but Option 2 is talking about people's preferences. In our hypothetical essay, we are never told the number of people who prefer one over the other.
***

These two answer choices are an illustration of one of the trickiest traps seen in MP Questions. There will be two tempting answer choices. One of them will be on topic, but seems incomplete; while the other covers all the bases but will have also made an unsupported/out of scope assertion.

If we really think back on what we had come up as potential main points of our hypothetical essay/passage, the ideal answer would have tied in all three of the sub key-points made in each paragraph. The ideal main point answer, we said, would have stated the superiority of democratic over authoritarian governments.

Option 1 does that. It is missing one of the key-points from one of the paragraphs, but it still captures the Main Point of the passage nicely. It's not the ideal answer we were looking for, but it is still acceptable.

Option 2; on the other hand, subverts the meaning the passage was trying to express. Just because A is better than or superior to B, doesn't mean more people prefer A to B. Salads are superior to junk food, but that doesn't mean more people prefer salads to junk food. So even though option 2 covers all the key-points in the passage, it is still the wrong answer.

This is a trend that has become more frequent in recent PTs, especially in the harder passages. Generally speaking, an answer choice that's missing some of the supporting information mentioned in the passage will be superior to an answer choice that appears complete on a first glance, but contains glaring errors.

Let's now look at some passages and their associated Main Point Questions. Like we did for purpose questions in the previous chapter, try to anticipate what the correct answer will look like before we even get to the answer choices.

Practice Questions

PT7 S3 Q15 (PT7 Passage 3)

Cultivation of a single crop on a given tract of land leads eventually to decreased yields. One reason for this is that harmful bacterial phytopathogens, organisms parasitic on plant hosts, increase in the soil surrounding plant roots. The problem can be cured by crop rotation, denying the pathogens a suitable host for a period of time. However, even if crops are not rotated, the severity of diseases brought on by such phytopathogens often decreases after a number or years as the microbial population of the soil changes and the soil becomes "suppressive" to those diseases. While there may be many reasons for this phenomenon, it is clear that levels of certain bacteria, such as Pseudomonas fluorescens, a bacterium antagonistic to a number of harmful phytopathogens, are greater in suppressive than in non-suppressive soil. This suggests that the presence of such bacteria suppresses phytopathogens. There is now considerable experimental support for this view. Wheat yield increases of 27 percent have been obtained in field trials by treatment of wheat seeds with fluorescent pseudomonads. Similar treatment of sugar beets, cotton, and potatoes has had similar results.

These improvements in crop yields through the application of Pseudomonas fluorescens suggest that agriculture could benefit from the use of bacteria genetically altered for specific purposes. For example, a form of phytopathogen altered to remove its harmful properties could be released into the environment in quantities favorable to its competing with and eventually excluding the harmful normal strain. Some experiments suggest that deliberately releasing altered non-pathogenic Pseudomonas syringae could crowd out the non-altered variety that causes frost damage. Opponents of such research have objected that the deliberate and large-scale release of genetically altered bacteria might have deleterious results. Proponents, on the other hand, argue that this particular strain is altered only by the removal of the gene responsible for the strain's propensity to cause frost damage, thereby rendering it safer than the phytopathogen from which it was derived.

Some proponents have gone further and suggest that genetic alteration techniques could create organisms with totally new combinations of desirable traits not found in nature. For example, genes responsible for production of insecticidal compounds have been transposed from other bacteria into pseudomonads that colonize corn roots. Experiments of this kind are difficult and require great care: such bacteria are developed in highly artificial environments and may not compete well with natural soil bacteria. Nevertheless, proponents contend that the prospects for improved agriculture through such methods seem excellent. These prospects lead many to hope that current efforts to assess the risks of deliberate release of altered microorganisms will successfully answer the concerns of opponents and create a climate in which such research can go forward without undue impediment.

Which one of the following best summarizes the main idea of the passage?

- A. Recent field experiments with genetically altered Pseudomonas bacteria have shown that releasing genetically altered bacteria into the environment would not involve any significant danger
- B. Encouraged by current research, advocates of agricultural use of genetically altered bacteria are optimistic that such use will eventually result in improved agriculture, though opponents remain wary
- C. Current research indicates that adding genetically altered Pseudomonas syringae bacteria to the soil surrounding crop plant roots will have many beneficial effects, such as the prevention of frost damage in certain crops
- D. Genetic alteration of a number of harmful phytopathogens has been advocated by many researchers who contend that these techniques will eventually replace such outdated methods as crop rotation
- E. Genetic alteration of bacteria has been successful in highly artificial laboratory conditions, but opponents of such research have argued that these techniques are unlikely to produce organisms that are able to survive in natural environments

Cultivation of a single crop on a given tract of land leads eventually to decreased yields. One reason for this is that harmful bacterial <u>phytopathogens</u>, organisms parasitic on plant hosts, increase in the soil surrounding plant roots. The problem can be cured by crop rotation, denying the pathogens a suitable host for a period of time. However, even if crops are not rotated, the severity of diseases brought on by such phytopathogens often decreases after a number or years as the microbial population of the soil changes and the soil becomes "suppressive" to those diseases. While there may be many reasons for this phenomenon, it is clear that levels of certain bacteria, such as <u>Pseudomonas fluorescens</u>, a bacterium antagonistic to a number of harmful phytopathogens, are greater in suppressive than in non-suppressive soil. This <u>suggests</u> that the presence of <u>such bacteria suppresses phytopathogens</u>. There is now <u>considerable experimental support</u> for this view. Wheat yield increases of 27 percent have been obtained in field trials by treatment of wheat seeds with fluorescent pseudomonads. Similar treatment of sugar beets, cotton, and potatoes has had similar results.

Back in Chapter 4 we talked about the importance of details: once you have a strong grasp of the passage's argument and structure, we need to be aware of certain details such as key terms.

The first passage starts off by talking about *phytopathogens*, which are "bad" bacteria. They can be decreased by crop rotation or suppressed by the presence of certain "good" bacteria in the soil. One of the "good" bacteria is the *Pseudomonas fluorescens*.

An additional detail we said to keep an eye out for is the author's opinion/attitude. What's the author's attitude towards this new finding about the *Pseudomonas fluorescens*? The author seems in general acceptance of the new experimental evidence ("*this suggests…there is now considerable experimental support…*"), but their tone seems fairly neutral and reserved at the same time.

These improvements in crop yields through the application of Pseudomonas fluorescens <u>suggest</u> that agriculture could benefit from the use of bacteria genetically altered for specific purposes. For example, a form of <u>phytopathogen altered to remove its harmful properties</u> could be released into the environment in quantities favorable to its competing with and eventually <u>excluding the harmful normal strain</u>. Some experiments <u>suggest</u> that deliberately releasing altered non-pathogenic <u>Pseudomonas syringae</u> could crowd out the non-altered variety that causes <u>frost damage</u>. <u>Opponents</u> of such research have objected that the deliberate and large-scale release of genetically altered bacteria might have <u>deleterious results</u>. <u>Proponents</u>, on the other hand, argue that this particular strain is altered only by the removal of the gene responsible for the strain's propensity to cause frost damage, thereby rendering it <u>safer</u> than the phytopathogen from which it was derived.

The author's tone is still fairly cautious coming into the second paragraph. The word "*suggest*" is used repeatedly. The author suggests that harmless genetically modified bacteria can be used to crowd out their regular counterparts. The *Pseudomonas syringae* was the example given.

The author then introduces some of the opponents' reservations, who are fearful of the consequences of large-scale release of genetically modified bacteria. The proponents' counter-argument is then stated.

It seems that the author has deliberately avoided taking a position on the debate up till now.

Some proponents have gone further and suggest that genetic alteration techniques could create organisms with <u>totally new combinations of desirable traits</u> not found in nature. For example, genes responsible for production of <u>insecticidal</u> compounds have been transposed from other bacteria into <u>pseudomonads</u> that colonize corn roots. Experiments of this kind are <u>difficult and require great care</u>: such bacteria are developed in highly artificial environments and may not compete well with natural soil bacteria. Nevertheless, <u>proponents</u> contend that the prospects for improved agriculture through such methods seem excellent. These prospects lead <u>many to hope</u> that current efforts to assess the risks of deliberate release of altered microorganisms will successfully <u>answer the concerns of opponents</u> and create a climate in which such research can go forward without undue impediment.

A more avant-garde position is introduced. No longer satisfied with simply removing the harmful traits from bacteria, some proponents now want to create organisms with desirable traits.

The author then restates their reservation about such an endeavor: *"experiments of this kind are difficult and require great care."*

Finally, the author reiterates the optimistic outlook of the proponents.

Which one of the following best summarizes the main idea of the passage?

What does the author do in this passage? They do several things. They start off by explaining how beneficial bacteria can fight off harmful bacteria. They then introduce the view held by proponents of genetic engineering, who believe that we can edit out the harmful genes in certain bacteria and use them to crowd out their harmful cousins, thereby helping plants.

The author then introduces the view held by the opponents of such a position, who are fearful of such activities' consequences. The author finally introduces a more extreme position held by the proponents, who are content not just with editing out harmful genes, but full-on genetic engineering of beneficial bacteria.

So the reading seems like a simple explanation/comparison hybrid passage. But as we mentioned earlier, we must always be mindful of the author's own position is, no matter how nuanced or subtle it is.

Is the author a "true believer" in the miracles of gene editing for bacteria? Not quite. Sure, the author devotes the majority of the passage to the proponents' position, but they also express their reservations regarding the whole endeavor. The author never considered the evidence conclusive, only that it "*suggests*" the possibility of beneficial effects. The author is also cautious of the more extreme position of those who advocate full on genetic engineering.

An ideal Main Point answer, in this case, would not only lay out the position of the proponents, but also factor in some of the author's reservations.

Let's take a look at the answer choices:

A. *Recent field experiments with genetically altered Pseudomonas bacteria* have shown that *releasing genetically altered bacteria into the environment* would not involve any significant danger

We know this is not exactly what the author thinks. This is probably the position of the proponents mentioned in the passage, but what we want is not only this, but also the author's own position.

B. *Encouraged by current research, advocates of agricultural use of genetically altered bacteria are* optimistic *that such use will eventually result in improved agriculture, though* opponents remain wary

Compared to Answer Choice A, this is more balanced and more reflective of both the makeup of the passage and the author's position. One party is optimistic, the other party is wary. A better answer would have touched upon the author's attitude and maybe also said that "great care is required," but I feel like this choice is still fairly representative. Let's see if there's a better choice.

C. *Current research indicates that adding genetically altered Pseudomonas syringae bacteria to the soil surrounding crop plant roots* will have many beneficial effects, *such as the prevention of frost damage in certain crops*

This answer is so close. It covers maybe 80% of the passage. But it's missing two important things.

First, even though the majority of the passage is devoted to the proponents' view, the Author's Purpose isn't a complete advocation/recommendation of that position. Even though limited coverage was given to the opponents, this passage is still comparing two opposing positions.

Secondly, the author's own attitude, as seen in the language they used throughout the passage, was not reflected in this answer choice. I would have wanted a more balanced answer choice, and this seems too one sided.

> D. *Genetic alteration of a number of harmful phytopathogens has been advocated by many researchers who contend that these techniques <u>will eventually replace</u> such outdated methods as crop rotation*

This is an unsupported linkage. The author suggests in the first paragraph that beneficial bacteria can achieve the same effect as crop rotation, but proponents never said these techniques will replace crop rotation.

> E. *Genetic alteration of bacteria has been successful in highly artificial laboratory conditions, but <u>opponents</u> of such research have argued that these techniques <u>are unlikely to produce organisms</u> that <u>are able to survive</u> in natural environments*

The opponents argue that the large-scale introduction of altered bacteria may have "deleterious" consequences. The author raises the possibility that genetically engineered bacteria may not compete with natural bacteria. This answer choice confuses the two positions. It also misses the proponents' stance entirely.

The best answer is B.

***

A rather tricky question, but it does present us with several take aways, many of which we have already covered earlier on in the chapter.

If the author's position, stance, or attitude is visible in a passage, then the correct answer will be reflective of that. So as we are reading through a passage, pay attention not just to its content and structure, but also to what the author actually thinks about the topic they are discussing.

> Try to come up with what the Author's Purpose might be before thinking about the Main Point of the passage. Thinking about *why* the author wrote this specific passage will force us to examine the author's position or attitude, and that in turn will help us with MP answer choice elimination.

Lastly, watch out for **one sided** answer choices, answer choices that make **unsupported connections** between ideas discussed in the passage, and answer choices that are **simple summaries** of content within the passage.

PT20 S2 Q23 (PT20 Passage 4)

In The Dynamics of Apocalypse, John Lowe attempts to solve the mystery of the collapse of the Classic Mayan civilization. Lowe bases his study on a detailed examination of the known archaeological record. Like previous investigators, Lowe relies on dated monuments to construct a step-by-step account of the actual collapse. Using the erection of new monuments as a means to determine a site's occupation span, Lowe assumes that once new monuments ceased to be built, a site had been abandoned. Lowe's analysis of the evidence suggests that construction of new monuments continued to increase between A.D. 672 and 751, but that the civilization stopped expanding geographically; new construction took place almost exclusively in established settlements. The first signs of trouble followed. Monument inscriptions indicate that between 751 and 790, long-standing alliances started to break down. Evidence also indicates that between 790 and 830, the death rate in Classic Mayan cities outstripped the birthrate. After approximately 830, construction stopped throughout the area, and within a hundred years, the Classic Mayan civilization all but vanished.

Having established this chronology, Lowe sets forth a plausible explanation of the collapse that accommodates the available archaeological evidence. He theorizes that Classic Mayan civilization was brought down by the interaction of several factors, set in motion by population growth. An increase in population, particularly within the elite segment of society, necessitated ever more intense farming. Agricultural intensification exerted stress on the soil and led to a decline in productivity (the amount of food produced through each unit of labor invested). At the same time, the growth of the elite class created increasing demands for ceremonial monuments and luxuries, diverting needed labor from the fields. The theory holds that these stresses were communicated— and amplified—throughout the area as Mayan states engaged in warfare to acquire laborers and food, and refugees fled impoverished areas. The most vulnerable states thus began to break down, and each downfall triggered others, until the entire civilization collapsed.

If there is a central flaw in Lowe's explanation, it is that the entire edifice rests on the assumption that the available evidence paints a true picture of how the collapse proceeded. However, it is difficult to know how accurately the archaeological record reflects historic activity, especially of a complex civilization such as the Mayans', and a hypothesis can be tested only against the best available data. It is quite possible that our understanding of the collapse might be radically altered by better data. For example, Lowe's assumption about monument construction and the occupation span of a site might well be disproved if further investigations of Classic Mayan sites established that some remained heavily settled long after the custom of carving dynastic monuments had ceased.

Which one of the following best expresses the main idea of the passage?

A. In The Dynamics of Apocalypse, John Lowe successfully proves that the collapse of Classic Mayan civilization was set in motion by increasing population and decreasing productivity.
B. In The Dynamics of Apocalypse, John Lowe breaks new ground in solving the mystery of the collapse of Classic Mayan civilization through his use of dated monuments to create a step-by-step account of the collapse.
C. In The Dynamics of Apocalypse, John Lowe successfully uses existing data to document the reduction and then cessation of new construction throughout Classic Mayan civilization.
D. Although John Lowe's study is based on a careful examination of the historical record, it does not accurately reflect the circumstances surrounding the collapse of Classic Mayan civilization.
E. While John Lowe's theory about the collapse of Classic Mayan civilization appears credible, it is based on an assumption that cannot be verified using the archaeological record.

Let's take a look at this passage:

In The Dynamics of Apocalypse, John Lowe attempts to solve the mystery of the collapse of the Classic Mayan civilization. Lowe bases his study on a detailed examination of the known archaeological record. Like previous investigators, Lowe relies on dated monuments to construct a step-by-step account of the actual collapse. Using the erection of new monuments as a means to determine a site's occupation span, Lowe assumes that once new monuments ceased to be built, a site had been abandoned. Lowe's analysis of the evidence suggests that construction of new monuments continued to increase between A.D. 672 and 751, but that the civilization stopped expanding geographically; new construction took place almost exclusively in established settlements. The first signs of trouble followed. Monument inscriptions indicate that between 751 and 790, long-standing alliances started to break down. Evidence also indicates that between 790 and 830, the death rate in Classic Mayan cities outstripped the birthrate. After approximately 830, construction stopped throughout the area, and within a hundred years, the Classic Mayan civilization all but vanished.

The first paragraph introduces JL's book, The Dynamics of Apocalypse. Lowe uses the date of monument construction as a timeline for the decline and collapse of Mayan civilization.

It will be helpful if we broke down the subsequent information. The details are arranged in chronological order, something we looked at in Chapter 4.

Prior to AD 672: Mayan civilization expanding geographically (We can infer this because the paragraph tells us that the Mayans stopped expanding between AD672 and AD751.)

672-751: New construction, but within existing settlements

751-790: Monuments tell us that alliances started to break down

790-830: Population decline

830 onwards: Construction stopped, eventual site abandonment? (we were told earlier that Lowe assumed that once new monuments ceased to be built, a site had been abandoned)

Prior to or in 930: Mayan civilization vanishes (within a hundred years of 830, so sometimes between 830 and 930 AD).

Having established this chronology, Lowe sets forth a plausible explanation of the collapse that accommodates the available archaeological evidence. He theorizes that Classic Mayan civilization was brought down by the interaction of several factors, set in motion by population growth. An increase in population, particularly within the elite segment of society, necessitated ever more intense farming. Agricultural intensification exerted stress on the soil and led to a decline in productivity (the amount of food produced through each unit of labor invested). At the same time, the growth of the elite class created increasing demands for ceremonial monuments and luxuries, diverting needed labor from the fields. The theory holds that these stresses were communicated— and amplified—throughout the area as Mayan states engaged in warfare to acquire laborers and food, and refugees fled impoverished areas. The most vulnerable states thus began to break down, and each downfall triggered others, until the entire civilization collapsed.

The author presents Lowe's hypothesis ("Lowe theorizes") in the second paragraph:

Increase in elite population ⇒ More intensive farming ⇒ Stress on soil ⇒ Decline in productivity

An additional effect of the increase in elite population is that:

Increase in elite population ⇒ More demand for monuments and luxuries ⇒ Less farmers

The result of decline in productivity (less food) and less labor is increased warfare to acquire food and labor, which led to civilizational collapse.

If there is a <u>central flaw</u> in Lowe's explanation, it is that the entire edifice rests on the assumption that the <u>available evidence paints a true picture</u> of how the collapse proceeded. However, it is difficult to know how <u>accurately the archaeological record reflects</u> historic activity, especially of a complex civilization such as the Mayans', and a hypothesis can be tested only against the best available data. It is quite possible that our understanding of the collapse <u>might be radically altered by better data</u>. For example, Lowe's assumption about monument construction and the occupation span of a site might well be disproved if further investigations of Classic Mayan sites established that some remained heavily settled long after the custom of carving dynastic monuments had ceased.

Does the author approve of or disapprove of Lowe's explanation? They point out a central flaw in Lowe's hypothesis. The author doesn't go to extremes and completely rejects Lowe's argument, only to point out a significant weakness in it.

So Lowe bases his understanding of the decline and collapse of the Mayan civilization on monuments. But our understanding of these monuments isn't complete. Maybe there are undiscovered monuments telling a different story, or maybe monuments were destroyed. Maybe even after the Mayans stopped building monuments, settlements still existed.

What is the purpose of this passage? I'd say it's two fold: to present a review of Lowe's new work, and to point out a central flaw in it.

With that in mind, we can come up with a potential main point for the passage:

While John Lowe presents a plausible (beginning of second paragraph) explanation of the Mayan collapse based on historical monuments in his book The Dynamics of Apocalypse, a central flaw in it is his over reliance on limited archaeological evidence.

***

Let's take a look at the answer choices:

A. *In The Dynamics of Apocalypse, John Lowe <u>successfully proves</u> that the collapse of Classic Mayan civilization was set in motion by increasing population and decreasing productivity.*

Based on the passage, Lowe doesn't "prove" anything. He presents a hypothesis, and the author even points out a central flaw with that hypothesis.

B. *In The Dynamics of Apocalypse, John Lowe breaks new ground in <u>solving the mystery</u> of the collapse of Classic Mayan civilization through his use of dated monuments to create a step-by-step account of the collapse.*

Same issue as Answer Choice A. To argue that Lowe had "solved the mystery" of Mayan collapse is too strong.

C. *In The Dynamics of Apocalypse, John Lowe <u>successfully</u> uses existing data to document the <u>reduction</u> and then <u>cessation</u> of new construction throughout Classic Mayan civilization.*

Does John Lowe do this? Sure, he makes note of the decrease and cessation of monuments being constructed. But he does this in order to present a chronology of the Mayan collapse.

He then comes up with an explanation for the collapse, which the author thinks contains a central flaw.

This answer choice really only covers what was discussed in the first paragraph.

D. *Although John Lowe's study is based on a careful examination of the historical record, it does not <u>accurately reflect the circumstances</u> surrounding the collapse of Classic Mayan civilization.*

Very tricky! What did the author think was the problem with John Lowe's book? The author thinks that it's overly depending on archaeological records which may or may not be accurate/complete. This is a very nuanced difference.

The author says, in the last paragraph, that Lowe's hypothesis may be overturned by new or better data. So in other words, maybe his study *does* accurately reflect on the collapse of the Mayan civilization *based on existing data,* but since existing data may be inaccurate or incomplete, his hypothesis does not rest on a solid foundation.

So the author isn't arguing that Lowe's conclusions are wrong, only that they are based on potentially weak evidence.

E. *While John Lowe's <u>theory</u> about the collapse of Classic Mayan civilization <u>appears</u> <u>credible</u>, it is based on an <u>assumption</u> that <u>cannot be verified</u> using the archaeological record.*

The first half of this answer is great. Words like "theory" and "appears credible" all closely mirror details found in the passage.

The second half is a little convoluted. Let's try to break it down.

What is John Lowe's assumption? We are told this way back in the first paragraph, and again in the last paragraph.

In the first paragraph, we are told that Lowe assumes that once monuments ceased to be built, sites are then abandoned. This concept is revisited in the last paragraph. The author tells us that if we ever found out that there were sites continuously inhabited, even after monuments ceased to be built, then Lowe's chronology of Mayan collapse would be overturned.

In other words, the author is suggesting that Lowe's whole argument rests upon data that may be incomplete. I wish the answer had been more direct and just said that, but Answer Choice E is still getting at that same idea, albeit super indirectly.

E is the best available answer choice.

***

Knowing exactly what the author's position is will help us on the harder MP questions. We saw that in PT7 S3 Q15, where the author's relatively neutral/balanced stance on genetically modified bacteria meant that the correct MP answer would take on a balanced tone as well.

It's the same situation here. The author's complaint about Lowe's book is that the data upon which it is based *may* be incomplete. Is Lowe wrong? Maybe, maybe not. But his hypothesis is based on data that *may* be inaccurate.

PT6 S1 Q21 (PT6 Passage 4)

Although the United States steel industry faces widely publicized economic problems that have eroded its steel production capacity, not all branches of the industry have been equally affected. The steel industry is not monolithic: it includes integrated producers, minimills, and specialty-steel mills. The integrated producers start with iron ore and coal and produce a wide assortment of shaped steels. The minimills reprocess scrap steel into a limited range of low-quality products, such as reinforcing rods for concrete. The specialty-steel mills are similar to minimills in that they tend to be smaller than the integrated producers and are based on scrap, but they manufacture much more expensive products than minimills do and commonly have an active in-house research-and-development effort.

Both minimills and specialty-steel mills have succeeded in avoiding the worst of the economic difficulties that are afflicting integrated steel producers, and some of the mills are quite profitable. Both take advantage of new technology for refining and casting steel, such as continuous casting, as soon as it becomes available. The minimills concentrate on producing a narrow range of products for sale in their immediate geographic area, whereas specialty-steel mills preserve flexibility in their operations in order to fulfill a customer's particular specifications.

Among the factors that constrain the competitiveness of integrated producers are excessive labor, energy, and capital costs, as well as manufacturing inflexibility. Their equipment is old and less automated, and does not incorporate many of the latest refinements in steelmaking technology. (For example, only about half of the United States integrated producers have continuous casters, which combine pouring and rolling into one operation and thus save the cost of separate rolling equipment.) One might conclude that the older, labor-intensive machinery still operating in United States integrated plants is at fault for the poor performance of the United States industry, but this cannot explain why Japanese integrated producers, who produce a higher-quality product using less energy and labor, are also experiencing economic trouble. The fact is that the common technological denominator of integrated producers is an inherently inefficient process that is still rooted in the nineteenth century.

Integrated producers have been unable to compete successfully with minimills because the minimills, like specialty-steel mills, have dispensed almost entirely with the archaic energy- and capital-intensive front end of integrated steelmaking: the iron-smelting process, including the mining and preparation of the raw materials and the blast-furnace operation. In addition, minimills have found a profitable way to market steel products: as indicated above, they sell their finished products locally, thereby reducing transportation costs, and concentrate on a limited range of shapes and sizes within a narrow group of products that can be manufactured economically. For these reasons, minimills have been able to avoid the economic decline affecting integrated steel producers.

Which one of the following best expresses the main idea of the passage?

A. United States steel producers face economic problems that are shared by producers in other nations.
B. Minimills are the most successful steel producers because they best meet market demands for cheap steel.
C. Minimills and specialty-steel mills are more economically competitive than integrated producers because they use new technology and avoid the costs of the iron-smelting process.
D. United States steel producers are experiencing an economic decline that can be traced back to the nineteenth century.
E. New steelmaking technologies such as continuous casting will replace blast-furnace operations to reverse the decline in United States steel production.

Although the United States steel industry faces widely publicized economic problems that have eroded its steel production capacity, not all branches of the industry have been equally affected. The steel industry is not monolithic: it includes <u>integrated producers</u>, <u>minimills</u>, and <u>specialty-steel mills</u>. The <u>integrated</u> <u>producers</u> start with iron ore and coal and produce a wide assortment of shaped steels. The <u>minimills</u> reprocess scrap steel into a limited range of low-quality products, such as reinforcing rods for concrete. The <u>specialty-steel</u> mills are similar to minimills in that they tend to be smaller than the integrated producers and are based on scrap, but they manufacture much more expensive products than minimills do and commonly have an active in-house research-and-development effort.

Three types of steel mills are introduced:

Integrated Producers (IP): uses iron ore and coal to produce a wide assortment of shaped steels

Minimills (MM): reprocess scrap steel into low quality products

Specialty Steel Mills (SM): similar to MM, but higher tier and do in house research

Both <u>minimills</u> and <u>specialty-steel mills</u> have succeeded in <u>avoiding</u> the worst of the economic difficulties that are afflicting integrated steel producers, and some of the mills are quite profitable. Both take advantage of <u>new technology</u> for refining and casting steel, such as continuous casting, as soon as it becomes available. The minimills concentrate on producing a narrow range of products for sale in their <u>immediate geographic area</u>, whereas specialty-steel mills preserve flexibility in their operations in order to fulfill a <u>customer's particular specifications</u>.

MM and SM make money, IP don't. For several reasons:

1. MM and SM take advantage of new technology.
2. MM focuses on a narrow range of products and serve local customers.
3. SM are flexible and fulfill special demands.

Among the factors that constrain the competitiveness of <u>integrated producers</u> are excessive <u>labor, energy, and capital costs, as well as manufacturing inflexibility</u>. Their <u>equipment</u> is old and less automated, and does not incorporate many of the latest refinements in steelmaking technology. (For example, only about half of the United States integrated producers have continuous casters, which combine pouring and rolling into one operation and thus save the cost of separate rolling equipment.) One might conclude that the older, labor-intensive machinery still operating in United States integrated plants is at fault for the poor performance of the United States industry, but this cannot explain why Japanese integrated producers, who produce a higher-quality product using less energy and labor, are also experiencing economic trouble. The fact is that the common technological denominator of integrated producers is an <u>inherently</u> <u>inefficient process</u> that is still rooted in the nineteenth century.

IP are disadvantaged by excessive costs and manufacturing inflexibility. Their equipment is old and outdated.

But old and outdated equipment is not the reason why they are losing money. Because Japanese IPs, which have higher quality products and less energy and labor, are also losing money.

The real reason is the outdated manufacturing process.

Integrated producers have been unable to compete successfully with minimills because the minimills, like specialty-steel mills, have dispensed almost entirely with the archaic energy- and capital-intensive front end of integrated steelmaking: <u>the iron-smelting process</u>, including the <u>mining</u> and <u>preparation</u> of the raw materials and the <u>blast-furnace operation</u>. In addition, minimills have found a profitable way to market steel products: as indicated above, they sell their finished products <u>locally</u>, thereby reducing transportation costs, and concentrate on a <u>limited range</u> of shapes and sizes within a narrow group of products that can be manufactured economically. For these reasons, minimills have been able to avoid the economic decline affecting integrated steel producers.

It's mining and preparation of iron ore and blast-furnace operations that's making IPs uncompetitive.

MM also sell locally, reduce transportation costs, and have more limited offerings.

A fairly straightforward passage with a lot of details. The purpose of the passage isn't hard to discern. It's to compare three types of mills and explain why MM and SM are able to make money while IP can't.

The Main Point of the passage might look something like this:

Minimills and Specialty Mills, due to their ability to take advantage of new technology, niche market specialization, and avoidance of the iron-smelting process, have been able to remain profitable while integrated producers, stymied by an inefficient and outdated labor process and excessive costs, have become uncompetitive.

***

Let's look at the answer choices:

    A.   *United States steel producers face economic problems that are shared by producers in other nations.*

There is literally one sentence that talks about this. We are told that US integrated producers and Japanese integrated producers both face problems. We are told this because the author wants to suggest that costs are not the real reason why IPs have not been competitive. Do not be led astray by answer choices that describe something that does happen in the passage but are not the Main Point.

    B.   *Minimills are the <u>most</u> successful steel producers because they best meet market demands for cheap steel.*

Not quite accurate. Minimills and Special Mills are more successful than Integrated Producers, and for a multitude of reasons.

    C.   *Minimills and specialty-steel mills are more economically competitive than integrated producers because they use new technology and avoid the costs of the iron-smelting process.*

This answer starts off looking great. But only two out of four reasons why MM and SM are competitive are mentioned. If you recall from the passage, the other two reasons are MM's focus on a smaller geographical area and narrower range of products; and SM's ability to cater to customers' special needs.

This is a classic example of a correct answer that doesn't cover all the bases. We know that the Main Point of the passage will tell us MM and SM are more competitive than IP, and for what reasons. Even though a few of the reasons listed in the passage were not mentioned here, it is still an acceptable answer if there isn't an alternative that's both accurate and more complete.

    D.   *United States steel producers are experiencing an <u>economic decline that can be traced back</u> to the nineteenth century.*

This passage is not talking about the historic origins of American steel producer decline.

    E.   *New steelmaking technologies such as continuous casting will <u>replace</u> blast-furnace operations to <u>reverse</u> the decline in United States steel production.*

We are concerned with MM/SM's competitive advantages over IP; not that new technology will save US steel production.

C is the best answer.

PT8 S3 Q7 (PT8 Passage 2)

Gray marketing, the selling of trademarked products through channels of distribution not authorized by the trademark holder, can involve distribution of goods either within a market region or across market boundaries. Gray marketing within a market region ("channel flow diversion") occurs when manufacturer-authorized distributors sell trademarked goods to unauthorized distributors who then sell the goods to consumers within the same region. For example, quantity discounts from manufacturers may motivate authorized dealers to enter the gray market because they can purchase larger quantities of a product than they themselves intend to stock if they can sell the extra units through gray market channels.

When gray marketing occurs across market boundaries, it is typically in an international setting and may be called "parallel importing." Manufacturers often produce and sell products in more than one country and establish a network of authorized dealers in each country. Parallel importing occurs when trademarked goods intended for one country are diverted from proper channels (channel flow diversion) and then exported to unauthorized distributors in another country.

Trademark owners justifiably argue against gray marketing practices since such practices clearly jeopardize the goodwill established by trademark owners: consumers who purchase trademarked goods in the gray market do not get the same "extended product," which typically includes pre and post sale service. Equally important, authorized distributors may cease to promote the product if it becomes available for much lower prices through unauthorized channels.

Current debate over regulation of gray marketing focuses on three disparate theories in trademark law that have been variously and confusingly applied to parallel importation cases: universality, exhaustion, and territoriality. The theory of universality holds that a trademark is only an indication of the source or origin of the product. This theory does not recognize the goodwill functions of a trademark. When the courts apply this theory, gray marketing practices are allowed to continue because the origin of the product remains the same regardless of the specific route of the product through the channel of distribution. The exhaustion theory holds that a trademark owner relinquishes all rights once a product has been sold. When this theory is applied, gray marketing practices are allowed to continue because the trademark owners' rights cease as soon as their products are sold to a distributor. The theory of territoriality holds that a trademark is effective in the country in which it is registered. Under the theory of territoriality, trademark owners can stop gray marketing practices in the registering countries on products bearing their trademarks. Since only the territoriality theory affords trademark owners any real legal protection against gray marketing practices, I believe it is inevitable as well as desirable that it will come to be consistently applied in gray marketing cases.

Which one of the following best expresses the main point of the passage?

A. Gray marketing is unfair to trademark owners and should be legally controlled.
B. Gray marketing is practiced in many different forms and places, and legislators should recognize the futility of trying to regulate it.
C. The mechanisms used to control gray marketing across markets are different from those most effective in controlling gray marketing within markets.
D. The three trademark law theories that have been applied in gray marketing cases lead to different case outcomes.
E. Current theories used to interpret trademark laws have resulted in increased gray marketing activity.

Gray marketing, the selling of trademarked products through channels of distribution not authorized by the trademark holder, can involve distribution of goods either <u>within a market region</u> or <u>across market boundaries</u>. Gray marketing within a market region ("channel flow diversion") occurs when manufacturer-authorized distributors sell trademarked goods to unauthorized distributors who then sell the goods to consumers within the same region. For example, quantity discounts from manufacturers may motivate authorized dealers to enter the gray market because they can purchase larger quantities of a product than they themselves intend to stock if they can sell the extra units through gray market channels.

Within a market region: authorized distributors sell to unauthorized distributors who then sell to consumers

When gray marketing occurs <u>across market boundaries</u>, it is typically in an international setting and may be called "<u>parallel importing</u>." Manufacturers often produce and sell products in more than one country and establish a network of authorized dealers in each country. Parallel importing occurs when trademarked goods intended for one country are diverted from proper channels (channel flow diversion) and then <u>exported to unauthorized distributors in another country</u>.

Across boundaries/parallel importing: trademarked goods destined for one country are diverted to be sold in another country.

Trademark owners <u>justifiably</u> argue against gray marketing practices since such practices clearly <u>jeopardize the goodwill</u> established by trademark owners: consumers who purchase trademarked goods in the gray market <u>do not get</u> the same "extended product," which typically includes pre and post sale <u>service</u>. Equally important, <u>authorized distributors may cease to promote the product</u> if it becomes available for much lower prices through unauthorized channels.

Trademark owners do not like such sales, for two reasons. One, consumers who buy unauthorized products do not get the same warranty or service. Two, if unauthorized sellers are undercutting authorized distributors, the authorized distributors may cease to promote a product.

Notice how the author thinks the trademark owners' position is "justified." We now know where the author stands.

Current debate over regulation of gray marketing focuses on three disparate <u>theories</u> in trademark law that have been <u>variously and confusingly applied to parallel importation cases</u>: universality, exhaustion, and territoriality. The theory of <u>universality</u> holds that a trademark is only an indication of the source or origin of the product. This theory does not recognize the goodwill functions of a trademark. When the courts apply this theory, gray marketing practices are <u>allowed to continue</u> because the origin of the product remains the same regardless of the specific route of the product through the channel of distribution. The <u>exhaustion</u> theory holds that a trademark owner <u>relinquishes all rights</u> once a product has been sold. When this theory is applied, gray marketing practices are allowed to continue because the trademark owners' <u>rights cease as soon as their products are sold</u> to a distributor. The theory of <u>territoriality</u> holds that a trademark is effective in the country in which it is registered. Under the theory of territoriality, trademark <u>owners can stop gray marketing practices</u> in the registering countries on products bearing their trademarks. Since only the territoriality theory affords trademark owners <u>any real legal protection</u> against gray marketing practices, <u>I believe</u> it is <u>inevitable</u> as well as <u>desirable</u> that it will come to <u>be consistently applied</u> in gray marketing cases.

In the last paragraph, the author introduces three legal theories that have been "variously and confusingly applied." Clearly, the author is dissatisfied with how the laws have been applied. We also know that earlier, the author called protection of owners' rights "justifiable." So we can infer that the author is frustrated at the lacklustre protection of owners' rights.

The three theories are:

Universality: Grey marketing is okay because these products are authentic products that came from the same place as the authorized products.

Exhaustion: When the goods are sold to a distributor, the owners relinquish their rights, so the distributors can subsequently resell to anyone else.

Territoriality: Owners retain their rights in countries where the trademarks are registered. So they have the right and legal means to stop grey marketing practices.

The author's view is quite evident in the last sentence. They believe that it is desirable as well as inevitable that Territoriality be applied, granting trademark owners more protection under the law.

***

What is the Author's Purpose in this passage, or why did they chose to write this?

I think there's two parts to this answer, the author *explains* what grey marketing is; and then *recommends* the legal theory that would bring maximum protection to trademark owners. So the Purpose of the passage would be *to explain a practice and to recommend an applicable legal theory to govern such a practice.*

As for the Main Point, it should look something like this:

Grey marketing involves the unauthorized sale of goods in the same market and abroad, the theory of territoriality provides the most legal protection to trademark owners, and should be more consistently applied.

***

Let's take a look at the answer choices:

A. *Gray marketing is unfair to trademark owners and should be legally controlled.*

This is definitely what the author is arguing for. But it's so general! It does not mention 90% of the things the passage talks about. It doesn't mention what gray marketing is; it doesn't mention parallel importing vs. unauthorized distribution locally; it doesn't mention the three legal theories…I both like and hate this answer simultaneously. Let's keep it and move on.

B. *Gray marketing is practiced in many different forms and places, and legislators should <u>recognize</u> the <u>futility</u> of trying to regulate it.*

This is the opposite of what the author is advocating. The author thinks it desirable as well as inevitable that gray marketing will be regulated.

C. *The mechanisms <u>used to control</u> gray marketing <u>across</u> markets are different from those most effective in controlling gray marketing <u>within</u> markets.*

We are told the difference between domestic and international gray marketing. But we don't really compare the mechanisms (rules, regulations, sanctions, etc.) used in both.

D. *The three trademark law theories that have been applied in gray marketing cases lead to different case outcomes.*

Yes, this is true. It's the message of the majority of the last paragraph. But the author's voice is non-existent in this answer. We need the answer to tell us that gray marketing should be regulated.

E. *Current theories used to interpret trademark laws have resulted in <u>increased</u> gray marketing activity.*

Nope, the passage tells us that two out of three legal theories don't do anything to prevent gray marketing activity; but to say that they result in increased gray marketing activity would be a stretch.

Furthermore, the answer choice is talking about "current theories," and doesn't specify which ones.

It looks like Answer Choice A is the best answer. I was wary of it initially, given how broad it was. I knew that the correct answer doesn't have to cover all the sub points in the paragraph; but this one barely covers *any of them*.

Nonetheless, it's the only answer that expresses what the author's opinion is. **Remember, if the author expresses their opinion in the passage, that opinion will appear in the correct answer choice.**

Summary

Every passage will have a Main Point Question, so it's crucial that we don't lose points on these. The majority of intermediate/advanced students will have a basic idea on how to approach these questions, so I will focus on the trickier aspects of Main Point Questions.

First, in passages where the author has expressed their personal opinions, this will be included in the correct answer choice. If the author was simply explaining a complex issue or scientific theory without expressing what they personally think about it, then it doesn't really matter. But if we can detect the author's voice, tone, attitude, stance, or opinion on what's being described in the passage, then the author's position **must** appear in the correct answer.

This is why when we are reading a passage, we start out by trying to decipher the Author's Purpose. We try to read the first sentences/paragraph of the passage with extra care and attention, in order to situate ourselves within the scope of the discussion, and to attempt to come up with a hypothesis of why the author is writing this passage.

We then use subsequent information to confirm or modify our hypothesis. Finally, once we have a clear idea of the Author's Purpose, we can use that to derive the Main Point of the passage.

I use the CEER framework as a crutch if I am at a loss or am having trouble with either of these questions.

The Main Point of a passage may need to be **inferred** sometimes. In easier passages it may be given to us either in the first or the last paragraph; but in more challenging passages, we may have to ask ourselves what are the key points the author makes in the passage, and what do they support, collectively.

Beware of answer choices that state one or multiple key points that appear in a passage. Again, the Main Point of a passage is its *central thesis*, we are not looking for a *partial description* of what happens in the passage, or even a *comprehensive description* of what happens in the passage. Be especially careful with **laundry list** type answers.

Continuing along that line of reasoning, the correct answer choice doesn't even have to cover all the points made in the passage. As we have seen in the practice earlier, the correct answer can appear **incomplete** at times, but as long as they express the author's opinion and no other answer choice does, it can be acceptable.

9. According to the Passage

9. According to the Passage

Textual Analysis and MBT Questions

We have mentioned back in the first part of the book that skills acquired when practicing Logical Reasoning questions can be invaluable when carried over into the Reading Comprehension section. We saw how Role Questions (which explores the relationship between different elements of an LR stimulus and the author's argument/conclusion) can serve as an inspiration for paragraph and passage structure analysis (Chapter 2 and 3), and even help us with certain types of Purpose Questions (Chapter 7).

We have already covered two of the "big four" question types. We have looked at **Purpose** and **Main Point** Questions, and the remaining two are **According to the Passage** Questions and **Inference** Questions.

The relationship between According to the Passage Questions and Inference Questions closely mirrors another pair of related question types in LR. Must be True Questions (MBT) and Most Strongly Supported Questions (MSS) share a relationship that is in many ways similar to the relationship between According to the Passage Questions and Inference Questions. We will look at how we can use MBT Questions as a source of inspiration for According to the Passage Questions in RC in this chapter; and how MSS Questions can help us think about Inference Questions in the next chapter.

If you recall from Chapter 17 of LR Perfection, MBT Questions must have textual proof. They must be certain, or 100% provable via the stimulus. In other words, for MBT Question Answers, we need to find the exact words that prove the answer choice, we must do this before we are justified in selecting it.

According to the Passage Questions are the same. 99% of the time, the correct answer choice will have proof/evidence from the passage itself.

I say 99% of the time because as questions and answer choices become vaguer, we learn to always watch out for exceptions to rules. Nothing is set in stone. But after going through all the RC Passages and their associated questions multiple times between PT 1 and PT 90, I can safely say that there were maybe 5-6 According to the Passage Questions where the support from the passage was non-explicit.

So for all intents and purposes, when you see an According to the Passage Question:

> Look for explicit support from the passage. This support **must be explicit**, meaning that you need to be able to underline or highlight it. We want evidence that is direct and textual, saying exactly what the answer choice is saying; rather than hinting at its possibility.

A great way to train ourselves if According to the Passage Questions are a particular weakness is to raise our standards when it comes to the answer choices. During drilling, don't worry too much about time. When you come to the answer choices, **don't pick an answer choice unless you have already highlighted or underlined the specific lines from the passage backing it up.** Try to do this for each of the answer choices, go back to the passage and try to search for the relevant material. Pick the answer choice with the most direct and explicit evidence that you have found in the passage.

Common Difficulties Associated with According to the Passage Questions

Because how we approach According to the Passage Questions is relatively straightforward, the biggest limiting factor here is usually how well we have understood the passage and grasped its details. As we saw in Chapter 4, once we have a strong understanding of the passage's overall structure, we must also pay special attention to certain types of details that appear in RC passages. An important reason why we keep an eye out for details is to prepare for According to the Passage Questions.

When looking at the answer choices, being able to remember if something had been mentioned in the passage will be immensely helpful. It will automatically help us see that answer choice as a contender, and all that's left to do is to find the exact location where it was discussed. On the other hand, if we see an answer choice but have no idea whether it had been mentioned in the passage, we are left with no choice but to go back to the passage itself, re-read it and try to look for any evidence or reference. This process is not only tedious and time-consuming, but will seriously damage our morale and lead to unnecessary stress.

Ideally, when we see an answer choice, we want to be able to remember if this concept/idea has been discussed in the passage, and if so, roughly in which paragraph did it appear. If we can do this, all that's left to do is to go to that general area of the passage, and try to locate such evidence, and evaluate it to see if it is actually direct evidence for the answer choice in question. Nice and straightforward, right?

But if our reading ability is a little weaker, then we may still recall that an answer choice was discussed in the passage, somewhere, but we don't know exactly where. This is more problematic, as we now have to go back to the passage to look for proof for each answer choice, sometimes parsing the passage five times, once for each answer choice. This will eat up significant amounts of time.

The worst case scenario; however, is when we see an answer choice, but have no idea whether it was mentioned in the passage. When this happens, we have to go back to the passage and look again. But even if we don't find such evidence, we can't be certain whether that's because such evidence doesn't exist in the passage; or because we were looking in the wrong place. Such an occurrence will throw even the most advanced test takers off balance and can negatively impact our performance on subsequent questions.

We saw back in Chapter 6 that an often ignored element in RC performance is our organic reading ability. Instructors, books, and test-prep agencies will downplay the importance of reading ability and try to focus on the actual techniques and test taking strategies to improve your RC score. But nowhere is the importance of reading ability more clearly demonstrated than when we are faced with According to the Passage Questions.

In order to navigate these questions quickly and accurately, we need to have an intimate grasp of the various details scattered within the passage. Because we can't really anticipate what the correct answer will look like in these types of questions, we are basically working with what we remember from the passage as we first look at the answer choices. To do that we would need to pay special attention to the details during our initial read of the passage. In order to devote more attention to the details in our reading, we need to have a good overall grasp of the passage and its structure. Since time is limited, all that really matters is how much of the passage you understood and how much you have remembered within that ~3 minute reading session.

Again, from our diagnostic in Chapter 6, if reading ability is something holding you back, jump straight to the end of the book and see how forcing yourself to read dense material on topics related to RC passages can drastically improve one's reading ability in a short time. I've trained many ESL students with such drills to great effect; so it will work with you too.

We will now look at a few more problems that are typically associated with According to the Passage Questions:

Hard to Find Details

Sometimes even when our reading ability is strong, certain details will still elude us. Fear not, this will happen to the best of us. We will devote significant attention and practice to this in an upcoming chapter on the tricky properties of harder questions. But for now, just be sure to check the very beginning of the passage, the very end of the passage, and take a closer look at the long, theoretical paragraphs if we just can't find the evidence needed to back up or eliminate an answer choice.

You see, the test makers are sharply aware of the shortcomings and pitfalls in our reading habits. When we begin to read a passage, we are still trying to figure out what is going on and what is the scope of the discussion. As a result, details hidden in the first few lines of the passage can easily be overlooked. Similarly, information that come at the very end of the passage are also frequently ignored by students. Being pressed for time, the typical student will usually already be thinking about the questions by the time they get to the last paragraph, skimming it as fast as they can, and moving to the questions. Lastly, when it comes to long paragraphs of an abstract or theoretical nature, many of us will skim or avoid them altogether, especially if we are pressed for time.

Synthesis of Information

Back in MBT Questions, we saw that an answer choice that synthesized two individual pieces of information from the stimulus can also be a valid answer. This is like combining two conditional rules to derive a third rule in the Logic Games section.

To use an oversimplified example, if we are told that *"John is the tallest student in the class,"* and that *"Peter is new to the class, he is taller than John,"* then we know that now, Peter is the tallest student in the class. Even though this was never explicitly mentioned, we know it to be true.

In According to the Passage Questions, synthesis answer choices are equally valid. Although we may never find direct and explicit evidence to back up such an answer choice, we need to go the additional step and realize that this answer choice can be derived by combining two pieces of information which are separately stated in the passage.

According to the Passage Questions with synthesized answer choices are brutally difficult, but luckily, they are a rare occurrence. Again, how in depth our understanding of the passage is will directly affect our ability to take on these questions. Another reason why they are difficult is because students almost never expect the correct answer to be synthesized. They are too used to a linear approach where we look at the answer choice, attempt to match it up with a statement from the passage, and then either eliminate or select it.

Pre-existing Knowledge and Bias

An interesting phenomenon that I've witnessed both during my own practice and among my former students is that sometimes we will end up underperforming on the passages with which we are supposed to be the most familiar with. Generally speaking, we will have an easier time with passages in topics close to our real-life experiences. Students who have studied the arts or music will have an easier time with art themed passages. Political science students will have an easier time with passages musing on government or international relations. Science majors will navigate science-based passages with ease, and students with a previous legal education (LLB or LLM) or who have worked in a legal environment will be more confident in legal themed passages.

But when it comes to According to the Passage Questions, pre-existing knowledge and biases can be a double-edged sword. On the one hand, our knowledge should make reading the passage easier and help fill in gaps in the writing itself; but on the other hand, when it comes to questions that must be backed by evidence from the passage, a tricky trap answer that relies more on common sense or industry knowledge may lead us astray.

Remember, the correct answer will only need to be correct, *according to the passage.* How things work in real life has no bearing on which answer choice we select. If the passage tells us that the earth is flat, then that will be the correct answer.

Practice Questions

Keep these traps in mind as we look at a few According to the Passage Questions and their corresponding passages:

PT22 S1 Q24 (PT22 Passage 4)

What it means to "explain" something in science often comes down to the application of mathematics. Some thinkers hold that mathematics is a kind of language—a systematic contrivance of signs, the criteria for the authority of which are internal coherence, elegance, and depth. The application of such a highly artificial system to the physical world, they claim, results in the creation of a kind of statement about the world. Accordingly, what matters in the sciences is finding a mathematical concept that attempts, as other language does, to accurately describe the functioning of some aspect of the world.

At the center of the issue of scientific knowledge can thus be found questions about the relationship between language and what it refers to. A discussion about the role played by language in the pursuit of knowledge has been going on among linguists for several decades. The debate centers around whether language corresponds in some essential way to objects and behaviors, making knowledge a solid and reliable commodity; or, on the other hand, whether the relationship between language and things is purely a matter of agreed-upon conventions, making knowledge tenuous, relative, and inexact.

Lately the latter theory has been gaining wider acceptance. According to linguists who support this theory, the way language is used varies depending upon changes in accepted practices and theories among those who work in a particular discipline. These linguists argue that, in the pursuit of knowledge, a statement is true only when there are no promising alternatives that might lead one to question it. Certainly this characterization would seem to be applicable to the sciences. In science, a mathematical statement may be taken to account for every aspect of a phenomenon it is applied to, but, some would argue, there is nothing inherent in mathematical language that guarantees such a correspondence. Under this view, acceptance of a mathematical statement by the scientific community— by virtue of the statement's predictive power or methodological efficiency—transforms what is basically an analogy or metaphor into an explanation of the physical process in question, to be held as true until another, more compelling analogy takes its place.

In pursuing the implications of this theory, linguists have reached the point at which they must ask: If words or sentences do not correspond in an essential way to life or to our ideas about life, then just what are they capable of telling us about the world? In science and mathematics, then, it would seem equally necessary to ask: If models of electrolytes or $E = mc2$, say, do not correspond essentially to the physical world, then just what functions do they perform in the acquisition of scientific knowledge? But this question has yet to be significantly addressed in the sciences.

According to the passage, mathematics can be considered a language because it

    A. conveys meaning in the same way that metaphors do
    B. constitutes a systematic collection of signs
    C. corresponds exactly to aspects of physical phenomena
    D. confers explanatory power on scientific theories
    E. relies on previously agreed-upon conventions

Typically, in According to the Passage Questions, the question stem will provide some hint as to where to look for the corresponding evidence to solve this question. Here, the question is asking us *why is mathematics considered a language.* Who was it that believed mathematics was considered a language? Was it either groups of the linguists in debate? Was it the author? Or was it someone else?

The details that we need to figure out the answer are tucked away discretely at the very beginning of the passage. Some thinkers consider mathematics a "*kind of language*" because it is a "*systematic contrivance of signs, the criteria for the authority of which are internal coherence, elegance, and depth.*"

I don't really know what this means. But we can try to simplify it without losing too much of its internal meaning. Let's just say "system" instead of "systematic contrivance." So math is a kind of language because it's a system of signs.

But how does the phrase "*the criteria for the authority of which are internal coherence, elegance, and depth*" link up with the concept that math is a language because it's a system of signs?

There are criteria for the authoritativeness of signs/language. So I think what is being suggested here is that math is system of signs, signs which are authoritative because of math's internal coherence, elegance, and depth. This makes math a language.

As you can see, I've tried to stay close to the original meaning and wording of the statement as much as I can. So even if there are a subtle loss of meaning in my translation, I am confident that it is not much.

So now I can anticipate that based on the textual evidence from the first paragraph, the correct answer will say that math is considered a language because it's a "system of signs, authoritative due to its internal coherence, elegance, and depth." This was the reason given in the passage precisely to answer this question.

Let's look at the answer choices:

    A.   *conveys meaning in the same way that metaphors do*

The author does talk about metaphors in the third paragraph. In that paragraph we are concerned with the second theory about what does language actually refer to.

Remember that one theory thinks language to refer to precise things; and the other theory thinks language to be a convention.

If language is a convention then it is not inherently true. It is more like an analogy or metaphor that is used to explain something until a better analogy or metaphor is found.

So really, what the author was trying to express is that mathematical language is like a metaphor because it's a temporary explanation of a physical process; and not that math is a language because it's like a metaphor.

It would have been very easy to pick this answer because the keywords found in the question (mathematics, language) also appear in the sentences where the word "metaphor" appears. If we had not known that there was a statement which provides an exact answer to the question, then we might have compromised and gone with A.

    B.   *constitutes a systematic collection of signs*

This is what we have found and predicted from the first paragraph. It doesn't really talk about the extra stuff that we found, the stuff about elegance and coherence. But I do like this answer choice, even though it's very short.

    C.   *corresponds exactly to aspects of physical phenomena*

This is also from the third paragraph. The author says that math may correspond to aspects of physical phenomena, but such correspondence is not guaranteed. In other words, math, like other languages, do not refer to exact and precise concepts. But this is not explaining why math is a language.

D.   confers explanatory power on scientific theories

This was never mentioned in the passage.

E.   relies on previously agreed-upon conventions

This is the position of the second group of linguists who believe this to be true about language. If math is a language, then it would also rely on such conventions. But the linguists never suggest that because math relies on such conventions, it is therefore a language.

B is the best answer, it's the most direct re-phrase of the evidence in the passage that provides the answer to this question.

Many students found this question extremely tricky. First, both the correct answer choice and a few of the trap answers were all located in **hard-to-find locations**. The correct answer was in the second sentence of the passage, something most students probably wouldn't remember as they are still trying to figure out what the passage was talking about, much less pay attention to the details. Similarly, a few of the trap answers were all situated in the third paragraph, the longest and most abstract paragraph of the passage.

If you didn't know where to look for the corresponding evidence for the correct answer choice, this question was as difficult as they came. But luckily, on the computer-based version of the test, we can search for keywords in the passage with the **search function**. I would start with words like "mathematics" and "language" and just quickly look over where in the passage were these two words mentioned in proximity. That should help us locate the detail at the very beginning of the passage if you didn't spot it in the first place.

We also saw how important it was to think about what the question is really asking for. Only when we know precisely what the question is asking, can we go about looking for and narrowing down potential evidence scattered throughout the passage. **Question stem analysis** is an extremely helpful, yet underrated skill. As we shall see in Chapter 14, it's a crucial skill in the repertoire of advanced test takers.

As you can see, if you couldn't find the evidence for the correct answer choice, there was pretty much no way that you could have gotten this question right, regardless of how well you understood the rest of the passage. According to the Passage Questions are among the few question types where you either know the answer or you don't. No matter how good you are at inferring, extrapolating ideas; no matter how much of the passage or Main Point you have grasped; the correct answer may lie in one single detail that you have conveniently missed. If that's the case, nothing else can help you.

This just to show how important it is to improve our innate reading ability. Only when you have become more confident in your reading skills and are able to retain more information, can you begin to pay more attention to the details in a passage, details that will prove crucial to According to the Passage questions.

PT22 S1 Q10 (PT22 Passage 2)

In recent years, a growing belief that the way society decides what to treat as true is controlled through largely unrecognized discursive practices has led legal reformers to examine the complex interconnections between narrative and law. In many legal systems, legal judgments are based on competing stories about events. Without having witnessed these events, judges and juries must validate some stories as true and reject others as false. This procedure is rooted in objectivism, a philosophical approach that has supported most <u>Western legal and intellectual systems</u> for centuries. Objectivism holds that there is a single neutral description of each event that is un-skewed by any particular point of view and that has a privileged position over all other accounts. The law's quest for truth, therefore, consists of locating this objective description, the one that tells what really happened, as opposed to what those involved thought happened. The serious flaw in objectivism is that there is no such thing as the neutral, objective observer. As psychologists have demonstrated, all observers bring to a situation a set of expectations, values, and beliefs that determine what the observers are able to see and hear. Two individuals listening to the same story will hear different things, because they emphasize those aspects that accord with their learned experiences and ignore those aspects that are dissonant with their view of the world. Hence there is never any escape in life or in law from selective perception, or from subjective judgments based on prior experiences, values, and beliefs.

The societal harm caused by the assumption of objectivist principles in traditional legal discourse is that, historically, the stories judged to be objectively true are those told by people who are trained in legal discourse, while the stories of those who are not fluent in the language of the law are rejected as false.

Legal scholars such as Patricia Williams, Derrick Bell, and Mari Matsuda have sought empowerment for the latter group of people through the construction of alternative legal narratives. Objectivist legal discourse systematically disallows the language of emotion and experience by focusing on cognition in its narrowest sense. These legal reformers propose replacing such abstract discourse with powerful personal stories. They argue that the absorbing, nonthreatening structure and tone of personal stories may convince legal insiders for the first time to listen to those not fluent in legal language. The compelling force of personal narrative can create a sense of empathy between legal insiders and people traditionally excluded from legal discourse and, hence, from power. Such alternative narratives can shatter the complacency of the legal establishment and disturb its tranquility. Thus, the engaging power of narrative might play a crucial, positive role in the process of legal reconstruction by overcoming differences in background and training and forming a new collectivity based on emotional empathy.

According to the passage, which one of the following is true about the intellectual systems? (Line 6)

    A.   They have long assumed the possibility of a neutral depiction of events.
    B.   They have generally remained un-skewed by particular points of view.
    C.   Their discursive practices have yet to be analyzed by legal scholars.
    D.   They accord a privileged position to the language of emotion and experience.
    E.   The accuracy of their basic tenets has been confirmed by psychologists.

Sometimes we get lucky and the question stem will tell us where the issue being discussed is located in the passage. Here, to make your job easier, I've opted to underline the location where the phrase appears in the passage.

The question is asking us "*which of the following is true*" about the intellectual systems. So we know that we are looking for a trait or characteristics about intellectual systems that will be mentioned in the passage. We will start by looking in the middle of the first paragraph where the words "intellectual systems" appear.

Now BE CAREFUL! Just because the question told you where to look doesn't mean that the correct answer will come from there. All the question has told you is that it's asking you something about "intellectual systems," which are discussed in line 6. But maybe "intellectual systems" are discussed again in line 26 or 46. The correct answer will be a feature or trait of these intellectual systems, and **they can come from anywhere in the passage.**

Another tip: I **always read the surrounding areas** of where I located the issue being discussed. For example, in this question, "intellectual systems" are discussed in line 6, but I will also check out lines 5 and lines 7 just to get a more complete idea of what is really being discussed.

With that in mind, let's take a look at the question:

The question asks us what is true of the intellectual systems mentioned in line 6. What do we know from line 6?

> This procedure is rooted in objectivism, a philosophical approach that has supported most <u>Western legal and intellectual systems</u> for centuries.

We know that most Western legal and intellectual systems have been backed by objectivism for centuries. So now the question remains, what is objectivism? Let's read on:

> Objectivism holds that there is a single neutral description of each event that is un-skewed by any particular point of view and that has a privileged position over all other accounts.

Objectivism holds that there is a single, neutral, authoritative, truthful version of events.

Does the passage mention any additional details about Western legal and intellectual systems later on in the passage?

I don't think so. I did a quick glance through the passage but didn't find any mention of these "systems." But we have enough information to work with. Let's try to pre-phrase an answer.

So the most obvious and direct correct answer can just be a repetition of what line 6 talked about. The correct answer can say that these intellectual systems "*were rooted in objectivism for centuries.*"

But that would be a little too obvious. We can also come up with a **synthesized** answer that combines both this and what we know about objectivism from the subsequent lines, we can say that these intellectual systems were "*rooted in a worldview that held that there is a single, neutral description of each event.*"

We might be able to go even a step further. We know that the passage/author believes objectivism to be flawed, so the correct answer choice might even say that intellectual systems were "*rooted in a flawed world view that held...*"

> A.   *They have long assumed the possibility of a neutral depiction of events.*

The wording of this answer choice is super indirect, but bear with me. We know that these intellectual systems have been supported by objectivism. In other words, objectivism is a central and perhaps fundamental tenet underlying these intellectual systems.

What does objectivism hold? That there is a neutral depiction of events.

If these intellectual systems are driven by objectivism, then they must accept or assume the possibility of a neutral depiction of events. Because otherwise, they would reject objectivism in the first place.

So this answer works.

> *B.   They have generally remained un-skewed by particular points of view.*

Objectivism holds that there is an un-skewed version of events, but believing in the existence of such theory doesn't mean you are un-skewed yourself. In other words, believing that objectivity exists doesn't make you objective. Just like believing in a black and white moral standard of right and wrong doesn't make you a righteous person.

> *C.   Their discursive practices have yet to be analyzed by legal scholars.*

The passage starts off by talking about how society's discursive practices on deciding what is true has led scholars to examine the relationship between law and narrative. I would in fact argue that the scholars mentioned in this passage are doing exactly what this answer is saying that they are not doing. Social practices emanate from assuming the existence of an objective truth, and scholars have been attempting to remedy that.

> *D.   They accord a privileged position to the language of emotion and experience.*

Another opposite answer. Objectivism disallows the language of emotion and experience. (Last paragraph.)

> *E.   The accuracy of their basic tenets has been confirmed by psychologists.*

Opposite answer again, later in the paragraph the author quotes psychologists to disaffirm the basic tenets of objectivism.

The best answer is A.

Here, we saw a few examples of answer choices that had **synthesized** different pieces of information from the passage. The correct answer had combined information from two sentences, just as we had come up in one of our pre-phrased answers. A was a fairly straightforward answer choice in the end. Had the passage gone into another discussion of these intellectual systems in a later paragraph, and the correct answer had been referring to that, then this question would have been much harder.

We just saw a question where the question stem provided hints as to where to find the relevant evidence for answer choice selection. But sometimes, the question stem can be tricky as well. Take a look at the following passage, read the question stem carefully, and ask yourself what exactly are you looking for in the passage.

PT10 S3 Q16 (PT10 Passage 3)

Currently, legal scholars agree that in some cases legal rules do not specify a definite outcome. These scholars believe that such indeterminacy results from the vagueness of language: the boundaries of the application of a term are often unclear. Nevertheless, they maintain that the system of legal rules by and large rests on clear core meanings that do determine definite outcomes for most cases. Contrary to this view, an earlier group of legal philosophers, called "realists," argued that indeterminacy pervades every part of the law.

The realists held that there is always a cluster of rules relevant to the decision in any litigated case. For example, deciding whether an aunt's promise to pay her niece a sum of money if she refrained from smoking is enforceable would involve a number of rules regarding such issues as offer, acceptance, and revocation. Linguistic vagueness in any one of these rules would affect the outcome of the case, making possible multiple points of indeterminacy, not just one or two, in any legal case.

For the realists, an even more damaging kind of indeterminacy stems from the fact that in a common-law system based on precedent, a judge's decision is held to be binding on judges in subsequent similar cases. Judicial decisions are expressed in written opinions, commonly held to consist of two parts: the holding (the decision for or against the plaintiff and the essential grounds or legal reasons for it, that is, what subsequent judges are bound by), and the dicta (everything in an opinion not essential to the decision, for example, comments about points of law not treated as the basis of the outcome). The realists argued that in practice the common-law system treats the "holding/dicta" distinction loosely. They pointed out that even when the judge writing an opinion characterizes part of it as "the holding," judges writing subsequent opinions, although unlikely to dispute the decision itself, are not bound by the original judge's perception of what was essential to the decision. Later judges have tremendous leeway in being able to redefine the holding and the dicta in a precedential case. This leeway enables judges to choose which rules of law formed the basis of the decision in the earlier case. When judging almost any case, then, a judge can find a relevant precedential case which, in subsequent opinions, has been read by one judge as stating one legal rule, and by another judge as stating another, possibly contradictory one. A judge thus faces an indeterminate legal situation in which he or she has to choose which rules are to govern the case at hand.

According to the passage, which one of the following best describes the relationship between a judicial holding and a judicial decision?

    A.   The holding is not commonly considered binding on subsequent judges, but the decision is.
    B.   The holding formally states the outcome of the case, while the decision explains it.
    C.   The holding explains the decision but does not include it.
    D.   The holding consists of the decision and the dicta.
    E.   The holding sets forth and justifies a decision.

The question is asking us to describe the relationship between a "judicial holding" and a "judicial decision." In order to do that, I would do three things: one, locate the descriptions of both terms in the passage and probably highlight them in different colors; two, think about their similarities and differences; and three, try to come up with a pre-phrased answer to the question before looking at the answer choices.

The word "decision" is mentioned in the first line of paragraph 2, but we aren't told what a judicial decision consists of. The real description of both terms appear in the first half of the third paragraph:

> *Judicial decisions* are expressed in *written opinions*, commonly held to consist of two parts: the *holding* (the decision for or against the plaintiff and the essential grounds or legal reasons for it, that is, what subsequent judges are bound by), and the dicta (everything in an opinion not essential to the decision, for example, comments about points of law not treated as the basis of the outcome).

So in a written opinion, there is the "holding" and the "dicta." The holding contains the actual judicial decision and its justification; whereas the dicta contain comments not related to the decision, such as policy considerations.

So the correct answer will probably tell us that the holding contains the decision and its justification.

> A. *The holding is not commonly considered binding on subsequent judges, but the decision is.*

Nope, depending on who you ask. The realists believe that decisions are not binding on subsequent judges, because there is much leeway in interpreting the decisions themselves. Furthermore, we were never told whether the holding itself is considered binding or not, per se.

> B. *The holding formally states the outcome of the case, while the decision explains it.*

The holding contains the decision, the decision states the outcome, and the rest of the holding explains it.

> C. *The holding explains the decision but does not include it.*

The decision is a part of the holding.

> D. *The holding consists of the decision and the dicta.*

Holding consists of the decision and its rationale. A written opinion consists of the holding and the dicta.

> E. *The holding sets forth and justifies a decision.*

This is the best answer, it lists the two functions of the holding. It contains the decision (sets forth), and provides the decision's explanation (justifies).

Overall, a rather tricky question. The problem was not, for most students, trying to find the relevant content needed to solve this question. Rather, it was thinking clearly about the relationship between the holding and the decision and not being led astray by wrong answer choices.

Whenever the question stem provides us with hints as to either the passage location or the concepts to be examined, we must take advantage of it. For this question, the key to finding the correct answer choice was quickly locating the relevant materials and clearly understanding the relationship between the key terms. (Opinion consists of holding and dicta, holding consists of the decision and justification for the decision.)

We saw how the question stem can act as a guide at times, but there are also instances where the question is sufficiently broad that we won't know for certain what the correct answer might look like. In questions like these, we would have no choice but to rely on our prior understanding of the passage.

PT12 S3 Q20 (PT12 Passage 3)

Although the legal systems of England and the United States are superficially similar, they differ profoundly in their approaches to and uses of legal reasons: substantive reasons are more common than formal reasons in the United States, whereas in England the reverse is true. This distinction reflects a difference in the visions of law that prevail in the two countries. In England the law has traditionally been viewed as a system of rules; the United States favors a vision of law as an outward expression of the community's sense of right and justice.

Substantive reasons, as applied to law, are based on moral, economic, political, and other considerations. These reasons are found both "in the law" and "outside the law," so to speak. Substantive reasons inform the content of a large part of the law: constitutions, statutes, contracts verdicts, and the like. Consider, for example, a statute providing that "no vehicles shall be taken into public parks." Suppose that no specific rationales or purposes were explicitly written into this statute, but that it was clear (from its legislative history) that the substantive purpose of the statute was to ensure quiet and safety in the park. Now suppose that a veterans' group mounts a World War II jeep (in running order but without a battery) as a war memorial on a concrete slab in the park, and charges are brought against its members. Most judges in the United States would find the defendants not guilty because what they did had no adverse effect on park quiet and safety.

Formal reasons are different in that they frequently prevent substantive reasons from coming into play, even when substantive reasons are explicitly incorporated into the law at hand. For example, when a document fails to comply with stipulated requirements, the court may render the document legally ineffective. A will requiring written witness may be declared null and void and, therefore, unenforceable for the formal reason that the requirement was not observed. Once the legal rule—that a will is invalid for lack of proper witnessing—has been clearly established, and the legality of the rule is not in question, application of that rule precludes from consideration substantive arguments in favor of the will's validity or enforcement.

Legal scholars in England and the United States have long bemused themselves with extreme examples of formal and substantive reasoning. On the one hand, formal reasoning in England has led to wooden interpretations of statutes and an unwillingness to develop the common law through judicial activism. On the other hand, freewheeling substantive reasoning in the United States has resulted in statutory interpretations so liberal that the texts of some statutes have been ignored altogether.

According to the passage, which one of the following statements about substantive reasons is true?

A. They may be written into laws, but they may also exert an external influence on the law.
B. They must be explicitly written into the law in order to be relevant to the application of the law.
C. They are legal in nature and determine particular applications of most laws.
D. They often provide judges with specific rationales for disregarding the laws of the land.
E. They are peripheral to the law, whereas formal reasons are central to the law.

The question asks us about "substantive reasons," and that's it. As we know from the passage, an entire paragraph was devoted to the discussion of substantive reasons! The correct answer could come from anywhere. We have no choice but to re-read that paragraph and see what we can extract.

We know that substantive reasons are "*based on moral, economic, political, and other considerations.*" In other words, they may be based on reasons not purely legal.

Substantive reasons are found within actual legal documents such as constitutions, statutes, contracts, etc.

They are also found "*outside the law.*" By this, I believe the author is talking about non-legal considerations that are considered and used to interpret a law.

We also know from the subsequent paragraph that substantive reasons are sometimes restricted by formal reasons. From the rest of the passage, we know that "*substantive reasons*" are also more accepted in the US than UK; and that this has led to interpretations and judgments that "*ignored altogether*" the actual text of the law.

***

It will be extremely difficult to pre-phrase or anticipate what the correct answer might look like, there are simply too many possibilities. We have found as many of those as we could. Hopefully, you would have been able to recall most of them from your initial readthrough, and only had to quickly glance over the passage to fill in the missing ones.

   A.   *They may be written into laws, but they may also exert an external influence on the law.*

This seems ok. We know that substantive reasons "*are found both in the law and outside the law.*" They can inform the content of constitutions, statutes, etc. (written into laws) They are also based on non-legal considerations and are used by American judges to justify their reasoning.

   B.   *They must be explicitly written into the law in order to be relevant to the application of the law.*

No, we are told that they are found "outside the law." We also know that they exert a significant influence on American legal reasoning.

   C.   *They are <u>legal</u> in nature and determine particular applications of <u>most</u> laws.*

Two words about which I am not certain. One, whether substantive reasonings are legal in nature. I know that they exert influence on the interpretation of laws. But just because something influences the law, is it legal in nature? We also know that substantive reasoning are based on non-legal considerations. So I really don't like the use of the word "*legal*" here.

Secondly, do they determine the application of "*most*" laws? We know that they are a significant influence in the US, but more than 50%? I can't be sure.

I would not pick this over A.

   D.   *They often provide judges with specific rationales for <u>disregarding the laws of the land</u>.*

The last paragraph tells us that substantive reasoning has resulted in the texts of some statutes being ignored all together.

I suppose you can make an argument that if you are ignoring the text of certain laws, you are disregarding the laws of the land. But again, I think we can also argue that this answer choice is overstretching the actual statement from the passage. I think that there is still a jump to go from "ignoring text of some statutes" to "disregarding the laws of the land." Exactly how big of a jump, I can't quantify.

But remember, our goal is to find the best answer, the one that most closely matches the evidence from the passage, and as such, I would still pick A over D.

> E. They are peripheral to the law, whereas formal reasons are central to the law.

Depends on where you are. If you are in the UK, formal reasons are central. But if you are in the US, substantive reasons are more central. This answer misses a key distinction discussed in the passage.

The best answer is A.

Let's take a look at a few more According to the Passage Questions. This time, be extra careful of tricky answer choices!

PT31 S4 Q24 (PT31 Passage 4)

Some of the philosophers find the traditional, subjective approach to studying the mind outdated and ineffectual. For them, the attempt to describe the sensation of pain or anger, for example, or the awareness that one is aware, has been surpassed by advances in fields such as psychology, neuroscience, and cognitive science. Scientists, they claim, do not concern themselves with how a phenomenon feels from the inside; instead of investigating private evidence perceivable only to a particular individual, scientists pursue hard data—such as the study of how nerves transmit impulses to the brain—which is externally observable and can be described without reference to any particular point of view. With respect to features of the universe such as those investigated by chemistry, biology, and physics, this objective approach has been remarkably successful in yielding knowledge. Why, these philosophers ask, should we suppose the mind to be any different?

But philosophers loyal to subjectivity are not persuaded by appeals to science when such appeals conflict with the data gathered by introspection. Knowledge, they argue, relies on the data of experience, which includes subjective experience. Why should philosophy ally itself with scientists who would reduce the sources of knowledge to only those data that can be discerned objectively?

On the face of it, it seems unlikely that these two approaches to studying the mind could be reconciled. Because philosophy, unlike science, does not progress inexorably toward a single truth, disputes concerning the nature of the mind are bound to continue. But what is particularly distressing about the present debate is that genuine communication between the two sides is virtually impossible. For reasoned discourse to occur, there must be shared assumptions or beliefs. Starting from radically divergent perspectives, subjectivists and objectivists lack a common context in which to consider evidence presented from each other's perspectives.

The situation may be likened to a debate between adherents of different religions about the creation of the universe. While each religion may be confident that its cosmology is firmly grounded in its respective sacred text, there is little hope that conflicts between their competing cosmologies could be resolved by recourse to the texts alone. Only further investigation into the authority of the texts themselves would be sufficient.

What would be required to resolve the debate between the philosophers of mind, then, is an investigation into the authority of their differing perspectives. How rational is it to take scientific description as the ideal way to understand the nature of consciousness? Conversely, how useful is it to rely solely on introspection for one's knowledge about the workings of the mind? Are there alternative ways of gaining such knowledge? In this debate, epistemology—the study of knowledge—may itself lead to the discovery of new forms of knowledge about how the mind works.

According to the passage, subjectivists advance which one of the following claims to support their charge that objectivism is faulty?

    A. Objectivism rests on evidence that conflicts with the data of introspection.
    B. Objectivism restricts the kinds of experience from which philosophers may draw knowledge.
    C. Objectivism relies on data that can be described and interpreted only by scientific specialists.
    D. Objectivism provides no context in which to view scientific data as relevant to philosophical questions.
    E. Objectivism concerns itself with questions that have not traditionally been part of philosophical inquiry.

The question is somewhat helpful. We know that we have to look for how the subjectivists attack the objectivists' position. But no line reference or location has been given to us. But if we had a good grasp of passage structure, we know that the subjectivists' attack on objectivism appears in the second paragraph. So let's start there:

In paragraph 2, the subjectivists argue that knowledge relies on the data of experience, which includes subjective experience. Objectivism, on the other hand, does not admit subjective experiences as sources of knowledge.

So I would say that this is the primary fault the subjectivists find with the objectivist position. Subjective experience are not admitted by objectivists as knowledge, even though they should be considered knowledge.

  A.   *Objectivism rests on evidence that conflicts with the data of introspection.*

Careful! The words "*conflict with the data of introspection*" appear in the same paragraph where the subjectivists attack the objectivist view. But are the subjectivists criticizing objectivism because it conflicts with introspection?

No, the subjectivists criticize objectivism for ignoring the data of introspection, not for conflicting with it.

What this sentence is actually saying in the paragraph is that when science conflicts with introspection, *the subjectivists do not believe the appeals to science.*

This was a tricky answer choice and it almost got me too. It's tempting for several reasons. First, there is a sentence that says something *very similar* right next to the actual evidence we need to answer this question. Second, the tone and scope of this answer choice is also nearly identical to what we are actually looking for.

This just goes to show how we must look at all answer choices and rank them in terms of preferability. It would have been so easy to have ticked off A and done a cursory glance and the other choices and moved on. But then you would have fallen into the trap laid out by the test makers.

  B.   *Objectivism restricts the kinds of experience from which philosophers may draw knowledge.*

This answer sounds a little vague, but it actually matches what the paragraph talks about.

What are the kinds of experiences from which philosophers may draw knowledge? Subjectivists believe that personal/subjective experiences constitutes one of them. Objectivism denies the admissibility of such knowledge.

Back in LR Perfection we talked about a common answer choice trap pattern. The test makers love to make the correct answer a little bit more vague or abstract, while slipping a close trap answer in right next to it. Looks like that's what they have done here as well.

  C.   *Objectivism relies on data that can be described and interpreted only by scientific specialists.*

The passage tells us that objectivism relies on data that can be measured and recorded, hard data. It was never said that objectivism relies on data that can only be interpreted by scientists.

  D.   *Objectivism provides no context in which to view scientific data as relevant to philosophical questions.*

Remember to not get carried away by answer choices that do not match up with our anticipated answer. The subjectivists have an issue with objectivism because it excludes the data of introspection, or the data of experience.

Whether or not scientific data are relevant to philosophical questions is out of scope.

   E.   *Objectivism concerns itself with questions that have not traditionally been part of philosophical inquiry.*

That objectivism is focused on non-philosophical questions (e.g. scientific ones) is not why the subjectivists are criticizing it. Again, they are criticizing it because objectivism dismisses the data of introspection, which subjectivists also believe to be knowledge.

I think for this question, the hardest thing was to distinguish between answer choices A and B.

The previous question (PT12 S3 Q20) was tricky because the textual evidence was a little convoluted, making it a little harder for those without legal background to understand the difference between holding, dicta, decision, and opinion.

For this question, however, the difficulty lies in the answer choice. Subtle shifts in answer choices are common features of trap answers. We must parse them carefully and compare them to the actual textual evidence from the passage.

If you struggled on this question, fear not. Answer choice differentiation is in fact the entire third part of this book. We will get to it soon.

Let's look at one final annoying variation of the According to the Passage Question type.

PT6 S1 Q22 (PT6 Passage 4)

Although the United States steel industry faces widely publicized economic problems that have eroded its steel production capacity, not all branches of the industry have been equally affected. The steel industry is not monolithic: it includes integrated producers, minimills, and specialty-steel mills. The integrated producers start with iron ore and coal and produce a wide assortment of shaped steels. The minimills reprocess scrap steel into a limited range of low-quality products, such as reinforcing rods for concrete. The specialty-steel mills are similar to minimills in that they tend to be smaller than the integrated producers and are based on scrap, but they manufacture much more expensive products than minimills do and commonly have an active in-house research-and-development effort.

Both minimills and specialty-steel mills have succeeded in avoiding the worst of the economic difficulties that are afflicting integrated steel producers, and some of the mills are quite profitable. Both take advantage of new technology for refining and casting steel, such as continuous casting, as soon as it becomes available. The minimills concentrate on producing a narrow range of products for sale in their immediate geographic area, whereas specialty-steel mills preserve flexibility in their operations in order to fulfill a customer's particular specifications.

Among the factors that constrain the competitiveness of integrated producers are excessive labor, energy, and capital costs, as well as manufacturing inflexibility. Their equipment is old and less automated, and does not incorporate many of the latest refinements in steelmaking technology. (For example, only about half of the United States integrated producers have continuous casters, which combine pouring and rolling into one operation and thus save the cost of separate rolling equipment.) One might conclude that the older, labor-intensive machinery still operating in United States integrated plants is at fault for the poor performance of the United States industry, but this cannot explain why Japanese integrated producers, who produce a higher-quality product using less energy and labor, are also experiencing economic trouble. The fact is that the common technological denominator of integrated producers is an inherently inefficient process that is still rooted in the nineteenth century.

Integrated producers have been unable to compete successfully with minimills because the minimills, like specialty-steel mills, have dispensed almost entirely with the archaic energy- and capital-intensive front end of integrated steelmaking: the iron-smelting process, including the mining and preparation of the raw materials and the blast-furnace operation. In addition, minimills have found a profitable way to market steel products: as indicated above, they sell their finished products locally, thereby reducing transportation costs, and concentrate on a limited range of shapes and sizes within a narrow group of products that can be manufactured economically. For these reasons, minimills have been able to avoid the economic decline affecting integrated steel producers.

The author mentions all of the following as features of minimills EXCEPT

    A. flexibility in their operations
    B. local sale of their products
    C. avoidance of mining operations
    D. use of new steel-refining technology
    E. a limited range of low-quality products

These questions are especially annoying because for EXCEPT questions, you have to find the item or concept that wasn't mentioned in the passage. In other words, unless you have an absolute command of the details within the passage, you have to search through the passage five times.

The search function on the electronic LSAT can be a great asset, but sometimes, the keywords used in the answer choices are **not exact replicas** of the words that originally appeared in the passage. For instance, the passage may have mentioned "tigers," whereas one of the answer choices is "large felines." A tiger is a large feline, so large felines are indeed mentioned in the passage. But if you just searched for "large felines" via the search function, you won't be able to find it.

The key to these types of questions, again, is a superior grasp of the passage's content, which translates into a stronger retention of the details. Outlining and notetaking while reading can help, but I highly recommend devoting time to improving one's general reading ability in step with RC practice. We will talk about this in one of the very last chapters.

Let's take a look at the answer choices:

    A.   *flexibility in their operations*

This is true of specialty steel mills, not minimills. (end of Paragraph 2)

    B.   *local sale of their products*

"The minimills concentrate on producing a narrow range of products for sale in their immediate geographic area" (Paragraph 2)

"they sell their finished products locally" (Paragraph 4)

    C.   *avoidance of mining operations*

"the minimills, like specialty-steel mills, have dispensed almost entirely with the archaic energy- and capital-intensive front end of integrated steelmaking: the iron-smelting process, including the mining…" (Paragraph 4)

    D.   *use of new steel-refining technology*

"Both take advantage of new technology for refining and casting steel, such as continuous casting, as soon as it becomes available." (Paragraph 2)

    E.   *a limited range of low-quality products*

"The minimills reprocess scrap steel into a limited range of low-quality products, such as reinforcing rods for concrete." (Paragraph 1)

The correct answer is A.

Summary

According to the Passage Questions test your ability to recall specific details from the passage. How they are solved are similar to Must be True Questions from the LR section.

These questions must be backed up by specific evidence from the passage, usually a sentence or a phrase. The correct answer choice is always supported by explicit information from the passage.

More difficult According to the Passage Questions can test your ability to locate details that are harder to find. Details from the very beginning or end of the passage, as well as details tucked away in a dense paragraph are common culprits in these questions.

Answer choices that synthesise or combine two pieces of information from the passage are also acceptable. Just because an answer choice was not found word for word in the passage is not automatic grounds for dismissal.

When tackling these questions, try to use the actual question stem to guide your thinking as much as you can.

If the question refers to a specific line in the passage, then read the sentence in that part of the passage extra carefully, read also the lines above and below it. Try to summarize this information in your own words and see if they provide the answer to the question.

If the question is asking you something very specific, take a moment to think about what the question is actually asking of you, and find the textual evidence that directly answers this question.

The correct answer doesn't have to be a word for word repetition of the evidence we found in the passage, as long as its expressing the same meaning, then it is acceptable. Sometimes, the authors will deliberately make the correct answer choice a little bit more vague than the original statement from the passage.

Ultimately, at the end of the day, the only systematic way to improve performance on these questions is to better retain key details scattered throughout the passage. In order to do that we must first have a strong grasp of the passage's structure and arguments, and to do that we must improve our reading ability through either targeted practice of passages, or external reading.

10. Inferences

Possibility, Probability, and MSS Questions

Out of the "big four" question types (Purpose, Main Point, According to the Passage, and Inference), we have already looked at three. Now we will turn to the last of the most frequently appearing question types, Inference Questions.

Just like how According to the Passage Questions closely mirror the reasoning and approach behind Must Be True LR Questions, so do Inference Questions have a counterpart in the LR world. How we approach Inference Questions in the RC section is *very similar* to how we approach MSS questions in the LR section.

For both types of questions (MSS and Inference), we are allowed to select an answer choice that is not fully backed up by the information in the stimulus/passage. The correct answer may contain information that cannot be fully proven by the text, or additional assumptions need to be made to hurdle the gap between the text and the correct answer choice.

This is what confuses many students. The LSAT is primarily a test of logic, and logic prefers certainty. We like to think in black and white terms, we love our conditional relationships because they are absolute. But when we don't have the luxury of certainty, many students become paralyzed and end up arbitrarily choosing an answer choice. Because uncertainty is permitted, they reason, it must mean that everything is arbitrary, so answer choice selection becomes essentially a freestyling process where the student picks something based on gut feeling.

This is one of the biggest obstacles top students face on the LSAT. When we don't have explicit evidence telling us which answer choice is correct for certain, many of us tend to lose our ability to differentiate between different answer choices, which will all have things that work for and against them. In other words, when we don't have a 100% answer, how do we rank the remaining answers on which one is more preferred over the rest?

To solve this problem, let us go back to MSS Questions. Let us retrace the differences between MBT and MSS Questions and see if that distinction can serve as an inspiration when we approach Inference Questions.

Below is a partial replication of the first part of the Chapter on MSS Questions from my other book, LR Perfection. Students interested in the original can find this and more in Chapter 18 of that book.

Truth vs. Speculation and the Distinction between Certainty and Probability

Bertrand Russell, one of my favorite authors, makes an interesting point in his book, The History of Western Philosophy. Russell makes a distinction between science and religion. On the one end of the spectrum of certainty lies immutable truth. This is the realm of science. On the other end lies religion, which is based on faith alone. Science requires hard facts as proof, while religion doesn't. Philosophy, according to Russell, lies somewhere in the middle.

Russell's distinction between science, which is provable, and religion, which he considers to be speculation, is something to note. The Must be True Questions we have studied in the previous chapter are akin to the scientific truths as described by Russell. Just like how science is based on real world evidence, data, and experimentation results, the correct MBT answer choice must also be based on evidence from the stimulus. The correct answer choice is true because the stimulus said so, or it can be deduced from the information in that stimulus.

We now turn to Most Strongly Supported Questions. Unlike MBT Questions, which must be provable via the stimulus, MSS questions can have correct answer choices that leave room for doubt. But this is where a lot of students stumble. They mistakenly assume that just because the correct answer isn't a "must be true" answer, all they need to do is select an answer choice that "could be true." Unfortunately, since the most difficult MSS questions can contain several answer choices that "could be true," they end up selecting an answer on a whim and end up making a mistake.

In reality, just about half of MSS Questions are no different from MBT questions. The correct answer choice in these questions is something that can be proven via the stimulus. If you think about it, it actually makes sense, MSS Questions ask us to find the *most strongly supported* answer choice, and an answer choice that is 100% supported, or provable via the stimulus, will obviously be the most supported answer.

So the **first step** to tackling any MSS question is to treat it as a MBT question. See if we can find a MBT answer choice that can be proven by the stimulus.

If we can find a suitable MBT answer, then great, that will be the correct answer. Only when there are no answers that are 100% provable by the stimulus do we look at the answer choices that are partially supported by the stimulus. This is the **second step** to MSS questions.

The alternate strategy, which we should avoid, is to look for answers that have some support from the stimulus. This was the mistake I made when I first started studying for the LSAT, and a mistake a lot of students still continue to make. What ends up happening is that there will be several answers that have a varying degree of support from the stimulus. As a result, we end up with a whole bunch of potential answer choices even after reading through all of them.

When there is no MBT answer, the **third step** to MSS questions is to find the *most probable answer* from a shortlist of *possible* answers.

Remember that in Strengthen/Weaken Questions we had the additional job of *comparing* answers in order to find the best choice available?

In MSS Questions, just like Strengthen/Weaken Questions, sometimes the best answer will not be perfect. It will have certain suspicious keywords or gaps that leave something to be desired. But remember in Strengthen Questions, the correct answer need not wholly justify the argument but only to be the most capable strengthener available. In Weaken questions, the correct answer also need not fully destroy the argument, it only needs to be the one that hurts the argument the most. The correct MSS answer choice, sometimes, will not be 100% certain. But it WILL be the *most certain* or *most reasonable* inference among the five answer choices.

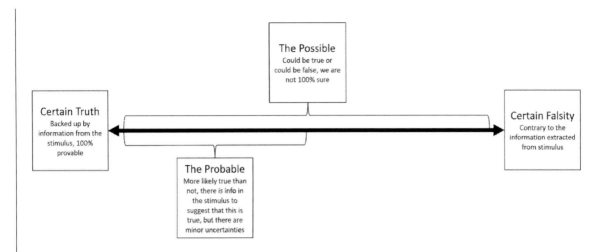

On our scales of certainty, on the very left are statements which **must be true**. These will be repetitions or synthesis of the information presented in the stimulus.

On the opposite end will be statements which **cannot be true/must be false**, they will run contrary to the information we have extracted or synthesized from the stimulus.

In the middle are statements which are **possible**, or in other words, **could be true**. Some are more likely to be true than others, but a common trait of could be true statements all possess is that we don't possess the absolute certainty as we do in MBT or MBF statements.

MBT Questions are relatively straightforward, we just have to find an answer choice that is a **Certain Truth**. No other answer choices are acceptable.

Solving MSS Questions takes multiple steps. We start by looking for an answer that is also a **Certain Truth**, and only when we can't find that among the answer choices, we take all the possible answers, and chose the **most probable** option.

Inference Questions vs. According to the Passage Questions

So, with MSS Questions, we treat it as a MBT Question first. Only when there aren't any MBT answers available do we move to the second phase of our problem-solving process, which is to rank the answer choices by the amount of support they have from the stimulus (finding the most probable answer).

The process is identical for Inference Questions. We try to solve it, initially, as an According to the Passage Question. If we were able to find explicit textual support from the passage for one of the answer choices to an Inference Question, then great, we have just solved it.

If there isn't such an answer, then we would need to start comparing answers. While it's easy to say that we want to pick the answer "most supported" by the information from the passage, the reality is that this process is a lot more nuanced and complicated. In this chapter, we will look at how "answer choice ranking" works for Inference Questions on the most fundamental level; and revisit the topic again in Part III of this book.

Practice Questions

<u>PT6 S1 Q25 (PT6 Passage 4)</u>

Although the United States steel industry faces widely publicized economic problems that have eroded its steel production capacity, not all branches of the industry have been equally affected. The steel industry is not monolithic: it includes integrated producers, minimills, and specialty-steel mills. The integrated producers start with iron ore and coal and produce a wide assortment of shaped steels. The minimills reprocess scrap steel into a limited range of low-quality products, such as reinforcing rods for concrete. The specialty-steel mills are similar to minimills in that they tend to be smaller than the integrated producers and are based on scrap, but they manufacture much more expensive products than minimills do and commonly have an active in-house research-and-development effort.

Both minimills and specialty-steel mills have succeeded in avoiding the worst of the economic difficulties that are afflicting integrated steel producers, and some of the mills are quite profitable. Both take advantage of new technology for refining and casting steel, such as continuous casting, as soon as it becomes available. The minimills concentrate on producing a narrow range of products for sale in their immediate geographic area, whereas specialty-steel mills preserve flexibility in their operations in order to fulfill a customer's particular specifications.

Among the factors that constrain the competitiveness of integrated producers are excessive labor, energy, and capital costs, as well as manufacturing inflexibility. Their equipment is old and less automated, and does not incorporate many of the latest refinements in steelmaking technology. (For example, only about half of the United States integrated producers have continuous casters, which combine pouring and rolling into one operation and thus save the cost of separate rolling equipment.) One might conclude that the older, labor-intensive machinery still operating in United States integrated plants is at fault for the poor performance of the United States industry, but this cannot explain why Japanese integrated producers, who produce a higher-quality product using less energy and labor, are also experiencing economic trouble. The fact is that the common technological denominator of integrated producers is an inherently inefficient process that is still rooted in the nineteenth century.

Integrated producers have been unable to compete successfully with minimills because the minimills, like specialty-steel mills, have dispensed almost entirely with the archaic energy- and capital-intensive front end of integrated steelmaking: the iron-smelting process, including the mining and preparation of the raw materials and the blast-furnace operation. In addition, minimills have found a profitable way to market steel products: as indicated above, they sell their finished products locally, thereby reducing transportation costs, and concentrate on a limited range of shapes and sizes within a narrow group of products that can be manufactured economically. For these reasons, minimills have been able to avoid the economic decline affecting integrated steel producers.

It can be inferred from the passage that United States specialty-steel mills generally differ from integrated steel producers in that the specialty-steel mills

    A. sell products in a restricted geographical area
    B. share the economic troubles of the minimills
    C. resemble specialty-steel mills found in Japan
    D. concentrate on producing a narrow range of products
    E. do not operate blast furnaces

Although this is an Inference Question, we should still strive to find as much explicit support for it as we can from the passage. The question is also very specific. We are looking for the differences between specialty steel mills and integrated steel producers. Not the difference between minimills and specialty steel mills or the differences between minimills and integrated steel producers.

Let's look at each answer choice in turn.

A.   sell products in a restricted geographical area

Remember what we are supposed to be comparing: specialty steel mills and integrated steel producers. Who sells products in a restricted geographical area? Minimills (paragraph 2). This information is irrelevant.

B.   share the economic troubles of the minimills

Specialty steel mills and minimills are doing well, it's the integrated producers that are suffering from economic troubles.

C.   resemble specialty-steel mills found in Japan

We have no idea how specialty mills are in Japan, they were never mentioned. The only time that the passage mentions Japan was to talk about integrated steel producers in Japan.

D.   concentrate on producing a narrow range of products

Again, it's the minimills that concentrate on producing a narrow range of products:

> *The minimills <u>concentrate on producing a narrow range of products</u> for sale in their immediate geographic area, whereas specialty-steel mills preserve flexibility in their operations in order to fulfill a customer's particular specifications.*

E.   do not operate blast furnaces

This is directly backed by textual support in the last paragraph. It's the correct answer.

> *because the minimills, <u>like specialty-steel mills</u>, have <u>dispensed</u> almost entirely with the archaic energy- and capital-intensive front end of integrated steelmaking: the iron-smelting process, <u>including</u> the mining and preparation of the raw materials and the <u>blast-furnace operation</u>.*

***

This question, while an Inference Question, required an approach **identical** to the approach we used on According to the Passage Questions in the previous chapter. We carefully examined the question stem to make sure we know what is being asked of us, and we went ahead to look for the relevant evidence from the passage. The correct answer, E, did not require a leap of faith to arrive at. It is explicitly backed by information already in the passage.

Let's look at another similar Inference Question.

PT40 S4 Q27 (PT40 Passage 4)

Leading questions—questions worded in such a way as to suggest a particular answer—can yield unreliable testimony either by design, as when a lawyer tries to trick a witness into affirming a particular version of the evidence of a case, or by accident, when a questioner unintentionally prejudices the witness's response. For this reason, a judge can disallow such questions in the courtroom interrogation of witnesses. But their exclusion from the courtroom by no means eliminates the remote effects of earlier leading questions on eyewitness testimony. Alarmingly, the beliefs about an event that a witness brings to the courtroom may often be adulterated by the effects of leading questions that were introduced intentionally or unintentionally by lawyers, police investigators, reporters, or others with whom the witness has already interacted.

Recent studies have confirmed the ability of leading questions to alter the details of our memories and have led to a better understanding of how this process occurs and, perhaps, of the conditions that make for greater risks that an eyewitness's memories have been tainted by leading questions. These studies suggest that not all details of our experiences become clearly or stably stored in memory—only those to which we give adequate attention. Moreover, experimental evidence indicates that if subtly introduced new data involving remembered events do not actively conflict with our stored memory data, we tend to process such new data similarly whether they correspond to details as we remember them, or to gaps in those details. In the former case, we often retain the new data as a reinforcement of the corresponding aspect of the memory, and in the latter case, we often retain them as a construction to fill the corresponding gap. An eyewitness who is asked, prior to courtroom testimony, "How fast was the car going when it passed the stop sign?" may respond to the query about speed without addressing the question of the stop sign. But the "stop sign" datum has now been introduced, and when later recalled, perhaps during courtroom testimony, it may be processed as belonging to the original memory even if the witness actually saw no stop sign.

The farther removed from the event, the greater the chance of a vague or incomplete recollection and the greater the likelihood of newly suggested information blending with original memories. Since we can be more easily misled with respect to fainter and more uncertain memories, tangential details are more apt to become constructed out of subsequently introduced information than are more central details. But what is tangential to a witness's original experience of an event may nevertheless be crucial to the courtroom issues that the witness's memories are supposed to resolve. For example, a perpetrator's shirt color or hairstyle might be tangential to one's shocked observance of an armed robbery, but later those factors might be crucial to establishing the identity of the perpetrator.

Which one of the following can be most reasonably inferred from the information in the passage?

    A. The tendency of leading questions to cause unreliable courtroom testimony has no correlation with the extent to which witnesses are emotionally affected by the events that they have observed.
    B. Leading questions asked in the process of a courtroom examination of a witness are more likely to cause inaccurate testimony than are leading questions asked outside the courtroom.
    C. The memory processes by which newly introduced data tend to reinforce accurately remembered details of events are not relevant to explaining the effects of leading questions.
    D. The risk of testimony being inaccurate due to certain other factors tends to increase as an eyewitness's susceptibility to giving inaccurate testimony due to the effects of leading questions increases.
    E. The traditional grounds on which leading questions can be excluded from courtroom interrogation of witnesses have been called into question by the findings of recent studies.

10. Inferences

This is a passage that we haven't covered before, so let's first take the time to read it through.

Leading questions—questions worded in such a way as to suggest a particular answer—can yield <u>unreliable</u> <u>testimony</u> either by <u>design</u>, as when a lawyer tries to trick a witness into affirming a particular version of the evidence of a case, or by <u>accident</u>, when a questioner unintentionally prejudices the witness's response. For this reason, a judge can disallow such questions in the courtroom interrogation of witnesses. But their <u>exclusion</u> from the courtroom <u>by no means eliminates the remote effects of earlier leading questions</u> on eyewitness testimony. Alarmingly, the beliefs about an event that a witness brings to the courtroom may often be <u>adulterated by the effects of leading questions</u> that were introduced intentionally or unintentionally by lawyers, police investigators, reporters, or others with whom the witness has already interacted.

Leading questions can mess with us. Judges can eliminate leading questions from the courtroom. But this doesn't entirely solve the problem. Because our memories may already have been diluted by leading questions asked by people that have interacted with us earlier. These people may have planted ideas or details in our minds. (Kind of like in Nolan's Inception movie…)

Recent studies have confirmed the ability of leading questions to <u>alter</u> the <u>details</u> of our memories and have led to a better understanding of how this process occurs and, perhaps, of the conditions that make for greater risks that an eyewitness's memories have been tainted by leading questions. These studies suggest that <u>not all details of our experiences become clearly or stably stored</u> in memory—only those to which we give adequate attention. Moreover, experimental evidence indicates that if subtly introduced <u>new data</u> involving remembered events <u>do not actively conflict</u> with our stored memory data, we tend to process such new data similarly whether they correspond to details as we remember them, or to gaps in those details. In the former case, we <u>often retain the new data as a reinforcement</u> of the corresponding aspect of the memory, and in the latter case, we often retain them as <u>a construction to fill the corresponding gap</u>. An eyewitness who is asked, prior to courtroom testimony, "How fast was the car going when it passed the stop sign?" may respond to the query about speed without addressing the question of the stop sign. But the "stop sign" datum has now been introduced, and when later recalled, perhaps during courtroom testimony, it may be processed as belonging to the original memory even if the witness actually saw no stop sign.

Additional expansions on what we talked about in the earlier paragraph. If we introduce new details that don't conflict with our pre-existing memory, we either use it to reinforce our existing memory, or use it to plug in the gaps.

The farther <u>removed</u> from the event, the <u>greater the chance</u> of a vague or incomplete recollection and the <u>greater the likelihood</u> of newly suggested information blending with original memories. Since we can be more easily misled with respect to fainter and more uncertain memories, <u>tangential details are more apt to become constructed</u> out of subsequently introduced information than are more central details. But what is <u>tangential</u> to a witness's original experience of an event may nevertheless be <u>crucial</u> to the courtroom issues that the witness's memories are supposed to resolve. For example, a perpetrator's shirt color or hairstyle might be tangential to one's shocked observance of an armed robbery, but later those factors might be crucial to establishing the identity of the perpetrator.

Farther removed ~ Greater the chance of incomplete memory ~ More easily led astray by leading questions.

Tangential ideas are more easily built out of false leads, but tangential ideas can significantly impact the case.

Purpose: the author is explaining the effects of leading questions on witness memory.

Main Point: Leading questions can manipulate witness memory, even when they are disallowed in the courtroom, especially when these memories are vague, and can significantly affect the outcome of a case.

***

Let's take a look at the answers:

A. *The tendency of leading questions to cause unreliable courtroom testimony has no correlation with the extent to which witnesses are <u>emotionally affected</u> by the events that they have observed.*

How emotional effects influence testimony accuracy was never mentioned in the passage.

B. *Leading questions asked in the process of a courtroom examination of a witness are <u>more likely to</u> cause inaccurate testimony than are leading questions asked outside the courtroom.*

Again, a comparison that we know nothing about. Both will affect testimony accuracy, but which one does so more is not mentioned or hinted at in the passage.

C. *The memory processes by which newly introduced data tend to reinforce <u>accurately remembered</u> details of events are <u>not relevant</u> to explaining the effects of leading questions.*

We don't know this. All we know is that newly introduced data reinforce pre-existing memories when there is no conflict. Are the pre-existing memories accurate? We don't know. Is this process relevant to explaining the effects of leading questions? We don't know either.

D. *The risk of testimony being inaccurate due to <u>certain other factors</u> tends to <u>increase</u> as an eyewitness's susceptibility to giving inaccurate testimony <u>due to the effects of leading questions</u> increases.*

This answer choice is strangely worded. So what we have to do is try to break it apart and come to a more relevant understanding of what it's trying to say, and what it's referring to in the passage.

Let's start with the second half of the answer choice: "*as an eyewitness's susceptibility to giving inaccurate testimony due to the effects of leading questions increases.*" When is a witness more suspect to give inaccurate testimony due to leading questions? When they have their memory manipulated by leading questions.

So this answer choice is essentially saying, the more you are likely to be misled by leading questions, the more likely your testimony is inaccurate due to other factors.

Take a look at the beginning of the last paragraph. There, we were told that there is a correlation between three different things.

Farther removed from the event ~ greater the chance of incomplete memory ~ more easily led astray by leading questions.

Now back to our answer choice, which is telling us that the more you are likely to be misled by leading questions (same as our last correlation from the passage), the more likely your testimony is inaccurate due to other factors. What other factors are there? I think that both your distance from the event and higher chances of incomplete memory both count as the other factors which causes inaccuracy.

So, this answer choice is essentially a super vaguely phrased restatement of the first sentence of the last paragraph.

E. *The traditional grounds on which leading questions <u>can be excluded</u> from courtroom interrogation of witnesses <u>have been called into question</u> by the findings of recent studies.*

This answer choice is tricky. It's not saying that recent studies have supported the exclusion of leading questions. Rather, it's saying that the recent studies are challenging the traditional criteria. This is not something discussed in the passage, and as a result, an out of scope answer.

10. Inferences

D is the best answer.

We saw in this question another instance of where the correct answer can be derived from the passage. Even though this time, the correct answer was worded so vaguely that you might not be able to recognize it as referring to something from the passage on a first glance.

 The **best** answer choice to an Inference Question are those explicitly supported by the passage. Even though answers that aren't fully supported by the passage are acceptable, we still start off by looking for something with explicit support.

Let's look at a few questions where the process gets a little more complicated.

PT32 S2 Q24 (PT32 Passage 4)

Most scientists who study the physiological effects of alcoholic beverages have assumed that wine, like beer or distilled spirits, is a drink whose only active ingredient is alcohol. Because of this assumption, these scientists have rarely investigated the effects of wine as distinct from other forms of alcoholic beverages. Nevertheless, unlike other alcoholic beverages, wine has for centuries been thought to have healthful effects that these scientists—who not only make no distinction among wine, beer, and distilled spirits but also study only the excessive or abusive intake of these beverages—have obscured.

Recently, a small group of researchers has questioned this assumption and investigated the effects of moderate wine consumption. While alcohol has been shown conclusively to have negative physiological effects—for example, alcohol strongly affects the body's processing of lipids (fats and other substances including cholesterol), causing dangerous increases in the levels of these substances in the blood, increases that are a large contributing factor in the development of premature heart disease—the researchers found that absorption of alcohol into the bloodstream occurs much more slowly when subjects drink wine than when they drink distilled spirits. More remarkably, it was discovered that deaths due to premature heart disease in the populations of several European countries decreased dramatically as the incidence of moderate wine consumption increased. One preliminary study linked this effect to red wine, but subsequent research has shown identical results whether the wine was white or red. What could explain such apparently healthful effects?

For one thing, the studies show increased activity of a natural clot-breaking compound used by doctors to restore blood flow through blocked vessels in victims of heart disease. In addition, the studies of wine drinkers indicate increased levels of certain compounds that may help to prevent damage from high lipid levels. And although the link between lipid processing and premature heart disease is one of the most important discoveries in modern medicine, in the past 20 years researchers have found several additional important contributing factors. We now know that endothelial cell reactivity (which affects the thickness of the innermost walls of blood vessels) and platelet adhesiveness (which influences the degree to which platelets cause blood to clot) are each linked to the development of premature heart disease. Studies show that wine appears to have ameliorating effects on both of these factors: it decreases the thickness of the innermost walls of blood vessels, and it reduces platelet adhesiveness. One study demonstrated a decrease in platelet adhesiveness among individuals who drank large amounts of grape juice. This finding may be the first step in confirming speculation that the potentially healthful effects of moderate wine intake may derive from the concentration of certain natural compounds found in grapes and not present in other alcoholic beverages.

It can be inferred from the passage that the author would most likely agree with which one of the following statements?

    A. Scientists should not attempt to study the possible healthful effects of moderate consumption of beer and distilled spirits.

    B. The conclusion that alcohol affects lipid processing should be questioned in light of studies of moderate wine consumption.

    C. Moderate consumption of wine made from plums or apples rather than grapes would be unlikely to reduce the risk of premature heart disease.

    D. Red wine consumption has a greater effect on reducing death rates from premature heart disease than does white wine consumption.

    E. Beer and distilled spirits contain active ingredients other than alcohol whose effects tend to be beneficial.

Most scientists who study the physiological effects of alcoholic beverages have <u>assumed</u> that wine, like beer or distilled spirits, is a drink whose only active ingredient is alcohol. Because of this assumption, these scientists have rarely investigated the effects of wine as distinct from other forms of alcoholic beverages. Nevertheless, unlike other alcoholic beverages, wine has for centuries been thought to have <u>healthful effects</u> that these scientists—who not only make no distinction among wine, beer, and distilled spirits but also study only the excessive or abusive intake of these beverages—have obscured.

It appears that wine has healthful effects hitherto overlooked by scientists.

Recently, a small group of researchers has <u>questioned</u> this assumption and investigated the effects of <u>moderate wine consumption</u>. While <u>alcohol</u> has been shown conclusively to have negative physiological effects—for example, alcohol strongly affects the body's processing of lipids (fats and other substances including cholesterol), causing dangerous increases in the levels of these substances in the blood, increases that are a large contributing factor in the development of premature heart disease—the researchers found that <u>absorption of alcohol into the bloodstream occurs much more slowly</u> when subjects drink wine than when they drink distilled spirits. More remarkably, it was discovered that deaths due to premature heart disease in the populations of several European countries <u>decreased dramatically</u> as the incidence of <u>moderate wine consumption</u> increased. One preliminary study linked this effect to red wine, but subsequent research has shown identical results whether the wine was white or red. What could explain such apparently healthful effects?

A small group of researchers began to study the effects of moderate wine consumption. I think the word "moderate" is key here. While alcohol is very bad for you, when you drink wine, alcohol absorption is actually slower than hard liquor. Data also shows that heart disease fatality rates decreased as wine consumption increased.

This got me thinking, are less people dying because wine is good for you, or is it because that when you drink wine, you are less likely to drink vodka, rum, etc.?

For one thing, the studies show <u>increased activity of a natural clot-breaking compound</u> used by doctors to restore blood flow through blocked vessels in victims of heart disease. In addition, the studies of wine drinkers indicate increased <u>levels of certain compounds that may help to prevent damage from high lipid levels</u>. And although the link between lipid processing and <u>premature heart disease</u> is one of the most important discoveries in modern medicine, in the past 20 years researchers have found several additional important contributing factors. We now know that <u>endothelial cell reactivity</u> (which affects the thickness of the innermost walls of blood vessels) and <u>platelet adhesiveness</u> (which influences the degree to which platelets cause blood to clot) are each linked to the <u>development of premature heart disease</u>. Studies show that wine appears to have ameliorating effects on both of these factors: it <u>decreases the thickness</u> of the innermost walls of blood vessels, and it <u>reduces platelet adhesiveness</u>. One study demonstrated a decrease in platelet adhesiveness among individuals who drank large amounts of <u>grape juice</u>. This finding may be the first step in confirming speculation that the potentially healthful effects of moderate wine intake <u>may</u> derive from the concentration of certain <u>natural compounds found in grapes</u> and <u>not present in other alcoholic beverages.</u>

This paragraph goes into depth talking about the reasons why wine decreases the risk of heart disease. There are increased levels of certain beneficial compounds in the blood of wine drinkers (clot breaking compound and lipid damage prevention compound). Further more, wine decreases blood vessels' wall thickness and reduces platelet adhesiveness, both of which are causes for heart disease.

The author believes the reason why wine is beneficial is due to grapes.

It can be inferred from the passage that the author would most likely agree with which one of the following statements?

    A.   *Scientists <u>should not attempt</u> to study the possible healthful effects of moderate consumption of beer and distilled spirits.*

We know that moderate wine consumption has healthful benefits. We have mostly assumed that other alcoholic drinks do not have healthful effects. *Nevertheless, unlike other alcoholic beverages, wine has for centuries been thought to have healthful effects.*

So if we don't think something is beneficial, does that mean we should not attempt to study its potential benefits?

There's certainly a pretty big jump here. Let's keep it and move on.

> B. The conclusion that alcohol affects lipid processing <u>should be questioned</u> in light of studies of moderate wine consumption.

This is contrary to what the passage says. The passage tells us that it has been conclusively shown how alcohol negatively affects lipid processing, wine consumption slows it down. So the author agrees with the conclusion about how alcohol affects lipid processing.

> C. Moderate consumption of wine made from plums or apples rather than grapes would be <u>unlikely</u> to reduce the risk of premature heart disease.

Initially, I did not like this answer choice very much. I thought it was out of scope, because the passage does not talk about plus or apples. What this answer choice is essentially saying that wine not made from grapes is unlikely to reduce premature heart disease.

Does this have any support? There's limited support at the end of the passage:

"...the potentially healthful effects of moderate wine intake may derive from the concentration of certain natural compounds found in grapes and not present in other alcoholic beverages."

So there is evidence from the passage that suggests "grapes reduce risk of heart disease."

But to go from that to "not grapes unlikely to reduce risk of heart disease" is such a big jump! We know from LR causal logic that just because grapes can reduce heart disease, doesn't mean grapes are the only thing that reduce heart disease. Maybe plums and apples contain other ingredients that can also reduce heart disease too?

Let's keep this one for now.

> D. Red wine consumption has a <u>greater effect</u> on reducing death rates from premature heart disease than does white wine consumption.

This is contrary to what the passage says. At the end of the second paragraph: *"but subsequent research has shown identical results whether the wine was white or red."*

> E. Beer and distilled spirits contain <u>active ingredients</u> other than alcohol whose effects tend to be <u>beneficial</u>.

First of all, we don't know whether beer and distilled spirits are beneficial in other ways. The passage just talks about the beneficial effects of wine. Second, there is no evidence whatsoever hinting at such a suggestion in the passage.

Now we are left with A and C. Let's look at them side by side:

	A	C
Passage Support	People thought beer/spirits had no health benefits for the longest time.	Grapes decrease heart disease.
Answer Choice	Scientists should not try to study their potential benefits.	If the wine doesn't contain grapes, it's unlikely to decrease heart disease.
Leap of Reasoning	Because we think something has no benefits, we should not try to study more to find out for sure.	If something has a certain effect, its absence means the likely absence of that effect.

This is a very tricky question and when I initially studied for the LSAT, I got this question wrong. But I deliberately picked it because it teaches us a very important lesson that will prove to be invaluable throughout the entirety of our RC experience.

Note how I underlined the word "likely" in our table. Remember that the answer choice itself read:

Moderate consumption of wine made from plums or apples rather than grapes would be <u>unlikely</u> to reduce the risk of premature heart disease.

The word "unlikely" is what gave answer choice C an advantage over answer choice A here. "Unlikely" is a rather weak word. If the answer had said that plum/apple wine *will not* reduce the risk of premature heart disease, then that would be too strong.

Had the answer said that plum/apple wine *may be less likely* to reduce the risk of heart disease, then it would have been a BETTER choice than what was given to us. Because there is certainly the *possibility* that without grapes as an active ingredient, the beneficial effects of wine are lowered.

When it comes to Inference Questions, the stronger the wording of the answer choice, the higher the **threshold of proof** I'll need from the passage in order for me to confidently select it as the right answer.

Let's look at A for a moment now. A is fairly certain in its language, "*scientists should not…*" If it had said "scientists *may* find it less helpful…" instead, then it would have been a better choice.

At the end of the day, what helped C win over A was the word "unlikely." It's not great, it's not perfect, and on an easier question it would surely have been the wrong answer to pick. But here, it's the most acceptable out of five very messed up answers.

This question gives us a glimpse into what truly makes RC difficult. It's the logical ambiguity and disconnect between claims made in the answer choices and the textual support you can find in the passage. There are two lessons that I want to emphasize from this question: **One**, develop a healthy suspicion of strongly worded answer choices; and **two**, when all answers are imperfect, pick the one that has the least amount of issues.

PT52 S4 Q18 (PT52 Passage 3)

Traditional theories of animal behavior assert that animal conflict within a species is highly ritualized and does not vary from contest to contest. This species-specific model assumes that repetitive use of the same visual and vocal displays and an absence of escalated fighting evolved to prevent injury. The contestant that exhibits the "best" display wins the contested resource. Galápagos tortoises, for instance, settle contests on the basis of height: the ritualized display consists of two tortoises facing one another and stretching their necks skyward; the tortoise perceived as being "taller" wins.

In populations of the spider Agelenopsis aperta, however, fighting behavior varies greatly from contest to contest. In addition, fighting is not limited to displays: biting and shoving are common. Susan Riechert argues that a recently developed model, evolutionary game theory, provides a closer fit to A. aperta territorial disputes than does the species specific model, because it explains variations in conflict behavior that may result from varying conditions, such as differences in size, age, and experience of combatants. Evolutionary game theory was adapted from the classical game theory that was developed by von Neumann and Morganstern to explain human behavior in conflict situations. In both classical and evolutionary game theory, strategies are weighed in terms of maximizing the average payoff against contestants employing both the same and different strategies. For example, a spider may engage in escalated fighting during a dispute only if the disputed resource is valuable enough to warrant the risk of physical injury. There are, however, two major differences between the classical and evolutionary theories. First, whereas in classical game theory it is assumed that rational thought is used to determine which action to take, evolutionary game theory assumes that instinct and long-term species advantage ultimately determine the strategies that are exhibited. The other difference is in the payoffs: in classical game theory, the payoffs are determined by an individual's personal judgment of what constitutes winning; in evolutionary game theory, the payoffs are defined in terms of reproductive success.

In studying populations of A. aperta in a grassland habitat and a riparian habitat, Riechert predicts that such factors as the size of the opponents, the potential rate of predation in a habitat, and the probability of winning a subsequent site if the dispute is lost will all affect the behavior of spiders in territorial disputes. In addition, she predicts that the markedly different levels of competition for web sites in the two habitats will affect the spiders' willingness to engage in escalated fighting. In the grassland, where 12 percent of the habitat is available for occupation by A. aperta, Riechert predicts that spiders will be more willing to engage in escalated fighting than in the riparian habitat, where 90 percent of the habitat is suitable for occupation.

The passage suggests which one of the following about the behavior of A. aperta in conflict situations?

    A. They exhibit variations in fighting behavior from contest to contest primarily because of the different levels of competition for suitable sites in different habitats.
    B. They may confine their fighting behavior to displays if the value of a disputed resource is too low and the risk of physical injury is too great.
    C. They exhibit variations in fighting behavior that are similar to those exhibited by members of most other species of animals.
    D. They are more likely to engage in escalated fighting during disputes than to limit their fighting behavior to visual and vocal displays.
    E. They are more willing to engage in escalated fighting during conflict situations than are members of most other species of animals.

We have seen this passage previously, so let's go directly to the answer choices.

The question stem doesn't really provide any hint as to what the potential answer might look like, or where to search for the relevant materials, so let's just bite the bullet and look at the ACs one by one.

> A. *They exhibit variations in fighting behavior from contest to contest <u>primarily</u> because of the different levels of competition for suitable sites in different habitats.*

We saw in the last question how conservative answer choices are preferred in Inference Questions. Why? Because conservatively worded answers would need a lower **threshold of proof**.

If this answer choice had said that the spiders exhibit variations in fighting *partially/potentially* because of the different levels of competition, then all we need to do is to find evidence in the passage that tells us that competition levels are a *partial* influence on fighting behavior. As long as there's one instance where competition levels did influence fighting behavior, even a tiny little bit, then this answer would be acceptable.

Similarly, if it had used the word "*potentially*," then that makes our job easy too. We just have to confirm that there is the possibility that competition levels influence fighting behavior. In other words, as long as there isn't explicit information to suggest that competition levels never influence fighting behavior, then it is a possibility, right? If it's a possibility, then an answer that called it a potential influence would be more than acceptable.

But alas, this answer choice chose the word "*primarily*" instead. That's a pretty high threshold of proof! In order to be able to select this answer choice, we would need evidence that competition levels were the *most significant cause* affecting fighting behavior. It can't be the second most important cause, or just one of the causes, it must be the most important cause. Otherwise, the use of the word "*primarily*" would be unjustified.

What does the passage tell us? "*In addition, she predicts that the markedly different levels of competition for web sites in the two habitats <u>will affect</u> the spiders' willingness to engage in escalated fighting.*"

The standard of proof is not met.

> B. *They <u>may</u> confine their fighting behavior to displays if the value of a disputed resource is too low and the risk of physical injury is too great.*

I like "may" a lot. Unlike answer choice A, the standard of proof here is much lower. All we have to do is show that whatever answer choice B is describing is indeed a possibility.

B is actually supported by a specific statement from the second paragraph: "*For example, a spider may engage in escalated fighting during a dispute only if the disputed resource is valuable enough to warrant the risk of physical injury.*" In other words, if the resource is not valuable or not valuable enough to warrant the risk of physical injury, the spider may not necessarily engage in fighting.

But even if you didn't locate this specific statement, modifier words like "may" should have meant this is a serious contender for the correct answer.

> C. *They exhibit variations in fighting behavior that are similar to those exhibited by members of <u>most</u> other species of animals.*

We don't know how "most" other species of animals behave. Some might engage in ritualistic fighting, some might fight for real. But we don't have the statistics to back up this claim. To select C, we need proof showing that the variations in spider fighting behavior is shared by >50% of all animal species.

> D. *They are <u>more likely</u> to engage in escalated fighting during disputes than to limit their fighting behavior to visual and vocal displays.*

The answer to this would be "it depends." I mean, that's kind of the whole point of the passage, right? They will fight if it's worth it, if resources are scarce, or if they are sure that they can take on their opponent. Otherwise, if it's not worth it, they won't fight. Further, we don't know if they resort to visual and vocal displays in cases when they choose not to fight.

> E.   They are _more willing to engage_ in escalated fighting during conflict situations than are members of _most_ other species of animals.

Sure, spiders are probably more willing to fight than animals that engage in ritualistic fights. But what percentage of animal species engage in actual fighting, and what percentage are avert to fighting? Without such information, we can't really select this answer.

We saw again that in Inference Questions, conservatively worded answer choices are "safer" than strongly worded answer choices. Answer choices worded weakly require a much lower standard of proof than answer choices containing more powerful verbs, adjectives, and adverbs.

Remember, our goal in Inference Questions is to find the answer choice with the *most support* that we can find in the passage. When we are looking at each answer choice, try to think about what kind of proof would I need in order to comfortably select it as the correct answer? Does the passage contain such proof?

Summary

In this chapter, we looked at the last of the "big four" question types, Inference Questions. Inference Questions can cause us a lot of trouble because of the potential imperfections even in correct answer choices. In the event that even the correct answer cannot be fully proven by the textual evidence, we are forced to deal with a lot of additional uncertainties during the answer choice elimination phase. In fact, this is a challenge that the majority of students will struggle with at one point, and an obstacle that most students never learn to fully overcome.

We began this chapter by emphasizing the need to find support from the passage for Inference Questions. **Just because some Inference Questions cannot be fully backed up by what we read in the passage doesn't mean that we can skip over this step and rely on our intuition.** In fact, a significant proportion of Inference Questions are no different from According to the Passage Questions. The correct answer choice actually doesn't need us to infer anything. It's fully supported and provable via the passage.

Back in LR Perfection, we talked about treating MSS Questions as MBT Questions to start, and only resorting to answer choice ranking/comparison when we cannot find a MBT answer choice. The process is similar for Inference Questions. We are allowed to make inferences and extrapolations *only when* no answer choice is fully backed by the text.

This is where many students fall short. The most important thing to realize is that for Inference Questions, even though answer choices that cannot be fully proven by the passage are *acceptable,* they should only be selected as a last resort.

For questions where none of the answer choices can be fully proven by the passage, we need to compare and rank them. Ranking answer choices is a habit we have devoted great attention to in LR Perfection, and it will come in handy in a lot of RC question types also. There are many strategies and exercises that we can drill when ranking the answer choices, most of which we will discuss in Part III of the book, Answer Choice Ranking and Elimination. But for now, know that one strategy that can be immensely helpful is to pick the answer with the **lowest threshold of proof requirement.**

We do this by focusing on the **verbs, adjectives, and adverbs** present in an answer choice. Are these words strong or weak words? Is the language conservative or moderate? Unless there is explicit support from the passage, we usually prefer the weakly/more conservatively worded answers.

A weakly worded answer would have a lower threshold of proof that needs to be met by information from the passage. For instance, if an AC said "some people like cheesecake," then all we need to gather from the passage is the evidence that at least one person likes cheesecake. However, if an AC said that "most people like cheesecake," then we would need the passage to say that more than 50% of people like cheesecakes.

So when ranking answer choices, weaker words are preferable most of the time.

We will look at how to eliminate, rank, and compare answer choices in more detail in Chapters 15 - 17. As we mentioned, this is probably the hardest skill to master in RC and the last obstacle to attaining perfection for the majority of us. But we will get there soon enough!

11. Attitude and Organization

Two Question Types that You should Already Know the Answer to.

Before we look at the more esoteric question types, I just wanted to get two commonly seen question types out of the way. They are **Author's Attitude Questions** and **Organization Questions**.

You might not know this, but if we had followed all the steps on how to read a passage properly from Part I, then we should already have all the information we need to answer these two questions.

Questions regarding the **Author's Attitude** will be asking us how the author feels about a specific position or group described in the passage. For these questions we need to think about what we learned in Chapter 4. In that chapter, we looked at some of the details we need to pay special attention to in a passage.

The author's attitude or opinion is something that we can decipher from their usage of specific words. Their choice of vocabulary, the meaning and connotation behind these words, as well as the times when they clearly make their positions known are all clues that will help us answer these questions. Go back to Chapter 4 and take a look at the passages in the first section of that chapter if you need to refresh your memory.

Organization Questions ask us about the structural organization of a passage. This was something that we looked at in Chapter 3. Basically, we have to figure out what are the roles, respectively, of each of the paragraphs. In order to answer this question, we need to know not only the Main Point of the passage, but the sub-point emphasized in each of the paragraphs. Again, revisit Chapter 3 if needed.

We will look at a few passages and their associated Author's Attitude Questions now, give a summary on how to approach these particular questions; then repeat the process with Organization Questions.

Author's Attitude

As we have mentioned earlier, Author's Attitude Questions will ask us how the author of the passage feels about a particular position, view, or argument. How the author feels about someone or something can usually be discerned from the passage during our initial read through. Either it will be explicitly stated in the passage; or we will have to find it from the specific words used; a strong grasp of the details within a passage will always come in handy when trying to solve these questions.

The answer choice format of the Author's Attitude Questions is also very particular. The answer choices will usually consist of two words: two adjectives, but sometimes an adjective and a noun. Our job is to find the answer that best describes how the author feels about the particular topic at hand.

With Author's Attitude Questions, I will attempt to solve the question via the following steps:

1.   **Locate** in passage the group, position, or view that the question is asking us for the author's attitude. If the question is asking us about how the author feels about something, what is this "something?"

2.   Read the portion of the passage again. If you had done a good job in the initial reading of the passage, you should have a general idea of how the author feels. But I always double check for **keywords** and explicit textual support just to make sure. Come up with your own **pre-phrased answer**.

3.   Compare your pre-phrased answer choice with the answer choices, **eliminate** answer choices that clearly conflict with your pre-phrased answer.

4.   By now, you should hopefully have two, maybe three answer choices left over. Take a look at the **second word** in each answer choice, separately. What do these words mean outside of the LSAT? What are their dictionary definitions? Which one is a better description of the author's feelings in the passage? Rank the remaining answer choices in terms of preferability based on the second word alone.

5.   Now, look at the **first word** of each remaining answer choice. Repeat Step 4 for the first word. Which answer choice is a more suitable description of the author's feelings? Pick that answer choice.

Let's look at a few Author's Attitude Questions:

PT32 S2 Q25 (PT32 Passage 4)

Most scientists who study the physiological effects of alcoholic beverages have assumed that wine, like beer or distilled spirits, is a drink whose only active ingredient is alcohol. Because of this assumption, these scientists have rarely investigated the effects of wine as distinct from other forms of alcoholic beverages. Nevertheless, unlike other alcoholic beverages, wine has for centuries been thought to have healthful effects that these scientists—who not only make no distinction among wine, beer, and distilled spirits but also study only the excessive or abusive intake of these beverages—have obscured.

Recently, a small group of researchers has questioned this assumption and investigated the effects of moderate wine consumption. While alcohol has been shown conclusively to have negative physiological effects—for example, alcohol strongly affects the body's processing of lipids (fats and other substances including cholesterol), causing dangerous increases in the levels of these substances in the blood, increases that are a large contributing factor in the development of premature heart disease—the researchers found that absorption of alcohol into the bloodstream occurs much more slowly when subjects drink wine than when they drink distilled spirits. More remarkably, it was discovered that deaths due to premature heart disease in the populations of several European countries decreased dramatically as the incidence of moderate wine consumption increased. One preliminary study linked this effect to red wine, but subsequent research has shown identical results whether the wine was white or red. What could explain such apparently healthful effects?

For one thing, the studies show increased activity of a natural clot-breaking compound used by doctors to restore blood flow through blocked vessels in victims of heart disease. In addition, the studies of wine drinkers indicate increased levels of certain compounds that may help to prevent damage from high lipid levels. And although the link between lipid processing and premature heart disease is one of the most important discoveries in modern medicine, in the past 20 years researchers have found several additional important contributing factors. We now know that endothelial cell reactivity (which affects the thickness of the innermost walls of blood vessels) and platelet adhesiveness (which influences the degree to which platelets cause blood to clot) are each linked to the development of premature heart disease. Studies show that wine appears to have ameliorating effects on both of these factors: it decreases the thickness of the innermost walls of blood vessels, and it reduces platelet adhesiveness. One study demonstrated a decrease in platelet adhesiveness among individuals who drank large amounts of grape juice. This finding may be the first step in confirming speculation that the potentially healthful effects of moderate wine intake may derive from the concentration of certain natural compounds found in grapes and not present in other alcoholic beverages.

Based on the passage, the author's attitude toward the scientists discussed in the first paragraph can most accurately be described as

    A. highly enthusiastic
    B. tacitly approving
    C. grudgingly accepting
    D. overtly critical
    E. clearly outraged

We start by examining the question stem itself. The question is asking us what the author's attitude is toward the scientists discussed in the first paragraph. This is an obvious hint and we should start there.

Who are the scientists discussed in the first paragraph? What do they think, what have they said?

These are the scientists that study the physiological effects of alcoholic beverages. So what have they, according to the author, done?

As we see in the first paragraph, these scientists have "assumed" that wine has no active ingredients besides alcohol; they have "rarely investigated" the effects of wine; they "make no distinction" between wine and other alcoholic beverages; and they "have obscured" the healthful effects of wine.

I think this is ample enough to start with. Note that on this question, we are lucky that the author's attitude can be deciphered from the location already alluded to by the question (first paragraph). We just had to look at the first paragraph itself.

But sometimes the question is slightly tricker. Hypothetically, we can have a question that is asking us what the author thinks about the scientists mentioned in the first paragraph. But then the first, second, and third paragraphs are just neutrally describing what the scientists do and believe. The author's opinion is only expressed in the last paragraph. If that were the case, even though the question is asking about "scientists mentioned in the first paragraph," the key to answer such a question actually lies in the last paragraph. **So use the question stems to guide our reading and thinking, but don't be tied down by it.**

So what is our pre-phrased answer here? How does the author feel about these scientists? Our author clearly thinks that they have overlooked something super important (the healthful effects of wine). The author also sees flawed thinking and problems with the scientists' methodologies. Let's take a look at the answer choices.

    A.   *highly enthusiastic*

Right away, this can be eliminated.

    B.   *tacitly approving*

I do not like the word "approving." I don't think the author approves of these scientists. In fact, the whole passage is directed at pointing out something that these scientists have overlooked. I want an answer choice that holds a negative view towards the scientists.

    C.   *grudgingly accepting*

Again, the word "accepting" is problematic. The author dose not accept the view of these scientists. Maybe an argument can be made for the word "grudgingly," in the sense that the author is unhappy about the flaw in research, but for attitude questions, we need **both** words to match, not just one of them.

Having one word that seems okay and one word that is problematic is a trait that frequently appears in Attitude Question trap answer.

That's why we have been looking at the words **one at a time**. Because sometimes if we look at two words simultaneously, our mind ends up focusing on the word that seems okay and forgets about the problematic word. Look at both words separately, choose an answer choice only if both words match up.

    D.   *overtly critical*

Is the author critical? Yes. Are they doing it in an overt way? Meaning that they are explicitly expressing their criticism? Yes.

E.   clearly outraged

In the previous chapter we introduced a concept called the "**threshold of proof**." In order to select this answer choice we must find evidence of the author's "outrage" in the passage. Which statement suggests that they are furious? Which sentences are permeated with rage? It's not there.

That's why conservatively worded answer choices are **usually** preferable in not just Inference Questions, but also Attitude Questions. Conservatively worded answers have a lower threshold of proof, one that is more easily satisfied.

However, we must also take this on a case-by-case basis. Sometimes the author expresses a very strong opinion in the passage, in such cases we would have no qualms selecting a strongly worded answer choice.

D is the correct/best answer.

In recent years, a growing belief that the way society decides what to treat as true is controlled through largely unrecognized discursive practices has led legal reformers to examine the complex interconnections between narrative and law. In many legal systems, legal judgments are based on competing stories about events. Without having witnessed these events, judges and juries must validate some stories as true and reject others as false. This procedure is rooted in objectivism, a philosophical approach that has supported most Western legal and intellectual systems for centuries. Objectivism holds that there is a single neutral description of each event that is un-skewed by any particular point of view and that has a privileged position over all other accounts. The law's quest for truth, therefore, consists of locating this objective description, the one that tells what really happened, as opposed to what those involved thought happened. The serious flaw in objectivism is that there is no such thing as the neutral, objective observer. As psychologists have demonstrated, all observers bring to a situation a set of expectations, values, and beliefs that determine what the observers are able to see and hear. Two individuals listening to the same story will hear different things, because they emphasize those aspects that accord with their learned experiences and ignore those aspects that are dissonant with their view of the world. Hence there is never any escape in life or in law from selective perception, or from subjective judgments based on prior experiences, values, and beliefs.

The societal harm caused by the assumption of objectivist principles in traditional legal discourse is that, historically, the stories judged to be objectively true are those told by people who are trained in legal discourse, while the stories of those who are not fluent in the language of the law are rejected as false.

Legal scholars such as Patricia Williams, Derrick Bell, and Mari Matsuda have sought empowerment for the latter group of people through the construction of alternative legal narratives. Objectivist legal discourse systematically disallows the language of emotion and experience by focusing on cognition in its narrowest sense. These legal reformers propose replacing such abstract discourse with powerful personal stories. They argue that the absorbing, nonthreatening structure and tone of personal stories may convince legal insiders for the first time to listen to those not fluent in legal language. The compelling force of personal narrative can create a sense of empathy between legal insiders and people traditionally excluded from legal discourse and, hence, from power. Such alternative narratives can shatter the complacency of the legal establishment and disturb its tranquility. Thus, the engaging power of narrative might play a crucial, positive role in the process of legal reconstruction by overcoming differences in background and training and forming a new collectivity based on emotional empathy.

Which one of the following most accurately describes the author's attitude toward proposals to introduce personal stories into legal discourse?

  A. strongly opposed
  B. somewhat skeptical
  C. ambivalent
  D. strongly supportive
  E. unreservedly optimistic

Here, for this question, we are not led to a specific spot in the passage to start looking for evidence. So we are a lot more dependent on our existing understanding of the passage. What does the author think about introducing personal stories into legal discourse?

The first part of the passage deals with subjectivist vs. objectivist discourse, and the last paragraph brings up the idea of introducing personal stories into legal discourse. This is where we find the author's attitude toward these proposals, in the second half of the last paragraph:

> The compelling force of personal narrative **can create a sense of empathy** between legal insiders and people traditionally excluded from legal discourse and, hence, from power. Such alternative narratives **can shatter the complacency** of the legal establishment and disturb its tranquility. Thus, the engaging power of narrative **might** play a crucial, positive role in the process of legal reconstruction by overcoming differences in background and training and forming a new collectivity based on emotional empathy.

The author has a very positive view towards this practice. They think it will be beneficial. But simultaneously, this positivity is not unabashed. Notice the use of words like "can" and "might." So overall, I would say that the author expresses "balanced support" for this proposal.

    A. strongly opposed

This is the opposite of what we want.

    B. somewhat skeptical

Like A, this can also be eliminated.

    C. ambivalent

We know that the author supports the proposal. "Ambivalent" means that they don't really care. This can also be eliminated.

    D. strongly supportive

The author is definitely supportive, no issues with that. But is this support strong? I suppose that words like "can" or "might" suggests that the support is tempered and a little reserved? I would like to take a look at E before committing.

    E. unreservedly optimistic

E is worse than D. Sure the author is optimistic, they think introducing personal stories will be great. But the word "unreservedly" is a little too strong. "Unreservedly" means 100%, going all out, putting all your chips on red, etc.

So D is the best answer choice here. I would have preferred an answer that had said "balanced support," or "reasoned support," but there is nothing wrong with "strongly" either. You can "strongly support" something without going all out, I suppose. Either way, it came down to choosing between D and E, and D wins, hands down. This is another question where **more conservative language** won over strong language.

PT32 S2 Q15 (PT32 Passage 3)

In studying the autobiographies of Native Americans, most scholars have focused on as-told-to life histories that were solicited, translated, recorded, and edited by non-Native American collaborators—that emerged from "bicultural composite authorship." Limiting their studies to such written documents, these scholars have overlooked traditional, preliterate modes of communicating personal history. In addition, they have **failed to address** the cultural constructs of the **highly diverse** Native American peoples, who prior to contact with nonindigenous cultures did not share with Europeans the same assumptions about self, life, and writing that underlie the concept of an autobiography— that indeed constitute the English word's root meaning.

The idea of self was, in a number of pre-contact Native American cultures, **markedly inclusive**: identity was not merely individual, but also relational to a society, a specific landscape, and the cosmos. Within these cultures, the expression of life experiences tended to be oriented toward current events: with the participation of fellow tribal members, an individual person would articulate, re-enact, or record important experiences as the person lived them, a mode of autobiography **seemingly more fragmented** than the European custom of writing down the recollections of a lifetime. Moreover, expression itself was not a matter of writing but of language, which can include speech and signs. Oral autobiography comprised songs, chants, stories, and even the process whereby one repeatedly took on new names to reflect important events and deeds in one's life. Dance and drama could convey personal history; for example, the advent of a vision to one person might require the enactment of that vision in the form of a tribal pageant.

One can view as autobiographical the elaborate tattoos that symbolized a warrior's valorous deeds, and such artifacts as a decorated shield that communicated the accomplishments and aspirations of its maker, or a robe that was emblazoned with the pictographic history of the wearer's battles and was sometimes used in re-enactments. Also autobiographical, and indicative of high status within the tribe, would have been a tepee painted with symbolic designs to record the achievements and display the dreams or visions of its owner, who was often assisted in the painting by other tribal members.

A tribe would, then, have contributed to the individual's narrative not merely passively, by its social codes and expectations, but actively by joining in the expression of that narrative. Such intercultural collaboration may seem **alien to the European style** of autobiography, yet any autobiography is shaped by its creator's ideas about the audience for which it is intended; in this sense, autobiography is justly called a simultaneous individual story and cultural narrative. Autobiographical expressions by early Native Americans may additionally have been shaped by the cultural perspectives of the people who transmitted them.

Which one of the following phrases best conveys the author's attitude toward the earlier scholarship on Native American autobiographies that is mentioned in the passage?

    A. "failed to address"
    B. "highly diverse"
    C. "markedly inclusive"
    D. "seemingly more fragmented"
    E. "alien to the European style"

This question is slightly different from the previous questions that we have seen. Instead of having simple, straightforward descriptive words making up the answer choices, now we have actual phrases from the passage itself.

Our job, however; is still the same. We are still to identify the author's attitude from the passage itself and try to match it up with the closest answer choice.

So what is the author's attitude towards earlier Native American autobiographies?

The author shares their view on these works in the first paragraph:

> _Limiting_ their studies to such written documents, these scholars have _overlooked_ traditional, preliterate modes of communicating personal history. In addition, they have _failed to address_ the cultural constructs of the highly diverse Native American peoples…

The author finds these autobiographies limiting in scope, and overlooks significant factors that would contribute to a fully understanding of indigenous diversity. The author is clearly not satisfied with these works.

A.   "failed to address"

This answer is great for a number of reasons. First, it appears in the same sentence as where the author's actual attitude towards earlier autobiographies is actually expressed in the passage. Two, it's one of the key phrases that we have marked out as implying the author's attitude.

The earlier autobiographies "failed to address" the complexity histories and cultural methods alien to Europeans but native to Indigenous peoples.

B.   "highly diverse"

Does the author think these works to be highly diverse? No, they think them to be not diverse enough as they (the works) express a purely Eurocentric perspective.

C.   "markedly inclusive"

Does the author think of these works as markedly inclusive? No, on the contrary, these earlier autobiographies exclude Indigenous views and expressions.

D.   "seemingly more fragmented"

This is talking about the Indigenous style of narration, rather than the European style of autobiographies.

E.   "alien to the European style"

Opposite answer, the earlier style is the European style .

A is the correct/best answer.

Organization

We now turn to Organization Questions. Organization Questions are straightforward in the sense that they are testing us on the relationship between individual paragraphs within a passage; and in some rarer questions, on the relationships between different sentences within a paragraph.

The ardent student will have noticed that this formed a majority of the discussion back in Chapters 2 and 3. In Chapter 2, we looked at how to break down an individual paragraph, how to find the key point of that paragraph, isolate that key point's supporting elements, thinking about individual paragraphs as a mini LR argument in its own. In Chapter 3, we took what we learned in Chapter 2 and applied it to the passage as a whole. We came up with the Main Point of the Passage and we thought about the role each paragraph played in relation to that MP. Which paragraph is background information? Which paragraph is presenting the opponents' view? Which paragraph is supporting the Main Point?

For Organization Questions, there are two main areas of difficulty:

In the first place, it's hard for many students to keep track of what each paragraph talked about. We end up forgetting what we've just read as soon as we launch into the next paragraph. Secondly, in some cases, we may not be able to decipher clearly what a paragraph is talking about. It may contain too many details or not have a clearly stated key point. As a result, we have trouble trying to summarize it or trying to find its role.

There are two things that we can do to remedy these difficulties. The first is **active recall**. When we are trying to actively recall something, we are essentially training our short-term memory to quickly recollect something that we have just read. Basically, when you are reading either an RC passage or external readings recommended at the end of this book, every time you finish a paragraph, put the book/passage down and immediately ask yourself, "what did I just read?"

This will be difficult initially, but the more you practice the more efficient you will get. Ultimately, you will be able to read a paragraph, immediately come up with a one sentence that best expresses what you've just read, keep that in mind and move to the next paragraph.

The second thing we can do is to **take notes** as we read. Writing things down forces us to confront our fuzzy thoughts and really express them in a coherent manner. I was able to gradually improve my ability to process and vocalize what I have just read via note taking. Initially I would have very detailed notes which took me a long time to write, but as my reading ability improved, I needed to write down less and less, as I was able to keep more and more in my head.

Organization Questions' answer choices can also be tricky because the correct answer often hinges on a minor detail. So focusing on the answer choices and their associated keywords is crucial. Ask yourself whether the things being described in the answer choice **really happen** in the passage? Do they occur in the **sequence** described in the answer choice? (Take a look at the Role Questions Chapter in LR Perfection for additional drills on how to extract information from abstract answer choices.)

PT25 S1 Q13 (PT25 Passage 2)

While a new surge of critical interest in the ancient Greek poems conventionally ascribed to Homer has taken place in the last twenty years or so, it was nonspecialists rather than professional scholars who studied the poetic aspects of the Iliad and the Odyssey between, roughly, 1935 and 1970. During these years, while such nonacademic intellectuals as Simone Weil and Erich Auerbach were trying to define the qualities that made these epic accounts of the Trojan War and its aftermath great poetry, the questions that occupied the specialists were directed elsewhere: "Did the Trojan War really happen?" "Does the bard preserve Indo- European folk memories?" "How did the poems get written down?" Something was driving scholars away from the actual works to peripheral issues. Scholars produced books about archaeology, and gift exchange in ancient societies, about the development of oral poetry, about virtually anything except the Iliad and the Odyssey themselves as unique reflections or distillations of life itself—as, in short, great poetry. The observations of the English poet Alexander Pope seemed as applicable in 1970 as they had been when he wrote them in 1715: according to Pope, the remarks of critics "are rather Philosophical, Historical, Geographical . . . or rather anything than Critical and Poetical."

Ironically, the modern manifestation of this "nonpoetical" emphasis can be traced to the profoundly influential work of Milman Parry, who attempted to demonstrate in detail how the Homeric poems, believed to have been recorded nearly three thousand years ago, were the products of a long and highly developed tradition of oral poetry about the Trojan War. Parry proposed that this tradition built up its diction and its content by a process of constant accumulation and refinement over many generations of storytellers. But after Parry's death in 1935, his legacy was taken up by scholars who, unlike Parry, forsook intensive analysis of the poetry itself and focused instead on only one element of Parry's work: the creative limitations and possibilities of oral composition, concentrating on fixed elements and inflexibilities, focusing on the things that oral poetry allegedly can and cannot do. The dryness of this kind of study drove many of the more inventive scholars away from the poems into the rapidly developing field of Homer's archaeological and historical background.

Appropriately, Milman Parry's son Adam was among those scholars responsible for a renewed interest in Homer's poetry as literary art. Building on his father's work, the younger Parry argued that the Homeric poems exist both within and against a tradition. The Iliad and the Odyssey were, Adam Parry thought, the beneficiaries of an inherited store of diction, scenes, and concepts, and at the same time highly individual works that surpassed these conventions. Adam Parry helped prepare the ground for the recent Homeric revival by affirming his father's belief in a strong inherited tradition, but also by emphasizing Homer's unique contributions within that tradition.

Which one of the following best describes the organization of the passage?

A. A situation is identified and its origins are examined.
B. A series of hypotheses is reviewed and one is advocated.
C. The works of two influential scholars are summarized.
D. Several issues contributing to a current debate are summarized.
E. Three possible solutions to a long-standing problem are posed.

If we were to summarize each paragraph with one sentence, it would probably look something like this:

- Paragraph 1: Critics gradually moved away from literary analysis of the Homeric epics and focused on the non-poetic elements of Homeric poetry in the twentieth century.
- Paragraph 2: This phenomenon occurred as predecessors of Milman Perry focused on only one aspect of his analysis, and this drove away a lot of scholars from poetic analysis.
- Paragraph 3: Perry's son led a interest revival in the poetic elements of Homer's poetry.

To put it abstractly, the first paragraph describes a phenomenon, the second paragraph explains what caused its occurrence, and the last paragraph describes its resolution.

A.   *A situation is identified and its origins are examined.*

This answer covers paragraphs 1 and 2. The return of interest in the poetic elements of Homeric poems as described in the last paragraph isn't mentioned. As a result, this answer choice is incomplete. But an incomplete answer is not automatic grounds for dismissal, as we saw in Chapter 8.

I don't love it, but let's keep it for now.

B.   *A series of hypotheses is reviewed and one is advocated.*

A "hypothesis" is an explanatory theory that is proposed but not yet backed up by experimental evidence.

A great tactic that I like to use when comparing answer choices is something called "**reverse confirmation.**"

Essentially, in a question where the answer is derived from the passage, we look at each answer choice, and ask ourselves this:

if this was indeed the correct answer choice, and I was designing the perfect passage to fit this answer, what would that passage look like?"

In this case, we would have a passage that gives us several hypotheses, each one is talked about in detail. Finally, the author choses one over the others. In the context of this passage, the ideal passage for answer choice B would look something like this:

Paragraph 1: Critics no longer studying the poetic elements of Homer
Paragraph 2: Maybe its because of A (hypothesis A is reviewed)
Paragraph 3: Maybe its because of B (hypothesis B is reviewed)
Paragraph 4: We believe it's because of A (hypothesis A is advocated)

The structure proposed by B is very different from the passage in reality.

C.   *The works of two influential scholars are summarized.*

If this was the correct answer, the passage would probably be a summary of Milman's works; and then Adam's works.

D.   *Several issues contributing to a current debate are summarized.*

Is there a "current debate" present in the passage? We know that in the present day (current), there's a revival of interest in the poetic elements of Homer. But is there a debate between the old school critics and Adam Milman? If so I do not see it mentioned in the passage.

E. *Three possible solutions* to a long-standing problem are posed.

With Organization Questions, if you select an answer choice, you'd better be able to back it up with evidence. If the long standing problem was the loss of focus in Homer's poetic qualities, then what are the three solutions?

Furthermore, if this was the correct answer, then the passage would probably be organized thus:

Paragraph 1: Problem
Paragraph 2: Solution 1
Paragraph 3: Solution 2
Paragraph 4: Solution 3

Ultimately, answer choice A, although incomplete, is the closest to describing what actually happened in the passage. Answer choice A is the correct/best answer.

PT28 S4 Q25 (PT28 Passage 4)

As one of the most pervasive and influential popular arts, the movies feed into and off of the rest of the culture in various ways. In the United States, the star system of the mid-1920s—in which actors were placed under exclusive contract to particular Hollywood film studios—was a consequence of studios' discovery that the public was interested in actor's private lives, and that information about actors could be used to promote their films. Public relations agents fed the information to gossip columnists, whetting the public's appetite for the films—which, audiences usually discovered, had the additional virtue of being created by talented writers, directors, and producers devoted to the art of storytelling. The important feature of this relationship was not the benefit to Hollywood, but rather to the press; in what amounted to a form of cultural cross-fertilization, the press saw that they could profit from studios' promotion of new films.

Today this arrangement has mushroomed into an intricately interdependent mass-media entertainment industry. The faith by which this industry sustains itself is the belief that there is always something worth promoting. A vast portion of the mass media— television and radio interviews, magazine articles, even product advertisements—now does most of the work for Hollywood studios attempting to promote their movies. It does so not out of altruism but because it makes for good business: If you produce a talk show or edit a newspaper, and other media are generating public curiosity about a studio's forthcoming film, it would be unwise for you not to broadcast or publish something about the film, too, because the audience for your story is already guaranteed.

The problem with this industry is that it has begun to affect the creation of films as well as their promotion. Choices of subject matter and actors are made more and more frequently by studio executives rather than by producers, writers, or directors. This problem is often referred to simply as an obsession with turning a profit, but Hollywood movies have almost always been produced to appeal to the largest possible audience. The new danger is that, increasingly, profit comes only from exciting an audience's curiosity about a movie instead of satisfying its desire to have an engaging experience watching the film. When movies can pull people into theaters instantly on the strength of media publicity rather than relying on the more gradual process of word of mouth among satisfied moviegoers, then the intimate relationship with the audience—on which the vitality of all popular art depends—is lost. But studios are making more money than ever by using this formula, and for this reason it appears that films whose appeal is due not merely to their publicity value but to their ability to affect audiences emotionally will become increasingly rare in the U.S. film industry.

Which one of the following most accurately describes the organization of the passage?

    A. description of the origins of a particular aspect of a popular art; discussion of the present state of this aspect; analysis of a problem associated with this aspect; introduction of a possible solution to the problem

    B. description of the origins of a particular aspect of a popular art; discussion of the present state of this aspect; analysis of a problem associated with this aspect; suggestion of a likely consequence of the problem

    C. description of the origins of a particular aspect of a popular art; analysis of a problem associated with this aspect; introduction of a possible solution to the problem; suggestion of a likely consequence of the solution

    D. summary of the history of a particular aspect of a popular art; discussion of a problem that accompanied the growth of this aspect; suggestion of a likely consequence of the problem; appraisal of the importance of avoiding this consequence

    E. summary of the history of a particular aspect of a popular art; analysis of factors that contributed to the growth of this aspect; discussion of a problem that accompanied the growth of this aspect; appeal for assistance in solving the problem

This is a passage that we haven't seen before, so let's go through its content quickly:

As one of the most pervasive and influential popular arts, the <u>movies feed into and off of</u> the rest of the culture in various ways. In the United States, the <u>star system</u> of the mid-1920s—in which actors were placed under exclusive contract to particular Hollywood film studios—was a consequence of studios' discovery that the public was interested in actor's <u>private lives</u>, and that information about actors could be used to <u>promote their films</u>. Public relations agents fed the information to gossip columnists, whetting the public's appetite for the films—which, audiences usually discovered, had the additional virtue of being created by talented writers, directors, and producers devoted to the art of storytelling. The important feature of this relationship was not <u>the benefit</u> to Hollywood, but rather <u>to the press</u>; in what amounted to a form of cultural cross-fertilization, the press saw that they could profit from studios' promotion of new films.

The first paragraph introduces a relationship between movies and the press. Movie studios shared information about the stars' private lives to promote their films. The press benefited from these stories, and in turn brought publicity to the movies.

Today this arrangement has mushroomed into an intricately <u>interdependent mass-media entertainment industry</u>. The faith by which this industry sustains itself is the belief that there is always something worth promoting. A <u>vast portion of the mass media</u>— television and radio interviews, magazine articles, even product advertisements—now does most of the work for Hollywood studios attempting to <u>promote</u> their movies. It does so <u>not out of altruism</u> but because it makes for good business: If you produce a talk show or edit a newspaper, and other media are generating public curiosity about a studio's forthcoming film, it would be unwise for you not to broadcast or publish something about the film, too, because the audience for your story is already guaranteed.

Today, there's hundreds if not thousands of media outlets that promote Hollywood movies. This is done out of business interest.

The <u>problem</u> with this industry is that it has begun to <u>affect the creation</u> of films as well as their promotion. Choices of subject matter and actors are made more and more frequently by studio executives rather than by producers, writers, or directors. This problem is often referred to simply as an obsession with turning a profit, but Hollywood movies have almost always been produced to appeal to the largest possible audience. The <u>new danger</u> is that, increasingly, profit comes only from <u>exciting an audience's curiosity about a movie instead of satisfying its desire to have an engaging experience</u> watching the film. When movies can pull people into theaters instantly on the <u>strength of media publicity</u> rather than relying on the more gradual process of word of mouth among satisfied moviegoers, then the <u>intimate relationship</u> with the audience—on which the vitality of all popular art depends—<u>is lost</u>. But studios are making more money than ever by using this formula, and for this reason it appears that films whose appeal is due not merely to their publicity value but to their ability to affect audiences emotionally will become increasingly rare in the U.S. film industry.

Movies are more driven by marketing ability than by their own inherent qualities. This has led to a degradation of the relationship between movies and the audience. This is a negative effect of the massive marketing machine that has been built up around Hollywood.

So in short, I would argue that the MP of the passage is stressing how the media machine has hurt the inherent value of movies. As a result, the first paragraph retraces the origins of the mass media industry; the second paragraph talks about its current condition; and the last paragraph talks about the effect it has had on the movie industry.

Let's take a look at the answers:

    A.   *description of the origins of a particular aspect of a popular art; discussion of the present state of this aspect; analysis of a problem associated with this aspect; <u>introduction of a possible solution to the problem</u>*

The passage never provides a solution to the problem, everything else looks good though.

   B. *description of the origins of a particular aspect of a popular art; discussion of the present state of this aspect; analysis of a problem associated with this aspect; suggestion of a likely consequence of the problem*

Each of the statements can be matched up with what happened in the passage. The origins of mass media promotion of movies in the 1920s is discussed; how present-day media companies promote movies for profit is mentioned; how movies are being sold based on marketing rather than quality is mentioned; and lastly, movies suffering and losing the connection to the audience is mentioned as a likely consequence.

   C. *description of the origins of a particular aspect of a popular art; analysis of a problem associated with this aspect; introduction of a possible solution to the problem; suggestion of a likely consequence of the solution*

Again, no solution was introduced in the passage, neither was there a likely consequence of the solution mentioned.

   D. *summary of the history of a particular aspect of a popular art; discussion of a problem that accompanied the growth of this aspect; suggestion of a likely consequence of the problem; appraisal of the importance of avoiding this consequence*

"Appraisal" means to assess. So this last statement is talking about trying to "figure out how important it is to avoid the loss of the relationship between viewers and movies."

We know that the author thinks this to be a unfortunate consequence, but they never really talk about if and how important it is to avoid this consequence. This is close, but not as good as B.

   E. *summary of the history of a particular aspect of a popular art; analysis of factors that contributed to the growth of this aspect; discussion of a problem that accompanied the growth of this aspect; appeal for assistance in solving the problem*

The author did not appeal for assistance in the passage.

B is the correct answer.

***

As we saw in the last question, the correct answer consisted of four statements, but there were only three paragraphs in the passage. So obviously not every statement corresponds with a paragraph. But the sequence in which the statements were presented in the answer choice has to match up with the order in which these ideas appeared in the passage. Matching up the chronological order is important as well as matching up the content!

Occasionally, we get a question that asks us about the organization of a paragraph, rather than a passage. Let's take a look:

PT26 S4 Q17 (PT26 Passage 3)

Between June 1987 and May 1988, the bodies of at least 740 bottlenose dolphins out of a total coastal population of 3,000 to 5,000 washed ashore on the Atlantic coast of the United States. Since some of the dead animals never washed ashore, the overall disaster was presumably worse; perhaps 50 percent of the population died. A dolphin die-off of this character and magnitude had never before been observed; furthermore, the dolphins exhibited a startling range of symptoms. The research team that examined the die-off noted the presence of both skin lesions and internal lesions in the liver, lung, pancreas, and heart, which suggested a massive opportunistic bacterial infection of already weakened animals.

Tissues from the stricken dolphins were analyzed for a variety of toxins. Brevetoxin, a toxin produced by the blooming of the alga Ptychodiscus brevis, was present in eight out of seventeen dolphins tested. Tests for synthetic pollutants revealed that polychlorinated biphenyls (PCBs) were present in almost all animals tested.

The research team concluded that brevetoxin poisoning was the most likely cause of the illnesses that killed the dolphins. Although P. brevis is ordinarily not found along the Atlantic coast, an unusual bloom of this organism—such blooms are called "red tides" because of the reddish color imparted by the blooming algae— did occur in the middle of the affected coastline in October 1987. These researchers believe the toxin accumulated in the tissue of fish and then was ingested by dolphins that preyed on them. The emaciated appearance of many dolphins indicated that they were metabolizing their blubber reserves, thereby reducing their buoyancy and insulation (and adding to overall stress) as well as releasing stores of previously accumulated synthetic pollutants, such as PCBs, which further exacerbated their condition. The combined impact made the dolphins vulnerable to opportunistic bacterial infection, the ultimate cause of death.

For several reasons, however, this explanation is not entirely plausible. First, bottlenose dolphins and P. brevis red tides are both common in the Gulf of Mexico, yet no dolphin die-off of a similar magnitude has been noted there. Second, dolphins began dying in June, hundreds of miles north of and some months earlier than the October red tide bloom. Finally, the specific effects of brevetoxin on dolphins are unknown, whereas PCB poisoning is known to impair functioning of the immune system and liver and to cause skin lesions; all of these problems were observed in the diseased animals. An alternative hypothesis, which accounts for these facts, is that a sudden influx of pollutants, perhaps from offshore dumping, triggered a cascade of disorders in animals whose systems were already heavily laden with pollutants. Although brevetoxin may have been a contributing factor, the event that actually precipitated the die-off was a sharp increase in the dolphins' exposure to synthetic pollutants.

Which one of the following most accurately describes the organization of the last paragraph?

A. One explanation is criticized and a different explanation is proposed.
B. An argument is advanced and then refuted by means of an opposing argument.
C. Objections against a hypothesis are advanced, the hypothesis is explained more fully, and then the objections are rejected.
D. New evidence in favor of a theory is described, and then the theory is reaffirmed.
E. Discrepancies between two explanations are noted, and a third explanation is proposed.

Since the question is asking us about the structure of the last paragraph, let's take a look at that in detail:

For several reasons, however, this explanation is <u>not entirely plausible</u>. <u>First</u>, bottlenose dolphins and P. brevis red tides are both common in the Gulf of Mexico, yet no dolphin die-off of a similar magnitude has been noted there. <u>Second</u>, dolphins began dying in June, hundreds of miles north of and some months earlier than the October red tide bloom. <u>Finally</u>, the specific effects of brevetoxin on dolphins are unknown, whereas PCB poisoning is known to impair functioning of the immune system and liver and to cause skin lesions; all of these problems were observed in the diseased animals. <u>An alternative</u> hypothesis, which accounts for these facts, is that a sudden influx of pollutants, perhaps from offshore dumping, triggered a cascade of disorders in animals whose systems were already heavily laden with pollutants. Although brevetoxin may have been a contributing factor, the event that actually precipitated the die-off was a sharp increase in the dolphins' exposure to synthetic pollutants.

The author offers a different opinion: rather than brevetoxins being the main cause and PCBs being a minor cause, they thinks it's the opposite. PCBs are the main cause and perhaps brevetoxins were a contributing factor.

The author lists three reasons for this: first, algae blooms associated with brevetoxin spikes have happened before, but dolphins didn't die then. Second, the algae bloom started after the dolphins started to die. Lastly, we don't know how brevetoxins affect dolphins, but PCBs definitely can lead to the result we are seeing.

In short, the author disputes one cause for the die off of dolphins; the author then provides three reasons why that cause is not the real cause. The author then offers up an alternative cause as a hypothesis.

    A.   One <u>explanation</u> *is criticized and a different explanation is proposed.*

We know that in LR, the word "explanation" just means "causation." So what this answer is essentially saying is that the author is criticizing one cause and proposing a different cause.

Does this happen? Yes. Brevetoxin as a cause for the dolphin die off is criticized, and pollution is proposed as an alternative cause. Although this answer is not as detailed as our pre-phrased answer, it covers all the bases.

    B.   *An argument is <u>advanced</u> and then <u>refuted</u> by means of an <u>opposing argument</u>.*

There is certainly the possibility of a refutation happening in the paragraph. Although I still think that word is way too strong. A refutation basically means disproving an opponent's argument or position. I don't think the first explanation has been disproven, only weakened.

Secondly, the author rejects the Brevetoxin cause right away, no argument was advanced for it.

Finally, the author provides a hypothesis, rather than an opposing argument.

    C.   *Objections against a hypothesis are advanced, the hypothesis is explained more fully, <u>and then the objections are rejected.</u>*

The last paragraph doesn't defend the Brevetoxin hypothesis, rather, an alternative hypothesis is proposed.

    D.   *New <u>evidence</u> in favor of a theory is described, and then the theory is <u>reaffirmed</u>.*

If we wanted to fix up this answer choice, it would say: "old theory attacked, new theory proposed." To reaffirm something, it must have been proposed earlier. Instead, a new theory was proposed.

Further, it's debatable whether the support the author gave to the pollutants theory could be considered "evidence." What we have instead is a hypothesis.

    E.   *Discrepancies between two explanations are noted, and a <u>third</u> explanation is proposed.*

Only two explanations here, one is rejected in favor of an alternative.

***

For this question, I think the biggest takeaway would be to carefully read the keywords that appear in each answer choice. Think about what they mean, specifically on the LSAT.

Practice the art of **keyword extraction**. Take a look at the chapter on Role Questions in LR Perfection, it includes many drills that deals exclusively with taking apart abstract answer choices and deciphering the meaning behind certain keywords.

Summary

Like the According to the Passage and Inference Questions we have seen, the first step to solving **Attitude Questions** would be to discover the relevant parts of a passage that can help us answer the question. Sometimes we get lucky and the question will give us a hint, other times we have to rely on our memory of the passage and our grasp of its details. Being able to locate the details, words, and phrases that shed light upon the author's views and feelings is crucial to solving this type of question. *Again, if your reading ability is not up to standard, you will have a hard time with these questions, regardless of how clear you are on the steps needed to tackle this question type.*

We follow a multi-step process to solve these questions. We start by locating the relevant materials in the passage, followed by pre-phrasing what the correct answer might look like. Then we try to eliminate the obviously mistaken answer choices, the ones that are either out of scope, or the opposite of what we want. Finally, we take the remaining answer choices and think about the suitability of each word of that answer choice. Beware of half right half wrong answers. All the words have to match up for the correct answer.

Sometimes the correct answer might not match up exactly with your anticipated answer. Fear not, pick the answer choice that is closest in meaning to your pre-phrased answer. Also be aware that without explicit support from the passage, conservatively worded answers are usually the safer bet.

***

Organization Questions test your ability to recall the role each paragraph plays relative to the Passage's Main Point. For these questions, our job is to know what each paragraph talked about, and if and how they advanced the author's argument.

Practice information recall and notetaking during reading, and our ability to pre-phrase the correct answer for these questions will improve drastically.

Finally, Role Questions from the Logical Reasoning Section can serve as an invaluable source of inspiration for Organization Questions, both in teaching us how to think about the relationship between paragraphs and the passage as a whole, as well as helping us decipher hard to understand answer choices.

12. Restricted Scope Questions

POV Questions

Definition Questions

Principle Questions

Title Questions

Assumption Questions

Continue the Passage Questions

Restricted Scope vs. Unrestricted Scope

We have already looked at the most common questions to appear in the RC section. We looked at multiple variations of the Purpose Question, the Main Point Question, According to the Passage/MBT Questions, and Inference/MSS Questions. These four question types are present in nearly every passage and together, form just over half of all the questions to appear in the RC section.

We then looked at Organization and Author's Attitude Questions. These two question types, while less common than the "big four," are still nonetheless frequent. Moreover, these questions can be solved in a relatively straightforward manner if we have an in-depth grasp of the passage. If we were aware of what each paragraph talked about, as well as how these points relate to the passage's Main Point, then we should have no problems with Organization Questions. Similarly, if we kept track of the details and keywords that gave us a hint of what the author thinks, then we should have no issues with Attitude Questions.

In the next two chapters, we will look at the rarer question types to appear in the RC section. There are 10 question types in total, and I've divided them into two camps: restricted scope and unrestricted scope questions.

"Scope" is a concept that we have discussed before, and it's something that we shall revisit again and again throughout this book. It's something that you are probably already very familiar with. The scope restricts what is being discussed from going off topic. It limits the topic that we are examining. If something is "out of scope," then it is either outside of the boundaries of what is being discussed, or it's a topic that is irrelevant.

For instance, if the passage was talking about common law in seventeenth century England, then any discussion about something else (common law in present day America, civil law in seventeenth century France, etc.) would be out of scope.

On the LSAT, scope is a concept that we examine in both the LR and RC sections. In LR and RC questions, an answer choice that's talking about something that was not mentioned in the stimulus/passage would be out of scope.

> Out of scope answer choices are ***not automatically wrong.*** Whether they are acceptable or not depends on the question type.

In LR, for instance, if the question type was "Find the Conclusion," then a out of scope answer choice will be unacceptable. If the stimulus was an argument about the benefits of wine drinking. Then an answer choice talking about the benefits of beer will automatically be wrong.

But in a Strengthen or Weaken Question, an out of scope answer is not automatic grounds for dismissal. If the argument was about how David is this super intelligent person because he scored a 180 on the LSAT, then an answer choice about David being a member of MENSA (the high IQ organization) would be an acceptable Strengthen answer, even though MENSA was never mentioned in the stimulus.

In RC, the idea is similar. For some questions, the correct answer must be derivable from the passage itself. Answer choices that have outside information appearing in them will be unacceptable. We call these "**restricted scope questions**." We will look at these in this chapter.

POV Questions

Point of View, or POV Questions, are a regular staple in RC. These questions will ask us for a particular view. This can either be the author's view, or a third party (someone else who was discussed in the passage) view.

The evidence for the correct answer choices **must** be derived from the passage itself. Sometimes there is explicit information backing up one of the answer choices, sometimes we need to make a reasonable leap as we have done in inference questions. The scope of the correct answer choice, in other words, is restricted.

POV Questions will usually look like this:

With which of the following would the author most likely agree with?

What is Tolstoy's view of historical determinism? (The hypothetical passage would have discussed both Tolstoy and historical determinism as well as Tolstoy's view towards historical determinism)

Author POV Questions

Author POV Questions are similar to Author's Attitude Questions in the sense that we have to think about what the author thinks and how the author feels about a particular topic for both question types. But while the Author's Attitude Questions ask us to describe the author's feelings in a string of adjectives; Author POV Questions will actually ask us to locate what the author actually thinks, in detail.

I like to think of these questions as a hybrid of Author's Attitude Questions and Inference Questions. First, we need to be able to locate the author's voice from the passage. Second, we need to find the correct answer by comparing the answer choices to the textual support that we have located.

These questions can be difficult if we are not proficient at locating the details that indicate the author's view or stance. The author's position can usually be inferred from their tone, use of words, and argument/purpose. But occasionally, we'll need to make an educated guess based on the limited evidence that we have.

PT33 S2 Q19 (PT33 Passage 3)

Experts anticipate that global atmospheric concentrations of carbon dioxide (CO_2) will have doubled by the end of the twenty-first century. It is known that CO_2 can contribute to global warming by trapping solar energy that is being reradiated as heat from the Earth's surface. However, some research has suggested that elevated CO_2 levels could enhance the photosynthetic rates of plants, resulting in a lush world of agricultural abundance, and that this CO_2 fertilization effect might eventually decrease the rate of global warming. The increased vegetation in such an environment could be counted on to draw more CO_2 from the atmosphere. The level of CO_2 would thus increase at a lower rate than many experts have predicted.

However, while a number of recent studies confirm that plant growth would be generally enhanced in an atmosphere rich in CO_2, they also suggest that increased CO_2 would differentially increase the growth rate of different species of plants, which could eventually result in decreased agricultural yields. Certain important crops such as corn and sugarcane that currently have higher photosynthetic efficiencies than other plants may lose that edge in an atmosphere rich in CO_2. Patterson and Flint have shown that these important crops may experience yield reductions because of the increased performance of certain weeds. Such differences in growth rates between plant species could also alter ecosystem stability. Studies have shown that within rangeland regions, for example, a weedy grass grows much better with plentiful CO_2 than do three other grasses. Because this weedy grass predisposes land to burning, its potential increase may lead to greater numbers of and more severe wildfires in future rangeland communities.

It is clear that the CO_2 fertilization effect does not guarantee the lush world of agricultural abundance that once seemed likely, but what about the potential for the increased uptake of CO_2 to decrease the rate of global warming? Some studies suggest that the changes accompanying global warming will not improve the ability of terrestrial ecosystems to absorb CO_2. Billings' simulation of global warming conditions in wet tundra grasslands showed that the level of CO_2 actually increased. Plant growth did increase under these conditions because of warmer temperatures and increased CO_2 levels. But as the permafrost melted, more peat (accumulated dead plant material) began to decompose. This process in turn liberated more CO_2 to the atmosphere. Billings estimated that if summer temperatures rose four degrees Celsius, the tundra would liberate 50 percent more CO_2 than it does currently. In a warmer world, increased plant growth, which could absorb CO_2 from the atmosphere, would not compensate for this rapid increase in decomposition rates. This observation is particularly important because high-latitude habitats such as the tundra are expected to experience the greatest temperature increase.

The author would be most likely to agree with which one of the following statements about the conclusions drawn on the basis of the research on plant growth mentioned in the first paragraph of the passage?

A. The conclusions are correct in suggesting that increased levels of CO_2 will increase the photosynthetic rates of certain plants.
B. The conclusions are correct in suggesting that increased levels of CO_2 will guarantee abundances of certain important crops.
C. The conclusions are correct in suggesting that increased plant growth will reverse the process of global warming.
D. The conclusions are incorrect in suggesting that enhanced plant growth could lead to abundances of certain species of plants.
E. The conclusions are incorrect in suggesting that vegetation can draw CO_2 from the atmosphere.

The question is asking us about the author's POV regarding a specific topic. These questions are easier to approach because they give us a hint as to where to start searching.

We are asked how the author feels about the "*conclusions drawn on the basis of the research on plant growth mentioned in the first paragraph.*"

Think about this question, in order to solve it, we actually have to do so in three steps:

1. What does the research on plant growth say in the first paragraph?
2. What is the conclusion drawn based on this research? Is the conclusion also in the first paragraph?
3. What is the author's view of this conclusion? Where is the author's view presented in the passage?

So even though the question is sending us to look for textual support starting in the first paragraph, the actual evidence needed to solve this question might be elsewhere.

So what does the first paragraph tell us about the research on plant growth?

some research has suggested that elevated CO2 levels could enhance the photosynthetic rate of plants, resulting in a lush world of agricultural abundance, and that this CO2 fertilization effect might eventually decrease the rate of global warming...increased vegetation...level of CO2 would thus increase at a lower rate...

So the research is essentially telling us that

More CO2 $\Rightarrow$ Faster Photosynthesis $\Rightarrow$ More Vegetation $\Rightarrow$ Lower Global Warming + Slowed Increase of CO2

The conclusion of the research appears to be that elevated CO2 levels could lower global warming rates and slow down the growth of CO2 levels.

What does the author think about all this?

They aren't buying it. We see this in the last paragraph. The author thinks that the CO2 fertilization effect will lead to neither "*the lush world of agricultural abundance that once seemed likely,*" nor would increased plant growth "*compensate for this rapid increase in decomposition rates.*"

Again, like we said, even though the question stem is asking about something in the first paragraph, the potential evidence for the question is actually in the last paragraph. So my anticipated answer for this question would be that "the author disagrees with the conclusions drawn based on research presented in the first paragraph."

A. *The conclusions are <u>correct</u> in suggesting that increased levels of CO2 will increase the photosynthetic rates of <u>certain plants</u>.*

Initially, I wanted to eliminate this answer choice because we know that the author disagrees with the overall conclusions drawn in the first paragraph. But as always, we need to read the answer to see what it's actually saying.

Did the experts anticipate an increase in the photosynthetic rates of certain plants? Yes. Does the author agree with this? The author's beliefs are more nuanced. On the one hand, the author doesn't think that important plants like corn and sugarcane would benefit; but on the other hand, the author claims that harmful weeds would benefit from increased photosynthetic rates.

So judging from just the text of this answer choice, it isn't wrong *per se*. Let's see if there is a better choice lurking around.

B. *The conclusions are correct in suggesting that increased levels of CO2 will guarantee abundances of certain important crops.*

This does not match the author's beliefs. The author argues the opposite. Increased levels of CO2 would hurt important crops because they actually benefit weeds.

C. *The conclusions are correct in suggesting that increased plant growth will reverse the process of global warming.*

This is also the opposite of what the author is claiming. Increased plant growth resulting from warmer temperatures and higher levels of CO2 did absorb some CO2, but higher temperatures led to permafrost melting, which released even greater amounts of CO2, which ultimately led to even greater global warming.

D. *The conclusions are incorrect in suggesting that enhanced plant growth could lead to abundances of <u>certain species</u> of plants.*

Enhanced plant growth would lead to an abundance of weeds. The problem with this answer choice is that we don't know what "certain species of plants is referring to."

The author would agree that enhanced plant growth would lead to an abundance of weeds, but hurt beneficial crops. In order for us to select this answer, the author must hold the belief that *"enhanced plant growth could NOT lead to abundances of certain species of plants."*

As a result, this answer is unclear.

E. *The conclusions are incorrect in suggesting that vegetation can draw CO2 from the atmosphere.*

The author agrees with the view, the author's actual belief is that even though vegetation can draw CO2 from the atmosphere, it's not enough to offset the increased CO2 released from the permafrost/tundra.

Let's take a look at answer choice A again:

The conclusions are <u>correct</u> in suggesting that increased levels of CO2 will increase the photosynthetic rates of <u>certain plants</u>.

Would the author agree with this? Yes, the author would say that "I agree that increased levels of CO2 would increase the photosynthetic rates of certain plants, such as weeds"

This was a really tricky question, and I think what ultimately helped me get this question right were the habits developed in LR. Back in the Chapter on Role Questions in LR Perfection, we saw how sometimes the correct answer did not match up with our pre-phrased answer; but rather, was correct simply because we could find no fault with its wording.

It's the same thing here. We anticipated an answer that told us the author disagreed with the conclusion. But instead we got an answer that told us that the author agreed with an aspect of the opponent's claim. The opposing experts claimed that increased CO2 would lead to an abundance of plants. The author would respond and say, "yes, but not the plants you think: increased CO2 would lead to an abundance of weeds."

PT38 S3 Q23 (PT38 Passage 4)

One of the greatest challenges facing medical students today, apart from absorbing volumes of technical information and learning habits of scientific thought, is that of remaining empathetic to the needs of patients in the face of all this rigorous training. Requiring students to immerse themselves completely in medical coursework risks disconnecting them from the personal and ethical aspects of doctoring, and such strictly scientific thinking is insufficient for grappling with modern ethical dilemmas. For these reasons, aspiring physicians need to develop new ways of thinking about and interacting with patients. Training in ethics that takes narrative literature as its primary subject is one method of accomplishing this.

Although training in ethics is currently provided by medical schools, this training relies heavily on an abstract, philosophical view of ethics. Although the conceptual clarity provided by a traditional ethics course can be valuable, theorizing about ethics contributes little to the understanding of everyday human experience or to preparing medical students for the multifarious ethical dilemmas they will face as physicians. A true foundation in ethics must be predicated on an understanding of human behavior that reflects a wide array of relationships and readily adapts to various perspectives, for this is what is required to develop empathy. Ethics courses drawing on narrative literature can better help students prepare for ethical dilemmas precisely because such literature attaches its readers so forcefully to the concrete and varied world of human events.

The act of reading narrative literature is uniquely suited to the development of what might be called flexible ethical thinking. To grasp the development of characters, to tangle with heightening moral crises, and to engage oneself with the story not as one's own but nevertheless as something recognizable and worthy of attention, readers must use their moral imagination. Giving oneself over to the ethical conflicts in a story requires the abandonment of strictly absolute, inviolate sets of moral principles. Reading literature also demands that the reader adopt another person's point of view—that of the narrator or a character in a story— and thus requires the ability to depart from one's personal ethical stance and examine moral issues from new perspectives.

It does not follow that readers, including medical professionals, must relinquish all moral principles, as is the case with situational ethics, in which decisions about ethical choices are made on the basis of intuition and are entirely relative to the circumstances in which they arise. Such an extremely relativistic stance would have as little benefit for the patient or physician as would a dogmatically absolutist one. Fortunately, the incorporation of narrative literature into the study of ethics, while serving as a corrective to the latter stance, need not lead to the former. But it can give us something that is lacking in the traditional philosophical study of ethics—namely, a deeper understanding of human nature that can serve as a foundation for ethical reasoning and allow greater flexibility in the application of moral principles.

It can be inferred from the passage that the author would most likely agree with which one of the following statements?

A. The heavy load of technical coursework in today's medical schools often keeps them from giving adequate emphasis to courses in medical ethics.
B. Students learn more about ethics through the use of fiction than through the use of nonfictional readings.
C. The traditional method of ethical training in medical schools should be supplemented or replaced by more direct practical experience with real-life patients in ethically difficult situations.
D. The failings of an abstract, philosophical training in ethics can be remedied only by replacing it with a purely narrative-based approach.
E. Neither scientific training nor traditional philosophical ethics adequately prepares doctors to deal with the emotional dimension of patients' needs.

Another passage that we have already seen at the beginning of the book. Let's jump straight to the answer choices.

A. *The heavy load of technical coursework in today's medical schools often keeps them from giving adequate emphasis to courses in medical ethics.*

This is a tricky answer, it builds an **unwarranted connection** between two concepts that are both mentioned in the passage. Yes, there's a lot of technical coursework; and yes, the training in ethics is inadequate; but it's not the former resulting in the latter.

B. *Students learn more about ethics through the use of fiction than through the use of nonfictional readings.*

This is too much of an extrapolation. The passage talks about the benefits of using narrative as a form of ethics training. Narrative literature is unique and offers special benefits. But the author doesn't say it's a *better tool* than nonfictional readings.

C. *The traditional method of ethical training in medical schools should be <u>supplemented or replaced</u> by <u>more direct practical experience</u> with real-life patients in ethically difficult situations.*

"Supplement" is good, "replace" isn't. But since the answer choice is saying "supplemented OR replaced," I guess that's ok.

A bigger concern is the talk about "more direct practical experience." This is out of scope. The passage is advocating the use of narrative literature, rather than hands on clinical experience.

D. *The failings of an abstract, philosophical training in ethics can be remedied <u>only by</u> replacing it with a purely narrative-based approach.*

This is too much, the author never said a purely narrative based approach is the only way, just that it's one way help.

E. *Neither scientific training nor traditional philosophical ethics adequately prepares doctors to deal with the emotional dimension of patients' needs.*

The passage talks about the need to remain empathetic to the needs of the patients, and that's why the author recommended a narrative literature based approach. If the scientific training or traditional training in ethics were adequate, then we wouldn't need a new approach, right?

This answer choice's truthfulness, while not backed up by a specific sentence from the passage, is nonetheless inferable from a synthesis of information from the passage, as well as being in line with the text's general theme.

Compare this to answer choice A from the previous passage. The correct answer choice from the previous passage is **explicitly backed** by a statement from the passage, while this answer needs to be **inferred**. Both are valid methods to derive the correct answer for Author POV Questions.

Another feature of this question is that we couldn't really anticipate what the answer choice might look like or know where to look for the relevant materials from the passage before we looked at the answer choices. We had to check each answer choice, consider it on its own merits, and go back to the passage five times to check for support. As a result, this type of Author POV Questions are much more time consuming.

Third-Party POV Questions

We now look at Third Party POV Questions. Similar to Author POV Questions, we are being asked what someone's position is regarding something specific. But unlike Author POV Questions, the person that we are concerned with is someone who is mentioned in the passage, but isn't the author.

I find these questions easier than Author POV Questions because the locations where you can go look for relevant evidence to confirm/reject answer choices are much more limited. If the question is asking about what A thinks, then we don't need to look at the areas in the passage where it's talking about what B's position is. So for these questions, I would start by reading the question stem and try to think about what it's asking of me. Then I would go into the passage and try to isolate/highlight all the bits and pieces that are describing what the subject's views are. Thirdly I would either pre-phrase an answer if I can, or start eliminating answer choices if I cannot.

A primary source of difficulty for Third Party POV Questions occurs when the passage discusses multiple parties in quick succession, or scatters the views of one speaker throughout the entire passage. This makes the relevant details difficult to locate. We may easily overlook a piece of crucial evidence or confuse the person of interest with someone else.

Second, the structure of the passage can be a source of misdirection when approaching these questions. For example, perhaps the majority of the discussion about a certain speaker and their views are located in paragraph 3, with only a brief mention of one of their views in the first paragraph. Naturally, we spend our time re-reading paragraph 3 in order to derive the correct answer. Ironically, the correct answer was based on the seemingly insignificant piece of evidence all the way back in paragraph 1.

PT30 S3 Q18 (PT30 Passage 3)

Philosopher Denise Meyerson views the Critical Legal Studies (CLS) movement as seeking to debunk orthodox legal theory by exposing its contradictions. However, Meyerson argues that CLS proponents tend to see contradictions where none exist, and that CLS overrates the threat that conflict poses to orthodox legal theory.

According to Meyerson, CLS proponents hold that the existence of conflicting values in the law implies the absence of any uniquely right solution to legal cases. CLS argues that these conflicting values generate equally plausible but opposing answers to any given legal question, and, consequently, that the choice between the conflicting answers must necessarily be arbitrary or irrational. Meyerson denies that the existence of conflicting values makes a case irresolvable, and asserts that at least some such cases can be resolved by ranking the conflicting values. For example, a lawyer's obligation to preserve a client's confidences may entail harming other parties, thus violating moral principle. This conflict can be resolved if it can be shown that in certain cases the professional obligation overrides ordinary moral obligations.

In addition, says Meyerson, even when the two solutions are equally compelling, it does not follow that the choice between them must be irrational. On the contrary, a solution that is not rationally required need not be unreasonable. Meyerson concurs with another critic that instead of concentrating on the choice between two compelling alternatives, we should rather reflect on the difference between both of these answers on the one hand, and some utterly unreasonable answer on the other—such as deciding a property dispute on the basis of which claimant is louder. The acknowledgment that conflicting values can exist, then, does not have the far-reaching implications imputed by CLS; even if some answer to a problem is not the only answer, opting for it can still be reasonable.

Last, Meyerson takes issue with the CLS charge that legal formalism, the belief that there is a quasi- deductive method capable of giving solutions to problems of legal choice, requires objectivism, the belief that the legal process has moral authority. Meyerson claims that showing the law to be unambiguous does not demonstrate its legitimacy: consider a game in which participants compete to steal the item of highest value from a shop; while a person may easily identify the winner in terms of the rules, it does not follow that the person endorses the rules of the game. A CLS scholar might object that legal cases are unlike games, in that one cannot merely apply the rules without appealing to, and therefore endorsing, **external considerations** of purpose, policy, and value. But Meyerson replies that such considerations may be viewed as part of, not separate from, the rules of the game.

It can be inferred from the passage that Meyerson would be most likely to agree with which one of the following statements about "external considerations"?

A. How one determines the extent to which these considerations are relevant depends on one's degree of belief in the legal process.
B. The extent to which these considerations are part of the legal process depends on the extent to which the policies and values can be endorsed.
C. When these considerations have more moral authority than the law, the former should outweigh the latter.
D. If one uses these considerations in determining a legal solution, one is assuming that the policies and values are desirable.
E. Whether these considerations are separate from or integral to the legal process is a matter of debate.

Here, we are concerned with what Meyerson thinks, rather than what the author thinks. Luckily, the question is very specific. The term in question (external considerations) appear in the last paragraph of the passage. That's where we shall start our search:

> Meyerson claims that showing the law to be unambiguous does not demonstrate its legitimacy: consider a game in which participants compete to steal the item of highest value from a shop; while a person may easily identify the winner in terms of the rules, it does not follow that the person endorses the rules of the game. A CLS scholar might object that legal cases are unlike games, in that one cannot merely apply the rules without appealing to, and therefore endorsing, **external considerations** of purpose, policy, and value. But Meyerson replies that such considerations may be viewed as part of, not separate from, the rules of the game.

CLS scholars argue that if you believe the law to be a system of rules that follows logic, you are endorsing the legal system's moral authority. Meyerson states that this is not necessarily the case. According to Meyerson, you can be clear about the rules of a game without agreeing that it's a good game.

Meyerson, in other words, is separating understanding the rules of the game from endorsing the game. CLS scholars would respond by saying even though the two are separable for games, they are not separable for laws. If you are applying the law, you are endorsing the values and policies behind that piece of legislation.

But for Meyerson, these so called "external considerations" are not external at all. They "may be viewed" as a part of the rules. "Purpose, policy, and value" are all part of the law itself.

So Meyerson's view towards these "external considerations" would be that they are not actually external considerations after all. They are an internal part of the law.

Another thing that I would note is the language Meyerson uses: "*such considerations may be viewed as part of the rules of the game.*" This is rather weak language at best, so I would be careful of strongly worded answer choices.

A. *How one determines the extent to which these considerations are relevant depends on one's degree of belief in the legal process.*

For Meyerson, these considerations may be considered a part of the legal process. We don't have to believe in the legal process in order to apply the rules, nor determine how relevant these considerations are.

B. *The extent to which these considerations are part of the legal process depends on the extent to which the policies and values can be endorsed.*

Again, Meyerson simply states that they can be considered a part of the legal process. Meyerson did talk about "endorsement," but in the context that you can apply the law without endorsing it.

C. *When these considerations have more moral authority than the law, the former should outweigh the latter.*

There is no comparison between the law and the considerations and which is more important.

D. *If one uses these considerations in determining a legal solution, one is assuming that the policies and values are desirable.*

This is probably closer to the CLS view. They believe that these considerations are inseparable from the law, and that if you apply the law, you are endorsing the policies.

E. Whether these considerations are separate from or integral to the legal process is a matter of debate.

This is literally a paraphrase of the last sentence of the passage. CLS scholars think these considerations are separate from the legal process, calling them "external considerations." Meyerson, on the other hand; says that they <u>may be</u> considered a part of the game. (i.e. integral to the legal process)

Not a great answer, but the only answer that is remotely supported by the text.

Again, as always, chose the answer choice that has the most direct support from the passage, support that you can point to.

Only when such an answer choice doesn't exist, are we permitted to infer and extrapolate on POV Questions.

Definition Questions

Definition Questions will ask us for the meaning of a word or phrase that appears in the passage. It's important to note that for these questions, the test makers want the meaning of the word **according to the passage**. In other words, what we need to find is the meaning of the word in the context of the passage. There is either an explicit definition given in the passage, or it's something that we need to figure out by reading the passage itself.

The dictionary definition, or surface meaning of the word can help us sometimes, but more often, the word will have a special connotation that is directly tied to how it is used in the passage. In other words, if the passage tells you that a "pig" is a giant bird that flies around, then that's the definition we need to pick from the answer choices. **I would only use real life knowledge to supplement what I have learned from the passage; and never rely on my previous understanding of the word alone.**

This is how I would approach these questions:

1.   I look at the word in question and think about what it means and its dictionary definition. Don't worry if it's a word that you don't recognize.

2.   I go back to the passage to where the word appears, and read the entire sentence that contains this word. What is the author trying to express with this sentence? Can I use a different word to replace this word without a material change to the sentence's meaning?

3.   I read a few lines above and a few lines below where the sentence/word had appeared, does my understanding of the word change? Do I now have a clearer understanding of what the author is trying to express by picking this particular word? Does this word appear elsewhere in the passage? I would use the search function to do a quick double check.

4.   I will now go to the answer choices and try to find the answer choice that most closely conforms to my understanding. If I'm stuck between two answer choices, I take each answer and plug it back into the passage, replacing the original word, and pick the AC that is a closer replica of the original sentence.

PT40 S4 Q18 (PT40 Passage 3)

According to the theory of gravitation, every particle of matter in the universe attracts every other particle with a force that increases as either the mass of the particles increases, or their proximity to one another increases, or both. Gravitation is believed to shape the structures of stars, galaxies, and the entire universe. But for decades cosmologists (scientists who study the universe) have attempted to account for the finding that at least 90 percent of the universe seems to be missing: that the total amount of observable matter—stars, dust, and miscellaneous debris—does not contain enough mass to explain why the universe is organized in the shape of galaxies and clusters of galaxies. To account for this discrepancy, cosmologists hypothesize that something else, which they call "dark matter," provides the gravitational force necessary to make the huge structures cohere.

What is dark matter? Numerous exotic entities have been postulated, but among the more attractive candidates—because they are known actually to exist—are neutrinos, elementary particles created as a by-product of nuclear fusion, radioactive decay, or catastrophic collisions between other particles. Neutrinos, which come in three types, are by far the most numerous kind of particle in the universe; however, they have long been assumed to have no mass. If so, that would disqualify them as dark matter. Without mass, matter cannot exert gravitational force; without such force, it cannot induce other matter to **cohere**.

But new evidence suggests that a neutrino does have mass. This evidence came by way of research findings supporting the existence of a long-theorized but never observed phenomenon called oscillation, whereby each of the three neutrino types can change into one of the others as it travels through space. Researchers held that the transformation is possible only if neutrinos also have mass. They obtained experimental confirmation of the theory by generating one neutrino type and then finding evidence that it had oscillated into the predicted neutrino type. In the process, they were able to estimate the mass of a neutrino at from 0.5 to 5 electron volts.

While slight, even the lowest estimate would yield a lot of mass given that neutrinos are so numerous, especially considering that neutrinos were previously assumed to have no mass. Still, even at the highest estimate, neutrinos could only account for about 20 percent of the universe's "missing" mass. Nevertheless, that is enough to alter our picture of the universe even if it does not account for all of dark matter. In fact, some cosmologists claim that this new evidence offers the best theoretical solution yet to the dark matter problem. If the evidence holds up, these cosmologists believe, it may add to our understanding of the role elementary particles play in holding the universe together.

Which one of the following phrases could replace the word "cohere" without substantively altering the author's meaning? (End of second paragraph)

- A. exert gravitational force
- B. form galactic structures
- C. oscillate into another type of matter
- D. become significantly more massive
- E. fuse to produce new particles

So the dictionary definition of "cohere" is "to be united, to form a whole."

But be careful, a **common trick** test makers use is to use a word that has one dictionary meaning, but a slightly different meaning when it comes to the passage. So let's try to figure out how the author uses the word "cohere" in the passage.

The question stem tells us that the word "cohere" appears at the end of the second paragraph. But it's easy to **overlook** the fact that the word also appears at the end of the first paragraph! It may be difficult to decipher what the author truly means by "cohere" from just one location, but with two locations, our job becomes much easier.

Let's look at both:

> that the total amount of observable matter—stars, dust, and miscellaneous debris—does not contain enough mass to explain why the universe is organized in the shape of galaxies and clusters of galaxies. To account for this discrepancy, cosmologists hypothesize that something else, which they call "dark matter," provides the gravitational force necessary to make the huge structures **cohere**.

> Without mass, matter cannot exert gravitational force; without such force, it cannot induce other matter to **cohere**.

As you can see, the first paragraph actually provides us with more evidence as to what the author means by "cohere." The author is talking about how the universe is formed into galaxies and clusters of galaxies. So to make the huge structures (galaxies) "cohere," the author is talking about how *matter comes together to form galaxies*.

With this in mind, let's look at the answer choices. Let's now **plug each answer choice** back into the original sentence and see which one most closely matches up with our understanding.

A.   *exert gravitational force*

Without mass, matter cannot exert gravitational force; without such force, it cannot induce other matter to *exert gravitational force*.

Gravitational force does not make other matter also have gravitational force.

B.   *form galactic structures*

Without mass, matter cannot exert gravitational force; without such force, it cannot induce other matter to *form galactic structures*.

This is close to the meaning of "cohere" as used in the first paragraph.

C.   *oscillate into another type of matter*

Without mass, matter cannot exert gravitational force; without such force, it cannot induce other matter to *oscillate into another type of matter*

We are not talking about transforming one element into another, that would be a nuclear reaction.

D.   *become significantly more massive*

Without mass, matter cannot exert gravitational force; without such force, it cannot induce other matter to *become significantly more massive*

Galaxies are massive, causing matter to come together to become galaxies is a process of enlargement. But is this the same as "inducing other matter to become significantly more massive?"

I find this answer choice unclear. Also, it's not just about becoming more massive, it's about forming galaxies, as we saw in the first paragraph.

     E. *fuse to produce new particles*

Without mass, matter cannot exert gravitational force; without such force, it cannot induce other matter to *fuse to produce new particles*

Fusing together is closer to the dictionary definition of "cohere," but we are not creating new particles! We are combining matter to build galaxies.

Ultimately, given the aid we had from how the author used the word "cohere" from paragraph 1, answer choice B is the best answer.

There are three takeaways from this tricky question: **First**, the correct answer may not match the dictionary definition of a word, we are more interested in how the word is used in context. **Second**, look for instances of the word appearing elsewhere in the passage, this may give us additional clues. **Lastly**, examine the answer choices by plugging the AC back into the sentence in question, and see if the original meaning has been preserved.

PT55 S2 Q27 (PT55 Passage 4)

In economics, the term "speculative bubble" refers to a large upward move in an asset's price driven not by the asset's fundamentals—that is, by the earnings derivable from the asset—but rather by mere speculation that someone else will be willing to pay a higher price for it. The price increase is then followed by a dramatic decline in price, due to a loss in confidence that the price will continue to rise, and the "bubble" is said to have burst. According to Charles Mackay's classic nineteenth-century account, the seventeenth-century Dutch tulip market provides an example of a speculative bubble. But the economist Peter Garber challenges Mackay's view, arguing that there is no evidence that the Dutch tulip market really involved a speculative bubble.

By the seventeenth century, the Netherlands had become a center of cultivation and development of new tulip varieties, and a market had developed in which rare varieties of bulbs sold at high prices. For example, a Semper Augustus bulb sold in 1625 for an amount of gold worth about U.S.$11,000 in 1999. Common bulb varieties, on the other hand, sold for very low prices. According to Mackay, by 1636 rapid price rises attracted speculators, and prices of many varieties surged upward from November 1636 through January 1637. Mackay further states that in February 1637 prices suddenly collapsed; bulbs could not be sold at 10 percent of their peak values. By 1739, the prices of all the most prized kinds of bulbs had fallen to no more than one two-hundredth of 1 percent of Semper Augustus's peak price.

Garber acknowledges that bulb prices increased dramatically from 1636 to 1637 and eventually reached very low levels. But he argues that this episode should not be described as a speculative bubble, for the increase and eventual decline in bulb prices can be explained in terms of the fundamentals. Garber argues that a **standard pricing pattern** occurs for new varieties of flowers. When a particularly prized variety is developed, its original bulb sells for a high price. Thus, the dramatic rise in the price of some original tulip bulbs could have resulted as tulips in general, and certain varieties in particular, became fashionable. However, as the prized bulbs become more readily available through reproduction from the original bulb, their price falls rapidly; after less than 30 years, bulbs sell at reproduction cost. But this does not mean that the high prices of original bulbs are irrational, for earnings derivable from the millions of bulbs descendent from the original bulbs can be very high, even if each individual descendent bulb commands a very low price. Given that an original bulb can generate a reasonable return on investment even if the price of descendent bulbs decreases dramatically, a rapid rise and eventual fall of tulip bulb prices need not indicate a speculative bubble.

The phrase "standard pricing pattern" as used in the passage most nearly means a pricing pattern

- A. against which other pricing patterns are to be measured
- B. that conforms to a commonly agreed-upon criterion
- C. that is merely acceptable
- D. that regularly recurs in certain types of cases
- E. that serves as an exemplar

I'll admit, I was overjoyed when I first read this passage. It talks about MacKay's famous work, "Extraordinary Popular Delusions and the Madness of Crowds," a book I have read.

In fact, my graduation thesis was on the Subprime Mortgage Crisis of 2008. I consulted MacKay's work, as well as similar books such as Reinhart and Rogoff's "This Time is Different: Eight Centuries of Financial Folly," and Charles Kindleberger's "History of Financial Crises," among others. So I felt confident and knowledgeable about the subject.

Things were looking good until I got to the last question, the question on "*standard pricing patterns.*" For some reason that escapes me now, my immediate reaction upon seeing this term was to think about something I learned in finance class, maybe the Capital Asset Pricing Model, which calculates the expected risk premium on a stock.

Now I think about it, it's probably because of the term "*pricing.*" And a "*standard pricing pattern*" made me think about a financial model with a standard equation. I ended up going with Answer Choice B, because it seemed so obvious, given my own knowledge. How can it be anything else? I never bothered checking the passage and was pretty confident about my choice.

But if you had gone to the passage and read the information immediately following the term "*standard pricing pattern,*" we saw that what Garver meant was simply that the rise and fall of the prices followed a recurring pattern. New varieties mean an increase in price, but as supplies saturate the market, prices gradually fall. The correct answer is D.

If I hadn't relied on my previous knowledge, and simply tried to base my understanding only on the information from the passage, I would probably have selected D. Because I would have looked at B and thought, what is the "commonly agreed-upon criterion" that this answer talks about? I would go back to the passage but would not have been able to find a standard that is agreed upon by many people/sources. That would have been enough reason to eliminate B in favor of D.

***

I wanted to bring this up to emphasize a trend I've seen many times since I started teaching the LSAT. I've had students with legal backgrounds struggle with certain legal passages, and art/music majors struggle with passages dealing with an art/music passage. As we see a passage on a topic we are familiar with, we tend to draw increasingly upon our own experiences, understanding, inferences, and analogies. But there will be times when the passages themselves will not be accurate depictions of the topic being discussed:

I've had one student who actually encountered a passage about an academic who happened to be a professor emeritus at his university in the field that he was specializing in. He found the passage inaccurate and actually went to meet with the professor who was discussed in the passage. The professor himself was very critical of that RC passage.

So I just wanted to emphasize that even when the passage is on a topic with which we are intimately familiar, try to base our understanding and judgment **entirely on the content of the passage itself**.

Principle Questions

We have encountered Principle Questions in the Logical Reasoning section. They have occasionally appeared in RC as well. So what is a principle?

Let's borrow again from the Principles Chapter of LR Perfection:

> The Merriam Webster dictionary defines a "principle" as a "fundamental law governing the rule of conduct," or a "general theorem that has numerous applications across a wide field."
>
> For the purposes of the LSAT, there are three characteristics of "principles" that we need to be aware of. If you see a statement in the stimulus or answer choices possessing these three characteristics, chances are that you are dealing with a principle.
>
> **A principle should have multiple and general applicability**
>
> In the first place, a principle has widespread applicability. It holds true not just for one specific instance, but across a wide range of situations and scenarios.
>
> The statement "John is a corrupt government official and he should be prosecuted" is NOT a principle. It pertains to John, who is one single person. But the statement "corrupt government officials should be prosecuted" IS a principle, because it applies to corrupt government officials in general, regardless of who you are. If this principle holds true, then it doesn't matter how many years of experience you have, which department you work for, or your position, if you are a corrupt government official, you should be prosecuted.
>
> **A principle should apply equally across the board and at all times**
>
> When we say "as a matter of principle," we mean something that is non-negotiable. If honesty is one of my principles, then that means I strive to be honest all the time, not only when it provides me with advantages or only when I feel like it. I should be honest even if it could get me in trouble. Similarly, even if there are extenuating circumstances and exceptions, by being dishonest, I would still have violated my principle.
>
> **A principle should be the expression of a rule or standard, it can be both descriptive and   prescriptive.**
>
> Behind every principle there is a standard. A principle should tell us what is or ought to be. For example, scientific laws such as the Theory of Relativity or the Law of Thermodynamics should be considered principles. A principle can also govern our actions, it can have a moral component to it, as we can be held accountable to moral standards/principles.

***

Now that we have a clearer idea of what constitutes a principle, let's begin the discussion of Principle Questions in RC.

RC Principle Questions closely conform to **Principle Extraction Questions** from the LR section. So take a look at those questions (Section 2.2 of the Principle Questions Chapter in LR Perfection) if you happen to struggle a little.

Most of the time, the principle had **not been explicitly** stated in the passage. So our job, first and foremost, is to extract it from the text.

Remember, a principle can be either **descriptive or prescriptive**. So when we come up with our versions of the principle, it can either read like a description, telling us how something is; or like a prescription, telling us how something should be.

The answer choices to these questions will come in two variations:

In the first variation, the five answer choices will all contain different principles. It's our job to find the answer that matches up most closely with what we believe to be the principle derivable from the passage.

In the second variation, the five answer choices will contain different scenarios. It's our job to extract the principle from the passage and see which scenario most closely matches the principle that we have in mind.

***

PT21 S4 Q11 (PT21 Passage 2)

What is "law"? By what processes do judges arrive at opinions, those documents that justify their belief that the "law" dictates a conclusion one way or the other? These are among the oldest questions in jurisprudence, debate about which has traditionally been dominated by representatives of two schools of thought: proponents of natural law, who see law as intertwined with a moral order independent of society's rules and mores, and legal positivists, who see law solely as embodying the commands of a society's ruling authority.

Since the early 1970s, these familiar questions have received some new and surprising answers in the legal academy. This novelty is in part a consequence of the increasing influence there of academic disciplines and intellectual traditions previously unconnected with the study of law. Perhaps the most influential have been the answers given by the Law and Economics school. According to these legal economists, law consists and ought to consist of those rules that maximize a society's material wealth and that abet the efficient operation of markets designed to generate wealth. More controversial have been the various answers provided by members of the Critical Legal Studies movement, according to whom law is one among several cultural mechanisms by which holders of power seek to legitimate their domination. Drawing on related arguments developed in anthropology, sociology, and history, the critical legal scholars contend that law is an expression of power, but not, as held by the positivists, the power of the legitimate sovereign government. Rather, it is an expression of the power of elites who may have no legitimate authority, but who are intent on preserving the privileges of their race, class, or gender.

In the mid-1970s, James Boyd White began to articulate yet another interdisciplinary response to the traditional questions, and in so doing spawned what is now known as the Law and Literature movement. White has insisted that law, particularly as it is interpreted in judicial opinions, should be understood as an essentially literary activity. Judicial opinions should be read and evaluated not primarily as political acts or as attempts to maximize society's wealth through efficient rules, but rather as artistic performances. And like all such performances, White argues, each judicial opinion attempts in its own way to promote a particular political or ethical value.

In the recent Justice as Translation, White argues that opinion-writing should be regarded as an act of "translation," and judges as "translators." As such, judges find themselves mediating between the authoritative legal text and the pressing legal problem that demands resolution. A judge must essentially "re-constitute" that text by fashioning a new one, which is faithful to the old text but also responsive to and informed by the conditions, constraints, and aspirations of the world in which the new legal problem has arisen.

Which one of the following statements is most compatible with the principles of the Critical Legal Studies movement as that movement is described in the passage?

A. Laws governing the succession of power at the death of a head of state represent a synthesis of legal precedents, specific situations, and the values of lawmakers.
B. Laws allowing income tax deductions for charitable contributions, though ostensibly passed by lawmakers, were devised by and are perpetuated by the rich.
C. Laws governing the tariffs placed on imported goods must favor the continuation of mutually beneficial trade arrangements, even at the expense of long-standing legal precedent.
D. Laws governing the treatment of the disadvantaged and powerless members of a given society are an accurate indication of that society's moral state.
E. Laws controlling the electoral processes of a representative democracy have been devised by lawmakers to ensure the continuation of that governmental system.

What are the principles of CLS? Let's revisit the second half of the second paragraph and see if we can come up with a coherent expression of that principle.

> *More controversial have been the various answers provided by members of the Critical Legal Studies movement, according to whom law is <u>one among several cultural mechanisms by which holders of power seek to legitimate their domination</u>. Drawing on related arguments developed in anthropology, sociology, and history, the critical legal scholars contend that law is an expression of power, but not, as held by the positivists, the power of the legitimate sovereign government. Rather, it is <u>an expression of the power of elites who may have no legitimate authority, but who are intent on preserving the privileges of their race, class, or gender.</u>*

The principle here is descriptive. It is telling us what CLS proponents think the law *is*. For them, the law is *a tool used by the powerful to preserve their power, domination, and privileges.*

Let's look at the answer choices, the answer choices here are all scenarios rather than explicit principles. So we have to find a scenario that best matches up with what we had come up with. We want a scenario where the powerful are using the law to perpetuate their power, maybe a president modifying the constitution to stay in power for a third term?

> A. *Laws governing the succession of power at the death of a head of state represent a synthesis of legal precedents, specific situations, and the values of lawmakers.*

It's unclear whether this application of the law represents an attempt to perpetuate the system, and to continuously benefit the elites by extending to them the benefits of power. The promotion of the "values of lawmakers" could potentially be describing a feature of the "Law and Literature" movement mentioned in the third paragraph, where "each judicial opinion attempts in its own way to promote a particular political or ethical value."

> B. *Laws allowing income tax deductions for charitable contributions, though ostensibly passed by lawmakers, were devised by and are perpetuated by the rich.*

This is a closer fit, the rich are gaming the law to get richer. I was looking for an answer that talks about the powerful using the law to stay powerful. So I don't know if this answer is slightly off scope. Let's keep on going.

> C. *Laws governing the tariffs placed on imported goods must favor the continuation of mutually beneficial trade arrangements, even at the expense of long-standing legal precedent.*

Have the powerful benefitted? We don't know. This might be closer to the ideas upheld by the "law and economics" school mentioned in the second paragraph.

> D. *Laws governing the treatment of the disadvantaged and powerless members of a given society are an accurate indication of that society's moral state.*

Have the powerful benefitted? We are looking for an answer that tells us the elites are using the law to perpetuate their power.

> E. *Laws controlling the electoral processes of a representative democracy have been devised by lawmakers to ensure the continuation of that governmental system.*

This answer also kind of matches the principle we had in mind. The ruling elite are using the laws to protect the system.

Let's take a closer look at B and E:

Remember, the principle we have in mind is that the powerful are using the law as a tool to stay powerful. If legislators are using the law to protect a democratic system, will these legislators continuous get elected? I don't think so. Whether these legislators maintain power is up to the election process, I don't think upholding a democracy will ensure that they stay in power.

The issue with B, on the other hand; is that it's talking about the rich staying rich. What we had in mind was the powerful using the law to stay powerful. This may seem off tangent at first, but remember that "class" was also cited by the author as an indicator of power. So "the upper class using the law to maintain their class status" would also be an acceptable answer. In other words, based on the evidence we have from the passage, I think B is a better fit. For CLS, the elites may have no legitimate authority, and answer choice B appears to better highlight this distinction.

B is the correct answer.

PT25 S1 Q26 (PT25 Passage 4)

Scientists typically advocate the analytic method of studying complex systems: systems are divided into component parts that are investigated separately. But nineteenth-century critics of this method claimed that when a system's parts are isolated its complexity tends to be lost. To address the perceived weaknesses of the analytic method these critics put forward a concept called organicism, which posited that the whole determines the nature of its parts and that the parts of a whole are interdependent.

Organicism depended upon the theory of internal relations, which states that relations between entities are possible only within some whole that embraces them, and that entities are altered by the relationships into which they enter. If an entity stands in a relationship with another entity, it has some property as a consequence. Without this relationship, and hence without the property, the entity would be different— and so would be another entity. Thus, the property is one of the entity's defining characteristics. Each of an entity's relationships likewise determines a defining characteristic of the entity.

One problem with the theory of internal relations is that not all properties of an entity are defining characteristics: numerous properties are accompanying characteristics—even if they are always present, their presence does not influence the entity's identity. Thus, even if it is admitted that every relationship into which an entity enters determines some characteristic of the entity, it is not necessarily true that such characteristics will define the entity; it is possible for the entity to enter into a relationship yet remain essentially unchanged.

The ultimate difficulty with the theory of internal relations is that it renders the acquisition of knowledge impossible. To truly know an entity, we must know all of its relationships; but because the entity is related to everything in each whole of which it is a part, these wholes must be known completely before the entity can be known. This seems to be a prerequisite impossible to satisfy.

Organicists' criticism of the analytic method arose from their failure to fully comprehend the method. In rejecting the analytic method, organicists overlooked the fact that before the proponents of the method analyzed the component parts of a system, they first determined both the laws applicable to the whole system and the initial conditions of the system; proponents of the method thus did not study parts of a system in full isolation from the system as a whole. Since organicists failed to recognize this, they never advanced any argument to show that laws and initial conditions of complex systems cannot be discovered. Hence, organicists offered no valid reason for rejecting the analytic method or for adopting organicism as a replacement for it.

Which one of the following is a principle upon which the author bases an argument against the theory of internal relations?

    A. An adequate theory of complex systems must define the entities of which the system is composed.
    B. An acceptable theory cannot have consequences that contradict its basic purpose.
    C. An adequate method of study of complex systems should reveal the actual complexity of the systems it studies.
    D. An acceptable theory must describe the laws and initial conditions of a complex system.
    E. An acceptable method of studying complex systems should not study parts of the system in isolation from the system as a whole.

The author criticizes the theory of internal relations in paragraphs 3 and 4 of the passage. In paragraph 3, the author says that "*not all properties of an entity are defining characteristics.*" So a problem with organicists is that they overlook the fact that there are "defining characteristics" and "non-defining characteristics."

It's more difficult to formulate this as a principle, but perhaps we can say that "an acceptable theory will differentiate between defining and non-defining characteristics?"

The second criticism is that the theory of internal relations "*renders the acquisition of knowledge impossible.*" As a principle, perhaps we can say that "an acceptable theory must allow for the successful acquisition of knowledge."

A. *An adequate theory of complex systems must define the entities of which the system is composed.*

This is a subtle variation of our first principle. We wanted an answer that said "an adequate theory must distinguish between characteristics that define the entities, and characteristics that don't define the entities."

B. *An acceptable theory cannot have consequences that contradict its basic purpose.*

This answer choice requires additional translation on our part. What is the purpose of the Theory of Internal Relations? It's to study complex systems. What happens when a theory makes the acquisition of knowledge impossible? It would also mean that we would get nowhere in our goal of studying complex systems with this theory. In other words, the Theory of Internal Relations, whose goal is to acquire new knowledge, is contradicting this basic purpose as it actually makes knowledge acquisition impossible.

C. *An adequate method of study of complex systems should reveal the actual complexity of the systems it studies.*

The Theory of Internal Relations does this: it shows how complex the systems are, so complex that it would be impossible to know how these complex systems actually work.

D. *An acceptable theory must describe the laws and initial conditions of a complex system.*

Remember, we are looking for the principle behind the author's criticism of the Theory of Internal Relations. This answer choice is actually describing the analytical method.

E. *An acceptable method of studying complex systems should not study parts of the system in isolation from the system as a whole.*

We are told that the analytical method *did not* study the system in isolation from the system as a whole. But we are never told that the Theory of Internal Relations is problematic because of this.

The correct answer is B.

Title Questions

We now turn to Title Questions, these questions will ask us to chose an appropriate title for the passage you have just read.

For these questions, the correct answer doesn't have to cover everything that was mentioned in the passage. Think back on our approach to Passage Purpose and Main Point Questions. For those two question types, our job was to find the *primary reason* why the author wrote the passage, and the *central thesis* behind the passage. We were not looking for shopping list type answer choices that covered everything, we wanted answers that get to the point.

For Title Questions, since I will already have come up with answers to the Purpose and Main Point of the Passage, I will use these two answers as inspiration. The correct title should in many ways link back to the Purpose and Main Point of the passage.

But again, it's really difficult to pre-phrase/anticipate what the title of a passage might be. More often than not, what we come up with will be different from what the correct answer choice actually is. So for Title Questions, after reminding myself of the Purpose and Main Point of the passage, and quickly thinking about what are some possible topics, I go straight to the answer choices.

Answer choice elimination and ranking will be the most important step to help you navigate these questions. I almost exclusively use the Process of "**Reverse Confirmation.**" It's a process that we saw briefly in Chapter 11, and something that we will devote greater attention to in a subsequent chapter on Advanced Answer Choice Ranking Tactics.

Basically, I would look at each answer choice and ask myself, "*if this was the topic assigned to me, and my job is to write an essay, how would I go about doing it? What kind of information would I include in the essay, how would I set it up structurally, and what would be my thesis statement?*"

This process helps me to expand upon the answer choices, giving them more substance. I am forcing myself to think about what these ACs are really discussing. Once I have done this, I go back to the passage and compare my imagined passage based on the answer choice to the real passage. I will pick the answer choice whose imagined passage most closely matches the actual passage as the best answer.

Let's look at an example and I will give you a demonstration of this process in action:

PT40 S4 Q14 (PT40 Passage 3)

According to the theory of gravitation, every particle of matter in the universe attracts every other particle with a force that increases as either the mass of the particles increases, or their proximity to one another increases, or both. Gravitation is believed to shape the structures of stars, galaxies, and the entire universe. But for decades cosmologists (scientists who study the universe) have attempted to account for the finding that at least 90 percent of the universe seems to be missing: that the total amount of observable matter—stars, dust, and miscellaneous debris—does not contain enough mass to explain why the universe is organized in the shape of galaxies and clusters of galaxies. To account for this discrepancy, cosmologists hypothesize that something else, which they call "dark matter," provides the gravitational force necessary to make the huge structures cohere.

What is dark matter? Numerous exotic entities have been postulated, but among the more attractive candidates—because they are known actually to exist—are neutrinos, elementary particles created as a by-product of nuclear fusion, radioactive decay, or catastrophic collisions between other particles. Neutrinos, which come in three types, are by far the most numerous kind of particle in the universe; however, they have long been assumed to have no mass. If so, that would disqualify them as dark matter. Without mass, matter cannot exert gravitational force; without such force, it cannot induce other matter to cohere.

But new evidence suggests that a neutrino does have mass. This evidence came by way of research findings supporting the existence of a long-theorized but never observed phenomenon called oscillation, whereby each of the three neutrino types can change into one of the others as it travels through space. Researchers held that the transformation is possible only if neutrinos also have mass. They obtained experimental confirmation of the theory by generating one neutrino type and then finding evidence that it had oscillated into the predicted neutrino type. In the process, they were able to estimate the mass of a neutrino at from 0.5 to 5 electron volts.

While slight, even the lowest estimate would yield a lot of mass given that neutrinos are so numerous, especially considering that neutrinos were previously assumed to have no mass. Still, even at the highest estimate, neutrinos could only account for about 20 percent of the universe's "missing" mass. Nevertheless, that is enough to alter our picture of the universe even if it does not account for all of dark matter. In fact, some cosmologists claim that this new evidence offers the best theoretical solution yet to the dark matter problem. If the evidence holds up, these cosmologists believe, it may add to our understanding of the role elementary particles play in holding the universe together.

Which one of the following titles most completely and accurately expresses the contents of the passage?

A. "The Existence of Dark Matter: Arguments For and Against"
B. "Neutrinos and the Dark Matter Problem: A Partial Solution?"
C. "Too Little, Too Late: Why Neutrinos Do Not Constitute Dark Matter"
D. "The Role of Gravity: How Dark Matter Shapes Stars"
E. "The Implications of Oscillation: Do Neutrinos Really Have Mass?"

We have encountered this passage previously:

Purpose: to explain how neutrinos may be some of the missing pieces behind the universe's unaccountable mass.

Main Point: There is a very high likelihood that neutrinos constitute some of the dark matter/missing mass that would be required for the level of gravitational force in the universe.

With this information in mind, what could be a potential title for this passage? We can potentially call it "Neutrinos: Potential Missing Pieces of the Universe?"

Let's look at the answer choices, we will practice Reverse Confirmation as a way to evaluate them.

   A. *"The Existence of Dark Matter: Arguments For and Against"*

If this was the topic given to us, our essay would probably be comparative in nature. On the one hand we would discuss arguments for why dark matter exist; on the other hand, why dark matter doesn't exist.

   B. *"Neutrinos and the Dark Matter Problem: A Partial Solution?"*

Recall that the dark matter problem is that a large part of the universe's mass is unaccounted for. If this was the topic of an essay, I would describe the problem, describe what neutrinos are, and why neutrinos might constitute the dark matter that we are looking for. I would finally end the essay by conceding that neutrinos do not offer a complete solution.

   C. *"Too Little, Too Late: Why Neutrinos Do Not Constitute Dark Matter"*

An essay with this topic would argue that neutrinos are not dark matter.

   D. *"The Role of Gravity: How Dark Matter Shapes Stars"*

If this was the topic, the essay would be explanatory in nature. It would go into details explaining how gravity and dark matter work together to construct celestial bodies.

   E. *"The Implications of Oscillation: Do Neutrinos Really Have Mass?"*

An essay with this topic would examine whether neutrinos have mass or not, it would probably look at experimental results, consider both sides of the argument, and finally come to the conclusion that "yes, neutrinos do have mass," or "no, neutrinos don't have mass."

B is the correct answer.

Assumption Questions

We will now look at a rarer type of Restricted Scope Questions. These questions have not appeared in RC for quite a long time. Nonetheless, in the unlikely event that they decide to show up again, we'll quickly study them.

Assumption Questions are like NA Questions that are found in the LR section. We are asked, *"which of the following is an assumption made by the author?"* or *"In arguing X, the scientist mentioned in the first paragraph assumes which one of the following?"*

Our approach to these questions is similar to our approach for NA Questions. We need to isolate the argument/position in question, and examine each answer choice, asking, "If the subject holds the position described in the passage, which one of these answer choices MUST be assumed/MUST be true?"

The **Assumption Negation Technique** works wonders with these types of answers. The ANT is a tried-and-true tactic that works on the majority of NA Questions and you should already be familiar with it. Negate each of the answer choices and see which negated version will attack the author/third party's position or argument.

PT30 S3 Q12 (PT30 Passage 2)

Tragic dramas written in Greece during the fifth century B.C. engender considerable scholarly debate over the relative influence of individual autonomy and the power of the gods on the drama's action. One early scholar, B. Snell, argues that Aeschylus, for example, develops in his tragedies a concept of the autonomy of the individual. In these dramas, the protagonists invariably confront a situation that paralyzes them, so that their prior notions about how to behave or think are dissolved. Faced with a decision on which their fate depends, they must re-examine their deepest motives, and then act with determination. They are given only two alternatives, each with grave consequences, and they make their decision only after a tortured internal debate. According to Snell, this decision is "free" and "personal" and such personal autonomy constitutes the central theme in Aeschylean drama, as if the plays were devised to isolate an abstract model of human action. Drawing psychological conclusions from this interpretation, another scholar, Z. Barbu, suggests that **"[Aeschylean] drama is proof of the emergence within ancient Greek civilization of the individual as a free agent."**

To A. Rivier, Snell's emphasis on the decision made by the protagonist, with its implicit notions of autonomy and responsibility, misrepresents the role of the superhuman forces at work, forces that give the dramas their truly tragic dimension. These forces are not only external to the protagonist; they are also experienced by the protagonist as an internal compulsion, subjecting him or her to constraint even in what are claimed to be his or her "choices." Hence all that the deliberation does is to make the protagonist aware of the impasse, rather than motivating one choice over another. It is finally a necessity imposed by the deities that generates the decision, so that at a particular moment in the drama necessity dictates a path. Thus, the protagonist does not so much "choose" between two possibilities as "recognize" that there is only one real option.

A. Lesky, in his discussion of Aeschylus' play Agamemnon, disputes both views. Agamemnon, ruler of Argos, must decide whether to brutally sacrifice his own daughter. A message from the deity Artemis has told him that only the sacrifice will bring a wind to blow his ships to an important battle. Agamemnon is indeed constrained by a divine necessity. But he also deeply desires a victorious battle: "If this sacrifice will loose the winds, it is permitted to desire it fervently," he says. The violence of his passion suggests that Agamemnon chooses a path—chosen by the gods for their own reasons—on the basis of desires that must be condemned by us, because they are his own. In Lesky's view, tragic action is bound by the constant tension between a self and superhuman forces.

The quotation at the end of the first paragraph suggests that Barbu assumes which one of the following about Aeschylean drama?

A. Aeschylean drama helped to initiate a new understanding of the person in ancient Greek society.
B. Aeschylean drama introduced new ways of understanding the role of the individual in ancient Greek society.
C. Aeschylean drama is the original source of the understanding of human motivation most familiar to the modern Western world.
D. Aeschylean drama accurately reflects the way personal autonomy was perceived in ancient Greek society.
E. Aeschylean drama embodies the notion of freedom most familiar to the modern Western world.

So since the question is asking us about Barbu's assumptions, we just have to focus on parts of the passage where Barbu's views are discussed. This only happens at the end of the first paragraph. Let's take a quick look at the first paragraph:

*Tragic dramas written in Greece during the fifth century B.C. engender considerable scholarly debate over the relative <u>influence of individual autonomy</u> and the <u>power of the gods</u> on the drama's action. One early scholar, B. **Snell**, argues that Aeschylus, for example, develops in his tragedies a concept of the <u>autonomy of the individual</u>. In these dramas, the protagonists invariably confront a situation that paralyzes them, so that their prior notions about how to behave or think are dissolved. Faced with a decision on which their fate depends, they must re-examine their deepest motives, and then act with determination. They are given only two alternatives, each with grave consequences, and they make their decision only after a tortured internal debate. According to Snell, <u>this decision is "free" and "personal"</u> and such personal autonomy constitutes the central theme in Aeschylean drama, as if the plays were devised to isolate an abstract model of human action. Drawing psychological conclusions from this interpretation, another scholar, Z. Barbu, suggests that **"[Aeschylean] drama is proof of the emergence within ancient Greek civilization of the individual as a free agent."***

There is significant debate on what influences a drama's actions, individual autonomy vs. power of the gods.

Snell believes in individual autonomy. For Snell, the protagonist's decision is free and personal.

Barbu goes a step further in his analysis. He believes that the dramas, which portray individuals as free agents, is proof that in ancient Greek society too, the individual is viewed as a free agent.

In other words, Zevedei Barbu believes that the ancient Greek dramas are an accurate reflection of views held in society at the time.

The correct answer is D. If Aeschylean dramas *are not* an accurate reflection of the way personal autonomy was perceived in ancient Greek society, then what these dramas portray cannot be argued to be proof of views held in society at the time.

Continue the Passage Questions

We now come to the final question type of the Restricted Scope Questions Chapter, Continue the Passage Questions.

These rare questions will ask you to find a sentence to graft to the end of the passage, a sentence of statement that would best continue the passage.

Continue the Passage Questions are peculiar because the correct answer can describe a wide variety of things. So without looking at the answer choices, we don't really know what the next sentence of the passage might be. As I result, I tend not to try to anticipate or pre-phrase what the correct answer might look like, but rather try to jump straight into the process of elimination.

In general, these are the criteria that I consider when eliminating Continue the Passage Questions:

1.   Answer choices that introduces new ideas previously unseen in the passage are a *red flag*. While it's okay for the correct answer to introduce an additional implication of a view already discussed, or go deeper on a previously examined point, we should be careful with **out of scope** answers. Answers that talk about an entirely new topic or relationship are probably wrong.

2.   Answer choices that introduces a **new POV but does not go off topic** are *acceptable* answers. For instance, if the topic of the passage was health care reform and what its advocates believe. An answer choice about what critics think is okay. What's not okay; however, is an answer that talks about gun reform.

3.   Answer choices that contradict the author's **tone**, **attitude**, **purpose**, and **main point** are *not okay*. If the author holds a positive attitude towards a certain position, the correct answer will not be attacking that position (unless its describing what opponents believe). Similarly, answers that are contrary to the Author's Purpose or Main Point will be suspect. If the Author's Purpose is to recommend moderate wine consumption, the correct answer choice, unless describing an opposing viewpoint, will not urge us to abstain from wine, or suggest that hard liquor is equally beneficial.

4.   The correct answer **will not contradict** information explicitly stated in the passage.

5.   Finally, the correct answer will most likely mirror the **strength of the language** of the passage. Answer choices too strong or too weak are suspect. So if the passage told us that dieting is one of the ways to lose weight, an answer choice that suggests dieting is the only way or the best way to lose weight will be wrong.

PT38 S3 Q16 (PT38 Passage 3)

In explaining the foundations of the discipline known as historical sociology—the examination of history using the methods of sociology—historical sociologist Philip Abrams argues that, while people are made by society as much as society is made by people, sociologists' approach to the subject is usually to focus on only one of these forms of influence to the exclusion of the other. Abrams insists on the necessity for sociologists to move beyond these one-sided approaches to understand society as an entity constructed by individuals who are at the same time constructed by their society. Abrams refers to this continuous process as "structuring."

Abrams also sees history as the result of structuring. People, both individually and as members of collectives, make history. But our making of history is itself formed and informed not only by the historical conditions we inherit from the past, but also by the prior formation of our own identities and capacities, which are shaped by what Abrams calls "contingencies"—social phenomena over which we have varying degrees of control. Contingencies include such things as the social conditions under which we come of age, the condition of our household's economy, the ideologies available to help us make sense of our situation, and accidental circumstances. The ways in which contingencies affect our individual or group identities create a structure of forces within which we are able to act, and that partially determines the sorts of actions we are able to perform.

In Abrams's analysis, historical structuring, like social structuring, is manifold and unremitting. To understand it, historical sociologists must extract from it certain significant episodes, or events, that their methodology can then analyze and interpret. According to Abrams, these events are points at which action and contingency meet, points that represent a cross section of the specific social and individual forces in play at a given time. At such moments, individuals stand forth as agents of history not simply because they possess a unique ability to act, but also because in them we see the force of the specific social conditions that allowed their actions to come forth. Individuals can "make their mark" on history, yet in individuals one also finds the convergence of wider social forces. In order to capture the various facets of this mutual interaction, Abrams recommends a fourfold structure to which he believes the investigations of historical sociologists should conform: first, description of the event itself; second, discussion of the social context that helped bring the event about and gave it significance; third, summary of the life history of the individual agent in the event; and fourth, analysis of the consequences of the event both for history and for the individual.

Given the passage's argument, which one of the following sentences most logically completes the last paragraph?

A. Only if they adhere to this structure, Abrams believes, can historical sociologists conclude with any certainty that the events that constitute the historical record are influenced by the actions of individuals.

B. Only if they adhere to this structure, Abrams believes, will historical sociologists be able to counter the standard sociological assumption that there is very little connection between history and individual agency.

C. Unless they can agree to adhere to this structure, Abrams believes, historical sociologists risk having their discipline treated as little more than an interesting but ultimately indefensible adjunct to history and sociology.

D. By adhering to this structure, Abrams believes, historical sociologists can shed light on issues that traditional sociologists have chosen to ignore in their one-sided approaches to the formation of societies.

E. By adhering to this structure, Abrams believes, historical sociologists will be able to better portray the complex connections between human agency and history.

Let's quickly summarize the passage prior to tackling the question.

In the first paragraph, Abrams espouses the view that society influences people as much as people influence society. Traditional sociologists have usually only considered one or the other, but not both relationships. Abrams calls this "structuring."

Social structuring is the mutual influential relationship between the individual and society. Historical structuring is the relationship between the individual and history. Special conditions made individuals the way they are, and they, in turn, made their marks on history.

In order to fully study this relationship between the individual and history, Abrams proposed a four fold structure.

    A.   *Only if they adhere to this structure, Abrams believes, can historical sociologists conclude with <u>any certainty</u> that the events that constitute the historical record are <u>influenced by the actions of individuals.</u>*

Abrams recommends using the four fold analysis to help historical sociologists better understand the interaction between the individual and wider social forces.

This answer is not only too strong, but only emphasizes one side of the relationship.

    B.   *<u>Only if</u> they adhere to this structure, Abrams believes, will historical sociologists be able to counter the <u>standard sociological assumption</u> that there is <u>very little connection between history and individual agency</u>.*

The passage never mentions such "standard sociological assumption." Sociologists have not examined both sides of the relationship between society and the individual. What they think about the relationship between history and individual agency is unknown.

    C.   *<u>Unless</u> they can agree to adhere to this structure, Abrams believes, historical sociologists risk having their discipline <u>treated as little more than an interesting but ultimately indefensible</u> adjunct to history and sociology.*

This answer is saying that if historical sociologists were to have any relevancy at all, they *must* adopt his model. This is too strong. All we know from the passage is that adopting this four fold model will *help* historical sociologists better understand the relationship between the individual and social forces.

    D.   *By adhering to this structure, Abrams believes, historical sociologists can shed light on issues that <u>traditional sociologists have chosen to ignore</u> in their one-sided approaches to the <u>formation</u> of societies.*

Traditional sociologists have tended to examine only a part of the relationship between the individual and society. But have they "chosen" to do so?

The words "formation of societies" is also suspect. Is that something traditional sociologists studied according to the passage?

Finally, we must remember that traditional sociologists and historical sociologists study two different phenomena. Traditional sociologists look at the relationship between society and the individual; while historical sociologists study the relationship between the individual and historical contingencies.

E. By adhering to this structure, Abrams believes, historical sociologists <u>will be able to better portray</u> the complex connections between human agency and history.

The wording of this answer choice does not conflict with the strength of the original text's language. The "complex connections between human agency and history" can be interpreted as the "relationship between individual action and history" with no material change in meaning. This answer most closely adheres to the original meaning in the passage.

E is the correct answer.

13. Unrestricted Scope Questions

Strengthen Questions

Weaken Questions

Analogy Questions

Exemplify Questions

Unrestricted Scope

Simply put, "unrestricted scope" questions allow correct answer choices to contain new and previously unseen information. The correct answer choice can bring in outside information, content not seen in the passage, and information that cannot be synthesized/inferred based on the text.

Some of the correct answers of Strengthen/Weaken Questions from the Logical Reasoning section are perfect examples of what Unrestricted Scope Questions can look like. For these questions, the correct answer can appear to have nothing to do with the content of the stimulus on a first glance. But they will still help or hurt the argument's conclusion.

Let's look at a very basic example of a Strengthen Question with a seemingly "out of scope" answer as the correct answer choice:

John graduated from law school with no debt, John must be wealthy.

What are the ways in which we can strengthen this argument?

Typical answers will address the gap between "graduating law school with no debt" and "being wealthy." For instance, we can say that "only the rich graduate from law school with no debt," or that "John did not have any scholarships." Both of these answers will make the reader more likely to believe that John is rich or has high spending power.

However, there's a second type of answer choices that are equally valid for Strengthen/Weaken Questions. In LR Perfection we call these "Type II" answer choices. These are answer choices that *independently add to the plausibility/viability* of the main conclusion in Strengthen Questions, or *independently* attack the plausibility of the main conclusion in Weaken Questions.

For the question above, something that has nothing to do with law school, tuition, debt, or scholarships; but still show us that John is wealthy, would be such an answer. For example:

John owns multiple properties.

John owns a yacht.

John sits courtside at NBA games.

All of these answer choices make it more likely that John is wealthy. They don't prove anything (maybe someone else is getting him the tickets), but they are independent information that make the conclusion (*John must be wealthy)* more believable.

"Yachts" and "courtside seats" have nothing to do with the content of our original stimulus, and they are definitely out of scope. But here, they are acceptable answers.

For Unrestricted Scope Questions, the correct answer can be derived from the passage, but this is not necessary. It can also contain new and previously unseen information.

Strengthen and Weaken Questions

Pre-phrasing or anticipating what the correct answer might look like is extremely important in RC Strengthen and Weaken Questions. Here is a guide to my thinking process when I encounter these types of questions:

For **Strengthen Questions**, I take the following steps:

1. Read the question stem carefully, what is the position that I'm trying to strengthen? Is it the view of a specific person, school, or the author?

2. What kind of support was given in the passage for the position that I'm trying to strengthen? Are there ways to make this supporting material stronger?

3. Were there any objections to the position mentioned in the passage? What are some ways in which I can eliminate these objections?

These are the most common ways in which we can strengthen a position or argument on the RC section. We look for outside information that can potentially make the position more believable, make the argument more watertight, or eliminate potential objections to the argument.

***

We do the opposite if it's a **Weaken Question**:

1. Isolate the position or argument that I'm trying to weaken. *Negate it*. What are some ways in which I can make the *negated position* more believable?

2. Are there ways in which I can attack the argument's support, as expressed in the passage? Can I suggest that the support provided are inaccurate or based on faulty reasoning?

3. Does the passage itself offer up objections or criticisms of the position? I can weaken the position by helping these criticisms instead. Can I think of additional ways to object to the position?

***

Strengthening/Weakening Causal Relationships

Sometimes the position we need to strengthen or weaken is a causal relationship, with A causing B, or A $\Rightarrow$ B.

There are standard ways in which we can weaken a causal relationship. Think of these methods as "standard operating procedures" you could apply whenever you see causation at work.

Given A causes B, or A $\Rightarrow$ B, what can we do to weaken this causal relationship?

We can propose an alternative cause. We can say that C also causes B, or its more likely that C $\Rightarrow$ B rather than A $\Rightarrow$ B. This is the first way to weaken a causal line of reasoning.

We can also demonstrate that when the cause is present, the effect is not present; or when the cause is not present, the effect is still present. (A, B̶; or A̶, B) This does *not* disprove the existence of a causal relationship between A and B, but still manages to weaken it.

We can suggest that the causal relationship is actually reversed, and that it should be B $\Rightarrow$ A instead.

We can suggest that a third cause, C, is responsible for causing both A and B. So C $\Rightarrow$ A + B.

***

To strengthen a causal relationship, A $\Rightarrow$ B, all we need to do is to eliminate all the possibilities listed above:

We can say that there is no alternative cause, or ~~C $\Rightarrow$ B~~.

We can suggest that whenever there is A, there is B; or vice versa.

We can eliminate the possibility of reverse causation, or ~~B $\Rightarrow$ A~~.

We can also rule out the possibility of a third common cause for both A and B, so ~~C $\Rightarrow$ A + B~~.

Strengthening/weakening causal relationships is a topic that we discuss at length in LR Perfection, Chapters 13-14.

PT38 S3 Q11 (PT38 Passage 2)

Intellectual authority is defined as the authority of arguments that prevail by virtue of good reasoning and do not depend on coercion or convention. A contrasting notion, institutional authority, refers to the power of social institutions to enforce acceptance of arguments that may or may not possess intellectual authority. The authority wielded by legal systems is especially interesting because such systems are institutions that nonetheless aspire to a purely intellectual authority. One judge goes so far as to claim that courts are merely passive vehicles for applying the intellectual authority of the law and possess no coercive powers of their own.

In contrast, some critics maintain that whatever authority judicial pronouncements have is exclusively institutional. Some of these critics go further, claiming that intellectual authority does not really exist—i.e., it reduces to institutional authority. But it can be countered that these claims break down when a sufficiently broad historical perspective is taken: Not all arguments accepted by institutions withstand the test of time, and some well-reasoned arguments never receive institutional imprimatur. The reasonable argument that goes unrecognized in its own time because it challenges institutional beliefs is common in intellectual history; intellectual authority and institutional consensus are not the same thing.

But, the critics might respond, intellectual authority is only recognized as such because of institutional consensus. For example, if a musicologist were to claim that an alleged musical genius who, after several decades, had not gained respect and recognition for his or her compositions is probably not a genius, the critics might say that basing a judgment on a unit of time— "several decades"—is an institutional rather than an intellectual construct. What, the critics might ask, makes a particular number of decades reasonable evidence by which to judge genius? The answer, of course, is nothing, except for the fact that such institutional procedures have proved useful to musicologists in making such distinctions in the past.

The analogous legal concept is the doctrine of precedent, i.e., a judge's merely deciding a case a certain way becoming a basis for deciding later cases the same way—a pure example of institutional authority. But the critics miss the crucial distinction that when a judicial decision is badly reasoned, or simply no longer applies in the face of evolving social standards or practices, the notion of intellectual authority is introduced: judges reconsider, revise, or in some cases throw out the decision. The conflict between intellectual and institutional authority in legal systems is thus played out in the reconsideration of decisions, leading one to draw the conclusion that legal systems contain a significant degree of intellectual authority even if the thrust of their power is predominantly institutional.

Which one of the following, if true, most challenges the author's contention that legal systems contain a significant degree of intellectual authority?

A. Judges often act under time constraints and occasionally render a badly reasoned or socially inappropriate decision.

B. In some legal systems, the percentage of judicial decisions that contain faulty reasoning is far higher than it is in other legal systems.

C. Many socially inappropriate legal decisions are thrown out by judges only after citizens begin to voice opposition to them.

D. In some legal systems, the percentage of judicial decisions that are reconsidered and revised is far higher than it is in other legal systems.

E. Judges are rarely willing to rectify the examples of faulty reasoning they discover when reviewing previous legal decisions.

From the question, we know that the author believes legal systems to *contain a significant degree of intellectual authority*. This is the position that we are trying to weaken, so let's find the location in the passage where the author argues this.

This happens near the end of the passage. The author believes that when judges "*reconsider, revise, or in some cases throw out the decision*," the intellectual authority of the law is demonstrated.

Why is this the case? Earlier in the paragraph the author argues that by following precedents, judges are following institutional authority. But judges can and do reverse decisions, which means that they are not tied down to institutional authority. This, by extension, means that they enjoy a significant degree of intellectual authority as well.

How would we go about weakening this position? We could attack the author's reasoning by suggesting that when judges reconsider, revise, or overturn decisions, this was still driven by institutional authority. Essentially, we are taking the evidence the author had used to support their position, and showing that it's actually supporting the opposite position.

We can also look for an answer choice that flat out tells us that judges/legal systems have no intellectual authority.

> A.   *Judges often act under time constraints and occasionally render a badly reasoned or socially inappropriate decision.*

A crucial habit that we emphasized back in LR Perfection was to think about the **implications** of each answer choice when faced with Strengthen/Weaken Questions. Ask yourself, "so what if this answer choice is true, does it make the position we are trying to attack less believable?"

So what if judges render "bad" decisions? If they are later overturned, then perhaps it goes to show that the legal system holds intellectual authority after all. This answer choice doesn't have a clear effect.

> B.   *In <u>some</u> legal systems, the percentage of judicial decisions that contain faulty reasoning is far higher than it is in other legal systems.*

Some legal systems have more faulty reasoning than other legal systems. So do these bad legal systems have less intellectual authority? The author tells us in the last paragraph that the reconsideration of faulty decisions is a sign of intellectual authority. But we do not know whether these erroneously reasoned cases are reconsidered. Our goal is to say that legal systems don't have intellectual authority. So in this sense, answer B is incomplete and does not have the direct effect that we want.

> C.   *Many socially inappropriate legal decisions are thrown out by judges only after citizens begin to voice opposition to them.*

This goes to show that judges/legal systems are not immune to social pressure. If a legal system is influenced by social pressure, does that weaken its intellectual or institutional authority? It is unclear. Perhaps an argument can be made that the intellectual foundations of a ruling can't be all that strong if social opposition can sway judicial opinions. But you can also say that the institutional authority is also weak if popular opinion is so powerful.

This answer choice is **open to interpretation**, depending on your assumptions. I like to avoid these answer choices if you remember from LR Perfection, Weaken Chapter, Difficult Trait #2.

D.   *In some legal systems, the percentage of judicial decisions that are reconsidered and revised is far higher than it is in other legal systems.*

Again, similar to answer choice B, this answer doesn't really tell us anything. So there's more judicial revisions in some legal systems, does that mean some legal systems have more intellectual authority than others? A has a higher percentage than B is the same as B having a lower percentage than A.

E.   *Judges are <u>rarely</u> willing to rectify the examples of <u>faulty reasoning</u> they discover when reviewing previous legal decisions.*

So judges don't care about faulty reasoning. It's not the reasoning that's causing them to overturn these decisions. What's driving them then? Well it can't be intellectual authority, because a sign of intellectual authority would be adherence to well reasoned arguments and opposition to those that aren't.

This answer choice is hinting at the lack of intellectual authority among judges who are reviewing decisions. It's not as strong as we'd liked. We were hoping an answer that told us either "revising decisions is based on institutional, rather than intellectual authority," or "when judges revise or throw out cases, it's not a sign of intellectual authority."

In the last paragraph of the passage, the author stated that "judges consider, revise, or even in some cases throw out decisions." This was taken as a sign of intellectual authority contained in legal systems. This answer is essentially attacking the premise of the author's argument. Premise attackers (or Type III answers, as we called them in LR Perfection, are acceptable answer choices.)

E is the best/correct answer.

Another thing to note:

> While we saw that conservatively worded answer choices are preferable for questions whose answers needs to be derived/inferred from the text, we usually lean towards **more strongly worded** ACs in Strengthen and Weaken Questions. This is because for these questions, strongly worded answers tend to have a more direct effect.
>
> For instance, words like "some" are red flags to me in Strengthen/Weaken Questions. Because depending on your assumptions, the statement "some people enjoy cold showers" can be construed to imply a wide range of possibilities. Two people out of a hundred enjoying cold showers means one thing, and ninety-nine out of a hundred persons enjoying cold showers means something else entirely.

PT32 S2 Q13 (PT32 Passage 2)

Many educators in Canada and the United States advocate multicultural education as a means of achieving multicultural understanding. There are, however, a variety of proposals as to what multicultural education should consist of. The most modest of these proposals holds that schools and colleges should promote multicultural understanding by teaching about other cultures, teaching which proceeds from within the context of the majority culture. Students should learn about other cultures, proponents claim, but examination of these cultures should operate with the methods, perspectives, and values of the majority culture. These values are typically those of liberalism: democracy, tolerance, and equality of persons.

Critics of this first proposal have argued that genuine understanding of other cultures is impossible if the study of other cultures is refracted through the distorting lens of the majority culture's perspective. Not all cultures share liberal values. Their value systems have arisen in often radically different social and historical circumstances, and thus, these critics argue, cannot be understood and adequately appreciated if one insists on approaching them solely from within the majority culture's perspective.

In response to this objection, a second version of multicultural education has developed that differs from the first in holding that multicultural education ought to adopt a neutral stance with respect to the value differences among cultures. The values of one culture should not be standards by which others are judged; each culture should be taken on its own terms. However, the methods of examination, study, and explanation of cultures in this second version of multicultural education are still identifiably Western. They are the methods of anthropology, social psychology, political science, and sociology. They are, that is, methods which derive from the Western scientific perspective and heritage.

Critics of this second form of multicultural education argue as follows: The Western scientific heritage is founded upon an epistemological system that prizes the objective over the subjective, the logical over the intuitive, and the empirically verifiable over the mystical. The methods of social-scientific examination of cultures are thus already value laden; the choice to examine and understand other cultures by these methods involves a commitment to certain values such as objectivity. Thus, the second version of multicultural education is not essentially different from the first. Scientific discourse has a privileged place in Western cultures, but the discourses of myth, tradition, religion, and mystical insight are often the dominant forms of thought and language of non-Western cultures. To insist on trying to understand non-scientific cultures by the methods of Western science is not only distorting, but is also an expression of an attempt to maintain a Eurocentric cultural chauvinism: the chauvinism of science. According to this objection, it is only by adopting the (often non-scientific) perspectives and methods of the cultures studied that real understanding can be achieved.

Which one of the following, if true, would provide the strongest objection to the criticism in the passage of the second version of multicultural education?

A. It is impossible to adopt the perspectives and methods of a culture unless one is a member of that culture.
B. Many non-Western societies have value systems that are very similar to one another.
C. Some non-Western societies use their own value system when studying cultures that have different values.
D. Students in Western societies cannot understand their culture's achievements unless such achievements are treated as the subject of Western scientific investigations.
E. Genuine understanding of another culture is necessary for adequately appreciating that culture.

Many educators in Canada and the United States advocate <u>multicultural education</u> as a means of achieving multicultural understanding. There are, however, a <u>variety of proposals</u> as to what multicultural education should consist of. <u>The most modest</u> of these proposals holds that schools and colleges should promote multicultural understanding by teaching about other cultures, teaching which proceeds from <u>within the context of the majority culture</u>. Students should learn about other cultures, proponents claim, but examination of these cultures should operate with the methods, perspectives, and values of the majority culture. These values are typically those of <u>liberalism</u>: democracy, tolerance, and equality of persons.

So one way to teach about different cultures is through the lens of Western liberalism.

<u>Critics</u> of this first proposal have argued that genuine understanding of other cultures is impossible if the study of other cultures is refracted through the distorting lens of the majority culture's perspective. Not all cultures share liberal values. Their value systems have arisen in often radically different social and historical circumstances, and thus, these critics argue, cannot be understood and adequately appreciated if one insists on approaching them solely from within the majority culture's perspective.

Critics argue that adopting a Eurocentric framework in learning about different cultures is problematic.

In response to this objection, a <u>second version of multicultural education</u> has developed that differs from the first in holding that multicultural education ought to adopt a <u>neutral stance</u> with respect to the value differences among cultures. The values of one culture should not be standards by which others are judged; each culture should be taken on its own terms. However, the methods of examination, study, and explanation of cultures in this second version of multicultural education are <u>still identifiably Western</u>. They are the methods of anthropology, social psychology, political science, and sociology. They are, that is, methods which derive from the Western scientific perspective and heritage.

A second way to study foreign cultures is devised, but the author still finds it problematic: even though we are no longer making value judgments, our methodology is still Eurocentric.

<u>Critics</u> of this second form of multicultural education argue as follows: The Western scientific heritage is founded upon an epistemological system that prizes the objective over the subjective, the logical over the intuitive, and the empirically verifiable over the mystical. The <u>methods</u> of social-scientific examination of cultures are thus <u>already value laden</u>; the choice to examine and understand other cultures by these methods involves a commitment to certain values such as objectivity. Thus, the second version of multicultural education is not essentially different from the first. Scientific discourse has a privileged place in Western cultures, but the discourses of myth, tradition, religion, and mystical insight are often the dominant forms of thought and language of non-Western cultures. To insist on trying to understand non-scientific cultures by the methods of Western science is not <u>only distorting, but is also an expression of an attempt to maintain a Eurocentric cultural chauvinism</u>: the chauvinism of science. According to this objection, it is only by adopting the (often non-scientific) perspectives and methods of the cultures studied that real understanding can be achieved.

Criticisms of the second approach is expanded upon. In this passage, the author introduces two ways to study non-Western cultures and the criticisms levelled against them. I think the Comparison-Evaluation framework works well here. While the author's stance is not explicit, we can sense from paragraph 2 and 3 that they seem more on the side of the critics.

We are attacking a specific criticism voiced in the passage. The question stem is a little complicated so let's simplify it.

The passage describes a second version of multicultural education. A criticism is voiced against it. Our job is to weaken that criticism. In other words, we are trying to defend the second version of multicultural education.

What is the second version of multicultural education, and what is the criticism levelled against it?

We know from the passage that the second version of multicultural education does not view the minority culture from the majority culture's perspective but strives to adopt a neutral stance. Critics attack it for using Western methodologies, for using the "*methods of anthropology, social psychology, political science, and sociology.*"

For the critics, Western methods are still flawed because of their commitment to objectivism and science. In order to achieve a real understanding of the cultures studied, we must adopt the non-scientific perspectives and methods of the local cultures.

How can we weaken this position?

We can suggest that it will be extremely hard to shed our objective and scientific methods when studying minority cultures, or that even though these methods have their shortcomings, we really have no alternatives. We can also suggest that we cannot realistically adopt the non-scientific perspectives and methods of local cultures without compromising the validity of the studies.

    A.   *It is impossible to adopt the perspectives and methods of a culture unless one is a member of that culture.*

This strongly worded answer is directly attacking the last sentence of the passage, which is a view held by the critics. The critics would like to adopt the perspectives and methods of the culture being studied. This answer is telling us that what they propose is impossible.

    B.   *Many non-Western societies have value systems that are very similar to one another.*

If they are similar, can they be studied via the scientific method? Do these value systems contain elements of objectivity? The effect of this answer choice is unclear.

    C.   *Some non-Western societies use their own value system when studying cultures that have different values.*

And should they be criticized for doing so? If so, then we are actually supporting the critics' position. Because no one should use their own value systems while studying a different culture.

Or is it okay? If it's okay for them, perhaps it's also ok for Westerners? Again, an unclear answer choice.

    D.   *Students in Western societies cannot understand their culture's achievements unless such achievements are treated as the subject of Western scientific investigations.*

This has no effect on the critics' argument. The critics are saying that we cannot use western scientific methods to study non-western cultures. This answer is saying that we need to use western methods to study western culture.

    E.   *Genuine understanding of another culture is necessary for adequately appreciating that culture.*

Yes, you need genuine understanding, but can that be achieved via western methodology? We don't know.

The correct answer is A.

In both questions, we saw the importance of pre-phrasing what a potential answer/answers might look like. To do this we had to dissect the question, know exactly what position we are supposed to attack, locate the source material, and brainstorm potential objections.

PT22 S1 Q23 (PT22 Passage 4)

What it means to "explain" something in science often comes down to the application of mathematics. Some thinkers hold that mathematics is a kind of language—a systematic contrivance of signs, the criteria for the authority of which are internal coherence, elegance, and depth. The application of such a highly artificial system to the physical world, they claim, results in the creation of a kind of statement about the world. Accordingly, what matters in the sciences is finding a mathematical concept that attempts, as other language does, to accurately describe the functioning of some aspect of the world.

At the center of the issue of scientific knowledge can thus be found questions about the relationship between language and what it refers to. A discussion about the role played by language in the pursuit of knowledge has been going on among linguists for several decades. The debate centers around whether language corresponds in some essential way to objects and behaviors, making knowledge a solid and reliable commodity; or, on the other hand, whether the relationship between language and things is purely a matter of agreed-upon conventions, making knowledge tenuous, relative, and inexact.

Lately the latter theory has been gaining wider acceptance. According to linguists who support this theory, the way language is used varies depending upon changes in accepted practices and theories among those who work in a particular discipline. These linguists argue that, in the pursuit of knowledge, a statement is true only when there are no promising alternatives that might lead one to question it. Certainly this characterization would seem to be applicable to the sciences. In science, a mathematical statement may be taken to account for every aspect of a phenomenon it is applied to, but, some would argue, there is nothing inherent in mathematical language that guarantees such a correspondence. Under this view, acceptance of a mathematical statement by the scientific community— by virtue of the statement's predictive power or methodological efficiency—transforms what is basically an analogy or metaphor into an explanation of the physical process in question, to be held as true until another, more compelling analogy takes its place.

In pursuing the implications of this theory, linguists have reached the point at which they must ask: If words or sentences do not correspond in an essential way to life or to our ideas about life, then just what are they capable of telling us about the world? In science and mathematics, then, it would seem equally necessary to ask: If models of electrolytes or $E = mc^2$, say, do not correspond essentially to the physical world, then just what functions do they perform in the acquisition of scientific knowledge? But this question has yet to be significantly addressed in the sciences.

Which one of the following statements, if true, lends the most support to the view that language has an essential correspondence to the things it describes?

A. The categories of physical objects employed by one language correspond remarkably to the categories employed by another language that developed independently of the first.
B. The categories of physical objects employed by one language correspond remarkably to the categories employed by another language that derives from the first.
C. The categories of physical objects employed by speakers of a language correspond remarkably to the categories employed by other speakers of the same language.
D. The sentence structures of languages in scientifically sophisticated societies vary little from language to language.
E. Native speakers of many languages believe that the categories of physical objects employed by their language correspond to natural categories of objects in the world.

We know that there are two theories of language. Theory 1 says that language has an essential connection to the object it refers to. Theory 2 says that language is purely a matter of agreed upon conventions.

Take the letters "d," "o," and "g." Why do these three letters, when combined, refer to a four-legged canine? Is it because there's a real connection between the sound/spelling of the word and the actual animal species itself (Theory 1); or is it because we simply chose these letters, and people all decided to go along with it? (Theory 2)

If the second theory is true, does this mean that as long as there is consensus, we can use different words/language to refer to different things and no meaning would be lost?

To strengthen the first theory, we would want an answer that shows us that language and words do indeed refer to concrete objects. Alternatively, we can have an answer that weakens the plausibility of Theory 2, and that would indirectly strengthen Theory 1. So we can also have an answer choice that tells us that language isn't purely a matter of convention/consensus.

>   A.   *The categories of physical objects employed by one language correspond remarkably to the categories employed by another language that developed independently of the first.*

So two languages, evolving independently from each other, use similar words to refer to the same thing. Why is this the case? The likelihood of both languages choosing the categories arbitrarily is lower, because both languages came to these categories independently.

Think of the following analogy: if two teams of scientists working independently from each other both come to the conclusion that there is water on Mars, then the likelihood of such an occurrence is increased. Maybe there is water on Mars after all.

So this answer is increasing the likelihood that the categories in languages actually do refer to physical objects in real life.

>   B.   *The categories of physical objects employed by one language correspond remarkably to the categories employed by another language that derives from the first.*

If one language is derived from the first, then there's the possibility that the categories were transferred from one language to the other. But how did these categories come to being in the first place? Was it because the speakers of the first language developed a consensus, or because the categories referred to real objects? It's unclear.

>   C.   *The categories of physical objects employed by speakers of a language correspond remarkably to the categories employed by other speakers of the same language.*

Same language, same categories, we still don't know if Theory 1 or 2 offers a better explanation for this.

>   D.   *The sentence structures of languages in scientifically sophisticated societies vary little from language to language.*

Advanced societies have similar sentence structure. Why is that? Does having advanced sentence structure mean that their language refers to concrete objects, or are based on conventions? We don't know.

>   E.   *Native speakers of many languages <u>believe</u> that the categories of physical objects employed by their language correspond to natural categories of objects in the world.*

> Many people believe in Theory 1. But is this belief justified? We don't know, we wanted an answer choice to support Theory 1's plausibility. This answer starts to lead us in that direction, but leaves a pretty big gap unfilled.

A is the correct answer.

In this question, it was basically impossible to have come up with a pre-phrased answer that resembled the actual correct answer. The best we could have done was to think about the general ways in which we could have strengthened Theory 1, or perhaps weakened Theory 2.

Once we got to the answer choices, we really had to think about the distinctions between each answer choice. We also had to think about the implications of each answer and how they would impact the plausibility of Theory 1 vs. Theory 2.

So in conclusion, dissect the question stem, isolate the position we are meant to strengthen/weaken, come up with potential answers, and compare actual answer choices for their impacts.

***

Let's look at one more Strengthen Question:

PT32 S2 Q23 (PT32 Passage 4)

Most scientists who study the physiological effects of alcoholic beverages have assumed that wine, like beer or distilled spirits, is a drink whose only active ingredient is alcohol. Because of this assumption, these scientists have rarely investigated the effects of wine as distinct from other forms of alcoholic beverages. Nevertheless, unlike other alcoholic beverages, wine has for centuries been thought to have healthful effects that these scientists—who not only make no distinction among wine, beer, and distilled spirits but also study only the excessive or abusive intake of these beverages—have obscured.

Recently, a small group of researchers has questioned this assumption and investigated the effects of moderate wine consumption. While alcohol has been shown conclusively to have negative physiological effects—for example, alcohol strongly affects the body's processing of lipids (fats and other substances including cholesterol), causing dangerous increases in the levels of these substances in the blood, increases that are a large contributing factor in the development of premature heart disease—the researchers found that absorption of alcohol into the bloodstream occurs much more slowly when subjects drink wine than when they drink distilled spirits. More remarkably, it was discovered that deaths due to premature heart disease in the populations of several European countries decreased dramatically as the incidence of moderate wine consumption increased. One preliminary study linked this effect to red wine, but subsequent research has shown identical results whether the wine was white or red. What could explain such apparently healthful effects?

For one thing, the studies show increased activity of a natural clot-breaking compound used by doctors to restore blood flow through blocked vessels in victims of heart disease. In addition, the studies of wine drinkers indicate increased levels of certain compounds that may help to prevent damage from high lipid levels. And although the link between lipid processing and premature heart disease is one of the most important discoveries in modern medicine, in the past 20 years researchers have found several additional important contributing factors. We now know that endothelial cell reactivity (which affects the thickness of the innermost walls of blood vessels) and platelet adhesiveness (which influences the degree to which platelets cause blood to clot) are each linked to the development of premature heart disease. Studies show that wine appears to have ameliorating effects on both of these factors: it decreases the thickness of the innermost walls of blood vessels, and it reduces platelet adhesiveness. One study demonstrated a decrease in platelet adhesiveness among individuals who drank large amounts of grape juice. This finding may be the first step in confirming speculation that the potentially healthful effects of moderate wine intake may derive from the concentration of certain natural compounds found in grapes and not present in other alcoholic beverages.

Which one of the following, if true, would most strengthen the passage's position concerning the apparently healthful effects of moderate wine consumption?

- A. Subjects who consumed large amount of grape juice exhibited decreased thickness of the innermost walls of their blood vessels.
- B. Subjects who were habitual drinkers of wine and subjects who were habitual drinkers of beer exhibited similar lipid levels in their bloodstreams.
- C. Subjects who drank grape juice exhibited greater platelet adhesiveness than did subjects who drank no grape juice.
- D. Subjects who drank excessive amounts of wine suffered from premature heart disease at roughly the same rate as moderate wine drinkers.
- E. Subjects who possess a natural clot-breaking compound were discovered to have a certain gene that is absent from subjects who do not possess the compound.

We know from the passage that there were several healthful benefits of wine consumption:

1. slower absorption of alcohol into the bloodstream (paragraph 2)
2. increased activity of a natural clot-breaking compound (paragraph 3)
3. increased level of certain compounds that may help prevent damage from high lipid levels (paragraph 3)
4. decreased thickness of the innermost walls of blood vessels (paragraph 3)
5. reduced platelet adhesiveness (paragraph 3)

I assume that the correct answer will reiterate one of the above.

> A. *Subjects who consumed large amount of grape juice exhibited decreased thickness of the innermost walls of their blood vessels.*

Grape juice leads to Beneficial Effect #4. This is definitely strengthening the argument.

> B. *Subjects who were habitual drinkers of wine and subjects who were habitual drinkers of beer exhibited similar lipid levels in their bloodstreams.*

This is actually weakening the argument. The whole point of the argument is that moderate assumption of wine is better than other alcoholic drinks. This answer tells us that wine is perhaps no better than beer.

> C. *Subjects who drank grape juice exhibited greater platelet adhesiveness than did subjects who drank no grape juice.*

Be careful! Greater platelet adhesiveness causes platelets to stick together, which causes blood to clot. This is the opposite of what we want.

> D. *Subjects who drank <u>excessive amounts</u> of wine suffered from premature heart disease at roughly the <u>same rate as moderate wine drinkers</u>.*

So moderate wine drinkers and binge wine drinkers suffered from the same rate of premature heart disease. That can tell us one of two things, either it's okay to drink a lot of wine; or it's not okay to drink even a moderate amount of wine.

This answer choice is **open to interpretation**, and we would like an answer that shows a definitive benefit resulting from "moderate" wine consumption.

> E. *Subjects who possess a natural clot-breaking compound were discovered to have a certain gene that is absent from subjects who do not possess the compound.*

People who have the clot breaking compound are due to genetics. So maybe it's not due to wine consumption after all, so wine isn't as great as we had thought. This answer weakens.

Analogies and Examples

Let's look at two more closely related question types: Analogy Questions and Exemplify Questions. Before we do that let's go over the nuanced differences between an Analogy and an Example.

Again, we are turning to an excerpt from LR Perfection:

An **analogy** is, according to the dictionary definition, *"a comparison between two things, typically for the purpose of clarification."* In other words, it is an advanced form of a comparison. For instance, physicists have used the analogy of a gun shooting bullets to better describe the process of radiation, where energy is "shot" out in the form of particles. The two processes are similar enough so that we can visualize one to better understand the other.

An **example**, on the other hand, is a specific instance that illustrates a general principle, theory, or concept. A pistol is an example of a gun; nuclear radiation is an example of radiation, and solar energy is an example of energy.

Try to think about the differences between these two concepts. When you are giving an analogy to a concept, you are using something else that works in a similar way to illustrate how the concept works. When you are giving an example, you are finding a specific instance that fits the description or requirements of the concept in question.

Analogy Questions

For many students, Analogy Questions are probably one of the hardest questions to encounter, because the process of problem solving for these questions is non-linear. In a lot of previous question types, we simply had to interpret the question stem, find the relevant textual support, and find the most strongly supported answer choice. For Analogy Questions, on the other hand, we not only have to **locate** the relevant material, we have to **summarize** the concept in our own language, and finally we need to **brainstorm** possible parallel comparisons.

The brainstorming aspect is the hardest, because it's something that we will not have encountered in other question types. Some students have found Parallel Questions from the LR section a helpful aid in thinking about Analogy Questions. I am personally ambivalent. But it's something you can look at if you find these questions especially challenging.

It's very difficult to explain how to "brainstorm" without actually going through the motions ourselves. So let's jump straight to some Analogy Questions, and use my explanations as a guide after you have selected an answer choice.

PT28 S4 Q7 (PT28 Passage 2)

Long after the lava has cooled, the effects of a major volcanic eruption may linger on. In the atmosphere a veil of fine dust and sulfuric acid droplets can spread around the globe and persist for years. Researchers have generally thought that this veil can block enough sunlight to have a chilling influence on Earth's climate. Many blame the cataclysmic eruption of the Indonesian volcano Tambora in 1815 for the ensuing "year without a summer" of 1816—when parts of the northeastern United States and southeastern Canada were hit by snowstorms in June and frosts in August.

The volcano-climate connection seems plausible, but, say scientists Clifford Mass and Davit Portman, it is not as strong as previously believed. Mass and Portman analyzed global temperature data for the years before and after nine volcanic eruptions, from Krakatau in 1883 to El Chichón in 1982. In the process they tried to filter out temperature changes caused by the cyclic weather phenomenon known as the El Niño-Southern Oscillation, which warms the sea surface in the equatorial Pacific and thereby warms the atmosphere. Such warming can mask the cooling brought about by an eruption, but it can also mimic volcanic cooling if the volcano happens to erupt just as an El Niño induced warm period is beginning to fade.

Once El Niño effects had been subtracted from the data, the actual effects of the eruptions came through more clearly. Contrary to what earlier studies had suggested, Mass and Portman found that minor eruptions have no discernible effect on temperature. And major, dust-spitting explosions, such as Krakatau or El Chichón, cause a smaller drop than expected in the average temperature in the hemisphere (Northern or Southern) of the eruption—only half a degree centigrade or less—a correspondingly smaller drop in the opposite hemisphere.

Other researchers, however, have argued that even a small temperature drop could result in a significant regional fluctuation in climate if its effects were amplified by climatic feedback loops. For example, a small temperature drop in the northeastern U.S. and southeastern Canada in early spring might delay the melting of snow, and the unmelted snow would continue to reflect sunlight away from the surface, amplifying the cooling. The cool air over the region could, in turn, affect the jet stream. The jet stream tends to flow at the boundary between cool northern air and warm southern air, drawing its power from the sharp temperature contrast and the consequent difference in pressure. An unusual cooling in the region could cause the stream to wander farther south than normal, allowing more polar air to come in behind it and deepen the region's cold snap. Through such a series of feedbacks a small temperature drop could be blown up into a year without a summer.

Not taking the effects of El Niño into account when figuring the effect of volcanic eruptions on Earth's climate is most closely analogous to not taking into account the

A. weight of a package as a whole when determining the weight of its contents apart from the packing material
B. monetary value of the coins in a pile when counting the number of coins in the pile
C. magnification of a lens when determining the shape of an object seen through the lens
D. number of false crime reports in a city when figuring the average annual number of crimes committed in that city
E. ages of new immigrants to a country before attributing a change in the average age of the country's population to a change in the number of births

Let's take a deep breath and look at this question. We want an analogy for not taking into account the effects of El Nino when figuring the effect of volcanic eruptions on Earth's climate.

So what is the effect of El Nino on how volcanic eruptions influence temperature?

Scientists originally thought that volcanic eruptions cause a drastic fall in temperature. But this was because they forgot to take into the effects of El Nino.

El Nino raises temperatures, so how can the El Nino account for a fall in temperature as well?

As the passage stated at the end of paragraph 2, "*but [El Nino] can also mimic volcanic cooling if the volcano happens to erupt just as an El Nino induced warm period is beginning to fade.*"

So what happens is that El Nino raised temperatures, but when El Nino ended, temperature started to drop. This is when the volcanoes erupted. The scientists mistakenly attributed the temperature drop to volcanic eruptions, when the real cause was in fact El Nino ending.

So if we were looking for an analogy, we should look for a case of where something is really caused by A, but we overlooked that, and mistakenly thought the cause to be B. **It really helps to summarize the relationship before looking at the answer choices.**

    A.   *weight of a package as a whole when determining the weight of its contents apart from the packing material*

This is really confusingly worded. I had to read it a few times before I figured out what it's trying to say. So you are trying to figure the weight of the contents and the packing material. But you overlook the total weight of the package.

In other words, you forget to look at the whole when trying to determine the parts. Is El Nino the overall cause of temperature drop? If El Nino is the overall cause, then what about Volcanic Eruptions?

I think if the answer had said something like "forgetting to look at the weight of the packing material when trying to determine the overall weight of a package," that would make more sense. That would be like saying forgetting to think about El Nino's effects when trying to figure out what really caused the temperature drop.

This answer is weird. But I would keep it for now.

    B.   *monetary value of the coins in a pile when counting the number of coins in the pile*

Number of coins and monetary value of coins are two different concepts, we are looking for two items of a similar nature (i.e. overlooking the real cause of temperature falling and thinking it's caused by something else).

    C.   *magnification of a lens when determining the shape of an object seen through the lens*

The shape wouldn't change with the magnification, it would only appear bigger or smaller. So maybe this answer is trying to suggest overlooking something that might amplify a cause?

This might work, because we did overlook the importance of El Nino. Let's keep this too for now. Between this and A, I think I can safely eliminate A.

    D.   *number of false crime reports in a city when figuring the average annual number of crimes committed in that city*

This is the opposite of what we want. In the passage, we overlooked the real cause (El Nino). Here, we are overlooking the false positives.

> E. *ages of new immigrants to a country before attributing a change in the average age of the country's population to a change in the number of births*

Here, we are overlooking another contributing factor, an alternative cause/influence. This results in a false conclusion.

This matches up with the nature of overlooking El Nino (the real cause behind temperature drops) and thinking the temperature drops are caused by volcanic eruptions.

E is a lot clearer to me in replicating the relationship as described in the passage than both C and A. I would go with E.

E is the correct answer.

As we saw in the previous question, **summarizing** the relationship upon which the analogy is based into **abstract terms**, and then doing the same with answer choices is a very helpful process. This process allows us to compare two discrete relationships from a different perspective.

In the following passage, we shall try an additional technique that can help us during the process of answer choice elimination, it's a tactic that we have encountered before – **reverse confirmation**.

According to the theory of gravitation, every particle of matter in the universe attracts every other particle with a force that increases as either the mass of the particles increases, or their proximity to one another increases, or both. Gravitation is believed to shape the structures of stars, galaxies, and the entire universe. But for decades cosmologists (scientists who study the universe) have attempted to account for the finding that at least 90 percent of the universe seems to be missing: that the total amount of observable matter—stars, dust, and miscellaneous debris—does not contain enough mass to explain why the universe is organized in the shape of galaxies and clusters of galaxies. To account for this discrepancy, cosmologists hypothesize that something else, which they call "dark matter," provides the gravitational force necessary to make the huge structures cohere.

What is dark matter? Numerous exotic entities have been postulated, but among the more attractive candidates—because they are known actually to exist—are neutrinos, elementary particles created as a by-product of nuclear fusion, radioactive decay, or catastrophic collisions between other particles. Neutrinos, which come in three types, are by far the most numerous kind of particle in the universe; however, they have long been assumed to have no mass. If so, that would disqualify them as dark matter. Without mass, matter cannot exert gravitational force; without such force, it cannot induce other matter to cohere.

But new evidence suggests that a neutrino does have mass. This evidence came by way of research findings supporting the existence of a long-theorized but never observed phenomenon called oscillation, whereby each of the three neutrino types can change into one of the others as it travels through space. Researchers held that the transformation is possible only if neutrinos also have mass. They obtained experimental confirmation of the theory by generating one neutrino type and then finding evidence that it had oscillated into the predicted neutrino type. In the process, they were able to estimate the mass of a neutrino at from 0.5 to 5 electron volts.

While slight, even the lowest estimate would yield a lot of mass given that neutrinos are so numerous, especially considering that neutrinos were previously assumed to have no mass. Still, even at the highest estimate, neutrinos could only account for about 20 percent of the universe's "missing" mass. Nevertheless, that is enough to alter our picture of the universe even if it does not account for all of dark matter. In fact, some cosmologists claim that this new evidence offers the best theoretical solution yet to the dark matter problem. If the evidence holds up, these cosmologists believe, it may add to our understanding of the role elementary particles play in holding the universe together.

As described in the last paragraph of the passage, the cosmologists' approach to solving the dark matter problem is most analogous to which one of the following?

A. A child seeking information about how to play chess consults a family member and so learns of a book that will instruct her in the game.
B. A child seeking to earn money by delivering papers is unable to earn enough money for a bicycle and so decides to buy a skateboard instead.
C. A child hoping to get a dog for his birthday is initially disappointed when his parents bring home a cat but eventually learns to love the animal.
D. A child seeking money to attend a movie is given some of the money by one of his siblings and so decides to go to each of his other siblings to ask for additional money.
E. A child enjoys playing sports with the neighborhood children but her parents insist that she cannot participate until she has completed her household chores.

What is the cosmologists' approach?

We know that they are trying to account for dark matter. Even if neutrinos are dark matter, they only account for 20%. So the approach is to look for something, but only finding a part of it.

Secondly, the cosmologists are actually okay with this partial discovery. Because it may add to our understanding of the universe. In other words, it's a good start.

Put into more abstract terms, the approach involves a partial discovery and continued optimism for the future.

> A. *A child seeking information about how to play chess consults a family member and so learns of a book that will instruct her in the game.*

Someone learns from a family member and a book. This is nowhere close to what we are looking for.

> B. *A child seeking to earn money by delivering papers is unable to earn enough money for a bicycle and so decides to buy a skateboard instead.*

This is looking better, the child is unable to earn enough money (cosmologists unable to find enough neutrinos), but the second part is suspect.

Instead of finding enough money for a bicycle they settle for a skateboard instead.

Let's try the tactic of Reverse Confirmation here. If this was the correct answer, what would the hypothetical passage look like?

Instead of finding enough neutrinos (money) to account for dark matter (bicycle), our cosmologists stop looking for dark matter and decide to come up with a new explanation/material (skateboard).

The cosmologists will keep on looking. They don't give up on their original goal or decides to give up on dark matter and settles for something else.

> C. *A child hoping to get a dog for his birthday is initially disappointed when his parents bring home a cat but eventually learns to love the animal.*

The second part of this answer choice might work with the passage. The scientists remain optimistic despite not finding enough neutrinos. But wanting a dog but getting a cat is like wanting something but getting something else. I think it's not quite getting some of what you wanted but not enough (i.e. neutrinos).

If this was the correct answer, then the passage should tell us that scientists were looking for neutrinos, but ended up finding quarks or some other cosmic element. They end up accepting quarks and decide on a new theory.

I don't particularly like either, but I would keep B and C as contenders as I go through the rest of the ACs.

> D. *A child seeking money to attend a movie is given some of the money by one of his siblings and so decides to go to each of his other siblings to ask for additional money.*

Someone who doesn't get enough, but keeps on looking. Cosmologists don't find enough neutrinos, but keep on looking. This works better than B and C.

> E. *A child enjoys playing sports with the neighborhood children but her parents insist that she cannot participate until she has completed her household chores.*

The child cannot play until she has finished her chores, so cosmologists cannot X until they do Y? This doesn't really make sense either.

The correct answer is D.

Whenever you are stuck on different answers in Analogy Questions, pretend each answer is correct, and ask yourself, how would you now redesign the passage around this answer choice?

Once you have figured out what the ideal passage would look like in relation to the answer choice in question, you will have an easier time figuring out which answer choice lies closer to the actual passage.

The answer choice whose ideal passage most closely resembles the actual passage will be the correct answer. This is what I call "**reverse confirmation**," and it allows us to see the discrepancies between answer choice and passage from a different perspective. We will examine this in greater detail in Chapter 17.

Exemplify Questions

As we mentioned earlier, Exemplify Questions will ask us to give an example based on a theory or practice mentioned in the passage. For these questions, we start with dissecting the question stem. What are we giving an example of? Once you know the specific idea or view that we are to exemplify, go back to the passage and isolate all descriptions of that idea or view. **Find as many details as you can**, because these details will serve as the criteria for matching or eliminating answer choices down the road.

Once we have these traits or descriptions of the idea or view to be exemplified, it's time to visit the answer choices. I don't try to pre-phrase what the correct answer might look like, because for these questions, the scope of the answer choice is essentially unlimited.

Instead, I proceed via the process of elimination, read each answer choice and ask myself whether they come into conflict with the traits I've isolated in the passage. If there is conflict, then that's reason for dismissal.

PT31 S4 Q27 (PT31 Passage 4)

Some of the philosophers find the traditional, subjective approach to studying the mind outdated and ineffectual. For them, the attempt to describe the sensation of pain or anger, for example, or the awareness that one is aware, has been surpassed by advances in fields such as psychology, neuroscience, and cognitive science. Scientists, they claim, do not concern themselves with how a phenomenon feels from the inside; instead of investigating private evidence perceivable only to a particular individual, scientists pursue hard data—such as the study of how nerves transmit impulses to the brain—which is externally observable and can be described without reference to any particular point of view. With respect to features of the universe such as those investigated by chemistry, biology, and physics, this objective approach has been remarkably successful in yielding knowledge. Why, these philosophers ask, should we suppose the mind to be any different?

But philosophers loyal to subjectivity are not persuaded by appeals to science when such appeals conflict with the data gathered by introspection. Knowledge, they argue, relies on the data of experience, which includes subjective experience. Why should philosophy ally itself with scientists who would reduce the sources of knowledge to only those data that can be discerned objectively?

On the face of it, it seems unlikely that these two approaches to studying the mind could be reconciled. Because philosophy, unlike science, does not progress inexorably toward a single truth, disputes concerning the nature of the mind are bound to continue. But what is particularly distressing about the present debate is that genuine communication between the two sides is virtually impossible. For reasoned discourse to occur, there must be shared assumptions or beliefs. Starting from radically divergent perspectives, subjectivists and objectivists lack a common context in which to consider evidence presented from each other's perspectives.

The situation may be likened to a debate between adherents of different religions about the creation of the universe. While each religion may be confident that its cosmology is firmly grounded in its respective sacred text, there is little hope that conflicts between their competing cosmologies could be resolved by recourse to the texts alone. Only further investigation into the authority of the texts themselves would be sufficient.

What would be required to resolve the debate between the philosophers of mind, then, is an investigation into the authority of their differing perspectives. How rational is it to take scientific description as the ideal way to understand the nature of consciousness? Conversely, how useful is it to rely solely on introspection for one's knowledge about the workings of the mind? Are there alternative ways of gaining such knowledge? In this debate, epistemology—the study of knowledge—may itself lead to the discovery of new forms of knowledge about how the mind works.

Based on the passage, which one of the following is most clearly an instance of the objectivist approach to studying the mind?

A.   collecting accounts of dreams given by subjects upon waking in order to better understand the nature of the subconscious

B.   interviewing subjects during extremes of hot and cold weather in order to investigate a connection between weather and mood

C.   recording subjects' evaluation of the stress they experienced while lecturing in order to determine how stress affects facility at public speaking

D.   analyzing the amount of a certain chemical in subjects' bloodstreams in order to investigate a proposed link between the chemical and aggressive behavior

E.   asking subjects to speak their thoughts aloud as they attempt to learn a new skill in order to test the relationship between mental understanding and physical performance

The objectivist approach is described in the first paragraph. It does not concern itself with how an individual feels, how a phenomenon feels from the inside. Instead, it's backed by hard data, data that can be observed by all and do not depend on individual POVs. It's the scientific approach applied in chemistry, biology, and physics.

    A.   collecting accounts of dreams <u>given by subjects</u> upon waking in order to better understand the nature of the subconscious

This is based on individual accounts, not hard data.

    B.   <u>interviewing subjects</u> during extremes of hot and cold weather in order to investigate a connection between weather and <u>mood</u>

Again, based on individual interviews, not hard data.

    C.   recording subjects' <u>evaluation of the stress they experienced</u> while lecturing in order to determine how stress affects facility at public speaking

Also based on personalized accounts of people's own experiences.

    D.   analyzing the amount of a certain chemical in subjects' bloodstreams in order to investigate a proposed link between the chemical and aggressive behavior

Finally, chemical levels of the blood, something that can be measured. This is hard data.

    E.   asking subjects to <u>speak their thoughts aloud</u> as they attempt to learn a new skill in order to test the relationship between mental understanding and physical performance

Again, this is based on individual accounts, or "how a phenomenon feels from the inside."

The correct answer is D.

PT50 S1 Q28 (PT50 Passage 4)

One of the foundations of scientific research is that an experimental result is credible only if it can be replicated—only if performing the experiment a second time leads to the same result. But physicists John Sommerer and Edward Ott have conceived of a physical system in which even the least change in the starting conditions—no matter how small, inadvertent, or undetectable—can alter results radically. The system is represented by a computer model of a mathematical equation describing the motion of a particle placed in a particular type of force field.

Sommerer and Ott based their system on an analogy with the phenomena known as riddled basins of attraction. If two bodies of water bound a large landmass and water is spilled somewhere on the land, the water will eventually make its way to one or the other body of water, its destination depending on such factors as where the water is spilled and the geographic features that shape the water's path and velocity. The basin of attraction for a body of water is the area of land that, whenever water is spilled on it, always directs the spilled water to that body.

In some geographical formations it is sometimes impossible to predict, not only the exact destination of the spilled water, but even which body of water it will end up in. This is because the boundary between one basin of attraction and another is riddled with fractal properties; in other words, the boundary is permeated by an extraordinarily high number of physical irregularities such as notches or zigzags. Along such a boundary, the only way to determine where spilled water will flow at any given point is actually to spill it and observe its motion; spilling the water at any immediately adjacent point could give the water an entirely different path, velocity, or destination.

In the system posited by the two physicists, this boundary expands to include the whole system: i.e., the entire force field is riddled with fractal properties, and it is impossible to predict even the general destination of the particle given its starting point. Sommerer and Ott make a distinction between this type of uncertainty and that known as "chaos"; under chaos, a particle's general destination would be predictable but its path and exact destination would not.

There are presumably other such systems because the equation the physicists used to construct the computer model was literally the first one they attempted, and the likelihood that they chose the only equation that would lead to an unstable system is small. If other such systems do exist, **metaphorical examples of riddled basins of attraction** may abound in the failed attempts of scientists to replicate previous experimental results—in which case, scientists would be forced to question one of the basic principles that guide their work.

Which one of the following is most clearly one of the "metaphorical examples of riddled basins of attraction" mentioned?

A. A scientist is unable to determine if mixing certain chemicals will result in a particular chemical reaction because the reaction cannot be consistently reproduced since sometimes the reaction occurs and other times it does not despite starting conditions that are in fact exactly the same in each experiment.

B. A scientist is unable to determine if mixing certain chemicals will result in a particular chemical reaction because the reaction cannot be consistently reproduced since it is impossible to bring about starting conditions that are in fact exactly the same in each experiment.

C. A scientist is unable to determine if mixing certain chemicals will result in a particular chemical reaction because the reaction cannot be consistently reproduced since it is impossible to produce starting conditions that are even approximately the same from one experiment to the next.

D. A scientist is able to determine that mixing certain chemicals results in a particular chemical reaction because it is possible to consistently reproduce the reaction even though the starting conditions vary significantly from one experiment to the next.

E. A scientist is able to determine that mixing certain chemicals results in a particular chemical reaction because it is possible to consistently reproduce the reaction despite the fact that the amount of time it takes for the reaction to occur varies significantly depending on the starting conditions of the experiment.

Let's think about what is meant by the "Riddled Basin of Attraction."

In an RBA, "*it is impossible to predict even the general destination of the particle given its starting point.*" The only way to determine the destination is to actually "*spill [the water] and observe its motion; spilling the water at any immediately adjacent point could give the water an entirely different path, velocity, or destination.*"

We also know from the first paragraph that "*the least change in the starting conditions – no matter how small, inadvertent, or undetectable – can alter the results radically.*"

So essentially, we are looking for an example where we don't know how the results will turn out. Tiny changes to the starting conditions will lead to drastically different results.

> A. *A scientist is unable to determine if mixing certain chemicals will result in a particular chemical reaction because the reaction cannot be consistently reproduced since sometimes the reaction occurs and other times it does not despite starting conditions that are in fact exactly the same in each experiment.*

We want an answer that tells us even if the starting conditions changed a little bit, the results will be completely off.

> B. *A scientist is unable to determine if mixing certain chemicals will result in a particular chemical reaction because the reaction cannot be consistently reproduced since it is impossible to bring about starting conditions that are in fact exactly the same in each experiment.*

So the starting conditions are not exactly the same, and as a result, the results are never the same.

> C. *A scientist is unable to determine if mixing certain chemicals will result in a particular chemical reaction because the reaction cannot be consistently reproduced since it is impossible to produce starting conditions that are even approximately the same from one experiment to the next.*

This is too much. We know from the passage that we are looking for something that tells us "*even the tiniest changes to the starting conditions lead to different results.*"

> D. *A scientist is able to determine that mixing certain chemicals results in a particular chemical reaction because it is possible to consistently reproduce the reaction even though the starting conditions vary significantly from one experiment to the next.*

This is the opposite of what we want. If we can replicate the experiment and the results, then the Riddled Basin of Attraction doesn't apply.

> E. *A scientist is able to determine that mixing certain chemicals results in a particular chemical reaction because it is possible to consistently reproduce the reaction despite the fact that the amount of time it takes for the reaction to occur varies significantly depending on the starting conditions of the experiment.*

Changes to the starting conditions only affect the timing of the experiment, but not the actual results. This is not what we are looking for. The correct answer is B.

14. Advanced Question Tactics

Question Stem Analysis

Now that we have taken a look at the 16 different types of RC Questions (19 if you count each of the 4 Purpose sub-types), we will practice some of the habits that will make your job on the exam a lot easier. Not only are these skills and habits crucial for the advanced test taker, they are also priceless for any student who is attempting to tackle more challenging questions in general.

The first skill is something that we have already seen in practice before, I call it **Question Stem Analysis**. In many previous questions, we saw that the question stem itself gave us many hints on what we should look for from the passage and where to look for it. If we thought long and hard about what the question is asking of us, it may even offer us insights on what the correct answer might look like.

Just as we have used to first paragraph of the passage as a tool to situate ourselves within the scope of the discussion and help us get ready to fully focus on the purpose and content of the passage, we can use the individual question stems to guide us in approaching that particular question.

Question Stem Analysis will make our RC experience a lot smoother once you start to do it out of habit. It's the essential step linking our reading of the passage and our comparison of the answer choices. In a way, it will help us mentally arrange the information just read, and anticipate what the correct answer could look like. This makes tackling the answer choices a lot easier.

***

Take a look at the following question stems, what can they tell us? Can we derive any guidance from them on how to approach the question, what to look for in the passage, and how to pre-phrase a potential answer?

With which one of the following statements about the views held by the medievalists mentioned in line 1 would the author of the passage most probably agree?

Which one of the following, if true, would most clearly undermine a portion of Ringer's argument as the argument is described in the passage?

It can be inferred from the author's discussion of McLoughlin's views that the author thinks that Cherokee acculturalization in the 1820s.

- *With which one of the following statements about the views held by the medievalists mentioned in line 1 would the author of the passage most probably agree?*

So this is an Author POV Question. We are being asked what the author's perspective towards the views held by the medievalists is mentioned in line 1.

In order to solve this problem, we must first try to clear up the following:

Who are the medievalists mentioned in line 1? Are they mentioned anywhere else?

What are the views held by these medievalists? Are these views also described in line 1? Are they described elsewhere? Do these medievalists hold multiple views? If so, what are they? (Remember, the question is asking us what the author thinks about the views held by the medievalists. If the medievalists hold several views, the correct AC can be about any one of those. **Just because the medievalists are mentioned in line 1, it doesn't mean that the answer choice will be about a view also described in line 1**.)

What is the author's stance on each of the views attributed to the medievalists? Is the author's stance explicit (with textual support), or implicit (inferred from words that express tone and attitude)?

As you can see, there is so much preparation that goes into truly understanding a more complicated question stem.

- *Which one of the following, if true, would most clearly undermine a portion of Ringer's argument as the argument is described in the passage?*

Ok, so this is a Weaken Question.

What is Ringer's argument? Are there multiple arguments? Can I structurally break down the argument into premises and a conclusion?

Can I divide Ringer's argument into "portions?"

What are some ways in which I can attack each of these individual "portions?"

- *It can be inferred from the author's discussion of McLoughlin's views that the author thinks that Cherokee acculturalization in the 1820s.*

Inference Question, so explicit support if I can find it, but slight gap in reasoning is acceptable if there's no better alternative answer.

So I have to find the author's discussion of McLoughlin's views. Where are these views discussed?

Also, the question is not asking about what McLoughlin thinks! It's asking about what the author thinks!

So after locating discussions of McLoughlin's views, I now have to try to figure out what the author personally thinks. I have to pay special attention to words that express the author's voice, attitude, tone, or opinion.

Finally, we are looking for what the author thinks about Cherokee acculturalization in the 1820s. Where is this discussed? Not the 1830s, not the 1810s, the 1820s.

PT23 S4 Q7 (PT23 Passage 2)

Medievalists usually distinguished medieval public law from private law: the former was concerned with government and military affairs and the latter with the family, social status, and land transactions. Examination of medieval women's lives shows this distinction to be overly simplistic. Although medieval women were legally excluded from roles thus categorized as public, such as soldier, justice, jury member, or professional administrative official, women's control of land—usually considered a private or domestic phenomenon—had important political implications in the feudal system of thirteenth-century England. Since land equaled wealth and wealth equaled power, certain women exercised influence by controlling land. Unlike unmarried women (who were legally subject to their guardians) or married women (who had no legal identity separate from their husbands), women who were widows had autonomy with respect to acquiring or disposing of certain property, suing in court, incurring liability for their own debts, and making wills.

Although feudal lands were normally transferred through primogeniture (the eldest son inheriting all), when no sons survived, the surviving daughters inherited equal shares under what was known as partible inheritance. In addition to controlling any such land inherited from her parents and any bridal dowry— property a woman brought to the marriage from her own family—a widow was entitled to use of one-third of her late husband's lands. Called "dower" in England, this grant had greater legal importance under common law than did the bridal dowry; no marriage was legal unless the groom endowed the bride with this property at the wedding ceremony. In 1215 Magna Carta guaranteed a widow's right to claim her dower without paying a fine; this document also strengthened widows' ability to control land by prohibiting forced remarriage. After 1272 women could also benefit from jointure: the groom could agree to hold part or all of his lands jointly with the bride, so that if one spouse died, the other received these lands.

Since many widows had inheritances as well as dowers, widows were frequently the financial heads of the family; even though legal theory assumed the maintenance of the principle of primogeniture, the amount of land the widow controlled could exceed that of her son or of other male heirs. Anyone who held feudal land exercised authority over the people attached to the land—knights, rental tenants, and peasants—and had to hire estate administrators, oversee accounts, receive rents, protect tenants from outside encroachment, punish tenants for not paying rents, appoint priests to local parishes, and act as guardians of tenants' children and executors of their wills. Many married women fulfilled these duties as deputies for husbands away at court or at war, but widows could act on their own behalf. Widows' legal independence is suggested by their frequent appearance in thirteenth-century English legal records. Moreover, the scope of their sway is indicated by the fact that some controlled not merely single estates, but multiple counties.

With which one of the following statements about the views held by the medievalists mentioned in line 1 would the author of the passage most probably agree?

    A. The medieval role of landowner was less affected by thirteenth-century changes in law than these
        medievalists customarily have recognized.
    B. The realm of law labeled public by these medievalists ultimately had greater political implications than
        that labeled private.
    C. The amount of wealth controlled by medieval women was greater than these medievalists have
        recorded.
    D. The distinction made by these medievalists between private law and public law fails to consider some
        of the actual legal cases of the period.
    E. The distinction made by these medievalists between private and public law fails to address the political
        importance of control over land in the medieval era.

What were the views held by the medievalists? They made a clear-cut distinction between public and private law. Government and military affairs were under the jurisdiction of public law, while family, social status, and land transactions were categorized under private law.

A quick glance through the rest of the passage confirmed for me that no additional positions attributed to the medievalists were introduced. So now I focus on the author's attitude toward the medievalists' distinction between the public and private spheres.

The author's opinion is that this distinction is overly simplistic. Perhaps the correct answer will just say that the "distinction is too simple." But that would probably be too easy.

Let's expand on the author's position a little bit more. If the author thinks the distinction too simplistic, that must mean that in reality, there is a lot of overlap between the two.

This is what the author suggests. Women, while nominally a part of the private sphere, could control land, which meant that they exercised power and influence, which had important political implications. Women's control of land, we learned throughout the passage, granted them a certain degree of legal independence.

So given all this information, what could a potential correct answer look like? The author would probably agree that the view is too simple, it doesn't account for women's control of land, or that it overlooks how women can gain power and influence through possession of land.

    A.   *The medieval role of landowner was less affected by thirteenth-century changes in law than these medievalists customarily have recognized.*

When it comes to more complex questions as this one, it is **crucial** to have a strong pre-phrased answer before you look at the answer choices. Otherwise we will have to give each answer equal attention, and for the answer choices with which we are not familiar, we have to repeat the process of interpreting it and going back to the passage to find evidence for it.

This answer does not look like what we had in mind, but what is it saying?

If the author thinks that the medieval role of the landowners was less affected by the changes in law than what the medievalists have recognized, then that means the medievalists have been overemphasizing the influences of legal changes on the role of the landowner.

Does the passage suggest that? What do we know about thirteenth century changes in the law?

We know that women could benefit from some of the legal reforms. If we take the term "landowner" to mean women, does the author think them to be less affected?

No. The whole point of the passage is to suggest that women were able to gain power and influence through possession of land, and legal changes in the thirteenth century aided in that.

Notice how time consuming that whole process was? If we had a clear idea of what the correct answer might look like; however, we could have skipped over this answer and looked through the rest of the answer choices to see if we can find what we had in mind first. That would save us a lot of time.

    B.   *The realm of law labeled public by these medievalists ultimately had greater political implications than that labeled private.*

This is an unsupported comparison of two concepts mentioned in the passage. The author would say that the distinction between the two are not as clear cut as the medievalists like to think; because a group (women) nominally governed by private law also interacted with what was governed by public law.

But the author never argued that public law had greater political implications than private law. This might be true intuitively, since public law dealt with government and military affairs, but it's not a view held by the author, at least not mentioned or inferable from the passage.

C. *The amount of wealth controlled by medieval women was greater than these medievalists have recorded.*

This might be true, but again, it's not a point of contention the author would dispute over with the medievalists.

Even though the author would probably agree that women held more property than previously thought, We don't know if the medievalists kept an accurate record of the amount of wealth controlled by women.

D. *The distinction made by these medievalists between private law and public law fails to consider some of the actual legal cases of the period.*

Again, this is possible. Maybe the medievalists thought the distinctions were so clear cut because they didn't look into public cases that involved women. But again, remember what this question is asking us! The correct answer choice will identify a view of the medievalists and the author's opinion towards that view.

As such, the correct answer choice will satisfy two requirements:

One, it's indeed concerning a view held by the medievalists, as supported by text from the passage.

Two, the position is something that would be agreed to by the author, also needing support from the passage.

But the author never once suggests that the shortcomings of the medievalists was due to their failure to consider the legal cases of the period.

E. *The distinction made by these medievalists between private and public law fails to address the political importance of control over land in the medieval era.*

This is essentially the author's central thesis. The distinction is an oversimplification because it overlooks the women who exerted political influence via control over land.

E is the correct answer.

PT21 S4 Q4 (PT21 Passage 1)

Musicologists concerned with the "London Pianoforte school," the group of composers, pedagogues, pianists, publishers, and builders who contributed to the development of the piano in London at the turn of the nineteenth century, have long encountered a formidable obstacle in the general unavailability of music of this "school" in modern scholarly editions. Indeed, much of this repertory has more or less vanished from our historical consciousness. Granted, the sonatas and Gradus ad Parnassum of Muzio Clementi and the nocturnes of John Field have remained familiar enough (though more often than not in editions lacking scholarly rigor), but the work of other leading representatives, like Johann Baptist Cramer and Jan Ladislav Dussek, has eluded serious attempts at revival.

Nicholas Temperley's ambitious new anthology decisively overcomes this deficiency. What underscores the intrinsic value of Temperley's editions is that the anthology reproduces nearly all of the original music in facsimile. Making available this cross section of English musical life—some 800 works by 49 composers—should encourage new critical perspectives about how piano music evolved in England, an issue of considerable relevance to our understanding of how piano music developed on the European continent, and of how, finally, the instrument was transformed from the fortepiano to what we know today as the piano.

To be sure, the concept of the London Pianoforte school itself calls for review. "School" may well be too strong a word for what was arguably a group unified not so much by stylistic principles or aesthetic creed as by the geographical circumstance that they worked at various times in London and produced pianos and piano music for English pianos and English markets. Indeed, Temperley concedes that their "variety may be so great as to cast doubt on the notion of a 'school.'"

The notion of a school was first propounded by Alexander Ringer, who argued that laws of artistic survival forced the young, progressive Beethoven to turn outside Austria for creative models, and that he found inspiration in a group of pianists connected with Clementi in London. Ringer's proposed London Pianoforte school did suggest a circumscribed and fairly unified group—for want of a better term, a school—of musicians whose influence was felt primarily in the decades just before and after 1800. After all, Beethoven did respond to the advances of the Broadwood piano—its reinforced frame, extended compass, triple stringing, and pedals, for example—and it is reasonable to suppose that London pianists who composed music for such an instrument during the critical phase of its development exercised no small degree of influence on Continental musicians. Nevertheless, perhaps the most sensible approach to this issue is to define the school by the period (c. 1766–1873) during which it flourished, as Temperley has done in the anthology.

Which one of the following, if true, would most clearly undermine a portion of Ringer's argument as the argument is described in the passage?

A. Musicians in Austria composed innovative music for the Broadwood piano as soon as the instrument became available.
B. Clementi and his followers produced most of their compositions between 1790 and 1810.
C. The influence of Continental musicians is apparent in some of the works of Beethoven.
D. The pianist-composers of the London Pianoforte school shared many of the same stylistic principles.
E. Most composers of the London Pianoforte school were born on the Continent and were drawn to London by the work of Clementi and his followers.

What is Ringer's argument?

Ringer treats the LPS as a "school." Remember that Temperley had created an anthology that very roughly categorized a series of composers of the same geographic region and period.

Ringer thinks of this group as a tightly knit "school," because they were all connected to Clementi, and that Beethoven came specifically to this group for help and inspiration. Beethoven was forced to turn outside Austria for inspiration.

Secondly, there was the Broadwood piano, which was an earlier forerunner of the modern piano. The LPS composers composed music for this instrument, and the instrument was influential on mainland European musicians. We are also told that Beethoven responded to the advances of the Broadwood piano, which means that the LPS probably composed music for the Broadwood piano, influenced Beethoven, and other continental European musicians.

How can we weaken this argument, or just a "portion" of it?

Ringer's argument consists of two parts: one, LPS was a tight knit group that influenced Beethoven; two, LPS influences on the Broadwood piano in turn influenced continental musicians. So if I was trying to weaken Ringer's argument, it would probably attack one of these two propositions.

   A.   *Musicians in Austria composed innovative music for the Broadwood piano as soon as the instrument became available.*

We know that Beethoven is from Austria. Ringer thinks that when Beethoven went to London, he was influenced by these composers who worked with the Broadwood piano. Beethoven subsequently learned about the Broadwood piano from the LPS guys. The innovation pioneered by the LPS was a significant influence on both Beethoven and continental musicians.

This answer weakens the link between Austria and the LPS. Ringer had said that Beethoven was forced to turn to the LPS for artistic survival. But if the influences of the Broadwood piano were clearly felt in Austria as soon as the instrument became available, then Beethoven wouldn't have been forced to go to London to learn about it.

Ultimately, this answer choice isn't what we were looking for, but it does attack one aspect of the author's argument, namely that Beethoven had no choice but to leave Austria.

   B.   *Clementi and his followers produced most of their compositions between 1790 and 1810.*

This is Ringer's view. Ringer believed that LPS influence was felt primarily in the decades just before and after 1800 (i.e. 1790 – 1810).

   C.   *The influence of Continental musicians is apparent in some of the works of Beethoven.*

Ringer thinks that LPS influenced Beethoven and continental musicians. But this answer does not conflict with that. Maybe Beethoven was influenced by both the LPS and continental musicians.

   D.   *The pianist-composers of the London Pianoforte school shared many of the same stylistic principles.*

This strengthens Ringer's argument, if they shared many principles, they are more likely to be a close knit school.

E. *Most composers of the London Pianoforte school were born on the Continent and were drawn to London by the work of Clementi and his followers.*

This strengthens Ringer's argument. So the LPS is not just a random group of composers, but people who shared the same network and stylistic vision.

PT18 S3 Q21 (PT18 Passage 3)

Until recently, it was thought that the Cherokee, a Native American tribe, were compelled to assimilate Euro-American culture during the 1820s. During that decade, it was supposed, White missionaries arrived and, together with their part Cherokee intermediaries, imposed the benefits of "civilization" on Cherokee tribes while the United States government actively promoted acculturalization by encouraging the Cherokee to switch from hunting to settled agriculture. This view was based on the assumption that the end of a Native American group's economic and political autonomy would automatically mean the end of its cultural autonomy as well.

William G. McLoughlin has recently argued that not only did Cherokee culture flourish during and after the 1820s, but the Cherokee themselves actively and continually reshaped their culture. Missionaries did have a decisive impact during these years, he argues, but that impact was far from what it was intended to be. The missionaries' tendency to cater to the interests of an acculturating part-Cherokee elite (who comprised the bulk of their converts) at the expense of the more traditionalist full-Cherokee majority created great intratribal tensions. As the elite initiated reforms designed to legitimize their own and the Cherokee Nation's place in the new republic of the United States, anti-mission Cherokee reacted by fostering revivals of traditional religious beliefs and practices. However, these revivals did not, according to McLoughlin, undermine the elitist reforms, but supplemented them with popular, traditionalist counterparts.

Traditionalist Cherokee did not reject the elitist reforms outright, McLoughlin argues, simply because they recognized that there was more than one way to use the skills the missionaries could provide them. As he quotes one group as saying, "We want our children to learn English so that the White man cannot cheat us." Many traditionalist Cherokee welcomed the missionaries for another reason: they perceived that it would be useful to have White allies. In the end, McLoughlin asserts, most members of the Cherokee council, including traditionalists, supported a move which preserved many of the reforms of the part-Cherokee elite but limited the activities and influence of the missionaries and other White settlers. According to McLoughlin, the identity and culture that resulted were distinctively Cherokee, yet reflected the larger political and social setting in which they flourished.

Because his work concentrates on the nineteenth century, McLoughlin unfortunately overlooks earlier sources of influence, such as eighteenth-century White resident traders and neighbors, thus obscuring the relative impact of the missionaries of the 1820s in contributing to both acculturalization and resistance to it among the Cherokee. However, McLoughlin is undoubtedly correct in recognizing that culture is an ongoing process rather than a static entity, and he has made a significant contribution to our understanding of how Cherokee culture changed while retaining its essential identity after confronting the missionaries.

It can be inferred from the author's discussion of McLoughlin's views that the author thinks that Cherokee acculturalization in the 1820s

- A. was reversed in the decades following the 1820s
- B. may have been part of an already-existing process of acculturalization
- C. could have been the result of earlier contacts with missionaries
- D. would not have occurred without the encouragement of the United States government
- E. was primarily a result of the influence of White traders living near the Cherokee

What does the author think about Cherokee acculturalization in the 1820s?

Remember, it's what the author thinks, not what McLoughlin thinks.

The author's views of McLouglin's views are in the last paragraph of the passage: McLoughlin unfortunately overlooks earlier sources of influence, thus obscuring the relative impact of the missionaries of the 1820s in contributing to both acculturalization and resistance to it among the Cherokee.

Remember, McLouglin believed that the role of the missionaries was limited, their efforts were limited to Cherokee elites and were often used by the Cherokee for their own ends.

Here, the author is suggesting that the impact of the missionaries has been obscured, meaning that the missionaries actually had a bigger impact. Why is that? Because McLouglin overlooked earlier sources of influence, such as traders and neighbors. Perhaps the earlier traders and neighbors paved the way for the missionaries?

So the correct answer choice may suggest that Cherokee acculturalization in the 1820s was in fact more dependent on missionaries, and that it was impacted by earlier contact with traders and neighbors.

> A.   *was reversed in the decades following the 1820s*

This is unsupported by the passage.

> B.   *<u>may</u> have been part of an already-existing process of acculturalization*

Yes, this matches up with one of our anticipated answers. The earlier impact from traders and neighbors was overlooked; in other words, acculturalization may have been a part of an already existing process.

> C.   *could have been the result of earlier contacts with missionaries*

Not the result of earlier contacts with missionaries, but traders and neighbors.

> D.   *<u>would not</u> have occurred <u>without</u> the encouragement of the United States government*

This answer choice is stating a conditional relationship, Acculturalization → US government encouragement. We know that the US government encouraged acculturalization, but is it necessary?

> E.   *was <u>primarily a result</u> of the influence of White traders living near the Cherokee*

The author thinks that M overlooks the influences of traders and neighbors, so the traders probably had some influence. But to say it's the primary influence is probably a stretch.

The correct answer is B.

Hard to Find Evidence

We now move to the second most common reason that makes certain questions more difficult than we expected. This primarily applies to questions whose answers must be derived or inferred from the passage. For these questions (According to the Passage, Infer, Restricted Scope), the test makers will often hide the essential details needed to solve the question in easily overlooked places, such as at the very beginning or very end of the passage.

Details from the **very beginning of the passage** are quite often overlooked because as we are just getting started with the passage, we are still trying to wrap our minds around what the passage is about, its scope, and its purpose.

Similarly, details from the **very end of the passage** can be overlooked also. A bad habit during the passage reading that plagues many of us, myself included, is that by the time we get to the last few lines of the passage, we tend to skip it in anticipation of the questions that are coming next. In other words, we can miss important details situated at the very end of a passage because we are no longer focused on the reading, but rather, thinking about getting to the questions as fast as we can. The test makers know about this, and will often ask a question whose correct answer is backed by evidence from the very end of a passage, evidence that many of us have conveniently overlooked.

Another way the test makers can confuse us is by trying to get us to **misattribute details** associated with one POV with another. Let me explain:

Assume in a hypothetical passage there were three different speakers, each with their own views. Let's call them Washington, Jefferson, and Franklin. Washington talked about issues A, B, C in the passage, while the other two people talked about issues B, C, and D.

A question will then ask us *which of the following issues was NOT discussed by Washington.*

While it's fairly clear that the correct answer will be "D," if this happened on a real passage in a real question, it might be much more difficult. First of all, D will look really familiar to us as it will have appeared in the passage. So we will have trouble eliminating it right away. Rather than simply eliminating the answer choice that did not appear in the passage, we now have to figure out which person said what, and which person *didn't* say what.

Finally, beware of questions where the correct answer choice is backed by evidence that must be **synthesized**. We have seen synthesized information already in previous questions. Just remember that sometimes the correct answer can be derived by combining information from different parts of the passage. Even if there isn't explicit word for word backing for an answer choice, it may still be correct.

***

PT25 S1 Q23 (PT25 Passage 4)

Scientists typically advocate the analytic method of studying complex systems: systems are divided into component parts that are investigated separately. But nineteenth-century critics of this method claimed that when a system's parts are isolated its complexity tends to be lost. To address the perceived weaknesses of the analytic method these critics put forward a concept called organicism, which posited that the whole determines the nature of its parts and that the parts of a whole are interdependent.

Organicism depended upon the theory of internal relations, which states that relations between entities are possible only within some whole that embraces them, and that entities are altered by the relationships into which they enter. If an entity stands in a relationship with another entity, it has some property as a consequence. Without this relationship, and hence without the property, the entity would be different— and so would be another entity. Thus, the property is one of the entity's defining characteristics. Each of an entity's relationships likewise determines a defining characteristic of the entity.

One problem with the theory of internal relations is that not all properties of an entity are defining characteristics: numerous properties are accompanying characteristics—even if they are always present, their presence does not influence the entity's identity. Thus, even if it is admitted that every relationship into which an entity enters determines some characteristic of the entity, it is not necessarily true that such characteristics will define the entity; it is possible for the entity to enter into a relationship yet remain essentially unchanged.

The ultimate difficulty with the theory of internal relations is that it renders the acquisition of knowledge impossible. To truly know an entity, we must know all of its relationships; but because the entity is related to everything in each whole of which it is a part, these wholes must be known completely before the entity can be known. This seems to be a prerequisite impossible to satisfy.

Organicists' criticism of the analytic method arose from their failure to fully comprehend the method. In rejecting the analytic method, organicists overlooked the fact that before the proponents of the method analyzed the component parts of a system, they first determined both the laws applicable to the whole system and the initial conditions of the system; proponents of the method thus did not study parts of a system in full isolation from the system as a whole. Since organicists failed to recognize this, they never advanced any argument to show that laws and initial conditions of complex systems cannot be discovered. Hence, organicists offered no valid reason for rejecting the analytic method or for adopting organicism as a replacement for it.

According to the passage, organicists' chief objection to the analytic method was that the method

    A. oversimplified systems by isolating their components
    B. assumed that a system can be divided into component parts
    C. ignored the laws applicable to the system as a whole
    D. claimed that the parts of a system are more important than the system as a whole
    E. denied the claim that entities enter into relationships

The evidence for the correct answer choice lies squarely in the first paragraph:

> *Scientists typically advocate the analytic method of studying complex systems: systems are divided into component parts that are investigated separately. But nineteenth-century* **critics** *of* **this method** *claimed that* **when a system's parts are isolated its complexity tends to be lost**. *To address the perceived weaknesses of the analytic method these critics put forward a concept called organicism, which posited that the whole determines the nature of its parts and that the parts of a whole are interdependent.*

What was the organicists' chief criticism of the analytic method? The nineteenth century critics of the analytic method came up with organicism. Their criticism of the analytic method was that the analytic system led to a loss of a system's complexity.

The correct answer is A, which says that the analytic system led to an "oversimplification" of a system.

Were you able to remember to look in the first paragraph and select A as the correct answer? It's the only answer choice with direct textual support.

PT22 S1 Q14+Q15 (PT22 Passage 2)

In recent years, a growing belief that the way society decides what to treat as true is controlled through largely unrecognized discursive practices has led legal reformers to examine the complex interconnections between narrative and law. In many legal systems, legal judgments are based on competing stories about events. Without having witnessed these events, judges and juries must validate some stories as true and reject others as false. This procedure is rooted in objectivism, a philosophical approach that has supported most Western legal and intellectual systems for centuries. Objectivism holds that there is a single neutral description of each event that is unskewed by any particular point of view and that has a privileged position over all other accounts. The law's quest for truth, therefore, consists of locating this objective description, the one that tells what really happened, as opposed to what those involved thought happened. The serious flaw in objectivism is that there is no such thing as the neutral, objective observer. As psychologists have demonstrated, all observers bring to a situation a set of expectations, values, and beliefs that determine what the observers are able to see and hear. Two individuals listening to the same story will hear different things, because they emphasize those aspects that accord with their learned experiences and ignore those aspects that are dissonant with their view of the world. Hence there is never any escape in life or in law from selective perception, or from subjective judgments based on prior experiences, values, and beliefs.

The societal harm caused by the assumption of objectivist principles in traditional legal discourse is that, historically, the stories judged to be objectively true are those told by people who are trained in legal discourse, while the stories of those who are not fluent in the language of the law are rejected as false.

Legal scholars such as Patricia Williams, Derrick Bell, and Mari Matsuda have sought empowerment for the latter group of people through the construction of alternative legal narratives. Objectivist legal discourse systematically disallows the language of emotion and experience by focusing on cognition in its narrowest sense. These legal reformers propose replacing such abstract discourse with powerful personal stories. They argue that the absorbing, nonthreatening structure and tone of personal stories may convince legal insiders for the first time to listen to those not fluent in legal language. The compelling force of personal narrative can create a sense of empathy between legal insiders and people traditionally excluded from legal discourse and, hence, from power. Such alternative narratives can shatter the complacency of the legal establishment and disturb its tranquility. Thus, the engaging power of narrative might play a crucial, positive role in the process of legal reconstruction by overcoming differences in background and training and forming a new collectivity based on emotional empathy.

The passage suggests that Williams, Bell, and Matsuda would most likely agree with which one of the following statements regarding personal stories?

A. Personal stories are more likely to adhere to the principles of objectivism than are other forms of discourse.
B. Personal stories are more likely to de-emphasize differences in background and training than are traditional forms of legal discourse.
C. Personal stories are more likely to restore tranquility to the legal establishment than are more adversarial forms of discourse.
D. Personal stories are more likely to lead to the accurate reconstruction of facts than are traditional forms of legal narrative.
E. Personal stories are more likely to be influenced by a person's expectations, values, and beliefs than are other forms of discourse.

***

Which one of the following statements about legal discourse in legal systems based on objectivism can be inferred from the passage?

A. In most Western societies' the legal establishment controls access to training in legal discourse.
B. Expertise in legal discourse affords power in most Western societies.
C. Legal discourse has become progressively more abstract for some centuries.
D. Legal discourse has traditionally denied the existence of neutral, objective observers.
E. Traditional legal discourse seeks to reconcile dissonant world views.

PT22 S1 Q14: The discussion of Williams, Bell and Matsuda is in the last paragraph of the passage. Unfortunately, the question is so open ended that it's quite difficult to pre-phrase what the correct answer might look like.

All three would agree that the inclusion of personal stories in legal narratives would empower those without the legal training, or that personal stories would focus on recognition in the wider sense. Personal stories can convince legal insiders to listen to outsiders, and include people traditionally excluded from legal discourse and power.

They would also agree that personal stories would shatter the complacency of legal establishments, and they would overcome the differences in background and training between the traditional participants in legal discourse and the outsiders.

> A. Personal stories *are more likely to adhere to the principles of objectivism* than are other forms of discourse.

This is the opposite of what we want. Objectivist principles are found in traditional legal discourse. Personal stories emphasize the individual, hence subjectivist principles.

> B. Personal stories are *more likely* to de-emphasize differences in background and training than are traditional forms of legal discourse.

Yes, this is supported by the **last sentence** of the passage, *"the engaging power of narrative might play a crucial, positive role…by overcoming differences in background and training…"*

We know that traditional legal discourse requires training and a specialized background. Personal stories level the playing field. In other words, personal stories are more likely to de-emphasize differences in background and training.

> C. Personal stories are more likely to *restore* tranquility to the legal establishment than are more adversarial forms of discourse.

Opposite answer, personal stories are more likely to disturb legal establishments' tranquility.

> D. Personal stories are more likely to lead to the *accurate* reconstruction of facts than are traditional forms of legal narrative.

The whole point of personal stories is to emphasize that there isn't a single, objectivist version of what is accurate.

> E. Personal stories are more likely to be influenced by a person's expectations, values, and beliefs than are other forms of discourse.

This is never mentioned in the last paragraph; furthermore, the author says that there is *never any escape from selective perception* in the last sentence of the first paragraph. So all forms of discourse are influenced by a person's expectations, values, and beliefs. Whether personal stories are more likely to be influenced by these factors is unknown.

The correct answer is B.

***

14. Advanced Question Tactics

<u>PT22 S1 Q15</u>: Another open-ended question, with possible supporting evidence that could come from anywhere in the passage.

The legal discourse in systems based on objectivism favors the interpretations and testimonies of those who are trained in such discourse. They disallow the language of emotion and experience, they focus on recognition in its narrowest sense.

We can also argue that such legal discourse has prevented or hindered the reconciliation of those who are included and those who are excluded; and has been contributory to the legal system's complacency and tranquility. Inclusion in traditional objectivist legal discourse is also a pathway to power.

  A. *In most Western societies' the legal establishment controls access to training in legal discourse.*

This is probably true, but it's not backed by evidence from the passage.

  B. *Expertise in legal discourse affords power in most Western societies.*

So we know that in "most" Western legal systems, the approach is rooted in objectivism. (Middle of first paragraph)

We also know that exclusion from the objectivist legal discourse leads to exclusion from power. (Near the end of the last paragraph)

If we combine these two pieces of information, B has ample support.

Answer choice B is a good example of an answer choice whose evidence/support needs to be combined or **synthesized** from two different areas of the passage; with a key piece of evidence found near the **very end of the paragraph**.

  C. *Legal discourse has become progressively more abstract for some centuries.*

We know that objectivist legal discourse has underlined Western systems for centuries, and that such discourse is abstract. But has it become more abstract for some centuries? We do not know.

  D. *Legal discourse has traditionally denied the existence of neutral, objective observers.*

This is the opposite of what we want. Objectivist legal discourse believes in the existence of neutral, objective observers.

  E. *Traditional legal discourse seeks to reconcile dissonant world views.*

Again, an opposite answer. Traditional legal discourse holds that there is a singular, accurate description of what happened.

The correct answer is B.

PT27 S3 Q13 (PT27 Passage 2)

Personal names are generally regarded by European thinkers in two major ways, both of which deny that names have any significant semantic content. In philosophy and linguistics, John Stuart Mill's formulation that "proper names are meaningless marks set upon…persons to distinguish them from one another" retains currency; in anthropology, Claude Lévi-Strauss's characterization of names as being primarily instruments of social classification has been very influential. Consequently, interpretation of personal names in societies where names have other functions and meanings has been neglected. Among the Hopi of the southwestern United States, names often refer to historical or ritual events in order both to place individuals within society and to confer an identity upon them. Furthermore, the images used to evoke these events suggest that Hopi names can be seen as a type of poetic composition.

Throughout life, Hopis receive several names in a sequence of ritual initiations. Birth, entry into one of the ritual societies during childhood, and puberty are among the name-giving occasions. Names are conferred by an adult member of a clan other than the child's clan, and names refer to that name giver's clan, sometimes combining characteristics of the clan's totem animal with the child's characteristics. Thus, a name might translate to something as simple as "little rabbit," which reflects both the child's size and the representative animal.

More often, though, the name giver has in mind a specific event that is not apparent in a name's literal translation. One Lizard clan member from the village of Oraibi is named Lomayayva, "beautifully ascended." This translation, however, tells nothing about either the event referred to—who or what ascended—or the name giver's clan. The name giver in this case is from Badger clan. Badger clan is responsible for an annual ceremony featuring a procession in which masked representations of spirits climb the mesa on which Oraibi sits. Combining the name giver's clan association with the receiver's home village, "beautifully ascended" refers to the splendid colors and movements of the procession up the mesa. The condensed image this name evokes—a typical feature of Hopi personal names—displays the same quality of Western Apache place names that led one commentator to call them "tiny imagist poems."

Hopi personal names do several things simultaneously. They indicate social relationships—but only indirectly—and they individuate persons. Equally important, though, is their poetic quality; in a sense they can be understood as oral texts that produce aesthetic delight. This view of Hopi names is thus opposed not only to Mill's claim that personal names are without inherent meaning but also to Lévi-Strauss's purely functional characterization. Interpreters must understand Hopi clan structures and linguistic practices in order to discern the beauty and significance of Hopi names.

It can be inferred from the passage that each of the following features of Hopi personal names contributes to their poetic quality EXCEPT:

    A.   their ability to be understood as oral texts
    B.   their use of condensed imagery to evoke events
    C.   their capacity to produce aesthetic delight
    D.   their ability to confer identity upon individuals
    E.   their ability to subtly convey meaning

Essentially, we are looking for a feature of Hopi names that DOES NOT contribute to their poetic quality. Let's see what kind support can we gather from the passage.

   A.   their ability to be understood as oral texts

Hopi personal names do several things simultaneously. They indicate social relationships—but only indirectly—and they individuate persons. Equally important, though, is their **poetic quality**; in a sense they can be understood **as oral texts** that produce aesthetic delight.

   B.   their use of condensed imagery to evoke events

The **condensed image** this name **evokes**—a typical feature of Hopi personal names—displays the same quality of Western Apache place names that led one commentator to call them "tiny imagist **poems**."

   C.   their capacity to produce aesthetic delight

Equally important, though, is their **poetic quality**; in a sense they can be understood as oral texts that **produce aesthetic delight**.

   D.   their ability to confer identity upon individuals

This answer is tricky. The passage does mention a name's ability to confer identity upon individuals. Most students will see this and realize that it looks familiar. But remember what this question is asking of us!

Four of the incorrect answers should contribute to the poetic nature of Hopi names; while the correct answer will not. Does a name's ability to confer identity upon individuals contribute to a name's poetic nature?

At the end of the first paragraph, we are told that Hopi names not only confer identities upon individuals, but also have a poetic quality to them. These are two separate qualities of Hopi names, but one does not contribute to the other.

   E.   their ability to subtly convey meaning

This does not have explicit support like answer choices A through C. However, we know that names such as "beautifully ascended" refers to the splendid colors and movements of the procession up the mesa. So the poetic names do convey more meaning than just the words used.

The name "beautifully ascended" refers to an event "not apparent in a name's literal translation."

The correct answer is D.

Summary

In this chapter we looked at some of the ways in which the test makers can raise the difficulty level of a particular question.

We must pay special attention to the wording of the question stem. This is an extremely underrated skill but something that I found invaluable in improving our RC performance. Ask yourself always what each question entails:

What type of question are we looking at? What is the approach to this type of questions?

What kind of support/evidence would I need to find in order to come up with a pre-phrased answer? Where should I be looking for such evidence?

Whose views am I most concerned with? Is it someone mentioned in the passage, or is it the author's?

Once I've located the appropriate evidence, what should I do with it?

Once you become proficient at passage analysis (covered in Part I of the book), and answer choice ranking/elimination (something that we will cover in Part III of the book), the advanced scorer will devote a large portion of their focus to thinking about what exactly a particular question is asking of them. So stop and think about the implications of more complex questions!

***

For a lot of questions whose answers are to be derived from the passage, we need to find the relevant evidence to confirm/reject each of the answer choices. However, such evidence can be hard to discover. So look at the very beginning and very end of a passage if you are stuck.

Second, be aware that sometimes a correct answer choice will be supported by more than one piece of the text. As we saw in an earlier example, we can have multiple statements all converging to support the correct answer choice. So just because an answer appears to be only partially supported, don't rush to eliminate it. Ask yourself if the rest of the support is elsewhere.

Finally, just because an answer choice is backed by evidence from the passage, it doesn't mean that it's the correct answer. Always check back on the question and be sure of what is asked of us.

Part III: The Answers

DRAGON TEST

15. Answer Choice Elimination

A Systematic and Step-by-Step Approach to Answer Choice Selection

We have looked at how to analyze a passage during the initial reading in Part I of the book, and the different types of questions and all their associated quirks and strategies in Part II. Now we shall look at how to navigate the five answer choices and maximize our chances of picking the right one.

Rather than reading through all the answer choices and then picking the one that sounds right to you, the advanced test taker will follow a two-stage process.

The first step is to look through the answer choices and **eliminate** the ones that you know are **flawed**.

We do this by looking at the keywords in each answer choice, based on the requirements of the particular question and our pre-phrased answer, and eliminate all the problematic options.

Hopefully for easier questions, this step is enough to lead us to the correct answer. But for the harder questions, we are usually only able to eliminate three of the answers, leaving us with two equally attractive choices. Sometimes we might only be able to eliminate two out of five choices, and we'd have to go into round two with three answers.

This brings us to the second step of the answer choice selection process:

We rank the remaining two or three answer choices based on specific criteria, and pick the answer choice with the least/smallest problems. We do this by **ranking** the remaining answer choices.

In this chapter we will look at the first step to the answer choice selection process, or Answer Choice Elimination. We will look at the specific standards that we use to determine whether an answer choice is flawed, as well as the systematic approach we apply to the answer choices to ensure that we don't miss anything. In the following two chapters we will focus on the second step, Answer Choice Ranking.

Does a flea have a mouth?

Yes, it's a legitimate question. Do fleas have mouths?

Unless you are intimately familiar with a flea's biological anatomy, you probably didn't know. But I would bet that as you thought about this question, an image of a flea with a mouth flashed across your mind.

This was a question raised by Dr. Steven Pinker, the world-famous cognitive psychologist in his book, "How the Mind Works." Humans have the tendency to try to build connections between pieces of information, mentally and visually, when we are faced with a question that we don't know the answer to. We don't know whether fleas have mouths, but no matter how hard we try to think about this question, we cannot shake the image of a flea with a mouth from our mind.

This illustrates an important takeaway about human cognition. When we are confronted with a confusing or difficult problem, our minds will subconsciously try to help it make sense. Nowhere is this better exemplified in our RC answer selection process:

Imagine that we have just read the passage, and because it was a rather difficult passage we only have a rudimentary understanding of its structure and a vague recollection of its details. Now as we are going through the answer choices, not knowing what the correct answer might look like, most if not all of the answers are starting to seem like they might be right. Depending on how we interpret them, they all seem to make sense.

When we are unsure of what to look for, our mind will begin to try to "help." It does so by connecting whatever information we remember from the passage to the answer choices that we are currently looking at, and try to "fit" the information to the answer choice.

Just like how our brain will try to graft a mouth on to a flea in our mind's eye, so it will subtly reinterpret the things that we have read, and make it appear that the answer choice is a good contender. Now repeat the process for several answer choices, and we are just running in circles.

Don't Stop Nitpicking

As a result, instead of asking ourselves whether "this answer choice could be the correct answer?" (Because our brain will eagerly tell us "Yes it could!") Ask yourself, **what is wrong with this answer choice?**

How we approach answer choices should be completely different from how we approach relationships. We want to be overly critical and nitpicking instead of being gracious and accepting. We want to look at each answer choice, go through its exact wording, and ask ourselves, "*do any of the words in this answer choice have problems with them? If so, are they grounds for elimination?*"

Scope, Strength, Opposite Answers, Improper Relationships

Generally speaking, answer choices are wrong for **four major reasons**: they can be out of scope, they can be too strong or too weak for our purposes, do the opposite of what we want; or they can formulate a relationship between two concepts mentioned in the passage when such a relationship is non-existent. Of course, whether an answer choice is right or wrong also depends on the type of question that we are dealing with, so it's crucial that we have done a proper job with question stem analysis and have tried, to the best of our ability, to pre-phrase what the correct answer might look like.

Since the majority of RC questions will be restricted scope questions, or questions whose correct answer must be derived from the passage, **out of scope** answers are the most prominent culprits among wrong answer choices. We have already seen legions of out of scope answer choices throughout the book, so these trap answers should be very familiar to us, but it's always important to remember to check the topic of discussion described in the answer choice, and make sure that it aligns with the topic being discussed in the passage.

For questions that ask us for the Main Point, Purpose, or Author's Attitude, beware of answer choices whose scope are **too narrow**. (*Just remember from the MP Chapter that a narrow-scope answer that reflects the author's opinion is preferable to an answer choice that covers all the content but leaves out what the author thinks.*)

For non-restricted scope questions such as Strengthen/Weaken, Analogy, or Exemplify Questions, scope is less of an issue. Although you still want to pick an answer choice that closely mirrors what has been described in the passage as an analogy or example. Similarly, even if we can select an answer choice that appears out of scope for Strengthen/Weaken Questions, we still want to check to make sure that the answer has a tangible effect on the specific issue that we are trying to strengthen or weaken.

***

The second type of issues that frequent wrong answer choices are answers that are either **too strong** or **too weak**. Again, the criteria for answer choice elimination varies depending on the question type. For the majority of RC Questions, as we have mentioned in earlier chapters, we prefer more conservatively worded answer choices.

This is because more conservatively worded or more weakly worded answer choices require a lower **threshold of proof**. For questions whose correct answer must be proven or inferred from the text of the passage, a weakly worded AC will be easier to prove. Thus, strong adjectives/adverbs or powerful verbs are a red flag to me in the answer choices.

However, for questions asking us about the author's attitude or Author/Third Party POV questions, make sure the correct answer is an accurate reflection of what we were told in the passage. Answers that are either too weak or too strong would be suspect.

But again, this doesn't really apply to Strengthen/Weaken, Analogy, and Exemplify Question types. For Strengthen/Weaken answer choices, strong answers are okay as long as *they have a direct and tangible effect.* In many ways, a more powerful answer is preferred to an ambiguous one. For Analogy and Exemplify Questions; on the other hand, we should be concerned with whether the analogy or example given in the answer choice is *an accurate reflection* of the original position.

***

The third type of wrong answers are the **Opposite Answers**, these are usually fairly easy to discover as long as you don't lose track of the question. A Strengthen answer in a Weaken Question, or an answer choice that says the polar opposite of what was mentioned in the passage in an Inference or According to the Passage Question would be such examples.

As long as you have a strong grasp of what the passage talked about as well as what the question is asking us to do, you should be fine.

***

Finally, we have the answer choices that contain **improper relationships**. The most common manifestation of this occurs when the answer choice extrapolates an unsupported relationship between different concepts mentioned in the passage.

For example, let's assume that in our hypothetical passage, the author had listed two causes for climate change: logging/deforestation and factory emissions. The passage never mentioned any linkages between the two, neither correlative nor causal. They may be independent or interconnected, but it's not a relationship touched upon in the passage.

In such an instance, a very attractive trap answer will suggest that factory emissions/manufacturing is in fact a cause for the acceleration of deforestation; or that a third common cause (maybe industrialization) is responsible for both deforestation and factory emissions. Such relationships are possible and perhaps even likely in the real world, but since it was never discussed in the passage, it would be improper to infer.

Another way improper relationship traps occur in answer choices is when an AC obfuscates different point of views. For instance, by misattributing a view belonging to speaker B to speaker A, when the passage contains multiple views and multiple perspectives, the test makers would have created a very attractive wrong answer choice.

***

Let's look now at a few sample questions:

PT21 S4 Q14 (PT21 Passage 2)

What is "law"? By what processes do judges arrive at opinions, those documents that justify their belief that the "law" dictates a conclusion one way or the other? These are among the oldest questions in jurisprudence, debate about which has traditionally been dominated by representatives of two schools of thought: proponents of natural law, who see law as intertwined with a moral order independent of society's rules and mores, and legal positivists, who see law solely as embodying the commands of a society's ruling authority.

Since the early 1970s, these familiar questions have received some new and surprising answers in the legal academy. This novelty is in part a consequence of the increasing influence there of academic disciplines and intellectual traditions previously unconnected with the study of law. Perhaps the most influential have been the answers given by the Law and Economics school. According to these legal economists, law consists and ought to consist of those rules that maximize a society's material wealth and that abet the efficient operation of markets designed to generate wealth. More controversial have been the various answers provided by members of the Critical Legal Studies movement, according to whom law is one among several cultural mechanisms by which holders of power seek to legitimate their domination. Drawing on related arguments developed in anthropology, sociology, and history, the critical legal scholars contend that law is an expression of power, but not, as held by the positivists, the power of the legitimate sovereign government. Rather, it is an expression of the power of elites who may have no legitimate authority, but who are intent on preserving the privileges of their race, class, or gender.

In the mid-1970s, James Boyd White began to articulate yet another interdisciplinary response to the traditional questions, and in so doing spawned what is now known as the Law and Literature movement. White has insisted that law, particularly as it is interpreted in judicial opinions, should be understood as an essentially literary activity. Judicial opinions should be read and evaluated not primarily as political acts or as attempts to maximize society's wealth through efficient rules, but rather as artistic performances. And like all such performances, White argues, each judicial opinion attempts in its own way to promote a particular political or ethical value.

In the recent Justice as Translation, White argues that opinion-writing should be regarded as an act of "translation," and judges as "translators." As such, judges find themselves mediating between the authoritative legal text and the pressing legal problem that demands resolution. A judge must essentially "re-constitute" that text by fashioning a new one, which is faithful to the old text but also responsive to and informed by the conditions, constraints, and aspirations of the world in which the new legal problem has arisen.

Proponents of the Law and Literature movement would most likely agree with which one of the following statements concerning the relationship between the law and judges' written opinions?

- A. The once-stable relationship between law and opinion-writing has been undermined by new and radical theoretical developments.
- B. Only the most politically conservative of judges continue to base their opinions on natural law or on legal positivism.
- C. The occurrence of different legal situations requires a judge to adopt diverse theoretical approaches to opinion-writing.
- D. Different judges will not necessarily write the same sorts of opinions when confronted with the same legal situation.
- E. Judges who subscribe to divergent theories of jurisprudence will necessarily render divergent opinions.

Let's start by looking at the question. It's a Third Party POV Question. We are asked about the beliefs/positions of the Proponents of the Law and Literature Movement.

The Law and Literature Movement was only introduced in the last two paragraphs of the passage, so that's where we will devote our attention. Remember, what we want to know is what this group thinks about the relationship between the law and judges' opinions.

Paragraph 3 tells us that judges' opinions are interpretations of the law, and they are essentially literary activity. They are not political acts or attempts to maximize social wealth, but "*artistic performances.*" These "*performances*" attempt to "*promote a particular political or ethical value.*"

In paragraph 4, we are told that opinion writing is an act of "*translation.*" So judges are "*interpreting*" and "*translating*" the legal text into something more applicable and relevant to the world.

This question is very open ended so it's hard to come up with a targeted pre-phrased answer. But armed with all this information, we should still have an easier time eliminating the ACs.

A. The <u>once-stable relationship</u> between law and opinion-writing has been <u>undermined</u> by new and <u>radical theoretical developments</u>.

Even if the Law and Literature movement consider themselves to be a new movement, are their theoretical developments radical? Was the relationship between law and opinion writing once "stable?" Has that relationship been undermined?

All of these are new ideas that do not appear in the passage, and are **out of scope**.

B. <u>Only the most</u> politically conservative of judges continue to base their opinions on natural law or on legal positivism.

We do not know how many judges base their opinions on natural law or legal positivism. We know these are traditional schools of thought. But what do proponents of the Law and Literature movement think? We don't know.

The wording of this answer is not only **too strong**, but the idea is also **out of scope**.

We don't know if it's the most political conservative judges, or any judges, for that matter, who hold these views. We also don't know what the position of the L&L movement is.

C. The occurrence of different legal situations requires a judge to adopt diverse theoretical approaches to opinion-writing.

The last paragraph tells us that judges need to "interpret," "translate," and "reconstitute" the legal text in order to deal with new situations.

Is this the same as adopting a "diverse theoretical approach?"

I'm not too sure at the moment. Let's keep this answer choice and keep on going.

D. Different judges <u>will not necessarily</u> write the same sorts of opinions when confronted with the same legal situation.

This makes sense, the words "not necessarily" are very **conservatively worded**. So as long as the passage never said that these people will always write the same sort of opinions, then we are good to select this answer.

What does the passage tell us? We know that opinions are "interpretations" and "translations." We are also told that opinions are "artistic performances." And that "each judicial opinion attempts in its own way to promote a particular political and ethical value."

In other words, each judicial opinion is a unique performance. If this is true, different performers will not necessarily have the same performance. That makes sense.

I think D has more support than C. D makes sense, but C needs a little more help. In order to select C, we need to assume that interpreting, translating, and reconstituting a text is the equivalent of adopting a theoretically diverse approach.

Remember what we said about AC elimination? We don't help the answers.

E.   *Judges who* <u>*subscribe to divergent theories*</u> *of jurisprudence* <u>*will necessarily*</u> *render divergent opinions.*

This again is really **strong**. Do judges who subscribe to divergent theories (e.g. natural law/law and economics/legal positivism) have no choice but to render divergent opinions?

The passage doesn't tell us. All we are told is that each judge will interpret and translate the legal text uniquely. This answer describes a position never mentioned by the L&L people, and it's certainty is a major red flag.

The best/correct answer is D.

PT32 S2 Q26 (PT32 Passage 4)

Most scientists who study the physiological effects of alcoholic beverages have assumed that wine, like beer or distilled spirits, is a drink whose only active ingredient is alcohol. Because of this assumption, these scientists have rarely investigated the effects of wine as distinct from other forms of alcoholic beverages. Nevertheless, unlike other alcoholic beverages, wine has for centuries been thought to have healthful effects that these scientists—who not only make no distinction among wine, beer, and distilled spirits but also study only the excessive or abusive intake of these beverages—have obscured.

Recently, a small group of researchers has questioned this assumption and investigated the effects of moderate wine consumption. While alcohol has been shown conclusively to have negative physiological effects—for example, alcohol strongly affects the body's processing of lipids (fats and other substances including cholesterol), causing dangerous increases in the levels of these substances in the blood, increases that are a large contributing factor in the development of premature heart disease—the researchers found that absorption of alcohol into the bloodstream occurs much more slowly when subjects drink wine than when they drink distilled spirits. More remarkably, it was discovered that deaths due to premature heart disease in the populations of several European countries decreased dramatically as the incidence of moderate wine consumption increased. One preliminary study linked this effect to red wine, but subsequent research has shown identical results whether the wine was white or red. What could explain such apparently healthful effects?

For one thing, the studies show increased activity of a natural clot-breaking compound used by doctors to restore blood flow through blocked vessels in victims of heart disease. In addition, the studies of wine drinkers indicate increased levels of certain compounds that may help to prevent damage from high lipid levels. And although the link between lipid processing and premature heart disease is one of the most important discoveries in modern medicine, in the past 20 years researchers have found several additional important contributing factors. We now know that endothelial cell reactivity (which affects the thickness of the innermost walls of blood vessels) and platelet adhesiveness (which influences the degree to which platelets cause blood to clot) are each linked to the development of premature heart disease. Studies show that wine appears to have ameliorating effects on both of these factors: it decreases the thickness of the innermost walls of blood vessels, and it reduces platelet adhesiveness. One study demonstrated a decrease in platelet adhesiveness among individuals who drank large amounts of grape juice. This finding may be the first step in confirming speculation that the potentially healthful effects of moderate wine intake may derive from the concentration of certain natural compounds found in grapes and not present in other alcoholic beverages.

In the passage, the author is primarily concerned with doing which one of the following?

    A. Advocating a particular method of treatment
    B. Criticizing popular opinion
    C. Correcting a scientific misconception
    D. Questioning the relevance of newly discovered evidence
    E. Countering a revolutionary hypothesis

If you recall, this passage talks about the health benefits of wine. Benefits that other alcoholic beverages don't possess. The Author's Purpose, as a result, is to highlight the potential health benefits of grape derived wine.

A. *Advocating a particular* <u>*method of treatment*</u>

Is the author advocating something? Sure, they are advocating wine. But wine is not a "method of treatment." That is out of scope.

B. *Criticizing* <u>*popular opinion*</u>

Perhaps there is an element of criticism towards scientists who have overlooked the healthful benefits of wine. But I'm not sure if that constitutes a "popular opinion." This is probably also out of scope. Because we don't know if what the scientists believe is also what most people believe.

C. *Correcting a* <u>*scientific misconception*</u>

Is the term "scientific misconception" also out of scope? We know that most scientists have overlooked the healthful benefits of wine, because they have assumed that the only active ingredient in wine is alcohol. This, according to the author, is a false "assumption." Is that the same as a "misconception?"

Most probably yes, but let's just look at the rest of the answer choices just to be safe.

D. <u>*Questioning the relevance*</u> *of newly discovered evidence*

This is the opposite of what we want. The author is accepting implicitly the newly discovered evidence of the healthful benefits of wine. They do not "question its relevancy."

E. <u>*Countering*</u> *a revolutionary* <u>*hypothesis*</u>

First, the "revolutionary hypothesis" would be referring to the benefits of wine. Does the author counter that? No, they are supporting it. Again, the opposite of what we want.

The correct answer is C.

PT9 S1 Q6 (PT9 Passage 1)

Many argue that recent developments in electronic technology such as computers and videotape have enabled artists to vary their forms of expression. For example, video art can now achieve images whose effect is produced by "digitalization": breaking up the picture using computerized information processing. Such new technologies create new ways of seeing and hearing by adding different dimensions to older forms, rather than replacing those forms. Consider Locale, a film about a modern dance company. The camera operator wore a Steadicam, an uncomplicated device that allows a camera to be mounted on a person so that the camera remains steady no matter how the operator moves. The Steadicam captures the dance in ways impossible with traditional mounts. Such new equipment also allows for the preservation of previously unrecordable aspects of performances, thus enriching archives.

By contrast, others claim that technology subverts the artistic enterprise: that artistic efforts achieved with machines pre-empt human creativity, rather than being inspired by it. The originality of musical performance, for example, might suffer, as musicians would be deprived of the opportunity to spontaneously change pieces of music before live audiences. Some even worry that technology will eliminate live performance altogether; performances will be recorded for home viewing, abolishing the relationship between performer and audience. But these negative views assume both that technology poses an unprecedented challenge to the arts and that we are not committed enough to the artistic enterprise to preserve the live performance, assumptions that seem unnecessarily cynical. In fact, technology has traditionally assisted our capacity for creative expression and can refine our notions of any given art form.

For example, the portable camera and the snapshot were developed at the same time as the rise of Impressionist painting in the nineteenth century. These photographic technologies encouraged a new appreciation for the chance view and unpredictable angle, thus preparing an audience for a new style of painting. In addition, Impressionist artists like Degas studied the elements of light and movement captured by instantaneous photography and used their new understanding of the way our perceptions distort reality to try to more accurately capture reality in their work. Since photos can capture the "moments" of a movement, such as a hand partially raised in a gesture of greeting, Impressionist artists were inspired to paint such moments in order to more effectively convey the quality of spontaneous human action. Photography freed artists from the preconception that a subject should be painted in a static, artificial entirety, and inspired them to capture the random and fragmentary qualities of our world. Finally, since photography pre-empted painting as the means of obtaining portraits, painters had more freedom to vary their subject matter, thus giving rise to the abstract creations characteristic of modern art.

It can be inferred from the passage that the author would agree with which one of the following statements regarding changes in painting since the nineteenth century?

A. The artistic experiments of the nineteenth century led painters to use a variety of methods in creating portraits, which they then applied to other subject matter.

B. The nineteenth-century knowledge of light and movement provided by photography inspired the abstract works characteristic of modern art.

C. Once painters no longer felt that they had to paint conventional portraits, they turned exclusively to abstract portraiture.

D. Once painters were less limited to the Impressionist style, they were able to experiment with a variety of styles of abstract art.

E. Once painters painted fewer conventional portraits, they had greater opportunity to move beyond the literal depiction of objects.

This is a new passage, let's go through the content and provide our usual Purpose, Main Point, and one sentence summary of each paragraph.

Many argue that recent developments in <u>electronic technology</u> such as computers and videotape have enabled artists <u>to vary their forms of expression</u>. For example, video art can now achieve images whose effect is produced by "digitalization": breaking up the picture using computerized information processing. Such new technologies create <u>new ways of seeing and hearing</u> by adding different dimensions to older forms, rather than replacing those forms. Consider Locale, a film about a modern dance company. The camera operator wore a Steadicam, an uncomplicated device that allows a camera to be mounted on a person so that the camera remains steady no matter how the operator moves. The Steadicam captures the dance in ways impossible with traditional mounts. Such new equipment also allows for the preservation of <u>previously unrecordable aspects</u> of performances, thus enriching archives.

The first viewpoint is presented: advances in technology enable artists, empowering them in new ways.

I am predicting that this passage will be comparing two viewpoints, with the author perhaps taking a position at the end.

<u>By contrast</u>, others claim that technology <u>subverts</u> the artistic enterprise: that artistic efforts achieved with machines <u>pre-empt human creativity</u>, rather than being inspired by it. The originality of musical performance, for example, might <u>suffer</u>, as musicians would be deprived of the opportunity to spontaneously change pieces of music before live audiences. Some even worry that technology will <u>eliminate live performance altogether</u>; performances will be recorded for home viewing, abolishing the relationship between performer and audience. <u>But</u> these negative views assume both that technology poses an unprecedented challenge to the arts and that we are not committed enough to the artistic enterprise to preserve the live performance, <u>assumptions that seem unnecessarily cynical</u>. In fact, technology has traditionally <u>assisted</u> our capacity for creative expression and <u>can refine</u> our notions of any given art form.

The second viewpoint is presented. These guys believe that technology is bad for artistic performances, and may even eliminate it.

We are given the author's opinion in the second half of the paragraph:

The author doesn't agree with the second viewpoint. The author thinks these people have made overly cynical assumptions (technology is an unprecedented challenge, we are not committed to live performances). In fact, the author thinks technology can help assist and refine art.

<u>For example</u>, the portable camera and the snapshot were developed at the same time as the rise of Impressionist painting in the nineteenth century. These photographic technologies <u>encouraged a new appreciation</u> for the chance view and unpredictable angle, thus preparing an audience for a new style of painting. In addition, Impressionist artists like Degas studied the elements of light and movement captured by instantaneous photography and <u>used their new understanding</u> of the way our perceptions distort reality to try to more accurately capture reality in their work. Since photos can capture the "moments" of a movement, such as a hand partially raised in a gesture of greeting, Impressionist artists were <u>inspired to paint such moments</u> in order to more effectively convey the quality of spontaneous human action. Photography <u>freed artists</u> from the preconception that a subject should be painted in a static, artificial entirety, and inspired them to capture the random and fragmentary qualities of our world. Finally, since photography pre-empted painting as the means of obtaining portraits, <u>painters had more freedom to vary their subject matter</u>, thus giving rise to the abstract creations characteristic of modern art.

The author gives examples of why technology can assist and refine art. The relationship between photography and impressionism is discussed. Photographic technology has inspired the impressionist painters and aided in art's evolution.

15. Answer Choice Elimination

In this passage, the Author's Purpose is not hard to discern. They compare the two views regarding the role and effect of technological advances on art and defend the first view.

It can be inferred from the passage that the author would agree with which one of the following statements regarding changes in painting since the nineteenth century?

The question stem gives us some hints as to where to look for the appropriate evidence. We know that the author uses changes in paintings since the nineteenth century as an example to illustrate the positive effects of technology.

A. *The artistic experiments of the nineteenth century led painters to use a variety of methods in <u>creating portraits</u>, which they then applied to <u>other subject matter</u>.*

The last paragraph does mention "portraits," but in the sense that since people took photos instead of commissioning paintings as portraits, painters were allowed to paint other subject matter.

This answer is saying that painters took the methods they used in portraits and used the same methods in other subject matter paintings. **This is an unwarranted connection.**

B. *The nineteenth-century knowledge of light and movement provided by photography <u>inspired the abstract works</u> characteristic of modern art.*

This answer is very tricky. We know that the knowledge provided by photography inspired impressionism. But it was not impressionism nor the knowledge provided by photography which inspired modern abstract art! It was because people no longer needed painters to do their portraits thanks to photography, that painters were able to experiment, which ultimately led to abstract modern art.

So in a way, it was the rise of photography which led to abstract modern art, but it was because they took the job formerly belonging to painters, and not because of the knowledge about light and movement they provided.

What this answer describes is an **unwarranted causal relationship**.

C. *Once painters no longer felt that they had to paint conventional portraits, they turned <u>exclusively</u> to abstract portraiture.*

This answer is too strong, did they turn exclusively to abstract portraiture? "Exclusively" means 100%. We don't have that kind of support from the passage.

D. *Once painters were <u>less limited to the Impressionist style</u>, they were able to experiment with a variety of styles of abstract art.*

Like answers A and B, this answer also confuses the two causal relationships mentioned in the last paragraph. We know that:

Photographic Advances → New Painting Techniques and Styles (e.g. Impressionism)

Photography Replacing Painting as Primary Sources of Portraits → Modern Art

D is again making an **unwarranted connection** between the two independent causal relationships.

E. *Once painters painted fewer conventional portraits, they had greater opportunity to move beyond the literal depiction of objects.*

This is the correct answer, it describes the second relationship, the one stated in the last sentence of the passage.

**

Nouns, Verbs, Adjectives/Adverbs

We have just seen how thinking about the scope, strength, and relationships described in an answer choice can help us eliminate many problematic answers. But no matter how careful we are with the answer choice selection process, there will be times when we miss something obvious, are pressed for time, or just simply do not understand what the answer choice is talking about.

In fact, when I was teaching the LSAT, I noticed how students' habits varied greatly when it came to the answer choice selection process. Some students, in the easier or earlier passages, will read the answer choices carefully, making justified eliminations. But when it came to harder passages or when time was limited, they automatically reverted back to their old habits, skimming the answers and making spontaneous selections as they went along.

Unsurprisingly, their accuracy plummeted. **Keyword driven answer choice elimination** was a habit that was really hard to foster, especially in a section where time is so restricted, and so much content needs to be covered.

The result that I came up with was "NVAA," or "**Nouns, Verbs, Adjectives and Adverbs**." (Like the NCAA but with a V) Basically, when we are drilling RC questions, make sure you've covered the nouns, verbs, adjectives and adverbs in every answer choice. This drill will force us to systematically consider every issue present in that answer choice, even the subtle and hidden ones that we would rather not face.

So, look at the nouns, and ask yourself, "is the scope of the subjects and objects mentioned in this answer choice too broad, too narrow, or simply unrelated?"

Look at the verbs, and ask yourself, "the actions described in this answer choice, are they an accurate description of the moves being made in the passage?"

Finally, look at the adjectives and adverbs, and ask yourself, "are these too strong or too weak? Are these the words I would use to describe what is going on?"

PT35 S2 Q22 (PT35 Passage 4)

Ronald Dworkin argues that judges are in danger of uncritically embracing an erroneous theory known as legal positivism because they think that the only alternative is a theory that they (and Dworkin) see as clearly unacceptable—natural law. The latter theory holds that judges ought to interpret the law by consulting their own moral convictions, even if this means ignoring the letter of the law and the legal precedents for its interpretation. Dworkin regards this as an impermissible form of judicial activism that arrogates to judges powers properly reserved for legislators.

Legal positivism, the more popular of the two theories, holds that law and morality are wholly distinct. The meaning of the law rests on social convention in the same way as does the meaning of a word. Dworkin's view is that legal positivists regard disagreement among jurists as legitimate only if it arises over what the underlying convention is, and it is to be resolved by registering a consensus, not by deciding what is morally right. In the same way, disagreement about the meaning of a word is settled by determining how people actually use it, and not by deciding what it ought to mean. Where there is no consensus, there is no legal fact of the matter. The judge's interpretive role is limited to discerning this consensus, or the absence thereof.

According to Dworkin, this account is incompatible with the actual practice of judges and lawyers, who act as if there is a fact of the matter even in cases where there is no consensus. The theory he proposes seeks to validate this practice without falling into what Dworkin correctly sees as the error of natural law theory. It represents a kind of middle ground between the latter and legal positivism. Dworkin stresses the fact that there is an internal logic to a society's laws and the general principles they typically embody. An interpretation that conforms to these principles may be correct even if it is not supported by a consensus. Since these general principles may involve such moral concepts as justice and fairness, judges may be called upon to consult their own moral intuitions in arriving at an interpretation. But this is not to say that judges are free to impose their own morality at will, without regard to the internal logic of the laws.

The positivist's mistake, as Dworkin points out, is assuming that the meaning of the law can only consist in what people think it means, whether these people be the original authors of the law or a majority of the interpreter's peers. Once we realize, as Dworkin does, that the law has an internal logic of its own that constrains interpretation, we open up the possibility of improving upon the interpretations not only of our contemporaries but of the original authors.

What is the main purpose of the second paragraph?

    A. To explain why legal positivism is so popular
    B. To evaluate the theory of legal positivism
    C. To discuss how judicial consensus is determined
    D. To identify the basic tenets of legal positivism
    E. To argue in favor of the theory of legal positivism

In this passage, the author describes natural law in the first paragraph, legal positivism in the second, and Dworkin's criticisms of legal positivism in paragraphs 3 and 4.

    A.   To <u>explain why</u> legal positivism is so popular

Sure, the beginning of the paragraph tells us that legal positivism is more popular than natural law. But does this paragraph "explain why?"

Is this something that the author does? No. This paragraph is explaining what legal positivism is, and not why it's popular.

    B.   To <u>evaluate</u> the theory of legal positivism

Again, think about the verb in this answer choice. What does it mean to evaluate something? Remember that "evaluate" is one of the four elements of CEER. To evaluate something means to look for its pros and cons, to determine if something is positive or negative.

Does the author do that? No, we are given a fairly neutral description of what legal positivism is.

    C.   To discuss <u>how judicial consensus is determined</u>

"To discuss" is a fairly neutral term, it can mean anything, so let's keep on looking. Does the paragraph discuss how judicial consensus is determined? Sure, but that's not the purpose of the paragraph. The purpose/function of the paragraph is to describe legal positivism. The scope of this answer is too narrow.

    D.   To <u>identify</u> the <u>basic tenets</u> of legal positivism

"Identify the basic tenets" can mean listing the basic rules of legal positivism. That's what this paragraph did. It talks about how the legal positivists view the law.

    E.   To <u>argue in favor</u> of the theory of legal positivism

The paragraph does not do that. If it did, it would conflict with the broader theme of the passage. The passage describes Dworkin's criticisms of legal positivism, and the second paragraph is only describing what legal positivism is.

The correct answer is D.

B was the most commonly selected trap answer. The only issue with it lies in the word "evaluate." To evaluate something means to consider its merits and flaws, and the paragraph never did that. Whenever we see a tempting answer choice and we don't find any issues with it on a first glance, run it through NVAA to see if we can find any additional gaps.

PT25 S1 Q21 (PT25 Passage 3)

Even in the midst of its resurgence as a vital tradition, many sociologists have viewed the current form of the powwow, a ceremonial gathering of native Americans, as a sign that tribal culture is in decline. Focusing on the dances and rituals that have recently come to be shared by most tribes, they suggest that an intertribal movement is now in ascension and claim the inevitable outcome of this tendency is the eventual dissolution of tribes and the complete assimilation of native Americans into Euro-American society. Proponents of this "Pan-Indian" theory point to the greater frequency of travel and communication between reservations, the greater urbanization of native Americans, and, most recently, their increasing politicization in response to common grievances as the chief causes of the shift toward inter-tribalism.

Indeed, the rapid diffusion of dance styles, outfits, and songs from one reservation to another offers compelling evidence that inter-tribalism has been increasing. However, these sociologists have failed to note the concurrent revitalization of many traditions unique to individual tribes. Among the Lakota, for instance, the Sun Dance was revived, after a forty-year hiatus, during the 1950's. Similarly, the Black Legging Society of the Kiowa and the Hethuska Society of the Ponca—both traditional groups within their respective tribes—have gained new popularity. Obviously, a more complex societal shift is taking place than the theory of Pan-Indianism can account for.

An examination of the theory's underpinnings may be critical at this point, especially given that native Americans themselves chafe most against the Pan-Indian classification. Like other assimilationist theories with which it is associated, the Pan-Indian view is predicated upon an a priori assumption about the nature of cultural contact: that upon contact minority societies immediately begin to succumb in every respect—biologically, linguistically, and culturally—to the majority society. However, there is no evidence that this is happening to native American groups.

Yet the fact remains that intertribal activities are a major facet of native American culture today. Certain dances at powwows, for instance, are announced as intertribal, others as traditional. Likewise, speeches given at the beginnings of powwows are often delivered in English, while the prayer that follows is usually spoken in a native language. Cultural borrowing is, of course, old news. What is important to note is the conscious distinction native Americans make between tribal and intertribal tendencies. Tribalism, although greatly altered by modern history, remains a potent force among native Americans: It forms a basis for tribal identity, and aligns music and dance with other social and cultural activities important to individual tribes. Intertribal activities, on the other hand, reinforce native American identity along a broader front, where this identity is directly threatened by outside influences.

In the passage, the author is primarily concerned with doing which one of the following?

    A. Identifying an assumption common to various assimilationist theories and then criticizing these theories by showing this assumption to be false
    B. Arguing that the recent revival of a number of tribal practices shows sociologists are mistaken in believing inter-tribalism to be a potent force among native American societies
    C. Questioning the belief that native American societies will eventually be assimilated into Euro-American society by arguing that inter-tribalism helps strengthen native American identity
    D. Showing how the recent resurgence of tribal activities is a deliberate attempt to counteract the growing influence of inter-tribalism
    E. Proposing an explanation of why the ascension of inter-tribalism could result in the eventual dissolution of tribes and complete assimilation of native American into Euro-American society

What is the Author's Purpose? I would say that the author is criticizing the Pan Indian Theory and proposing an alternative way to look at the effects of inter-tribalism on tribal identity.

Main Point? I would propose something like this:

Contrary to the belief of Pan-Indian theorists, the rise of inter-tribalism will not weaken tribal identity and lead to complete assimilation; tribalism and intertribal activities both have their roles in reinforcing native American identity and defending its integrity.

>   A. *Identifying an <u>assumption</u> common to various assimilationist theories and then criticizing these theories by showing this assumption to be <u>false</u>*

Does the author identify such an assumption? Yes, in the third paragraph. Does the author show this assumption to be false? Yes, also in the third paragraph.

The assumption is that minority cultures are unable to survive contact with majority cultures, and the author declares that there is no evidence that this is happening.

The question is asking us what the Author's Purpose is for the passage, rather than the third paragraph. This answer is too limited in scope.

>   B. *Arguing that the recent revival of a number of tribal practices shows sociologists are <u>mistaken</u> in believing inter-tribalism to be a <u>potent force</u> among native American societies*

Is inter-tribalism a potent force? Yes. Do the sociologists believe inter-tribalism to be such a potent force? Actually they believe it will lead to complete assimilation.

The sociologists are mistaken, but not in the belief that inter-tribalism is a potent force; but rather that inter-tribalism will lead to the complete assimilation of minority cultures.

>   C. *Questioning the belief that native American societies will eventually be assimilated into Euro-American society by arguing that inter-tribalism helps strengthen native American identity*

Yes, this matches up with our pre-phrased answer. The sociologists believe inter-tribalism is bad, it's going to destroy Indigenous culture. The author disagrees. The author thinks that inter-tribalism has its own special role to play.

>   D. *Showing how the recent resurgence of tribal activities is a <u>deliberate attempt to counteract</u> the growing influence of inter-tribalism*

There is an **unsupported relationship** between two concepts in this answer choice. Yes, there is a resurgence of tribal activities. Yes, there is growing inter-tribalism. The sociologists believe the resurgence of tribal activities is a sign of the growth of inter-tribalism. The author never disputes that. Where the two parties differ is on the role of inter-tribalism on Indigenous identity.

Tribal activities are not an attempt to "counteract" inter-tribalism.

>   E. *Proposing an explanation of why the ascension of inter-tribalism could <u>result</u> in the eventual <u>dissolution</u> of tribes and complete <u>assimilation</u> of native American into Euro-American society*

Pay attention to the nouns and verbs here. This answer is the opposite of what we want. The author does not think inter-tribalism could lead to the dissolution of tribes, that's the view of the sociologists.

Summary

In this chapter we covered the first step to the answer choice selection process. After having examined the question stem and having found the relevant details and tried coming up with a potential answer to the best of our ability, it's time to dive into the answers.

We start with an **initial round** of elimination. Be on the look out of answers whose scope or strength are problematic, as well as answers that describe a relationship unsupported by information in the passage. Different types of questions will have different types of trap answers, so it's important to familiarize yourself with these through practice.

Focus on the nouns, verbs, and adjectives/adverbs in an answer choice to force yourself into developing a habit of eliminating answers based on keywords.

In the next two chapters we'll look at the second stage of the answer choice selection process, answer choice ranking.

Oh, and fleas don't have mouths.

16. Basic Answer Choice Ranking

16. Basic Answer Choice Ranking

We now approach perhaps what is the biggest obstacle in terms of attaining perfection in Reading Comprehension. The next two chapters will be entirely devoted to **Stage 2** of our answer choice selection process, or **Answer Choice Ranking**.

Most of us, especially the advanced student, will probably have encountered the following scenario:

We are moving through the answer choices, being able to eliminate a few that are obviously wrong or completely out of place. We are eventually left with two answer choices and stuck. We look at both answer choices, both may sound reasonable, both may have support from the passage, and both may have issues that we don't particularly like.

With time running out we end up picking one. The choice may have some justification, or maybe it was entirely arbitrary. But when we score the test, we realize that we have gotten the question wrong. This was probably not the first time that this happened, you are consistently making that same number of mistakes in RC, and with nearly every mistake, you are able to narrow it down to two answers, but nearly always pick the wrong one.

This experience is highly frustrating. Many students end up stuck in this purgatory and never end up seeing substantive improvement. For others, their accuracy rate fluctuates wildly, but being unable to pick the right answer out of two attractive choices consistently remains one of the biggest obstacles to perfecting their RC.

For readers of LR Perfection, this situation reminds us of the hardest Strengthen, Weaken, and MSS Questions. The need to rank answer choices based on their respective merits and shortcomings, rather than simply eliminating four wrong answers and ending up with the right one, was the key to success in those question types. The need to rank answers and adopt a relative comparison framework was so important that we devoted an entire chapter to it, and Ranking formed the last building block of the SLAKR Method which we learned in LR Perfection.

After working with hundreds of students in the past few years and reworking through all the RC sections from PT 1 to PT 90 in preparation for this book, one of the key questions that always came to the forefront was this: *"Is there a set of objective criteria that can be applied consistently to the remaining two or three answer choices to determine what the correct answer is?"* In other words, when none of the answer choices are perfect, when none of them match up with what we really want, what is **the standard** that we apply to our answer choice selection process?

The answer to this question, unfortunately, is complicated. The ability to pick the correct answer is dependent on a multitude of factors including our understanding of the passage, our ability to locate hard to find details in the passage, our grasp of the Author's Purpose and Main Point, our familiarity with the question type, our ability to discover the meaning behind the wording of the answer choices, and the gaps between what was said in the passage and what was stated in the answer choice.

In other words, there exists, in the LSAT RC universe, multiple ways to determine whether the answer choice you have your eyes on is in fact the most suitable. Some of these methods will be fairly straightforward, some other ones will be more troublesome to apply. Some of these methods will work on certain answer choices, but there is no one method fits all approach. It is only through encountering and practicing tricky questions that we become more at ease with the methods that I'm about to show you. So try to incorporate these skills and habits into your answer ranking repertoire, and try to apply them when you are stuck.

Finding the Most Textual Support

Since the majority of RC Questions are asking us to derive the correct answer via information from the passage, one of the most straightforward and intuitive things we can do when stuck on two answer choices is to go back to the passage and look at the support each of these answers have, respectively.

For Inference Questions and similar question types, this requires minimal effort but can still be quite effective. Instead of comparing the two prospective answer choices in isolation, we go back to the passage, identify their purported support, and ask ourselves this:

> Based on the information in the passage, and based on each answer choice's respective textual evidence, which answer has **more explicit backing** from the passage?

For instance, if we were able to eliminate answer choices B, C, and E in a question, that would leave us with only A and D. Now we would read A and D, and go back to the passage to see if there is information supporting either answer choice.

Chances are that both would have partial support, otherwise we should have been able to solve this question during the first stage of the Answer Choice Selection process, the elimination stage. So our job now is to isolate the supporting evidence for both A and D, and to consider the relationship between each answer choice and their respective supporting material.

Let's say that Answer Choice A seems to be supported by a sentence from the beginning of the second paragraph; and Answer Choice D seems to be supported by a statement from the end of the third paragraph; our job now is to look at the support, and look at the answer choices, and ask ourselves which answer choice is *most strongly supported* by their respective textual evidence?

This process can be tricky because sometimes we might miss the purported textual support for an AC entirely and thereby eliminating it. There might be multiple pieces of the text backing an AC but we did not find all of them and as a result deemed it lacking in support. If this is frequently happening to you, then the only thing to do really is to pay more attention to the details of a passage during the initial reading, and in order to do that we need to be fully comfortable with the reading habits developed in Part I of the book.

Let's look at a few questions and see how this test operates in reality:

PT25 S1 Q10 (PT25 Passage 2)

While a new surge of critical interest in the ancient Greek poems conventionally ascribed to Homer has taken place in the last twenty years or so, it was nonspecialists rather than professional scholars who studied the poetic aspects of the Iliad and the Odyssey between, roughly, 1935 and 1970. During these years, while such nonacademic intellectuals as Simone Weil and Erich Auerbach were trying to define the qualities that made these epic accounts of the Trojan War and its aftermath great poetry, the questions that occupied the specialists were directed elsewhere: "Did the Trojan War really happen?" "Does the bard preserve Indo- European folk memories?" "How did the poems get written down?" Something was driving scholars away from the actual works to peripheral issues. Scholars produced books about archaeology, and gift exchange in ancient societies, about the development of oral poetry, about virtually anything except the Iliad and the Odyssey themselves as unique reflections or distillations of life itself—as, in short, great poetry. The observations of the English poet Alexander Pope seemed as applicable in 1970 as they had been when he wrote them in 1715: according to Pope, the remarks of critics "are rather Philosophical, Historical, Geographical . . . or rather anything than Critical and Poetical."

Ironically, the modern manifestation of this "nonpoetical" emphasis can be traced to the profoundly influential work of Milman Parry, who attempted to demonstrate in detail how the Homeric poems, believed to have been recorded nearly three thousand years ago, were the products of a long and highly developed tradition of oral poetry about the Trojan War. Parry proposed that this tradition built up its diction and its content by a process of constant accumulation and refinement over many generations of storytellers. But after Parry's death in 1935, his legacy was taken up by scholars who, unlike Parry, forsook intensive analysis of the poetry itself and focused instead on only one element of Parry's work: the creative limitations and possibilities of oral composition, concentrating on fixed elements and inflexibilities, focusing on the things that oral poetry allegedly can and cannot do. The dryness of this kind of study drove many of the more inventive scholars away from the poems into the rapidly developing field of Homer's archaeological and historical background.

Appropriately, Milman Parry's son Adam was among those scholars responsible for a renewed interest in Homer's poetry as literary art. Building on his father's work, the younger Parry argued that the Homeric poems exist both within and against a tradition. The Iliad and the Odyssey were, Adam Parry thought, the beneficiaries of an inherited store of diction, scenes, and concepts, and at the same time highly individual works that surpassed these conventions. Adam Parry helped prepare the ground for the recent Homeric revival by affirming his father's belief in a strong inherited tradition, but also by emphasizing Homer's unique contributions within that tradition.

The passage suggests which one of the following about scholarship on Homer that has appeared since 1970?

A. It has dealt extensively with the Homeric poems as literary art.
B. It is more incisive than the work of the Parrys.
C. It has rejected as irrelevant the scholarship produced by specialists between 1935 and 1970.
D. It has ignored the work of Simone Weil and Erich Auerbach.
E. It has attempted to confirm that the Iliad and the Odyssey were written by Homer.

We know from the passage that between 1935 and 1970, it was the non-specialists who studied the poetic aspects of the Homeric epics. Since the question is asking about developments post-1970, I think it's safe to assume that the years since 1970 marked the return of the specialists to the literary qualities of the Iliad and the Odyssey.

What else happened since 1970? Well, now that we know the specialists returned to the literary tradition, we can take another look at the last paragraph. We know Milman's son was one of the people responsible for this revival.

The passage seems to be supporting a potential answer that tells us there was a return to the literary tradition by specialists since 1970. Let's see if such an answer exists.

  A. It has _dealt extensively_ with the Homeric poems as literary art.

I didn't like this answer very much, the language seemed a little strong for my preferences. We know that scholars returned to the literary tradition, does that mean they are "dealing extensively" with the Homeric poems as literary art?

  B. It is more _incisive_ than the work of the _Parrys._

Being incisive means to be clear and focused. Can we argue that a return to the literary traditions was more focused? Possibly.

But we also know that Parry Jr. was also part of the movement, so this answer is saying that "the analysis of the post 1970 group, of which Parry Jr. was a part of, was more incisive than the work of both Parry Sr. and Parry Jr."

If the answer had said "it was more incisive than the work of scholars between 1935 and 1970," then maybe it would have been a contender.

  C. It has rejected as irrelevant the scholarship produced by specialists between 1935 and 1970.

There is a return to the literary aspects of Homer, but does a change in research direction = rejection of past research?

This is a fairly big gap. But let's keep it for now.

  D. It has ignored the work of Simone Weil and Erich Auerbach.

SW and EA were mentioned in the first paragraph. They were non-specialists who focused on the literary aspects of Homer. What this answer is saying is that the "specialists who focused on Homer as literature ignored the earlier non-specialists who did the same thing."

Nowhere is this contention supported in the passage, I think it's a safe elimination.

  E. It has attempted to confirm that the Iliad and the Odyssey were written by Homer.

Scholars returned to literary analysis of Homer, we don't know if they examined the epics' authorship.

We are now left with answer choices A and C. Let's look at each of them in turn, and see which answer is more supported by the relevant evidence from the passage:

- A: We know from the passage that scholars returned to literary analysis, can we infer that this means they are now dealing extensively with literary analysis?

- C: The scholars returned to literary analysis, does this mean that they are rejecting past scholarship?

Let's use an analogy to help us see the leap in reasoning in both answers:

Let's say that *you moved back home to live with your parents during COVID*. What would be the more reasonable inference?

You are now dealing extensively with your parents?

Or

You are rejecting your friends?

Here, changing the focus of your research probably means that you are "dealing extensively" with the topic and scope of your new research. Answer choice A is stronger than the support from the passage, but I think it's a reasonable inference.

Whereas for Answer C, we have no evidence to suggest that research on the literary aspects of Homer necessitates a wholesale rejection of the non-literary studies of Homer in the past.

The correct answer is A.

PT27 S3 Q11 (PT27 Passage 2)

Personal names are generally regarded by European thinkers in two major ways, both of which deny that names have any significant semantic content. In philosophy and linguistics, John Stuart Mill's formulation that "proper names are meaningless marks set upon…persons to distinguish them from one another" retains currency; in anthropology, Claude Lévi-Strauss's characterization of names as being primarily instruments of social classification has been very influential. Consequently, interpretation of personal names in societies where names have other functions and meanings has been neglected. Among the Hopi of the southwestern United States, names often refer to historical or ritual events in order both to place individuals within society and to confer an identity upon them. Furthermore, the images used to evoke these events suggest that Hopi names can be seen as a type of poetic composition.

Throughout life, Hopis receive several names in a sequence of ritual initiations. Birth, entry into one of the ritual societies during childhood, and puberty are among the name-giving occasions. Names are conferred by an adult member of a clan other than the child's clan, and names refer to that name giver's clan, sometimes combining characteristics of the clan's totem animal with the child's characteristics. Thus, a name might translate to something as simple as "little rabbit," which reflects both the child's size and the representative animal.

More often, though, the name giver has in mind a specific event that is not apparent in a name's literal translation. One Lizard clan member from the village of Oraibi is named Lomayayva, "beautifully ascended." This translation, however, tells nothing about either the event referred to—who or what ascended—or the name giver's clan. The name giver in this case is from Badger clan. Badger clan is responsible for an annual ceremony featuring a procession in which masked representations of spirits climb the mesa on which Oraibi sits. Combining the name giver's clan association with the receiver's home village, "beautifully ascended" refers to the splendid colors and movements of the procession up the mesa. The condensed image this name evokes—a typical feature of Hopi personal names—displays the same quality of Western Apache place names that led one commentator to call them "tiny imagist poems."

Hopi personal names do several things simultaneously. They indicate social relationships—but only indirectly—and they individuate persons. Equally important, though, is their poetic quality; in a sense they can be understood as oral texts that produce aesthetic delight. This view of Hopi names is thus opposed not only to Mill's claim that personal names are without inherent meaning but also to Lévi-Strauss's purely functional characterization. Interpreters must understand Hopi clan structures and linguistic practices in order to discern the beauty and significance of Hopi names.

The primary function of the second paragraph is to

- A. Present reasons why Hopi personal names can be treated as poetic compositions.
- B. Support the claim that Hopi personal names make reference to events in the recipients life.
- C. Argue that the fact that Hopis receive many names throughout life refutes European theories about naming.
- D. Illustrate ways in which Hopi personal names may have semantic content.
- E. Demonstrate that the literal translation of Hopi personal names often obscures their true meaning.

We know that the entire passage is a challenge towards European theories of naming conventions. JSM thinks that names are meaningless, while CLS thinks names are tools of social classification. The author uses Hopi names as examples of exceptions to these theories. Hopi names not only confer an identity upon them, situate them in society, but can also be seen as poetic compositions.

The second paragraph describes how Hopi names confer an identity upon the named, ("little rabbit") and situate them within society. ("names refer to the name giver's clan")

Let's find an answer that tells us that.

   A.   *Present reasons why Hopi personal names can be treated as poetic compositions*

This is the subject matter of paragraph 3. We can eliminate it.

   B.   *Support the claim that Hopi personal names make reference to events in the recipients life*

We are told that Hopis receive names to mark events in their lives (birth, entry into society, puberty, etc.)

But do names refer to these events? Let's keep this one for now.

   C.   *Argue that the fact that Hopis receive many names throughout life refutes European theories about naming*

I think the content in the second paragraph refutes JSM, who thinks are names meaningless. But it's not because that Hopis receive many names, but rather that names like "little rabbit" actually do have meaning.

I don't think the information in the second paragraph refutes CLS though. Because Hopi names also refer to the child's name giver's clan, so there is a social aspect to Hopi naming conventions as well.

Too many issues with this answer, I think it can be eliminated.

   D.   *Illustrate ways in which Hopi personal names may have semantic content*

"Semantic content" just means words with meaning, I think. I suppose that by giving names that "refer to that name giver's clan, the clan's totem animal, and the child's characteristics," the paragraph is demonstrating that Hopi names have "semantic content."

The answer I was looking for is a little more specific though, if the answer had said "conferred identity," it would have been perfect. Let's keep this one for now.

   E.   *Demonstrate that the literal translation of Hopi personal names often obscures their true meaning*

Paragraph 3 talks about Hopi names being imagist poems that may not be apparent in their literal translations. We are being asked about paragraph 2.

***

So again, we are left with two answer choices: B and D. Let's see which one has more support from the text.

In order for answer choice B to stand, we must believe that receiving a new name on your thirteenth birthday is means that the name itself will refer to your thirteenth birthday.

This doesn't sound right to me. If you had spent your 13th birthday with your family at Yosemite, then your new name would be Yosemite, or perhaps El Capitan. That's what answer B is saying.

In paragraph 3, we know that names can refer to processions up the Mesa, but this procession doesn't happen on the special day during which the child receives their name, either.

Let's look at answer D.

Is having "semantic content" something that happens in paragraph 2? Yes, but is it too narrow in scope to be the purpose of the paragraph?

On a first glance, yes. Our anticipated purpose was to show that Hopi names have meaning, as well as fulfill a social purpose. This answer only covers the "meaning" part. Having "semantic content," I think, is the same as having meaning. So it is rejecting JSM's characterization of what names are, but leaving CLS's views untouched. So the problem with this answer choice is that it's incomplete.

But if you take a broad enough perspective on the term "semantic content," then perhaps "social classification" also constitutes a part of the meaning of names.

But at the end of the day, even though D was not what we were looking for originally, it can be supported amply by the text of the passage. It's not a perfect match with our anticipated answer choice, but there is a high level of overlap.

That's more than what I can say for answer choice B.

The correct answer is D.

Unexpected Wording

In the previous question, we saw the correct answer as something that was totally unexpected. That threw us off during the initial answer choice elimination process. Indeed, as we have encountered before, the correct answer may often be worded in a more vague and abstract manner than we'd like. This is not a random coincidence, the test makers do this on purpose to entrap you. As we saw in Role and Method Questions back in LR Perfection, **do not eliminate an answer choice simply because you don't understand it.** Only eliminate an answer if you can point to an exact reason why it is wrong.

When we are left with two answer choices and one or both of them are incomprehensible, fear not. Rather than trying to come to a hasty conclusion on what the correct answer might be, seek first to understand what the AC is really saying.

When it comes to ranking answer choices, unexpected, abstract, or vague answers **should not be penalized**.

PT33 S2 Q15 (PT33 Passage 3)

Experts anticipate that global atmospheric concentrations of carbon dioxide (CO_2) will have doubled by the end of the twenty-first century. It is known that CO_2 can contribute to global warming by trapping solar energy that is being reradiated as heat from the Earth's surface. However, some research has suggested that elevated CO_2 levels could enhance the photosynthetic rates of plants, resulting in a lush world of agricultural abundance, and that this CO_2 fertilization effect might eventually decrease the rate of global warming. The increased vegetation in such an environment could be counted on to draw more CO_2 from the atmosphere. The level of CO_2 would thus increase at a lower rate than many experts have predicted.

However, while a number of recent studies confirm that plant growth would be generally enhanced in an atmosphere rich in CO_2, they also suggest that increased CO_2 would differentially increase the growth rate of different species of plants, which could eventually result in decreased agricultural yields. Certain important crops such as corn and sugarcane that currently have higher photosynthetic efficiencies than other plants may lose that edge in an atmosphere rich in CO_2. Patterson and Flint have shown that these important crops may experience yield reductions because of the increased performance of certain weeds. Such differences in growth rates between plant species could also alter ecosystem stability. Studies have shown that within rangeland regions, for example, a weedy grass grows much better with plentiful CO_2 than do three other grasses. Because this weedy grass predisposes land to burning, its potential increase may lead to greater numbers of and more severe wildfires in future rangeland communities.

It is clear that the CO_2 fertilization effect does not guarantee the lush world of agricultural abundance that once seemed likely, but what about the potential for the increased uptake of CO_2 to decrease the rate of global warming? Some studies suggest that the changes accompanying global warming will not improve the ability of terrestrial ecosystems to absorb CO_2. Billings' simulation of global warming conditions in wet tundra grasslands showed that the level of CO_2 actually increased. Plant growth did increase under these conditions because of warmer temperatures and increased CO_2 levels. But as the permafrost melted, more peat (accumulated dead plant material) began to decompose. This process in turn liberated more CO_2 to the atmosphere. Billings estimated that if summer temperatures rose four degrees Celsius, the tundra would liberate 50 percent more CO_2 than it does currently. In a warmer world, increased plant growth, which could absorb CO_2 from the atmosphere, would not compensate for this rapid increase in decomposition rates. This observation is particularly important because high-latitude habitats such as the tundra are expected to experience the greatest temperature increase.

Which one of the following best states the main point of the passage?

A. Elevated levels of CO_2 would enhance photosynthetic rates, thus increasing plant growth and agricultural yields.

B. Recent studies have yielded contradictory findings about the benefits of increased levels of CO_2 on agricultural productivity.

C. The possible beneficial effects of increased levels of CO_2 on plant growth and global warming have been overstated.

D. Increased levels of CO_2 would enhance the growth rates of certain plants, but would inhibit the growth rates of other plants.

E. Increased levels of CO_2 would increase plant growth, but the rate of global warming would ultimately increase.

We have encountered this passage before, the Main Point of the passage is that increased levels of CO_2 will neither lead to an increase in beneficial plants nor gradually slow down the rate of further CO_2 increase and global warming. To put it succinctly, the CO_2 increase that we are witnessing will not have the positive benefits some research has suggested.

A. *Elevated levels of CO2 would enhance photosynthetic rates, thus increasing plant growth and agricultural yields.*

This is wrong. The passage states that the growth rate of weeds will increase but agricultural yields will not.

B. *Recent studies have yielded contradictory findings about the benefits of increased levels of CO2 on agricultural productivity.*

Yes, this describes the second paragraph, but it's incomplete at best, since we are looking for the Main Point of the entire passage.

An incomplete MP answer is not automatically wrong, so I won't just eliminate this one yet.

C. *The possible beneficial effects of increased levels of CO2 on plant growth and global warming have been overstated.*

This one talks about both plant growth and global warming, but instead of saying that the benefits of both are non-existent, the word "overstated" is used. It's not exactly an accurate reflection of the author's tone, but I suppose that thinking CO_2 had agricultural and global warming benefits when it doesn't is a form of "overstatement."

So other than its weak wording, there's nothing factually wrong with this AC. Let's keep it for now.

D. *Increased levels of CO2 would enhance the growth rates of certain plants, but would inhibit the growth rates of other plants.*

Yes, this is also factually correct, but extremely limited in scope. It's almost the same as B.

E. *Increased levels of CO2 would increase plant growth, but the rate of global warming would ultimately increase.*

This, on its surface, is not wrong per se. But I feel like it's an oversimplification of the actual message of the passage.

The passage tells us that increased levels of CO_2 would lead to increased growth of weeds and not "good plants," while global warming would continue and release more CO_2 into the atmosphere, and the initial increase in CO_2 levels would not slow this process down.

It does cover (partially) the content of the second paragraph, as well as the third paragraph. So in that sense its better than B and D.

So let's take a look at C and E.

The passage tells us the CO_2 will not lead to positive plant growth and lessened global warming. Answer choice C tells us that the "beneficial effects…have been overstated."

Is it an "overstatement?" To put it mildly, yes. Let's say that you met someone on Tinder whose photos had them sitting in a Rolls Royce and in private jets. But in real life they are unemployed and are trying to scam you. Would you say that they have "overstated" their wealth?

That would be a bit of an understatement, although it would technically be correct.

Let's look at answer E. The issue I had with this answer was that the passage was talking about not just increased plant growth, but increased growth of weeds at the expense of agricultural yields. So E is an oversimplification that is actually quite misleading.

The choice boils down to C, which is an overly modest but factually correct answer; and E, which is an oversimplified and potentially misleading answer.

I think C wins over E. C is the better answer here.

PT25 S1 Q12 (PT25 Passage 2)

While a new surge of critical interest in the ancient Greek poems conventionally ascribed to Homer has taken place in the last twenty years or so, it was nonspecialists rather than professional scholars who studied the poetic aspects of the Iliad and the Odyssey between, roughly, 1935 and 1970. During these years, while such nonacademic intellectuals as Simone Weil and Erich Auerbach were trying to define the qualities that made these epic accounts of the Trojan War and its aftermath great poetry, the questions that occupied the specialists were directed elsewhere: "Did the Trojan War really happen?" "Does the bard preserve Indo- European folk memories?" "How did the poems get written down?" Something was driving scholars away from the actual works to peripheral issues. Scholars produced books about archaeology, and gift exchange in ancient societies, about the development of oral poetry, about virtually anything except the Iliad and the Odyssey themselves as unique reflections or distillations of life itself—as, in short, great poetry. The observations of the English poet Alexander Pope seemed as applicable in 1970 as they had been when he wrote them in 1715: according to Pope, the remarks of critics "are rather Philosophical, Historical, Geographical . . . or rather anything than Critical and Poetical."

Ironically, the modern manifestation of this "nonpoetical" emphasis can be traced to the profoundly influential work of Milman Parry, who attempted to demonstrate in detail how the Homeric poems, believed to have been recorded nearly three thousand years ago, were the products of a long and highly developed tradition of oral poetry about the Trojan War. Parry proposed that this tradition built up its diction and its content by a process of constant accumulation and refinement over many generations of storytellers. But after Parry's death in 1935, his legacy was taken up by scholars who, unlike Parry, forsook intensive analysis of the poetry itself and focused instead on only one element of Parry's work: the creative limitations and possibilities of oral composition, concentrating on fixed elements and inflexibilities, focusing on the things that oral poetry allegedly can and cannot do. The dryness of this kind of study drove many of the more inventive scholars away from the poems into the rapidly developing field of Homer's archaeological and historical background.

Appropriately, Milman Parry's son Adam was among those scholars responsible for a renewed interest in Homer's poetry as literary art. Building on his father's work, the younger Parry argued that the Homeric poems exist both within and against a tradition. The Iliad and the Odyssey were, Adam Parry thought, the beneficiaries of an inherited store of diction, scenes, and concepts, and at the same time highly individual works that surpassed these conventions. Adam Parry helped prepare the ground for the recent Homeric revival by affirming his father's belief in a strong inherited tradition, but also by emphasizing Homer's unique contributions within that tradition.

According to the passage, which one of the following is true of Milman Parry's immediate successors in the field of Homeric studies?

    A. They reconciled Homer's poetry with archaeological and historical concerns.
    B. They acknowledged the tradition of oral poetry, but focused on the uniqueness of Homer's poetry within the tradition.
    C. They occupied themselves with the question of what qualities made for great poetry.
    D. They emphasized the boundaries of oral poetry.
    E. They called for a revival of Homer's popularity.

We just keep on returning to this passage. **In many ways I think it's better to re-use the same passage, because our energy will be focused on the nuances of the answer choices, as opposed to trying to understand the reading itself.**

What do we know about MP's immediate successors? This information is found in the latter part of the second paragraph:

> *But after Parry's death in 1935, his legacy was taken up by scholars who, unlike Parry, forsook intensive analysis of the poetry itself and focused instead on only one element of Parry's work: the creative limitations and possibilities of oral composition, concentrating on fixed elements and inflexibilities, focusing on the things that oral poetry allegedly can and cannot do.*

They stopped analyzing the poetry itself. They focused on the limitations and possibilities of oral poetry.

The correct answer is D, *"they emphasized the boundaries of oral poetry."*

That's just another way of saying "they focused on the limitations of oral poetry."

***

We saw in this section two questions where the correct answer choice was something we weren't expecting. When we are ranking answer choices based on their desirability, it's important to remember that just because an answer is worded awkwardly or in an unexpected way is not grounds for dismissal.

Read these answers word for word and try to interpret them into more comprehensible language, then compare them to the text of the passage. Only eliminate an answer choice if it contains a specific error or flaw.

We saw two such correct answer choices just now. In both of these answers, we were resistant to them more because of the way they were phrased rather than any gaps or mistakes they contained. Perhaps they were worded too vaguely and not as specific as we'd have liked; perhaps we felt that the strength of the wording was a little off. But they were not wrong, per se. Furthermore, if you compared them to the next best alternative, you'll find that the other answers had even more issues.

Incomplete Answers

Let's look at another type of correct answer choice that is quickly eliminated or discarded during answer choice ranking. We have seen these answer choices before, in Chapter 8, and they feature predominantly in **Main Point Questions**. For a lot of more recent MP questions, the correct answer choice may have skipped over a significant portion of the passage. But as long as the overall central thesis of the passage is expressed in that answer choice, and there are no better alternatives, an incomplete Main Point answer choice is acceptable. **However, if there are MP answer choices that offer more holistic coverage of the argument and its components, those should be picked first.**

Scientists typically advocate the analytic method of studying complex systems: systems are divided into component parts that are investigated separately. But nineteenth-century critics of this method claimed that when a system's parts are isolated its complexity tends to be lost. To address the perceived weaknesses of the analytic method these critics put forward a concept called organicism, which posited that the whole determines the nature of its parts and that the parts of a whole are interdependent.

Organicism depended upon the theory of internal relations, which states that relations between entities are possible only within some whole that embraces them, and that entities are altered by the relationships into which they enter. If an entity stands in a relationship with another entity, it has some property as a consequence. Without this relationship, and hence without the property, the entity would be different— and so would be another entity. Thus, the property is one of the entity's defining characteristics. Each of an entity's relationships likewise determines a defining characteristic of the entity.

One problem with the theory of internal relations is that not all properties of an entity are defining characteristics: numerous properties are accompanying characteristics—even if they are always present, their presence does not influence the entity's identity. Thus, even if it is admitted that every relationship into which an entity enters determines some characteristic of the entity, it is not necessarily true that such characteristics will define the entity; it is possible for the entity to enter into a relationship yet remain essentially unchanged.

The ultimate difficulty with the theory of internal relations is that it renders the acquisition of knowledge impossible. To truly know an entity, we must know all of its relationships; but because the entity is related to everything in each whole of which it is a part, these wholes must be known completely before the entity can be known. This seems to be a prerequisite impossible to satisfy.

Organicists' criticism of the analytic method arose from their failure to fully comprehend the method. In rejecting the analytic method, organicists overlooked the fact that before the proponents of the method analyzed the component parts of a system, they first determined both the laws applicable to the whole system and the initial conditions of the system; proponents of the method thus did not study parts of a system in full isolation from the system as a whole. Since organicists failed to recognize this, they never advanced any argument to show that laws and initial conditions of complex systems cannot be discovered. Hence, organicists offered no valid reason for rejecting the analytic method or for adopting organicism as a replacement for it.

Which one of the following most completely and accurately summarizes the argument of the passage?

A. By calling into question the possibility that complex systems can be studied in their entirety, organicists offered an alternative to the analytic method favored by nineteenth century scientists.
B. Organicists did not offer a useful method of studying complex systems because they did not acknowledge that there are relationships into which an entity may enter that do not alter the entity's identity.
C. Organicism is flawed because it relies on a theory that both ignores the fact that not all characteristics of entities are defining and ultimately makes the acquisition of knowledge impossible.
D. Organicism does not offer a valid challenge to the analytic method both because it relies on faulty theory and because it is based on a misrepresentation of the analytic method.
E. In criticizing the analytic method, organicists neglected to disprove that scientists who employ the method are able to discover the laws and initial conditions of the systems they study.

We have encountered this passage before, recall our takeaways from this passage during an earlier read:

- Paragraph 1: Scientists break systems into components in order to study them, but organicists believe that you can't understand parts without understanding the whole.
- Paragraph 2: Organicists believe in the theory of internal relations, which states that you can't take the parts out of a whole when trying to understand a problem. (Parts are defined by their relationship to the whole, and parts change when they interact as a part of a whole.)
- Paragraph 3: But a problem with this theory is that even though parts can change, these changes may be inconsequential.
- Paragraph 4: This theory also creates a slippery slope that makes acquiring knowledge impossible.
- Paragraph 5: The scientific method doesn't really study parts in full isolation, the organicists overlook this, and they were wrong.

***

Overall, the relationship between each paragraph and the passage as a whole is pretty clear. Paragraph 1 provides background information, paragraph 2 explains the theory underlining the organicists' argument (opposing viewpoint). Paragraphs 3-5 provides critiques of the organicists' position, with the passage's Main Point is the last sentence of the passage.

If this passage were a massive LR argument, then paragraph 1 would be background information, paragraph 2 the opposing viewpoint, paragraphs 3-4 the argument's premises, and paragraph 5 containing an additional premise and the main conclusion.

The purpose of this passage is rather straight forward as well: to provide a critique/attack the organicists' position.

***

Let's now look at the question:

Which one of the following most completely and accurately <u>summarizes</u> the argument of the passage?

Something important to note here: even though the question stem makes it seem like its asking for a "summary" of the argument of the passage, this is still essentially a **Main Point Question**. I had to learn the hard way that the correct answer is not a detailed summary of what happens in every paragraph.

A.   *By calling into question the possibility that complex systems can be studied in their entirety, <u>organicists offered an alternative</u> to the analytic method favored by nineteenth century scientists.*

We know that this is contrary to the idea expressed by the passage. The passage is criticizing the organicists' alternative. This answer can be eliminated in the first round.

B.   *Organicists did not offer a useful method of studying complex systems because they did not acknowledge that there are relationships into which an entity may enter that do not alter the entity's identity.*

This answer choice talks about the first problem with organicists, but not the second. But like we said, an incomplete MP answer choice is okay if there are none better, so let's keep it for now.

C.   *Organicism is flawed because it relies on a theory that <u>both</u> ignores the fact that not all characteristics of entities are defining <u>and</u> ultimately makes the acquisition of knowledge impossible.*

This answer covers both the point made in Answer Choice B, as well as the sub-point of the fourth paragraph. This is better than B, so let's eliminate B and keep C.

> D. *Organicism does not offer a valid challenge to the analytic method both because it relies on faulty theory <u>and</u> because it is based on a misrepresentation of the analytic method.*

This answer is very similar to C, the direction of the answer choice is fine, and it describes two of the sub-points mentioned in the passage. Let's keep this one for now as well.

> E. *In criticizing the analytic method, organicists <u>neglected to disprove</u> that scientists who employ the method are able to discover the laws and initial conditions of the systems they study.*

This one is confusing, what does it mean to "neglect to disprove?" Does it mean that they should have disproven something, but didn't? What should they have disproven?

Organicists should have disproven the idea that analytic method scientists are able to discover the laws and initial conditions of the systems they study.

In other words, organicists should have shown that analytic scientists cannot discover the laws and initial conditions.

But this is contrary to the information from the last paragraph, where we are told that the analytic scientists are in fact able to discover the laws and initial conditions of the systems they study.

Furthermore, the idea should be that "the organicists are wrong because they ignore the fact that analytic scientists are able to discover the laws and initial conditions."

This answer also only covers a part of the last paragraph.

So we saw that Answers B is a partial answer, whereas answer choices C and D were more complete. So let's look at C and D to see which is a better option.

Remember, the Main Point of the passage was that "the organicist criticism of the analytic method is flawed." The support for this is three-fold:

One, the Theory of IR (upon which organicism depends) overlooks that not all properties will define or change an entity.

Two, the Theory of IR makes the acquisition of knowledge impossible, and

Three, the organicists misunderstand the analytic method.

Answer C covers #1 and #2 criticisms.

Answer D covers #3 for sure, but does it cover #1 and #2? Remember, both #1 and #2 are attacking the underlying theory of organicism, the theory of internal relations. Answer D offers a very generalized description of this: "it relies on faulty theory."

Even though it's not as specific as we would have liked, both the first and second points made in criticism of organicism are in fact pointing out the faults behind the theory of internal relations.

So answer choice D has in fact covered all three criticisms.

The correct answer is D.

PT51 S2 Q8 (PT51 Passage 2)

A vigorous debate in astronomy centers on an epoch in planetary history that was first identified by analysis of rock samples obtained in lunar missions. Scientists discovered that the major craters on the Moon were created by a vigorous bombardment of debris approximately four billion years ago—the so-called late heavy bombardment (LHB). Projectiles from this bombardment that affected the Moon should also have struck Earth, a likelihood with profound consequences for the history of Earth since, until the LHB ended, life could not have survived here.

Various theoretical approaches have been developed to account for both the evidence gleaned from samples of Moon rock collected during lunar explorations and the size and distribution of craters on the Moon. Since the sizes of LHB craters suggest they were formed by large bodies, some astronomers believe that the LHB was linked to the disintegration of an asteroid or comet orbiting the Sun. In this view, a large body broke apart and peppered the inner solar system with debris. Other scientists disagree and believe that the label "LHB" is in itself a misnomer. These researchers claim that a cataclysm is not necessary to explain the LHB evidence. They claim that the Moon's evidence merely provides a view of the period concluding billions of years of a continuous, declining heavy bombardment throughout the inner solar system. According to them, the impacts from the latter part of the bombardment were so intense that they obliterated evidence of earlier impacts. A third group contends that the Moon's evidence supports the view that the LHB was a sharply defined cataclysmic cratering period, but these scientists believe that because of its relatively brief duration, this cataclysm did not extend throughout the inner solar system. They hold that the LHB involved only the disintegration of a body within the Earth- Moon system, because the debris from such an event would have been swept up relatively quickly.

New support for the hypothesis that a late bombardment extended throughout the inner solar system has been found in evidence from the textural features and chemical makeup of a meteorite that has been found on Earth. It seems to be a rare example of a Mars rock that made its way to Earth after being knocked from the surface of Mars. The rock has recently been experimentally dated at about four billion years old, which means that, if the rock is indeed from Mars, it was knocked from the planet at about the same time that the Moon was experiencing the LHB. This tiny piece of evidence suggests that at least two planetary systems in the inner solar system experienced bombardment at the same time. However, to determine the pervasiveness of the LHB, scientists will need to locate many more such rocks and perhaps obtain surface samples from other planets in the inner solar system.

Which one of the following most accurately expresses the main point of the passage?

    A.   The LHB is an intense meteorite bombardment that occurred about four billion years ago and is responsible for the cratering on the Moon and perhaps on other members of the inner solar system as well.

    B.   Astronomers now believe that they may never collect enough evidence to determine the true nature of the LHB.

    C.   If scientists continue to collect new clues at their current rate, the various LHB hypotheses can soon be evaluated and a clear picture will emerge.

    D.   The Moon's evidence shows that the LHB was linked to a small body that disintegrated while in solar orbit and sprayed the inner solar system with debris.

    E.   New evidence has been found that favors the view that the LHB was widespread, but before competing theories of the LHB can be excluded, more evidence needs to be gathered.

We have seen this passage before, the author presents three theories/hypotheses on the LHB, and offers tentative evidence that seems to support the first theory.

> A. *The LHB is an intense meteorite bombardment that occurred about four billion years ago and is responsible for the cratering on the Moon and perhaps on other members of the inner solar system as well.*

Ok, this sounds like background information to me. The core of the passage is talking about the three theories and how theory #1 seems to have some evidence. This answer is too narrow in focus.

> B. *Astronomers now believe that they <u>may never collect enough</u> evidence to determine the true nature of the LHB.*

This is contrary to the passage, the passage tells us that there is some support for theory #1, but to be sure, we need additional evidence.

> C. *If scientists continue to collect new clues at their current rate, the various LHB hypotheses can soon be evaluated and a clear picture will emerge.*

This is a corruption of the last sentence of the passage. The passage says that in order to determine the pervasiveness of LHB, scientists will need more evidence. This answer is saying that if scientists collect new evidence, they will be able to determine the pervasiveness of LHB. Take a look at the following analogy:

To find out who the culprit is, we must conduct additional investigation. (Find culprit → Additional Investigation)

If we conduct additional investigation, we will find out who the culprit is. (Additional Investigation → Find culprit)

> D. *The Moon's evidence <u>shows that</u> the LHB was linked to a small body that disintegrated while in solar orbit and sprayed the inner solar system with debris.*

This is both too strong and too partial. It's talking about the third hypothesis only, and the word "show" is too strong. In the passage, we are told that this is only a view of what could have happened.

> E. *New evidence has been found that favors the view that the LHB was widespread, but before competing theories of the LHB can be excluded, more evidence needs to be gathered.*

This answer choice perfectly encapsulates what the last paragraph is telling us. I was initially weary of selecting it, however.

The majority of the passage is devoted to comparing the three different hypotheses on the LHB. The correct answer, I thought, would at least have to cover that. But then again, as we have witnessed many times on Main Point Questions, the correct answer will *only* cover the most important points in a passage, or the ideas that the author is trying to get across. For this passage, there were three points I would have liked to see in the correct answer, and in order of significance, they are:

1. New evidence seems to support theory #1. (This is most clearly an idea that the author is trying to convey)

2. But we need additional evidence. (Also clearly the author's opinion)

3. There were three theories regarding the LHB. (Even though they take up a large portion of the passage, it can be argued that this is background information, or laying the groundwork for the author's opinion in the last paragraph)

This answer only covers #1 and #2. Is there an answer that covers all three points? Unfortunately there isn't. So we have no choice but to select E.

Recall in the last passage (PT25 Passage 4) that even though there were several answers that all covered the most central issues of the passage, we picked the most **complete answer choice available**. *If no complete answer was available, we pick the best of the bunch*. This is a habit that we shall re-emphasize in the next two chapters.

Conservatively Worded Answers

Finally, let's revisit another feature of more desirable answers that are specific to According to the Passage, Inference, and Restricted Scope Questions: **Conservatively Worded Answer Choices**.

We saw earlier in the Inference Questions Chapter that the **threshold of proof** is something that we must consider when comparing answer choices. A neutral, weakly worded, ambiguous, or conservatively phrased answer is going to have a lower threshold of proof. That means it will be easier to prove given the passage.

Since the correct answer must be backed up by the text as much as possible, answers whose wording is easier to prove will be more attractive. For instance, if an answer said that the author "hated" a certain opponent's position, then we would need to find evidence of this "hatred" within the text of the passage. But if an answer said that the author "disapproved" of the opposing position, then as long as there is any evidence of aversion, no matter how mild, then this answer can possibly be proven.

Similarly, if an answer choice stated that "the majority" of legislators approved of the amendment, then we'll need evidence that >50% of all legislators have given their approval. But if the wording was "some" legislators approved of the amendment, then all we need is for one legislator to have approved. That's something much easier to find from the passage.

But of course, your job is to **find the most accurate answer choice in the first place**. So if the author is actually displaying "hatred" for an opponent, as evident from the text of the passage, by all means select that answer instead. If the passage stated that 150/200 legislators voted to approve the amendment, then select the answer that said "most" legislators without further consternation.

It is when we are unclear about the exact support each answer choice has that we would want to err on the side of caution, and that means choosing the option with the lowest threshold of proof to maximize our chances.

Lastly, this rule for ranking answers only applies to questions that **derive their answers from the passage**. If we are faced with a non-restricted scope question like a Strengthen or a Weaken Question, then we would be looking for the answer with the clearest impact instead. (See Chapter 13 for additional details)

Summary

After an initial round of eliminations, if we still have several potential candidates for the correct answer choice, it's time to rank them in terms of preferability. In this chapter we looked at some of the ways in which we determine preferability, and certain things that we must remind ourselves of during this ranking phase.

We saw that in harder RC questions, more than one answer choice can ostensibly have support from the passage. Hence it is our job to identify the location of the textual support, and compare the answers again in light of the support they depend on. Is one answer only partially supported by the text, while another is fully supported? Does one answer require us to make a lengthy inference, while another answer is more explicitly backed by a specific sentence? Our job is to *choose the answer choice that is more fully and explicitly supported by the information found in the passage.*

Several additional factors to consider when ranking answer choices:

Just because an answer doesn't match what we were anticipating doesn't make it wrong. As we have seen in multiple instances, the correct answer choice to a question turned out to be very different from what we were expecting. Maybe it was worded in an unfamiliar or vague manner, or perhaps it was indirect and convoluted. But in order to maximize our chances for success, we should do our best to parse these answers, try to understand what they are saying, and see if the answer can still be matched up with what we were looking for in the first place.

Finally, for Main Point Questions, if there are multiple contenders that all happen to encapsulate the passage's central thesis, go with the answer that offers the most complete coverage of the reading's key points.

For questions that derive their answers from the passage, a general rule of thumb is that *conservatively worded answer choices* are usually safer bets. If none of the remaining answer choices contravene the content of the passage, and you can't find one specific answer that most accurately mirrors the text, pick the answer choice with the lowest threshold of proof.

These are habits that I found useful in helping me and my students when it comes to answer choice ranking. But for the hardest questions, this may not be enough. We'll look at advanced ranking techniques reserved for the hardest RC questions in the next chapter.

16. Basic Answer Choice Ranking

17. Advanced Answer Choice Ranking

Taming the Unknown

In an ideal world, when we approach the questions of a particular RC section, we would have a very clear and detailed understanding of the information from the passage already. This way, when we compare and rank the various answer choices, we can be confident that the answers we eliminated are in fact less desirable. They have been discarded because they contained errors, or did not match up with what was discussed in the passage.

But in reality, we will *not* have a 100% grasp of the passage when we are selecting answer choices. Sometimes, we may have eliminated an answer because we thought it was out of scope, when in reality it was actually stated in the passage and we missed it. This is especially troublesome because having only a partial understanding of the reading will be detrimental to our answer selection process. Because now, no matter how efficient and systematic our answer choice ranking/elimination skills are, coming up with the correct answer choice can no longer be guaranteed because we are now basing the process on partial and potentially faulty information.

An analogy or equivalent can be found in the world of accounting/computer science. The acronym "garbage in, garbage out" refers to systems where even though the model/algorithm may be impeccable, but if you feed it with "garbage" data/input, the result will be "garbage" as well.

In RC, similarly, if our understanding of the passage is flawed and incomplete, then no matter how careful we are looking at and comparing answers, our answers will still be riddled with flaws. One way to improve is to "read better." Unfortunately, this kind of advice doesn't really help us very much. We can improve our reading ability organically via outside reading (Chapter 21), and focus on the habits and techniques fostered in Part I of the book, but that is something that will take time and energy to see results.

Luckily for us, there is another way to address this problem.

Bayesian Inspirations

Students familiar with probability and statistics will understand that our calculations of the likelihood of an occurrence will change depending on the new evidence that is introduced. This is called "updating our priors." Whenever we receive new data/evidence, we must incorporate that to turn our "prior" belief into a "posterior" belief. Let me give you an example:

You are Jason Bourne living in a cabin in the woods of Wyoming, hiding from assassins. You have been hiding here for a few years now, and you have perimeter alarms set up to warn you of potential intruders. Nine times out of ten, what triggers your alarm has been wolves, and the alarms never give off a false warning when something is not there. As you are going hiking this morning, your alarm goes off.

At this point, the chances that it's the wolves again is 90%. So you take your silenced pistol out of your backpack and begin to walk back to your property. But as you get closer to your property, something feels off. Wolves normally come out at night but it's early morning now. The last few times when the wolves triggered the alarms you heard the howls and your dog was especially anxious. None of that is happening this time. So the likelihood that it's the wolves rather than a genuine threat is dropping. Let's say that now, with the additional information, wolves being the culprit is only 70% likely.

When you finally get to the edge of your property, you notice footprints in the dirt. The markings don't match your shoes. The probability that it's the wolves that triggered the alarms is now at 40%...

We can see that as new evidence is introduced, our beliefs and predictions will also change. New data would and should make us see events and probabilities in a different light, and this is an idea that will help us in RC as well.

Reverse Confirmation

When we are approaching a question, there will be gaps or missing bits of information that will dilute our understanding of the passage, and subsequently our answer choice selection process. These are details or parts of the passage that we have either missed or didn't fully understand.

But because we are not even aware of the existence of such information, it's not like we will know where to look in the passage to fill in the missing pieces. For instance, if a question asked you to define the word "serendipity." You didn't know what the word meant but knew that it appeared in the third paragraph, you would be able to go there and try to discover the word's meaning in context. But if there was an answer choice discussing a concept which had appeared in the passage but you were not aware of, you would have probably eliminated it for being out of scope, and being none the wiser for it.

We have already seen that our calculus should change when new evidence enters the equation, and that quite often, our knowledge of the passage is incomplete when we start looking at the questions. So the question is:

Is there a way to use the answer choices as guides to help us hunt down what we don't know from the passage, thereby allowing us to make more informed decisions when it comes to answer choice selection?

The answer is yes.

It's a process that we have looked at in a limited sense in some earlier questions, namely the process of **reverse confirmation**.

***

We saw Reverse Confirmation at work in both Chapters 11 and 12. Basically, we took the keywords extracted from each answer choice as hints and used them to guide our second reading of the passage. For example, if Answer Choice A talks about a "theory," and we don't remember anything about any theory, instead of eliminating this answer outright, we think about what the word theory means, and we go back to the passage to see if we can find a mention of a theory or any semblance of a theory.

In other words, we are using the wording of the answer choices to help us discover any potential gaps or unknowns left over from our initial reading of the passage, and in doing so improve our understanding of the passage even as we are working through the answer choices.

As we uncover more information and details, our ability to rank answer choices will improve, since we have essentially updated our priors and have accounted for the missing information from the passage.

We will now look at several questions where Reverse Confirmation can help us find the better answer choice.

PT21 S4 Q7 (PT21 Passage 1)

Musicologists concerned with the "London Pianoforte school," the group of composers, pedagogues, pianists, publishers, and builders who contributed to the development of the piano in London at the turn of the nineteenth century, have long encountered a formidable obstacle in the general unavailability of music of this "school" in modern scholarly editions. Indeed, much of this repertory has more or less vanished from our historical consciousness. Granted, the sonatas and Gradus ad Parnassum of Muzio Clementi and the nocturnes of John Field have remained familiar enough (though more often than not in editions lacking scholarly rigor), but the work of other leading representatives, like Johann Baptist Cramer and Jan Ladislav Dussek, has eluded serious attempts at revival.

Nicholas Temperley's ambitious new anthology decisively overcomes this deficiency. What underscores the intrinsic value of Temperley's editions is that the anthology reproduces nearly all of the original music in facsimile. Making available this cross section of English musical life—some 800 works by 49 composers—should encourage new critical perspectives about how piano music evolved in England, an issue of considerable relevance to our understanding of how piano music developed on the European continent, and of how, finally, the instrument was transformed from the fortepiano to what we know today as the piano.

To be sure, the concept of the London Pianoforte school itself calls for review. "School" may well be too strong a word for what was arguably a group unified not so much by stylistic principles or aesthetic creed as by the geographical circumstance that they worked at various times in London and produced pianos and piano music for English pianos and English markets. Indeed, Temperley concedes that their "variety may be so great as to cast doubt on the notion of a 'school.'"

The notion of a school was first propounded by Alexander Ringer, who argued that laws of artistic survival forced the young, progressive Beethoven to turn outside Austria for creative models, and that he found inspiration in a group of pianists connected with Clementi in London. Ringer's proposed London Pianoforte school did suggest a circumscribed and fairly unified group—for want of a better term, a school—of musicians whose influence was felt primarily in the decades just before and after 1800. After all, Beethoven did respond to the advances of the Broadwood piano—its reinforced frame, extended compass, triple stringing, and pedals, for example—and it is reasonable to suppose that London pianists who composed music for such an instrument during the critical phase of its development exercised no small degree of influence on Continental musicians. Nevertheless, perhaps the most sensible approach to this issue is to define the school by the period (c. 1766–1873) during which it flourished, as Temperley has done in the anthology.

The author of the passage is primarily concerned with

A. explaining the influence of the development of the pianoforte on the music of Beethoven
B. describing Temperley's view of the contrast between the development of piano music in England and the development of piano music elsewhere in Europe
C. presenting Temperley's evaluation of the impact of changes in piano construction on styles and forms of music composed in the era of the London Pianoforte school
D. considering an alternative theory to that proposed by Ringer concerning the London Pianoforte school
E. discussing the contribution of Temperley's anthology to what is known of the history of the London Pianoforte school

The passage discusses Temperley's new anthology. This passage basically feels like a positive book review. Let's look at the answer choices, we will use each of the answers to practice Reverse Confirmation:

 A.   *explaining* the *influence* of the development of the pianoforte *on the music of Beethoven*

When practicing Reverse Confirmation, we take the keywords out of the answer choice, think about what the answer is trying to say, and ask ourselves, "**what kind of information would the passage need to contain in order to justify this answer?**"

Then we go to the passage and check to see if it indeed contains such information.

If the purpose of the passage is to explain the influence of pianoforte on Beethoven, we would be looking at a passage that tells us "how the pianoforte influenced Beethoven's music." In other words, the passage would tell us how Beethoven was inspired by the pianoforte, what he learned from the pianoforte, how it influenced his style, etc.

The actual passage is very different, it's talking about Temperley's anthology. Influences of the pianoforte on Beethoven was mentioned in the passage in passing, only to describe a view on the coherence of the London Pianoforte School.

 B.   describing Temperley's view of the *contrast* between the development of piano music in *England* and the development of piano music elsewhere in *Europe*

If this was indeed the purpose of the passage, the passage would go into detail on how piano music developed in England, and how piano music developed in Europe. The passage would tell us what Temperley thought the differences were.

Imagine this was the topic given to you by your professor. How would you organize the passage? What would you write in the first, second, and third paragraphs?

The entire passage would be "describing" what Temperley believes to be the contrast between the development of piano music in England and Europe. Paragraph 1 would talk about Temperley, while Paragraphs 2 – 4 would talk about the three main contrasts according to Temperley.

At least that's how I would organize the passage. Once you think about the passage in that light, you will realize how different it is from reality.

 C.   *presenting* Temperley's *evaluation* of the *impact of changes* in piano construction on *styles* and *forms of music* composed in the era of the London Pianoforte school

This answer choice is talking about how changes in piano construction influenced music styles and forms. Furthermore, it's talking about Temperley's "evaluation" of these influences.

In other words, if this was the purpose of the passage, then the passage will have to talk about some of the following topics:

What were the changes made to piano construction?

How did these changes influence music styles and forms?

What does Temperley think about these changes? What is his evaluation? Are these changes positive or negative?

 D.   considering an *alternative theory* to that proposed by Ringer concerning the London Pianoforte school

Does Ringer propose a theory? I'm not too sure. Ringer labels the LPS a "school," but I don't know if this constitutes a theory in itself.

Is there an alternative theory? We know that Temperley categorizes the "school" by period, but would this constitute an "alternative theory?"

Remember what we are looking for: what Temperley did, and why his work is great.

>   E.   *discussing the contribution of Temperley's anthology to what is known of the history of the London Pianoforte school*

If the purpose of this passage was to discuss Temperley's contributions, then the passage should be organized in such a way that different paragraphs will talk about something positive about Temperley's work, and how they aid us in the understanding of the LPS. Is this so?

Paragraph 1 talks about how there is limited scholarship on the LPS.

Paragraph 2 talks about how comprehensive Temperley's work is at addressing this problem.

Paragraph 3 talks about whether the term "school" is appropriate.

Paragraph 4 talks about the origin of the term "school," and finally reaffirms Temperley's more flexible, more sensible approach to defining the school by period.

Answer Choice E is the correct answer. The passage, while going into details describing Temperley's anthology, is also aimed at highlighting its positive "contributions."

PT21 S4 Q13 (PT21 Passage 2)

What is "law"? By what processes do judges arrive at opinions, those documents that justify their belief that the "law" dictates a conclusion one way or the other? These are among the oldest questions in jurisprudence, debate about which has traditionally been dominated by representatives of two schools of thought: proponents of natural law, who see law as intertwined with a moral order independent of society's rules and mores, and legal positivists, who see law solely as embodying the commands of a society's ruling authority.

Since the early 1970s, these familiar questions have received some new and surprising answers in the legal academy. This novelty is in part a consequence of the increasing influence there of academic disciplines and intellectual traditions previously unconnected with the study of law. Perhaps the most influential have been the answers given by the Law and Economics school. According to these legal economists, law consists and ought to consist of those rules that maximize a society's material wealth and that abet the efficient operation of markets designed to generate wealth. More controversial have been the various answers provided by members of the Critical Legal Studies movement, according to whom law is one among several cultural mechanisms by which holders of power seek to legitimate their domination. Drawing on related arguments developed in anthropology, sociology, and history, the critical legal scholars contend that law is an expression of power, but not, as held by the positivists, the power of the legitimate sovereign government. Rather, it is an expression of the power of elites who may have no legitimate authority, but who are intent on preserving the privileges of their race, class, or gender.

In the mid-1970s, James Boyd White began to articulate yet another interdisciplinary response to the traditional questions, and in so doing spawned what is now known as the Law and Literature movement. White has insisted that law, particularly as it is interpreted in judicial opinions, should be understood as an essentially literary activity. Judicial opinions should be read and evaluated not primarily as political acts or as attempts to maximize society's wealth through efficient rules, but rather as artistic performances. And like all such performances, White argues, each judicial opinion attempts in its own way to promote a particular political or ethical value.

In the recent Justice as Translation, White argues that opinion-writing should be regarded as an act of "translation," and judges as "translators." As such, judges find themselves mediating between the authoritative legal text and the pressing legal problem that demands resolution. A judge must essentially "re-constitute" that text by fashioning a new one, which is faithful to the old text but also responsive to and informed by the conditions, constraints, and aspirations of the world in which the new legal problem has arisen.

Which one of the following can be inferred from the passage about the academic study of jurisprudence before the 1970s?

A. It was concerned primarily with codifying and maintaining the privileges of elites.
B. It rejected theories that interpreted law as an expression of a group's power.
C. It seldom focused on how and by what authority judges arrived at opinions.
D. It was concerned primarily with the study of law as an economic and moral agent.
E. It was not concerned with such disciplines as anthropology and sociology.

The question stem here affords us some guidance on where to look for the relevant information needed. The question is asking about the academic study of jurisprudence before the 1970s.

The passage is laid out in chronological order. Paragraph 2 talks about events since the early 1970s. If we are concerned about information from prior to the 1970s, then we'll have to look in paragraph 1.

We see in paragraph 1 that earlier academic studies have been dominated by two schools: the natural law proponents and the legal positivists. So perhaps the answer choice will say something about these two schools.

> A. It was concerned _primarily_ with _codifying and maintaining_ the privileges of elites.

Two words/phrases stand out to me: "primarily" and "codifying and maintaining." I couldn't find any support for either natural law proponents or legal positivists "codifying and maintaining the privileges of elites." That felt more like what the Critical Legal Theorists think of the law.

> B. It _rejected_ theories that interpreted law as an _expression of a group's power_.

Again, both the CLS movement and the legal positivists interpreted law as an expression of a group's power. So what this answer is saying is that _pre-1970 scholarship (natural law and legal positivists) rejected CLS and legal positivism._

This is self contradictory. Legal positivists did not reject themselves, and we don't know how both they and the natural law proponents felt about the CLS movement.

> C. It _seldom_ focused on how and by what authority judges arrived at opinions.

Both the theory of natural law and legal positivism are concerned with "by what process do judges arrive at opinions."

> D. It was _concerned primarily_ with the study of law as an _economic_ and _moral agent_.

Perhaps natural law is primarily concerned with the study of law as a moral agent. But what about legal positivism? In order to select this answer choice, the two schools mentioned in the first paragraph will have to be the natural law school and the law and economics school. This answer is partially out of scope.

> E. It was not concerned with such disciplines as _anthropology_ and _sociology_.

This answer looks out of scope at a first glance, because the first paragraph never mentions disciplines such as anthropology and sociology.

But remember, what is the question asking us?

It's asking us what is true about the academic study of the law pre-1970. Does the passage talk about subjects like anthropology and sociology? Yes, but in later parts of the passage.

If I were to select this answer, what kind of evidence would I need to see from the passage?

Either direct evidence telling me that _the theory of natural law and legal positivism are not concerned with disciplines such as anthropology and sociology_, or

Interdisciplinary studies of the law that included topics like anthropology and sociology only appeared in the 1970s or later.
Both kinds of evidence are sufficient for me to select E as the right answer.

Indirect evidence can be found in the second paragraph. We know that the CLS movement appeared since the early 1970s, and CLS draws upon anthropology and sociology.

Of course, we must admit that the textual support for answer choice E is weak at best. If we wanted to be super strict about our standards, then just because a new theory drew upon anthropology and sociology doesn't necessarily mean that older theories didn't.

By adopting a ranking mentality, where we pick the answer with the most support, rather than trying to chase the perfect answer choice, we can maximize our accuracy rate on RC questions. Also, by using the strategy of Reverse Confirmation, where we try to discover whatever evidence the passage contained for each answer, we can come to the realization that answer choice E is the only answer where we can find even *indirect* or *partial* support.

E is the correct answer.

PT71 S4 Q15 (PT71 Passage 3)

In certain fields of human endeavor, such as music, chess, and some athletic activities, the performance of the best practitioners is so outstanding, so superior even to the performance of other highly experienced individuals in the field, that some people believe some notion of innate talent must be invoked to account for this highest level of performance. Certain psychologists have supported this view with data concerning the performance of prodigies and the apparent heritability of relevant traits. They have noted, for example, that most outstanding musicians are discovered by the age of six, and they have found evidence that some of the qualities necessary for exceptional athletic performance, including superior motor coordination, speed of reflexes, and hand-eye coordination, can be inborn.

Until recently, however, little systematic research was done on the topic of superior performance, and previous estimates of the heritability of traits relevant to performance were based almost exclusively on random samples of the general population rather than on studies of highly trained superior performers as compared with the general population. Recent research in different domains of excellence suggests that exceptional performance arises predominantly from acquired complex skills and physiological adaptations, rather than from innate abilities. For example, it has been found that the most accomplished athletes show a systematic advantage in reaction time or perceptual discrimination only in their particular fields of performance, not in more general laboratory tests for these factors. Similarly, superior chess players have exceptional memory for configurations of chess pieces, but only if those configurations are typical of chess games.

The vast majority of exceptional adult performers were not exceptional as children, but started instruction early and improved their performance through sustained high-level training. Only extremely rarely is outstanding performance achieved without at least ten years of intensive, deliberate practice. With such intensive training, chess players who may not have superior innate capacities can acquire skills that circumvent basic limits on such factors as memory and the ability to process information. Recent research shows that, with the clear exception of some traits such as height, a surprisingly large number of anatomical characteristics, including aerobic capacity and the percentage of muscle fibers, show specific changes that develop from extended intensive training.

The evidence does not, therefore, support the claim that a notion of innate talent must be invoked in order to account for the difference between good and outstanding performance, since it suggests instead that extended intense training, together with that level of talent common to all reasonably competent performers, may suffice to account for this difference. Since sustained intense training usually depends on an appropriate level of interest and desire, and since those who eventually become superior performers more often show early signs of exceptional interest than early evidence of unusual ability, motivational factors are more likely to be effective predictors of superior performance than is innate talent.

Which one of the following most accurately represents the primary function of the final paragraph?

A. It makes proposals for educational reform based on the evidence cited by the author
B. It demonstrates that two consequences of the findings regarding superior performance are at odds with one another
C. It recapitulates the evidence against the supposed heritability of outstanding talent and advocates a particular direction to be taken in future research on the topic
D. It raises and answers a possible objection to the author's view of the importance of intense training
E. It draws two inferences regarding the explanatory and predictive roles of possible factors in the development of superior performance

Let's take a look at the passage, as it is new to us.

In certain fields of human endeavor, such as music, chess, and some athletic activities, the performance of the best practitioners is so outstanding, so superior even to the performance of other highly experienced individuals in the field, that some people believe <u>some notion of innate talent</u> must be invoked to account for this highest level of performance. Certain psychologists have supported this view with data concerning the performance of prodigies and the apparent heritability of relevant traits. They have noted, for example, that most outstanding <u>musicians</u> are discovered by the <u>age of six</u>, and they have found evidence that some of the qualities necessary for exceptional athletic performance, including superior motor coordination, speed of reflexes, and hand-eye coordination, <u>can be inborn</u>.

The top performers in some fields are so good that some believe this talent to be innate. Some psychologists have supported this view with data.

Until recently, however, <u>little systematic research</u> was done on the topic of superior performance, and previous estimates of the heritability of traits relevant to performance were based almost exclusively on <u>random samples of the general population</u> rather than on studies of highly trained superior performers as compared with the general population. <u>Recent research</u> in different domains of excellence suggests that exceptional performance <u>arises predominantly from acquired complex skills and physiological adaptations, rather than from innate abilities</u>. For example, it has been found that the most accomplished athletes show a systematic advantage in reaction time or perceptual discrimination <u>only in their particular fields of performance</u>, not in more general laboratory tests for these factors. Similarly, superior chess players have exceptional memory for <u>configurations of chess pieces</u>, but only if those configurations are typical of chess games.

Previous studies have been limited and flawed.

New research suggest that excellence comes predominantly from acquired skills and adaptations, rather than from innate abilities.

The vast majority of exceptional adult performers were <u>not exceptional as children</u>, but started instruction early and improved their performance through <u>sustained high-level training</u>. Only extremely rarely is outstanding performance achieved without at least ten years of intensive, deliberate practice. With such intensive training, chess players who may not have superior innate capacities <u>can acquire skills</u> that circumvent basic limits on such factors as memory and the ability to process information. Recent research shows that, with the clear exception of some traits such as height, a surprisingly large number of anatomical characteristics, including aerobic capacity and the percentage of muscle fibers, show specific changes that develop from <u>extended intensive training</u>.

Training can lead to exceptional performance and compensate for a lack of superior innate capacity.

The evidence does not, therefore, support the claim that a notion of innate talent must be invoked in order to account for the difference between good and outstanding performance, since it suggests instead that <u>extended intense training</u>, together with that level of <u>talent common to all reasonably</u> competent performers, may suffice to account for this difference. Since sustained intense training usually depends on an appropriate level of interest and desire, and since those who eventually become superior performers more often show early signs of exceptional interest than early evidence of unusual ability, <u>motivational factors</u> are more likely to be effective predictors of superior performance than is innate talent.

Here, we are told that to achieve outstanding performance, training and reasonable talent is all you need. But since training requires a high level of interest, motivation is more important than innate talent.

In this passage, the author examines a new study that casts doubt on existing beliefs about the role of innate talent in exceptional performance. Training as well as motivation, according to the author, are better predictors of exceptional performance.

Which one of the following most accurately represents the primary function of the final paragraph?

We mentioned earlier in Chapter 7 that Purpose/Function Questions are like Role Questions in LR. It helps to think of the entire passage as one giant LR argument, and each paragraph as premise, conclusion, opposing viewpoint, concession, or background info. In this passage, I think the last paragraph can be considered the "conclusion" paragraph. Paragraph 1 presents background info and the opposing view, whereas paragraphs 2 and 3 are the support/premises of the author's argument.

So I will look for an answer that says something like "the final paragraph summarizes the key point of the new search."

   A.   It makes <u>proposals for educational reform</u> based on the evidence cited by the author

What would be considered a "proposal for educational reform?" I'm thinking that it would look something like this:

"Schools should incorporate more X subjects into its curriculum"

This does not happen in the last paragraph.

   B.   It demonstrates that <u>two consequences of the findings</u> regarding superior performance <u>are at odds with one another</u>

What are the two consequences of the findings? One, extensive training and reasonable talent may suffice to lead to superior performance. Two, motivation rather than talent is more important. Both of these consequences suggest that innate talent is not that important, they are not at odds with each other, they complement each other.

   C.   It <u>recapitulates the evidence</u> against the supposed heritability of outstanding talent and <u>advocates</u> a particular direction to be taken in future research on the topic

What does it mean to "recapitulate evidence?" I'm under the impression that it means a "restatement of evidence."

Does the last paragraph "restate" evidence? I don't think so, I think what it does can be more suitably labelled as a "summarization" of the evidence. This paragraph feels like a conclusion after all, and when applying **reverse confirmation**, I couldn't find a "restatement" of the different pieces of evidence mentioned earlier in the passage.

A second issue is regarding what this supposed evidence is for. As we see from the passage, the evidence suggests that innate talent is not necessary for superior performance. The evidence suggests that training is a bigger factor.

But here, according to this particular answer choice, its evidence "against the supposed heritability of outstanding talent." That means evidence which demonstrates that outstanding talent cannot be inherited.

So that would be like evidence showing us that Michael Jordan couldn't pass his basketball skills to his sons, or that Federer couldn't have kids who were also really good at tennis.

That's NOT what the evidence mentioned in the last paragraph is about. The evidence actually in the passage is telling us that to become great like MJ, we need a reasonable level of talent, and we need to train super hard.

Finally, I think the word "advocate" is a little too strong/out of scope. The author does mention "motivation" as a more effective predictor, but never explicitly calls for research into the role of motivation.

    D. It <u>raises</u> and <u>answers</u> a possible objection to the author's view of the importance of intense training

Does the last paragraph raise an objection? Since we know that the author believes intense training to be crucial, a possible objection would have to tell us that training isn't as important as we thought.

This doesn't happen in the last paragraph.

    E. It draws <u>two inferences</u> regarding the <u>explanatory</u> and <u>predictive</u> roles of <u>possible factors</u> in the development of superior performance

This answer choice is super vague! Let's see if **reverse confirmation** can help us again with deciphering what it's trying to say.

"Possible factors": what are the possible factors in the development of superior performance?

We know it's not innate talent. It's sustained training and motivation.

Since we know that motivation is a factor, and we know that the author did call it likely to be an "effective predictor," let's substitute one of the factors for "motivation," and see if the answer choice will make more sense.

"it draws an inference regarding the predictive role of motivation in the development of superior performance."

Can we match this up with the content from the last paragraph? I believe so. The author did suggest that motivation is likely to be an effective predictor of superior performance than innate talent.

So let's try to plug in the other factor, sustained training:

"it draws an inference regarding the explanatory role of sustained training in the development of superior performance."

What is the inference drawn in the passage? Namely that innate talent need not be invoked, since sustained training and normal talent may be enough.

Recall Advanced Trap #4 for Role Questions in **LR Perfection**, sometimes a vaguely worded trait can be acceptable as the correct answer, something different from our pre-phrased answer. This answer choice is similar. It is vaguely worded, and doesn't really describe the paragraph's role in relation to the entire passage or the passage's Main Point. Nonetheless, it is an accurate description of what occurs in the last paragraph, and since it's the only one that does so, it is the correct answer.

Equal Standards Test

We now come to a last resort strategy for answer choice ranking. Given its rather time-consuming nature, this is a tactic reserved for only the most advanced test-takers. Before we fully delve into the strategy itself, let's speak a little more on human psychology and how that factors into our answer choice selection process.

Students of behavioural psychology and those of us who have encountered PT37 Passage 4 will have a notion of what Nobel Laureate Dr. Daniel Kahneman calls "Prospect Theory."

Prospect theory states that people are naturally risk averse, so when faced with a potential loss they want to avoid, they subconsciously take on more risk. In other words, we are willing to risk more to avoid a loss than a potential gain.

Imagine now that you are stuck between two RC answer choices, you are leaning towards one but are afraid to choose it. You examine that answer, analyze it, pick at its potential issues, and suffer over it. You so desperately want to pick it but it just doesn't feel perfect. You are frustrated and end up picking another answer, almost spontaneously.

The answer you picked, unfortunately, was wrong. With the benefit of hindsight, you see that the wrong answer indeed has more problems than the right one, but because you were so suspicious of the correct answer, you have lowered the standard and chosen the wrong answer instead.

Our fear of getting the question wrong made us risk averse, we were so afraid of making a mistake on the correct answer choice that we ended up running to another answer for refuge, in the process subconsciously lowering our standards, without realizing that the answer we picked instead contained more gaps.

If we had only applied the same level of suspicion and examination to both answer choices, we would have seen that the "correct" answer had a smaller number of problems.

As a result, a habit of human nature that we must resist when conducting answer choice ranking is when we take a critical view of one answer choice (as you should) but end up being overly forgiving with another choice.

> *The uneven application of scrutiny to answer choices is the single greatest obstacle for advanced RC students.*

After working with several hundred students, most eventually attaining a 170/175+ score, we saw this "uneven scrutiny" habit prevalent even among the most advanced test takers. In many ways, it's even harder to break an undesirable habit in an advanced student. The advanced test taker will be confident in their abilities, and after having witnessed their method's effectiveness so far, will be resistant to suggestions of change. In order to address and overcome this "stubbornness" I devised the **Equal Standards Test**:

Answer Choice Fixing

The Equal Standards Test, at its core, is about *quantifying* the gaps each answer choice contains. In the hardest questions, no answer choice will be perfect. So our job instead is to pick the answer with **the least number of problems**. In order to do this we must have a clear idea of exactly what's wrong with each answer choice, as well as being able to objectively compare them to determine which answer is, relatively speaking, the better choice.

Applying the Equal Standards Test, as I mentioned earlier, is something reserved for the advanced student. This is because the test requires us to have an intimate understanding of the passage. If we only have a fragmented and partial understanding of the passage, its content, and its details, we will not be able to effectively apply this test.

For the Equal Standards Test, the question we are asking ourselves after looking at each answer choice is this:

What would I change about this answer choice to make it into a perfect answer? What parts would I modify about this answer choice that would make me comfortable in selecting it as the right answer?

Essentially, we are trying to "fix" the answer choices. By trying to close the gaps present in each answer choice, we are forcing ourselves to isolate and list any and all the issues an answer may have. If an answer choice contained three problems, and another answer had only one problem that needed fixing, then the latter answer choice would be the preferred answer since it needs the least amount of work.

Take a look at the following passages and their associated questions. When you narrow your answers down to two possibilities, ask yourself the following questions:

What is it exactly that you don't like about these answers?

What would you change to make either answer acceptable as the correct answer?

Which answer needs a greater amount of work, or which answer contains more numerous and/or significant issues?

***

Take a look at the following passage (PT 35 Passage 4), with which you should be very familiar by now, and answer the following questions:

Ronald Dworkin argues that judges are in danger of uncritically embracing an erroneous theory known as legal positivism because they think that the only alternative is a theory that they (and Dworkin) see as clearly unacceptable—natural law. The latter theory holds that judges ought to interpret the law by consulting their own moral convictions, even if this means ignoring the letter of the law and the legal precedents for its interpretation. Dworkin regards this as an impermissible form of judicial activism that arrogates to judges powers properly reserved for legislators.

Legal positivism, the more popular of the two theories, holds that law and morality are wholly distinct. The meaning of the law rests on social convention in the same way as does the meaning of a word. Dworkin's view is that legal positivists regard disagreement among jurists as legitimate only if it arises over what the underlying convention is, and it is to be resolved by registering a consensus, not by deciding what is morally right. In the same way, disagreement about the meaning of a word is settled by determining how people actually use it, and not by deciding what it ought to mean. Where there is no consensus, there is no legal fact of the matter. The judge's interpretive role is limited to discerning this consensus, or the absence thereof.

According to Dworkin, this account is incompatible with the actual practice of judges and lawyers, who act as if there is a fact of the matter even in cases where there is no consensus. The theory he proposes seeks to validate this practice without falling into what Dworkin correctly sees as the error of natural law theory. It represents a kind of middle ground between the latter and legal positivism. Dworkin stresses the fact that there is an internal logic to a society's laws and the general principles they typically embody. An interpretation that conforms to these principles may be correct even if it is not supported by a consensus. Since these general principles may involve such moral concepts as justice and fairness, judges may be called upon to consult their own moral intuitions in arriving at an interpretation. But this is not to say that judges are free to impose their own morality at will, without regard to the internal logic of the laws.

The positivist's mistake, as Dworkin points out, is assuming that the meaning of the law can only consist in what people think it means, whether these people be the original authors of the law or a majority of the interpreter's peers. Once we realize, as Dworkin does, that the law has an internal logic of its own that constrains interpretation, we open up the possibility of improving upon the interpretations not only of our contemporaries but of the original authors.

PT35 S2 Q25 (PT35 Passage 4)

The passage suggests that Dworkin would be most likely to agree with which one of the following statements?

A. Judges and lawyers too often act as though there is a fact of the matter in legal cases.
B. Judges should not use their moral intuition when it conflicts with the intentions of those legislators who authored the law being interpreted.
C. Legal positivism is a more popular theory than natural law theory because legal positivism simplifies the judge's role.
D. If there is consensus about how to interpret a law, then jurists should not examine the internal logic of the law being interpreted.
E. Legal positivists misunderstand the role of moral intuition in legal interpretation.

PT35 S2 Q26 (PT35 Passage 4)

It can be inferred that legal positivists, as described in the passage, agree with which one of the following statements?

A. Judges sometimes ought to be allowed to use personal moral convictions as a basis for a legal interpretation.
B. Disagreements about the meaning of a law are never legitimate.
C. The ultimate standard of interpretation is the logic of the law itself, not moral intuition.
D. The meaning of a law derives from jurists' interpretations of that law.
E. There is no legal fact of the matter when jurists have differing moral convictions about an issue

Let's look at each of the questions in turn:

Q25 asks us what Dworkin would most likely agree with, a Third Party POV Question. So, let's see what we can find from the passage that may provide us with some hints.

From the first paragraph, we can gather that Dworkin considers legal positivism to be erroneous. Dworkin also sees natural law as unacceptable too.

Dworkin believes that judges are making a mistake in believing these two theories to be the only options available.

Dworkin also considers judicial activism to be something impermissible.

In the second paragraph, we are given Dworkin's view of what legal positivism is. According to Dworkin, legal positivists don't believe that there is an objective standard behind the law. The law is about what we all agree upon.

In the third paragraph, we are told that Dworkin thinks that in reality, judges and lawyers act like there is an objective standard. So the theory of legal positivism doesn't bear out in reality.

Dworkin believes in a middle ground between natural law and legal positivism.

Dworkin believes in an internal logic and principles behind the law. These principles may involve moral concepts.

Judges may apply their own morality but within the limits set by the internal logic of the laws.

Finally, in the last paragraph, we are told that Dworkin believes the law to contain both objective and subjective meanings, and the objective meaning (the law's internal logic) limits the scope of our subjective understanding (interpretation).

Lastly, Dworkin believes that interpretations of the law can improve upon both the original authors' and our contemporaries' understandings.

***

Now that's a lot of information, let's look at the answer choices:

A. Judges and lawyers *too often* act as though there is a fact of the matter in legal cases.

Do judges and lawyers act as though there is a fact of the matter even when there is no consensus? Yes they do.

Does Dworkin believe that they do so "too often?" No, Dworkin is not critical of the frequency at which judges and lawyers act in such a way. Instead, Dworkin tries to come up with a theory that accounts for this actual practice.

B. Judges *should not* use their moral intuition when it *conflicts* with the intentions of those legislators who authored the law being interpreted.

The third paragraph tells us that judges may use their own moral intuition. Furthermore, the last sentence tells us that we may improve upon the interpretation of the original authors.

C. Legal positivism is a more popular theory than natural law theory because legal positivism simplifies the judge's role.

This is out of scope, we are never told why legal positivism is more popular.

> D. *If there is consensus about how to interpret a law, then jurists should not examine the internal logic of the law being interpreted.*

This would be the view of the legal positivists, consensus > internal logic. This would not be Dworkin's view.

> E. *Legal positivists __misunderstand__ the role of moral intuition in legal interpretation.*

Dworkin stresses that moral intuition has a role in legal interpretation, legal positivists don't think so. But is this because legal positivists "misunderstand" the role of moral intuition?

***

I think C and D can be safely eliminated, leaving us with A, B, and E.

Let's see what the problems are with these three answers, and if we wanted to fix them up, how much work is needed.

For answer choice A, if we said *"judges and lawyers ~~too often~~ act as though there is a fact of the matter in legal cases,"* then it would be fine.

For answer choice B, it should read as *"judges __should not__ use their moral intuition when it __conflicts__ with ~~the intentions of those legislators who authored the law being interpreted~~ the internal logic of the laws.*

For answer choice E, instead of saying that legal positivists "misunderstand," if the answer had said *"legal positivists __overlook__ the role of moral intuition in legal interpretation,"* then I would be okay with it.

I think answer B is clearly the one that has the biggest problems, it can be eliminated. That leaves us with A and E.

Both answers do not 100% reflect the original meaning as expressed in the passage, but which answer contains the bigger gap?

Think about the following analogy:

"I eat ice cream" vs. *"I eat ice cream too often."*

The inclusion of the words "too often" turns an observation into a judgment. That's a pretty big jump. We know that Dworkin did not look critically upon how frequently judges act like there is a fact of the matter.

How about this:

"some parents misunderstand the role they play in their children's emotional development" vs. *"some parents overlook the role they play in their children's emotional development."*

I think that if you overlook something, you are ignoring its significance. Whereas if you misunderstand something, you may either overemphasize or underemphasize its significance. The two terms are not equivalent, far from it, but I do think that there is some minor overlap.

I would say that answer choice E is closer/slightly more inferable from the original text.

Answer E also happens to be the correct/better answer.

***

Q26 asks us with what the legal positivists would agree. Another open-ended question that we need to go back to the passage to search for answers.

The view of the legal positivists is revealed in the second paragraph:

They hold that law and morality are wholly distinct.

The meaning of the law rests upon social convention/consensus.

Disagreement in law is about what the consensus is, and not about what is objectively right or wrong.

Judges should limit their roles to figuring out what the consensus is.

***

> A. *Judges sometimes ought to be allowed to use personal moral convictions as a basis for a legal interpretation.*

This is Dworkin's view, and to an extent the natural law perspective. We are being asked for the legal positivists' view.

> B. *Disagreements about the meaning of a law are never legitimate.*

Disagreements are legitimate, according to legal positivists, only if it arises over what the underlying convention is.

> C. *The ultimate standard of interpretation is the logic of the law itself, not moral intuition.*

This answer confuses different strands of ideas. According to the legal positivists, the standard of interpretation is the underlying consensus.

For Dworkin, the ultimate standard is the logic of the law itself, supplemented by moral intuition.

> D. *The meaning of a law derives from jurists' interpretations of that law.*

This answer choice is confusing. The passage tells us that for the legal positivists, the meaning of the law rests on social convention.

How does that relate to the jurists' interpretations of that law?

Take a look at the last sentence of the second paragraph.

We are told that the judge's interpretive role is limited to discerning the consensus.
In the middle of the second paragraph we are also told that "*legal positivists regard disagreement among jurists as legitimate only if it arises over what the underlying convention is, and it is to be resolved by registering a consensus.*"

So essentially, what this paragraph is telling us is that the legal positivists believe that *the meaning of the law rests on social convention, which is to be resolved by registering a consensus, and the judges' role is limited to discerning that consensus through interpretation.*

That's quite a handful, can we simplify that?

What about "an element essential to the meaning of the law needs to be interpreted by judges?"

A consensus is essential to determining what the social convention behind a law is. The judges must interpret what that consensus is.

So if the answer choice had said, "*consensus is essential to the meaning of the law, and judges are limited to interpreting what the consensus is,*" I think that would be a great answer.

Instead, we got "*meaning of the law derives from the jurists' interpretation of the law.*"

If you look at it now, I think there is significant overlap between the content of the passage and what the actual answer choice said.

     E.   *There is no legal fact of the matter when jurists have differing moral convictions about an issue.*

There is no fact of the matter when there is no consensus.

D is the only answer that did not contain information that contradicted the passage. It had parts which were unclear, and may even be considered an oversimplification of the information from the passage, but the other four answers all had erroneous parts. So D ended up being the best of the bunch.

D is the best/correct answer.

Let's now look at how Answer Choice Fixing would work in a Strengthen Question.

A vigorous debate in astronomy centers on an epoch in planetary history that was first identified by analysis of rock samples obtained in lunar missions. Scientists discovered that the major craters on the Moon were created by a vigorous bombardment of debris approximately four billion years ago—the so-called late heavy bombardment (LHB). Projectiles from this bombardment that affected the Moon should also have struck Earth, a likelihood with profound consequences for the history of Earth since, until the LHB ended, life could not have survived here.

Various theoretical approaches have been developed to account for both the evidence gleaned from samples of Moon rock collected during lunar explorations and the size and distribution of craters on the Moon. Since the sizes of LHB craters suggest they were formed by large bodies, some astronomers believe that the LHB was linked to the disintegration of an asteroid or comet orbiting the Sun. In this view, a large body broke apart and peppered the inner solar system with debris. Other scientists disagree and believe that the label "LHB" is in itself a misnomer. These researchers claim that a cataclysm is not necessary to explain the LHB evidence. They claim that the Moon's evidence merely provides a view of the period concluding billions of years of a continuous, declining heavy bombardment throughout the inner solar system. According to them, the impacts from the latter part of the bombardment were so intense that they obliterated evidence of earlier impacts. A third group contends that the Moon's evidence supports the view that the LHB was a sharply defined cataclysmic cratering period, but these scientists believe that because of its relatively brief duration, this cataclysm did not extend throughout the inner solar system. They hold that the LHB involved only the disintegration of a body within the Earth- Moon system, because the debris from such an event would have been swept up relatively quickly.

New support for the hypothesis that a late bombardment extended throughout the inner solar system has been found in evidence from the textural features and chemical makeup of a meteorite that has been found on Earth. It seems to be a rare example of a Mars rock that made its way to Earth after being knocked from the surface of Mars. The rock has recently been experimentally dated at about four billion years old, which means that, if the rock is indeed from Mars, it was knocked from the planet at about the same time that the Moon was experiencing the LHB. This tiny piece of evidence suggests that at least two planetary systems in the inner solar system experienced bombardment at the same time. However, to determine the pervasiveness of the LHB, scientists will need to locate many more such rocks and perhaps obtain surface samples from other planets in the inner solar system.

Which one of the following, if true, would lend the most support to the view that the LHB was limited to Earth and the Moon?

A. An extensive survey of craters on Mars shows very little evidence for an increase in the intensity of projectiles striking Mars during the period from three billion to five billion years ago.
B. Scientists discover another meteorite on Earth that they conclude had been knocked from the surface of the Moon during the LHB.
C. A re-analysis of Moon rocks reveals that several originated on Earth during the LHB.
D. Based on further testing, scientists conclude that the rock believed to have originated on Mars actually originated on the Moon.
E. Excavations on both Earth and the Moon yield evidence that the LHB concluded billions of years of heavy bombardment.

Remember, for the Equal Standards Test/Answer Choice Fixing process, we are essentially trying to come up with what the *ideal* answer would look like, and then comparing the tricky answer choices to that ideal standard to see how much they have fallen short.

The correct answer will be the one that's closest to the *ideal answer*.

For this question, we are trying to find an answer that strengthens the idea that the LHB was limited to the earth and moon. What would the ideal answer look like?

An answer choice that tells us that no craters were found in the inner solar system besides on the earth and moon would be great. If there were no craters on Mercury, Venus, and Mars, then it's pretty strong evidence that the LHB occurred only on the Earth and on the Moon.

Similarly, if we had conclusive evidence that the craters on Mercury, Venus, and Mars were caused by something else, then that would be a really strong answer too.

> A. *An extensive survey of craters on Mars shows very little evidence for an increase in the intensity of projectiles striking Mars during the period from three billion to five billion years ago.*

This is pretty good, it's very close to the ideal answer we had in our mind. Mars didn't see heavy bombardment, Mars is a part of the inner solar system, so maybe the bombardment was limited to the Earth and Moon after all.

> B. *Scientists discover another meteorite on Earth that they conclude had been knocked from the surface of the Moon during the LHB.*

This only tells us that the Moon got hit during LHB. We want an answer that tells us Mars, Mercury, and Venus *didn't* get hit during LHB.

> C. *A re-analysis of Moon rocks reveals that several originated on Earth during the LHB.*

Same problem with B, this tells us that the Earth got it but says nothing about the other planets.

> D. *Based on further testing, scientists conclude that the rock believed to have originated on Mars actually originated on the Moon.*

This answer definitely strengthens the possibility that Mars didn't get hit. It is directly attacking the evidence provided in the passage for the theory that LHB extended to the inner solar system.

But let's stop and think for a moment. What was our ideal answer? We want an answer that tells us that Mars never got hit.

What does this answer tell us? Namely that this one rock didn't come from Mars.

A better answer choice would say that no rocks originated from Mars, ever. But an even better answer would tell us that Mars was never bombarded.

> E. *Excavations on both Earth and the Moon yield evidence that the LHB concluded billions of years of heavy bombardment.*

This answer is talking about the length of the LHB but says nothing about other planets in the inner solar system.

Take a look at answer choices A and D. Which answer does more to convince us that the LHB meteor strikes didn't impact Mars?

It's A.

Even though D seemed more relevant as it directly addresses something mentioned in the passage, we must remember that for Unrestricted Scope Questions like Strengthen, scope doesn't really matter.

By having a general idea of what the idea answer could look like, we can then find the answer with the most definitive and similar effect as our ideal answer. This helps us determine what the correct answer is.

PT81 S1 Q20 (PT81 Passage 3)

Dowsing is the practice of detecting resources of objects beneath the ground by passing handheld, inert tools such as forked sticks, pendulums, or metal rods over a terrain. For example, dowsers typically determine prospective water well drilling locations by walking with a horizontally held forked tree branch until it becomes vertical, claiming the branch is pulled to this position. The distance to the water from the surface and the potential well's flow rate are then determined by holding the branch horizontally again and either walking in place or backwards while the branch is pulled vertical again. The number of paces indicates the distance to the water, and the strength of the pull felt by the dowser correlates with the potential well's flow rate.

Those skeptical of dowsing's efficacy point to the crudeness of its methods as a self-evident reason to question it. They assert that dowsers' use of inert tools indicates that the dowsers themselves actually make subconscious determinations concerning the likely location of groundwater using clues derived from surface conditions; the tools' movements merely reflect the dowsers' subconscious thoughts. Further, the skeptics say, numerous studies show that while a few dowsers have demonstrated considerable and consistent success, the success rate for dowsers generally is notably inconsistent. Finally, skeptics note, dowsing to locate groundwater is largely confined to areas where groundwater is expected to be ubiquitous, making it statistically unlikely that a dowsed well will be completely dry.

Proponents of dowsing point out that it involves a number of distinct techniques and contend that each of these techniques should be evaluated separately. They also note that numerous dowsing studies have been influenced by a lack of care in selecting the study population; dowsers are largely self-proclaimed and self-certified, and verifiably successful dowsers are not well represented in the typical study. Proponents claim that successful dowsers may be sensitive to minute changes in Earth's electromagnetic field associated with variations in subsurface conditions. They also claim that these dowsers have higher success rates than geologists and hydrologists who use scientific tools such as electromagnetic sensors or seismic readings to locate groundwater.

The last two claims were corroborated during a recent and extensive study that utilized teams of the most successful dowsers, geologists, and hydrologists to locate reliable water supplies in various arid countries. Efforts were concentrated on finding groundwater in narrow, tilted fracture zones in bedrock underlying surface sediments. The teams were unfamiliar with the areas targeted, and they agreed that no surface clues existed that could assist in pinpointing the locations of fracture zones. The dowsers consistently made significantly more accurate predictions regarding drill sites, and on request even located a dry fracture zone, suggesting that dowsers can detect variations in subsurface conditions.

The passage provides the most support for inferring which one of the following statements?

    A.   Narrow, tilted fracture zones in underlying bedrock are more likely to be found in arid regions than in other regions.

    B.   There are no reliable studies indicating that dowsers are consistently able to locate subsurface resources other than groundwater.

    C.   A dowser attempting to locate a dry fracture zone would not use the same tools as a dowser attempting to locate groundwater.

    D.   Geologists and hydrologists participating in the groundwater-locating study described in the final paragraph could not locate a dry fracture zone upon request.

    E.   The groundwater-locating study described in the final paragraph was not a typical dowsing study.

Dowsing is the practice of detecting resources of objects beneath the ground by passing handheld, inert tools such as forked sticks, pendulums, or metal rods over a terrain. For example, dowsers typically determine prospective water well drilling locations by walking with a horizontally held forked tree branch until it becomes vertical, claiming the branch is pulled to this position. The distance to the water from the surface and the potential well's flow rate are then determined by holding the branch horizontally again and either walking in place or backwards while the branch is pulled vertical again. The number of paces indicates the distance to the water, and the strength of the pull felt by the dowser correlates with the potential well's flow rate.

The first paragraph explains to us what "dowsing" is.

Those skeptical of dowsing's efficacy point to the crudeness of its methods as a self-evident reason to question it. They assert that dowsers' use of inert tools indicates that the dowsers themselves actually make subconscious determinations concerning the likely location of groundwater using clues derived from surface conditions; the tools' movements merely reflect the dowsers' subconscious thoughts. Further, the skeptics say, numerous studies show that while a few dowsers have demonstrated considerable and consistent success, the success rate for dowsers generally is notably inconsistent. Finally, skeptics note, dowsing to locate groundwater is largely confined to areas where groundwater is expected to be ubiquitous, making it statistically unlikely that a dowsed well will be completely dry.

The second paragraph points to some of the criticisms levelled at dowsing. It's crude, dowsers actually make subconscious thoughts, most dowsers do not enjoy consistent success, and that where dowsers are looking for water are usually places with lots of groundwater anyway.

Proponents of dowsing point out that it involves a number of distinct techniques and contend that each of these techniques should be evaluated separately. They also note that numerous dowsing studies have been influenced by a lack of care in selecting the study population; dowsers are largely self-proclaimed and self-certified, and verifiably successful dowsers are not well represented in the typical study. Proponents claim that successful dowsers may be sensitive to minute changes in Earth's electromagnetic field associated with variations in subsurface conditions. They also claim that these dowsers have higher success rates than geologists and hydrologists who use scientific tools such as electromagnetic sensors or seismic readings to locate groundwater.

Proponents respond to criticisms: dowsers have a number of distinct techniques; the dowser population is not vetted carefully, so that successful dowsers are not well represented in studies. Proponents also believe that dowsers can sense changes in the Earth's electromagnetic field and subsurface variations. They also believe that dowsers are more successful than geologists and hydrologists.

The last two claims were corroborated during a recent and extensive study that utilized teams of the most successful dowsers, geologists, and hydrologists to locate reliable water supplies in various arid countries. Efforts were concentrated on finding groundwater in narrow, tilted fracture zones in bedrock underlying surface sediments. The teams were unfamiliar with the areas targeted, and they agreed that no surface clues existed that could assist in pinpointing the locations of fracture zones. The dowsers consistently made significantly more accurate predictions regarding drill sites, and on request even located a dry fracture zone, suggesting that dowsers can detect variations in subsurface conditions.

In the final paragraph, we see a new study that seems to add weight to the supporters' argument. The study addresses some of the concerns listed by the proponents of dowsing (successful dowsers well represented, arid locations rather than locations with ubiquitous underground water). The results suggest that dowsers can in fact locate water. The author seems to find this plausible, as evident in the last sentence of the passage.

The Purpose of the Passage can be thought of as an evaluation of the credibility of dowsing, with the author taking a fairly neutral but supportive stance on the practice.

As for the Main Point, I would come up with something like "dowsing appears to be a viable practice at finding groundwater, as suggested by a new study."

A. *Narrow, tilted fracture zones in underlying bedrock are <u>more likely</u> to be found in arid regions than in other regions.*

This is an **improper relationship** and ample grounds for elimination. The passage tells us that in the study conducted in arid regions, the region also happened to have these fracture zones. But that doesn't mean these zones are more likely to be found in arid regions than other regions.

To use an analogy, if I said "fish are found in lakes," does that mean fish are more likely to be found in lakes than other bodies of water? Not necessarily.

B. *There are <u>no reliable studies</u> indicating that dowsers are consistently able to locate subsurface resources other than groundwater.*

The words "no reliable studies" are really strong. In order to select this answer we need to find evidence in the passage that tells us the number of reliable studies is zero. Using **reverse confirmation** to search the passage, we cannot find such evidence.

Remember that strongly worded answers require a very high threshold of proof when it comes to Inference Questions.

C. *A dowser attempting to locate a dry fracture zone <u>would not use the same tools</u> as a dowser attempting to locate groundwater.*

What kind of tools does a dowser use to locate groundwater? Sticks, pendulums, or metal rods. What kind of tools does a dowser use to locate a dry fracture zone? We don't know. This answer is unsupported.

D. *Geologists and hydrologists participating in the groundwater-locating study described in the final paragraph could not locate a dry fracture zone upon request.*

There seems to be some support for this, albeit non-explicitly. We know from the last paragraph that the dowsers were more successful than the geologists and hydrologists. Dowsers "even located a dry fracture zone on request."

So I'm assuming that the geologists and hydrologists couldn't do it?

Think about the following analogy:

In a shooting contest between Steph Curry and Lebron James, Curry has shown himself to be the more accurate shot. He scored more baskets than James, and even scored a three-pointer blind-folded upon request.

What can we infer from this analogy? Curry being able to score a three-pointer blind folded is used as evidence that he is a better shooter than James. So I guess we are assuming that James wouldn't be able to do it?

But was the request made to James, and if so, did he fail to score?

Now I think there are multiple possibilities. Perhaps James also scored, but this is unlikely, since the analogy is basically talking about why Curry is better.

Perhaps the request was made to James, but he missed. This is certainly a possibility.

But there is also the possibility that the request was never made to James? Perhaps after demonstrating his superior shooting skills, Curry got a little cocky and decided to show off?

Back to our answer choice, there is no direct support for answer choice D, but I would say that it's a possibility. Let's keep it for now.

  E. *The groundwater-locating study described in the final paragraph was <u>not a typical dowsing study.</u>*

Let's use **reverse confirmation** to examine this answer. What is a typical dowsing study?

We know from the third paragraph that "verifiably successful dowsers are not well represented in the typical study."

So in order to select this answer choice we must find evidence that successful dowsers *are* well represented in the groundwater-locating study.

Do we have that kind of support?

Yes, in the first sentence of the last paragraph, we are told that the recent study utilized teams of the "most successful dowsers."

So there is explicit support for Answer Choice E, it just had to be **synthesized**.

***

This question was challenging for many students, you may still be unconvinced. Let's use the Equal Standards Test/Answer Choice Fixing just to make sure.

How would you make Answer Choice E better? So the passage talks about the typical study not being representative of the most successful dowsers, while this study is representative, so if we added the element of representation into the answer, it would probably be a lot more acceptable to most people.

So let's change Answer E to

"<u>The participants of</u> the groundwater-locating study described in the final paragraph were not <u>representative of</u> a typical dowsing study."

If the nature of the sample studied is drastically different (successful vs. unsuccessful dowsers), could you say that the studies themselves were also drastically different? I think so. If the participants were not representative of the participants from a typical study, then I think its safe to say that the study itself was not typical.

I don't think there is a significant gap to be hurdled for Answer Choice E.

Now let's go back and look at D.

How do you know for sure that the experts could not locate a dry fracture upon request? We don't. The best we can do is to argue that since the author is talking about why dowsers are better, and since dowsers could locate a dry fracture zone upon request, it's less likely that the geologists were able to do so. Maybe they were asked to do so and failed, but maybe they were never asked in the first place.

I think if you changed Answer Choice D to

"Geologists and hydrologists participating in the groundwater-locating study described in the final paragraph <u>were probably less likely to be able to</u> locate a dry fracture zone upon request.

I think it would be much more acceptable.

However, to go from "less likely to" to "unable to" is a significant jump. The strength of the language is going from the possible to the definite. So the gap/problems Answer D has are bigger than Answer E.

Answer Choice E is the correct answer.

Summary

In the last three chapters, we looked at the answer choice selection process. The entire process can be divided into two phases.

In the initial phase, we want to **eliminate** answers that are clearly wrong. We can do this based on the keywords in the answers, our understanding of the passage/question stem, and our anticipation of what the correct answer might look like.

You will not be able to eliminate four answers and have one answer choice left when it comes to harder questions. We must learn to accept imperfect answers that are convoluted, vague, and quite often unclear. We must learn to **rank** the answer choices that we cannot eliminate outright, based on support from the passage, and according to the requirements of the question type.

Reverse Confirmation and Answer Choice Fixing are two strategies that we can apply when we are really stuck. **Reverse Confirmation** works with questions whose correct answer must be derived from the passage. Take the answer choice, think about its keywords and overall meaning, and ask yourself whether what this answer describes in fact occurs in the passage. If this was the correct answer, what would the passage look like? Is that what the passage *actually* looks like?

Answer Choice Fixing is harder to apply because it would require an unrivaled grasp of the content of the passage. But for the advanced test taker, when you are stuck on two answer choices with no hopes of moving forward, ask yourself this: *what changes would you make to each of these answers to make them acceptable to choose? Which answer choice required less fixes?* That would be the better answer.

Lastly, we must remember that when approaching RC questions, we no longer have the luxury of that sense of logical certainty that accompany us in the Logic Games. In LG, all answers are either must be true, or cannot be true. There will not be two answers that could both work as the correct answer. In RC, on the other hand, just like LR, it's crucial to adopt a *relativist* mentality when it comes to answer choice selection. We are picking the **best** answer, rather than picking the **correct** answer.

But occasionally, even the habit of ranking is not enough to come to the correct answer. From my experiences tutoring the LSAT, this happens most frequently when you have skipped over the correct answer choice in your first passthrough. Perhaps you went with your gut feeling and quickly eliminated three ACs without truly thinking about their implications. Perhaps the correct answer is worded in such an abstract and vague way that you just didn't understand what it was trying to express. Either way, you are ranking the answers, except that you are looking in the wrong place.

So whenever I end up with **two imperfect/problematic answer choices**, I will quickly check the three ACs that I have already eliminated. I will make sure I didn't eliminate a contender without fully understanding it, before I zone in on the two ACs that truly need to be compared.

Similarly, if you are left with **two answer choices that both look good**, chances are that you have missed a keyword here and there. Think about the implications of every noun, verb, and adjective/adverb with a critical mindset if this is the case.

This habit is so important that we devoted an entire chapter to it in LR Perfection, take a look at Chapter 19 of LR Perfection for additional info.

Part IV: Passage-Specific Strategies

18. Comparative Passages: Reading Strategies

Agree/Disagree?

Near the end of LR Perfection, we encountered a very specific type of LR Question, or Point of Disagreement Questions. In these questions, the stimulus would have two speakers engaged in a conversation. Each person would present their viewpoint, which could either be in argument form, with supporting evidence; or simply a statement stating their position. Our job was to find the specific issue on which these two speakers disagreed or agreed.

Comparative Passages can be viewed as Point of Disagreement/Agreement Questions on a much larger scale. Instead of two arguments each comprising of two or three sentences, we now have two passages each consisting of two or three paragraphs. But despite this sudden increase in volume and content, the goal is the same. We are trying to compare the views expressed by one speaker with that of the other, and look for similarities, differences, and overlaps.

There will be questions that ask us about only one of the passages, but in a majority of times, the questions will ask us about something that is either common to both passages, or about what is different between the passages. I would say that in more than 80% the times, the questions we encounter will ask us to compare or contrast the views or details presented in both passages.

Everything is Relative

Since our goal is to successfully answer the questions, and we know that most of the questions ask us to *compare* the passages, it doesn't make sense to read the passages in isolation. Instead of reading Passage A and B and then comparing the two passages, a more efficient method is to **read Passage A first, then read Passage B in light of what we have learned in Passage A.**

In other words, we want to read Passage A as a regular passage, but as we read Passage B, think about everything *relative* to what we have just learned in Passage A. For example, as we are figuring out the Author's Purpose for Passage B, ask yourself, *"how does this compare to the Author's Purpose in Passage A?"* As we are trying to decide the scope of Passage B's discussion, think about *how it compares to the scope of Passage A?* Is there overlap? If so, by how much? Are they examining the same issue, or are they examining two different problems that emanated from the same source?

The details also matter heavily in Comparison Passages. Questions asking, *"Which one of the following concepts appeared in both passages,"* or *"Which one of the following words appeared in Passage B but not Passage A"* have been the bane of many students' existence. So, as we are reading Comparative Passages, make a note of the terms and concepts that appear in both passages.

Note Taking

If you have ever thought about taking notes on paper during RC, now is the time. I have always recommended that students use scrap paper to take structured, shorthand notes during Reading Comprehension, but when it comes to Comparative Passages, notes are especially helpful.

Because having two separate passages will naturally break the logical coherence and flow that develops as we read, our understanding of both passages can be disjointed and disconnected. Having read two shorter passages can be harder than one long passage because there isn't enough time or depth for our ideas to fully develop and our understanding to fully form. Just as we are getting a clearer idea of what Passage A is talking about, it ends, and we have to move to Passage B and start all over again.

Furthermore, because the scope of both passages may not entirely overlap, even a slight change in the topic of discussion can fracture our train of thought. We may end up confusing what was discussed in Passage A for something that occurred in Passage B; or mix up the positions and streams of ideas discussed in both passages.

I have *always* approached Comparative Passages with pen and paper ready. I will take notes in conjunction with the highlighting function available in the online LSAT testing interface. I will use the highlighter on screen to highlight terms, concepts and nouns that stood out to me; while writing down the Purpose, Main Point, and one sentence summaries of each paragraph for both passages. Having these ideas on paper will force me to think about them in relationship to each other, how they are connected, and how they differ. After having finished both reading and note taking, I will quickly review my notes, and try to make a mental note of the similarities and differences between the two passages.

Purpose, Scope, and Main Point

When you have finished reading Passage A, you should already have a decent grasp of that passage's Purpose, Scope of Discussion, and Main Point. These are skills that we have focused on developing back in Part I of the book.

As soon as you start reading Passage B, we should be thinking about the same questions that we used to guide our reading in regular passages: *what is the Author's Purpose? What is the scope of the discussion here? And how will the passage most likely develop in the following paragraphs?*

The only difference is that as soon as we come up with an answer for these questions, we must think about it *in conjunction* with the same question from Passage A. For example, if I realized that the **purpose** of Passage B was to "highlight the failures of the government's environmental policy," I need to compare this to Passage A's purpose. Perhaps Passage A's purpose was to defend the government's environmental policy, or perhaps it was simply outlining the factors that led to the formulation of that policy, or maybe it was to echo Passage B's criticisms but offer suggestions for improvement. Is one passage echoing, supporting, or contradicting the other passage? Is one passage exploring a ramification or implication introduced by the other passage?

Comparing the purposes of both passages is only the first step though. We also need to think about how the **scope of the discussion** of both passages relate to each other. In all the passages that have appeared on the LSAT so far (until PT90), there has been a degree of overlap between the scope of both passages. Sometimes the overlap is great, sometimes its limited, but it has always existed. As we will see later in this chapter, sometimes the scope overlap is not obvious on a first glance; for example, the first passage can describe a theory, and the second passage is an example of the application of that theory.

So think about the content overlap between the two passages, as well as the areas where they differ. Maybe both passages are talking about works of Russian literature, but while one passage talks about Tolstoy's struggles with faith as exemplified by Prince Bolkonsky in *War and Peace*, the other passage talks about Dostoevsky's interplay of faith and doubt manifested in Alyosha's personage from *The Brothers Karamazov*. In this example, overlap in scope would be the discussions of the concept of faith as expressed by an author of Russian literature; the differences would be that each passage is talking about a different author and a different work.

Differences in scope can also be very easy to grasp. We can have one passage talk about elephants in Africa, and the other passage talk about elephants in Asia. Both passages talk about elephants, in this sense their scope is shared. But the location and habitats of these elephants are different, so their scope differs in that way. Differences in population, location, chronology, and topic of discussion are all manifestations of variations in scope between the two passages.

Upon finishing our initial reading of each passage, we should be able to come up with a tentative **Main Point** for both. Building upon what we have learned via earlier comparisons of Purpose and Scope, it should not be too hard to formulate an answer for the Main Point of Passage B, as well as how it compares to the Main Point of Passage A. The Main Point of each passage can be related to each other, but they don't have to be. They may be in conflict, in accordance, simply acknowledge each other without further commitment, or completely unrelated. We need to come up with the Main Point for each passage, then manually compare them with each other.

Take a look at the following passages, and think about how their purpose, scope, and main points relate to or differ from one another:

PT56 Passage 3

Passage A

There is no universally accepted definition within international law for the term "national minority." It is most commonly applied to (1) groups of persons—not necessarily citizens—under the jurisdiction of one country who have ethnic ties to another "homeland" country, or (2) groups of citizens of a country who have lasting ties to that country and have no such ties to any other country, but are distinguished from the majority of the population by ethnicity, religion, or language. The terms "people" and "nation" are also vaguely defined in international agreements. Documents that refer to a "nation" generally link the term to the concept of "nationalism," which is often associated with ties to land. It also connotes sovereignty, for which reason, perhaps, "people" is often used instead of "nation" for groups subject to a colonial power.

While the lack of definition of the terms "minority," "people," and "nation" presents difficulties to numerous minority groups, this lack is particularly problematic for the Roma (Gypsies). The Roma are not a colonized people, they do not have a homeland, and many do not bear ties to any currently existing country. Some Roma are not even citizens of any country, in part because of their nomadic way of life, which developed in response to centuries of fleeing persecution. Instead, they have ethnic and linguistic ties to other groups of Roma that reside in other countries.

Passage B

Capotorti's definition of a minority includes four empirical criteria—a group's being numerically smaller than the rest of the population of the state; their being nondominant; their having distinctive ethnic, linguistic, or religious characteristics; and their desiring to preserve their own culture—and one legal criterion, that they be citizens of the state in question. This last element can be problematic, given the previous nomadic character of the Roma, that they still cross borders between European states to avoid persecution, and that some states have denied them citizenship, and thus minority status. Because this element essentially grants the state the arbitrary right to decide if the Roma constitute a minority without reference to empirical characteristics, it seems patently unfair that it should be included in the definition.

However, the Roma easily fulfill the four objective elements of Capotorti's definition and should, therefore, be considered a minority in all major European states. Numerically, they are nowhere near a majority, though they number in the hundreds of thousands, even millions, in some states. Their nondominant position is evident—they are not even acknowledged as a minority in some states. The Roma have a number of distinctive linguistic, ethnic, and religious characteristics. For example, most speak Romani, an Indo-European language descended from Sanskrit. Roma groups also have their own distinctive legal and court systems, which are group oriented rather than individual-rights oriented. That they have preserved their language, customs, and identity through centuries of persecution is evidence enough of their desire to preserve their culture.

Passage A

The first paragraph talks about how the term "national minority" does not have a universally accepted definition.

Two common definitions are given: First, ties to another homeland, and second, distinguished from majority population. Terms like "people" or "nation" are also vaguely defined.

The second paragraph talks about how this lack of a clearcut definition is problematic for the Roma.

Because they do not fit the categories mentioned in the first paragraph.

***

One benefit about Comparative Passages is that each of the passage will be relatively short and will therefore not go to great theoretical depth as some regular passages can. Passage A gives us some commonly used definitions for the term "national minority," and shows how they are problematic for the Roma.

The Purpose of the passage, I would say, is to highlight how a lack of clear definitions has been especially problematic for the Roma.

Passage B

Let's read the second passage while keeping in mind the content of Passage A.

A definition for "minority" is given here also. Is the term "minority" used interchangeably with the term "national minority" from Passage A? We shall see.

There are 4+1 rules to determine who is a minority:

1. smaller than the rest (*matches the second definition from Passage A*)
2. non-dominance
3. distinct ethnic, linguistic, or religious characteristics (*this matches the second definition from Passage A*)
4. desire to preserve own culture

5. citizens of state (*matches second definition of Passage A, but not the first definition*)

The #5 legal criterion is difficult for the Roma, because they are nomadic (*also mentioned in Passage A*). Because the Roma are not citizens, they are not considered minorities.

Looking back on Passage A, I can tell that Capotorti's definition is probably the same as the second definition mentioned there.

The author of Passage B thinks that the Roma do not fit under the legal criteria. But they should still be considered a minority because they fulfill the first four criteria.

In this passage, the author argues that even though the Roma do not fit the definition of minorities in its strictest sense, the Roma should nonetheless still be considered a minority and be entitled to the protections granted.

Both passage are sympathetic to the plight of the Roma and highlight the problems they face due to definitions of what constitutes a minority. But while Passage A only highlights these problems, the author of Passage B is more forceful in arguing that such definitions should cover the Roma.

Passage A mentions two definitions of "minority," and it seems that the definition used in Passage B is the second one from Passage A. The first definition from Passage A was not mentioned in Passage B. Terms such as "ethnicity," "religion," "language," and "nomadic" appear in both passages.

PT81 Passage 4

Passage A

Why do some trial courts judges oppose conducting independent research to help them make decisions? One of their objections is that it distorts the adversarial system by requiring an active judicial role and undermining the importance of evidence presented by the opposing parties. Another fear is that judges lack the wherewithal to conduct first rate research and may wind up using outlier or discredited scientific materials.

While these concerns have some merit, they do not justify an absolute prohibition of the practice. First, there are reasons to sacrifice adversarial values in the scientific evidence context. The adversarial system is particularly ill-suited to handling specialized knowledge. The two parties pre-screen and compensate expert witnesses, which virtually ensures conflicting and partisan testimony. At the same time, scientific facts are general truths not confined to the immediate cases. Because scientific admissibility decisions can exert considerable influence over future cases, erroneous decisions detract from the legitimacy of the system. Independent research could help judges avoid such errors.

Second, a trial provides a structure that guides any potential independent research, reducing the possibility of a judge's reaching outlandish results. Independent research supplements, rather than replaces, the parties' presentation of the evidence, so the parties always frame the debate.

Passage B

Regardless of what trial courts may do, appellate courts should resist the temptation to conduct their own independent research of scientific literature.

As a general rule, appellate courts do not hear live testimony. Thus these courts lack some of the critical tools available at the trial level for arriving at a determination of the facts: live testimony and cross-examination. Experts practicing in the field may have knowledge and experience beyond what is reflected in the available scientific literature. And adverse parties can test the credibility and reliability of proffered literature by subjecting the expert witness to the greatest legal engine ever invented for the discovery of truth – cross-examination. The trial judge may even participate in the process by questioning live witnesses. However, these events can only occur at the trial level.

Literature considered for the first time at the appellate level is not subject to live comment by practicing experts and cannot be tested in the crucible of the adversarial system. Thus one of the core criticisms against the use of such sources by appellate courts is that doing so usurps the trial court's fact-finding function. Internet sources, in particular, have come under criticism for their potential unreliability.

When an appellate court goes outside the record to determine case facts, it ignores its function as a court of review, and it substitutes its own questionable research results for evidence that should have been tested in the trial court. This criticism applies with full force to the use of outside-the-record texts and treatises, regardless of the medium in which they are found.

Passage A

The first paragraph tells us why some TRIAL judges oppose doing independent research themselves, instead choosing to rely on expert testimony.

One, active participation is not the proper role for judges, and two, judges may not be smart enough to do scientific research.

The second paragraph presents the author's opinion. The author thinks judges should be allowed to conduct research themselves. The author also gives two reasons:

One, the adversarial court system is not good for handling specialized information due to its conflicting nature. Scientific evidence, on the other hand, are truths and facts. Judges' own research can mean less wrong decisions and more fair outcomes.

Two, trial structure will be a form of quality control on the research produced by judges.

In this passage, the author addresses two of the concerns opponents use as reasons for why judges shouldn't conduct research. The author's Main Point is that "trial judges should be allowed to conduct independent research."

Passage B

The second passage is about APPELLATE courts (higher court). Remember that the first passage was about TRIAL courts (lower court).

The author here doesn't take a position on what the trial court should do, thereby *sidestepping the discussion of Passage A*. But they think that the appellate court should not conduct independent research.

In the second paragraph, the author says that because the appellate court doesn't hear live testimony and doesn't conduct cross-examination, it's much harder for judges to determine the facts. The author believes that cross-examination is great for discovering the truth. *Remember that in Passage A the author thinks the adversarial system is partisan and not suited to handling specialized knowledge.*

The third paragraph says that the appellate court shouldn't steal the trial court's job of fact finding.

The last paragraph is a summary of the author's argument, namely that the appellate court should not try to determine the facts.

Even though the scope of discussion for these two passages is different, Passage A is talking about trial courts, while Passage B is talking about appellate courts, there are still some discernable connections between the two.

The author of Passage B seems to be aware of the debate mentioned in Passage A, on whether trial courts should conduct independent scientific research. Something really fascinating is how each author views the adversarial nature of the trial court. For the author of Passage A, the trial court system is not suited to handling specialized information and scientific truths/facts, hence judges must undertake this role. The author of Passage B, however, seems to think that the trial court is great for discovering the truth through cross-examinations. So both authors definitely have **conflicting assumptions** underlying their arguments.

PT76 Passage 4

Passage A

Karl Popper's main contribution to the philosophy of science concerns the power of negative evidence. The fundamental point is simple: No number of white swans, for example, can ever prove that all swans are white, but a single black swan disproves the hypothesis. Popper gives this logical asymmetry between positive and negative evidence hyperbolic application, maintaining that positive evidence has no value as evidence and that negative evidence is tantamount to disproof. Moreover, Popper takes the search for negative evidence to be at the heart of scientific research; that is, for Popper, scientific research involves not only generating bold theories, but also searching for evidence that would disprove them. Indeed, for him, a theory counts as scientific only if it makes predictions that are testable in this way.

However, Popper's use of the logical asymmetry does not adequately capture the actual situation scientists face. If a theory deductively entails a false prediction, then the theory must be false as well. But a scientific theory rarely entails predictions on its own. When scientists actually derive a theory's predictions, they almost always need diverse additional "auxiliary" premises, which appeal to other theories, to the correct functioning of instrumentation, to the absence of disturbing forces, etc. When a prediction fails, logic indicates that at least one of the premises must be false, but it does not indicate which one. When an experiment does not work out as predicted, there is usually more than one possible explanation. Positive evidence is never conclusive. But negative evidence rarely is either.

Passage B

When the planet Uranus was discovered, astronomers attempted to predict its orbit. They based their predictions on Newton's laws and auxiliary assumptions about the mass of the sun and the masses, orbits, and velocities of other planets. One of the auxiliary assumptions was that no planets existed in the vicinity of Uranus. When the astronomers made their observations, they found that the orbit they had predicted for Uranus was incorrect. One possible explanation for the failure of their prediction was that Newton's laws were incorrect. Another was that there was an error in the auxiliary assumptions. The astronomers changed their assumptions about the existence of other planets, concluding that there must be another planet close enough to Uranus to produce the observed orbit. Not long afterward, scientists discovered the planet Neptune in the precise place it would have to be to bring their calculations into alignment with their observations.

Later astronomers, again using Newton's laws, predicted the orbit of Mercury. Once again, the predictions were not borne out. They hypothesized the existence of another planet in the vicinity, which they called Vulcan. However, Vulcan was never found, and some scientists began to think that perhaps Newton's laws were in error. Finally, when Einstein's general theory of relativity was introduced, astronomers discovered that calculations based on that theory and the old auxiliary assumptions predicted the observed orbit of Mercury, leading to the rejection of Newton's theory of gravity and to increased confidence in Einstein's theory.

Passage A	Passage B
What is negative evidence? One piece of negative evidence is enough to disprove something, but positive evidence is not enough to prove something. For Karl Popper, science is all about generating theories and finding negative evidence to disprove these theories. The author introduces their own opinion in the second paragraph. The author thinks KP's ideas are not representative of reality. When negative theory is generated, it can be due to many factors, external circumstances, or extenuating reasons. So you can't simply disprove a theory because of negative evidence. KP's argument is too strong. In this passage, the author criticizes Karl Popper's theory of negative evidence.	This passage, unlike the previous one we've seen, does not mention Karl Popper at all. On the surface, it appears that the scope of both passages are entirely different, but let's read on. The term "auxiliary assumptions" appear in the first paragraph, a term we also saw in Passage A. A prediction based on Newton's Theory did not turn out. There are two possibilities: Newton's laws were incorrect, or that there was an error in the auxiliary assumptions. *The first possibility would be something KP would believe in, while the second possibility was something raised by the author of Passage A.* *So Passage B seems to be an example illustrating Passage A.* Discovering Neptune due to a wrong prediction of Uranus' orbit is an example of a piece of negative evidence not disproving a theory (Newton's Laws), but due to wrong auxiliary assumptions. The first paragraph illustrates the point made by the author of Passage A. The second paragraph gives another example of the power of negative evidence. This time, a faulty prediction overturned a theory, rather than leading to the discovery of a faulty auxiliary assumption. This example would align with Karl Popper's understanding of how negative evidence works.

While Passages A and B appears to be talking about different topics, Passage B is actually an **illustration/example** of the concepts discussed in Passage A. Passage A talks about negative evidence. Karl Popper thinks negative evidence disproves a theory, but the author says it doesn't. Negative evidence can occur due to many factors, and not necessarily because the theory is wrong.

Passage B gives two examples, one of each. When Newton's laws could not predict Uranus' orbit, it didn't mean Newton's laws were wrong. It was because auxiliary assumptions were wrong. Scientists thought there was no other planet in the vicinity, but Neptune was there all along.

When Newton's laws couldn't predict the orbit of Mercury, it was not because the auxiliary assumptions were wrong. There was no Vulcan. Rather, it was as Karl Popper would have us believe, that the theory itself was inadequate.

Views towards each other

We saw in the earlier passages how the relationship between the two passages can take on a variety of formats. Both passages can be discussing the same problem (Roma people's minority status); they may be discussing related, but distinct issues (trial court research vs. appellate court research); or one passage may be an example of a theory described in another (negative evidence and the prediction of Uranus and Mercury's orbits).

Even when the scope of the discussion does not entirely overlap, it can be helpful to think about what position, if any, do the authors of each passage hold towards the other. Does one passage display an awareness of the arguments made in the other passage, but not vice versa? Or are both passages aware of the arguments made in the other passage? Perhaps each passage is just doing their own thing, displaying neither awareness nor acknowledgement of the other passage?

If there was an awareness of the arguments made in the other passage (as Passage B's author was aware of the debate on the role of scientific research in trial courts, which was the topic of Passage A), does the author commit to a position? Do they simply acknowledge the existence of the other passage's argument/views, or do they take a more direct position? If they do take an explicit position, are they supporting or objecting? Do they have a neutral stance? If they are supporting or objecting to the Main Point of the other passage, is the passage devoted entirely to supporting or attacking the other passage, or is the support/objection partial?

Take a look at the following passages, ask yourself what the author of Passage A would say if they met the author of Passage B, and vice versa.

PT55 Passage 2

Passage A

Purple loosestrife (Lythrum salicaria), an aggressive and invasive perennial of Eurasian origin, arrived with settlers in eastern North America in the early 1800s and has spread across the continent's midlatitude wetlands. The impact of purple loosestrife on native vegetation has been disastrous, with more than 50 percent of the biomass of some wetland communities displaced. Monospecific blocks of this weed have maintained themselves for at least 20 years. Impacts on wildlife have not been well studied, but serious reductions in waterfowl and aquatic furbearer productivity have been observed. In addition, several endangered species of vertebrates are threatened with further degradation of their breeding habitats. Although purple loosestrife can invade relatively undisturbed habitats, the spread and dominance of this weed have been greatly accelerated in disturbed habitats. While digging out the plants can temporarily halt their spread, there has been little research on long-term purple loosestrife control. Glyphosate has been used successfully, but no measure of the impact of this herbicide on native plant communities has been made.

With the spread of purple loosestrife growing exponentially, some form of integrated control is needed. At present, coping with purple loosestrife hinges on early detection of the weed's arrival in areas, which allows local eradication to be carried out with minimum damage to the native plant community.

Passage B

The war on purple loosestrife is apparently conducted on behalf of nature, an attempt to liberate the biotic community from the tyrannical influence of a life-destroying invasive weed. Indeed, purple loosestrife control is portrayed by its practitioners as an environmental initiative intended to save nature rather than control it. Accordingly, the purple loosestrife literature, scientific and otherwise, dutifully discusses the impacts of the weed on endangered species—and on threatened biodiversity more generally. Purple loosestrife is a pollution, according to the scientific community, and all of nature suffers under its pervasive influence.

Regardless of the perceived and actual ecological effects of the purple invader, it is apparent that popular pollution ideologies have been extended into the wetlands of North America. Consequently, the scientific effort to liberate nature from purple loosestrife has failed to decouple itself from its philosophical origin as an instrument to control nature to the satisfaction of human desires. Birds, particularly game birds and waterfowl, provide the bulk of the justification for loosestrife management. However, no bird species other than the canvasback has been identified in the literature as endangered by purple loosestrife. The impact of purple loosestrife on furbearing mammals is discussed at great length, though none of the species highlighted (muskrat, mink) can be considered threatened in North America. What is threatened by purple loosestrife is the economics of exploiting such preferred species and the millions of dollars that will be lost to the economies of the United States and Canada from reduced hunting, trapping, and recreation revenues due to a decline in the production of the wetland resource.

Passage A

In the first paragraph, we are told how disastrous purple loosestrife has been for the North American ecology. It has destroyed local vegetation and adversely affected animal species. There has been little research on long term control.

In the second paragraph, the author calls for "integrated control" of purple loosestrife, namely early detection and local eradication.

The author's views and purpose are obvious. Purple loosestrife is very bad, it must be controlled.

Passage B

The author describes the stance of Passage A's author in the first paragraph *("purple loosestrife control is portrayed by its practitioners…")* Passage B is clearly aware of Passage A.

In the second paragraph, the author criticizes the people described earlier. These people, such as the author of Passage A, are trying to control purple loosestrife because of their underlying desire to control and subjugate nature.

Passage B also contradicts Passage A directly. Passage A had told us that *"serious reductions in waterfowl productivity have been observed."* Here, in Passage B, we are told that *"no bird species other than the canvasback has been identified…as endangered."* Similarly, the author disputes Passage A's account of the negative influence on furbearing animals.

For the author of Passage B, it's underlying economic concerns which are driving the campaign to eradicate purple loosestrife, rather than any innate concern for nature.

Here, Passage B feels like a direct response and rebuttal to Passage A.

Passage A, on the other hand, does not seem to be aware of the criticism it faces.

Passage A calls for the control of purple loosestrife, while Passage B attacks the motives of people like the author of Passage A.

Some details reappear in both passages, such as discussions of birds/waterfowls and furbearing animals.

PT85 Passage 3

Passage A

Music does not always gain by association with words. Like images, words can excite the deepest emotions but are inadequate to express the emotions they excite. Music is more adequate, and hence will often seize an emotion that may have been excited by images or words, deepen its expression, and, by so doing, excite still deeper emotion. That is how words can gain by being set to music.

But to set words to music-as in opera or song--is in fact to mix two arts together. A striking effect may be produced, but at the expense of the purity of each art. Poetry is a great art; so is music. But as a medium for emotion, each is greater alone than in company, although various good ends arise from linking the two, providing that the words are subordinated to the more expressive medium of music. What good could any words do for Beethoven's Fifth Symphony? So too an opera is largely independent of words, and depends for its aesthetic value not upon the poetry of the libretto (the words of the opera), or even the plot or scenery, but upon its emotional range-a region dominated by the musical element.

Passage B

Throughout the history of opera, two fundamental types may be distinguished: that in which the music is primary, and that in which there is, essentially, parity between music and other factors. The former, sometimes called "singer's opera"-a term which has earned undeserved contempt-is exemplified by most Italian operas, while the latter, exemplified by the operas of German composer Richard Wagner, depend for their effect on a balance among many factors of which music is only one, albeit the most important. Theoretically, it would seem that there should be a third kind of opera, in which the music is subordinated
to the other features. While the earliest operas were of this kind, their appeal was limited, and a fuller participation of music was required to establish opera on a secure basis.

In any event, in any aesthetic judgment of opera, regardless of the opera's type, neither the music nor the poetry of the libretto should be judged in isolation. The music is good not if it would make a good concert piece but if it serves the particular situation in the opera in which it occurs, contributing something not supplied by other elements. Similarly, the poetry is good not because it reads well by itself but primarily if, while embodying a sound dramatic idea, it furnishes opportunity for effective musical and scenic treatment. True, the elements of music and poetry may be considered separately, but only for purposes of analyzing their formal features. In actuality these elements are as united as hydrogen and oxygen are united in water. It is this union-further enriched and clarified by the visual action-that results in opera's inimitable character.

Passage A

In the first paragraph, the author tells us that music is better than words at expressing emotion. Adding music to words (such as adding music to a poem to make it a song) will excite deeper emotion.

But to add words to a piece of music is not good. Both arts are sacrificed.

Passage B

The author starts off talking about opera. Right away I recall that Passage A also talked about the opera. What did Passage A say? Basically that *adding words to an opera doesn't make it more awesome, an opera's aesthetic value is largely dependent upon its music.* Let's see if Passage B thinks the same.

Two types of opera are mentioned: Singer's opera, where music > other factors (Italian); and another kind where music is equal to other factors (German). In both kinds of opera, music is the most important element. The author also talks about a third kind of opera where words are more important, but these have limited appeal.

So these observations seem to confirm the views described in Passage A: Music is more important than words in most operas.

But in the second paragraph, the author starts to contradict somewhat the views of Passage A. Remember that Passage A had said that "*each is greater alone than in company...opera is largely independent of words...depends not upon the poetry...*"

The author of Passage B; however, is telling us that neither the music nor the poetry "*should be judged in isolation.*" The author concedes that both words and music may be considered separately, but they are in actuality inseparable.

Unlike PT55 Passage 2, the positions both passages hold towards each other is more subtle here. The author of Passage A makes it clear that music is more important than words in operas, and we should examine each element alone.

Passage B starts off by describing different types of operas, and it seems that music is indeed the most important element. Perhaps Passage B is supporting the views espoused in Passage A, after all.

But instead, Passage B goes on to talk about how both the music and words are essential elements and must be considered in conjunction.

So in this passage, while the authors of both passages hold differences in opinion, their views are not diametrically opposed as was the case in the previous passage.

18. Comparative Passages: Reading Strategies

Details

In Chapter 4 we looked at the type of details we should watch out for when reading a passage. We said that paying attention to the details of a passage should only be emphasized *after* you have become proficient at understanding the macroscopic elements of a passage, such as its structure, main point, and purpose. In other words, think of your training for passage reading as comprising of two phases.

In **Phase I**, we practice active reading. We try to hypothesize what the purpose of the passage may be and use the subsequent content to validate or revise our hypothesis. We treat the passage as one giant argument, assign roles to individual paragraphs, determine whether they are supporting the argument, describing an opposing view, conceding a point, or providing background information. We break down hard to follow paragraphs into sub-sections, or along different POVs. Finally, we try to formulate what the Main Point of the passage might be.

Consistently time yourself when reading, if you can do all of the above within 3:00, instinctively, involuntarily, subconsciously, then it's time to pay attention to the details. This is **Phase II** of our RC passage reading training process. You see, our attention and mental capacity are limited. So the more we spend on trying to understand the passage, the less we will have to decipher the subtle aspects of a passage such as a specific word's connotation, or the author's attitude. Get really good at the fundamentals so we can focus on the more esoteric. Because at the end of the day, it's the grasp of the details that will set apart a high 170s scorer from a high 160s/low 170s scorer.

***

Details matter too in Comparative Passages, but the process is much more straightforward. In traditional passages we had to watch out for a myriad of things, such as the author's opinion, dates, key persons, etc. In Comparative Passages, all we really have to worry about are **key terms that have appeared in either or both passages**. We have already witnessed this in earlier passages: terms like "nomadic" in PT56, "auxiliary assumptions" in PT76, "furbearing animals" in PT55, and "libretto" in PT85. Our job is to make a note of the words or terms that appear in both passages, because questions that ask us "which term appears in both passages" are quite common.

A variation of this question will ask us *"which of the following terms appeared in Passage A but not Passage B, or vice versa."* These are even tricker. Our job is now to eliminate all the answers that appear in both passages, or in a manner not described by the question. Success with these detail-oriented questions really depend on our ability to retain information, and how much detail can we grasp and recall.

So get really good at figuring out the purpose, scope, the Main Point of each passage, and how the passages relate to each other and view each other. Then, start making a note of potential keywords (usually nouns) that stand out to you in a passage, highlight them or underline them, and see if they turn up in just one or both passages.

PT54 Passage 2

Passage A

Drilling fluids, including the various mixtures known as drilling muds, play essential roles in oil-well drilling. As they are circulated down through the drill pipe and back up the well itself, they lubricate the drill bit, bearings, and drill pipe; clean and cool the drill bit as it cuts into the rock; lift rock chips (cuttings) to the surface; provide information about what is happening downhole, allowing the drillers to monitor the behavior, flow rate, pressure, and composition of the drilling fluid; and maintain well pressure to control cave-ins.

Drilling muds are made of bentonite and other clays and polymers, mixed with a fluid to the desired viscosity. By far the largest ingredient of drilling muds, by weight, is barite, a very heavy mineral of density 4.3 to 4.6. It is also used as an inert filler in some foods and is more familiar in its medical use as the "barium meal" administered before X-raying the digestive tract.

Over the years individual drilling companies and their expert drillers have devised proprietary formulations, or mud "recipes," to deal with specific types of drilling jobs. One problem in studying the effects of drilling waste discharges is that the drilling fluids are made from a range of over 1,000, sometimes toxic, ingredients—many of them known, confusingly, by different trade names, generic descriptions, chemical formulae, and regional or industry slang words, and many of them kept secret by companies or individual formulators.

Passage B

Drilling mud, cuttings, and associated chemicals are normally released only during the drilling phase of a well's existence. These discharges are the main environmental concern in offshore oil production, and their use is tightly regulated. The discharges are closely monitored by the offshore operator, and releases are controlled as a condition of the operating permit.

One type of mud—water-based mud (WBM)—is a mixture of water, bentonite clay, and chemical additives, and is used to drill shallow parts of wells. It is not particularly toxic to marine organisms and disperses readily. Under current regulations, it can be dumped directly overboard. Companies typically recycle WBMs until their properties are no longer suitable and then, over a period of hours, dump the entire batch into the sea.

For drilling deeper wells, oil-based mud (OBM) is normally used. The typical difference from WBM is the high content of mineral oil (typically 30 percent). OBMs also contain greater concentrations of barite, a powdered heavy mineral, and a number of additives. OBMs have a greater potential for negative environmental impact, partly because they do not disperse as readily. Barite may impact some organisms, particularly scallops, and the mineral oil may have toxic effects. Currently only the residues of OBMs adhering to cuttings that remain after the cuttings are sieved from the drilling fluids may be discharged overboard, and then only mixtures up to a specified maximum oil content.

Passage A

Drilling fluids, including the various mixtures known as <u>drilling muds</u>, play essential roles in oil-well drilling. As they are circulated down through the drill pipe and back up the <u>well</u> itself, they lubricate the drill bit, bearings, and drill pipe; clean and cool the drill bit as it cuts into the rock; lift rock chips (<u>cuttings</u>) to the surface; provide information about what is happening downhole, allowing the drillers to <u>monitor</u> the behavior, flow rate, pressure, and composition of the drilling fluid; and maintain well pressure to control cave-ins.

Drilling muds are made of <u>bentonite</u> and other <u>clays</u> and polymers, <u>mixed</u> with a fluid to the desired viscosity. By far the largest ingredient of drilling muds, by weight, is <u>barite</u>, a very heavy mineral of density 4.3 to 4.6. It is also used as an inert filler in some foods and is more familiar in its medical use as the "barium meal" administered before X-raying the digestive tract.

Over the years individual drilling companies and their expert drillers have devised proprietary formulations, or mud "recipes," to deal with specific types of drilling jobs. One problem in studying the effects of drilling waste discharges is that the drilling fluids are made from a range of over 1,000, sometimes toxic, ingredients—many of them known, confusingly, by different trade names, generic descriptions, chemical formulae, and regional or industry slang words, and many of them kept secret by companies or individual formulators.

Passage B

<u>Drilling mud</u>, <u>cuttings</u>, and associated chemicals are normally released only during the drilling phase of a <u>well's</u> existence. These discharges are the main environmental concern in offshore oil production, and their use is tightly regulated. The discharges are closely <u>monitored</u> by the offshore operator, and releases are controlled as a condition of the operating permit.

One type of mud—water-based mud (WBM)—is a <u>mixture</u> of water, <u>bentonite clay</u>, and chemical additives, and is used to drill shallow parts of wells. It is not particularly toxic to marine organisms and disperses readily. Under current regulations, it can be dumped directly overboard. Companies typically recycle WBMs until their properties are no longer suitable and then, over a period of hours, dump the entire batch into the sea.

For drilling deeper wells, oil-based mud (OBM) is normally used. The typical difference from WBM is the high content of mineral oil (typically 30 percent). OBMs also contain greater concentrations of <u>barite</u>, a powdered heavy mineral, and a number of additives. OBMs have a greater potential for negative environmental impact, partly because they do not disperse as readily. <u>Barite</u> may impact some organisms, particularly scallops, and the mineral oil may have toxic effects. Currently only the residues of OBMs adhering to cuttings that remain after the cuttings are sieved from the drilling fluids may be discharged overboard, and then only mixtures up to a specified maximum oil content.

I have underlined some of the recurring terms in both passages above. With so much going on, it would be easy to lose track of some of these. Passage A talks about how drilling fluids/muds are used in the first paragraph, their content is described in the second paragraph, and a difficulty associated with studying the effects of drilling waste discharges is mentioned in the third paragraph.

Passage B talks about the regulation and environmental impact of drilling muds. The second paragraph talks about the content, usage, effects, and environmental impact of water-based mud. The third paragraph talks about the content, impact, and current disposal practices for oil-based mud.

PT62 Passage 3

Passage A

Because dental caries (decay) is strongly linked to consumption of the sticky, carbohydrate-rich staples of agricultural diets, prehistoric human teeth can provide clues about when a population made the transition from a hunter-gatherer diet to an agricultural one. Caries formation is influenced by several factors, including tooth structure, bacteria in the mouth, and diet. In particular, caries formation is affected by carbohydrates' texture and composition, since carbohydrates more readily stick to teeth.

Many researchers have demonstrated the link between carbohydrate consumption and caries. In North America, Leigh studied caries in archaeologically derived teeth, noting that caries rates differed between indigenous populations that primarily consumed meat (a Sioux sample showed almost no caries) and those heavily dependent on cultivated maize (a Zuni sample had 75 percent carious teeth). Leigh's findings have been frequently confirmed by other researchers, who have shown that, in general, the greater a population's dependence on agriculture is, the higher its rate of caries formation will be.

Under some circumstances, however, non-agricultural populations may exhibit relatively high caries rates. For example, early non-agricultural populations in western North America who consumed large amounts of highly processed stone-ground flour made from gathered acorns show relatively high caries frequencies. And wild plants collected by the Hopi included several species with high cariogenic potential, notably pinyon nuts and wild tubers.

Passage B

Archaeologists recovered human skeletal remains interred over a 2,000-year period in prehistoric Ban Chiang, Thailand. The site's early inhabitants appear to have had a hunter-gatherer-cultivator economy. Evidence indicates that, over time, the population became increasingly dependent on agriculture.

Research suggests that agricultural intensification results in declining human health, including dental health. Studies show that dental caries is uncommon in pre-agricultural populations. Increased caries frequency may result from increased consumption of starchy-sticky foodstuffs or from alterations in tooth wear. The wearing down of tooth crown surfaces reduces caries formation by removing fissures that can trap food particles. A reduction of fiber or grit in a diet may diminish tooth wear, thus increasing caries frequency. However, severe wear that exposes a tooth's pulp cavity may also result in caries.

The diet of Ban Chiang's inhabitants included some cultivated rice and yams from the beginning of the period represented by the recovered remains. These were part of a varied diet that also included wild plant and animal foods. Since both rice and yams are carbohydrates, increased reliance on either or both should theoretically result in increased caries frequency.

Yet comparisons of caries frequency in the Early and Late Ban Chiang Groups indicate that overall caries frequency is slightly greater in the Early Group. Tooth wear patterns do not indicate tooth wear changes between Early and Late Groups that would explain this unexpected finding. It is more likely that, although dependence on agriculture increased, the diet in the Late period remained varied enough that no single food dominated. Furthermore, there may have been a shift from sweeter carbohydrates (yams) toward rice, a less cariogenic carbohydrate.

Passage A

Cavities are a sign of when prehistoric humans started eating carbs, so when cavities appear in fossils can tell us when humans switched from hunters to farmers.

The second paragraph reinforces the causal relationship between carb consumption and cavities. Several studies are mentioned.

An exception is mentioned. Non-agricultural populations can also have high rates of cavities. Some populations who gathered plants and made flour (carbs) from it also had a high level of cavities. (*So these people, even though they didn't farm, they still ate a lot of carbs, hence the cavities.*)

Passage B

The first paragraph talks about a population who went from hunters to being farmers. *If the theory mentioned in Passage A is correct, we should see more cavities in their fossils?*

The second paragraph talks about how agricultural diets lead to more cavities.

Paragraph three tells us that theoretically, we should have seen more cavities in later populations at Ban Chiang.

Paragraph 4 gives us the unexpected results: after the population of Ban Chiang became farmers, they did not have more cavities. The author proposes an explanation: no single food dominated, and the carbs they ate were less cavity causing.

There were a multitude of terms that appeared in both passages, terms such as "hunter-gatherer," "cultivator," "agriculture," "caries," "starchy-sticky," "wild plant," "carbohydrates," etc. all appear in both passages.

Both authors seem to hold in high regard the belief that an agricultural lifestyle leads to a higher incidence of caries. Both are also aware of the exceptions. In Passage A, the author cites indigenous populations who were hunter-gatherers but nonetheless had high caries rates thanks to their diet. In Passage B, the author also tried to explain why the Ban Chiang population did not witness a commiserate rise in caries rates as they became agrarian as an exception rather than challenge to the theory.

19. Comparative Passages: The Questions

19. Comparative Passages: The Questions

Main Point and Purpose Questions

Passage A

Karl Popper's main contribution to the philosophy of science concerns the power of negative evidence. The fundamental point is simple: No number of white swans, for example, can ever prove that all swans are white, but a single black swan disproves the hypothesis. Popper gives this logical asymmetry between positive and negative evidence hyperbolic application, maintaining that positive evidence has no value as evidence and that negative evidence is tantamount to disproof. Moreover, Popper takes the search for negative evidence to be at the heart of scientific research; that is, for Popper, scientific research involves not only generating bold theories, but also searching for evidence that would disprove them. Indeed, for him, a theory counts as scientific only if it makes predictions that are testable in this way.

However, Popper's use of the logical asymmetry does not adequately capture the actual situation scientists face. If a theory deductively entails a false prediction, then the theory must be false as well. But a scientific theory rarely entails predictions on its own. When scientists actually derive a theory's predictions, they almost always need diverse additional "auxiliary" premises, which appeal to other theories, to the correct functioning of instrumentation, to the absence of disturbing forces, etc. When a prediction fails, logic indicates that at least one of the premises must be false, but it does not indicate which one. When an experiment does not work out as predicted, there is usually more than one possible explanation. Positive evidence is never conclusive. But negative evidence rarely is either.

Passage B

When the planet Uranus was discovered, astronomers attempted to predict its orbit. They based their predictions on Newton's laws and auxiliary assumptions about the mass of the sun and the masses, orbits, and velocities of other planets. One of the auxiliary assumptions was that no planets existed in the vicinity of Uranus. When the astronomers made their observations, they found that the orbit they had predicted for Uranus was incorrect. One possible explanation for the failure of their prediction was that Newton's laws were incorrect. Another was that there was an error in the auxiliary assumptions. The astronomers changed their assumptions about the existence of other planets, concluding that there must be another planet close enough to Uranus to produce the observed orbit Not long afterward, scientists discovered the planet Neptune in the precise place it would have to be to bring their calculations into alignment with their observations.

Later astronomers, again using Newton's laws, predicted the orbit of Mercury. Once again, the predictions were not borne out. They hypothesized the existence of another planet in the vicinity, which they called Vulcan. However, Vulcan was never found, and some scientists began to think that perhaps Newton's laws were in error. Finally, when Einstein's general theory of relativity was introduced, astronomers discovered that calculations based on that theory and the old auxiliary assumptions predicted the observed orbit of Mercury, leading to the rejection of Newton's theory of gravity and to increased confidence in Einstein's theory.

PT76 S1 Q20

Which one of the following is a central topic of both passages?

A. The logical asymmetry of positive and negative evidence
B. The role of auxiliary assumptions in predicting planetary orbits
C. The role of negative evidence in scientific research
D. The proper technique for confirming a scientific theory
E. The irrelevance of experimentation for disproving a scientific theory

Main Point Questions are harder in Comparative Passages simply because it's more difficult to "pre-phrase" the correct answer. If the question is asking for the main point/central topic of just one of the passages, then we approach them just as we would a regular passage, as we have done back in Chapter 8. However, it's when the question is asking for the main point to *both* passages that troubles arise. We can pre-phrase an answer for Passage A and another answer for Passage B, but now we have to find an answer choice that best encapsulates both of these.

Answer choices in questions that ask us for the main point to *both* passages will be deliberately vague, and will not be a perfect match for either passages. This is to be expected. The topic/main point of passages A and B will not be exactly the same, and in order to fit both passages under one correct answer, some compromises have to be made. Our job, when approaching these "both passage" MP questions, is to try to find any **common ground** between the main points of both passages.

When the answers are especially vague, **reverse confirmation** (Chapter 17) should be applied. Ask yourself what is this specific answer referring to, and where do the authors do this in each of the passages?

***

We know that Passage A discusses Popper's view of the role of negative evidence and how negative evidence can disprove a scientific theory. The author, on the other hand, argues that reality is much more complicated than this. Passage B illustrates/exemplifies the two scenarios discussed in Passage A, both where a theory was disproven and when auxiliary assumptions were revised.

The correct answer won't be talking about Karl Popper (Passage A only), or Uranus or Mercury (Passage B only). Instead, expect an answer that tells us "*negative evidence can both disprove a theory or lead to a revision of one's assumptions.*"

A. The <u>logical asymmetry</u> of positive and negative evidence

This was discussed in Passage A exclusively, Karl Popper thinks that positive evidence cannot prove a theory, but one piece of negative evidence is enough to disprove a theory.

B. The role of auxiliary assumptions in predicting <u>planetary orbits</u>

Planetary orbits were never mentioned in Passage A.

C. The role of negative evidence in scientific research

Yes, both passages talk about negative evidence. Passage A compares Popper and the author's views on the impact of negative evidence on scientific theories; while Passage B demonstrates the role negative theory played in predicting the orbit of Uranus and Mercury.

D. The <u>proper technique</u> for confirming a scientific theory

Using **reverse confirmation**, if this was indeed the correct answer choice, then we should be able to answer the question, "so what is the proper technique for confirming a scientific theory?"

Unfortunately even though the language of answer choice D sounds tempting because its closely related to the topics discussed, we cannot come up with a straightforward answer to this question.

E. The <u>irrelevance of experimentation</u> for disproving a scientific theory

This answer is essentially saying that to disprove a theory, experiments don't matter. This runs contrary to the theme of both passages.

The correct answer is C, an answer choice that is a little vaguer than what we are used to. But as we mentioned, the correct answer to *both passage* MP questions cannot be too specific. As long as it covers the most important aspects of both passages and is the most comprehensive answer out of the bunch, it will be an acceptable choice.

PT54 S1 Q6

Passage A

Drilling fluids, including the various mixtures known as drilling muds, play essential roles in oil-well drilling. As they are circulated down through the drill pipe and back up the well itself, they lubricate the drill bit, bearings, and drill pipe; clean and cool the drill bit as it cuts into the rock; lift rock chips (cuttings) to the surface; provide information about what is happening downhole, allowing the drillers to monitor the behavior, flow rate, pressure, and composition of the drilling fluid; and maintain well pressure to control cave-ins.

Drilling muds are made of bentonite and other clays and polymers, mixed with a fluid to the desired viscosity. By far the largest ingredient of drilling muds, by weight, is barite, a very heavy mineral of density 4.3 to 4.6. It is also used as an inert filler in some foods and is more familiar in its medical use as the "barium meal" administered before X-raying the digestive tract.

Over the years individual drilling companies and their expert drillers have devised proprietary formulations, or mud "recipes," to deal with specific types of drilling jobs. One problem in studying the effects of drilling waste discharges is that the drilling fluids are made from a range of over 1,000, sometimes toxic, ingredients—many of them known, confusingly, by different trade names, generic descriptions, chemical formulae, and regional or industry slang words, and many of them kept secret by companies or individual formulators.

Passage B

Drilling mud, cuttings, and associated chemicals are normally released only during the drilling phase of a well's existence. These discharges are the main environmental concern in offshore oil production, and their use is tightly regulated. The discharges are closely monitored by the offshore operator, and releases are controlled as a condition of the operating permit.

One type of mud—water-based mud (WBM)—is a mixture of water, bentonite clay, and chemical additives, and is used to drill shallow parts of wells. It is not particularly toxic to marine organisms and disperses readily. Under current regulations, it can be dumped directly overboard. Companies typically recycle WBMs until their properties are no longer suitable and then, over a period of hours, dump the entire batch into the sea.

For drilling deeper wells, oil-based mud (OBM) is normally used. The typical difference from WBM is the high content of mineral oil (typically 30 percent). OBMs also contain greater concentrations of barite, a powdered heavy mineral, and a number of additives. OBMs have a greater potential for negative environmental impact, partly because they do not disperse as readily. Barite may impact some organisms, particularly scallops, and the mineral oil may have toxic effects. Currently only the residues of OBMs adhering to cuttings that remain after the cuttings are sieved from the drilling fluids may be discharged overboard, and then only mixtures up to a specified maximum oil content.

A primary purpose of each of the passages is to

    A. Provide causal explanations for a type of environmental pollution
    B. Describe the general composition and properties of drilling muds
    C. Point out possible environmental impacts associated with oil drilling
    D. Explain why oil-well drilling requires the use of drilling muds
    E. Identify difficulties inherent in the regulation of oil-well drilling operations

If you recall, Passage A talks about the use, content, and a difficulty associated with the studying of drilling fluids/muds. Passage B talks about the content and regulations controlling WBM and OBM.

What is the **purpose** of each passage?

Both passages seem largely explanatory in nature (recall the CEER framework). Passage A points out a difficulty associated with the study of drilling muds but doesn't really offer any recommendations. Passage B also talks about the content and makeup of drilling muds but makes an additional observation about dumping regulations.

So if the question is asking us the "primary purpose of each/both of the passages," then we just take the common ground between the two passages. The correct answer won't mention the difficulties associated with studying drilling muds, neither will it mention dumping regulations, as both only appear in one of the passages.

The correct answer will probably say that both passages *"outline the content and usage of drilling oils/muds."*

   A.   *Provide causal explanations for a type of environmental pollution*

Providing a causal explanation means to give a reason why. So this answer is saying that both passages' goal is to tell us why a type of environmental pollution occurred. If this was indeed the purpose of both passages, then both passages should be highlighting environmental pollution, then pointing the finger at drilling/drilling muds as the culprit.

   B.   *Describe the general composition and properties of drilling muds*

This is close to "content" and "usage" of drilling muds, as we anticipated. "Describe" is also a neutral term and close to the original purpose of the passage, since there were no evaluations and no recommendations made in either of the passages.

   C.   *Point out possible environmental impacts associated with oil drilling*

Passage B does this. The only thing remotely related to this in Passage A is the one-word reference to the word "toxic" in the last paragraph. Remember, the question is asking for the "primary purpose."

   D.   *Explain why oil-well drilling requires the use of drilling muds*

Only the first paragraph of Passage A addresses this. (To lubricate, clean, cool, lift rock chips, provide information, etc.)

   E.   *Identify difficulties inherent in the regulation of oil-well drilling operations*

This was something only mentioned by the author of Passage A and appears in the last paragraph of that passage.

The correct answer is B. When it comes to **Primary Purpose** Questions, be especially careful of answer choices that describe something that does appear in both passages, but isn't the main reason why the passage was written. Just finding limited textual evidence in both passages isn't enough, as we saw in answer choice C.

Views towards each other

In the previous chapter we saw that thinking about the relationship between passages and how the author of each passage would view their opponent is a crucial step to understanding comparative passages on a deeper level. Is one passage supporting the other? Do they acknowledge each others' positions? Are they exploring the same topic?

***

Passage A

Purple loosestrife (Lythrum salicaria), an aggressive and invasive perennial of Eurasian origin, arrived with settlers in eastern North America in the early 1800s and has spread across the continent's midlatitude wetlands. The impact of purple loosestrife on native vegetation has been disastrous, with more than 50 percent of the biomass of some wetland communities displaced. Monospecific blocks of this weed have maintained themselves for at least 20 years. Impacts on wildlife have not been well studied, but serious reductions in waterfowl and aquatic furbearer productivity have been observed. In addition, several endangered species of vertebrates are threatened with further degradation of their breeding habitats. Although purple loosestrife can invade relatively undisturbed habitats, the spread and dominance of this weed have been greatly accelerated in disturbed habitats. While digging out the plants can temporarily halt their spread, there has been little research on long-term purple loosestrife control. Glyphosate has been used successfully, but no measure of the impact of this herbicide on native plant communities has been made.

With the spread of purple loosestrife growing exponentially, some form of integrated control is needed. At present, coping with purple loosestrife hinges on early detection of the weed's arrival in areas, which allows local eradication to be carried out with minimum damage to the native plant community.

Passage B

The war on purple loosestrife is apparently conducted on behalf of nature, an attempt to liberate the biotic community from the tyrannical influence of a life-destroying invasive weed. Indeed, purple loosestrife control is portrayed by its practitioners as an environmental initiative intended to save nature rather than control it. Accordingly, the purple loosestrife literature, scientific and otherwise, dutifully discusses the impacts of the weed on endangered species—and on threatened biodiversity more generally. Purple loosestrife is a pollution, according to the scientific community, and all of nature suffers under its pervasive influence.

Regardless of the perceived and actual ecological effects of the purple invader, it is apparent that popular pollution ideologies have been extended into the wetlands of North America. Consequently, the scientific effort to liberate nature from purple loosestrife has failed to decouple itself from its philosophical origin as an instrument to control nature to the satisfaction of human desires. Birds, particularly game birds and waterfowl, provide the bulk of the justification for loosestrife management. However, no bird species other than the canvasback has been identified in the literature as endangered by purple loosestrife. The impact of purple loosestrife on furbearing mammals is discussed at great length, though none of the species highlighted (muskrat, mink) can be considered threatened in North America. What is threatened by purple loosestrife is the economics of exploiting such preferred species and the millions of dollars that will be lost to the economies of the United States and Canada from reduced hunting, trapping, and recreation revenues due to a decline in the production of the wetland resource.

PT55 S2 Q10

Which one of the following most accurately describes the attitude expressed by the author of passage B toward the overall argument represented by passage A?

- A. Enthusiastic agreement
- B. Cautious agreement
- C. Pure neutrality
- D. General ambivalence
- E. Pointed skepticism

***

PT55 S2 Q12

Which one of the following is true about the relationship between the two passages?

- A. Passage A presents evidence that directly counters claims made in passage B.
- B. Passage B assumes what passage A explicitly argues for.
- C. Passage B displays an awareness of the arguments touched on in passage A, but not vice versa.
- D. Passage B advocates a policy that passage A rejects.
- E. Passage A downplays the seriousness of claims made in Passage B.

We recall that while Passage A calls for controlling purple loosestrife, Passage B is adamantly against it. In fact, Passage B is devoted to attacking the motives and assumptions of people like the author of Passage A.

Let's look at Q10 first: the correct answer is E.

We know that the author of Passage B disagrees with the author of Passage A. E is the only answer that expresses disagreement.

Normally, if the author's attitude or position isn't clear, we tend to prefer a more neutral or ambivalent answer, such as D. But that's not the case here! The author of Passage B has made their views perfectly clear; their entire passage is devoted to attacking the positions of someone like the author of Passage A.

***

Let's look at Q12: *Which one of the following is true about the relationship between the two passages?*

My anticipated answer here would be that "Passage B attacks Passage A." Notice how we don't really have a back and forth debate between the two authors. Passage A advocates a position, and Passage B attacks the sources of that position.

> A.   *Passage A presents evidence that directly counters claims made in passage B.*

I think it's the other way around. Passage A claims that birds and furbearing animals are seriously endangered. Passage B says that only one species has seen reductions.

> B.   *Passage B assumes what passage A explicitly argues for.*

A argues for the preservation of the wetlands and combatting purple loosestrife. B doesn't assume this. B is against this position.

> C.   *Passage B displays an awareness of the arguments touched on in passage A, but not vice versa.*

Passage B does display an awareness of the arguments from Passage A, as we can see from Passage B's rebuttals of Passage A's claims. (Passage A claims that purple loosestrife is damaging birds and animals, B disputes that; Passage A calls for control, B calls this type of control misguided.)

But can we argue that Passage A is *unaware* of the arguments from Passage B?

Does the author of Passage A know that there is someone out there being super critical? I don't think so. Passage A does not address any potential counterarguments, does not acknowledge opposing views, and did not make any concessions. So answer choice C is technically correct in this sense.

> D.   *Passage B advocates a policy that passage A rejects.*

Again, it's the other way around. A call for control, B rejects that.

> E.   *Passage A downplays the seriousness of claims made in Passage B.*

Also the other way around. A says purple loosestrife is dangerous, B says it's not that bad.

C is the correct answer. We may not have been expecting an answer choice like C, but as long as we can match it up with the actual passages themselves using **reverse confirmation**, then it's an acceptable answer.

Detail Dependent Questions

These questions require us to locate details from either or both passages. Sometimes the question will just ask us, *"which of the following words appear in both passages/in only one of the passages?"* To answer these questions correctly, we must have a clear awareness of the details and keywords that have appeared in the passages. We also need to be aware of terms or concepts that only appear in one passage and terms or concepts that appear in both passages.

As we have seen in the previous chapter, it is extremely time consuming to try to solve these questions if you didn't pay enough attention to the details during the initial readthrough. Because now, for each answer choice, you have to go back to both passages and look for them. Furthermore, you can't skim the passages because we are looking for a specific keyword. Going back to both passages five times, once for each answer choice will take significant amounts of time, time we can't afford to lose on the actual test.

Even though we can't know what details will be asked about in the questions when we are first reading, we can still pay attention to certain keywords that may be of potential interest. Get into the habit of making a note of words (usually nouns) that stand out to you in Passage A, and when you are reading Passage B, check to see if those words have reappeared.

The second type of "detail dependent questions" that we see in comparative passages are basically **According to the Passage Questions** we saw back in Chapter 9. The exception is that this time, we might need to find textual evidence from both passages. We may even need to compare the relevant details from both passages or even combine them to derive a synthesized answer.

Passage A

Drilling fluids, including the various mixtures known as drilling muds, play essential roles in oil-well drilling. As they are circulated down through the drill pipe and back up the well itself, they lubricate the drill bit, bearings, and drill pipe; clean and cool the drill bit as it cuts into the rock; lift rock chips (cuttings) to the surface; provide information about what is happening downhole, allowing the drillers to monitor the behavior, flow rate, pressure, and composition of the drilling fluid; and maintain well pressure to control cave-ins.

Drilling muds are made of bentonite and other clays and polymers, mixed with a fluid to the desired viscosity. By far the largest ingredient of drilling muds, by weight, is barite, a very heavy mineral of density 4.3 to 4.6. It is also used as an inert filler in some foods and is more familiar in its medical use as the "barium meal" administered before X-raying the digestive tract.

Over the years individual drilling companies and their expert drillers have devised proprietary formulations, or mud "recipes," to deal with specific types of drilling jobs. One problem in studying the effects of drilling waste discharges is that the drilling fluids are made from a range of over 1,000, sometimes toxic, ingredients—many of them known, confusingly, by different trade names, generic descriptions, chemical formulae, and regional or industry slang words, and many of them kept secret by companies or individual formulators.

Passage B

Drilling mud, cuttings, and associated chemicals are normally released only during the drilling phase of a well's existence. These discharges are the main environmental concern in offshore oil production, and their use is tightly regulated. The discharges are closely monitored by the offshore operator, and releases are controlled as a condition of the operating permit.

One type of mud—water-based mud (WBM)—is a mixture of water, bentonite clay, and chemical additives, and is used to drill shallow parts of wells. It is not particularly toxic to marine organisms and disperses readily. Under current regulations, it can be dumped directly overboard. Companies typically recycle WBMs until their properties are no longer suitable and then, over a period of hours, dump the entire batch into the sea.

For drilling deeper wells, oil-based mud (OBM) is normally used. The typical difference from WBM is the high content of mineral oil (typically 30 percent). OBMs also contain greater concentrations of barite, a powdered heavy mineral, and a number of additives. OBMs have a greater potential for negative environmental impact, partly because they do not disperse as readily. Barite may impact some organisms, particularly scallops, and the mineral oil may have toxic effects. Currently only the residues of OBMs adhering to cuttings that remain after the cuttings are sieved from the drilling fluids may be discharged overboard, and then only mixtures up to a specified maximum oil content.

PT54 S1 Q7

Which one of the following is a characteristic of barite that is mentioned in both of the passages?

    A. It does not disperse readily in seawater.
    B. It is not found in drilling muds containing bentonite.
    C. Its use in drilling muds is tightly regulated.
    D. It is the most commonly used ingredient in drilling muds.
    E. It is a heavy mineral.

***

PT54 S1 Q9

Which one of the following can be most reasonably inferred from the two passages taken together, but not from either one individually?

    A. Barite is the largest ingredient of drilling muds, by weight, and also the most environmentally damaging.
    B. Although barite can be harmful to marine organisms, it can be consumed safely by humans.
    C. Offshore drilling is more damaging to the environment than is land based drilling.
    D. The use of drilling muds needs to be more tightly controlled by government.
    E. If offshore drilling did not generate cuttings, it would be less harmful to the environment.

Let's look at Q7 first. What do we know about barite?

From Passage A, we know that barite is a "heavy mineral," the largest ingredient; it is used in some "foods," and is digested for medical purposes (paragraph 2).

From Passage B, we know that barite is a "powdered heavy mineral," it may impact some organisms such as scallops negatively (paragraph 3).

Since the question asks us for a characteristic that is mentioned in *both* passages, the correct answer will talk about barite being a "heavy mineral." The correct answer is E.

***

Q9 is an open-ended question, so we can't really try to pre-phrase. Let's read each answer choice and see if it requires a **synthesis** of information from both passages.

> A.   Barite is the <u>largest</u> ingredient of drilling muds, by weight, and also the <u>most</u> environmentally damaging

We know that barite is the largest ingredient from Passage A, but we don't know if it's the "most" damaging. All we are told from Passage B is that barite has negative effects on marine organisms, such as scallops.

> B.   Although barite can be harmful to marine organisms, it can be consumed safely by humans

Yes, this answer requires information from both passages. Passage B tells us that barite is harmful to scallops, Passage A tells us that it's a food additive and consumed before X-Rays.

> C.   Offshore drilling is more damaging to the environment than is land based drilling

This comparison was not made in either passage.

> D.   The use of drilling muds <u>needs to be more</u> tightly controlled by government

Passage A talks about a difficulty with studying drilling muds, government control was not mentioned. Passage B talks about their negative effects. Perhaps the author of Passage B would agree with this, we are not 100% sure. But we don't have any support suggesting that the author of Passage A would also agree with this.

> E.   If offshore drilling did not generate cuttings, it would be less harmful to the environment

Passage A doesn't talk about cuttings or their damage to the environment. Passage B talks about certain OBMs that adhere to the cuttings causing environmental damage. If there were no cuttings, would the OBMs still be present? We are not sure.

The correct answer is B.

Passage A

There is no universally accepted definition within international law for the term "national minority." It is most commonly applied to (1) groups of persons—not necessarily citizens—under the jurisdiction of one country who have ethnic ties to another "homeland" country, or (2) groups of citizens of a country who have lasting ties to that country and have no such ties to any other country, but are distinguished from the majority of the population by ethnicity, religion, or language. The terms "people" and "nation" are also vaguely defined in international agreements. Documents that refer to a "nation" generally link the term to the concept of "nationalism," which is often associated with ties to land. It also connotes sovereignty, for which reason, perhaps, "people" is often used instead of "nation" for groups subject to a colonial power.

While the lack of definition of the terms "minority," "people," and "nation" presents difficulties to numerous minority groups, this lack is particularly problematic for the Roma (Gypsies). The Roma are not a colonized people, they do not have a homeland, and many do not bear ties to any currently existing country. Some Roma are not even citizens of any country, in part because of their nomadic way of life, which developed in response to centuries of fleeing persecution. Instead, they have ethnic and linguistic ties to other groups of Roma that reside in other countries.

Passage B

Capotorti's definition of a minority includes four empirical criteria—a group's being numerically smaller than the rest of the population of the state; their being nondominant; their having distinctive ethnic, linguistic, or religious characteristics; and their desiring to preserve their own culture—and one legal criterion, that they be citizens of the state in question. This last element can be problematic, given the previous nomadic character of the Roma, that they still cross borders between European states to avoid persecution, and that some states have denied them citizenship, and thus minority status. Because this element essentially grants the state the arbitrary right to decide if the Roma constitute a minority without reference to empirical characteristics, it seems patently unfair that it should be included in the definition.

However, the Roma easily fulfill the four objective elements of Capotorti's definition and should, therefore, be considered a minority in all major European states. Numerically, they are nowhere near a majority, though they number in the hundreds of thousands, even millions, in some states. Their nondominant position is evident—they are not even acknowledged as a minority in some states. The Roma have a number of distinctive linguistic, ethnic, and religious characteristics. For example, most speak Romani, an Indo-European language descended from Sanskrit. Roma groups also have their own distinctive legal and court systems, which are group oriented rather than individual-rights oriented. That they have preserved their language, customs, and identity through centuries of persecution is evidence enough of their desire to preserve their culture.

PT56 S4 Q18

Which one of the following claims about the Roma is NOT made in Passage A?

A. Those living in one country have ethnic ties to Roma in other countries.
B. Some of them practice a nomadic way of life.
C. They, as a people, have no recognizable homeland.
D. In some countries, their population exceeds one million.
E. The lack of a completely satisfactory definition of "minority" is a greater problem for them than for most.

This question is difficult because it throws us off balance. Whenever we see a Detail Question, we are almost always expecting the question to ask us what term appears in both passages. These are the questions we prepared for by locating recurring terms in both passages.

However, this question is asking us for something that does NOT appear in Passage A. The correct answer can either appear in Passage B only, or have never appeared at all in either passage. That makes this question basically impossible to anticipate. The best we can do is to go through the answer choices, eliminate the answers that we know Passage A has discussed, and double check Passage A to verify the remaining answers.

    A.   *Those living in one country have ethnic ties to Roma in other countries.*

This is mentioned in the last sentence of Passage A.

    B.   *Some of them practice a nomadic way of life.*

Second to last sentence of the passage: "…in part because of their nomadic way of life…"

    C.   *They, as a people, have no recognizable homeland.*

Also mentioned in the last paragraph: "The Roma are not a colonized people; they do not have a homeland."

    D.   *In some countries, their population exceeds one million.*

This is actually mentioned in of Passage B, "…number in the…even millions, in some states."

    E.   *The lack of a completely satisfactory definition of "minority" is a greater problem for them than for most.*

This is mentioned in the first sentence of the last paragraph of Passage A: "lack of definitions…particularly problematic for the Roma."

The correct answer is D.

Passage A

Music does not always gain by association with words. Like images, words can excite the deepest emotions but are inadequate to express the emotions they excite. Music is more adequate, and hence will often seize an emotion that may have been excited by images or words, deepen its expression, and, by so doing, excite still deeper emotion. That is how words can gain by being set to music.

But to set words to music-as in opera or song--is in fact to mix two arts together. A striking effect may be produced, but at the expense of the purity of each art. Poetry is a great art; so is music. But as a medium for emotion, each is greater alone than in company, although various good ends arise from linking the two, providing that the words are subordinated to the more expressive medium of music. What good could any words do for Beethoven's Fifth Symphony? So too an opera is largely independent of words, and depends for its aesthetic value not upon the poetry of the libretto (the words of the opera), or even the plot or scenery, but upon its emotional range-a region dominated by the musical element.

Passage B

Throughout the history of opera, two fundamental types may be distinguished: that in which the music is primary, and that in which there is, essentially, parity between music and other factors. The former, sometimes called "singer's opera"-a term which has earned undeserved contempt-is exemplified by most Italian operas, while the latter, exemplified by the operas of German composer Richard Wagner, depend for their effect on a balance among many factors of which music is only one, albeit the most important. Theoretically, it would seem that there should be a third kind of opera, in which the music is subordinated
to the other features. While the earliest operas were of this kind, their appeal was limited, and a fuller participation of music was required to establish opera on a secure basis.

In any event, in any aesthetic judgment of opera, regardless of the opera's type, neither the music nor the poetry of the libretto should be judged in isolation. The music is good not if it would make a good concert piece but if it serves the particular situation in the opera in which it occurs, contributing something not supplied by other elements. Similarly, the poetry is good not because it reads well by itself but primarily if, while embodying a sound dramatic idea, it furnishes opportunity for effective musical and scenic treatment. True, the elements of music and poetry may be considered separately, but only for purposes of analyzing their formal features. In actuality these elements are as united as hydrogen and oxygen are united in water. It is this union-further enriched and clarified by the visual action-that results in opera's inimitable character.

<u>PT85 S1 Q16</u>

Which one of the following issues is addressed by the author of Passage A but not by the author of Passage B?

    A.   The importance of music to any aesthetic judgment of an operatic work.
    B.   How music is affected when it is combined with words.
    C.   The ability of music to evoke an emotional response in the listener.
    D.   Whether music should ever be subordinated to words with which it is combined.
    E.   Whether music should be judged in isolation from the libretto in opera.

***

<u>PT85 S1 Q17</u>

Passage B, but not passage A, includes which one of the following topics in its discussion of opera?

    A.   The importance of plot and scenery to an opera's aesthetic value.
    B.   The ability of images and words to excite deep emotion.
    C.   The consequences of combining poetry and music into a single art form.
    D.   The relative roles of music and libretto in opera.
    E.   The differences among different types of opera.

We will start with Q16: another question that we can't really pre-phrase the answer to. Let's take a look at the answers, be especially careful with answers that describe something mentioned by both authors, or only by Passage B. Remember, the correct answer will describe an issue that's only described by Passage A!

A. *The importance of music to any aesthetic judgment of an operatic work*

This is discussed in Passage B. At the beginning of the second paragraph, it says, "in any aesthetic judgment of opera…neither the music nor the poetry should be judged in isolation."

B. *How music is affected when it is combined with words*

This is not explicitly stated in Passage B, but at the end of the last paragraph, the author states that the elements of music and poetry…are as united as hydrogen and oxygen are united in water…this union…results in opera's inimitable character.

The author of Passage B, in other words, considers music and words to be inseparable and essential to the nature of an opera.

C. *The ability of music to evoke an emotional response in the listener*

"Emotional response" is talked about in the first paragraph of Passage A ("excite still deeper emotion"), emotional response was not discussed in Passage B.

D. *Whether music should ever be subordinated to words with which it is combined*

B talks about this, a third kind of opera, where music is subordinate to the other features (words). In the author's opinion, their lack of appeal seems to suggest that music *shouldn't* be subjugated to the words.

E. *Whether music should be judged in isolation from the libretto in opera*

The "libretto" just means words. Passage B talks about this. Music and words are inseparable.

The correct answer is C.

***

Q17 is asking the opposite as Q16. This time, we need to find something that Passage B talks about, but not Passage A. If an answer mentions something discussed by both passages, or only in Passage A, or neither, then it would be wrong.

A. *The importance of plot and scenery to an opera's aesthetic value*

The last sentence of Passage A discusses this.

B. *The ability of images and words to excite deep emotion*

Passage A talks about this in the second sentence of the first paragraph.

C. *The consequences of combining poetry and music into a single art form*

Passage A thinks that each is better off alone, mixing the two arts together causes both to suffer.

D. *The relative roles of music and libretto in opera*

Passage A talks about this near the end of the passage. The role of music is more important than that of the libretto.

E. *The differences among different types of opera*

Passage A does not talk about the different types of opera. Passage B talks about Italian, German, and the third type of opera where music is subordinate to words.

The correct answer is E.

19. Comparative Passages: The Questions

Passage A

Because dental caries (decay) is strongly linked to consumption of the sticky, carbohydrate-rich staples of agricultural diets, prehistoric human teeth can provide clues about when a population made the transition from a hunter-gatherer diet to an agricultural one. Caries formation is influenced by several factors, including tooth structure, bacteria in the mouth, and diet. In particular, caries formation is affected by carbohydrates' texture and composition, since carbohydrates more readily stick to teeth.

Many researchers have demonstrated the link between carbohydrate consumption and caries. In North America, Leigh studied caries in archaeologically derived teeth, noting that caries rates differed between indigenous populations that primarily consumed meat (a Sioux sample showed almost no caries) and those heavily dependent on cultivated maize (a Zuni sample had 75 percent carious teeth). Leigh's findings have been frequently confirmed by other researchers, who have shown that, in general, the greater a population's dependence on agriculture is, the higher its rate of caries formation will be.

Under some circumstances, however, non-agricultural populations may exhibit relatively high caries rates. For example, early non-agricultural populations in western North America who consumed large amounts of highly processed stone-ground flour made from gathered acorns show relatively high caries frequencies. And wild plants collected by the Hopi included several species with high cariogenic potential, notably pinyon nuts and wild tubers.

Passage B

Archaeologists recovered human skeletal remains interred over a 2,000-year period in prehistoric Ban Chiang, Thailand. The site's early inhabitants appear to have had a hunter-gatherer-cultivator economy. Evidence indicates that, over time, the population became increasingly dependent on agriculture.

Research suggests that agricultural intensification results in declining human health, including dental health. Studies show that dental caries is uncommon in pre-agricultural populations. Increased caries frequency may result from increased consumption of starchy-sticky foodstuffs or from alterations in tooth wear. The wearing down of tooth crown surfaces reduces caries formation by removing fissures that can trap food particles. A reduction of fiber or grit in a diet may diminish tooth wear, thus increasing caries frequency. However, severe wear that exposes a tooth's pulp cavity may also result in caries.

The diet of Ban Chiang's inhabitants included some cultivated rice and yams from the beginning of the period represented by the recovered remains. These were part of a varied diet that also included wild plant and animal foods. Since both rice and yams are carbohydrates, increased reliance on either or both should theoretically result in increased caries frequency.

Yet comparisons of caries frequency in the Early and Late Ban Chiang Groups indicate that overall caries frequency is slightly greater in the Early Group. Tooth wear patterns do not indicate tooth wear changes between Early and Late Groups that would explain this unexpected finding. It is more likely that, although dependence on agriculture increased, the diet in the Late period remained varied enough that no single food dominated. Furthermore, there may have been a shift from sweeter carbohydrates (yams) toward rice, a less cariogenic carbohydrate.

PT62 S1 Q16

Which one of the following distinguishes the Ban Chiang populations discussed in passage B from the populations discussed in the last paragraph of passage A?

    A. While the Ban Chiang populations consumed several highly cariogenic foods, the populations discussed in the last paragraph of passage A did not.
    B. While the Ban Chiang populations ate cultivated foods, the populations discussed in the last paragraph of passage A did not.
    C. While the Ban Chiang populations consumed a diet consisting primarily of carbohydrates, the populations discussed in the last paragraph of passage A did not.
    D. While the Ban Chiang populations exhibited very high levels of tooth wear, the populations discussed in the last paragraph of passage A did not.
    E. While the Ban Chiang populations ate certain highly processed foods, the populations discussed in the last paragraph of passage A did not.

Q16: *Which one of the following distinguishes the Ban Chiang populations discussed in passage B from the populations discussed in the last paragraph of passage A?*

A more specific question than the ones we have encountered so far, let's see if the question itself offers any guidance. We are asked the differences between the Ban Chiang population and the "*early non-agricultural populations in western North America and the Hopi population.*"

What do we know about the Ban Chiang population? We know that they turned from a hunter-gatherer lifestyle to become increasingly dependent on agriculture. But contrary to expectations, the Ban Chiang population did not witness an increase in cavities, in fact, there was a decrease.

What do we know about the Indigenous population from Passage A? We are told that even though they were non-agricultural, they still had relatively high cavity rates. This is because they still ate a diet of carbs derived from gathered acorns and wild plants.

What distinguishes these two groups? I would say that one group is a hunter gatherer society, and the other group went from hunting/gathering to an agricultural lifestyle. One group (Indigenous peoples) had relatively high cavity rates despite being hunter gatherers; while the other group (Ban Chiang) had lower cavity rates despite adopting an agricultural lifestyle.

   A. *While the Ban Chiang populations consumed several highly cariogenic foods, the populations discussed in the last paragraph of passage A did not.*

The indigenous people did consume cariogenic foods, such as pinyon nuts and wild tubers.

   B. *While the Ban Chiang populations ate cultivated foods, the populations discussed in the last paragraph of passage A did not.*

The Ban Chiang population eventually settled into an agricultural lifestyle (i.e. ate cultivated foods). The Indigenous population remained hunter gatherers, which means that they did not cultivate foods.

   C. *While the Ban Chiang populations consumed a diet consisting primarily of carbohydrates, the populations discussed in the last paragraph of passage A did not.*

We know both groups consumed carbohydrates, but we don't know what proportion of carbs their diet consisted of. How much of it was protein, or fat?

   D. *While the Ban Chiang populations exhibited very high levels of tooth wear, the populations discussed in the last paragraph of passage A did not.*

This is the opposite of what we are looking for. The Ban Chiang population saw a decrease in tooth wear. (We don't know whether it was very high to begin with.) The populations from Passage A exhibited "relatively high caries rates."

   E. *While the Ban Chiang populations ate certain highly processed foods, the populations discussed in the last paragraph of passage A did not.*

Those discussed in Passage A ate processed flour made from acorns. The correct answer is B.

Inference Questions

Inference Questions in Comparative Passages, like their cousins from regular passages, are first and foremost, *according to the passage* questions. This means that during the answer choice selection process, we want the answer choice with the most explicit support from the text. It is only when we cannot find an answer that's 100% backed up by the passage that we are allowed to make inferences. And even when we do make inferences, our reasoning must remain conservative and as close to the original text as possible.

When it comes to Inference Questions, just like in Detail Dependent Questions, the correct answer will often draw upon evidence from both passages.

***

Passage A

Why do some trial courts judges oppose conducting independent research to help them make decisions? One of their objections is that it distorts the adversarial system by requiring an active judicial role and undermining the importance of evidence presented by the opposing parties. Another fear is that judges lack the wherewithal to conduct first rate research and may wind up using outlier or discredited scientific materials.

While these concerns have some merit, they do not justify an absolute prohibition of the practice. First, there are reasons to sacrifice adversarial values in the scientific evidence context. The adversarial system is particularly ill-suited to handling specialized knowledge. The two parties pre-screen and compensate expert witnesses, which virtually ensures conflicting and partisan testimony. At the same time, scientific facts are general truths not confined to the immediate cases. Because scientific admissibility decisions can exert considerable influence over future cases, erroneous decisions detract from the legitimacy of the system. Independent research could help judges avoid such errors.

Second, a trial provides a structure that guides any potential independent research, reducing the possibility of a judge's reaching outlandish results. Independent research supplements, rather than replaces, the parties' presentation of the evidence, so the parties always frame the debate.

Passage B

Regardless of what trial courts may do, appellate courts should resist the temptation to conduct their own independent research of scientific literature.

As a general rule, appellate courts do not hear live testimony. Thus these courts lack some of the critical tools available at the trial level for arriving at a determination of the facts: live testimony and cross-examination. Experts practicing in the field may have knowledge and experience beyond what is reflected in the available scientific literature. And adverse parties can test the credibility and reliability of proffered literature by subjecting the expert witness to the greatest legal engine ever invented for the discovery of truth – cross-examination. The trial judge may even participate in the process by questioning live witnesses. However, these events can only occur at the trial level.

Literature considered for the first time at the appellate level is not subject to live comment by practicing experts and cannot be tested in the crucible of the adversarial system. Thus one of the core criticisms against the use of such sources by appellate courts is that doing so usurps the trial court's fact-finding function. Internet sources, in particular, have come under criticism for their potential unreliability.

When an appellate court goes outside the record to determine case facts, it ignores its function as a court of review, and it substitutes its own questionable research results for evidence that should have been tested in the trial court. This criticism applies with full force to the use of outside-the-record texts and treatises, regardless of the medium in which they are found.

PT81 S1 Q22

It can be inferred that each author would agree that if judges conduct independent research, that research

    A. Should be constrained by the structure of a trial.
    B. Is typically confined to standard, reliable sources.
    C. Replaces, rather than supplements, party-presented evidence.
    D. Should be conducted at the trial level but not at the appellate level.
    E. Usurps the trial court's fact-finding function.

***

PT81 S1 Q24

Given the statements about cross-examination in the passage, the author of passage B would be most likely to take issue with which one of the following claims by the author of Passage A?

    A. An absolute prohibition of independent research by trial judges is not justified.
    B. The adversarial system is particularly ill-suited to handling specialized knowledge.
    C. Scientific admissibility decisions exert considerable influence over future cases.
    D. Erroneous decisions can be readily exposed by third parties.
    E. A trial provides a structure that guides any potential independent research.

Q22: Seeing that the question is about "*independent research*," let's see what each author says about the issue, and whether there's any overlap between their views.

The author of Passage A argues that "independent research" should be permitted. Because at the trial court level, the format of the trial hinders the truth. So "independent research" can be really helpful.

Further, the structure of the trial will prevent the judge from coming up with crazy results.

The author of Passage B thinks that "independent research" shouldn't be permitted at the appellate level. But since we are looking for areas where both authors will *agree*, we have to look deeper.

Passage B thinks that judges should not hear testimony at the appellate level because judges do not have the tools available at the trial court level: live testimony and cross-examination. These are parts of the adversarial system that the author thinks will help us arrive at the truth.

Can we potentially infer that certain elements of the trial court format makes it more acceptable for independent research? Yes, because even though the author never says it's ok for lower-level judges to conduct independent research per se, they do think it's *more acceptable* to do so at the lower level than at the higher level.

> A. *Should be constrained by the structure of a trial.*

Passage A would agree, as they say that the structure of a trial should guide the judge's independent research.

Passage B kind of agrees too. They do think that the adversarial system (part of the structure of a trial) is better suited to handling independent research.

I don't like this answer too much, but it can be construed to refer to something from the text, let's keep it for now.

> B. *Is typically confined to standard, reliable sources.*

Using the search function will help us locate certain keywords from the passages. And the word "sources" appear in the third paragraph of Passage B. The author of Passage B thinks judges may end up using reliable sources.

> C. *Replaces, rather than supplements, party-presented evidence.*

Both authors would disagree with this, the author of Passage A explicitly says: "independent research supplements, rather than replaces...evidence."

> D. *Should be conducted at the trial level but not at the appellate level.*

This one is tricky. The author of Passage A would say: trial level yes, appellate level unknown. The author of Passage B would say: regardless of what happens at the trial level (no comment for trial level), appellate level no. So we don't know what the author of Passage A thinks about research at the appellate level. This is out of scope.

> E. *Usurps the trial court's fact-finding function.*

Passage A would argue against this. Passage A advocates the use of independent research.

The correct answer is A.

***

Let's look at Q24:

Given the statements about cross-examination in the passage, the author of passage B would be most likely to take issue with which one of the following claims by the author of Passage A?

What do we know about cross-examination from the passages?

Passage A thinks that it hinders the truth: "the two parties pre-screen and compensate expert witnesses, which virtually ensures conflicting and partisan testimony." Also that "the adversarial system is particularly ill-suited to handling specialized knowledge."

What does Passage B think?

Passage B thinks that "cross-examination" is the greatest legal engine ever invented for the discovery of truth.

In other words, the two authors have opposing views of the impact of cross-examinations.

So the correct answer will need to fulfill the following requirements:

One, it's something actually claimed by author A; and two, it's something that author B disagrees with. So the correct answer will either say that cross-examinations lead to conflicting/partisan testimony; or such a trial system is not friendly to scientific truths; or that the system is not suited to handling specialized knowledge.

The correct answer is B.

For Inference Questions, if the question stem is giving us hints or clues on where to look for the relevant evidence, we must do our best to **pre-phrase**. Armed with several potential iterations of what the correct answer might look like, our job will be drastically easier, and we are much less likely to be fooled or carried away by a trap answer.

Passage A
Because dental caries (decay) is strongly linked to consumption of the sticky, carbohydrate-rich staples of agricultural diets, prehistoric human teeth can provide clues about when a population made the transition from a hunter-gatherer diet to an agricultural one. Caries formation is influenced by several factors, including tooth structure, bacteria in the mouth, and diet. In particular, caries formation is affected by carbohydrates' texture and composition, since carbohydrates more readily stick to teeth.

Many researchers have demonstrated the link between carbohydrate consumption and caries. In North America, Leigh studied caries in archaeologically derived teeth, noting that caries rates differed between indigenous populations that primarily consumed meat (a Sioux sample showed almost no caries) and those heavily dependent on cultivated maize (a Zuni sample had 75 percent carious teeth). Leigh's findings have been frequently confirmed by other researchers, who have shown that, in general, the greater a population's dependence on agriculture is, the higher its rate of caries formation will be.

Under some circumstances, however, non-agricultural populations may exhibit relatively high caries rates. For example, early non-agricultural populations in western North America who consumed large amounts of highly processed stone-ground flour made from gathered acorns show relatively high caries frequencies. And wild plants collected by the Hopi included several species with high cariogenic potential, notably pinyon nuts and wild tubers.

Passage B
Archaeologists recovered human skeletal remains interred over a 2,000-year period in prehistoric Ban Chiang, Thailand. The site's early inhabitants appear to have had a hunter-gatherer-cultivator economy. Evidence indicates that, over time, the population became increasingly dependent on agriculture.

Research suggests that agricultural intensification results in declining human health, including dental health. Studies show that dental caries is uncommon in pre-agricultural populations. Increased caries frequency may result from increased consumption of starchy-sticky foodstuffs or from alterations in tooth wear. The wearing down of tooth crown surfaces reduces caries formation by removing fissures that can trap food particles. A reduction of fiber or grit in a diet may diminish tooth wear, thus increasing caries frequency. However, severe wear that exposes a tooth's pulp cavity may also result in caries.

The diet of Ban Chiang's inhabitants included some cultivated rice and yams from the beginning of the period represented by the recovered remains. These were part of a varied diet that also included wild plant and animal foods. Since both rice and yams are carbohydrates, increased reliance on either or both should theoretically result in increased caries frequency.

Yet comparisons of caries frequency in the Early and Late Ban Chiang Groups indicate that overall caries frequency is slightly greater in the Early Group. Tooth wear patterns do not indicate tooth wear changes between Early and Late Groups that would explain this unexpected finding. It is more likely that, although dependence on agriculture increased, the diet in the Late period remained varied enough that no single food dominated. Furthermore, there may have been a shift from sweeter carbohydrates (yams) toward rice, a less cariogenic carbohydrate.

PT62 S1 Q19

It is most likely that both authors would agree with which one of the following statements about dental caries?

   A. The incidence of dental caries increases predictably in populations over time.
   B. Dental caries is often difficult to detect in teeth recovered from archaeological sites.
   C. Dental caries tends to be more prevalent in populations with a hunter-gatherer diet than in populations with an agricultural diet.
   D. The frequency of dental caries in a population does not necessarily correspond directly to the population's degree of dependence on agriculture.
   E. The formation of dental caries tends to be more strongly linked to tooth wear than to the consumption of a particular kind of food.

Again, a fairly open-ended question, these are a lot harder to anticipate, so I will quickly remind myself of the key arguments in each passage before jumping to the answer choices.

Passage A told us that generally speaking, the higher the dependency on agriculture, the higher the rate of cavities. (With exceptions, of course.)

Passage B is a case study of the Ban Chiang population. Contrary to expectations outlined in Passage A, the Ban Chiang people did not have more cavities after settling down to become farmers. The author then provides some potential reasons for why this was the case.

> A. The incidence of dental caries increases _predictably_ in populations over time.

Passage B would point to the Ban Chiang people as an exception.

> B. Dental caries is often _difficult_ to detect in teeth recovered from archaeological sites.

This was never mentioned in either passage.

> C. Dental caries tends to be more prevalent in populations with a hunter-gatherer diet than in populations with an agricultural diet.

Both authors would agree with the opposite, dental caries are more prevalent, generally speaking, in agricultural populations.

> D. The frequency of dental caries in a population _does not necessarily correspond directly_ to the population's degree of dependence on agriculture.

Would both authors agree with this? Yes, author A would point to the Indigenous hunter gatherer tribes who had no dependency on agriculture but still had a high degree of cavities. The author of Passage B would also point to the Ban Chiang population as a case in point.

> E. The formation of dental caries tends to be more strongly linked to tooth wear than to the consumption of a particular kind of food.

Passage B does talk about tooth wear and consumption of certain foods as reasons why cavities are formed. But there was never a comparison between the two. Passage A never talks about this.

The correct answer is D.

Passage A

Purple loosestrife (Lythrum salicaria), an aggressive and invasive perennial of Eurasian origin, arrived with settlers in eastern North America in the early 1800s and has spread across the continent's midlatitude wetlands. The impact of purple loosestrife on native vegetation has been disastrous, with more than 50 percent of the biomass of some wetland communities displaced. Monospecific blocks of this weed have maintained themselves for at least 20 years. Impacts on wildlife have not been well studied, but serious reductions in waterfowl and aquatic furbearer productivity have been observed. In addition, several endangered species of vertebrates are threatened with further degradation of their breeding habitats. Although purple loosestrife can invade relatively undisturbed habitats, the spread and dominance of this weed have been greatly accelerated in disturbed habitats. While digging out the plants can temporarily halt their spread, there has been little research on long-term purple loosestrife control. Glyphosate has been used successfully, but no measure of the impact of this herbicide on native plant communities has been made.

With the spread of purple loosestrife growing exponentially, some form of integrated control is needed. At present, coping with purple loosestrife hinges on early detection of the weed's arrival in areas, which allows local eradication to be carried out with minimum damage to the native plant community.

Passage B

The war on purple loosestrife is apparently conducted on behalf of nature, an attempt to liberate the biotic community from the tyrannical influence of a life-destroying invasive weed. Indeed, purple loosestrife control is portrayed by its practitioners as an environmental initiative intended to save nature rather than control it. Accordingly, the purple loosestrife literature, scientific and otherwise, dutifully discusses the impacts of the weed on endangered species—and on threatened biodiversity more generally. Purple loosestrife is a pollution, according to the scientific community, and all of nature suffers under its pervasive influence.

Regardless of the perceived and actual ecological effects of the purple invader, it is apparent that popular pollution ideologies have been extended into the wetlands of North America. Consequently, the scientific effort to liberate nature from purple loosestrife has failed to decouple itself from its philosophical origin as an instrument to control nature to the satisfaction of human desires. Birds, particularly game birds and waterfowl, provide the bulk of the justification for loosestrife management. However, no bird species other than the canvasback has been identified in the literature as endangered by purple loosestrife. The impact of purple loosestrife on furbearing mammals is discussed at great length, though none of the species highlighted (muskrat, mink) can be considered threatened in North America. What is threatened by purple loosestrife is the economics of exploiting such preferred species and the millions of dollars that will be lost to the economies of the United States and Canada from reduced hunting, trapping, and recreation revenues due to a decline in the production of the wetland resource.

It can be inferred that the authors would be most likely to disagree about which one of the following?

A. Purple loosestrife spreads more quickly in disturbed habitats than in undisturbed habitats.
B. The threat posed by purple loosestrife to local aquatic furbearer populations is serious.
C. Most people who advocate that eradication measures be taken to control purple loosestrife are not genuine in their concern for the environment.
D. The size of the biomass that has been displaced by purple loosestrife is larger than is generally thought.
E. Measures should be taken to prevent other non-native plant species from invading North America.

***

It can be inferred that both authors would be most likely to agree with which one of the following statements regarding purple loosestrife?

A. As it increases in North America, some wildlife populations tend to decrease.
B. Its establishment in North America has had a disastrous effect on native North American wetland vegetation in certain regions.
C. It is very difficult to control effectively with herbicides.
D. Its introduction into North America was a great ecological blunder.
E. When it is eliminated from a given area, it tends to return to that area fairly quickly.

For Q9, we are asked what the authors would most likely *disagree* about. There are many issues on which they disagree. For instance, whether we should try to control purple loosestrife, whether purple loosestrife really poses a danger to the environment, what's the motivation behind the attempts to control purple loosestrife, etc. Since there's so many possibilities, let's look at the answer choices. For this question, the correct answer needs to have one author agreeing, and the other author disagreeing.

>   A.   *Purple loosestrife spreads more quickly in disturbed habitats than in undisturbed habitats.*

Author A would agree, but we have no evidence that author B would disagree.

>   B.   *The threat posed by purple loosestrife to local aquatic furbearer populations is serious.*

Author A thinks so: "*Serious reductions in aquatic furbearer productivity have been observed.*"

Author B doesn't think so: "*None of the species [of furbearing mammals] can be considered threatened in North America.*"

>   C.   *Most people who advocate that eradication measures be taken to control purple loosestrife are not genuine in their concern for the environment.*

Most means >50%. Think about the **threshold of proof** for this answer choice (See Chapters 10 and 16 for a refresher). In order to select this answer, we need one party to say, "yes, its greater than 50%," and the other party to say, "no, its less than 50%."

>   D.   *The size of the biomass that has been displaced by purple loosestrife is larger than is generally thought.*

We only know that >50% of biomass has been displaced from Passage A, we don't know what people "generally think" it is. Similarly, we don't know what people think it is from Passage B, as it's never mentioned there.

>   E.   *Measures should be taken to prevent other non-native plant species from invading North America.*

This answer is out of scope, we don't know what each author thinks about other species. Maybe author A would agree with this, since they are so against purple loosestrife. But again, we are just guessing and do not have any textual evidence to back us up here.

The correct answer is B.

***

Q11 is rather difficult to pre-phrase. While we know that Author A considers purple loosestrife to be dangerous and should be eradicated. Author B considers such attempts to be misguided. We know what these two authors *disagree* about. But there seems to be little common ground between the two.

This is where the habit of reading Passage B and constantly comparing it to what we have already learned in Passage A may help. After reading a few sentences from Passage B, I would pause and ask myself, "is this something also touched upon by Author A? If so, what is their opinion/attitude towards this concept?" I would do this as I move through Passage B. By the time I have finished, I will have come to an in-depth understanding of Passage B relative to Passage A. Understanding how the two passages **relate** to each other is fundamental to success in comparative passages.

The author of Passage B decries the attitude and prejudices of the scientific community, many of whom are bent on eradicating purple loosestrife. So they would at least agree with the statement that *"some people believe the Purple Loosestrife to be a harmful species."* Would the author of Passage A agree with this statement? Sure, their own position stands in testimony to this statement. So perhaps the correct answer choice will not be about Purple Loosestrife *per se*, but rather an observation about a view held by some members of the scientific community.

Author A also concedes the effects of purple loosestrife on animals have not been well studied. Author B also complains that the effect of purple loosestrife on birds other than the canvasback have not been identified. So perhaps we can make an argument that both authors would agree that the research and literature on purple loosestrife are incomplete.

> A. *As it increases in North America, <u>some</u> wildlife populations tend to decrease.*

Author A would certainly agree with this. On the other hand, Author B had stated that furbearing animals are not threatened by purple loosestrife. Many students would recall this and automatically eliminate this answer choice.

But wait, remember the lessons we learned throughout the book. In an answer choice that is worded weakly/conservatively, it would require a lower **threshold of proof**. The word *"some"* can mean anywhere from one to all. So if we can find evidence that purple loosestrife can hurt just one type of animal in Passage B, this would be a good enough answer for me.

This is where the power of **Reverse Confirmation** shines through. You may recall that the canvasback is in fact endangered by purple loosestrife (in a concession made by Author B in the last paragraph). But if you didn't, you can quickly skim through Passage B again, asking yourself, "is there an animal that has been harmed by the purple loosestrife? If so, what is it?" Hopefully you would have discovered the statement about the canvasback. Even Author B would not deny the detrimental effect of purple loosestrife on the canvasback.

A is the correct answer.

> B. *Its establishment in North America has had a <u>disastrous</u> effect on native North American wetland vegetation in certain regions.*

We can use the same strategy we used to confirm A to eliminate B. Author A would agree with this statement, but in order to select this answer, we need to find evidence in Passage B for a "disastrous effect on vegetation." Is there such evidence? No.

> C. *It is very difficult to control effectively with herbicides.*

Author A tells us that glyphosate has been used successfully, so this actually runs contrary to what answer choice C is telling us. Herbicides were not mentioned in Passage B.

> D. *Its introduction into North America was a <u>great</u> ecological blunder.*

Author A would probably agree with this, but it runs contrary to the spirit of Author B's argument. Author B, if you recall, argues that the negative effects of purple loosestrife on the ecosystem are minimal. Author B is more concerned with attacking the motives of those who are advocating for the control and eradication of this plant. Given this information, would Author B agree that purple loosestrife's introduction into North America was a great ecological blunder? Probably not.

> E. *When it is eliminated from a given area, it tends to return to that area fairly quickly.*

Again, it's possible that Author A would agree with this. They claim that purple loosestrife can be "temporarily" halted. This is a bit of a stretch but let's see what Author B has to say about this.

There are no mentions of how stubborn purple loosestrife is in Passage B.

***

Passage A

Karl Popper's main contribution to the philosophy of science concerns the power of negative evidence. The fundamental point is simple: No number of white swans, for example, can ever prove that all swans are white, but a single black swan disproves the hypothesis. Popper gives this logical asymmetry between positive and negative evidence hyperbolic application, maintaining that positive evidence has no value as evidence and that negative evidence is tantamount to disproof. Moreover, Popper takes the search for negative evidence to be at the heart of scientific research; that is, for Popper, scientific research involves not only generating bold theories, but also searching for evidence that would disprove them. Indeed, for him, a theory counts as scientific only if it makes predictions that are testable in this way.

However, Popper's use of the logical asymmetry does not adequately capture the actual situation scientists face. If a theory deductively entails a false prediction, then the theory must be false as well. But a scientific theory rarely entails predictions on its own. When scientists actually derive a theory's predictions, they almost always need diverse additional "auxiliary" premises, which appeal to other theories, to the correct functioning of instrumentation, to the absence of disturbing forces, etc. When a prediction fails, logic indicates that at least one of the premises must be false, but it does not indicate which one. When an experiment does not work out as predicted, there is usually more than one possible explanation. Positive evidence is never conclusive. But negative evidence rarely is either.

Passage B

When the planet Uranus was discovered, astronomers attempted to predict its orbit. They based their predictions on Newton's laws and auxiliary assumptions about the mass of the sun and the masses, orbits, and velocities of other planets. One of the auxiliary assumptions was that no planets existed in the vicinity of Uranus. When the astronomers made their observations, they found that the orbit they had predicted for Uranus was incorrect. One possible explanation for the failure of their prediction was that Newton's laws were incorrect. Another was that there was an error in the auxiliary assumptions. The astronomers changed their assumptions about the existence of other planets, concluding that there must be another planet close enough to Uranus to produce the observed orbit. Not long afterward, scientists discovered the planet Neptune in the precise place it would have to be to bring their calculations into alignment with their observations.

Later astronomers, again using Newton's laws, predicted the orbit of Mercury. Once again, the predictions were not borne out. They hypothesized the existence of another planet in the vicinity, which they called Vulcan. However, Vulcan was never found, and some scientists began to think that perhaps Newton's laws were in error. Finally, when Einstein's general theory of relativity was introduced, astronomers discovered that calculations based on that theory and the old auxiliary assumptions predicted the observed orbit of Mercury, leading to the rejection of Newton's theory of gravity and to increased confidence in Einstein's theory.

PT76 S1 Q26

It can be inferred that the author of passage B would be likely to be most skeptical of which one of the following ideas mentioned in passage A?

 A. Popper's main contribution to the philosophy of science concerned the power of negative evidence.
 B. Positive evidence plays no role in supporting a theory.
 C. Auxiliary premises are usually needed in order to derive predictions from a scientific theory.
 D. There is a logical asymmetry between positive and negative evidence.
 E. Scientific research involves generating bold theories and attempting to refute them.

This question is asking for what Author B would be skeptical about from Passage A. In order to solve this question, we have to know clearly the positions held by Author B, then we have to find an answer that states something from Passage A, and then we have to make sure that these two are contradictory to each other, maybe explicitly, maybe by inference. (Review *Chapter 14: Advanced Question Tactics* to further practice question stem analysis if you are struggling with this part.)

So what do we know about Author B's position? This is a little difficult to come up with, as Passage B is a predominantly explanatory passage, and the author's views are not super clear. But we know that the author would agree that negative evidence is not tantamount to disproof, as auxiliary assumptions may need to be revised instead.

But Author B would also agree that negative evidence is enough to overturn a theory, in the event that there are no auxiliary assumptions to take the blame.

What are some positions from Passage A? There's Popper's position that negative evidence is tantamount to disproof. This is something that the author of Passage B would probably be skeptical about.

The author of Passage B would probably *agree* with author A's view that negative evidence can be due to faulty assumptions, so this would probably not be something they would be skeptical about.

Finally, perhaps author B would be skeptical of author A's claim that "negative evidence is rarely conclusive either." Negative evidence did overturn Newtonian physics, as we saw in Passage B.

When we do not have a clear anticipated answer, we'll use the answer choices to guide us. Again, **reverse confirmation** can be potentially very helpful.

For each of the answer choices, they need to satisfy two requirements:

- **One, is it an idea mentioned in Passage A?**
- **Two, would the author of Passage B disagree with it and where is the evidence?**

A. Popper's main contribution to the philosophy of science concerned the power of negative evidence

We don't know what author B thinks about Popper, they never mention Karl Popper in Passage B.

B. Positive evidence plays no role in supporting a theory

This is a view espoused by author A. What does author B think about positive evidence?

Positive evidence (Einstein's Theory correctly predicting Mercury's orbit) was seen as having a positive role in supporting that theory. It led "to an increased confidence in Einstein's theory."

This answer matches both of our requirements for the correct answer.

C. Auxiliary premises are <u>usually</u> needed in order to <u>derive predictions</u> from a scientific theory

Author A does say this, "when scientists derive predictions…they almost always need auxiliary premises."

Does author B disagree with this? Do we have support from Passage B suggesting that "auxiliary premises are *usually NOT* needed?"

We do not have such evidence.

D. There is a logical asymmetry between positive and negative evidence

This is Popper's view, even though it's not author A's view, it still appears in Passage A, so I will allow it.

Does author B disagree with this? Does author B think there to be non-asymmetry or equality between positive and negative evidence?

We know that for the author of Passage B, both positive and negative evidence have their roles to play, but are these roles "equal?" We do not know.

E.   *Scientific research involves generating bold theories and attempting to refute them*

Passage B never talks about what scientific research involves.

***

Definition Questions

Definition Questions will ask us for the meaning of a keyword, as it is used in the passage. In Comparative Passages, the question will usually ask us to select an answer choice that also happens to be another word used in one of the passages. Our goal is to find the word that most resembles the word from the question stem in meaning.

These questions can be solved by thinking about the **dictionary definition** of the word, then the meaning of the word **in context**. Does the word's meaning change subtly when it's used in the passage, as compared to what it means in the real world?

Once we have thought about this, we can look at each one of the answer choices, and the context in which they appear in. I will ask myself which answer choice, as it is used in the passage, most closely resembles the word in question?

As a final step to test my preferred answer, I will **substitute** it back into the passage and replace the original word in question. When I'm reading the passage with the new word, does the meaning of the sentence/paragraph change in any way?

> **Definition Questions** (Chapter 12), as well as **Purpose Questions** (Chapter 7) and **Attitude Questions** (Chapter 11) to a lesser extent, can be especially difficult for students whose first language is not English, or students with a limited vocabulary. Because solving these questions do depend to a certain extent on our pre-existing understanding of the word's dictionary definition, guessing an unknown word's meaning purely based on context can lead to uncertainties. So if you are an ESL student, pay special attention to these three types of questions, and make a note of the unknown words that appear.

Passage A

Why do some trial courts judges oppose conducting independent research to help them make decisions? One of their objections is that it distorts the adversarial system by requiring an active judicial role and undermining the importance of evidence presented by the opposing parties. Another fear is that judges lack the wherewithal to conduct first rate research and may wind up using outlier or discredited scientific materials.

While these concerns have some merit, they do not justify an absolute prohibition of the practice. First, there are reasons to sacrifice adversarial values in the scientific evidence context. The adversarial system is particularly ill-suited to handling specialized knowledge. The two parties pre-screen and compensate expert witnesses, which virtually ensures conflicting and partisan testimony. At the same time, scientific facts are general truths not confined to the immediate cases. Because scientific admissibility decisions can exert considerable influence over future cases, erroneous decisions detract from the legitimacy of the system. Independent research could help judges avoid such errors.

Second, a trial provides a structure that guides any potential independent research, reducing the possibility of a judge's reaching outlandish results. Independent research supplements, rather than replaces, the parties' presentation of the evidence, so the parties always frame the debate.

Passage B

Regardless of what trial courts may do, appellate courts should resist the temptation to conduct their own independent research of scientific literature.

As a general rule, appellate courts do not hear live testimony. Thus these courts lack some of the critical tools available at the trial level for arriving at a determination of the facts: live testimony and cross-examination. Experts practicing in the field may have knowledge and experience beyond what is reflected in the available scientific literature. And adverse parties can test the credibility and reliability of proffered literature by subjecting the expert witness to the greatest legal engine ever invented for the discovery of truth – cross-examination. The trial judge may even participate in the process by questioning live witnesses. However, these events can only occur at the trial level.

Literature considered for the first time at the appellate level is not subject to live comment by practicing experts and cannot be tested in the crucible of the adversarial system. Thus one of the core criticisms against the use of such sources by appellate courts is that doing so usurps the trial court's fact-finding function. Internet sources, in particular, have come under criticism for their potential unreliability.

When an appellate court goes outside the record to determine case facts, it ignores its function as a court of review, and it substitutes its own questionable research results for evidence that should have been tested in the trial court. This criticism applies with full force to the use of outside-the-record texts and treatises, regardless of the medium in which they are found.

<u>PT81 S1 Q23</u>

Which one of the following phrases is used by the author of passage B to express a concern that is most closely related to the concern expressed by the author of passage A using the phrase "lack the wherewithal?"

    A.   Experience beyond what is reflected
    B.   May even participate in the process
    C.   Subject to live comment
    D.   Questionable research results
    E.   Outside the record texts

***

<u>PT81 S1 Q25</u>

Which one of the following words as used in passage B comes closest to having the same reference as the word "crucible" in the passage?

    A.   Temptation
    B.   Credibility
    C.   Engine
    D.   Function
    E.   Medium

Q23: I actually didn't know what "wherewithal" meant. (Checking the dictionary afterwards told me that it literally meant "means." So lacking the wherewithal just meant "lacking the means.")

Without knowing what the word meant, I went back to the location where the phrase appeared. In the first paragraph of Passage A, it said that *judges lacked the wherewithal to conduct first rate research.*"

If judges lacked something to conduct first rate research, then that something is probably going to be something like "ability," or "experience," or "expertise." Maybe they lacked the resources to conduct first rate research, but that is unlikely. Similarly, we probably won't get an answer that says the judges lacked the money, time, or patience to conduct research.

The answers for this question are actually all phrases from Passage B, so we now have to read each statement and think about their meaning in Passage B.

   A.   *Experience beyond what is reflected*

This is talking about experts who know more from experience than what's in the books.

This is the opposite to what Passage A thinks about judges. Judges lack something that would make their research first rate.

   B.   *May even participate in the process*

This is talking about judges questioning witnesses. Remember, we want an answer that tells us judges are doing bad research.

   C.   *Subject to live comment*

This is from the part of Passage B where we are told appellate court literature is not subject to live comment by experts. We are looking for something that describes the research conducted by judges.

   D.   *Questionable research results*

This is talking about courts that do their own research and come up with questionable results.

"Judges lacking the wherewithal" is talking about the same thing: judges don't have what it takes to come up with first rate results.

   E.   *Outside the record texts*

"Outside the record texts" are something that the author thinks should be limited, just like independent research should be. But since answer choice D also talks about the negative impression conveyed by the term "lack the wherewithal," D is a better answer.

D is the correct answer.

***

Q25: Again, some students might not know what a "crucible" is. This presents us with difficulties. A crucible is basically a melting pot used for the melting and purification of metals. It's often used to describe something that is difficult, but it made us stronger if we came out successful. (USMC Bootcamp would probably be considered as such.) But if we didn't know what it meant, we would only be able to infer that it meant something like "arena," or a place where the validity of testimony can be tested and examined.

What had the function of purifying or fortifying after many difficulties? The only thing that comes remotely close in Passage B is the use of cross-examination. It is an intense, arduous process used to arrive at the truth. Cross-examination, in Passage B, is also called the "greatest legal engine" ever invented.

The correct answer is C.

Ultimately, this was one of those questions where you will be severely disadvantaged if you didn't know what a "crucible" was. You may have made an educated guess based on context, and have realized that both the "crucible" and the "legal engine" were referring to the same thing, the adversarial, cross-examination system.

***

Attitude Questions

How we approach Attitude Questions in Comparative Passages is no different from the approach we learned in Chapter 11. The only difference is that now we have to consider the attitude of both authors.

So try to come up with a pre-phrased answer for author A's attitude, then do the same for author B, and finally think about how their attitudes differ or align.

Refer back to Chapter 11 for a step-by-step process to solving Attitude Questions.

Let's look at another question from PT81:

PT81 S1 Q27

The stances of the authors of passage A and passage B, respectively, toward independent research on the part of trial judges are most accurately described as?

A. Resigned acceptance and implicit disapproval
B. Cautious ambivalence and strict neutrality
C. Reasoned skepticism and veiled antipathy
D. Qualified approval and explicit noncommitment
E. Forceful advocacy and tentative opposition

We know from the passage that author A supports independent research on the part of trial judges. Author B is against research from *appellate judges* but didn't really say anything about trial judges ("regardless of what trial courts may do").

So let's look for an answer that says "support from A, and neutrality from B."

   A.   *Resigned* acceptance and implicit *disapproval*

Author A advocates for independent research, "resigned acceptance" would be like saying "it's fine, since there's nothing else we can do about it."

Author B doesn't really offer an opinion on how trial courts should act. I think "implicit disapproval" is an overstretch.

   B.   *Cautious ambivalence and strict neutrality*

Author A is not "cautiously ambivalent." They do commit explicitly to a position.

Passage B is a good match though.

   C.   *Reasoned skepticism and veiled antipathy*

Again, wrong for both. A is not skeptical; and B does not display antipathy.

   D.   *Qualified* approval and explicit noncommitment

This answer looks good, the only issue I have would be with the word "qualified." Because in my mind, A was pretty forthcoming in their advocation for independent research. But then again, I went back to the passage to look for a sense that A's approval was "qualified." (**reverse confirmation**)

Then I saw the first sentence of the second paragraph, which stated that "while these concerns have some merit, they do not justify an absolute prohibition of the practice."

Ok, so the approval was "qualified" after all, I have no further issues with this answer.

   E.   *Forceful* advocacy and tentative *opposition*

Now that I have a deeper understanding of the passage after studying answer choice D, I can tell that "forceful" is too strong. Similarly, B is more neutral than opposed.

The correct answer is D.

This question is interesting because it gives us a glimpse of something superstar test takers will do. They will engage with the answer choices and use them as a way to **continue to better understand the passage**.

My awareness of author A's attitude was not complete until I read answer choice D, at which point I went back to the passage for a deeper read. That improved understanding actually helped me eliminate E.

Just like with LR Questions, after the initial reading of the stimulus/passage, the process of solving each question is **never linear**. Don't be afraid to go back and forth between the text and the answer choices, and use this process to further guide our understanding of the passage itself.

Principle Questions

The Principle Questions we encounter in Comparative Passages will be slightly different from the Principle Questions we saw back in Chapter 12. Now, with two passages, most Principle Questions will ask us for *"a principle underlying both passages,"* or *"a principle with which both authors would agree."*

In my experience, for Comparative Passage based Principle Questions, the questions are less about locating a principle from the passage; but more about finding a principle based answer choice with which both authors would agree with. In other words, these Principle Questions are very similar to Inference Questions, with the only major difference being that the answer choices are worded as principles.

For these questions, I would focus on the answer choices and ask myself whether both authors would agree with each statement. Remember, like Inference Questions, the correct answer to these questions MUST have support from the passage. We want to locate support from both Passages A and B to support the correct answer choice. Answer choices where we cannot locate support will usually be wrong. Do not select an answer simply because it "sounds reasonable."

Another type of Principle Questions will occur in passages where the authors do not agree with each other. The question will ask us *"what is a principle behind/underlying Passage A, but one with which Passage B would not agree with?"*

It takes two steps to solve such questions. In the first step, we make sure that the principle described in the answer is in fact a principle underlying Passage A. (We can do this by doing a quick scan of Passage A while conducting **Principle Extraction**, as seen in Chapter 12 and also in LR Perfection.) In the second step, we confirm whether the principle is in fact something Passage B would disagree with. If you think it is, then it's essential that you are able to point to the exact textual support you are basing your views on. Again, evidence is needed.

We'll look at such a question now:

Passage A

Music does not always gain by association with words. Like images, words can excite the deepest emotions but are inadequate to express the emotions they excite. Music is more adequate, and hence will often seize an emotion that may have been excited by images or words, deepen its expression, and, by so doing, excite still deeper emotion. That is how words can gain by being set to music.

But to set words to music-as in opera or song--is in fact to mix two arts together. A striking effect may be produced, but at the expense of the purity of each art. Poetry is a great art; so is music. But as a medium for emotion, each is greater alone than in company, although various good ends arise from linking the two, providing that the words are subordinated to the more expressive medium of music. What good could any words do for Beethoven's Fifth Symphony? So too an opera is largely independent of words, and depends for its aesthetic value not upon the poetry of the libretto (the words of the opera), or even the plot or scenery, but upon its emotional range-a region dominated by the musical element.

Passage B

Throughout the history of opera, two fundamental types may be distinguished: that in which the music is primary, and that in which there is, essentially, parity between music and other factors. The former, sometimes called "singer's opera"-a term which has earned undeserved contempt-is exemplified by most Italian operas, while the latter, exemplified by the operas of German composer Richard Wagner, depend for their effect on a balance among many factors of which music is only one, albeit the most important. Theoretically, it would seem that there should be a third kind of opera, in which the music is subordinated to the other features. While the earliest operas were of this kind, their appeal was limited, and a fuller participation of music was required to establish opera on a secure basis.

In any event, in any aesthetic judgment of opera, regardless of the opera's type, neither the music nor the poetry of the libretto should be judged in isolation. The music is good not if it would make a good concert piece but if it serves the particular situation in the opera in which it occurs, contributing something not supplied by other elements. Similarly, the poetry is good not because it reads well by itself but primarily if, while embodying a sound dramatic idea, it furnishes opportunity for effective musical and scenic treatment. True, the elements of music and poetry may be considered separately, but only for purposes of analyzing their formal features. In actuality these elements are as united as hydrogen and oxygen are united in water. It is this union-further enriched and clarified by the visual action-that results in opera's inimitable character.

PT85 S1 Q19

Which one of the following is a principle that is implicit in the argument made by the author of passage B but that would most likely be rejected by the author of passage A?

- A. An opera's non-musical elements are essential to the opera's aesthetic value.
- B. Even in operas where there is relative parity among the various elements, the music is the most important element.
- C. An opera cannot be artistically successful unless it skillfully balances many factors.
- D. In order for an opera to be artistically successful, the music should not be subordinated to other features of the opera.
- E. An opera's libretto has formal features that can be analyzed independently of the opera's music.

The question stem gives us a lot to work with. Recall what we learned about **question stem analysis** back in Chapter 14. So there's three takeaways from just the question alone that I can deduce.

First, the correct answer will contain an *implicit* principle that underlies the argument of Passage B. An implicit principle will not be *explicitly* stated, so we won't find word-for-word support for it in Passage B, but it will be something that we can read and say, "yes, the author of Passage B definitely agrees with this."

Second, it has to be a view that the author of Passage A would reject. This implicit principle would run contrary to the views and positions of the author of Passage A.

Lastly, the question said it is something that would *"most likely"* be rejected by the author of Passage A, so maybe a degree of inference is needed. Maybe the author of Passage A will not explicitly deny the truth of the correct answer, but we can deduce their opposition from the rest of the passage.

What are some implicit principles underlying Passage B?

The author of Passage B considers music to be an important part of an opera. (Three types of operas, only those where music is important have survived.)

Second, neither music nor words should be judged in isolation in any aesthetic judgment of opera.

Lastly, music and words can be considered in isolation. But they are inseparable and contribute together to the opera in reality.

With which one of these would the author of Passage A most likely disagree?

We know that the author of Passage A also firmly believes that music to be the most important element of an opera. It's superior to words. So they would not disagree with Passage B's first principle.

Passage A declares that music and words should be considered in isolation; and thinking about them together lessens each. Each is greater alone than in company.

Finally, Passage A says that an opera is really only dependent on its music. Words or plot are not that important.

Thus, it appears that the correct answer will either talk about author B's view that "music and words are inseparable," or that "music and words together add to the value of an opera."

    A.   *An opera's non-musical elements are essential to the opera's aesthetic value.*

Is this an implicit principle in Passage B's argument? *"Non-musical elements"* can refer to words, so yes, it is one of author B's beliefs. They think that words and music are inseparable and should not be considered in isolation when judging an opera's aesthetic value.

Is this something author A would disagree with?

Yes, author A says it's better to look at words and music separately, and only music matters for an opera. (Words and plot don't matter.)

    B.   *Even in operas where there is relative parity among the various elements, the music is the most important element.*

Both would agree with this. Author B says that for this type of opera (Wagner's) music is only one, albeit the most important factor.

The author of Passage A, on the other hand, believes music is the most important element, period.

    C.   *An opera cannot be artistically successful unless it skillfully balances many factors.*

B would disagree with this. An opera that balances many factors is exemplified by Wagner's operas. But we know directly from the passage that Italian operas do not have this quality. The author of Passage B never says that Italian operas are not artistically successful.

    D.   *In order for an opera to be artistically successful, the music <u>should not be subordinated</u> to other features of the opera.*

Passage B probably agrees with this. Passage B talks about a third type of opera where music is subordinate, and these failed.

But Passage A would not disagree with this. Both authors could conceivably agree with this.

    E.   *An opera's libretto has formal features that <u>can</u> be analyzed independently of the opera's music.*

Passage B says that we may consider words and music in isolation (this is not ideal), so Passage B probably agrees with this.

But Passage A agrees too! The author of Passage A thinks words and music are better off being separate.

The correct answer is A.

***

Analogy Questions

Analogy Questions in Comparative Passages will usually test us on our understanding of the relationship between the two passages or two ideas presented in the passages. The most typical Analogy Question will give us several pairings, and ask us which one of them is the most analogous to the relationship between Passage A and Passage B.

For these questions, the first step is to go back to the two passages and think about how they are similar and different. These are questions that we struggled with back in Chapter 18, when we considered how two passages can differ from each other on Purpose, Scope, and Main Point. Think about these similarities and differences, list them out if you need to, and then look at the answer choices.

Think back on the passages from PT81. Passage A was advocating the use of independent research in trial courts; while Passage B argued against its use in appellate court. So the Purpose/Main Point of these two passages are diametrically opposed. However, their scope is also not completely overlapping. Both are talking about judges, but one is talking about trial court judges, and the other is talking about appellate court judges.

***

Take a look at the following question, and if you have trouble, review Chapter 13: Unrestricted Scope Questions, with a special emphasis towards the section on Analogies and Examples.

Passage A

Why do some trial courts judges oppose conducting independent research to help them make decisions? One of their objections is that it distorts the adversarial system by requiring an active judicial role and undermining the importance of evidence presented by the opposing parties. Another fear is that judges lack the wherewithal to conduct first rate research and may wind up using outlier or discredited scientific materials.

While these concerns have some merit, they do not justify an absolute prohibition of the practice. First, there are reasons to sacrifice adversarial values in the scientific evidence context. The adversarial system is particularly ill-suited to handling specialized knowledge. The two parties pre-screen and compensate expert witnesses, which virtually ensures conflicting and partisan testimony. At the same time, scientific facts are general truths not confined to the immediate cases. Because scientific admissibility decisions can exert considerable influence over future cases, erroneous decisions detract from the legitimacy of the system. Independent research could help judges avoid such errors.

Second, a trial provides a structure that guides any potential independent research, reducing the possibility of a judge's reaching outlandish results. Independent research supplements, rather than replaces, the parties' presentation of the evidence, so the parties always frame the debate.

Passage B

Regardless of what trial courts may do, appellate courts should resist the temptation to conduct their own independent research of scientific literature.

As a general rule, appellate courts do not hear live testimony. Thus these courts lack some of the critical tools available at the trial level for arriving at a determination of the facts: live testimony and cross-examination. Experts practicing in the field may have knowledge and experience beyond what is reflected in the available scientific literature. And adverse parties can test the credibility and reliability of proffered literature by subjecting the expert witness to the greatest legal engine ever invented for the discovery of truth – cross-examination. The trial judge may even participate in the process by questioning live witnesses. However, these events can only occur at the trial level.

Literature considered for the first time at the appellate level is not subject to live comment by practicing experts and cannot be tested in the crucible of the adversarial system. Thus one of the core criticisms against the use of such sources by appellate courts is that doing so usurps the trial court's fact-finding function. Internet sources, in particular, have come under criticism for their potential unreliability.

When an appellate court goes outside the record to determine case facts, it ignores its function as a court of review, and it substitutes its own questionable research results for evidence that should have been tested in the trial court. This criticism applies with full force to the use of outside-the-record texts and treatises, regardless of the medium in which they are found.

PT81 S1 Q26

It can be inferred, based on their titles, that the relationship between which one of the following pairs of documents is most analogous to the relationship between passage A and B, respectively?

A. "Negative Effects of Salt Consumption" and "Unhealthy Amounts of Salt in the Diet"
B. "Salt can be beneficial for some people" and "People with high blood pressure should avoid salt"
C. "Debunking the alleged danger posed by salt" and "Inconclusive research results on the health effects of salt consumption"
D. "Substitutes for dietary salt" and "Salt substitutes come under fire"
E. "The health effects of salt consumption" and "Salt deficiency in a sample population"

Without knowing anything about the answer choices, we can surmise that the correct answer will have two qualities. One, the first word/phrase will be advocating something, while the second word/phrase will be against something.

Secondly, while both may be talking about the same general topic, the exact issue will not be the same. Just like in our original passages, where one passage was about trial courts and the other passage about appellate courts; I suspect that the scope of the word pairings in the correct answer will be slightly different too.

Let's take a look at the answer choices:

A.   "Negative Effects of Salt Consumption" and "Unhealthy Amounts of Salt in the Diet"

Both of these phrases are talking about how bad salt is. Remember, we are looking for two phrases where one thinks salt is good, and the other one thinks its bad.

B.   "Salt can be beneficial for some people" and "People with high blood pressure should avoid salt"

This one matches our initial anticipation. One says salt is good, the other says salt is bad/should be avoided. There is a slight variance in scope as well. One is talking about "some people," the other talks about "people with high blood pressure."

Everything looks good, let's look at the other answers.

C.   "Debunking the alleged danger posed by salt" and "Inconclusive research results on the health effects of salt consumption"

The first one looks ok, "debunking the danger" means it's not dangerous, just like independent research by trial judges is fine.

The second one is more problematic, here salt consumption is said to have "inconclusive research results." But in Passage B, the author is adamantly against research at the appellate court level.

D.   "Substitutes for dietary salt" and "Salt substitutes come under fire"

The first one is too neutral, if it had said "substitutes for dietary salt are great," then it would have been better.

E.   "The health effects of salt consumption" and "Salt deficiency in a sample population"

Again, both topics are neutral. We want something that better expresses the authors' attitudes.

B is the correct answer.

Passage A

Karl Popper's main contribution to the philosophy of science concerns the power of negative evidence. The fundamental point is simple: No number of white swans, for example, can ever prove that all swans are white, but a single black swan disproves the hypothesis. Popper gives this logical asymmetry between positive and negative evidence hyperbolic application, maintaining that positive evidence has no value as evidence and that negative evidence is tantamount to disproof. Moreover, Popper takes the search for negative evidence to be at the heart of scientific research; that is, for Popper, scientific research involves not only generating bold theories, but also searching for evidence that would disprove them. Indeed, for him, a theory counts as scientific only if it makes predictions that are testable in this way.

However, Popper's use of the logical asymmetry does not adequately capture the actual situation scientists face. If a theory deductively entails a false prediction, then the theory must be false as well. But a scientific theory rarely entails predictions on its own. When scientists actually derive a theory's predictions, they almost always need diverse additional "auxiliary" premises, which appeal to other theories, to the correct functioning of instrumentation, to the absence of disturbing forces, etc. When a prediction fails, logic indicates that at least one of the premises must be false, but it does not indicate which one. When an experiment does not work out as predicted, there is usually more than one possible explanation. Positive evidence is never conclusive. But negative evidence rarely is either.

Passage B

When the planet Uranus was discovered, astronomers attempted to predict its orbit. They based their predictions on Newton's laws and auxiliary assumptions about the mass of the sun and the masses, orbits, and velocities of other planets. One of the auxiliary assumptions was that no planets existed in the vicinity of Uranus. When the astronomers made their observations, they found that the orbit they had predicted for Uranus was incorrect. One possible explanation for the failure of their prediction was that Newton's laws were incorrect. Another was that there was an error in the auxiliary assumptions. The astronomers changed their assumptions about the existence of other planets, concluding that there must be another planet close enough to Uranus to produce the observed orbit. Not long afterward, scientists discovered the planet Neptune in the precise place it would have to be to bring their calculations into alignment with their observations.

Later astronomers, again using Newton's laws, predicted the orbit of Mercury. Once again, the predictions were not borne out. They hypothesized the existence of another planet in the vicinity, which they called Vulcan. However, Vulcan was never found, and some scientists began to think that perhaps Newton's laws were in error. Finally, when Einstein's general theory of relativity was introduced, astronomers discovered that calculations based on that theory and the old auxiliary assumptions predicted the observed orbit of Mercury, leading to the rejection of Newton's theory of gravity and to increased confidence in Einstein's theory.

PT76 S1 Q25

In passage B's description of the developments leading to the rejection of Newton's theory of gravity, which one of the following astronomical bodies plays a role most analogous to the black swan discussed in passage A?

A. Mercury
B. Uranus
C. Neptune
D. Venus
E. The Sun

We are looking for something analogous to the "black swan" discussed in Passage A.

"Black swans" are mentioned as examples of negative evidence in Passage A. According to Popper, no matter how many white swans you see, you cannot confirm the theory that "all swans are white." But if you saw just one black swan, the theory "all swans are white" has been overturned.

Popper thinks negative evidence is tantamount to disproof. The author doesn't agree, the author of Passage A thinks negative evidence is rarely conclusive.

What constitutes as negative evidence in Passage B? Newton's theory of gravity failed to predict both Uranus and Mercury's orbit. So both Uranus and Mercury could constitute negative evidence, or the so called "black swan."

However, the question is asking us for the "black swan" that led to the rejection of Newtonian physics. We know that it was during the search for Vulcan and the prediction of Mercury's orbit that Newton was rejected. So the correct answer would be Mercury.

The correct answer is A.

Many students selected B or C. But both Uranus and Neptune were from an earlier study where Newtonian physics wasn't rejected. So both these answers are out of scope. Furthermore, even though Uranus can be considered a black swan, Neptune is the auxiliary assumption that explained why Newton's theory didn't work. None of these led to the overturning of Newton's theory of gravity.

Misc. Questions

The following question types have also appeared occasionally in Comparative Reading Passages. We will study them briefly as well as look at an example for each.

Strengthen/Weaken Questions

Strengthen/Weaken Questions in Comparative Passages have appeared infrequently. But when they have appeared, they have been a source of consternation for many students. The typical question will ask you to locate a statement from one passage, and use it to strengthen/weaken a position in another passage. So compared to the regular Strengthen/Weaken Questions (Chapter 13), the extra steps involved end up throwing some of us off balance.

With Strengthen/Weaken Questions, it's important to follow a step-by-step process. It's crucial to know **exactly the position that we are trying to help/attack**. So start by locating this position. If it's a Strengthen Question, ask yourself what would make this position more believable. If it's a Weaken Question, ask yourself what would make this position more unlikely.

Let's look at one more question from PT76:

PT76 S1 Q24

The author of passage A would be most likely to take which one of the following results mentioned in passage B as support for the claim made in the last sentence of passage A?

A. The discovery of Uranus
B. The initial failure of Newton's laws to correctly predict Uranus' orbit
C. The ultimate failure of Newton's laws to correctly predict Mercury's orbit
D. The failure to find Vulcan
E. The success of Einstein's general theory of relativity at predicting Mercury's orbit

We are trying to strengthen the claim made in the last sentence of passage A, which says that "*negative evidence rarely is [conclusive] either.*"

In other words, we are trying to find evidence that tells us negative evidence is not enough to disprove a theory by itself.

Think back on Passage B, there were two appearances of negative evidence. In the first case, failure to predict Uranus' orbit was not enough to disprove Newtonian physics. In the second case, failure to predict Mercury's orbit was. Since we are looking for an instance where negative evidence *couldn't* disprove a theory, then the correct answer will discuss the failure to predict Uranus' orbit.

The correct answer is B.

Method and Role Questions

We haven't seen these questions yet, but students who have read LR Perfection will no doubt be familiar with them. For Method Questions, we are trying to find the best description of how the author/authors advance their argument. For these questions, we should pay special attention to the wording of the answer choices. We need to first **extract** the keywords from potential answer choices and come to an understanding of what these answers are describing. We then use the **reverse confirmation** technique to try to match these answers up with the actual passages themselves.

For additional practice please take a look at Chapters 4 and 6 of LR Perfection.

PT63 S4 Q27

Passage A

Central to the historian's profession and scholarship has been the ideal of objectivity. The assumptions upon which this ideal rests include a commitment to the reality of the past, a sharp separation between fact and value, and above all, a distinction between history and fiction.

According to this ideal, historical facts are prior to and independent of interpretation: the value of an interpretation should be judged by how well it accounts for the facts; if an interpretation is contradicted by facts, it should be abandoned. The fact that successive generations of historians have ascribed different meanings to past events does not mean, as relativist historians claim, that the events themselves lack fixed or absolute meanings.

Objective historians see their role as that of a neutral judge, one who must never become an advocate or, worse, propagandist. Their conclusions should display the judicial qualities of balance and even-handedness. As with the judiciary, these qualities require insulation from political considerations, and avoidance of partisanship or bias. Thus objective historians must purge themselves of external loyalties; their primary allegiance is to objective historical truth and to colleagues who share a commitment to its discovery.

Passage B

The very possibility of historical scholarship as an enterprise distinct from propaganda requires of its practitioners that self-discipline that enables them to do such things as abandon wishful thinking, assimilate bad news, and discard pleasing interpretations that fail elementary tests of evidence and logic. Yet objectivity, for the historian, should not be confused with neutrality. Objectivity is perfectly compatible with strong political commitment. The objective thinker does not value detachment as an end in itself but only as an indispensable means of achieving deeper understanding. In historical scholarship, the ideal of objectivity is most compellingly embodied in the powerful argument—one that reveals by its every twist and turn its respectful appreciation of the alternative arguments it rejects. Such a text attains power precisely because its author has managed to suspend momentarily his or her own perceptions so as to anticipate and take into account objections and alternative constructions—not those of straw men, but those that truly issue from the rival's position, understood as sensitively and stated as eloquently as the rival could desire. To mount a telling attack on a position, one must first inhabit it. Those so habituated to their customary intellectual abode that they cannot even explore others can never be persuasive to anyone but fellow habitués. Such arguments are often more faithful to the complexity of historical interpretation—more faithful even to the irreducible plurality of human perspectives— than texts that abjure position-taking altogether. The powerful argument is the highest fruit of the kind of thinking I would call objective, and in it neutrality plays no part. Authentic objectivity bears no resemblance to the television newscaster's mechanical gesture of allocating the same number of seconds to both sides of a question, editorially splitting the difference between them, irrespective of their perceived merits.

The argument described in passage A and the argument made by the author of passage B are both advanced by

   A. Citing historical scholarship that fails to achieve objectivity.
   B. Showing how certain recent developments in historical scholarship have undermined the credibility of the profession.
   C. Summarizing opposing arguments in order to point out their flaws.
   D. Suggesting that historians should adopt standards used by professionals in certain other fields.
   E. Identifying what are seen as obstacles to achieving objectivity.

Passage A	Passage B
The ideal of objectivity (there being a single version of the truth) is essential to historians. Interpretations are secondary to the facts. Even though there are different interpretations of the same facts, the facts themselves do not change in meaning. Objective historians are like neutral judges, they must not take sides. They must avoid biases and loyalties to other causes.	History is not propaganda, and historians must strive to maintain objectivity. (*Here the author is echoing Passage A.*) But objectivity is NOT the same as neutrality. (*Here the two authors depart from each other's views.*) You can have political commitment and be objective at the same time. Objectivity is instead embodied in the "powerful argument." The powerful argument is a forceful rebuttal of one's opponent precisely because one inhabits the opponent's positions. (*You have to walk a mile in someone else's shoes in order to truly understand their position, by occupying their position, you are not being neutral.*) You can be objective yet still take a position.

Both passages believe that the historian must be objective. However, this is where their similarities end. Passage A believes that in order to be objective, you have to be neutral, you cannot take sides. Passage B believes that to be objective, you can take sides. You don't have to be neutral. As long as you truly consider the opponent's argument, truly understand their position, and do it full justice in your rebuttals instead of oversimplifying it, then you are being objective.

***

The argument described in passage A and the argument made by the author of passage B are both advanced by

I found this question hard to pre-phrase. Passage A is basically telling us what objectivism entails. (Historians should be neutral judges.) Passage B is saying the opposite. (Historians should be objective, but they don't have to be neutral.) I really can't think of any similarities in their method of reasoning off the top of my head.

This means going into the answer choices and performing **keyword extraction** (Chapter 15) and **reverse confirmation** (Chapter 17) as we try to eliminate the answer choices.

    A.   *Citing historical scholarship that fails to achieve objectivity*

"Citing historical scholarship" means quoting or referring to historians. For instance, the author could have mentioned Edward Gibbon's "Decline and Fall of the Roman Empire," or Tacitus, or Livy's works; or works by WWII historians such as A.J.P Taylor or Shirer…the list goes on and on.

The point is, neither passage cite historical scholarship.

    B.   *Showing how certain recent developments in historical scholarship have undermined the credibility of the profession*

This means that something that happened in the last little while has made people skeptical of historians. This doesn't happen either.

C. *Summarizing opposing arguments in order to point out their flaws*

I think Passage B does this, to an extent. Passage B does say that "you can be objective without being neutral." Passage B also attacks the neutral historian as akin to the superficial newscaster.

Passage A doesn't mention anything about opposing arguments, which is Passage B's position.

D. *Suggesting that historians should adopt standards used by professionals in certain other fields*

Perhaps Passage A's comparison of historian objectivity to judicial neutrality could be an instance of this? But I'm not sure whether that amounts to adopting the standards used by judges. (Is "be more like neutral judges" the equivalent of "adopting judicial standards?")

Passage B does not mention this.

E. *Identifying what are seen as obstacles to achieving objectivity*

Do the authors do this? I think so. In the last paragraph of Passage A, the author says that "*insulation from political considerations, and avoidance of partisanship or bias* [are required.]" Furthermore, the objective historian must "*purge themselves of external loyalties*" – these are all obstacles to achieving objectivity.

In the very first paragraph of Passage B, the author declares that the objective historian must "*abandon wishful thinking, assimilate bad news, and discard pleasing interpretations that fail elementary tests of evidence and logic.*"

So Answer Choice E is the only answer that matches up with the content of the passages. While typically, for Method Questions, we would like an answer choice that *actually* describes how the author advances their argument, such as by eliminating alternatives or by appealing to an expert. But an answer choice that only describes something that happens in the passage is fine too. (See LR Perfection Chapter 4 Difficult Trait #4 for more information.)

The correct answer is E.

PT52 S4 Q11

Passage A

Readers, like writers, need to search for answers. Part of the joy of reading is in being surprised, but academic historians leave little to the imagination. The perniciousness of the historiographic approach became fully evident to me when I started teaching. Historians require undergraduates to read scholarly monographs that sap the vitality of history; they visit on students what was visited on them in graduate school. They assign books with formulaic arguments that transform history into an abstract debate that would have been unfathomable to those who lived in the past. Aimed so squarely at the head, such books cannot stimulate students who yearn to connect to history emotionally as well as intellectually.

In an effort to address this problem, some historians have begun to rediscover stories. It has even become something of a fad within the profession. This year, the American Historical Association chose as the theme for its annual conference some putative connection to storytelling: "Practices of Historical Narrative." Predictably, historians responded by adding the word "narrative" to their titles and presenting papers at sessions on "Oral History and the Narrative of Class Identity," and "Meaning and Time: The Problem of Historical Narrative." But it was still historiography. intended only for other academics. At meetings of historians, we still encounter very few historians telling stories or moving audiences to smiles, chills, or tears.

Passage B

Writing is at the heart of the lawyer's craft, and so, like it or not, we who teach the law inevitably teach aspiring lawyers how lawyers write. We do this in a few stand-alone courses and, to a greater extent, through the constraints that we impose on their writing throughout the curriculum. Legal writing, because of the purposes it serves, is necessarily ruled by linear logic, creating a path without diversions, surprises, or reversals. Conformity is a virtue, creativity suspect, humor forbidden, and voice mute.

Lawyers write as they see other lawyers write, and, influenced by education, profession, economic constraints, and perceived self-interest, they too often write badly. Perhaps the currently fashionable call for attention to narrative in legal education could have an effect on this. It is not yet exactly clear what role narrative should play in the law, but it is nonetheless true that every case has at its heart a story—of real events and people, of concerns, misfortunes, conflicts, feelings. But because legal analysis strips the human narrative content from the abstract, canonical legal form of the case, law students learn to act as if there is no such story.

It may well turn out that some of the terminology and public rhetoric of this potentially subversive movement toward attention to narrative will find its way into the law curriculum, but without producing corresponding changes in how legal writing is actually taught or in how our future colleagues will write. Still, even mere awareness of the value of narrative could perhaps serve as an important corrective.

The phrase "scholarly monographs that sap the vitality of history" in passage A plays a role in that passage's overall argument that is most analogous to the role played in passage B by which one of the following phrases?

    A. "Writing is at the heart of the lawyer's craft"
    B. "Conformity is a virtue, creativity suspect, humor forbidden, and voice mute"
    C. "Lawyers write as they see other lawyers write"
    D. "Every case has at its heart a story"
    E. "Still, even mere awareness of the value of narrative could perhaps serve as an important corrective"

Passage A	Passage B
The author is very critical of academic historians. Their writing is boring, abstract and does not engage the student. There's been an attempt to incorporate stories in the study and writing of history. But most historians are only paying lip service to this, and still resort to boring and abstract prose.	Legal writing is very logical, strict, and emotionless. Lawyers learn to write this way, and this is bad writing. (*Both authors consider voiceless and logical writing negatively.*) *So there is also a move to incorporate narrative into legal writing, similar to the move to incorporate more stories into the study of history mentioned in Passage A.* The author seems optimistic about the effect stories can have on legal writing. The author also acknowledges that perhaps no real changes will occur. (*Just like how the author of Passage A is saying that most historians just pay lip service to the idea of stories.*) But the author still says that it's worth a shot.

The scope of these two passages is not perfectly aligned. Passage A talks about writing history; while Passage B talks about legal writing. In both passages, the authors believe the current state of the writing to be dry, abstract, overly logical, and tedious. Both authors saw the incorporation of stories/narration into their respective fields as an attempt to remedy this. Both authors think that the effects have been limited, and author B seems to be a tad more hopeful about the positive effects of narration on the legal field.

***

The phrase "scholarly monographs that sap the vitality of history" in passage A plays a role in that passage's overall argument that is most analogous to the role played in passage B by which one of the following phrases?

This was mentioned in the first paragraph of Passage A. It's an example of the boring, abstract writing that should be addressed/fixed in the study of history.

So the correct answer will mention a kind of boring, abstract *legal* writing mentioned in Passage B, the kind that the author believes should be remedied/redressed.

    A.   *"Writing is at the heart of the lawyer's craft"*

This emphasizes the importance of writing for lawyers. We are looking for something that describes a negative aspect of legal writing.

    B.   *"Conformity is a virtue, creativity suspect, humor forbidden, and voice mute"*

This describes what is wrong with legal writing, what needs to be remedied. It has the same role/function as the statement from the question stem.

    C.   *"Lawyers write as they see other lawyers write"*

This can potentially also be pointing to a negative trait of legal writing, but it is much less direct than answer choice B.

In addition, the statement from the question stem is a description of the qualities of a piece of writing. So our ideal answer should also fulfill a similar function. It should be describing a specific piece or pieces of legal writing.

    D.   *"Every case has at its heart a story"*

This is emphasizing the importance of narration to legal writing. It is not what we are looking for. We are looking for a statement that tells us how bad legal writing currently is.

    E.   *"Still, even mere awareness of the value of narrative could perhaps serve as an important corrective"*

Similarly, this is talking about why narratives can be a valuable addition to legal writing.

The correct answer is B.

***

Title and Audience Questions

Finally, we come to Title and Audience Questions. These questions have only appeared two or three times in the history of Comparative Passages. Still, since we are striving to write a complete guide to RC, we shouldn't miss them.

For Title Questions, we are asked to pick a most suitable title for the passages we've just read. I will use my pre-phrased **Main Point** of the passage as a guide, going through the answer choices, **eliminating** answers that are either out of scope, contradictory to the author's views, or do not accurately reflect the author's attitude. This is usually enough to derive the correct answer. Let me expand upon what to look for during the process of elimination:

Out of scope: if the prospective title is describing something that did not get mentioned in the passage, that's automatic grounds for dismissal.

Contradictory to the author's views: this can be explicit or implicit. If the author is advocating for the adoption of electric vehicles, the title of the passage will reflect that. The title of the passage will not be called "EVs, the hidden danger" or something like that. Sure, perhaps the author did offer up a concession and talked about some of the hidden dangers of EVs, but the title of the passage should reflect the Main Point. So if you see an answer choice like that, it can be quickly dismissed.

Does not accurately reflect the author's attitude: this is more about the strength of the language used in the answer choice. If the author is fairly neutral throughout the passage, the topic will not be a wholehearted endorsement of whatever position that was described. Be aware of the author's attitude and specific positions.

***

For Audience Questions, we are asked who the intended audience of a passage/passages are. Look for details scattered in the passage that may give us a hint as to the **occupation** of the author. Is the author an academic or something else?

Second, think about the Author's Purpose in writing. Use CEER from Chapter 1 if you need to. Is the author making a recommendation or evaluation? If so, who is it being made to? Is the author explaining something? Who is it being explained to?

Lastly, think about the **language** used in the passage. Is the language/diction vernacular? Is it full of laypersons' terms or colloquial English? Or does the language appear polished and professional sounding?

***

Passage A

Millions of people worldwide play multiplayer online games. They each pick, say, a medieval character to play, such as a warrior. Then they might band together in quests to slay magical beasts; their avatars appear as tiny characters striding across a Tolkienesque land.

The economist Edward Castronova noticed something curious about the game he played: it had its own economy, a bustling trade in virtual goods. Players generate goods as they play, often by killing creatures for their treasure and trading it. The longer they play, the wealthier they get.

Things got even more interesting when Castronova learned about the "player auctions." Players would sometimes tire of the game and decide to sell off their virtual possessions at online auction sites.

As Castronova stared at the auction listings, he recognized with a shock what he was looking at. It was a form of currency trading! Each item had a value in the virtual currency traded in the game; when it was sold on the auction site, someone was paying cold hard cash for it. That meant that the virtual currency was worth something in real currency. Moreover, since players were killing monsters or skinning animals to sell their pelts, they were, in effect, creating wealth.

Passage B

Most multiplayer online games prohibit real-world trade in virtual items, but some actually encourage it, for example, by granting participants intellectual property rights in their creations.

Although it seems intuitively the case that someone who accepts real money for the transfer of a virtual item should be taxed, what about the player who only accumulates items or virtual currency within a virtual world? Is "loot" acquired in a game taxable, as a prize or award is? And is the profit in a purely in-game trade or sale for virtual currency taxable? These are important questions, given the tax revenues at stake, and there is pressure on governments to answer them, given that the economies of some virtual worlds are comparable to those of small countries.

Most people's intuition probably would be that accumulation of assets within a game should not be taxed even though income tax applies even to noncash accessions to wealth This article will argue that income tax law and policy support that result. Loot acquisitions in game worlds should not be treated as taxable prizes and awards, but rather should be treated like other property that requires effort to obtain, such as fish pulled from the ocean, which is taxed only upon sale. Moreover, in-game trades of virtual items should not be treated as taxable barter.

By contrast, tax doctrine and policy counsel taxation of the sale of virtual items for real currency, and, in games that are intentionally commodified, even of in-world sales for virtual currency, regardless of whether the participant cashes out. This approach would leave entertainment value untaxed without creating a tax shelter for virtual commerce.

PT71 S4 Q7

Which one of the following pairs of titles would be most appropriate for passage A and B, respectively?

- A. "The Economic Theories of Edward Castronova" and "Intellectual Property Rights in Virtual Worlds"
- B. "An Economist Discovers New Economic Territory" and "Taxing Virtual Property"
- C. "The Surprising Growth of Multiplayer Online Games" and "Virtual Reality and the Law"
- D. "How to Make Money Playing Games" and "Closing Virtual Tax Shelters"
- E. "A New Economic Paradigm" and "An Untapped Source of Revenue"

***

PT71 S4 Q11

The passages were most likely taken from which one of the following pairs of sources?

- A. Passage A: a magazine article addressed to a general audience; Passage B: a law journal article
- B. Passage A: a technical journal for economists; Passage B: a magazine article addressed to a general audience
- C. Passage A: a science-fiction novel; Passage B: a technical journal for economists
- D. Passage A: a law journal article; Passage B: a speech delivered before a legislative body
- E. Passage A: a speech delivered before a legislative body; Passage B: a science-fiction novel

Passage A

MMORPGs (think World of Warcraft) are described. An economist realizes that these games have their own economy.

Castronova realizes that when players sell weapons and skins from within the game on websites for cash, it's a form of currency trading (trading virtual currency for real legal tender currency).

Another observation is made that players are creating wealth in video games. They can farm for items and then sell them for real money.

Passage B

Most games prohibit trading of game items in real life, but some encourage it.

So if you sell an item in a game for USD, you should be taxed. But what if you never cash out? What if you become wealthy in the game itself by accumulating gold or items?

If you sell armor for gold within a game, should you be taxed? These are all important questions.

(*Passage B makes a distinction between players who cash out and players who don't cash out. While Passage A really only talks about the former.*)

Most people and the author believe that as long as you don't cash out for real world money, you shouldn't be taxed.

But if you do decide to cash out, or in games that are intentionally commodified, even if you don't cash out, you should still be taxed for earning gold or items.

Both passages are talking about the economics of multiplayer online games. Passage A talks about the discoveries of an economist, who considers it currency trading when players sell items/gold for dollars. Passage B makes an additional distinction between those who sell items for dollars, and those who keep their wealth in the game. Those who cash out should be taxed, according to author B, but not those who keep their wealth in game, no matter how much items or gold they accumulate.

Which one of the following pairs of titles would be most appropriate for passage A and B, respectively?

  A.   "The Economic <u>Theories</u> of Edward Castronova" and "<u>Intellectual Property</u> Rights in Virtual Worlds"

Both titles are out of scope. We are never told what the theories are, only that EC considers the sale of game items to be a form of currency trading. Similarly, the second passage is about taxation, not IP.

  B.   "An Economist Discovers New Economic Territory" and "Taxing Virtual Property"

This works, Castronova discovers an interesting phenomenon, and the second passage is about taxation.

  C.   "The <u>Surprising</u> <u>Growth</u> of Multiplayer Online Games" and "<u>Virtual Reality</u> and the Law"

We know that millions play MMORPGs, but the passage is not about why this is surprising; similarly, VR and the law is out of scope.

  D.   "<u>How to Make Money</u> Playing Games" and "<u>Closing</u> Virtual Tax Shelters"

Sure, Passage A talks about trading items for real money; but Passage A is not an instruction manual teaching you how to make money. Passage B argues that in-game transactions shouldn't be taxed, only out-game transactions. So the second part of this answer is not entirely accurate either.

E.   *"A New Economic <u>Paradigm</u>" and "An Untapped Source of Revenue"*

Maybe it's a new paradigm, but the term "phenomenon" would probably be more appropriate. I will let this slide. But the second part is contradictory to Passage B, just like Answer D.

The correct answer is B.

***

Q11 is asking us about the source from which both passages are drawn. These questions can be difficult because we don't have much information to go off on. Sometimes the author will give us a hint about their professions in the passage, so if we know that the author is a professor, then we can venture to guess that the source is an academic journal. Sometimes we can guess who the intended audience is, in that case we can also try to guess the source of the passages.

Unfortunately, it doesn't seem like we can deduce any of that in these passages. But it does seem that the second passage was harder to read than the first passage. The language of the second passage sounded more academic, more in depth. It also mentioned "tax laws and policies" repeatedly. So I'm going to venture out and guess that the second passage is intended for an audience with a legal background, perhaps in tax law. If that's not the case then perhaps policymakers at a thinktank or perhaps Treasury officials. Perhaps it's tailored towards an academic audience. But either way, I think the source would be a policy briefing, a legal article, or something similar.

By contrast, the source of Passage A will be less esoteric and academically inclined. Perhaps it's from a blogpost, news article, or something tailored towards a less sophisticated audience. That's all I got for now.

A.   *Passage A: a magazine article addressed to a general audience; Passage B: a law journal article*

This works, A is less sophisticated than B, and B is either a policy briefing or law journal article.

B.   *Passage A: a technical journal for economists; Passage B: a magazine article addressed to a general audience*

Order is reversed. A is less technical than B.

C.   *Passage A: <u>a science-fiction novel</u>; Passage B: a technical journal for economists*

Science fiction novel? Remember that A is talking about how an economist views the trading of video game items for cash in real life.

D.   *Passage A: a law journal article; Passage B: a speech delivered before a legislative body*

A feels like its geared towards a generalized audience. Passage B could be aimed at the government, as we have anticipated. Passage A does not match in this answer.

E.   *Passage A: a speech delivered before a legislative body; Passage B: a science-fiction novel*

Passage B could have been a speech delivered before a legislative body; rather than a science fiction novel.

The correct answer is A.

20. Topic Specific Reading Strategies

20. Topic Specific Reading Strategies

Reading Strategies for Difficult Passages

In this second to last chapter of the book, we will look at some of the specialized reading techniques and habits that have served me well in the hardest RC passages. Many students have also found these techniques helpful, and I hope they may be of service to you!

It's important to note that these techniques may not be applicable to every passage that you encounter. When it comes to the hardest passages, each passage is unique in terms of the difficulties it presents. It can be difficult because of an overwhelming amount of details, or it can be hard because of the abstract nature of its argument. The techniques we look at here will be powerful tools that we can depend on for the most typical and representative passages of each topic, but it's still up to us to come to a personal understanding of the passage.

Science

Visualization

Some of the hardest details within science-based passages can be aided by visualization. What a thousand words cannot succinctly explain, oftentimes a simple picture can. Whenever I'm going through a science-based passage, I will often use diagrams or illustrations to supplement my understanding of the passage.

Take a look at the following passage:

<u>PT57 Passage 4</u>

Fractal geometry is a mathematical theory devoted to the study of complex shapes called fractals. Although an exact definition of fractals has not been established, fractals commonly exhibit the property of self-similarity: the reiteration of irregular details or patterns at progressively smaller scales so that each part, when magnified, looks basically like the object as a whole. The Koch curve is a significant fractal in mathematics and examining it provides some insight into fractal geometry. To generate the Koch curve, one begins with a straight line. The middle third of the line is removed and replaced with two line segments, each as long as the removed piece, which are positioned so as to meet and form the top of a triangle. At this stage, the curve consists of four connected segments of equal length that form a pointed protrusion in the middle. This process is repeated on the four segments so that all the protrusions are on the same side of the curve, and then the process is repeated indefinitely on the segments at each stage of the construction.

Self-similarity is built into the construction process by treating segments at each stage the same way as the original segment was treated. Since the rules for getting from one stage to another are fully explicit and always the same, images of successive stages of the process can be generated by computer. Theoretically, the Koch curve is the result of infinitely many steps in the construction process, but the finest image approximating the Koch curve will be limited by the fact that eventually the segments will get too short to be drawn or displayed. However, using computer graphics to produce images of successive stages of the construction process dramatically illustrates a major attraction of fractal geometry: simple processes can be responsible for incredibly complex patterns.

A worldwide public has become captivated by fractal geometry after viewing astonishing computer generated images of fractals; enthusiastic practitioners in the field of fractal geometry consider it a new language for describing complex natural and mathematical forms. They anticipate that fractal geometry's significance will rival that of calculus and expect that proficiency in fractal geometry will allow mathematicians to describe the form of a cloud as easily and precisely as an architect can describe a house using the language of traditional geometry. Other mathematicians have reservations about the fractal geometers' preoccupation with computer-generated graphic images and their lack of interest in theory. These mathematicians point out that traditional mathematics consists of proving theorems, and while many theorems about fractals have already been proven using the notions of pre-fractal mathematics, fractal geometers have proven only a handful of theorems that could not have been proven with pre-fractal mathematics. According to these mathematicians, fractal geometry can attain a lasting role in mathematics only if it becomes a precise language supporting a system of theorems and proofs.

This passage was difficult for many students because of the abstract description of the Koch curve in the first paragraph. Let's take a look at that information, and see if simple diagramming can clear things up for us:

To generate the Koch curve, one begins with a straight line.

The middle third of the line is removed

replaced with two line segments, each as long as the removed piece

which are positioned so as to meet and form the top of a triangle... At this stage, the curve consists of four connected segments of equal length that form a pointed protrusion in the middle

This process is repeated on the four segments so that all the protrusions are on the same side of the curve, and then the process is repeated indefinitely on the segments at each stage of the construction.

Does that make sense? Whenever there is detailed description of some kind of visualization or imagery in a science passage, I always slow down, diagram or visualize what the author is describing step by step. Only when I have fully understood what the author is trying to depict do I move forward into the more theoretical stuff. Diagramming can be extremely helpful.

Take a look at the following passage, see if diagramming can help you understand some of the details

PT85 Passage 4

According to the generally accepted theory of plate tectonics, the earth's crust consists of a dozen or so plates of solid rock moving across the mantle-the slightly fluid layer of rock between crust and core. Most earthquakes can then be explained as a result of the grinding of these plates against one another as they collide. When two plates collide, one plate is forced under the other until it eventually merges with the underlying mantle. According to this explanation, this process, called subduction, causes an enormous build-up of energy that is abruptly released in the form of an earthquake. Most earthquakes take place in the earth's seismic "hot zones" – regions with very high levels of subduction. Contrary to expectations, however, global seismic data indicate that there are also regions with high levels of subduction that are nonetheless nearly free of earthquakes. Thus, until recently, there remained a crucial question for which the plate tectonics theory had no answer-how can often intense subduction take place at certain locations with little or no seismic effect?

One group of scientists now proposes that the relative quiet of these zones is tied to the nature of the collision between the plates. In many seismic hot zones, the plates exhibit motion in opposite directions-that is, they collide because they are moving toward each other. And because the two plates are moving in opposite directions, the subduction zone is relatively motionless relative to the underlying mantle. In contrast, the plate collisions in the quiet subduction zones occur between two plates that are moving in the same general direction-the second plate's motion is simply faster than that of the first, and its leading edge therefore becomes subducted. But in this type of subduction, the collision zone moves with a comparatively high velocity relative to the mantle below. Thus, rather like an oar dipped into the water from a moving boat, the overtaking plate encounters great resistance from the mantle and is forced to descend steeply as it is absorbed into the mantle. The steep descent of the overtaking plate in this type of collision reduces the amount of contact between the two plates, and the earthquake-producing friction is thereby reduced as well. On the other hand, in collisions in which the plates move toward each other the subducted plate receives relatively little resistance from the mantle, and so its angle of descent is correspondingly shallow, allowing for a much larger plane of contact between the two plates. Like two sheets of sandpaper pressed together, these plates offer each other a great deal of resistance.

This proposal also provides a warning. It suggests that regions that were previously thought to be seismically innocuous-regions with low levels of subduction-may in fact be at a significant risk of earthquakes, depending on the nature of the subduction taking place.

We have seen this passage previously, let's see if we can use some simple diagramming to make things easier to understand:

According to the generally accepted theory of plate tectonics, the earth's crust consists of a dozen or so plates of solid rock moving across the mantle-the slightly fluid layer of rock between crust and core. Most earthquakes can then be explained as a result of the grinding of these plates against one another as they collide. When two plates collide, one plate is forced under the other until it eventually merges with the underlying mantle. According to this explanation, this process, called subduction, causes an enormous build-up of energy that is abruptly released in the form of an earthquake. Most earthquakes take place in the earth's seismic "hot zones" – regions with very high levels of subduction. Contrary to expectations, however, global seismic data indicate that there are also regions with high levels of subduction that are nonetheless nearly free of earthquakes. Thus, until recently, there remained a crucial question for which the plate tectonics theory had no answer-how can often intense subduction take place at certain locations with little or no seismic effect?

Generally Accepted Theory: Two plates collide and one plate gets subducted.

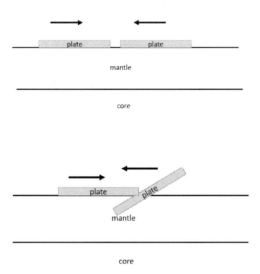

In the second paragraph, a group of scientists propose a theory on how subduction can occur in areas with little seismic activity:

In contrast, the plate collisions in the quiet subduction zones occur between two plates that are moving in the same general direction-the second plate's motion is simply faster than that of the first, and its leading edge therefore becomes subducted. But in this type of subduction, the collision zone moves with a comparatively high velocity relative to the mantle below. Thus, rather like an oar dipped into the water from a moving boat, the overtaking plate encounters great resistance from the mantle and is forced to descend steeply as it is absorbed into the mantle.

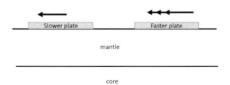

What subsequently happens is that the faster plate catches up, but dips below the back of the slower plate:

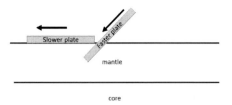

So subduction does not only occur when two plates collide, it also occurs when one plate catches up with another, and gets buried behind the earlier plate. When two plates collide, the angle is shallow and there is a lot of friction. But when one catches up to the other, the angle of descent is steep and there is less friction.

That's essentially all the technical information from the passage! Notice how as soon as we are able to visualize the process, as soon as we are able to translate the abstract language into an easily understandable image, our understanding of the passage gains exponentially.

So don't hesitate to diagram the process in science passages, especially if you are a visual learner.

Keeping Track of Different Ideas

Most science-based passages will go into depth on a specific topic or idea, so from the moment we start to read until the time when we finish the passage, we are able to form an uninterrupted train of the thought on the topic and gradually come to a deeper understanding of what has been discussed. However, there will be passages where several concepts are discussed. These passages are difficult because we need to keep track of the multiple issues talked about in the passage. It's not enough just to know what the Author's Purpose or Main Point is, but we must also be aware of the sub-topic of each paragraph.

For example, if the passage discussed three related yet slightly different issues (let's call them A, B, and C) in three paragraphs, then knowing the content of each paragraph is going to help us quickly locate the appropriate text when it comes to the questions. If a question is asking about issue C, then we can quickly turn to the third paragraph to look for the relevant support. Similarly, if a question was asking us to compare issues A and B, then we can focus the majority of our attention on the relationship between paragraphs one and two.

Read the following passage, and see if you can summarize the main point not just of the passage, but of each paragraph as well:

PT56 Passage 2

Mechanisms for recognizing kin are found throughout the plant and animal kingdoms, regardless of an organism's social or mental complexity. Improvements in the general understanding of these mechanisms have turned some biologists' attention to the question of why kin recognition occurs at all. One response to this question is offered by the inclusive fitness theory, which was developed in the 1960s. The theory is based on the realization that an organism transmits its genetic attributes to succeeding generations not solely through its offspring, but more generally through all of its close relatives. Whereas the traditional view of evolution held that natural selection favors the continued genetic representation of individuals within a species that produce the greatest number of offspring, the inclusive fitness theory posits that natural selection similarly favors organisms that help their relatives, because doing so also increases their own total genetic representation. The theory has helped to explain previously mysterious phenomena, including the evolution of social insect species like the honeybee, most of whose members do not produce offspring and exist only to nurture relatives.

Inclusive fitness theory has also been applied usefully to new findings concerning cannibalism within animal species. Based on the theory, cannibals should have evolved to avoid eating their own kin because of the obvious genetic costs of such a practice. Spadefoot toad tadpoles provide an illustration. Biologists have found that all tadpoles of that species begin life as omnivores, feeding mainly on organic debris in their soon-to-be-dry pool in the desert, but that occasionally one tadpole eats another or eats a freshwater shrimp. This event can trigger changes in the tadpole's physiology and dietary preference, causing the tadpole to become larger and exclusively carnivorous, feasting on other animals including members of its own species. Yet the cannibals have a procedure of discrimination whereby they nip at other tadpoles, eating non siblings but releasing siblings unharmed. This suggests that the inclusive fitness theory offers at least a partial answer to why kin recognition develops. Interestingly, a cannibal tadpole is less likely to avoid eating kin when it becomes very hungry, apparently putting its own unique genetic makeup ahead of its siblings'.

But there may be other reasons why organisms recognize kin. For example, it has recently been found that tiger salamander larvae, also either omnivorous or cannibalistic, are plagued in nature by a deadly bacterium. Furthermore, it was determined that cannibal larvae are especially likely to be infected by eating diseased species members. The fact that this bacterium is more deadly when it comes from a close relative with a similar immune system suggests that natural selection may favor cannibals that avoid such pathogens by not eating kin. For tiger salamanders then, kin recognition can be explained simply as a means by which an organism preserves its own life, not as a means to aid in relatives' survival.

The passage can be broken down by paragraph:

In the first paragraph, the author **introduces** Inclusive Fitness Theory, a theory that attempts to answer the question of why animals recognize their relatives. The theory posits that animals strive to help their relatives, and this is also considered a form of evolutionary success, rather than purely trying to help themselves pass on their own genes.

The second paragraph discusses an **application** of IFT. The paragraph discusses how tadpoles do not eat their own kin. IFT is offered as a potential explanation.

Finally, the third paragraph provides **alternative reasons** why animals do not eat their own kin. These are theories or explanations competing with IFT.

***

Recognizing the **function** of each paragraph can help us come to a more coherent and lean understanding of the passage as a whole. This will improve our clarity and ability to search for the relevant textual evidence.

So if different ideas are discussed in the passage, or if each paragraph serves a different function, make sure we are aware of the changes or shifts in the passage that are occurring.

Gradual Buildup of an Idea

We just saw a passage where distinct ideas were discussed, now we will look at another type of passage where only one idea is discussed, but at greater depth. In these passages, there will be a gradual buildup of an idea or theory, and the further you get in the passage, the more difficult it gets. For instance, the first paragraph will introduce a theory, the second paragraph will talk about the theory in fuller detail, and the third paragraph will talk about the more abstract aspects of the theory. It would be extremely difficult to understand what the latter part of such a passage is talking about if you didn't pay attention earlier.

As always, start slow, make sure you understand what is going on and the full implications of the information that you've just read before moving on, especially if it's the third or last passage of the section.

***

PT28 Passage 2

Long after the lava has cooled, the effects of a major volcanic eruption may linger on. In the atmosphere a veil of fine dust and sulfuric acid droplets can spread around the globe and persist for years. Researchers have generally thought that this veil can block enough sunlight to have a chilling influence on Earth's climate. Many blame the cataclysmic eruption of the Indonesian volcano Tambora in 1815 for the ensuing "year without a summer" of 1816—when parts of the northeastern United States and southeastern Canada were hit by snowstorms in June and frosts in August.

The volcano-climate connection seems plausible, but, say scientists Clifford Mass and Davit Portman, it is not as strong as previously believed. Mass and Portman analyzed global temperature data for the years before and after nine volcanic eruptions, from Krakatau in 1883 to El Chichón in 1982. In the process they tried to filter out temperature changes caused by the cyclic weather phenomenon known as the El Niño-Southern Oscillation, which warms the sea surface in the equatorial Pacific and thereby warms the atmosphere. Such warming can mask the cooling brought about by an eruption, but it can also mimic volcanic cooling if the volcano happens to erupt just as an El Niño induced warm period is beginning to fade.

Once El Niño effects had been subtracted from the data, the actual effects of the eruptions came through more clearly. Contrary to what earlier studies had suggested, Mass and Portman found that minor eruptions have no discernible effect on temperature. And major, dust-spitting explosions, such as Krakatau or El Chichón, cause a smaller drop than expected in the average temperature in the hemisphere (Northern or Southern) of the eruption—only half a degree centigrade or less—a correspondingly smaller drop in the opposite hemisphere.

Other researchers, however, have argued that even a small temperature drop could result in a significant regional fluctuation in climate if its effects were amplified by climatic feedback loops. For example, a small temperature drop in the northeastern U.S. and southeastern Canada in early spring might delay the melting of snow, and the un-melted snow would continue to reflect sunlight away from the surface, amplifying the cooling. The cool air over the region could, in turn, affect the jet stream. The jet stream tends to flow at the boundary between cool northern air and warm southern air, drawing its power from the sharp temperature contrast and the consequent difference in pressure. An unusual cooling in the region could cause the stream to wander farther south than normal, allowing more polar air to come in behind it and deepen the region's cold snap. Through such a series of feedbacks a small temperature drop could be blown up into a year without a summer.

In the first paragraph, we are introduced to the belief that volcanic eruptions cause a drop in temperature. The dust and acid drops that result from a volcanic eruption block out sunlight, and chills the earth. Several examples are given.

The second paragraph contains two scientists' doubts about the relationship discussed in the first paragraph. They looked over the data, but also took into consideration the effect of El Nino on the temperature. When El Nino ends, temperature will also drop.

After taking El Nino into consideration, the scientists find that minor volcanic eruptions do not lower temperatures. Major volcanic eruptions cause a smaller drop in temperature than previously thought.

Other researchers responded to these findings by saying that even though the drop in temperature due to a volcanic eruption may be smaller than previously thought, it can still lead to a series of chain effects that ultimately cool the earth significantly.

***

Unlike PT56 Passage 2, PT28 Passage 2's argument follows a linear logical progression. A theory is introduced, an attempt to overturn that theory is described, the findings of that attempt are described, and finally opposing viewpoints are introduced. The topic/content of each paragraph builds upon the previous paragraph, and we really have to understand the previous paragraph before we can understand the later paragraphs. (We won't understand the data presented in the third paragraph if we didn't know the relationship between El Nino, volcanic eruptions, and temperature change, which were discussed in the first and second paragraphs, for example.)

Logical Relationships

When we studied LR, we paid special attention to the logical relationships contained in stimulus arguments. We saw that the three main ways in which arguments are advanced are via conditional logic, causal reasoning, and analogies.

Causal relationships frequent science themed passages. In fact, if we can identify the causal chains present, our understanding of the passage and our retention of the details will be much easier.

Read the following passage, and see if you can isolate the logical relationships present.

PT36 Passage 3

Discussions of how hormones influence behavior have generally been limited to the effects of gonadal hormones on reproductive behavior and have emphasized the parsimonious arrangement whereby the same hormones involved in the biology of reproduction also influence sexual behavior. It has now become clear, however, that other hormones, in addition to their recognized influence on biological functions, can affect behavior. Specifically, peptide and steroid hormones involved in maintaining the physiological balance, or homeostasis, of body fluids also appear to play an important role in the control of water and salt consumption. The phenomenon of homeostasis in animals depends on various mechanisms that promote stability within the organism despite an inconstant external environment; the homeostasis of body fluids, whereby the osmolality (the concentration of solutes) of blood plasma is closely regulated, is achieved primarily through alterations in the intake and excretion of water and sodium, the two principal components of the fluid matrix that surrounds body cells. Appropriate compensatory responses are initiated when deviations from normal are quite small, thereby maintaining plasma osmolality within relatively narrow ranges.

In the osmoregulation of body fluids, the movement of water across cell membranes permits minor fluctuations in the concentration of solutes in extracellular fluid to be buffered by corresponding changes in the relatively larger volume of cellular water. Nevertheless, the concentration of solutes in extracellular fluid may at times become elevated or reduced by more than the allowed tolerances of one or two percent. It is then that complementary physiological and behavioral responses come into play to restore plasma osmolality to normal. Thus, for example, a decrease in plasma osmolality, such as that which occurs after the consumption of water in excess of need, leads to the excretion of surplus body water in the urine by inhibiting secretion from the pituitary gland of vasopressin, a peptide hormone that promotes water conservation in the kidneys. As might be expected, thirst also is inhibited then, to prevent further dilution of body fluids. Conversely, an increase in plasma osmolality, such as that which occurs after one eats salty foods or after body water evaporates without being replaced, stimulates the release of vasopressin, increasing the conservation of water and the excretion of solutes in urine. This process is accompanied by increased thirst, with the result of making plasma osmolality more dilute through the consumption of water. The threshold for thirst appears to be slightly higher than for vasopressin secretion, so that thirst is stimulated only after vasopressin has been released in amounts sufficient to produce maximal water retention by the kidneys—that is, only after osmotic dehydration exceeds the capacity of the animal to deal with it physiologically.

Discussions of how <u>hormones influence behavior</u> have generally been limited to the effects of gonadal hormones on reproductive behavior and have emphasized the parsimonious arrangement whereby the same <u>hormones</u> involved in the biology of reproduction also influence <u>sexual behavior</u>. It has now become clear, however, that other hormones, in addition to their recognized influence on biological functions, can affect behavior. Specifically, <u>peptide and steroid hormones</u> involved in maintaining the physiological balance, or homeostasis, of body fluids also appear to play an important role in the control of <u>water and salt consumption</u>. The phenomenon of homeostasis in animals depends on various mechanisms that promote stability within the organism despite an inconstant external environment; the <u>homeostasis of body fluids</u>, whereby the osmolality (the concentration of solutes) of <u>blood plasma</u> is closely regulated, is achieved primarily through alterations in the <u>intake and excretion of water and sodium</u>, the two principal components of the fluid matrix that surrounds body cells. Appropriate compensatory responses are initiated when deviations from normal are quite small, thereby maintaining plasma osmolality within relatively narrow ranges.

In the first paragraph, we are told that certain hormones play an important role in maintaining homeostasis.

More specifically, these hormones regulate the intake and secretion of water and sodium, which in turn regulates the concentration of blood plasma, which ultimately controls the homeostasis of body fluids.

In the osmoregulation of body fluids, the movement of water across cell membranes permits minor fluctuations in the concentration of solutes in extracellular fluid to be buffered by corresponding changes in the relatively larger volume of cellular water. Nevertheless, the concentration of solutes in extracellular fluid may at times become elevated or reduced by more than the allowed tolerances of one or two percent. It is then that complementary physiological and behavioral responses come into play to restore plasma osmolality to normal. Thus, for example, a decrease in plasma osmolality, such as that which occurs after the consumption of <u>water</u> in excess of need, <u>leads</u> to the <u>excretion</u> of surplus body water in the urine by <u>inhibiting secretion from the pituitary gland of vasopressin</u>, a peptide <u>hormone</u> that <u>promotes water conservation</u> in the kidneys. As might be expected, thirst also is inhibited then, to prevent further dilution of body fluids. Conversely, an <u>increase</u> in plasma osmolality, such as that which occurs after one eats salty foods or after body water evaporates without being replaced, <u>stimulates</u> the release of <u>vasopressin</u>, <u>increasing</u> the conservation of water and the <u>excretion</u> of solutes in urine. This process is accompanied by <u>increased thirst</u>, with the result of making plasma osmolality more dilute through the consumption of water. The threshold for thirst appears to be slightly higher than for vasopressin secretion, so that thirst is stimulated only after vasopressin has been released in amounts sufficient to produce maximal water retention by the kidneys—that is, only after osmotic dehydration exceeds the capacity of the animal to deal with it physiologically.

If you drink too much water, that leads to a decrease in plasma osmolality, that in turn leads to a repression of a peptide hormone called vasopressin, which lowers water conservation in the kidneys, which ultimately lead to excretion of the extra water.

To put this into a causal relationship:

Drank too much water ⇒ Decrease in plasma osmolality ⇒ Repression of vasopressin (which conserves water) ⇒ Less water conserved ⇒ Extra water released

Alternatively,

Eating too much salty foods ⇒ Increase in plasma osmolality ⇒ Release of vasopressin ⇒ Conserve water + Excrete solutes in urine + Thirst

On the surface, this was an extremely challenging passage, but by grasping the causal chain within the second paragraph, we have made the passage much more manageable.

A Scientific Discovery/Finding a Solution to a Scientific Problem

A final trend/trait worth noting in science passages is the recurring theme of finding a solution to a problem or highlighting a scientific discovery. In fact, there are so many science passages on the LSAT that discuss either the origins and conditions surrounding a scientific discovery or outlines how a solution was found for a pressing problem, that whenever I encounter a science passage, I will **automatically ask myself if this is something that the author does or talk about in the passage.**

If there is indeed a discovery mentioned in the passage, then I will ask myself the following questions:

- What exactly did our scientist discover?
- What's so special about it?
- What are the conditions surrounding that discovery or what did they do to come to this discovery?

***

PT44 Passage 3

The survival of nerve cells, as well as their performance of some specialized functions, is regulated by chemicals known as neurotrophic factors, which are produced in the bodies of animals, including humans. Rita Levi-Montalcini's discovery in the 1950s of the first of these agents, a hormonelike substance now known as NGF, was a crucial development in the history of biochemistry, which led to Levi-Montalcini sharing the Nobel Prize for medicine in 1986.

In the mid-1940s, Levi-Montalcini had begun by hypothesizing that many of the immature nerve cells produced in the development of an organism are normally programmed to die. In order to confirm this theory, she conducted research that in 1949 found that, when embryos are in the process of forming their nervous systems, they produce many more nerve cells than are finally required, the number that survives eventually adjusting itself to the volume of tissue to be supplied with nerves. A further phase of the experimentation, which led to Levi-Montalcini's identification of the substance that controls this process, began with her observation that the development of nerves in chick embryos could be stimulated by implanting a certain variety of mouse tumor in the embryos. She theorized that a chemical produced by the tumors was responsible for the observed nerve growth. To investigate this hypothesis, she used the then new technique of tissue culture, by which specific types of body cells can be made to grow outside the organism from which they are derived. Within twenty-four hours, her tissue cultures of chick embryo extracts developed dense halos of nerve tissue near the places in the culture where she had added the mouse tumor. Further research identified a specific substance contributed by the mouse tumors that was responsible for the effects Levi-Montalcini had observed: a protein that she named "nerve growth factor" (NGF).

NGF was the first of many cell-growth factors to be found in the bodies of animals. Through Levi-Montalcini's work and other subsequent research, it has been determined that this substance is present in many tissues and biological fluids, and that it is especially concentrated in some organs. In developing organisms, nerve cells apparently receive this growth factor locally from the cells of muscles or other organs to which they will form connections for transmission of nerve impulses, and sometimes from supporting cells intermingled with the nerve tissue. NGF seems to play two roles, serving initially to direct the developing nerve processes toward the correct, specific "target" cells with which they must connect, and later being necessary for the continued survival of those nerve cells. During some periods of their development, the types of nerve cells that are affected by NGF—primarily cells outside the brain and spinal cord—die if the factor is not present or if they encounter anti-NGF antibodies.

The survival of <u>nerve cells</u>, as well as their performance of some specialized functions, is regulated by <u>chemicals</u> known as neurotrophic factors, which are produced in the bodies of animals, including humans. Rita Levi-Montalcini's discovery in the 1950s of the first of these agents, a hormonelike substance now known as NGF, was a crucial development in the history of biochemistry, which led to Levi-Montalcini sharing the Nobel Prize for medicine in 1986.

RLM's discoveries of neurotrophic factors, or NGF is going to be the topic of this passage. Perhaps the author will talk about what led to this discovery, what difficulties RLM faced, and what are the implications of such a discovery? Let's read on.

In the mid-1940s, Levi-Montalcini had begun by hypothesizing that many of the immature nerve cells produced in the development of an organism are <u>normally programmed to die</u>. In order to confirm this theory, she conducted research that in 1949 found that, when embryos are in the process of forming their nervous systems, they produce many <u>more nerve cells than are finally required</u>, the number that survives eventually adjusting itself to the volume of tissue to be supplied with nerves. A further phase of the experimentation, which led to Levi-Montalcini's identification of the substance that controls this process, began with her observation that the development of nerves in chick embryos could be stimulated by implanting a certain variety of mouse tumor in the embryos. She theorized that a <u>chemical</u> produced by the tumors <u>was responsible for the observed nerve growth</u>. To investigate this hypothesis, she used the then new technique <u>of tissue culture</u>, by which specific types of body cells can be made to grow outside the organism from which they are derived. Within twenty-four hours, her tissue cultures of chick embryo extracts developed dense halos of nerve tissue near the places in the culture where she had added the mouse tumor. Further research identified a specific substance contributed by the mouse tumors that was responsible for the effects Levi-Montalcini had observed: a protein that she named "nerve growth factor" (NGF).

RLM hypothesized that nerve cells are programmed to die. More are produced than finally required.

RLM saw that implanting a mouse tumor in chick embryos led to the development of nerves. She thought it was due to a chemical present in the mouse tumor.

She was able to isolate NGF using the technique of tissue culture.

NGF was the <u>first of many</u> cell-growth factors to be found in the bodies of animals. Through Levi-Montalcini's work and other subsequent research, it has been determined that this substance is present in many tissues and biological fluids, and that it is especially concentrated in <u>some organs</u>. In developing organisms, nerve cells apparently receive this growth factor locally from the <u>cells of muscles</u> or other organs to which they <u>will form connections</u> for transmission of nerve impulses, and sometimes from supporting cells intermingled with the nerve tissue. NGF seems to play <u>two roles</u>, serving initially to <u>direct</u> the developing nerve processes toward the correct, specific "target" cells with which they must connect, and later being necessary for the <u>continued survival</u> of those nerve cells. During some periods of their development, the types of nerve cells that are affected by NGF—primarily cells outside the brain and spinal cord—die if the factor is not present or if they encounter anti-NGF antibodies.

There are other chemicals similar to NGF, and they are concentrated in certain organs. Nerve cells receive NGF from muscles or organs they eventually link up with.

NGF plays two roles: they guide the nerves toward the location where they must connect; and they ensure the survival of those nerve cells.

Arts

Artist's Unique Traits

In passages where the author is discussing an artist, painter, musician, or even movie director, a majority of the passage will be devoted to describing this person's work. As a result, we may end up with many details about where this artist learned to paint, what projects they completed, what kind of materials they used, or what kind of brushstrokes and what subjects they painted. In other words, we are left with an overwhelming amount of specifics about this artist, lots of facts, lots of observations.

But at the same time, we need to read between the lines to find what the author most values in this artist, what is the most special aspect of this artist's works and journey, what are their unique traits. Discovering what is truly unique about this artist will help us with the more macroscopic questions like Main Point or Purpose Questions, and help us recall what the passage is about when we are attempting the questions.

Take a look at the following passage:

PT59 Passage 3

The Japanese American sculptor Isamu Noguchi (1904–1988) was an artist who intuitively asked—and responded to—deeply original questions. He might well have become a scientist within a standard scientific discipline, but he instead became an artist who repeatedly veered off at wide angles from the well-known courses followed by conventionally talented artists of both the traditional and modern schools. The story behind one particular sculpture typifies this aspect of his creativeness.

By his early twenties, Noguchi's sculptures showed such exquisite comprehension of human anatomy and deft conceptual realization that he won a Guggenheim Fellowship for travel in Europe. After arriving in Paris in 1927, Noguchi asked the Romanian-born sculptor Constantin Brancusi if he might become his student. When Brancusi said no, that he never took students, Noguchi asked if he needed a stonecutter. Brancusi did. Noguchi cut and polished stone for Brancusi in his studio, frequently also polishing Brancusi's brass and bronze sculptures. Noguchi, with his scientist's mind, pondered the fact that sculptors through the ages had relied exclusively upon negative light—that is, shadows—for their conceptual communication, precisely because no metals, other than the expensive, nonoxidizing gold, could be relied upon to give off positive-light reflections.

Noguchi wanted to create a sculpture that was purely reflective. In 1929, after returning to the United States, he met the architect and philosopher R. Buckminster Fuller, offering to sculpt a portrait of him. When Fuller heard of Noguchi's ideas regarding positive-light sculpture, he suggested using chrome nickel steel, which Henry Ford, through automotive research and development, had just made commercially available for the first time in history. Here, finally, was a permanently reflective surface, economically available in massive quantities.

In sculpting his portrait of Fuller, Noguchi did not think of it as merely a shiny alternate model of traditional, negative-light sculptures. What he saw was that completely reflective surfaces provided a fundamental invisibility of surface like that of utterly still waters, whose presence can be apprehended only when objects—a ship's mast, a tree, or sky—are reflected in them. Seaplane pilots making offshore landings in dead calm cannot tell where the water is and must glide in, waiting for the unpredictable touchdown. Noguchi conceived a similarly invisible sculpture, hidden in and communicating through the reflections of images surrounding it. Then only the distortion of familiar shapes in the surrounding environment could be seen by the viewer. The viewer's awareness of the "invisible" sculpture's presence and dimensional relationships would be derived only secondarily.

Even after this stunning discovery, Noguchi remained faithful to his inquisitive nature. At the moment when his explorations had won critical recognition of the genius of his original and fundamental conception, Noguchi proceeded to the next phase of his evolution.

The majority of the passage is devoted to recounting Noguchi's development as a sculptor. We are told about his studies in Paris with Brancusi, his eventual creation of a portrait for Fuller, and the qualities of the statute he made for Fuller.

These descriptions take up over 90% of the passage, so it's easy to overlook some subtle, yet crucial elements of the passage.

Take a look at the latter part of the first paragraph:

but he instead became an artist who repeatedly <u>veered off</u> at wide angles from the <u>well-known courses</u> followed by conventionally talented artists of both the traditional and modern schools. The story behind one particular sculpture <u>typifies</u> this aspect of his <u>creativeness</u>.

The author is trying to emphasize Noguchi's unconventional path and his creativity. The story of the sculpture is in fact used as an example to illustrate this.

Take a look at the final paragraph:

Even after this stunning discovery, Noguchi remained faithful to his <u>inquisitive</u> nature. At the moment when his explorations had won critical recognition of the genius of his original and fundamental conception, Noguchi proceeded to the next phase of his <u>evolution</u>.

So the Author's Purpose and by extension Main Point, was to **highlight Noguchi's creativity and unconventional evolution**. It was not, as many students mistakenly assumed, to simply retrace Noguchi's career as a sculptor.

Overarching Themes/Linkages

Searching for what the author thinks about a specific artist is essential in these passages. In passages where the author discusses several phases of an artist's life, or several of the artist's works, try to think about what **commonalities** there are that span across the artist's career, or what are the **common themes** behind their works.

PT79 Passage 2

Best known for her work with lacquer, Eileen Gray (1878-1976) had a fascinating and multifaceted artistic career: she became a designer of ornaments, furniture, interiors, and eventually homes. Though her attention shifted from smaller objects to the very large, she always focused on details, even details that were forever hidden. In Paris she studied the Japanese tradition of lacquer, employing wood surfaces-e.g., bowls, screens, furniture-for the application of the clear, hard-drying liquid. It is a time-consuming craft, then little known in Europe, that superimposes layer upon layer, sometimes involving twenty layers or more. The tradition of lacquer fit well with her artistic sensibilities, as Gray eschewed the flowing, leafy lines of the Art Nouveau movement that had flourished in Paris, preferring the austere beauty of straight lines and simple forms juxtaposed.

In addition to requiring painstaking layering, the wood used in lacquer work must be lacquered on both sides to prevent warping. This tension between aesthetic demands and structural requirements, which invests Gray's work in lacquer with an architectural quality, is critical but not always apparent: a folding screen or door panel reveals more of the artist's work than does a flat panel, which hides one side. In Gray's early work she produced flat panels; later she made door panels and even unfolded the panels into screens. In a screen she made for the lobby of an apartment, she fully realizes the implications of this expansion from two to three dimensions: the screen juts out from a wall, and that wall visually disintegrates into panels of lacquered bricks on the screen. The screen thus becomes a painting, a piece of furniture, and an architectural element all at once. She subsequently became heavily invested in the design of furniture, often tailoring pieces to fit a particular interior environment. She often used modem materials, such as tubular steel, to create furniture and environments that, though visually austere, meet their occupants' needs.

Gray's work in both lacquer and interior design prefigures her work as an architect. She did not believe that one should divorce the structural design of the exterior from the design of the interior. She designed the interior elements of a house together with the more permanent structures, as an integrated whole. Architecture for her was like work in lacquer: it could only be achieved from the inside out. But in architecture we discover the hidden layers; in fact we inhabit them. We find storage cabinets in the recesses of a staircase, desks that are also cabinets, and tables that are set on pivots to serve different functions in different contexts. One such table can be positioned either outside, on a balcony, or inside the house. Gray placed a carpet underneath it in each location, as though to underscore that there is no important distinction between exterior and interior.

We should already be familiar with this passage. On the surface, it's talking about Eileen Gray's journey from a designer of ornaments to furniture to the interior and ultimately to homes. But on a deeper level, the passage is talking about the commonalities between her work in the four areas.

There's always that hidden element: layers of lacquer, hidden architectural qualities of her furniture, hidden layers of her architecture that we inhabit.

There's the tension between opposing demands that spans her journey as well: lacquer being lacquered on both sides, furniture's aesthetic demands and structural demands, structural design of the exterior of a house and the design of the interior.

These are all common themes and traits of Eileen Gray's work that are shared across her artistic journey.

***

Contributions and Influences

We will make a final mention of a common theme in art-based passages. Whenever the author is presenting an artist, musician, writer, etc. we should always strive to look at what contributions this person has made to their field or to society in general. Have they been influential in bringing about change? Many arts-based passages have highlighted the contributions of minority artists to not just their field, but to social justice on a broader perspective. So it's crucial not to overlook these if they are mentioned.

Law

For the uninitiated, law-themed passages can be a daunting task. **Key terms** loaded with meaning abound, and if we did not know what they referred to, our understanding may suffer.

Think back on the Comparative Passage about independent research by judges. One referred to the trial court, the other about appellate courts. If you didn't know that the trial court was the lower court and the appellate court was an intermediate court of appeals, our understanding of the passages would have been stymied no matter how carefully we read.

Abstract arguments can also be a source of pain for students. When faced with such an argument, there is little we can do except to read more carefully and try to brainstorm fitting analogies to help us better understand the idea that the author is trying to express.

Ultimately, legal passages are one area where a little external reading on our own time can potentially do wonders. Read up on the court system, brief history of the common law, and even some key figures of jurisprudence and their ideas. (More on this in the last chapter.)

***

Differentiating between Statutes and Cases

Another source of difficulty we encounter when reading law themed passages is the liability to confuse different laws and precisely what they entail. The author may list several laws, statutes, or legislation, each brought forward by a different agency, all with different effects and implications.

It's our job to distinguish them clearly and not confuse one for the other. If you see this happening in a passage, you can almost be certain that there will be tricky detail-oriented questions that try to entrap you with half right half wrong answers later on.

PT63 Passage 1

In Alaska, tradition is a powerful legal concept, appearing in a wide variety of legal contexts relating to natural-resource and public-lands activities. Both state and federal laws in the United States assign privileges and exemptions to individuals engaged in "traditional" activities using otherwise off-limits land and resources. But in spite of its prevalence in statutory law, the term "tradition" is rarely defined. Instead, there seems to be a presumption that its meaning is obvious. Failure to define "tradition" clearly in written law has given rise to problematic and inconsistent legal results.

One of the most prevalent ideas associated with the term "tradition" in the law is that tradition is based on long-standing practice, where "long-standing" refers not only to the passage of time but also to the continuity and regularity of a practice. But two recent court cases involving indigenous use of sea otter pelts illustrate the problems that can arise in the application of this sense of "traditional."

The hunting of sea otters was initially prohibited by the Fur Seal Treaty of 1910. The Marine Mammal Protection Act (MMPA) of 1972 continued the prohibition, but it also included an Alaska Native exemption, which allowed takings of protected animals for use in creating authentic native articles by means of "traditional native handicrafts." The U.S. Fish and Wildlife Service (FWS) subsequently issued regulations defining authentic native articles as those "commonly produced" before 1972, when the MMPA took effect. Not covered by the exemption, according to the FWS, were items produced from sea otter pelts, because Alaska Natives had not produced such handicrafts "within living memory."

In 1986, FWS agents seized articles of clothing made from sea otter pelts from Marina Katelnikoff, an Aleut. She sued, but the district court upheld the FWS regulations. Then in 1991 Katelnikoff joined a similar suit brought by Boyd Dickinson, a Tlingit from whom articles of clothing made from sea otter pelts had also been seized. After hearing testimony establishing that Alaska Natives had made many uses of sea otters before the occupation of the territory by Russia in the late 1700s, the court reconsidered what constituted a traditional item under the statute. The court now held that the FWS's regulations were based on a "strained interpretation" of the word "traditional," and that the reference to "living memory" imposed an excessively restrictive time frame. The court stated, "The fact that Alaskan natives were prevented, by circumstances beyond their control, from exercising a tradition for a given period of time does not mean that it has been lost forever or that it has become any less a 'tradition.' It defies common sense to define 'traditional' in such a way that only those traditions that were exercised during a comparatively short period in history could qualify as 'traditional.'"

This was not a difficult passage to understand from a theoretical perspective, what most students have trouble with is trying to differentiate between different laws and cases.

There was the Fur Seal Treaty which prevented the hunting of seals in 1910, the MMPA of 1972 with its Indigenous exemption, the FWS regulations, and the FWS' interpretations of what's covered and what's not covered under the exemptions.

There was also the Marina Katelnikoff case in 1986, and finally the Katelnikoff and Dickinson case in 1991.

In a passage like this, even as we are reading the passage, **we can already tell** that the harder questions will ask us about a specific ruling or statute and throw in answer choices describing another case/statute in order to confuse us.

Make sure you are differentiating between different laws and rulings.

Differentiating between different Viewpoints/Arguments

Let us revisit a passage from earlier:

This time, as you read, keep in mind the four different views on faculty inventions: The supra-maximalist, the maximalist, the resource provider model, and the faculty-oriented model. Recall also Chew's response to each of these different models.

Again, just like in the previous passage, it's crucial to recognize and remember the similarities and differences between the different viewpoints or arguments. Remember that in a passage with an overwhelming number of details, the harder questions will also test our ability to organize and differentiate between these details.

PT43 Passage 4

Faculty researchers, particularly in scientific, engineering, and medical programs, often produce scientific discoveries and invent products or processes that have potential commercial value. Many institutions have invested heavily in the administrative infrastructure to develop and exploit these discoveries, and they expect to prosper both by an increased level of research support and by the royalties from licensing those discoveries having patentable commercial applications. However, although faculty themselves are unlikely to become entrepreneurs, an increasing number of highly valued researchers will be sought and sponsored by research corporations or have consulting contracts with commercial firms. One study of such entrepreneurship concluded that "if universities do not provide the flexibility needed to venture into business, faculty will be tempted to go to those institutions that are responsive to their commercialized desires." There is therefore a need to consider the different intellectual property policies that govern the commercial exploitation of faculty inventions in order to determine which would provide the appropriate level of flexibility.

In a recent study of faculty rights, Patricia Chew has suggested a fourfold classification of institutional policies. A supramaximalist institution stakes out the broadest claim possible, asserting ownership not only of all intellectual property produced by faculty in the course of their employment while using university resources, but also for any inventions or patent rights from faculty activities, even those involving research sponsored by non-university funders. A maximalist institution allows faculty ownership of inventions that do not arise either "in the course of the faculty's employment [or] from the faculty's use of university resources." This approach, although not as all encompassing as that of the supramaximalist university, can affect virtually all of a faculty member's intellectual production. A resource-provider institution asserts a claim to faculty's intellectual product in those cases where "significant use" of university time and facilities is employed. Of course, what constitutes significant use of resources is a matter of institutional judgment.

As Chew notes, in these policies "faculty rights, including the sharing of royalties, are the result of university benevolence and generosity. [However, this] presumption is contrary to the common law, which provides that faculty own their inventions." Others have pointed to this anomaly and, indeed, to the uncertain legal and historical basis upon which the ownership of intellectual property rests. Although these issues remain unsettled, and though universities may be overreaching due to faculty's limited knowledge of their rights, most major institutions behave in the ways that maximize university ownership and profit participation.

But there is a fourth way, one that seems to be free from these particular issues. Faculty-oriented institutions assume that researchers own their own intellectual products and the rights to exploit them commercially, except in the development of public health inventions or if there is previously specified "substantial university involvement." At these institutions industry practice is effectively reversed, with the university benefiting in far fewer circumstances.

Humanities/Social Sciences

Gradual Buildup/Development of an Idea

Humanities and Social Sciences can touch upon difficult concepts. Topics like Kant's Categorical Imperative, Mill's Utilitarianism, and Aristotle's Nicomachean Ethics have appeared, directly or indirectly, in RC passages.

Like the more advanced science passages, harder humanities passages will analyze in depth a specific topic, as opposed to giving a generalized overview of many topics. In order to understand later paragraphs/sections of the passage, a more in depth understanding of the early sections is required. Do not try to rush your reading, it's important to be sure you understand each paragraph and can give a coherent account of what has been discussed before you proceed.

PT64 Passage 4

During Dostoyevsky's time there were two significant and opposing directions in Russian literary criticism. One position maintained that art stood high above the present and the everyday, while the radical view maintained that art had a right to exist only if it found its sources in concrete reality, and, through the exposure of want and injustice, it contributed to the creation of a new society; literature, in other words, should be useful. Dostoyevsky took a third position. As a realist, he never doubted that reality was literature's crucial source. But his understanding of reality went deeper than the one prevailing among radical critics, since for Dostoyevsky there was no distinction in principle between fantasy and reality, and reality was far more than the merely tangible.

The radical critics' demand that reality be depicted "as it is" was meaningless for Dostoyevsky; reality was necessarily shaped by the person who experienced it: what may not be reality for you may be reality for me. The task of the writer was to explode the boundaries of the so-called real world. Within perceptible "reality" exists another sphere, the fantastic, which is not in any way superfluous to a writer's concerns: "The fantastic must be so intimately bound up with the real that one almost believes in it."
The radical critics' insistence that art must serve a particular political view was for Dostoyevsky the equivalent of assigning to art "a shameful destiny." A literary work must stand or fall on its "artistic merit," he explained. The utilitarian claim that the formal aspects of a work were of secondary importance so long as its goal was good and its purpose clear struck Dostoyevsky as a contradiction in terms. Only fully realized artistic works could fulfill their goals. But what does it mean to say that a work is "artistic"? Dostoyevsky defined it thus: "To say that a novelist is 'artistic' means that he possesses a talent to express his thoughts in characters and images so that when the reader has finished the novel, he has fully understood the author's thoughts. Therefore, artistry is quite simply the ability to write well."

The radical critics' requirement that art must at all costs be "useful" to people and society seemed to Dostoyevsky unsatisfactory. How can we know what will show itself to be useful? Can we say with assurance how useful the Iliad has been to humankind? No, Dostoyevsky believed, when it comes to this we encounter breadths that cannot be measured with any precision; sometimes a work of art may appear to deviate from reality and serve no useful purpose because we cannot see clearly what paths it may take to become useful.

I think it is fitting to use a discussion of my favorite author as the last passage of the book. Here we go:

During Dostoyevsky's time there were two significant and opposing directions in Russian literary criticism. One position maintained that art stood high above the present and the everyday, while the radical view maintained that art had a right to exist only if it found its sources in concrete reality, and, through the exposure of want and injustice, it contributed to the creation of a new society; literature, in other words, should be useful. Dostoyevsky took a third position. As a realist, he never doubted that reality was literature's crucial source. But his understanding of reality went deeper than the one prevailing among radical critics, since for Dostoyevsky there was no distinction in principle between fantasy and reality, and reality was far more than the merely tangible.

There are two schools of literary criticism:

One school believes art is above daily life. (We weren't given a name for this group, but since the other group are called radicals, let's call this group the "conservatives.")

The radicals believe art must represent reality, and effect social change.

Dostoevsky takes a third position.

Many students will assume that these are three different positions and move to the next paragraph. However, they overlook a subtle point:

Dostoevsky's third position actually has a lot of common ground with the second, radical position. Dostoevsky is a "realist," the radicals are realists too. But Dostoevsky's understanding of reality is different from the radicals' understanding of reality, this is the difference between Dostoevsky and the second position.

The radical critics' demand that reality be depicted "as it is" was meaningless for Dostoyevsky; reality was necessarily shaped by the person who experienced it: what may not be reality for you may be reality for me. The task of the writer was to explode the boundaries of the so-called real world. Within perceptible "reality" exists another sphere, the fantastic, which is not in any way superfluous to a writer's concerns: "The fantastic must be so intimately bound up with the real that one almost believes in it."

For Dostoevsky reality is subjective. (We can probably infer that the radical critics believe reality to be objective.) Further, the idea of the "fantastic" is introduced. For Dostoevsky, it's a part of reality.

The radical critics' insistence that art must serve a particular political view was for Dostoyevsky the equivalent of assigning to art "a shameful destiny." A literary work must stand or fall on its "artistic merit," he explained. The utilitarian claim that the formal aspects of a work were of secondary importance so long as its goal was good and its purpose clear struck Dostoyevsky as a contradiction in terms. Only fully realized artistic works could fulfill their goals. But what does it mean to say that a work is "artistic"? Dostoyevsky defined it thus: "To say that a novelist is 'artistic' means that he possesses a talent to express his thoughts in characters and images so that when the reader has finished the novel, he has fully understood the author's thoughts. Therefore, artistry is quite simply the ability to write well."

Other than differing conceptions of what constitutes "reality," Dostoevsky differs from the radicals in the sense that he does not think literature should have political goals.

He disagrees with the view that goals are more important than the literary/aesthetic quality of a work. A work's paramount indicator of quality is that it's well written, and the reader can fully understand what the author is trying to say.

The radical critics' requirement that art must at all costs be "useful" to people and society seemed to Dostoyevsky unsatisfactory. How can we know what will show itself to be useful? Can we say with assurance how useful the Iliad has been to humankind? No, Dostoyevsky believed, when it comes to this we encounter breadths that cannot be measured with any precision; sometimes a work of art may appear to deviate from reality and serve no useful purpose because we cannot see clearly what paths it may take to become useful.

How do we know if something is useful or not? We can't say with certainty that a work is "useful" or not.

In this passage, if we didn't understand the distinctions between Dostoevsky and the Radicals, as mentioned in the first paragraph, then we will have a hard time understanding Dostoevsky's rebuttals of each successive radical position. It's important to develop a strong understanding of the foundations of a passage before moving to the more difficult parts.

20. Topic Specific Reading Strategies

21. Timing and Reading Ability Hacking

Timing

Timing is probably the trickiest element in RC for most students. It was also something that haunted me until the very end of my LSAT preparation journey. No matter how much time I was given, it never felt like it was enough.

There are two possible reasons why we are running out of time during RC. One possibility is that we are taking too long to read the passages. If you have been following the strategies on passage reading laid out in Part I of the book and in Chapter 20, a lack of speed is probably an indicator of weaker reading ability. Think back on the Diagnostic Section from Chapter 6, were you having trouble understanding the passage and coming up with the relevant answers within the given time slot? If that's the case, then we'll need to work on your general reading ability. We need to make you a better and faster reader in a short period of time. We do that by bringing in outside readings to "hack" our reading ability.

We will look at using outside reading to improve our general reading ability in the second half of this chapter.

But if you *are* able to read the passage in a three-minute window and know what the Main Point, Author's Purpose, and key point of each paragraph is; but are still pressed for time, then the timing issue can probably be attributed to your test taking habits. You may be spending too much time on the earlier, easier passages; you may be gradually losing momentum due to fatigue or a risk-averse test taking style; you may be too fixated on getting each question right and spending a disproportionate amount of time on the answer choice selection process.

Let's look at each of these in turn:

Milestones

There are four passages in an RC section, but not all of them are created equal. Generally speaking, the first passages will be the easiest, and will gradually increase in difficulty as we move towards the end of the section. A common mistake students make is to commit the same amount of time to each passage, so 8:45 for the first passage, 8:45 for the second passage, etc.

We saw back in LR Perfection how splitting the Logical Reasoning section into three phases akin to a chess game can do wonders for our section performance (opening, mid-game, endgame). For RC, I would recommend splitting the section into **two halves**. Passage 1 and 2, typically easier passages, make up the first half; while passages 3 and 4, probably slightly harder, make up the second half.

In terms of timing I am very strict. I am not only checking the clock to make sure that I'm reading the passage in three minutes, but I'm also timing myself so that I'm finishing the first passage and its questions in around 7 minutes, and the first two passages under 15 minutes. Think about RC (and LG too, for that matter) as a relay race: we are trying to save time from the earlier parts of the section to use as a buffer for the later, more challenging parts of the section.

So essentially, I'm trying to hit the following lap times/milestones on an RC section:

Start	Time Passed
Finish reading Passage 1	Under 3 minutes
Finish Passage 1 Questions	7-8 minutes
Finish Reading Passage 2	10-11 minutes
Finish Passage 2 Questions	Around 15-minute mark
Finish Reading Passage 3	Under 20 minutes
Finish Passage 3 Questions	Around 25-minute mark, if not sooner (definitely sooner if Passage 4 has 7-8 questions)
Finish Reading Passage 4	28-29 minutes, if not less
Complete section	Aim for 34 minutes

Planning out your timing strategy down to the most miniscule detail may seem like an overkill. But it's only by following a strict regimen that we are able to notice the exact moment when our practice begins to deviate from our plan. Find your bottleneck and focus on eliminating it.

Hardest First?

Finetuning our timing based on precise milestones can be helpful for many students. But since everyone is different, here is an alternative strategy you can try.

Start with the last passage, or the second to last passage, whichever one has the most questions. Often, there is a difficult passage with 7-8 questions near the end of the section, and it's on this passage that most students run out of time.

So I start with this passage, because it's the first passage that I'm encountering, my attention will be focused and my mind fresh. I give myself a maximum of 8 minutes to read the passage and go through the questions. Of course, 8 minutes is probably not enough, but I am not looking for absolute certainty on the questions here. Whenever there's a question that I'm unsure about, I make an educated guess, flag my selection and move on. What's the worst that can happen? Even if I get half the questions wrong on this passage, I'm only missing -3 or -4 questions.

After having "completed" the longest/hardest passage in only eight minutes, I am feeling confident. I start working through the rest of the passages. My mind is now operating at a higher capacity because of the difficult passage that I just finished, and because I'm working backwards, the passages are getting easier and easier. Furthermore, as long as I can maintain my speed I will have a few minutes to spare, and this is when I come back and review the questions I flagged.

This strategy works for some students because it's such a confidence booster if it works. It's also a gamble too. The typical high scoring student will have no issues with LG or LR, and the only thing troubling them are difficult RC passages and timing. So by getting the biggest obstacle out of the way first, you can crack the rest of the passages in a relatively straightforward manner and come back to the source of your problems and take another look in search of that elusive perfection.

Flagging/Maintaining Momentum During Answer Choice Selection

Another reason why we end up running out of time is mental fatigue. The LSAT is a long and tedious test. We will be exhausted at the end of it. If RC is coming in a later section then your mental sharpness will already have suffered. If you had back-to-back RC sections (RC experimental), your will be lethargic no matter what you do. This happens to the best of us.

For the most serious student we can escalate our practice intensity to further train our mental fortitude. Think of it as a stress-test that banks conduct to ensure they can weather financial crises. We know that the modern LSAT consists of four sections (3+1 experimental section). So why not train by doing five sections in a row? Deliberately place two RC sections back-to-back at the end of the test, as sections 4 and 5, or do three LR sections in a row.

Risk avoidant behavior during the answer choice selection process is another reason why we lose unnecessary time. This is especially true for the high scorer. The high scoring student knows that they can afford only a few mistakes, and they are also pretty good at guessing which questions they probably got wrong. As a result, the high performer will strive to be a perfectionist on the actual exam, and each unclear question will feel like the end of the world to them.

This will lead to risk-avoidant behavior and must be avoided at all costs. The student will be so fixated on getting a specific question right that they forget RC at its very core, is an exercise in the "**art of ranking**." They forget that the correct answer can contain imperfections, because they would like to find the "perfect" answer to put their mind at ease. As a result, they end up paralyzed between two answer choices, unable to chose. What ensues is that precious time passes, and they end up missing easier questions due to time running out.

Harder questions and easy questions are worth the same number of points. Getting the first 23 questions right means nothing if you had no time left for the remaining 4. With harder passages, maintain momentum. Flag questions about which you are uncertain and move on. Hit your preplanned timing milestones. Come back at the end and look at the question with fresh eyes. Run the **Reverse Confirmation Technique** or the **Equal Standards Test** (both Chapter 17) and make an educated guess about what the best answer may be.

A final note on flagging during the test:

Upon completing the test and seeing the results, always check to see if the mistakes you made had all been flagged. If there were mistakes which went un-flagged, what can you do to make sure similar mistakes are flagged the next time around? If a lot of your flagged questions ended up being correct? Then why are you flagging them? Was it just for peace of mind, or did you actually have reservations about the answer you picked?

Most of my top students are highly aware. They may flag 3-4 questions per RC Section, and almost without exception, whatever mistakes they've made will be contained to those 3-4 questions. This means that if they are able to finish the section a few minutes early, they only have to look at the questions flagged, knowing with confidence that if they made any mistakes, this is where they will be.

Blind Review and Learning from Your Mistakes

Blind Review in RC is not as straightforward as it is in LR. In LR, we can use SLAKR (structure, logic, assumptions, keywords, and ranking) to analyze a question from multiple perspectives. But there isn't a one size fits all method to blind reviewing RC questions.

Furthermore, because RC performance is so dependent on our prior understanding of the passage, blind reviewing RC questions doesn't really help us prevent further mistakes.

For example, if you got a question wrong because of insufficient understanding of the passage, then there isn't much you can take away from that question except to "read better." Let's say I got Question 10 wrong because I missed a specific adjective describing the author's opinion in line 3 of the second paragraph, how will this help me on another question, in another passage, at another time?

What blind review and wrong answer review for RC can do; however, is showing us in what general sector our problems lie. Are you making a lot of mistakes that are subsequently fixed up during blind review? That's probably because you now have more time to re-read the passage, and this enhanced understanding of the reading material has helped you overcome your mistakes. Your problem then, in this case, is that you are reading too slow. Whatever knowledge you took away from the passage under timed conditions was not enough to help you navigate the questions Speed up your reading and improve your ability to retain and recall key information.

At the very beginning of the book we said that success in RC depends on four factors:

1. The ability to reorganize the passage structurally during reading and remember key details.

2. The ability to draw hints from the questions and anticipate what the correct answer might look like.

3. The ability to parse answer choices, compare them, and rank them in preferability.

4. The ability to do all this within the allotted time.

Use blind review or wrong answer review to narrow down the source of our problems to one of these sub-categories and focus on improving that instead.

Fighting Your Intuition

The social psychologist Jonathan Haidt, who developed the social intuition model in moral psychology, believes that people make moral judgments based on intuition and rationalize them afterwards. Whether or not you agree with his theory, it's something that we must avoid on the LSAT.

Too often students will pick an answer choice based on intuition. During blind review, all they try to do is selectively look for evidence to back up their choice and eliminate the alternatives. Instead of using blind review to reaffirm our decision and feel good about ourselves, we need to re-examine each answer choice rationally and on equal footing. Using the criteria and techniques you have learned in this book, strive to compare each answer choice from a rational and holistic perspective.

Warming Up

Even the best students may tense up or get stressed out by the whole test day experience. Small things such as checking in to the test center or scanning your room with a webcam for the online proctor can be fear inducing if things don't go smoothly. I've had high scoring students whose computers ran into issues on test day, and although it was fixed eventually, the whole ordeal messed up their flow and prevented them from reaching their normal PT score range.

While unexpected delays and obstacles can and will occur, we can try to minimize their effects on us (and minimize the initial shock and stress that affects some students when they start the test) by warming up. For me personally, warming up 30 minutes to an hour before starting the test was crucial for me to hit the ground running, and it gave me the confidence to go in to the test composed and calm.

Warming up can be helpful for other students, but for some students perhaps meditation, practicing breathing techniques, or visualizing success will be more helpful. As with everything that we've tried to do in this book, take a few PTs with warmup and a few without. See for yourself which method is more effective, and have the data to back it up.

When I am warming up for a test, I would spend maybe 10 minutes and go over a super easy Logic Game, 3-5 super easy LR Questions (usually Q1 to Q5), and a super easy passage. I will usually just read the passage for structure and practice my active reading skills without looking at the questions. All these will be questions/content that I have seen and done before.

Outside Reading

Throughout this book, we saw that our innate reading ability still has an oversized role to play in determining how successfully we navigate the RC section. An extremely competent reader who might not be familiar with the ins and outs of different RC question types will struggle, but so will the student who knows how to solve each question type but does not have a commanding understanding of the passage itself.

However, improving our performance on the RC section will be much easier for the former student. As long as they familiarize themselves with how different questions differ and the steps taken to solve these questions, their success is ensured. However, the student with a relatively weaker reading ability will struggle for longer, as it's extremely difficult to improve our reading ability in a short time window and consistently.

But that is not to say that such a task is impossible. It will take longer and will require more effort and consistency, but developing a habit of reading external materials can do wonders for our overall performance on the RC section, even if you've only started reading a few months ago. The key is consistency: read daily, if only for thirty minutes a day.

Topic

RC Passages have recurring topics, and you have probably noticed that already. In fact, you probably saw that your performance on a given passage was much better if it happened to be a topic with which you are familiar with, even though you might not have developed the reading habits, question analysis habits, or the answer choice selection habits we talked about earlier. That is the power of a strong reading ability.

By familiarizing ourselves with potential topics that may appear or have appeared frequently in RC passages, we are effectively minimizing contingency scenarios where we are faced with a topic that we are completely ignorant of. It's true that the topics we face on the actual test will not be exactly identical to the topics we read about during practice, but it will still be helpful and relevant. To use an example, it will be much easier to understand Einstein's General Theory of Relativity if you had an understanding of Newtonian physics. Even indirect or off-tangent knowledge from a related field can help us with our understanding of a passage's topic.

RC passages, as we have seen in Chapter 20, can generally be divided into four categories: science, law, art, humanities. Here are some potential topics in each category:

Science: biology and/or evolutionary biology has been by far the post common topic, followed by passages on physics, geology, and astronomy. There's been limited exposure to papers on chemistry, but passages on biological processes have touched upon formulas and compounds.

Law: jurisprudence is a big one, passages covering the debate with natural law advocates and legal positivists; passages describing different schools of law, passages on law and ethics, etc. We have also seen passages on the development of the common law through history, how a particular institution came into existence, and the plight of women and minorities under different legal regimes.

Art: visual art, music, and film are probably the three biggest categories to appear in an art-based passage. I would focus, as we mentioned in the earlier chapter, on an artist's contributions to their field, craft, and society. Learning more about art history, especially African American, Hispanic American, or Native American art, can be an invaluable source of knowledge.

Humanities: Politics and History are the most common themes in earlier passages, with a dash of ethics and epistemology. More recent passages have seen topics of discussion on economics and psychology.

See my website for a list of the most difficult passages from PT1 to PT90 and their associated topics, and for a list of recommended books ranked according to content and difficulty.

Difficulty

In short, we want to read outside works that are much more difficult than our RC passages. To use an example, if you are having trouble understanding the debate with Dworkin and the legal positivists, jump straight into Dworkin's "A Model of Rules." (You will have to read it in law school, anyway.) In an ideal world, we would have years to gradually improve our reading ability, we would gradually build up our knowledge of a field, and slowly move to the more difficult materials.

But given that we are reading not just for the sake of reading but to prepare for RC, we probably only have a few months max to get our reading levels up. We are not concerned with developing a lifelong reading habit (although you should), but how to both gain knowledge in certain fields and process high density information efficiently. Time is of the essence. So find the most difficult papers on a topic that you found the most challenging, read them through several times, understand them, and build the confidence you need to tackle RC. If you can understand a paper on quantum mechanics written by a real physics professor, you will have no trouble navigating an RC passage on the topic.

Structure May Be Different

Because external readings are usually longer, they will not necessarily have a specific structure that we can follow, unlike many RC passages. As such, I'm reading not so much for structure but rather to train my other reading habits. (Reading for structure can be practiced on actual RC passages.) The other reading habits I'd like to emphasize are as follows:

Hypothesis Building

We covered this back in Part I. As we read, we want to anticipate what the author might discuss in subsequent paragraphs. I would come up with a hypothesis as I read and see if it indeed bears out in subsequent text. I am constantly hypothesizing and revising what I think the reading is talking about, and what the reading will talk about next. This process helps me remain engaged and focused on the information at hand.

Conceptual Link Back

We also saw in Part I that authors will often return to a topic or theme discussed earlier. So it's important to make the connection between what was talked about earlier with what was talked about now. For instance, if the author was talking about the views of Historian A on page 10, and then again on page 15, when we read the information on page 15 we would need to connect it with what we remember from page 10. Synthesize this information; it's not standalone.

Secondly, the author can and will use different nouns to refer to the same subject. (See our Kremlin example in Chapter 3.) Make sure you know who or what is being discussed.

Active Recall

The sign of a strong reader is how much information they are able to retain from their reading. This was something I struggled with the most as an LSAT student. You basically want to read a paragraph, immediately close the book, and be able to formulate what that paragraph was about into a coherent and concise sentence. Do this for every paragraph you read. There are different ways to train this:

At the **Beginner** level, you can take notes on each paragraph and write down the Key Point after you finish reading.

At the **Intermediate** level, you are using highlighters only and vocalizing the paragraph Key Point without writing it down.

At the **Advanced** level, you are just reading (no notetaking, no highlights) and can consistently come up with the Key Point of each paragraph as you read.

Finally, at the **Mastery** level, you can read three to four paragraphs in one go, close the book, and tell me what each paragraph was talking about.

Superstar RC students will be able to perform at the "Advanced" or "Mastery" levels. Of course, this is very content-dependent. It doesn't count if you are able to do this for a Wikipedia article, but if you are reading Foucault, Derrida, Habermas, or Geertz, and still pulling this off, then that is impressive.

For a complete list of books, articles, and journals that I have used for my students to train reading skills for RC, check out my website or send me an email if you are looking for more specific recommendations!

https://dragontest.org/rc-recommended-readings/

Final Thoughts

That's it! It's now time to start practicing. Train your reading ability with outside reading, and finetune your RC skills with drills of passages and questions.

Like the Logical Reasoning section, we improve in RC by isolating the source of our problems. Blindly PTing repeatedly without self-reflection will not be helpful.

If you are unsatisfied with your performance, ask yourself, "What is my biggest concern?" Is it timing? Is it not reading the answer choices carefully? Is it not comparing hard answer choices and ranking them? Is it not knowing the approach to specific question types and the traps to avoid?

Find the source of your problems. If it's due to bad habits, devise drills to overcome these bad habits. If it's due to a lack of knowledge, revisit the relevant chapters in this book and commit the knowledge to heart. If it's due to reading ability, bite the bullet and read as much as possible! Even a few months of uninterrupted reading of dense material can miraculously improve our reading ability.

Throughout the book, we have used a limited number of passages repeatedly. This is because I felt that re-using the same passage is more effective for illustrating and driving home the points I wanted to convey. Instead of spending our energy deciphering the meaning of a new passage, we can now focus on the nuanced subtleties of its questions and answer choices.

My website, www.dragontest.org, offers additional resources and guides for the high-scoring student. My discord server (https://discord.com/invite/2khvCBBRbk or discord.io/lsatdragon) is a welcoming community of advanced students who regularly discuss LSAT and law school-related questions. Me and other high scoring former students will answer any LSAT related questions that you might have, free of charge. :)

I also offer LSAT tutoring in Mandarin. My WeChat Account is Lsatdragon (中文咨询请加我微信)

Lastly, I have a small favor to ask. If you have indeed enjoyed this book or found it helpful, I would be grateful if you could leave a review on Amazon. Reviews drive exposure, which drives sales, which is crucial to an author like me. They help pay the bills and allow me to keep on offering content.

I am currently offering a free 30-minute tutoring session via Zoom to all my readers. **After finishing the book**, simply email me a screenshot of your Amazon order and we can set up a time. If you have also finished LR Perfection, that's 60 minutes in total. I ask that you finish the book first because its more efficient this way. There will be many questions that can be answered simply by reading the rest of the material, and we can use the time to work on more niche problems.

Yours very gratefully,

Joshua

Appendix: Recurring Topics in RC

Below are four tables detailing the hardest passages under each topic (law/science/social/arts), as well as their specific topics of discussion. If you are particularly troubled by certain topics, there's no harm in doing a bit of additional research to fortify yourself.

Even if you have only an elementary understanding of a certain topic or merely a related topic, you will have a much easier time when faced with a difficult RC passage. Not only can you leverage your existing knowledge to better understand what the author is trying to express; but your confidence levels will be heightened, which in turn allows you to dive into the material and practice active reading more confidently.

Refer to my website for a specific list of books I found helpful. (https://dragontest.org/rc-recommended-readings/) In addition, Oxford University Press's "Very Short Introduction" series are a great primer on some of these topics.

Law:

PT-Passage	Passage Topic
30-3	Jurisprudence
33-4	Historical Feature of Common Law
35-4	Jurisprudence
43-4	Intellectual Property Law
45-4	Property Law
46-4	Jurisprudence
53-2	Historical Feature of Common Law
58-3	Intellectual Property Law
60-4	Feature of Legal System
79-4	Contract Law
88-4	International Environmental Law
90-4	Criminal/Corporate Law

Science:

2-3	Insect Biology
19-3	Biology/Species Extinction
32-4	Biochemistry/Physiology
36-3	Biology/Chemistry
40-3	Physics
44-3	Biochemistry/Physiology
49-4	Agriculture
50-4	Geology/Philosophy of Science
52-3	Evolution
53-4	Agriculture
56-2	Evolutionary Biology
57-4	Math/Geometry
63-3	Geology
65-4	Agriculture
69-4	Bird Biology
71-4	Scientific Thinking
72-3	Medical Ethics
75-4	Chemistry
77-4	Evolutionary Biology
78-4	Chemistry/Ecology,
84-4	Evolutionary Biology
85-4	Geology
86-4	Physics/Astronomy

Arts:

12-1	Architecture
21-1	Classical Music
24-4	Art Theory
42-2	Popular Art
59-3	Sculptor
62-4	Literature
64-4	Literature
78-2	Art Theory
79-2	Architecture

Social Sciences:

10-4	Historical Socio-Economic Development
19-4	Historical Socio-Economic Development
22-4	Linguistics/Epistemology
25-4	Philosophy of Science/Epistemology
27-2	Anthropology
31-4	Philosophy/Epistemology
37-4	Behavioral Psychology
41-4	Socio-Economic Development
67-2	Anthropology
71-3	Developmental Psychology
73-3	Behavioral Psychology
74-4	Political Activism
78-3	Archaeology
81-2	Psychology
82-4	Philosophy
83-4	Social Darwinism

Comparative:

65-3	Feature of Legal System
68-4	Feature of Legal System
72-4	Tax Law
73-4	Property Law
75-3	Philosophy/Ethics
76-4	Philosophy of Science/Epistemology
81-4	Court System
82-3	Jurisprudence
87-4	Sociology/History/Music
89-4	Linguistics
90-3	Philosophy/Semantics/Literary Analysis/Ethics

Made in United States
Troutdale, OR
11/04/2024

24427247R10328